PROFILE
OF A
METROPOLIS

PROFILE
OF A
METROPOLIS
A CASE BOOK

ROBERT J. MOWITZ
Wayne State University

DEIL S. WRIGHT
State University of Iowa

Detroit / Wayne State University Press / 1962

Published simultaneously in Canada by
Ambassador Books, Limited, Toronto, Ontario, Canada

Library of Congress Catalog Card Number 62-14069

Grateful acknowledgment is made to the Ford Foundation for financial assistance in the publication of this volume.

Preface

The Detroit Metropolis, sprawled on the banks of the Detroit River in Midwest America, has characteristics and problems typical of sister metropolises as well as some unique features. Home of the automobile, it is a prime example of a core city blending with satellite cities and suburban areas to form a single metropolitan system—a development to which the automobile has contributed mightily.

The modern metropolis is a marvelously complex system of cultural, social, economic, and political institutions woven together by a network of channels for the movement of people and goods. The lure of the metropolis has attracted close to two-thirds of our national population, and the percentage is increasing. From now on most Americans will be born, educated, work, and die in a metropolitan area. If understanding one's environment is a condition for successful adaptation and survival, then understanding the modern metropolis has become imperative for most of us.

This book is a collection of ten case studies which examine in detail crucial decisions and events that took place in the Detroit metropolis during a critical period of growth and transformation—the period from 1945 to 1960. During these fifteen years core cities were faced with deterioration and depopulation of downtown residential and commercial areas, while suburbs faced problems brought about by phenomenal population growth. The cases focus upon decisions in problem areas that were thrust upon community decision-makers because of the changes occurring within a dynamic system. Slum clearance, urban renewal, new sources of water, expressway construction, suburban drains and sewers, airport construction, expansion of port facilities, annexation of fringe areas: these are key terms in the lexicon of metropolitan growth and transformation, and these are the subjects of our cases.

Of the ten cases in this book, Professor Wright is responsible for those on the City-County Building, the Metropolitan Airport, and the Ford Expressway. Professor Mowitz is responsible for the remaining seven cases, although Professor Wright collected the bulk of the material for the Farmington Township case.

We aim this work at all students of the modern metropolis, whether they are in classrooms or active participants in one of the many decision-making roles afforded the metropolitan citizen. This is indeed a broad audience, since every responsible citizen of the metropolis has decision-making opportunities and obligations, and few academic disciplines can ignore the metropolis as part of their relevant data.

R. J. M.

D. S. W.

Acknowledgments

Many hands have contributed to the collection of materials behind each case, and without their assistance this case book could not have been written. Special recognition must be given to the students whose Master's thesis research has made a major contribution to certain cases. They are Richard LeClair (The Gratiot Redevelopment Project), Philip Workman (Detroit's Metropolitan Airport), Donald Warren (The Urban Renewal of Corktown), David Livingston (The Extension of the Lodge Expressway), and Charles Sturtz (The Case of the Missing Port).

Next, we would like to thank the many government officials, businessmen, community leaders, and private citizens who granted us interviews and made available reports, correspondence, and the various records and documents indispensable to our research. There are for each case from fifteen to twenty persons who fit into this category. Perhaps we should address our thanks to the community at large for creating a climate in which both citizens and public officials feel free to discuss in detail their decisions and reasons for them.

The Municipal Reference Branch of the Detroit Public Library and Librarians Lawrence Wember and Doris Detwiler were a great help. This library is a repository for local governmental reports and other documents that are otherwise hard to track down, and its file of newspaper clippings from the major dailies is a timesaver. Local newspapers were most generous in granting us access to their "clips"; this was true not only of the major dailies but also of the neighborhood weeklies and suburban papers.

Some of our colleagues deserve a word of thanks. York Willbern has followed our project over the years and provided helpful counsel. William Wheaton's detailed analysis of the Gratiot Redevelopment case was more helpful than he probably realizes. Many of our immediate colleagues gave us aid and comfort in ways too numerous to mention. The one to whom we are most indebted is Maurice Ramsey, whose careful reading of the manuscript and sage advice has saved us many pitfalls. Special thanks go to our Press editor, Mrs. Faith S. Schmidt, for her skillful assistance.

The Inter-University Case Program and its staff director, Edwin A. Bock, worked out an arrangement whereby Professor Wright could devote the summer of 1960 to working on cases for publication both in the Case Program series and in this volume. We are also grateful to the Graduate School of the State University of Iowa and to Wayne State University for financial assistance for typing portions of the manuscript. For providing us with many of the maps, illustrations, and diagrams used in this volume, we are indebted to agencies of local and state government and to private organizations.

We have tried hard to be scrupulously fair and to avoid causing any person unnecessary embarrassment. Our cases deal with real people and real events. We have done our best to describe behavior as it was and events as they happened. The myriad of details raises the statistical odds that error has crept into this work. Where it has, we accept full responsibility for it. If error results in the miscasting of the role of some individual, we offer our apologies in advance, for this is precisely what we have done our best to avoid.

Contents

Maps

Illustrations

Tables

Introduction

The cases in this book deal with a single metropolis, Detroit. Rather than viewing it as essentially an economic system or as essentially a political system, we have taken the metropolis as a whole as our system. Economic and political variables and values are involved in all the cases, as are other variables and values. The case method permits us to deal with these plural aspects within the limits of our capacity to observe and report. By focusing upon the metropolis as our system, we take as our continuum problems afflicting areas ranging from the downtown core of the central city to the edge of the suburban fringe. Our object is to convey a sense of the whole through an examination of particular cases.

Since Harold Stein's case book, *Public Administration and Policy Development* (New York, 1952), a good deal, pro and con, has been written about the use of the case method in political science. There is no need to review that debate here.[1] Our use of the case method is evidence of our belief in its efficacy in spite of its possible drawbacks. As Stein so aptly pointed out in his Introduction, one limitation upon the case method is the capacity of

[1] An excellent review of the arguments in this debate will be found in Paul Tillett's "Case Studies in Practical Politics: Their Use and Abuse," a paper prepared for delivery at the 1959 Annual Meeting of the American Political Science Association, Washington, D.C. See also Herbert Kaufman, "The Next Step in Case Studies," *Public Administration Review*, XVIII (Winter, 1958), 52, and citations therein. Two other recent discussions of the case method which were written for the Inter-University Case Program are James Fesler's "The Case Method in Political Science," 32 pp., mimeographed (undated), and Dwight Waldo's "Five Perspectives on the Cases of the Inter-University Case Program," 33 pp., mimeographed (August, 1960).

the author to observe and to translate his observations into communicable language. Yet the unwary reader may gain the illusory impression that he has gotten the complete story by reading the case. We, too, must acknowledge this limitation but would add that the notion that there is a "whole story" to be had about any complex sequence of events is in itself an illusion. The compulsion to know the whole truth may be great, but it can only be partially satisfied by this or any other method.

The materials for this case book were collected over the past ten years. The research for most of the cases was begun while some phase of the events in the case was in the process of happening. Thus it was possible to interview participants and observe their behavior in the midst of events, which has minimized the necessity of relying upon *ex post facto* interviews exclusively. In reducing a wealth of information to a narrative of reasonable length, we have attempted to maintain the balance and objectivity necessary for preserving the "essential truth." We have avoided using footnotes as much as possible by including our references and sources in the body of the text. This is done as much to keep the reader aware of where the information is coming from as to avoid interrupting the reading rhythm.

A few cautions are in order concerning the use of the cases. The first has to do with the temptation to second-guess actions and decisions based upon information gleaned after the event or decision. Case studies describe events occurring in time. At the time the events are taking place, certain finite amounts of information are available to the various participants, and this information is not distributed equally among them. The most difficult task of the case writer is to keep each set of events within the information setting of the period during which the events occurred. It requires a positive act of cooperation on the reader's part to "follow along" at the information rate of the case, particularly during periods of intense activity when many events are occurring simultaneously. The dimensional limitations imposed by the printed page require that events be reported sequentially, and this presentation tends to flatten the perspective. To obtain a more accurate picture the reader must mentally reconstruct some events as simultaneous occurrences, which means mentally lifting them from the page and placing them back beside events reported earlier.

The same may be said of the cases themselves, which overlap each other in time and are often otherwise interconnected. Nonetheless, the data included in each case are sufficient for that case, so that the cases can be read separately or in an order different from that in which they are presented without undue sacrifice. The resulting repetition of information crucial to several cases is more than offset by the advantages of having each case stand on its own.

A final caution has to do with the tendency to reduce complex social phenomena to the dimensions of a morality play where the "good," after a frustrating struggle with "evil," finally prevails; or the more sophisticated twist where "evil" comes out the winner. The inherent drama in the case approach provides tempting opportunities for a subtle use of this technique. We have made every effort to avoid casting our cases in such a mold. We expect that the reader will prefer one side to the other in some of the controversies. As citizens we, too, take sides at the proper time and place, but as social scientists our task has been to deal as objectively as possible with the dynamics of the metropolis.

In examining adjustment to change in a system as complex as the modern metropolis, it is helpful to bear in mind the conditions that determine the limits and potentialities of adjustment. Since the individual is the basic unit in any metropolis, the limits and potentialities of the system are determined by the factors conditioning behavior—the physical environment, human biology, available science and technology, institutions (social, economic, and political), and values. These conditioning factors may appear self-evident, but a few words about them are in order.

The physical environment and human biology set the primary limits. Geography sets boundaries in the form of rivers, mountains, lakes, and oceans, and land, air, and water transportation must accommodate themselves to these boundaries. Structures must be designed to meet prevailing environmental conditions if the human need for shelter from the elements is to be fulfilled. Even the zealous suburban developer will occasionally admit defeat in the face of a bog that refuses to be converted into lakeside lots or soil that will not absorb another ounce from a septic tank. Facilities for disposal of waste (especially in densely populated areas), food, water, and shelter are elementary prerequisites of human survival which remain in force even though we take them for granted, and the physical environment promotes or inhibits the fulfillment of these conditions.

Available science and technology provide means by which adjustments can be made to conditions imposed by the physical environment and human biology, and by which other values may be achieved. Without question, the modern metropolis is the product of science and technology. Limitations upon space-time relationships prior to modern transportation and communications placed practical limits upon the optimum spatial distribution of persons within an urban area. But the automobile, airplane, telephone, and computer, among other present-day gadgets, have revolutionized space-time relationships, with consequent metropolitan spread. Scientific and technological developments have made possible the dramatic growth of the mid-twentieth-century metropolis and will mold its future development.

Integral to the metropolis is its elaborate institutional structure, composed of everything from the loosely organized and ephemeral neighborhood civic association to the highly formal and stable industrial corporations, labor unions, and governmental units. Because of the plural interests present in the metropolis, the organizational environment is pluralistic, and the mapping of the institutional structure is a major feat in itself. The governmental jurisdictions are varied—counties, cities, townships, villages, and school districts—each with a definite boundary limiting the geographic extent of its powers. The major organizations in the metropolis have a formal organizational structure with positions manned by full-time employees prepared to carry out the tasks of the organization. In other words, the bureaucratic type of organization prevails, and relationships among organizations tend to be relationships among bureaucracies. The institutional structure is the framework which limits and channels behavior within the metropolitan system.

A fifth and final conditioner of behavior in the metropolis is values, as they are reflected in the rating of alternative choices according to degrees of preference. This may or may not be a rational, self-conscious process; in either case, values motivate action. Individual values derive from a variety of sources, including conditioning and other learning processes, and institutions structure their values through rules and policies directing how choices should be made and which choices should be made in decision-making situations. For large numbers of individuals and groups, the metropolis is the medium through which they seek to attain their values, be they biological, economic, social, cultural, political, or combinations of these. Seeking to attain values, or goal-seeking, includes the behavior of the slum-area landlord and skid-row alcoholic as well as that of the patron of the symphony orchestra. The lure of the metropolis is that within it more different types of values can be obtained than in any other type of environment. The metropolis is the medium for our present-day civilization.

These five interrelated conditioners—the physical environment, human biology, science and technology, institutions, and values—influence each other in ways beyond the capacity of the cases to describe, but they do provide a useful framework through which to view both the particular case and the metropolis as a whole. For example, in the case dealing with Wayne County's attempt to build a water system to serve suburban areas of the county (Water for Southwestern Wayne County), the demand for water is a function of human biology; the location of the water source is a function of the physical environment; the sizing of the system and the determination of the purity of the water source involve science and technology; the struggle over who should provide the water takes place between two governmental organizations, one city and the other county, and the principal actors are part of the bureaucracy of these two organizations; the values vary with the participants—householders want water, real-estate developers want to open new areas for development, the county bureaucracy wants to expand its services, the city bureaucracy wants to extend its service into the county area and keep the county out of the water business, and so on. The dynamic factor is values. Someone has to value something in order to start the behavior chain, but once it has begun, the other factors come into play to condition behavior.

These conditioning factors not only influence change; they are also influenced by it, especially during a period of profound and rapid transformation. The years from 1945 to 1960 were such a period.

The end of World War II started a chain of events that by 1960 had transformed most American cities from self-contained islands of dense population to "cores" of population concentrations which spilled far beyond the core-city boundaries. Demands pent up during the depression years and postponed during the war years were satisfied during this period of relatively sustained economic well-being, and new demands were created that sought and found gratification. New homes, new cars, new families, more jobs, higher incomes, new factories, new expressways, larger families, bigger homes, new subdivisions, new shopping centers—these are some of the more obvious characteristics of the period. Not all metropolitan areas were equally affected, but for the Detroit metropolis this was a critical period.

Following a postwar spurt, the population of the core city (Detroit) rose to a peak of 1,910,000 (based upon local estimates) sometime in the mid-fifties, but by 1960 the city's population had declined to 1,670,144, which was 179,424 less than the 1950 census total of 1,849,568. Meanwhile the population of the metropolis had increased by 756,000 between 1950 and 1960, bringing the metropolitan total to 3,762,000. Thus, while the core city had to adjust to a declining population, the fringe areas had to adjust to rapid growth. One suburban city, Oak Park, increased from 5,267 to 36,616 in the decade. Outside the core city for the period from April 1957 through August 1958, the Detroit Metropolitan Area Regional Planning Commission reported 7,217 acres of new subdivisions with 19,535 new lots. These population changes indicate the different rates at which change was taking place in various parts of the metropolis.

A rapid change of conditions within a system stimulates efforts to adjust to the new state of affairs, efforts which put particular strains upon the adjustment capacity of the system. The changes occurring during this period were of a character that could not be ignored. More people demanding water and sewers is not a hypothetical demand any more than fewer people paying taxes is a hypothetical loss. The incapacity of a highway to handle rush-hour traffic is a demonstrable fact to the motorist using the highway during the rush hour. The strong pressure generated by the need to adjust to rapid change does result in some form of adjustive behavior. Whether the efforts at adjustment can be judged successful, adequate, or even appropriate to the situation varies from case to case and will no doubt vary also according to the values of the observer, but in each case something did "give." A look at the historical, economic, and political framework within which these adjustments were made will provide the necessary local perspective. A more detailed description of the Detroit metropolis appears in the Appendix.

Detroit was founded in 1701 by the Frenchman Antoine Cadillac, who decided that the site on the banks of the strait (Detroit River) linking Lakes St. Clair and Erie was a strategic location for a fur-trading post. It was a good choice, for the Great Lakes system has continued to nourish the economy of the city, providing an avenue for immigration, the channel through which raw materials such as iron ore and limestone could be fed to industry, an outlet for finished products, and, with the opening of the St. Lawrence Seaway, direct access to the ocean ports of the world. Starting from the river bank, the metropolis has fanned inland north, south, and west from the core, Detroit's central business district, which has remained attached to the river frontage. The Detroit River is the international boundary between the United States and Canada, and the city of Windsor, Ontario, with a population of approximately 130,000, occupies the Canadian side (east bank) of the river, opposite Detroit. While the Windsor economy is affected by the metropolis across the river, the reverse is not true: decisions and happenings in Windsor have little if any effect upon Detroit. Thus the whole area of the Detroit metropolis, as we shall define it, is within the state of Michigan.

The precise boundaries of a metropolis are always difficult to define, but for demographic purposes it is necessary to use the census boundaries. The U.S. Bureau of the Census defines the Detroit Standard Metropolitan Area (SMA) as consisting of three Michigan counties, Wayne, Oakland, and Macomb. Wayne County, with a land area of 607 square miles, includes within its boundaries all of the city of Detroit, the fifth largest city in the United States, with a population of 1,670,144 and land area of 140 square miles. Wayne County's total population is 2,666,297. Oakland County is due north of Wayne County and has a land area of 877 square miles and a population of 690,259. The eastern section of Oakland County's southern boundary line, Eight Mile Road, is also the northern boundary of Detroit. Oakland County is land-locked in the sense that none of its territory fronts on the Great Lakes system. Macomb County, north of Wayne County and east of Oakland County, has an area of 481 square miles. It also has a common boundary with Detroit along Eight Mile Road, and its eastern boundary is Lake St. Clair and the St. Clair River. Macomb County's population is 405,804. Summing up, the Detroit Standard Metropolitan Area has a land area of 1,965 square miles and a population of 3,762,360, but it would be misleading to assume that the metropolis is identical with the SMA. Ninety percent of the SMA population is concentrated in an area of about 500 square miles, which includes the city of Detroit and the areas immediately adjacent to it—southeastern Oakland County, southern Macomb County, and the Wayne County area bordering Detroit. This area is a single system, for the influence of the core city is felt throughout the whole area, and any significant changes in one part of the area will affect one or more other parts. This is the area to which we refer when we use the words "Detroit metropolis."

The dominant feature of the Detroit economy is the automobile. The 1950 census reported 28 percent of the metropolitan labor force engaged in motor vehicle manufacturing. The Detroit metropolis was the only major metropolitan area to have such a large percentage of its labor force devoted to a single product, and the percentage would be still more impressive if it were to include all those employed in allied industries. Constant effort is under way to diversify the economic base of the metropolis, but the automobile continues in the dominant role. Another major feature of the economy is the significant role played by organized labor. The United Auto Workers of America and its president, Walter Reuther, are well known nationally as symbols of Detroit unionism. Automobile manufacturing had its peak production year in 1955, and since that time it has dipped in the even years and moved upward in the odd years, but never again during the fifties was it to reach the 1955 summit. Dependent as it is upon automobile production, the economy of the metropolis sways with automobile production curves.

Within the Detroit metropolis, there are fifty-four different political jurisdictions (exclusive of school districts), including three counties, eight townships and forty-three cities and villages. As the metropolis spreads, it engulfs additional jurisdictions, and the remaining townships, if they follow precedent, will be carved up into new cities and villages which will swell the total number of jurisdictions. The smallest jurisdiction is Quakertown, an incorporated suburban village with a population of 482, and the largest is Wayne County.

Detroit is governed by a mayor and a Common Council of nine members elected at large on a non-partisan ballot for terms of four years. The city has a strong-mayor type of organization. For the remaining Wayne County cities, the pattern is mixed. Some have partisan ballots and the strong-mayor system, and some have non-partisan ballots and the council-manager plan. The cities of south Oakland County are uniform in that they all have the council-manager form of government and the non-partisan ballot. Each of the three counties is governed by a board of supervisors consisting of township supervisors and representation from each city pro-rated according to population. This arrangement results in a large board membership in the two large counties: in 1960 the Wayne County Board of Supervisors had 111 members, the Oakland County board, 83. County elections are partisan. Wayne and Macomb counties are most likely to return Democratic majorities, while in Oakland County Republicans hold the edge.

The mixture of partisan and non-partisan elections places political party organizations in an enigmatic position. Active during partisan elections, political parties are expected to be, and for the most part are, inactive during non-partisan contests. Furthermore, civil service regulations and professionalization of the metropolitan bureaucracy have deprived the parties of the extensive patronage and influence required to build a political machine. As a result, political parties in the Detroit metropolis are but one among a plurality of political forces involved in local issues, and in many instances the party's role is minor or nonexistent.

The representation of the metropolis in the Michigan state legislature does not correspond to its share of the state population, since the basis for representation in both houses of the state legislature favors rural areas. The cities and counties in the metropolis have been forced to rely upon lobbying tactics to obtain desired legislation, and evidence will be found in many of the cases that this has been an effective technique. But few would argue that effective lobbying is an adequate substitute for an equitable system of representation.

Is the Detroit metropolis unique? Any self-respecting metropolis would be properly insulted if it were not considered somewhat unique, but as one runs down the list of the twenty largest metropolitan areas in the United States, beginning with New York and including places such as Cleveland, Buffalo, Atlanta, and Pittsburgh, one is struck by the fact that most of the metropolises are in a stage of becoming more like Detroit in size than they are to becoming like New York. One can make a good case, in terms of population alone, that Detroit is more likely to be a prototype of the majority of the American metropolises of the next twenty years than are the super-metropolises, New York and Chicago; Detroit and Buffalo have more in common with each other than either has with New York. What is common and what is unique cannot be demonstrated from a set of cases that deal with one metropolis, but the problems, issues and decisions that we have dealt with will find their counterparts in other American metropolises.

1
The Gratiot
Redevelopment Project
Regenerating the Core City

Introduction

Urban deterioration and blight are physical conditions. They can be described in terms of numbers of human bodies occupying a given square footage of living-space. They can be seen in littered yards, peeling paint, broken steps, dead rats plastered to the pavement by passing cars, and children competing with traffic for control of the streets. Urban blight has a stench. On a hot, humid summer day the stale odor of fried foods hangs in the air, and the open doors of crowded homes emit a draft that reeks of neglected diapers and human sweat. More sophisticated signs—morbidity, mortality, crime and delinquency rates—show that the conditions we label "slum" do not provide a healthy environment for the human organism.

There is general agreement that these physical conditions should be eliminated. One aim of urban redevelopment is to remove the slum and put the site to a more desirable use. The means by which this can be accomplished and the end use for which the site is to be developed are conditioned by the prevailing institutional structure and the values that energize and shape it. This structure includes the business network consisting of lending institutions, real-estate brokers and developers, and the construction firms through which housing is provided. It also includes local governmental organization—in this case the mayor, the council, and the administrative agencies, Housing Commission and City Plan Commission, in which major responsibility for urban redevelopment had been placed. Because Congress has made housing and urban redevelopment a part of national policy, the Federal Housing and Home Finance Agency forms a part of the relevant structure. Added to these are various private organizations, such as labor organizations, organizations devoted to protecting the rights of minority groups, and trade associations consisting of builders and merchants in the central business district.

Certain end-values are institutionalized in these organizations. The building industry is designed to produce housing at a profit; trade associations and labor organizations are designed to look after the interests of their members. Each of the formal organizations involved has one or more institutionalized end-values that bear on some aspect of slum clearance and urban redevelopment. Some of these values are shared among the various organizations, and some are incompatible. Each of the individuals playing significant decision-making roles accepts in varying degrees the institutionalized values of the organization or group with which he identifies, depending upon his own value system. As environmental conditions change, both individual and institutional values may change. Issues hotly contested in 1950 may be forgotten or ignored by the same contestants in 1954. The Gratiot redevelopment project is a case that involves significant shifts in values over a period of time by individuals, organizations, and agencies.

"U.R. Mich. 1-1" was the official designation assigned to Detroit's first urban redevelopment project. Although completed under the Housing Act of 1949, the project had been planned and launched some years before. The time covered in the case is the thirteen years from 1946 through 1958. This is how long it took to condemn 129 acres of the city's worst slum, relocate 1,950 Negro families, prepare and receive approval for four different sets of plans for the re-use of the site (Plan Commission, Housing Commission, Common Council, Federal Housing Administration, and Division of Slum Clearance and Urban Redevelopment of the Housing and Home Finance Agency were the formal approval channels), sell the land to a private developer, and construct a twenty-two-story apartment building. It might seem that thirteen years is a long time to devote to these tasks, but the rebuilding of even as small a chunk of a city as 129 acres is a complex operation involving many decisions which affected crucial values and thousands of individuals.

Early Stages

The Detroit Plan. During and following World War II, the city of Detroit was beset by a number of problems that stemmed in part from the prewar depression and in part from wartime conditions. The depression had brought the construction of private dwellings to a virtual standstill, and the wartime influx of workers plus an increase in the number of births created a serious housing shortage. The results followed the pattern familiar in American urban centers: a high concentration of low-income families in the older residential sections near the central business district of the core city. At the same time middle- and upper-income families had begun the exodus to the suburbs as fast as available housing would permit. The "Detroit Plan" was designed to deal with these two conditions, urban slum and suburban flight.

The Detroit Plan was made public on November 18, 1946, by Mayor Edward J. Jeffries, Jr. The substance of his proposal was that the city acquire approximately one hundred acres of land a few blocks northeast of the central business district, later to be known as the Gratiot redevelopment area, demolish the slum residences and other buildings, and prepare the land for resale to private developers for residential use. This was an ambitious project for a city to undertake on its own financial initiative, but a look at the arithmetic of the financing reveals the reasoning behind it. It was estimated that the cost of acquiring and clearing the land would be $3,750,000 and that it could be sold to private builders at a fair land-use value of $860,000. This would leave the city with a net cost of $2,890,000 which was reduced another $950,000 by estimating that this amount would have to be spent on the area in any event for badly needed community improvements, such as parks, play space, and land required for an expressway. This reduced the net cost to slightly under $2,000,000. The city would recapture its $2,000,000 investment through a net annual gain in tax revenue amounting to $134,200 from the same hundred acres once redevelopment had been accomplished. Thus, the argument went, the city would recover its investment in fifteen years.

At the 1947 annual meeting of the American Society of Plan-

ning Officials, Charles F. Edgecomb, director-secretary of the Detroit Housing Commission, reviewed the above financing arrangements and pointed out that "the theory advanced by Mayor Jeffries
is that the city of Detroit should allocate $2,000,000, or 2 percent
of the total tax budget, each year for slum clearance. This sum
will be placed in a revolving fund. The proceeds from the resale
of these acquired properties would, of course, be left in or returned
to the revolving fund. All our studies in relation to the $2,000,000
annual contribution and the revolving fund theory indicate that
at the end of fifteen years, or in the year 1960–61 [*sic*], Detroit
will have reclaimed and redeveloped 1,325 acres of blighted area."
The housing director went on to point out that there had been
some misunderstanding that the intent of the plan was to demonstrate that cities had no need for federal assistance. Instead, he
urged the enactment of the then pending Wagner-Ellender-Taft
Housing Bill, which would provide aid to municipalities for
redevelopment.

The Detroit Plan was not the sudden brain-child of Mayor
Jeffries but the result of well over a year of discussion and committee activity aimed at bringing private enterprise into the business of slum clearance and of housing low-income families. Since
1933, when the first allocation for slum clearance and low-rent
housing was made to Detroit by the Federal Emergency Housing
Corporation, private builders and real-estate men had become
increasingly critical of the predominant role of government in this
program. The obvious rejoinder to this criticism was that private
enterprise could not provide housing within the financial reach of
low-income families. In March 1945, Eugene Greenhut, a New
York builder, submitted a proposal in which he offered to build
low-rent units on blighted land. Mayor Jeffries appointed a committee of city officials, consisting of the controller, the corporation
counsel, the director-secretary of the Housing Commission, and
the public utility analyst, to determine the possibility of implementing the "Greenhut Plan" under existing legislation and available funds. Late in 1945 the committee issued its report, which
presented a number of reasons for rejecting the Greenhut Plan.
Among them were these: since the plan would not serve the low-
income groups which the Public Housing Act was designed to

accommodate, financing under the act was of questionable legality; competitive bidding for construction of the project was not
contemplated, although it was required by the city charter; and
the proposal would not accomplish the redevelopment of blighted
areas by private enterprise "as that term [private enterprise] is
commonly understood."

The same committee that rejected the Greenhut Plan continued
to consider alternative measures for meeting the slum problem.
One alternative was to replace the slums with public housing
projects. This was objected to on the grounds that it ruled out the
use of private enterprise; that complete reliance upon public housing for slum removal would result in large segments of the city
devoted entirely to subsidized housing, with consequent loss in
tax revenue; and that the surrounding of the central business district with subsidized housing would have a depressing effect upon
the maintenance of that district. Certainly, the large department
stores would suffer if they had to rely upon the trade of the residents of public housing projects. The alternative of development
entirely through private investment was considered too costly to
attract investors. It was estimated that it would cost $4,000 to ac-
quire, clear, and develop a forty-foot lot. Since the planned re-use
of the area at this time called for dwelling units selling for about
$5,000 (these, of course, are 1944–45 dollars), the cost of acquir-
ing and preparing the land was prohibitive. It was therefore decided that the city should acquire and clear the land and provide
the private builder with sites at a price he could afford, with the
city absorbing the difference between actual cost and write-down
price. This was the substance of the committee's report early in
1946, which became known as the Detroit Plan upon its announcement by Mayor Jeffries later that year.

Many hands participated in the development of the Detroit
Plan. The mayor's committee sought and obtained the advice of
real-estate and building interests in the community both through
direct personal contact and through formal representative bodies
such as the Construction Industry Council and the Builders' Association of Metropolitan Detroit. City Treasurer Albert E. Cobo,
who later became mayor, had an active role, but it would be difficult to point to any one person as the author of this plan. What is

clear is that those with the greatest economic stake in the downtown area's future—the banking, investment, retail-business, real-
estate, and building interests—took an active part along with city
officials in developing this strategy for eliminating slums and for
stemming the tide of public housing with all of its feared consequences for each of the groups involved in the decision.

Although it appeared at the time that federal legislation might
be forthcoming to relieve cities from part of the net loss incurred
in selling reclaimed land at a write-down price, the fate of this
legislation was uncertain, and there was the feeling among some
supporters of the plan that Detroit should not be dependent upon
aid from Washington. The opportunity to attempt to put the plan
into effect without federal aid arose with the shelving of another
civic improvement project.

For some time consideration had been given to building an
international airport across the Detroit River in Windsor, Canada,
in order to establish a facility accessible to downtown Detroit.
In a report to the council on February 12, 1946, the mayor set
forth seven reasons why the building of the proposed airport was
unnecessary. He then recommended that the $2,000,000 set aside
in a capital outlay fund for this project be earmarked instead for
slum clearance at the Gratiot site. The council agreed with the
airport recommendation and allocated $1,500,000 to a capital im-
provement fund for the Gratiot project to be spent at the rate of
$500,000 a year for each of the three fiscal years beginning July 1,
1946. The $2,000,000 that had been earmarked for the airport was
identical with the net cost to the city of acquiring and clearing the
land after deducting proceeds from the sale of the land and cost
of required community services. The financial rationale thus jibed
with available funds almost to the penny. With this rather modest
financial backing, the way was cleared for the mayor to make his
November announcement that the city was ready to proceed with
the condemnation of the Gratiot site.

The selection of the Gratiot site for a pilot project for clearance and redevelopment was not difficult, since the area was unquestionably a slum. The original hundred-acre site was later
expanded to about 129 acres bounded by Gratiot Avenue on the
north, Lafayette Avenue on the south, Dequindre Road on the

east (this became the right-of-way of the Grand Trunk Western Railroad) and Hastings Street on the west. This was the central part of a larger area that had been designated for future redevelopment. Although plans were subsequently changed, at this time the area north of the Gratiot site was to be redeveloped for industrial use; the area south of it was to be put to the same use (residential) as the Gratiot site; the area to the east, on the other side of the Grand Trunk Western Railroad tracks, was to hold a large (3,800 units) public housing project; and to the west a central business district development was planned, separated from the Gratiot site by an expressway.

A survey of the Gratiot site supported the visual evidence of blight. It revealed that there were nearly twice as many dwelling units as there were structures in the area (705 structures and 1,355 dwelling units); that 8 percent of the dwelling units were occupied by the owners and 92 percent by renters; and that 51 percent of the dwelling units had been built before 1900 while only 5 percent had been built since 1920. Additional evidence showed that the average rent per month was $19.95, the lowest in the city, and that the area contained the greatest number of families on welfare and had the highest incidence of complaints against juveniles filed in the Juvenile Court. The 1945 survey identified 90 percent of the site population as Negro, while a 1950 survey estimated the Negro portion at 98 percent. Although the indicators used to determine "urban blight" were to be questioned in later redevelopment efforts (see the Corktown case), there was no question about Gratiot. It was a classic slum.

By the beginning of 1947, Detroit was ready to begin its urban face-lifting. A plan had been worked out that received the support of private enterprise, $500,000 was available for the purchase of land, and a ripe slum site was ready for plucking. All that remained to be done was to acquire, clear, and sell the land. But this was to take more time than even the most conservative backers of the Detroit Plan would have predicted.

Land Acquisition. In February 1947, condemnation proceedings were begun on the first ten of the site's forty-three blocks. As had been anticipated, a taxpayer's suit was filed in November of that year, and the suit halted further action until the legality of the condemnation was clarified by the court. Land acquisition for slum clearance and eventual resale to a private developer was an innovation, and no clear precedents existed in Michigan law. In October of 1948, eleven months after the case had been initiated in the lower courts, the Michigan Supreme Court handed down a decision upholding the right of the city to proceed with the condemnation (*General Development Corporation* v. *City of Detroit,* 322 Mich. 495, 33 N.W. 2d 919). Plaintiff had argued that under Michigan law, Act 250, Public Acts of 1941, acquisition of slum areas by cities and later disposal of such areas to private corporations required that the private developer reimburse a city in full for all funds expended in acquiring and preparing the land. It was claimed that the law did not permit a city to sell land at a loss and that such a loss would result in an illegal tax on the plaintiff and other taxpayers. Although the court disposed of the issue that slum clearance would result in an illegal tax, the pleadings did not permit a decision on the key issue as to whether or not it was legal to condemn slum property for eventual resale to private developers. This latter issue was decided by the Michigan Supreme Court in December 1951 (*in re* Slum Clearance between Hastings, Gratiot, Dequindre, and Mullett Streets, 331 Mich. 714, 50 N.W. 2d 340). Here the plaintiff did not dispute the city's right to acquire land for slum clearance under Michigan laws and the city charter but claimed that the condemnation was unconstitutional because the property, while taken for a public purpose, slum clearance, was to be used for redevelopment by private persons.

In upholding the action of the city, the court stated: "It seems to us that the public purpose of slum clearance is, in any event, the one controlling purpose of the condemnation. The jury were not asked to decide any necessity to condemn the parcels involved for any purpose of resale, but only for slum clearance." It went on to point out that condemnation of property for a permissible public use "will not be defeated by the mere fact that an incidental private benefit or use of some portion of such property will result." This decision did come to grips with the key issue and made it clear that slum removal per se was enough to justify public condemnation proceedings under the police power.

Although a clear-cut judicial decision was not forthcoming until December 1951, condemnation proceedings were resumed in March 1949, following the court's first decision the previous October. The first jury verdict covering ten of the forty-three blocks in the project area was rendered in May 1950 and confirmed a month later. Condemnation proceedings continued throughout 1950, and by the end of the year, the city had obtained title to thirty-three of the forty-three blocks in the project area. By September 1951, condemnation jury verdict awards had been made on the final ten blocks, and all litigation ceased with the Michigan Supreme Court decision in December.

The most publicized bit of litigation that was put to rest by the Supreme Court decision was an action brought by Michael Novak, president of the Wayne County CIO Council, together with the council's vice president and secretary, to restrain Mayor Cobo and the Detroit Housing Commission from selling any land in the Gratiot project to any private individuals or corporation. This action by labor leaders may seem strange in view of later events wherein Walter Reuther played a substantial role in expediting the sale of land in the Gratiot project to private developers. But late in 1951, labor leaders were convinced that Mayor Cobo and his new housing director, former builder and real-estate developer Harry J. Durbin, were involved in a plan to turn over the Gratiot site to private developers eager to exploit the land as soon as it became available. It was feared that this pattern would be followed in the future to the detriment of the development of public housing projects. The mayor's opposition to public housing was no secret and had been an issue in his successful election campaign. Soon after he took office in January 1950, not only was a new housing director (Durbin) named, but also three new commissioners were appointed by the mayor to the five-man Housing Commission. During the previous year the Housing Commission had submitted a plan to the Detroit Common Council for public housing on twelve new sites, eight of which were vacant land. Before 1950 was over, the "Cobo Commission" had recommended that the council abandon the eight vacant sites and two of the slum sites from further consideration. The council obligingly complied, leaving only two slum sites. It appeared that, unless the court intervened, the Detroit Plan would replace the public housing program. Since the case involving the Gratiot project was pending before the Michigan Supreme Court when the union officials initiated their case, the Wayne County Circuit Court withheld a decision until the Supreme Court had acted and dismissed the case after the decision.

It had taken almost five years to acquire 129 acres, but in the process clear legal precedents had been established which would facilitate future projects. The city had spent $6,284,000 to acquire the land. This was substantially more than the $3,750,000 estimate made in 1946, and the $1,500,000 that had been made available for this purpose in the capital improvement budget had been supplemented by the issuance of tax anticipation notes in the amount of $4,784,000. But by the end of 1951, no one was much concerned about the earlier calculations and discrepancies resulting from faulty estimates. The Detroit Plan, at least that part of it that projected the ability of the city to pay for its own redevelopment, never had to be put to the test. The long-pending federal legislation finally emerged from Congress as the Housing Act of 1949 and was signed by President Harry S. Truman on July 15, 1949. The city would not have to go it alone.

The Housing Act of 1949. The Housing Act of 1949 finally clarified the financial role the federal government was prepared to play in urban redevelopment, and before the first blocks had cleared the condemnation proceedings the city found itself relieved of the necessity to finance its own program. As early as mid-1944, the Subcommittee on Housing and Urban Redevelopment of the Senate Committee on Postwar Economic Policy and Planning had initiated a comprehensive study of the housing problem. A year later, in August 1945, this committee, in a unanimous report, recommended that the postwar housing program include an extension of the public housing program begun by the Housing Act of 1937 and the establishment of financial assistance to help cities eliminate slum and blighted areas. Senators Robert F. Wagner, Allen J. Ellender, and Robert A. Taft introduced in November 1945 a bill that included the subcommittee recommendations. The

bill passed the Senate but was bottled up in the House of Representatives at the close of the Seventy-ninth Congress. Again during the Eightieth Congress a similar housing measure was passed
by the Senate but failed to get through the House. The major
point of contention was the provision for public housing, which
was receiving the brunt of a powerful campaign waged by real-
estate and building interests to convince Congress and the public
that public housing should be defeated. During the Eighty-first
Congress, after the Democrats had regained control, the Housing
Act of 1949 was finally passed, authorizing aid to local communities for slum-clearance and urban redevelopment activities and
for the extension of the public housing program.

The link between slum clearance and public housing was a
vital one. A number of arguments and positions can be noted,
but since some of these violated popular myths, it is impossible to
trace them to published sources. Nevertheless, the whispered argument with the caveat, "Don't quote me," is as powerful an influence as a published broadside. In this category was the argument
that slum clearance and public housing should go hand in hand
in order to maintain the slum population in its place. This is sometimes referred to as the ghetto or containment policy. Since the
low-income eligibles in northern urban areas such as Detroit included a large number of Negroes, the provision of public housing
on the former slum site would prevent the Negro from migrating
within the city. There were those who agreed with the containment theory in principle, but who believed it could be accomplished by private development of low-rent housing if government
would underwrite acquisition and clearance of slum land. It was
contended that this was what some of the founders of the Detroit
Plan had in mind. Thus, both supporters and opponents of public
housing, depending upon their economic views, could hold to the
containment policy.

On the other hand, there were supporters of public housing
who saw in this an opportunity to extend the principles of liberal
democracy into the housing field by providing equal opportunity
for decent housing to those unable to afford the cost of acceptable
private housing. Those holding to this view would have the sites
distributed throughout the city, on vacant as well as slum sites, in

such a way as to discourage segregation on racial or other grounds. This position became less vocal and less effective during the 1950's, as cities tended to concentrate their public housing on former slum sites and a general slowdown in the building of public housing units set in.

Finally, there were those who felt that slum clearance and urban redevelopment were necessary for urban survival. This meant that the former slum area had to be put to some other use than housing the former slum dweller, for what did it profit a city to go to the expense of redevelopment only to end up with the same population group as before, making extraordinary demands for services and returning little in the way of tax revenue. If the area were to be redeveloped for residential use, this group argued that the housing should be such that only the middle- and upper-middle-income families would be attracted to it, for only in this way would the flight to the suburbs be stemmed. To some in this group, the fate of the former slum dweller was of no concern, and some hoped he could be made to disappear simply by redeveloping slums out from under him.

The impact of these positions and arguments upon the formulation of housing legislation and later events cannot be accurately assessed here. It is clear from the following quotation that the Senate Committee on Banking and Currency, which reported out the housing bill, did consider the relationship between slum clearance and public housing but decided to keep the two separate in the bill. The following is taken from the committee's report on the Housing Act of 1949 (Report No. 84, 81st Congress, 1st Session, p. 11).

> Your committee also concurs with the findings of previous investigations that while the problems of slum clearance and of the provision of decent housing for the low-income families now living in the slums are closely related and in fact inseparable, their solution can best be undertaken through independent but closely coordinated programs. This is particularly true in view of the desirability that enlarged opportunity be given to private enterprise to participate in the redevelopment of these areas. At the same time, your committee desires to emphasize that no slum-clearance program can successfully proceed without simultaneous provision for an adequate program of low-rent public housing for low-income families, such as is provided for in the bill.

Although separating the urban redevelopment from the public housing program, the committee went on to point out that it did not intend to separate redevelopment from human values:

> The pending bill limits federal financial assistance to the assembly and clearance of areas which either are predominantly residential or will be redeveloped primarily for residential use. This limitation is fully justified in view of the fact that *the primary purpose of federal aid in this field is to help remove the impact of the slums on human lives rather than simply to assist in the redevelopment or rebuilding of cities.* (italics added)

As enacted, the Housing Act of 1949 did deal separately with urban redevelopment and public housing, leaving it to the decision of local authorities as to how the two programs should be related, if at all. Detroit did take advantage of the public housing provisions to complete two projects that had been planned since 1940 and for which the city had already acquired the land. Both of these projects—Edward J. Jeffries Homes and Frederick Douglass Homes—were located on former slum sites and, when completed in 1955, added 3,176 dwelling units to the supply of public housing, 2,170 at Jeffries and 1,006 at Douglass. But "U.R. Mich. 1-11," the only new public housing project to be initiated under the act, was delayed time and again until it was abandoned in 1960. This project was located on a slum site adjacent to, but across the Grand Trunk Western Railroad tracks from, the Gratiot project. The fate of U.R. Mich. 1-11 was related to that of U.R. Mich. 1-1.

The urban redevelopment provisions of the Housing Act of 1949 were made to order for the Detroit Plan, and they were framed with the same values in mind, viz., the encouragement of private enterprise in urban redevelopment. This was to be accomplished by assisting cities in the financing of land acquisition and preparation so that the land could be sold to private developers, and, through the extension of credit with FHA guarantees, to potential developers. Specifically, Title I of the act provided for loans to local agencies for assembly, clearance, and preparation of land for sale or lease for redevelopment. The total amount of a loan could not exceed gross project costs, and advances were authorized for surveys and plans in preparation of the project. In addition, the new law provided that the administrator of the Housing and Home Finance Agency was authorized to make capital grants to local agencies amounting to two-thirds of the net cost of preparing the land for actual construction. The net cost, of course, referred to the gross cost minus the resale value of the land. In order to qualify for benefits under the act, local government was required to (1) designate a local public agency as a coordinating body through which all urban redevelopment activities, including the sale of land, should clear; (2) prepare a redevelopment plan for the area and have it approved by the local governing body; (3) prepare a plan for the relocation of all families displaced from the project area to "decent, safe, and sanitary" dwellings; and (4) provide a public hearing prior to the acquisition of project land.

A Change in Command. Between the enactment of the federal housing legislation in July 1949 and the filing of Detroit's request on January 16, 1950, for a capital grant reservation of $4,311,440, a major political change had taken place in Detroit. At this time Detroit elected its mayor for a two-year term in non-partisan elections held on the odd years. (The term was subsequently increased to four years, but the non-partisan ballot was retained.) City Treasurer Albert Cobo and Common Council President George Edwards were the two candidates who emerged from the September primary in which incumbent Mayor Eugene Van-Antwerp had been eliminated from the November race.

George Edwards was the recognized liberal candidate and received the open endorsement of the local CIO council. His rise to political prominence—the Common Council presidency went to the candidate polling the most votes in the council election—resulted from his identification with the liberal, social policies of the New Deal and Fair Deal and from the increased political power of the labor unions. Candidate Cobo, on the other hand, had been recruited from private business during the depression of the thirties to work on the city's fiscal problems. He was later elected city treasurer and continued to win this post until deciding to enter the race for mayor. His reputation was that of a fiscal expert, or, in the words of his more enthusiastic supporters, a "wizard," but in any event there was no doubt that he was much more conservative in his political views than was Edwards. Local newspapers, especially *The Detroit News,* supported Cobo.

Part of the convention of the non-partisan election is that candidates be coy about their party affiliation. But Edwards' identification with the Democratic party was no secret, whereas Cobo maintained a more rigid non-partisan posture. The newspapers and other groups that supported Republican candidates in partisan elections supported Cobo. (In 1956 Cobo ran on the Republican ticket for governor and was defeated by the incumbent Democrat, G. Mennen Williams. Edwards was subsequently elected to the Michigan Supreme Court, after having been nominated by the state Democratic party convention.)

At the time of the Cobo-Edwards campaign, Detroit city government was poised between an orientation of the New Deal–Fair Deal type and a more conservative orientation for which no handy label is available. The structure of Detroit government is such that it provides the opportunity for a mayor determined to exercise leadership to do so. Although on organization charts a number of boards and commissions appear, the appointive and removal power of the mayor is broad enough, in most cases, to provide him with the means of exercising leadership over the bureaucracy in policy matters. Thus the election of Mayor Cobo in the fall of 1949 had a direct bearing upon the future of urban redevelopment in the city. Specifically, it meant that public housing programs were to be de-emphasized and that slum clearance leading to private development of cleared land would receive the major emphasis.

This shift in emphasis is dramatically illustrated in the following excerpts from the "Chronology of Housing Events," reported in the annual report of the Detroit Housing Commission for the period July 1949 through June 1950:

July 15—President Harry S. Truman signs the Housing Act of 1949.
August 8—Housing Commission passes Resolution 88 approving application to PHA [Public Housing Administration] for a two-year reservation of 14,350 permanent low-rent units.
December 14—Housing Commission holds annual meeting, with Mayor VanAntwerp, Mayor-elect Cobo, and members of the newly elected Common Council as guests.

December 22—James H. Inglis resigns as director-secretary of the Housing Commission, effective January 3, 1950.

January 4—Harry J. Durbin appointed director-secretary of the Housing Commission.

January 19—Common Council authorizes Housing Commission to make application to Housing and Home Finance Agency for two-year program reservation of $4,311,440 in capital grants for slum clearance and urban redevelopment under Title I of the Housing Act of 1949.

January 24—Common Council deletes Site No. 11 from the city's public low-rent housing program.

February 3—Housing and Home Finance Agency grants Detroit a two-year reservation of $4,311,430 for slum clearance.

February 10—Mayor Cobo appoints Robert L. Berry and Walter J. Gessell to the Housing Commission to replace H. V. Babcock and Remie Cools, who resigned.

February 22—Housing Commission votes to recommend to Common Council deleting all remaining vacant sites from the city's low-rent housing program, approving Sites No. 1, 2, and 3 and making further study of Site No. 4.

March 8—Mayor Cobo appoints George A. Isabell to the Housing Commission to replace Rev. Robert L. Bradby, who was removed by the mayor on March 7.

March 14—Common Council, on recommendation of Housing Commission, deletes Sites No. 5, 6, 7, 7A, 8, 9, and 10 from the city's public housing program, approves No. 1, 2, and 3, and takes No. 4 under advisement.

April 17—Housing Commission requests preliminary site approval of Site No. 2 (Mich. 1-11) from the Public Housing Administration.

April 24—Common Council designates Housing Commission as the city's official agency to administer slum clearance and redevelopment under Housing Act of 1949.

May 2—Upon recommendation of Housing Commission, Common Council deletes Site No. 4 from the city's public housing program.

May 31—Public Housing Administration gives tentative site approval to Site No. 2 (Mich. 1-11) to provide for 3,840 public low-rent housing units.

June 1—City of Detroit takes title to first ten blocks of Gratiot redevelopment area.

June 29—Housing Commission recommends to Common Council deleting Site No. 3 from the city's low-rent housing program, designating it for private redevelopment under Title I of the Housing Act of 1949.

The deletion of the vacant sites for public housing, all of which were located in outlying areas of the city, meant that low-income families would continue to be concentrated in the city's core area, and the elimination of the projects slated for slum sites meant that public housing would not be used as a vehicle for slum clearance. Thus, these decisions meant that projects such as Gratiot would have to bear the brunt of urban redevelopment to accommodate low-income families.

With the federal approval of the capital grant reservation in hand, the designation of the Detroit Housing Commission as the Local Public Agency (the co-ordinating body for local dealings with the federal government on redevelopment), and an eager mayor at the helm, Detroit seemed all set to sail. But having accepted the federal capital grant reservation for the Gratiot project, a new dimension had been added to decision-making. Decisions from now on had to clear with the Housing and Home Finance Agency (HHFA) in Washington to assure that the conditions established by the Housing Act were fulfilled. The two conditions that were to prove most demanding to city officials were the requirement that a redevelopment plan be prepared that would receive local approval, meet federal standards, and at the same time create conditions of land use attractive to private capital, and the requirement that adequate provision be made for the relocation of families displaced through the demolition of slum dwellings. Although the efforts to satisfy these two conditions went on simultaneously, here they will be dealt with separately.

Relocation

Relocation Problems. On November 7, 1950, demolition began on the Gratiot site with the razing of two buildings on Mullett Street. With this activity begun, it was necessary to find new homes for the residents in the area; the responsibility for this was placed on the Detroit Housing Commission. This assignment involved a number of practical difficulties which were not eased by the federal requirement that local agencies submit a relocation plan acceptable to HHFA prior to the granting of funds. As a preliminary to the preparation of this plan, the commission staff conducted a survey of the area, interviewing 1,953 families and 989 single persons.

The survey was conducted in May 1950. In presenting the table on responses to questions concerning the relocation plans of families, the staff survey reported:

> It did not appear that plans for redevelopment of the area had progressed far enough to result in any feeling on the part of its residents that clearance of the area was imminent. The vast majority of families had not even begun to think about relocation. Many families, especially subtenants, did not know that the area was under condemnation, or at best had heard only vague rumors about it.

Relocation Plans	Number	Percentage
Total families	1,953	100.0
Definitely plan to buy a home	91	4.7
Public housing (eligible families only)	1,005	51.3
Not interested in public housing (but eligible)	60	3.1
Move in with relatives	11	.6
Leave town	5	.3
Other plans	8	.4
No plans, or expect to find private rental quarters	752	38.5
No record	21	1.1

From the above it will be seen that about three families in five are either eligible for public housing, plan to buy a home, or have other plans. The remaining two-fifths of the families—virtually all of whom are ineligible for public housing—form the most difficult part of the relocation problem, since most of them have incomes and assets too low to be able to purchase homes.

A most significant statistic missing from the above table is that virtually all of the familes were Negro. There seemed to be some official reluctance to report the racial composition of the area, although the most popular figure was "98 percent or more" Negro. The survey reported that 24 percent of the families had an annual income, including income from rentals, of less than $2,000, and 76 percent earned less than $3,500 a year. Nearly one-fifth of the families (18.5 percent) received public assistance.

These were the families for which the Housing Commission had to meet the conditions stipulated in Section 105(c) of the Housing Act of 1949, viz., that there be a feasible method for their relocation in housing that was "decent, safe, and sanitary . . . at rents and prices within [their] financial means . . . and reasonably accessible to their places of employment." This section further provided that in view of [the] existing acute housing shortage, each such contract entered into prior to July 1, 1951, shall further provide that there be no demolition of residential structures in connection with the project assisted under the contract prior to July 1, 1951, if the local governing body determines that the demolition thereof would reasonably be expected to create undue housing hardship in the locality.

The relocation provisions of Title I are indicative of conflicting values implicit in the urban redevelopment program. On the one hand, Congress was willing to assist local communities with their slum clearance for other than public housing, but on the other hand, Congress did not want the displaced slum dweller to suffer under this program. Presumably, Section 105(c) would take care of that.

The Detroit Housing Commission had had some experience in relocation with its public housing projects built on former slum sites, but most of this experience was prior to the acute housing shortage following World War II. Moreover, relocation in such cases was a temporary condition for many of the families, who would become eligible for the new public housing. The 1949–50 annual report of the commission described the relocation of families from the Jeffries and Douglass public housing sites: "The tools used for accomplishing this task were the simple ones of daily contact plus the pressure of written notices to vacate followed by court action." Here the main concern was to empty houses in order to proceed with demolition. What happened to former residents was of no official concern to the commission unless eligibility for public housing was involved. The commission staff did, however, attempt to assist families in their relocation efforts through conferences with them and through Negro community organizations, such as the Detroit Urban League. These efforts were, nevertheless, minimal. The relocation plan required in order to qualify for federal funds for the Gratiot project was the commission's first experience with detailed planning of relocation.

The Relocation Plan. According to those close to the administration of the relocation process, the relocation plan, which was prepared by the newly formed Redevelopment Division of the Housing Commission, had little relationship to what was actually taking place. The responsibility for carrying out relocation was assigned to another division of the commission. Nevertheless, a formal relocation program for the Gratiot project was prepared by February 26, 1951, and submitted to federal housing officials. The plan described what appeared to be insurmountable problems facing Negroes in search of housing in Detroit, but it ended on an optimistic note:

> It can be determined that there are or are being provided areas in the city of Detroit not generally less desirable in regard to public utilities and public and commercial facilities and at rents or prices within the financial means of the families displaced, decent, safe, and sanitary dwellings equal in number to the number of displaced families. . . .

The housing needs of the relocation families can be divided into three categories: public housing for those eligible, private homes for sale to those willing and able to buy, and rental units for the remainder. The commission survey showed that over half of the families were eligible for public housing and presumably would be so housed as units became available. It is, therefore, interesting to look at the summary of applications and placements in public housing units reported in the annual report of the Housing Commission for the eighteen-month period from July 1950 through December 1951. During this period 3,175 public housing units were leased to white families and 648 to Negro families. At the beginning of the period, the waiting list of eligibles contained 2,247 white families and 5,226 Negro. By the end of the period, the white waiting list had been reduced to 574, while the Negro waiting list had grown to 7,571. The Housing Commission was under fire from Negro organizations for maintaining racial segregation in its projects and thus preventing Negro eligibles from receiving an equitable share of available units. It was the expressed hope of the commission that the two public housing projects then in progress, Douglass and Jeffries, would absorb some of the relocation load. That the commission was giving priority to relocation families among the Negro eligibles is evident from the report that of the 648 Negro families granted leases, 550 were classified as relocation families. These data show that the need for public housing units for Negroes, as represented by the commission's own eligibility list, was very great, and that the policy of giving priority to relocation families was merely increasing the pressure. Perhaps these data help to explain why only 659 families from the Gratiot project site were eventually relocated in permanent public housing units.

The relocation plan submitted by the Housing Commission was more concerned with the availability of housing for the other two categories, i.e., those seeking to buy or rent homes. With regard to those intending to buy a home—ninety-one families had indicated this intent—it was pointed out in the plan that although some thirty-five thousand new homes had been built in the Detroit metropolitan area during 1950, their prices were beyond the reach of most relocation families, and the homes were located in areas not available for Negro occupancy. In spite of this, the plan went on to explain, available housing would trickle down to the Negro buyer.

In Detroit there is an ample supply of units provided from vacancies in housing which meet all the other conditions of the section (105[c]) . . . except for the one qualification of availability. These units have been occupied by white persons and because of restrictive covenants, subdivision restrictions, racial attitudes, or personal preference, were not available for Negro occupancy. Each year some of this housing supply has become available for Negro occupancy. . . . Since the Supreme Court ruling in 1949 regarding the legal unenforceability of restrictive covenants, the acquisition or possession by Negroes of homes formerly restricted to white occupancy has accelerated. It is reasonably estimated that over thirty thousand dwelling units were occupied by Negroes for the first time during the last decade. It is submitted that as diminishing segregation makes housing for the first time available to Negroes, it constitutes a provision of housing that meets the requirements of Section 105(c). The change in occupancy means that units, more than enough in number of families displaced, at rents or prices within the means of the families displaced, safe, decent, and sanitary, and accessible to places of employment, are being provided.

It was estimated in the plan that a two-bedroom house meeting the required standards would cost $8,500, require a down payment of $2,000, and that monthly costs, including principal, interest, taxes, and maintenance, would total $102. There were no accurate data available on the ability of the intended purchasers to pay for homes of this quality or better. This was due in part to the fact that the survey had been conducted before condemnation awards had been made, and for some families the ability to purchase would depend on the size of the condemnation award they would receive for their property. For the twenty or so families about whom there was information, the picture looked gloomy, since none of these reported being able to pay over $80.00 a month.

The rental outlook for the 752 families ineligible for public housing and not intending to buy homes was equally discouraging. The efforts of the commission to locate rentals were described in the relocation plan as follows:

> On May 6, 1950, the Detroit Real Estate Brokers Association, comprised of Negro real-estate brokers, was asked to give its cooperation and help to the Housing Commission in finding rental accommodations, for the large number of ineligible [for public housing] Negro families. . . . The association replied . . . [that] "the relocation job you have given us is an impossible one. We simply do not have the available vacancies. We not only do not have listings to make available to families displaced by slum clearance, we do not even have listings to take care of our own regular applicants who have been waiting for vacancies for many months. . . . It would be foolish and hypocritical for us to pretend that we are assisting the Housing Commission in this relocation job when in fact we find it impossible to do so. . . ."

Later that same year, in December 1950, the president of the Detroit Real Estate Brokers Association was contacted again and was asked if there had been any change in the Negro housing situation. He reported no change. There was no rental housing available, although there was a fifty-two-unit development under construction. The rentals in this project would begin at $80.00 per month for one-bedroom units.

The Housing Commission staff conducted a survey of sixteen major property-management companies and sixteen apartment buildings with a combined capacity of 11,378 dwelling units. It was found that only three vacancies existed. Six of the property-management companies and nine apartment buildings reported a combined total of 750 names on their waiting lists.

As the following information, obtained by the 1950 relocation survey, shows, the rent-paying ability of the families in the project area would put most of the families in a poor position when it came to bargaining for scarce rental units.

Monthly Rent-paying Ability	All Families	Families Ineligible for Public Housing
Total families	1953*	843
Less than $10	31	3
$10–19	217	13
20–29	258	15
30–39	198	14
40–49	317	96
50–59	381	275
60–69	260	211
70–79	112	86
80–89	52	38
90 and over	83	59
No record	44	33

*The figure for the total number of families that was used in Housing Commission records changed over succeeding years, as will be noted ·in later charts.

In the face of these apparent obstacles, the relocation plan submitted by the commission concluded that it would be possible for those ineligible for public housing to find acceptable housing from the following sources: new rental housing being built; conversion of existing housing; rental vacancies listed in newspapers and by agencies; listings for relocation families by special arrangement with real-estate brokers; unlisted vacancies through friends, relatives, etc.; merging with other families; new houses for sale; and finding used houses. The reasoning in the relocation plan must have been convincing to HHFA, for on April 18, 1952 that agency entered into a contract with the Detroit Housing Commission, acting as the Local Public Agency, for carrying out the Gratiot project under Title I of the Housing Act. Under the provisions of the act, the contract could not have been signed had not the HHFA approved the relocation plan. Federal officials were later to have some qualms over relocation.

The Relocation Process. The physical relocation of families from the Gratiot site did not await the filing of the relocation plan or the approval of federal authorities, although from the provisions of Title I it would seem that relocation should not have begun prior to the approval of the plan. The position assumed by Detroit officials was that since the Gratiot project antedated the

Housing Act, relocation was begun as if this were an exclusively local project; but the provisions of Section 105(c) would be followed, so that when the anticipated approval was forthcoming, it would be found that Detroit had complied with the conditions established by the act. This position could be defended on the grounds that Detroit was eager to get started, and since relocation under the conditions stipulated in the act was something new, it would require some experience on the part of local agencies before workable procedures could be developed. In any event, by the time the relocation plan was prepared in February 1951, close to four hundred families had been relocated, and by the time the contract was signed with HHFA in April 1952, over a thousand families had been relocated.

When relocation began on September 18, 1950, the prospect facing the Detroit Housing Commission Relocation Office staff was not very encouraging. Their orders were to move the residents, but no one said where, except that the new quarters should be decent, safe, and sanitary. In spite of the large number of eligibles, there were very few public housing units available to Negroes. In fact, the first eighteen units of the Douglass project were not occupied by Gratiot families until September 1951, and the first units of the Jeffries project were not completed until November 1952. To add to the public housing shortage, the dismantling of temporary units built during World War II had begun.

The staff member assigned to the relocation job had obtained his experience in relocating families from the Jeffries and Douglass sites, where the number of families was smaller than the number involved in Gratiot, and where temporary relocations were acceptable, since many families would be moving back into the scheduled public housing units. The Gratiot site was an entirely different problem. The official policy was that the Gratiot site would be redeveloped with apartments and homes within the financial reach of many of the area residents, but the Relocation Office staff did not take this very seriously, for they were well aware of the difference between rent-paying capacity of the residents and the rentals that would have to be charged under private development. It would have been possible to arrange on-site relocations for some families while part of the site was being

cleared and rebuilt for their occupancy if they could have afforded
to return. This was, in fact, one of the relocation techniques suggested in the plan filed with HHFA, but it was not feasible in
view of the probable cost of housing in the rebuilt area. As it
turned out, a number of on-site relocations were necessary in
order to make way for the demolition crews, but these relocations
had to be followed up with permanent relocations in order to
satisfy the conditions of the act.

While the relocation plan was being prepared, little effort was
made to relate the plan to what was actually taking place on the
site. One member of the Relocation Office staff stated that the plan
was confidential and that nothing about it was revealed to this
staff, except for the suggestion of on-site relocations. It appears
that the plan was more an argument designed to convince federal
officials of the feasibility of relocation than an operating plan for
the relocation staff. Apparently, there was no direct contact between the Redevelopment Division of the commission and the
Relocation Office staff, which was located in another division,
Tenant Selection. During the years 1950 and 1951, a number of
organizational and personnel shifts were made within the commission staff. This was due in part to the assumption of control
by Mayor Cobo's appointee Durbin and by the number of new
responsibilities that arose with the redevelopment programs. Since
the professional staff was small (about thirty people), personnel
shifts were as important as, if not commensurate to, shifts in organizational structure. With the de-emphasis of public housing
under Cobo and Durbin and the opening up of redevelopment
made possible by the Housing Act, it was easy to understand why
staff members were eager to assume key spots in the newer,
expanding program.

The relocation procedures were quite simple. The first step
was to notify residents by letter that the city was planning to clear
the area for redevelopment and to offer assistance to any who
needed it in seeking a new home. This was designed to motivate
the most mobile of the renters to find new quarters. After condemnation of a given area, each family in that area was notified
that the city was now their legal landlord and that rents were to
be paid to a management office located on the site. An attempt

was made to prohibit the acquiring of new subtenants, but it was unsuccessful because many of the families in the demolition blocks had to move to other on-site units for want of any other place to go. The rental notice advised tenants that they would be "notified in writing in ample time to vacate your unit." This letter, which was signed by the manager of the Gratiot Redevelopment Office, implied no urgency. (It was suggested that some officials wanted to keep tenants until as close to demolition time as possible in order to have some revenue to show for the area.)

There was no question concerning the urgency expressed in the letter sent over the signature of Director-Secretary Durbin to all residents of blocks designated for clearance. The letter began by informing the residents that their block would be cleared and that formal notice to vacate would be forthcoming, but went on to urge them to look for housing in the meantime. The letter continued:

We urge you to keep the following points in mind:
1. Income limits for permanent low-rent housing are:

Number of Children under 21 Years	Top Income Allowed (Yearly)
None	$2,480
1 or 2	2,760
3 or 4	2,980
5 or more	3,312

2. Veterans of World War II with incomes too high for permanent housing may be placed in veterans' projects located throughout the city. We must see the veteran's discharge papers or other proof of service if he is to be placed in this housing.
3. Vacancies becoming available in other areas of the redevelopment area will be utilized for temporary relocations if necessary. Assistance will be rendered all families temporarily relocated so that no undue hardships will result.
4. The city recognizes that there is a housing shortage. For this reason, the relocation staff will assist families in finding private housing. The Construction Industry Council will also cooperate in this respect.
5. We do not wish to "put anyone out on the street," and will make every effort to find a place for all our tenants. At the same time, we must tell you that there is not a wide choice of location or type of housing. All residents of the block you reside in should make every possible effort to find housing on the private market.
6. We urge that you move as soon as possible. Delay will only in-

crease your problem as vacancies in public housing projects are limited and only a few families can be placed during any one month.

7. In asking you to move, the city is clearly within its rights because it owns the houses in which you live. They were purchased in full accordance with proper legal procedure. The rights of all former owners and present tenants have been and will be observed.

SOME FACTS YOU SHOULD KNOW
ABOUT THE REDEVELOPMENT PROGRAM

The area you live in will be completely cleared. Some of the land will be set aside for parks, playfields, recreation centers, schools, expressways, and commercial facilities. The balance of the land will be sold to private industry for construction of new buildings in accordance with an approved plan. A new, modern community, designed to meet present-day standards for good living, will be erected on the site.

Many hundreds of new dwellings will be built. Some of it will be rental housing and some will be available for purchase. Many of you will undoubtedly move back into the area when redevelopment is completed, as either renters or owners of a dwelling.

Redevelopment of this area (and others also) is important to all the citizens of Detroit. The time is now here so that an area of substandard, obsolete, and hazardous houses, badly overcrowded and lacking in community facilities, can be removed and replaced by a new, modern, complete community built to present-day standards to meet present-day needs.

We are counting on your cooperation to bring about this important change.

Following this notice, a survey was made of the families living in the clearance blocks to determine how many were eligible for public housing. Eligible families were then given notice to appear at the Relocation Office to file an application for public housing. Failure to apply relieved the city of any further responsibility for that family. All families eligible for public housing but not filing an application, along with families ineligible for public housing, were sent a sixty-day eviction notice. (Commercial establishments in an immediate clearance area were given a thirty-day eviction notice.) At the end of the sixty-day period, families who had not moved were taken to court. Those who had been offered some housing and refused it were given a notice to terminate occupancy by a specific date. (The relocation staff reported that no one was evicted if the monthly rental fees were paid, but a few were evicted for non-payment.) Families who had not been offered housing were given an extension of time to find suitable quarters. Although there were numerous exceptions, this was the general procedure followed.

The Detroit Urban League, an organization concerned with preventing discriminatory practices against Negroes and including among its members prominent citizens of both races, assigned members of its staff to observe the relocation process. In April 1951, the league issued a report on the relocation of the first 258 families from a six-block section. The report concluded that (1) through court action seeking writs of eviction, the city had attempted "to pressure and harass the families into moving and accepting any type of accommodations"; (2) the Housing Commission had not only failed to notify site occupants of its responsibilities to assist them but had also circulated letters "implying" that they must move and had failed to offer housing opportunities; (3) families moving into other areas were transplanting the same doubling-up and sharing pattern that previously existed; (4) undue hardship was placed upon families who were living from one payday to the next and could not afford the expense of moving; (5) temporary relocation on-site placed families in units which were not safe, sanitary, and decent; and (6) the supply of "fair marginal" private housing available to families relocating themselves was so limited that it would prevent subsequent relocation. The league backed up its findings with a number of case studies.

Housing Director Durbin labeled the report biased and only half-true, and his assistant, Mark Herley, produced statistics showing that out of 450 families displaced at that date (April 5, 1951), the commission had discharged its responsibility for 320: 58 had purchased homes, 120 were placed in permanent public housing, 53 were given temporary housing, and 89 were unknown. But these denials and statistics did not deter the Urban League from directing its complaint to federal housing officials. In response to suggestions from Washington, the local housing staff prepared a letter stating in simple language the provisions of Section 105(c), which advised families not to move unless they could "move to a suitable place which is: Safe, decent, sanitary. At a cost they can afford. Within traveling distance of work. No doubling up." The letter urged everyone to look for a place on his own when the time came to move, but it went on to say:

> The Detroit Housing Commission Relocation Office will help people find places. The Relocation Office will visit everyone who should move to find out what help is needed. Then they will talk about other places, too. They will call again and again, as long as necessary, until a place is found. The Relocation Office is at 1510 Gratiot, and there is someone present to answer any question anyone may have.
>
> Sometimes people will have to make a temporary move. A temporary move is to any place which is not suitable and means that the family can move again when suitable housing can be had. But no one will be asked to move to worse housing. People should go and look at any place they know they can move to. They should take the place if it is suitable or take it on a temporary basis if it is livable and as good as where they are living.

To determine whether or not the Section 105(c) conditions were being met, the Relocation Office staff applied the following criteria: (1) There should be no sharing of kitchen or bath by more than one family unless it is impossible to do otherwise. (2) The rental fee should not be greater than 25 percent of gross income. (3) The dwelling unit should not be more than ten miles from the place of work of the head wage earner in the household. (4) The bathroom should have three pieces of plumbing. (5) No building violations should exist. (6) The dwelling unit must have hot and cold running water. The Relocation Office staff considered these to be ideal rather than practical standards, and they claimed that if they had followed them to the letter there would have been very little relocation. As was pointed out, if housing of this quality did exist at rents these families could afford, Detroit would have had no need for an elaborate slum-clearance program.

The new informational letter seemed to satisfy HHFA officials that relocation families were being notified of their rights under the Housing Act. Throughout 1951, the Relocation Office staff managed to keep ahead of the demolition crews, and in the fall the Housing Commission hired two real-estate men to work with the Relocation Office staff as housing expediters. Their specific task was to find private rentals "which families in the middle-income groups can afford and which meet the decent, safe, and sanitary standards necessary for relocation families." Summarizing the relocation progress as of the end of 1951, the commission reported:

> Fifty-one percent of the . . . families in the Gratiot redevelopment area had been relocated by the end of 1951. Approximately 30 percent of the families relocated were placed in permanent low-rent public housing. Eight percent were placed in temporary housing operated by the commission. The remaining 62 percent were relocated to private rental or sale housing. 11 percent of the total of 1,043 families purchased homes. 10 percent rented permanent quarters in privately owned units and 6 percent rented temporary quarters in private housing.
>
> Thirty-five percent of the total number of families relocated were classified as unknown. Some families refused to accept the assistance of the Housing Commission staff and found quarters for themselves without notifying the commission. Other families moved out of town in the wake of rising unemployment and some families just neglected to inform the staff at the time they moved. Vigorous efforts are made to follow up these unknown cases in order to ensure that the provisions of the 1949 Housing Act relating to safe and sanitary dwellings for relocatees are followed.

Early in 1952, federal officials became concerned over the large proportion (35 percent) of processed families that were classified as "unknown." How could assurance be given that these families had been rehoused as intended by the legislation? In order to answer this question, an intensive search was begun in the spring of 1952 and continued through June to locate as many as possible of the relocated families. This search confirmed the hunches of the Relocation Office staff that most of the displaced families had moved within a mile or so of the project site, viz., they had remained in the most densely populated Negro slum area of the city. Of the 540 families accounted for in this survey, 441 had moved into this adjacent area, where 224 rented units, 91 purchased homes, and 126 were classified as temporary relocations. All of the remaining 99 families had moved into established Negro neighborhoods more removed from the projected area. The commission reported the following relocation summary as of July 18, 1952:

Total Relocation Load	Number of Families
Total Families	1,952
Total families for whom relocation responsibility is discharged	1,301
A. On-site	
Refused suitable housing	47
B. Off-site	
(a) Refused suitable housing	130
(b) Rented permanent public housing	462
(c) Rented standard private housing	90
(d) Purchased homes	179
(e) Moved to avoid paying rent (more than one month)	39
(f) Unable to trace after diligent search	23
(g) Moved voluntarily after receipt of informational letter	331

During the latter part of 1952, HHFA provided a list of conditions of what constituted proper relocation, which included the following:

(1) Families relocated in standard housing, including low-rent permanent public housing and private rental units;
(2) Families purchasing homes;
(3) Families refusing offers of standard housing at moderate rentals in neighborhoods accessible to employment and community facilities;
(4) Families who moved to avoid paying rent for more than one month;
(5) Families moving after receipt of a registered letter informing them of their rights and privileges under the Housing Act; and
(6) Families who moved leaving no forwarding address and who cannot be located after a diligent search.

Although by the fall of 1952 the Division of Slum Clearance and Urban Redevelopment of HHFA had developed the above conditions of proper relocation, they had very little information at this time about how, in fact, relocation was working. This is indicated in a letter sent to Director-Secretary Durbin by C. L. Farris, acting for the director of the division. The letter, dated September 12, 1952, said in part:

The Division of Slum Clearance and Urban Redevelopment has from time to time received requests for information concerning the manner in which families being displaced from redevelopment project areas have been rehoused, and how such families had been affected by their removal from homes which they had formerly occupied.

As you know, this division has been very diligent in seeing to it that the provisions of Section 105(c) of Title I of the Housing Act of 1949 are fully adhered to. This should prevent any displaced families from being subject to undue hardship as a result of relocation. However, it has been made amply clear in many cities that families about to be displaced from project areas anticipate great inconvenience and hardship; as a result they frequently make appearances at public hearings to object to programs formulated by Local Public Agencies for their relocation.

In our judgment, the best way to find out whether or not there is any basis for such concern on the part of families to be displaced is by an impartial study of what has actually happened in the relocation of families from projects whether completed or well under way. Once the facts are ascertained, they will show either that fears are groundless or that additional steps need to be taken to eliminate evident weaknesses in the relocation process.

Your city is one of the few which have progressed far enough in urban redevelopment to justify objective review of its relocation operation. In our opinion, this review should be done locally and by the most reputable and impartial source possible. Probably a college or university conveniently located would be the most acceptable source.

The study should be set up to produce answers to at least the following questions:

(1) Do members of the displaced families feel they received proper counseling service prior to moving?

(2) Do they feel that they were put under undue pressure to move through threat of eviction or by any other means?

(3) Do they feel that they have suffered financial loss as a result of relocation; if so, in what respect?

(4) To what extent does their present housing conform to the provisions of Section 105(c)?

(5) Have they been forced to pay an excessive proportion of their income for rent or purchase of their new accommodations?

(6) Has relocation resulted in the overcrowding of the areas adjacent to the project area, thus creating the basis for future deterioration?

(7) Have aged single persons and couples encountered unusual difficulties in finding new dwellings?

(8) Have families found difficulty in continuing membership in their former churches or in joining new ones? Has rehousing resulted in depriving families of the use of public facilities formerly available, such as public libraries, social centers, and other recreational facilities?

(9) Are a substantial number now located at a much greater distance from their usual jobs?

(10) Have single persons and childless couples maintaining an independent housekeeping establishment been forced to move into single furnished rooms or to double up with married children or relatives?

(11) How has the sense of security of the displaced families been affected by relocation?

(12) Do they feel that their relocation was unnecessary or unjustified, or that it has placed upon them undue hardship of any kind? Do professional men or businessmen feel that they have been treated with unnecessary severity by the relocation process?

These and similar questions need to be answered in order that we may have a comprehensive view of how the displaced families have fared through relocation and what their attitude is toward the urban redevelopment program. Special care should be taken to secure detailed information from any racial minority families which may be involved. They are apt to have the greatest difficulty in finding satisfactory rehousing. Particular care should be exercised to ascertain whether or not these families were subject to greater hardship than others; and if so, what must be done to minimize such hardship in future relocation operations.

The letter raised the points that had been made by critics of the relocation process in Detroit, and it focused upon the problem areas faced by the relocation staff. If answers could be obtained to these questions, much of the conjecture and guesswork surrounding the relocation process would be dispelled.

Following the suggestion made in the letter, Durbin's assistant, Mark Herley, contacted Charles B. Brink, the dean of the School of Social Work at Wayne University (now Wayne State University), located in Detroit. Dean Brink arranged a meeting between members of the Housing Commission staff and a small group of faculty who, he thought, might be interested in such a project. After a number of meetings with commission staff members, including Durbin, and representatives of the Division of Slum Clearance and Urban Redevelopment of HHFA, the faculty group sent a letter to Durbin on December 30, 1952, proposing that two of its members undertake a study of the relocation process which would "focus primarily on the people who experienced the relocation process. . . . compare and evaluate the living conditions of these people before and after relocation. . . . examine the relocation process itself, and . . . attempt to appraise the attitudes toward relocation of those who were involved." A sociologist and a political scientist would staff the study. Durbin forwarded the proposal to Washington, and on January 22, 1953, the Division of Slum Clearance and Urban Redevelopment gave approval to expending the necessary funds to carry out the study. In order to justify the expenditure ($9,882), the study was considered "necessitated by the difficulty of relocating the 196 families still remaining in the Gratiot area which represent the hard core of the relocation problem for that project."

Following approval from Washington, a contract was drawn up between the City of Detroit and Wayne University for carrying out the study. At the insistence of the researchers and the university, a clause was included providing that "the university shall have full freedom of publication of the results of the research under this agreement." When first presented with this clause, the Housing Commission staff was somewhat disquieted, but it finally agreed to it. At the close of the contract sessions, the faculty personnel assumed that all disagreements had been settled and that all that remained was the formality of signing the document. Time was important, for the study was to begin during the semester beginning in February, and some adjustments in class scheduling had to be made to arrange for released staff time. It soon became apparent that the contract would not be signed by February, and then it became evident that it would never be signed.

The university received no official explanation of the city's decision not to sign the document. Members of the staff of the Housing Commission said that the Detroit corporation counsel refused to approve it because of the clause providing freedom of publication, but no official opinion to that effect was submitted to university officials. The most obvious deduction from these events was that some city official or officials balked at having a survey conducted, the results of which were certain to be made public regardless of the findings. The officials who would have been most affected by the study were the secretary-director of the Housing Commission, his top staff, the Housing Commission, and the mayor.

Washington's reaction to the scuttling of the study was unknown. One speculation was that the original request for the study was the result of pressure upon HHFA from Negro and various liberal groups, and that the Housing Commission staff went through the motions of complying but took the first opportunity to kill the project on a technicality, thus removing the onus from both the federal and the local agency. This strategy, it was conjectured, was related to the Republican victory in the November 1952 elections and an anticipated change in HHFA's attitude to one more congenial to the Detroit Plan. But none of this can be proven. The fact remains that no study was conducted by a "reputable and impartial source" to answer questions concerning relocation in Detroit.

By the end of 1952, all but 196 families had been moved from the project site. These were the families that represented the "hard core of the relocation problem" referred to above. Included were large families, those unable to purchase homes, or those generally unfavorable as tenants. By this time, haste was not necessary. It had become evident that no developer was going to snatch up the land and start rebuilding immediately. Time and normal attrition were now on the side of those responsible for relocation. By February 1956, the commission could report the site completely cleared, and there remained, on off-site locations, only eight families for whom the commission had some relocation responsibility. With the exception of these eight families, this was the final relocation scoreboard:

Refused suitable housing	483
Rented permanent public housing	659
Rented permanent private housing	116
Purchased homes	226
Moved to avoid paying rent (more than one month)	50
Unable to trace after diligent search	279
Moved off site owing money (less than one month rent)	137

Since the Housing Commission was not required by federal regulation to assume a similar relocation responsibility for single persons, no data were available on their relocation. Staff members were queried early in 1959 to determine if they had more complete data on the disposition of the Gratiot families, but they maintained that everything they had was contained in the above table. The urban renewal co-ordinator did add, however, that it was his guess that most of the former project residents lived within a radius of two miles of the Gratiot site. No one ever did get the answers to HHFA's questions as they applied to the Gratiot project. But if most of the relocated families, other than those in public housing, did move to the area immediately adjacent to the Gratiot site, they moved into slum dwellings comparable to those they left. That the City Plan Commission had designated much of this area for redevelopment testified to a state of deterioration and blight severe enough to qualify the area for redevelopment funds. If these redevelopment plans were to be carried out, some of the Gratiot families would have another crack at the relocation process.

The Redevelopment Plan

Redevelopment for Whom? The main objective of the Detroit Plan, an objective shared by Title I of the Housing Act of 1949, was to provide an opportunity for private enterprise to play a major role in urban redevelopment. This could be accomplished only if the permissible uses of the land to be made available would yield a profit to the developer. But profitable private development was not an unrestricted value. There were other values to be taken into account in order to provide acceptable living conditions and prevent a relapse to the former slum condition. A most important consideration from the point of view of the developer was the market for which he was to provide housing, since the housing purchasing power of his market would condition the amount of investment in each dwelling unit. If the market were to consist of low-income families, then the developer would have to manipulate densities and construction-cost factors in such a manner as to produce profitable housing on a given amount of land. If, in addition to the fixed market consisting of low-income families, density and quality restrictions were placed upon the developer, he might decide that these restrictions did not provide conditions under which he could produce profitable housing. On the other hand, if the restriction on the market were removed and the developer were free to build for any market he could attract, while at the same time meeting density and other restrictions, the developer must then consider whether the location and type of housing provided would be desired by the market for which it was intended. These were some of the elementary economic considerations involved in any investment in housing developments, and they were weighed by lending institutions providing loans as well as by FHA officials if their insuring facilities were involved.

That the Gratiot site should be redeveloped for residential use was never seriously questioned. The persistent question was, For whom? In his presentation of the Detroit Plan before the American Society of Planning Officials in 1947, the then director-secretary of the Housing Commission, Charles Edgecomb, said:

> As we face this problem realistically we must recognize that our first humane obligation is to rehouse those presently living in the area planned for redevelopment. This, of course, means low-rent housing, but there is another important factor that we must consider —that is the desire of many middle-income groups to live close to the downtown area. These people should be provided for, and, in doing so, we minimize the danger of establishing economic ghettos through our redevelopment program.

He also pointed out that although some "extremists" felt that the city should take out the property needed for municipal improvements and auction off the rest to the highest bidder for development without restrictions, he preferred to "set up a committee composed of representatives of the Building Department [Department of Building and Safety Engineering], the City Plan Commission, and the Housing Commission to check proposals of potential builders in the area to see that they conform with broad specifications as to density, architecture, and land coverage." The intention was to provide housing for both low- and middle-income families, and since almost all of the families on the site were Negro, the reference to avoiding "economic ghettos" could be interpreted as referring to racial ghettos. This view, then, contemplated mixed occupancy of the site in terms of income and race, but it was impossible to determine how many in the community agreed with this viewpoint. Some felt that a racial ghetto was precisely what was needed to keep the Negro population in place, and others felt that housing appealing to middle- and upper-income families was needed in order to insure an all-white development. Certainly, the views expressed by Edgecomb came closer to expressing publicly acceptable values than did the other two positions.

Prior to the passage of the Housing Act in 1949, no specific plans had been agreed upon for the area. Litigation had held up condemnation, so that by the time the city was ready to proceed, it was necessary to clear the redevelopment plans with federal officials in order to qualify for funds. The City Plan Commission was the city agency responsible for developing the plan. In structure, this agency was comparable to the Housing Commission. Its nine commissioners were appointed by the mayor, and the director-secretary was the executive officer responsible to the commission for the direction and performance of the staff. Since the Housing Commission had been designated by the Common Council as the Local Public Agency for dealing with Washington, the commission had to forward all plans to HHFA officials; but this channeling of documents did not place the Plan Commission staff in a subordinate position to the Housing Commission staff. On the contrary, the planning staff considered itself better qualified professionally to deal with the broad problems of urban redevelopment than the housing staff, which up to that time had been primarily engaged in building and managing public housing projects. During the period from 1949 to 1955, both agencies were undergoing important changes. Both obtained new directors (Housing in 1950, City Plan in 1953), and urban renewal became the principal concern of both.

The Plan Commission was responsible for formulating a redevelopment plan, which, together with the relocation plan drawn up by the Housing Commission, had to be accepted by HHFA if Detroit was to obtain the $4,311,440 capital grant reservation for slum clearance and urban redevelopment that had been approved by HHFA in February 1950. The redevelopment plan had to show that (1) the financial aid requested was necessary in order to redevelop the land in the project area according to the redevelopment plan; (2) maximum opportunity, "consistent with the sound needs of the locality as a whole" was being provided for redevelopment by private enterprise; and (3) the redevelopment plan conformed to a general plan for the development of the area as a whole. On the face of it, these mild, rather ambiguous statutory conditions could be easily satisfied; but they offered little substantive guidance and thus provided ample discretionary latitude to permit federal housing officials to become involved in the local controversy over what type of housing was to be built. The basic question underlying this controversy was: For whom were the housing units to be built?

The controversy broke into the open on June 6, 1950, when the chairman of the City Plan Commission, Willis Hall, told his fellow commissioners to "either get down to business or be fired." Chairman Hall's warning was provoked by the failure of the commission to approve a redevelopment plan. He pointed out that they had been given sixty days to do the job, and that ninety days had already gone by with no plan adopted. Mayor Cobo, Hall said, would not tolerate further delay, since the commission's failure to act was holding up the whole redevelopment program. The commission had before it a proposal from its staff that set aside about 49 acres of the 129-acre project site for residential use. (The net area available for development after subtracting streets and alleys, expressway and railroad right-of-way amounted to 88 acres.) The Plan Commission staff proposed that 40 acres be devoted to low-density, two-story, terrace, garden-type construction and the remaining eight and one-half acres be used for multi-story, high-density construction. This plan contemplated a reduction in density from the former level of approximately three thousand families to twelve hundred families.

The president of the Builders' Association of Metropolitan Detroit, John Weinhart, was present at this meeting of the commission, along with other builders, and questions were raised concerning their ability to build units with rents low enough for low-income families. One of the commissioners objected to the predominant use of two-story row housing and suggested that a more diversified plan be developed which would include single-story and single-residence units. This suggestion was overruled as being economically out of the question. Mr. Weinhart told the commission that the Builders' Association was prepared to develop the site so as to meet the needs of low-income families in the community, if no other plans were forthcoming. He reminded the commission, "we made a pledge years ago to former Mayor Jeffries that we would stand by to aid the city in this venture. We still mean to keep that promise." The commission decided to approve the staff proposals.

Mayor Cobo had his own ideas about how the site should be developed, and he was quick to voice them after learning of the commission's decision. The mayor immediately met with the commission and expressed his disapproval of their failure to include single-residence units in the plan. The builders reacted to this suggestion by arguing that the site was too small to permit inclusion of single residences. For that matter, they felt that the present plan calling for practically all row housing on small lots was a waste of land.

The Common Council, which had to approve the plan before it could be submitted to HHFA, began to be heard. Council President Louis Miriani cautioned the plan commissioners against too much haste and against being pressured to make a decision counter to their best judgment, and the mayor continued to voice disapproval that no single homes were being planned. In spite of the mayor's persistence, on July 19, the council approved the commission's preliminary plan for forwarding to HHFA.

Both the Slum Clearance and FHA staff of HHFA took a dim view of Mayor Cobo's insistence upon single-dwelling units. The Housing Commission staff discovered this when it sought informal approval of the mayor's suggestion from federal officials. Such approval would have strengthened the mayor's hand with the Plan Commission and especially with the builders, but the HHFA staff shared the builders' doubts about the economic feasibility of such a plan. The only type of single residence that a family of modest income would be likely to afford to rent or purchase would be of a size and quality that would soon return the Gratiot site to its pre-redevelopment condition. The mayor found little support for his plan.

HHFA officials also objected to the predominance of two-story row housing. This objection was based on the premise that such housing would only restore overcrowding and slum conditions. When the mayor, whose irritation over the slow pace of the project had been aggravated by the rejection of his own plan, was informed of these objections in September, he publicly stated that Detroit would proceed with slum clearance with or without federal aid. He cited the Detroit Plan as evidence that the city had been engaged in slum clearance on its own before the federal government got involved. However, no independent city action was forthcoming, and a year later, on October 19, 1951, the Common Council approved the final redevelopment plan for the Gratiot area, which was subsequently approved by HHFA.

During the year that elapsed from the time Mayor Cobo threatened to go it alone and the council approved an acceptable redevelopment plan, a number of events took place, including a shift in attitudes toward urban redevelopment, that had a bearing upon the Gratiot project. With the beginning of demolition and relocation in the fall of 1950, Negro housing problems had to be faced. Was the Gratiot site to be redeveloped for the former residents who could not qualify for public housing? All available evidence up to the end of 1950 indicated that providing housing for former Gratiot residents was a major goal of the project. This goal was clearly stated in the informational letter sent to families to be relocated. If facilities were to be built for this clientele, density standards had to be relatively high in order to make the building of low-rent units a profitable investment. Many of the local builders and real-estate men believed that low-cost housing, or at least Negro housing, was the only possible residential use for the site. They felt that since the site was almost completely surrounded by slum housing occupied by Negroes, only Negroes would live in the area, regardless of the type or quality of housing construction. Thus construction had to be for the Negro market, which was predominantly low-income. These businessmen felt that site planning had to recognize these circumstances in setting density and other restrictions in order to attract private investment.

The City Adopts a Plan. The professional planners on the Plan Commission staff recognized the goal of rehousing former residents, but they wanted to accomplish this in a way which would maintain "good planning" standards. These standards seem to defy explicit articulation, but they include population-density criteria as well as engineering and aesthetic considerations. The commission itself, which included by law an architect, civil engineer, structural engineer, real-estate dealer, builder, attorney, and physician, did not share all of the professional planners' values, but they tended to defend them. The chairman, Willis Hall, was secretary-manager of the Greater Detroit Board of Commerce and a proponent of measures that would protect the tax base of the city, such as redevelopment of the downtown area. The commissioners wanted to be practical. They didn't want to be accused of holding up progress, but on the other hand, they were not eager to endorse a plan that would re-create the evil they were trying to eliminate.

Since the redevelopment plan was the responsibility of the Plan Commission, the Housing Commission and its staff could remain on the sidelines. At least they could avoid a public official stand on the plan. This did not prevent Durbin from blaming the planners for delaying progress, but with the number of activities involved in determining the cost of moving utilities, of closing bridges, and of preparing maps and other minutiae of detailed planning, the planners were able to convince the council that they were not dragging their feet. The main objective of the Housing Commission, Durbin, and his staff, was to clear Gratiot and get something built on it by private enterprise. The Housing Commission staff was becoming convinced that it was going to be difficult, if not impossible, for private enterprise to develop the site for low-income families. Their experience during this period with construction costs on public housing projects combined with their relocation experience provided convincing evidence of the problems a developer would face in trying to produce at a profit housing for low-income families. It seemed to them that the only practical solution was to press for housing for middle-income families. It was recognized that in order to do this, it would be necessary to convince a developer that there was a middle-income market.

Federal housing officials were having their problems with Detroit during this period. They were receiving complaints concerning the relocation of Negro families, but since relocation had begun even before the relocation plan had been filed, to say nothing of being approved, no action other than warnings was taken. Durbin assured Washington that its fears were unwarranted, but HHFA was not completely defenseless. In November 1950, the Housing Commission submitted a development program for its one new public housing project, U.R. Mich. 1-11. By February 20, 1951, the Public Housing Administration had approved all aspects of this plan with the exception of the relocation plan. A year later the commission reported: "After several conferences and submittal and resubmittal of relocation plans, the most recent of which was sent to PHA on November 21 [1951], the commission is awaiting their approval." This delay may not have been a very severe sanction, since the commission's zeal for building public housing was notably slight; nevertheless it did rub some of the gloss off the claims of the Housing Commission staff that all was going well with relocation.

Relocation was only a symptom of the difficulty that faced federal housing officials. Urban redevelopment was a new program, and Detroit's head start provided an excellent vehicle for demonstrating what could be accomplished through a cooperative federal-local program. On the one hand, federal officials wanted to demonstrate that such a program did permit a degree of local discretion which would allow each community to design a program for its own needs, but on the other hand, they were wary of what might be demonstrated if local officials had too much their own way. Mayor Cobo's testy impatience of interference with his administration made him a difficult mayor with whom to work under these circumstances.

The concern of the Slum Clearance and Urban Redevelopment Division officials of HHFA with the racial problem was reflected not only in their relocation policies but also in their position on redevelopment of the site. Some felt very strongly that urban redevelopment should be a vehicle for desegregation in housing, by providing Negro families with an opportunity to obtain private rental housing without racial discrimination. Those who held these views were anxious to avert any local policy which might result in the redeveloped area becoming a reservoir of low-income Negro families. On the other hand, they wanted to avoid a policy which might result in a segregated high-income white neighborhood. The middle position, which they preferred, was a project that permitted mixed occupancy from both an income and a racial standpoint.

The redevelopment plan approved by the Detroit Common Council on October 19, 1951, was considered to be a mixed plan. In approving it, the council announced that it was designed primarily for middle-income families, but that provision would be made for a sufficient number of units for low-income families to accommodate former residents of the site who desired to return. The following April (1952), federal approval was obtained and a contract concluded between the Detroit Housing Commission and the United States of America, acting by and through the Housing and Home Finance Administration, for carrying out the Gratiot Slum Clearance and Urban Redevelopment Project, U.R. Mich. 1-1.

This plan, designed to accommodate both middle- and low-income families, seemed to satisfy the major values of those concerned with the project. Low-income Negro families would be taken care of as well as middle-income Negro and white families. Densities could be maintained at a relatively low level and at the same time attract investment, since middle-income families could afford higher rents. The following table shows the land use authorized by the plan:

Land Use	Acres	Percent
Net Area	88.19	100.0
Residential Area—Total	51.30	58.3
Low Density (two-story)	40.40	45.9
High Density (multi-story)	10.90	12.4
Commercial Area	3.10	3.5
Industrial Area (includes parking parcels and railroad property)	4.61	5.2
Churches	1.25	1.4
Schools and Yards	6.30	7.2
Playgrounds	11.30	12.8
Parks (open green areas; includes public walkways)	4.30	4.9
Wayne University (medical campus)*	5.80	6.5
Public Lighting Commission	.23	.2

*By mutual agreement of all parties, a portion of the site was set aside as part of a medical campus.

The net area was that remaining of the 129 acres after subtracting land used for streets, an expressway, and part of a railroad right-of-way. The original area had a net of 85.46 acres, since
a larger proportion of it was devoted to streets and alleys. The most
dramatic change between the original and the planned use was
the amount of land for schools and yards, playgrounds, and parks.
These uses totaled 2 acres on the original site and 21.9 acres in
the plan.

Although the formal approval was not forthcoming from Washington until April 1952, the City Plan Commission had completed
its work the previous August. The final document consisted of

> . . . a narrative text dealing with general community planning, a
> similar text describing the plan for redevelopment, a complete set of
> documentation drawings, a copy of the Detroit master plan and a set
> of photostatic copies of supporting documentation from city depart-
> ments and private utility companies, consisting of correspondence,
> cost estimates, etc.

The Housing Commission submitted this document informally for
review and approval to the Division of Slum Clearance and Urban
Redevelopment of HHFA before submittal to the council in October. Counting from the beginning of 1950, when detailed planning
to qualify for aid under Title I had begun, a little over two years
had been consumed in the planning and approval process.

The Reluctant Redevelopers.

> Since Common Council approval of the site and redevelopment plan
> of October 19, 1951, the Detroit Housing Commission has received
> numerous inquiries as to availability of land for redevelopment in
> the Gratiot project area from interested parties in Detroit, Chicago,
> New York City, and Phoenix, Arizona. Conferences have been held
> with local realtors and builders who have pledged support of the
> program since its inception. Some of the redevelopers are interested
> in purchasing the entire forty-three-acre block area, and have made
> independent studies of site layout and proposed residential designs
> and density.

This quotation from the Housing Commission's annual report
for the year 1951 reflects the optimism with which Harry Durbin
faced the prospect of finally placing the Gratiot parcels on the

auction block. The signing of the contract with HHFA in April
removed the last obstacle to the sale. Accordingly, a prospectus
was prepared, and the council approved the holding of an auction
at 2:00 P.M., July 30, 1952, in the council chambers of City Hall.
The auction came off on schedule. Some fifty builders and brokers
appeared, but all sat in silence when the call came for bids. No
bids were offered, and no property was sold.

Density standards were the main reason publicly cited for the
failure to offer bids. The builders and brokers claimed that these
standards would push building costs out of proportion to the
rentals which could be expected from the area. Durbin rejoined
by pointing out that the plan allowed densities of up to twenty-
six two-bedroom dwelling units or their equivalent per acre,
whereas the standard for public housing and most private multiple housing in Detroit was sixteen two-bedroom units per acre.
Another objection was that there was no provision for cooperative-
ownership arrangements. It was suggested that such arrangements
would be more attractive to prospective tenants and would make
the investment more attractive. There was also some grumbling
about close supervision from Washington and about the red tape
entailed in obtaining approval of all plans from both local and
federal officials. Some objection was also voiced to the terms of
the sale which, among other things, provided that 50 percent of
the deposit required of successful bidders would be retained by
the city in case the sale fell through.

Privately, other reasons for failure to bid were cited. Doubt
was expressed over the likelihood that middle-income whites
would move into the project area; therefore, to be realistic, construction had to be for the Negro market. To build for this market and still make a profit, it would be necessary to increase the
density in order to reduce unit costs. None of the builders who
were interviewed were optimistic about the chances of selling or
renting to both Negroes and whites in the same area. One thing
was clear from this first auction: selling the land was not going
to be as easy as had been anticipated.

In preparation for the second auction, which was scheduled
for May 6, 1953, the Housing Commission staff tried to make adjustments in the sale arrangements in order to attract purchasers.

Any changes involved discussions and clearances with a number of agencies. Since financing would probably have to be obtained through FHA facilities, this agency had to be consulted on details they would deem necessary in any arrangement; the council and the mayor had to be kept informed on all changes, since they ultimately had to approve them; the Detroit corporation counsel had to be consulted on all aspects of the purchase agreement; the Plan Commission and its staff had to initiate changes if any were to be made in the conditions on density and construction; and, finally, the Division of Slum Clearance and Urban Redevelopment of HHFA had to review and approve all changes. On December 14, 1952, *The Detroit News* reported the "slum-clearance deadlock broken." The "idealists" of the Plan Commission, finally yielding to the "realists" of the Housing Commission, had relaxed certain restrictions on distances between buildings for the Gratiot project, thereby permitting the developer more latitude in the development of his own plans. Density standards, however, remained unchanged. On January 20, 1953, a revised Declaration of Restrictions incorporating these changes was sent to the council, which approved it. On April 12, 1953, Mayor Cobo met with the local builders. He told them that they should tackle the slum redevelopment job in Detroit and suggested that the auction would be a good place to start.

The principal changes that were made to encourage a sale, in addition to those made by the Plan Commission, included provision for either rental or cooperative units or a combination of both. The most important change had to do with the purchase terms. It provided that the purchaser had thirty-six weeks from the signing of the purchase agreement in which to pay the balance of the purchase price to the city, but if the developer could not obtain financing commitments that were satisfactory to him, the city would cancel the agreement and return the deposit. In his letter to the council describing this provision Durbin said:

> In effect, this Agreement is a combination option and purchase agreement for a period of thirty-six (36) weeks rather than an outright purchase. To the writer, this appears to be a satisfactory arrangement, as we prefer to have a developer actively working toward the development of the property for the next thirty-six (36) weeks.

Durbin was doing his best to give private enterprise the opportunity to demonstrate initiative under conditions of minimum risk. Before requesting the second auction, Durbin attempted to make certain that he would have at least one bidder, preferably one who would agree to purchase all of the residential sites. When it became evident that local builders were not eager to take on even individual parcels, the search for a single developer intensified. On the grounds that a single developer should have some freedom in working out a plan for the whole site through his own architects, Durbin was able to convince the Plan Commission to relax its restrictions. The Warner-Kanter Company, a New York–Cincinnati combine, had expressed interest in the site and was prepared to bid on the whole project.

With a prospective buyer assured, the second auction was certain to produce action, and it did. The hopes of the supporters of the Detroit Plan were finally justified. Not only was the Warner-Kanter Company on hand to bid but also a local syndicate headed by Bert L. Smokler, a Detroit builder. The bidding was lively. Warner-Kanter's newly formed organization, the Housing Corporation of America, was the successful bidder, having obtained forty-seven acres of land for residential use and three acres of commercial land for a purchase price of $1,266,000. This was $340,-000 above the minimum sale price set by the city. It looked as if the Gratiot project would soon be under construction.

One of the conditions included in the purchase agreement signed by the Housing Corporation of America was that first preference for initial occupancy of its units, and for vacancies during the first year of operation, would be given to families from homes displaced by the project and second preference to those displaced from other redevelopment areas or to families evicted from permanent public housing units as a result of exceeding the income limits for eligibility. Providing housing for low-income families was thus an implied responsibility of the developer, and the early plans submitted by the Housing Corporation of America were designed to meet this need. Under the terms of the purchase agreement, the developer's plans had to be submitted to the Plan Commission for review to determine whether they met the established restrictions, and since financing was being sought through FHA, that agency had to review and approve plans.

The first signs of disenchantment with the plans became public in October 1953, when an advisory committee of architects appointed by the Plan Commission to review the developer's plans objected to them. The planning staff noted that the plans had been originally designed for a West Coast project rather than for the Gratiot site. Among the objectionable features pointed to by the architects were exposed outside wooden stairways leading to second-floor apartments. (In a revised Declaration of Restrictions for the project, issued sometime later, the Plan Commission added the sentence: "All stairways to and from the second floor shall be contained within the structural walls of the building proper.") The planners felt that the developer was trying to cut too many corners in terms of both space and quality of construction. FHA officials agreed, and the developer was requested to submit revised plans. The second set of plans, submitted a few months later, called for much more elaborate constructions and higher costs, which brought objections from FHA officials. The revised plans required rentals of approximately $125 to $135 a month.

On June 17, 1954, the Common Council accepted the cancellation of the purchase agreement with the Housing Corporation of America. The corporation invoked the escape clause by notifying the council that the statement of eligibility received from FHA was unsatisfactory and that "the developer hereby exercises his right to cancel the agreement without recourse and respectfully requests the city to return the deposit of $92,638 which he made to the City of Detroit." In a letter accompanying the formal withdrawal, Joseph Kanter, president of the corporation, said:

> The matter has developed into what we now feel is an irreconcilable conflict between the natural desire of all concerned to erect a large, elaborate, well-designed living area, and what we believe in the interest of practicality is required, i.e., smaller, less expensive units. Construction of apartments of the size and with the exterior appearance which seems now to be desired would, in our opinion, make the cost of the buildings so great and the rents so high as to jeopardize the ultimate success of the project.

Reassessment of the Market. The collapse of the agreement was greeted with disappointment and recriminations. Durbin, who had the most at stake since the developer was his find, aimed his fire at the board of trustees of the city pension fund. He was quoted in the *Detroit Times* for May 25, 1954, to the effect that if $4,000,000 or $5,000,000 of the $54,000,000 which the fund had available in various investments had been put into FHA-guaranteed mortgages, the city might have gotten started on the Gratiot project in 1953. Edmund Kuhlman, a member of the Plan Commission, blamed federal and local officials. His comment, reported in the *Detroit Times* of July 11, was:

> Any reputable builder would jump at the opportunity if he had to meet only standards of the city Department of Building and Safety Engineering. When he runs into the ivory tower ideas of the Plan and Housing Commission and FHA, no wonder he turns his back.

The mayor and various councilmen added their voices to the chorus, and there was much public viewing with alarm and many calls for action; but it was hard to fix the blame on any one person or agency. The dilemma faced by the developer was that in order to produce low-rent housing, construction costs had to be scaled to the potential rents, but such plans did not satisfy the professional planners and architects. On the other hand, the more elaborate plans met the disapproval of FHA, which was concerned over the potential market for the higher-cost units. The time had arrived to take a frank look at the cause of this dilemma.

On March 12, 1954, Gordon Howard, head of the Economics Section, Planning and Engineering Branch, Division of Slum Clearance and Urban Renewal of HHFA, received from two assistants a memorandum entitled "Racial Aspects of Housing Market Analysis." The memorandum pointed out that it was high time that an objective study was done of the racial aspects of housing which would, among other things, explore the "whole series of traditional racial stereotypes and unverified notions and assumptions as to the behavior of Negro housing consumers." It was hypothesized that if such a study were carefully designed and conducted so as to avoid built-in biases, the effective market demand for housing among Negroes would be discovered to be quite different from that expressed by the stereotypes. A copy of the memorandum was sent to the Detroit Housing Commission along with a suggestion that they look into the matter. Advice was sought from a local real-estate consultant, and the first three paragraphs of his memorandum were a candid summary of what was tying up the Gratiot project:

> The proper use of the Gratiot redevelopment site is one that presents some very complex problems. The correct evaluation and solution of these problems can only be done, in our opinion, after a complete factual survey is made in Detroit of the various issues at hand.
>
> Almost any problem that faces the builder, federal government, mortgagers, or city council will revert back to facts which would be brought out in such a survey as we are proposing. Examples of these are as follows:
>
> (a) A builder cannot intelligently plan the number of units to be built or the kind of units to be built until he knows *what is the market for Negro housing.*
>
> (b) The government cannot properly consider putting money into this development unless it knows that the requirements of the Negro population who will live in this community will be properly and adequately satisfied and that the rental charged will be in line with their ability to pay.
>
> (c) A mortgagee considering this loan either as an insuring agency like the FHA or as an insurance company considering the purchase of the mortgage, would have to be satisfied that the demand for housing of the type to be constructed in this location is sufficiently large to definitely insure full occupancy of the project, and particularly they must know if today's income of the prospective owners and/or tenants is sufficient to pay the rental that would have to be charged.
>
> (d) Before the city council approves both the plans and the builder it must know that the type of units which he will erect are those most likely to provide a successful operation.

The memorandum recommended that a personal interview survey be conducted to determine (1) the economic status of the Negro in Detroit; (2) conditions of the Negro housing market (type and size of units; rental or sale); (3) the size and nature of the market for housing on the Gratiot site (it was suggested Negroes might no longer wish to live in the area); and (4) the cost of housing which would be acceptable to people buying or renting in the Gratiot area.

Although the memorandum implied that the Gratiot site could

be considered only for Negro housing, the Housing Commission staff was still convinced that there was a market among whites as well. Undaunted by the earlier experience, W. Joseph Starrs, the commission's urban renewal co-ordinator, approached the Wayne University faculty members who had worked on the relocation research proposal and invited them to prepare a proposal for a study of the market problem. Having first established that publication rights would be guaranteed in the contract, the faculty researchers, also undaunted, prepared a proposal in which they agreed to provide:

1. An estimate, within the limits of the sampling error, of the number of families in the Detroit area interested in living in the Gratiot redevelopment area, with comparative data between white and nonwhite families.

2. Data on the capabilities of the interested families to pay economic rents at levels defined by the Local Public Agency.

3. Data on the conditions and amenities considered important to the interested families in determining the degree of attraction to housing in the Gratiot redevelopment area.

4. Descriptive data on the family characteristics of groups interested in living in the area, contrasted with characteristics of families not so interested.

5. Data concerning families with one or more members employed in the vicinity of the area, as to the degree of interest in housing quarters in the area and the conditions which would minimize or maximize such interest.

6. Data on the dwelling unit sizes and facilities desired by families interested in living in the area.

7. Recommendations, based upon these findings, concerning (a) the types of facilities for which an economic market may be most readily found, and (b) the groups in the Detroit area which would be most interested in alternative types of project.

The data were to be obtained by an area probability sample of 750 households in the metropolitan area and 450 interviews distributed among selected groups employed in the downtown area adjacent to the project site. Although aimed at the Gratiot project, the study was designed to provide basic data on attitudes and opinions relative to housing in the metropolis.

This time it was the federal agency that prevented the study.

The contract, drafted in the middle of June 1954, provided for completion by February 1955, but federal officials insisted that the information was required by the end of the summer. As the survey was to be financed under the Title I grant, federal approval was required. The Housing Commission then contracted with the Chicago Real Estate Research Corporation for a market analysis survey of the potential housing market among employees in the downtown area.

The market analysts' report was submitted to the Housing Commission in November 1955. (The Housing Commission staff was reluctant to discuss this survey and maintained that the findings could not be made public. A fairly complete report of the findings, however, was reported in the November 25, 1954, edition of the *Detroit Times*.) The analysts distributed 6,061 forms to employees in the central business district, 5 percent of those employed in the area. The key question stated that investors were considering a "fine, modern apartment development" on the Gratiot site, and respondents were asked if they would be interested in living in such a development, with rents ranging from $85 a month for an efficiency apartment to $145 for a three-bedroom unit. Twenty-three percent answered in the affirmative. The next question asked whether occupancy by both colored and white tenants would make the development less attractive, more attractive, or have no effect. Among those who said they were interested in the area, 1,244 were whites and 125 were Negroes. Seventy-six percent of the white respondents said that mixed occupancy would make the project less attractive to them, and so did 2 percent of the Negroes. The analysts concluded that the market in the Gratiot project area was restricted by prejudices against the area as such and by prejudices against biracial occupancy. They predicted that these attitudes would change in time but that it would be a gradual process. They recommended that the area be developed in installments so that attitudes would have an opportunity to change. By the time the market analysis was completed, the initiative for carrying out the Gratiot project had passed from the Housing Commission to the Citizens Redevelopment Committee. This committee was operating under its own head of steam and paid little, if any, attention to the analysts' report.

The Citizens Redevelopment Committee. The Citizens Redevelopment Committee traces its origin to the spring of 1953 when, in anticipation of the second auction, a brochure was prepared by Walter J. Gessell, mortgage broker and consultant, entitled "Constructive Housing Program for Detroit's Gratiot Redevelopment Area." The key person behind the brochure, however, was James W. Bell. Bell had become interested in urban redevelopment some time earlier when he served on the staff of the Plan Commission. Bell was not a professionally trained planner. In fact, his formal education had ended when he graduated from Cass Technical High School in 1932, but in addition to his job on the Plan Commission staff, his experience included work with a firm of architects and employment with one of Detroit's largest builders. The brochure prepared by Bell and Gessell, who was at that time a member of the Housing Commission, proposed that a non-profit corporation be formed for the purpose of acquiring and retaining control of the entire redevelopment area in order to "promote its redevelopment under highest standards of design and construction." The specific plan, illustrated with a map and photographs, called for a number of multi-story apartment buildings which would provide "high density without crowding the land." It was pointed out that high construction costs made cooperative ownership the best possible financing method.

The authors took their plan to Mayor Cobo, but he advised them to forget about it, since negotiations had cleared the way for a firm bid from the Housing Corporation of America. When this agreement fell through a year later, the time was ripe to revive the non-profit corporation plan. This time, instead of going to the mayor, Bell contacted *The Detroit News,* with the result that the plan which had been described in the brochure was a feature story in the Sunday, June 27, 1954 edition of the *News.* The next day the mayor and the council received a long telegram from Walter Reuther, president of the United Auto Workers, CIO. Reuther urged that action be taken to set up a citizens' committee to deal with the Gratiot project. "It is economically stupid and morally wrong for an industrial community with the wealth, the power, and the know-how of Detroit to tolerate the social cesspools of our slums, which breed crime and disease," he wrote.

The substance of the telegram reflected careful briefing on, and endorsement of, the Bell-Gessell plan. Reuther backed his interest with an offer of $10,000 from the UAW to help finance the work of a citizens' committee.

The council had scheduled a public hearing on the Gratiot project for July 7. The timing of the newspaper feature and the Reuther telegram focused attention on the Bell-Gessell plan as a way out of the embarrassment created by the cancelled purchase agreement. Prior to the hearing, Councilman Edward Connor suggested that control of Gratiot should remain with an official governmental agency, such as a redevelopment authority. He felt that the citizens' committee approach was too fleeting for the long-term haul of the eighteen-year redevelopment program drawn up by the Plan Commission. The Plan Commission staff endorsed Connor's appraisal of the *ad hoc* committee approach. Housing Director Durbin reminded one and all that his agency was the Local Public Agency designated to deal with federal agencies, and he questioned the value of a non-profit corporation whose only purpose was to buy land and resell it to a builder. These and other views were voiced and debated at the public hearing on July 7, but attention continued to center on the Bell-Gessell plan.

Following the hearing, Mayor Cobo found himself in a difficult position. Any endorsement of a citizens' committee authorized to dispose of the Gratiot site was public acknowledgment of lack of confidence in his housing director, Durbin. After all, sale of the land was the Housing Commission's responsibility. But the co-author of the citizens' committee plan, Walter Gessell, was also a Cobo appointee and currently president of the Housing Commission. Moreover, the mayor had recently appointed a Detroit Tomorrow Committee. This committee had a membership of well over a hundred and included the standard roster of distinguished citizens. The mayor had charged the committee with responsibility for saving the core city, but the committee was considered too large to be effective. Added to this was the Cobo distaste for being pressured into anything, compounded by the fact that the pressure was being applied by Walter Reuther, for whom Cobo had little liking. Nevertheless, the Gratiot site was now being referred to in the press as "Ragweed Acres" and privately as

"Cobo's Acres," so something had to be done.

On July 12, Housing Director Durbin recommended that the mayor and council jointly appoint a citizens' committee to study site lay-out, consider the creation of a non-profit corporation, and work out a redevelopment program for the Gratiot area as a whole, which would include the area to the east that had been designated for public housing and the area directly south that had been earmarked for an extension of the original project. The following day, the council passed a resolution authorizing the mayor and president of the council to appoint jointly a Citizens Redevelopment Committee of twelve members for the purpose of studying the best methods for the development of the Gratiot project. The resolution also provided that the committee include one ex officio member of the city government to maintain liaison with the various governmental agencies. This post went to Harry Durbin, who was also made committee chairman. The four key citizen appointees were Gessell, Reuther, Walter Gehrke, chairman of the board, First Federal Savings and Loan Association of Detroit, and Foster K. Winter, vice president, The J. L. Hudson Company. These four made up the executive board of the committee with the following assignments: Gessell, secretary-treasurer; Gehrke, chairman of the finance subcommittee; Winter, chairman of the legal subcommittee; and Reuther, chairman of the planning and design subcommittee. James Bell was appointed full-time co-ordinator.

By September 13, the Citizens Redevelopment Committee was ready with its first report. It informed the council of its organizing activities and reported that a working agreement had been reached with two Detroit architectural firms (Victor Gruen Associates and Leinweber, Yamasaki, and Hellmuth) along with the Philadelphia architect, Oskar Stonorov, to prepare a comprehensive plan for the Gratiot area. The committee requested an additional ninety days to complete the physical development plan and the necessary legal and financial studies and asked that during this period the council refrain from selling "or otherwise disposing of said land except upon advice from the committee, and only after alternate plans or programs have been subjected to review and study by the committee." The council granted the request.

Both the housing director and the planning director reacted

against the council's approval of the extension. Durbin argued that it placed the authority to dispose of the land in the hands of the committee, but the council countered that authority to approve or disapprove committee action remained with the council. The council's action did effectively limit Durbin and the Housing Commission from proceeding with any sale arrangements without the committee's approval. Plan Director Blessing complained that the committee had invaded his jurisdiction by taking over the planning function. He pointed to the months of planning that his staff had already devoted to the site and accused the committee and its architects of ignoring this labor. Durbin claimed to have a builder who was ready to purchase land and start construction of an apartment building. The mayor suggested that Durbin take up the offer with the committee, and if it were rejected, he could then go to the council with it. The mayor was obviously avoiding taking up the cause of either the committee or Durbin. Cobo soon left for a vacation in Arizona and was not on hand when the next crisis developed.

Late in October, Durbin received a request from the Bonwit Construction Company of New York for a six-month option on part of the site. Durbin was enthusiastic over the offer and was prepared to go to the council to request that the waiting period on the sale of the land granted to the committee be waived. The offer was submitted to the Citizens Committee, which decided to hold it up until the committee's own detailed planning could be completed. Since the committee's objective was to avoid piecemeal development, sale of a portion of the site had little appeal. The Bonwit offer permitted Durbin to decry publicly the delay imposed upon him by the committee. He withdrew as chairman and was succeeded by Gessell. In order to strengthen the committee's hand, Gessell, Gehrke, Reuther, and Bell went to Washington and met with HHFA Administrator Albert Cole on November 10. Cole gave them informal approval of the principles embodied in the committee's program and assurances of federal cooperation and support.

Upon his return to Detroit early in December, the mayor called a meeting in his office between the Housing Commission and the Citizens Redevelopment Committee. The committee accused Durbin of attempting to use the Bonwit offer as a tactic to impede the committee's efforts, and Durbin accused the committee of meeting with federal officials without clearing with either the Housing or the Plan Commission staffs. Bell announced that he had contacted the New York firms and found them agreeable to delaying their offer until the committee had completed its planning. The mayor's meeting gave Durbin a chance to let off steam, but the committee retained its firm control.

On December 20, 1954, the Citizens Redevelopment Committee unveiled its plan for the Gratiot area with appropriate ritual and fanfare. A model of the plan was put on display at the Veterans' Memorial Building, and it drew the anticipated exclamations of approval and delight from assembled officials and dignitaries. The theory behind the plan was summarized in the following paragraph from a report to the council:

> Our committee is convinced that a successful program—for now and in the future—is completely dependent upon the city obtaining an integrated residential community of the most advanced design, of the highest possible standards; a community that, on a completely competitive basis, can attract back to the heart of the city people who are finding their housing in the outlying sections of the city and its suburbs. Anything short of attaining that objective would be of dubious value from both an economic and social point of view.

The plan took in not only the original Gratiot site but also the area due east, referred to as the St. Aubin extension, and the area due south, the Lafayette extension. By an integrated community, the committee meant one that included people of varying income levels; thus, the plan included provision for two small public housing projects, one in the St. Aubin extension and one in the Lafayette extension. The St. Aubin extension had been earmarked for a public housing project since the beginning of planning for Gratiot; but the Redevelopment Committee's plan reversed the earlier plan to extend private development like that envisaged for Gratiot to the Lafayette extension. For the most part, the expanded site included "high-rise apartments in green fields" and "ingeniously planned complexes of single free-standing houses, three-bedroom rental row houses, semi-detached houses with enclosed yards and commons, and four-bedroom ownership-type houses."

The economic distribution was designed to locate the highest-priced housing in the center, with the less costly housing (including public housing) surrounding it. (A detailed treatment of the plan was published in *Architectural Forum,* Vol. CII, No. 3 [March, 1955], p. 116.)

This plan, along with other plans and discussions in which reference was made to "low-cost" housing, contained a certain ambiguity. With a continuing increase in construction costs, low-cost housing, i.e., housing at a price or rental that low-income families could afford without some form of public subsidy, was no longer a practical objective, if, indeed, it ever had been. Nevertheless, the early commitment to a policy for Gratiot that would accommodate low-income families resulted in continuing reference to "low-cost" housing even at a time when the lowest-cost housing was well beyond the economic grasp of low-income Gratiot families. But these distinctions were not always made when plans were proposed and discussed.

The committee reported that time had not permitted the prior review of its plans by the Plan Commission, but that the architects were eager to assist the Plan Commission staff in this process. The committee recommended that the original Gratiot area be developed by a single developer in not more than two stages and that the two extensions follow later. It was further recommended that a non-profit corporation be formed to purchase the land in order to control its development according to plan. The council enthusiastically endorsed the recommendations and prepared to adopt a resolution authorizing the formation of the non-profit corporation. At this point, Director J. W. Follin of HHFA questioned the legality, under the Housing Act, of selling the land to a middleman for resale to a developer. He further pointed out that the inclusion of public housing on the expanded Gratiot site, as called for in the plan, would violate the provisions of Title I. The mayor suggested that instead of forming a corporation to purchase land, the committee could continue to function as the city's agent to enforce its standards, but that the sale process could follow the original procedure through the Housing Commission. However, the committee members were not convinced that the legal problem was insurmountable. On January 4, 1955, Gessell, Gehrke, and Winter met in Washington with HHFA Administrator Cole and his Slum Clearance Division director, Follin, to try to resolve the legal problems. On January 13, Cole came to Detroit and met with city officials, and the legal tangles were unsnarled.

Under the arrangement approved by HHFA, the committee's plans for redevelopment had to pass through the same approval channels (the Plan Commission, the council, and HHFA), as if they had originated with a governmental agency. Mayor Cobo ordered the Plan Commission to get together with other governmental units and the committee staff and come up with a plan upon which they all agreed. This was accomplished in a little over a week. Relations were strained between the committee and the planners, since the planners felt that they should have been consulted in the earlier phases of the committee's planning. This attitude was shared by other government agencies which felt left out of the process. Nevertheless, the insistence of the mayor, echoed by the council, was sufficient to prevent any prolonged haggling over details, and the necessary adjustments in official redevelopment plans were made to accommodate the committee's recommendations. Among these adjustments were the removal of the restriction against single-story construction in the low-density areas and the addition of a third parcel to the high-density area, along with a reshuffling of the parcels to be devoted to high-rise apartments. The committee's plans carried the weight of having been developed by well-known, highly regarded architects, and they incorporated values generally shared by the Plan Commission staff.

Lafayette Park–University City. While planning details were being ironed out, organizational details were agreed upon. In a resolution adopted on February 1, the council approved in principle both the committee's plan for the Gratiot area and the organization of a non-profit corporation "with subsidiaries as proposed by the Citizens Redevelopment Committee for the purpose of acquiring and redeveloping the Gratiot Redevelopment area." Under this setup, which HHFA approved, a non-profit Citizens Redevelopment Corporation would purchase the land and retain over-all control of the project. Builders would become subsidiaries of the corporation by buying non-voting shares which would allow them to build under the supervision of the corporation. Upon satisfactory completion of the construction, the land and buildings would be sold to the builder. On April 6, 1955, the Citizens Redevelopment Corporation of Detroit was incorporated as a Michigan non-profit corporation, and James Bell was hired as its full-time co-ordinator. With the incorporation of the Citizens Redevelopment Corporation of Detroit, the responsibility for the Gratiot site passed from the Local Public Agency (the Housing Commission) to a private non-profit corporation.

The Citizens Committee, predecessor to Redevelopment Corporation, had operated on a modest budget of $60,000 obtained through contributions from banks, the UAW, and other local sources. The Redevelopment Corporation's original aim was to raise through local contributions a revolving fund of five hundred thousand dollars for the purchase of land. The fund would be reimbursed after the developer had completed construction and purchased the land from the Redevelopment Corporation. Contributions were slow in arriving. Since this was no doubt due to concern over whether the Redevelopment Corporation would be declared a non-profit, tax-exempt, charitable organization, Winter and Gessel, accompanied by lawyers, met with Treasury officials in Washington late in 1955 and obtained a favorable ruling. With the favorable tax ruling plus some local prompting, the contributions began to come in, and by early 1956 the Redevelopment Corporation had a little over $425,000, which was increased the following year to $450,000. The major contributors were:

Ford Motor Company	$80,000	National Bank of Detroit	$25,000
Chrysler Corporation	50,000	Michigan Bell Telephone	
General Motors Corporation	50,000	Company	16,000
The J. L. Hudson Company	50,000	Michigan Consolidated Gas	
Kresge Foundation	50,000	Company	10,000
United Automobile Workers		Burroughs Adding Machine	
(CIO)	50,000	Company	7,500
Detroit Edison Company	25,000	Parke, Davis & Company	7,500

In addition to Gessell, Gehrke, Reuther, and Winter, the officers and trustees of the Redevelopment Corporation included representatives from all the major contributors as well as religious and Negro leaders. A deliberate effort was made to have this group of twenty-one citizens representative of major interests in the community.

On July 2, 1956, the Citizens Redevelopment Corporation of Detroit, as redeveloper, entered into an "Agreement for Disposition of the Gratiot Area for Private Redevelopment" with the City of Detroit and Cities Redevelopment, Inc., as co-developer. This agreement was the culmination of the Redevelopment Corporation's efforts to find an acceptable developer. After assuming control of the Gratiot site, the corporation began to receive inquiries from potential developers, many of whom were interested in only a part of the site. The corporation soon decided that they would prefer to work through a single developer for the whole site, if one could be found. The proposals made by Cities Redevelopment, Inc., owned by Herbert S. Greenwald and Samuel N. Katzin, for total site development so impressed the trustees that early in November 1955 they decided that this firm would be the exclusive co-developer of the site, with Architect Ludwig Mies van der Rohe as the chief designer of the redevelopment construction. The developer's architect prepared a new plan for the site and submitted it to the corporation in January 1956. It "received the somewhat reluctant approval of the corporation." The Redevelopment Corporation had no wish to abandon the plan drafted by its own architects (it had won an award and had been given national publicity), but the trustees were eager to get on with construction. No developer had appeared with a proposal to carry out the committee's "integrated" project.

The Greenwald-Katzin plan called for "six skyscraper apartment houses which will flow together with two-story and one-story row houses." The plan would provide 2,000 dwelling units, whereas the Redevelopment Corporation's plan provided for 1,750. The high-rise apartments were to be rental units, and the low-rise, now more elegantly classified as town houses and terraces, were for cooperative ownership. What may have given Redevelopment Corporation some pause was the market at which the construction was aimed, since it would take more than a modest income for families to afford the proposed units. In the spring of 1956, the necessary clearances were obtained from the Plan Commission and the Common Council, paving the way for the formal disposition agreements in July.

Under the terms of the formal agreements, (1) the city agreed to sell the twelve parcels of the Gratiot site available for private development to the Redevelopment Corporation and Cities Redevelopment, Inc., for the prices stated in the agreement (total—$1,166,780); (2) the property had to be bought according to a schedule which provided that all parcels be purchased by the end of forty-five months; (3) the Redevelopment Corporation agreed to purchase the land from the city according to the schedule and pay to the city the carrying charges on all parcels not purchased; (4) for each parcel purchased, Cities Redevelopment would act as general contractor for all construction; and (5) upon the completion of construction on any parcel, the Redevelopment Corporation's interest would be sold to Cities Redevelopment upon payment of the land purchase price plus certain other overhead costs, including carrying charges paid by the Redevelopment Corporation. Under this arrangement, the Redevelopment Corporation retained control until construction was completed. Citizens Redevelopment Corporation made its first land purchase on July 30, 1956, and after one false start, construction on the first high-rise apartment began on January 14, 1957. By that time the name of the site had been changed to Lafayette Park–University City.

When the Citizens Redevelopment Committee first took over the Gratiot project, it was intent on preventing the area from becoming a low-income ghetto. In its various pronouncements it stressed the need for what it called an "integrated" community with a range of income levels. The award-winning plan of the committee's architects stressed low-cost housing, including public housing, integrated with more expensive housing. Title I restrictions forced the dropping of plans for public housing on the Gratiot site. The area due east, the St. Aubin extension, had been earmarked for public housing since 1949. Some 3,800 units were planned for this area. This prospect now disturbed the committee planners, for it would guarantee that one boundary of the Gratiot site would consist of a large, Negro public housing project. (It was taken for granted that the project would be Negro, since Negroes substantially outnumbered eligible white applicants for

public housing and since the area had been occupied by Negroes.)
This large public housing project was considered a threat to the
development of the desired integrated neighborhood, and the committee prevailed upon the council to reduce the number of authorized units for St. Aubin to about twelve hundred. By 1960, plans
for a public housing project had been dropped; the planned re-use
called for single dwellings in the $16,000-to-$18,000 price range.

As the market at which the redevelopment housing would be
aimed was decided, so was the fate of St. James Baptist Church.
The church had a Negro congregation and was located on the site.
It was originally decided to let the church remain intact since the
congregation was expected to return with the low-cost housing
to be provided. By the time the Greenwald-Katzin plans for Lafayette Park–University City were completed, it was obvious that
there would be no clientele for the church, nor would it fit in very
well with the architect's plan for a park-like setting. Citizens Redevelopment Corporation solved the problem by purchasing the
church for about $75,000, thus permitting the congregation to
build a new church more convenient to their place of residence.
The cost was prorated to the various parcels in the site, to be re-
captured by the corporation when it sold the land. The departure
of St. James Baptist Church from the Gratiot site was the final act
of disassociation from the earlier view that the area would be
redeveloped for low-income Negro families.

The first unit of Lafayette Park–University City, a twenty-two-
story apartment building, began receiving tenants in the fall of
1958. Monthly rents varied from $85 to $120 for efficiency apartments, and from $190 to $210 for two-bedroom apartments. "The
applications we have received thus far indicate that these buildings will service a most distinguished tenantry," proclaimed a
letter issued by the rental agency. By early 1959, construction was
begun on an expressway which would give the western side of the
site a new and secure physical boundary. Just east of the expressway, the new buildings of the Wayne State University Medical
School and Lafayette Clinic (a research unit of the Michigan Department of Mental Health) gave the site an institutional tone, the
reason for the "University City" part of the site's new name. Construction had also begun on ten two-story "town-house" apart-

ments, and the developer had filed an FHA application for another twenty-two-story apartment and was preparing to apply for an FHA-approved mortgage for three twenty-seven-story apartments. There was still a long way to go before the eighteen hundred to two thousand families contemplated for the area could move in, but the repopulation of the Gratiot site had begun.

Concluding Comments

The net project cost of U.R. Mich. 1-1 was $7,141,644, two-thirds of which was paid from a federal grant. The remaining $2,380,548 was the net cost to the city. With a big assist from the Housing Act, the actual cost to Detroit came close to the $2,000,000 anticipated in Mayor Jeffries' plan. If the $35,000,000 construction slated for the site is built and occupied according to plan, the city will have no difficulty in recapturing its investment with substantial dividends, by means of the increased tax yield from the former slum area.

Involving local builders in urban redevelopment was not accomplished. When the chips were down at the first auction, local bidders were silent. Although they did offer bids at the second auction, when the successful bidder withdrew from the purchase agreement, it was again necessary to go outside the area to find a developer. Local offers were made for individual parcels, but these offers were turned down to avoid piecemeal development. Local developers were not willing and/or able to take on the redevelopment chore in their own backyard, even though they had actively promoted and supported a plan that would provide them with such an opportunity. It takes more than civic loyalty to elicit a down payment in urban redevelopment from a local builder.

Three major plans were drafted for the site: the original redevelopment plan prepared by the City Plan Commission in compliance with Title I; the plan prepared by the Citizens Redevelopment Committee; and the Greenwald-Katzin plan. (In addition to these, of course, were the plans from the Housing Corporation of America and other interested potential developers. Someone said that at least 129 acres of maps had been prepared for the 129-acre site.) The original redevelopment plan had been drafted with the low-income family in mind; the Citizens Committee plan contemplated economically "mixed" or integrated occupancy; and the Greenwald-Katzin plan was designed for middle- and upper-income families. The bitterest battles were fought over the first official plan, with the Plan Commission insisting upon relatively low densities and control over construction design to prevent deterioration to the former slum condition. As the prospective population shifted from low-income Negro to middle- and upper-income families, over-all density standards for the site were relaxed. The original plan called for forty acres of low-density two-story construction and eleven acres of high-density, high-rise construction, with total accommodations for about twelve hundred families. The Greenwald-Katzin plan allocated twenty-two acres for high-rise apartments and twenty-seven acres for low-rise units, including one-story dwellings. This plan would provide units for two thousand families. In describing these plans, the Plan Commission literature emphasized "low land coverage" and "open-ness of plan" rather than low densities. Obviously, density was considered less relevant as the income level of the prospective population went up. A similar shift took place in regard to single-story units, which were specifically prohibited under the first plan but were permitted (now called "town houses") under the final plan.

A number of questions can be raised about the way in which Detroit's first urban redevelopment project was organized and administered. Was it a wise decision to designate the Housing Commission as the Local Public Agency for co-ordinating urban redevelopment efforts under the Housing Act? Would it have made more sense to place this responsibility with the Plan Commission, or would it have been better to set up a new agency, one without prior commitments to either housing or planning programs? Should Mayor Cobo have used his influence to sidetrack the Citizens Redevelopment Committee into an advisory position? Should the mayor have removed Durbin after the Housing Corporation of America deal fell through? Should Durbin have resigned when the council agreed to withhold the sale of the land until the Citizens Committee had had an opportunity to develop its own plan? Should he have resigned later when the Redevelopment Corporation was formed? Should HHFA have backed

Durbin and the Housing Commission and insisted that the Local Public Agency rather than the Redevelopment Corporation retain control of the site?

The role of James Bell, promoter of Citizens Redevelopment Committee, is worthy of special note. It is rather extraordinary for a private citizen to move in and take over control of a project from two major city agencies, the Housing and Plan Commissions, but Bell's excellent contacts at the operating level of the community decision-making system permitted him literally to play the role of co-ordinator. The interest of the department store executive, the mortgage consultant, and the banker in urban redevelopment was obvious, whereas labor's interest was less obvious. Bell knew, however, that Reuther and some of his top associates were eager to prevent the Gratiot site from becoming a receptacle for low-income Negro families. This, they felt, would result in restoring all of the evils of segregated slum housing, which the project was designed to eliminate. They welcomed the opportunity to aid in taking the initiative from Durbin and Cobo, in whom they had little confidence. Reuther was interested in the prospects of an integrated neighborhood which would include all income groups as well as racial groups. He felt that cooperative ownership arrangements would help achieve this. With the support of Reuther, combined with that of Winter, representing Detroit's largest department store, The J. L. Hudson Company, plus support from mortgage and banking circles through Gessell and Gehrke, Bell was able to put together a formidable combination, which, in fact, took over the Gratiot project.

There were other reasons for the Citizens Committee's success. Bell was careful to avoid stacking the committee with members who played the role of official ambassadors of various interests whenever citizens' committees were organized. The mayor's Detroit Tomorrow Committee, with over a hundred members, was filled with this kind of talent. Bell's committee was composed of decision-makers, not mere representatives of interests, whose ability to act decisively contributed to their success in getting HHFA to approve their organization, in resolving the tax-exempt status problem, in raising the $450,000 revolving fund, in working out an acceptable plan with a developer, and finally, when it looked as if the FHA financing of the first apartment unit of the Greenwald-Katzin development would delay construction, in arranging for temporary local financing of the construction. The committee's maneuverability was complimented by the unique freedom of movement enjoyed by Co-ordinator Bell. Unencumbered by the formal hierarchical commitments involved in any official governmental position, he was free to deal at that level of authority appropriate to the problem at hand.

Gains are seldom achieved without costs, although it is possible to create the impression that cost-free gains have been achieved by failing to account for all the costs. The prospective tax revenue from the redeveloped site will easily justify the city's cash investment, but a hidden cost involves the former residents. With the exception of those who were admitted to public housing and some who purchased private homes, the majority of the former residents, informed observers agree, are now living under slum conditions equal to, if not worse than, those they left. The original Detroit Plan was hopefully designed to cope with the problem of housing low-income families. Although racial attitudes conditioned the various plans for the Gratiot site, in the long run economic values prevailed. It proved economically impossible to obtain private development of housing units for low-income families, regardless of their race. Even the "integrated" plan of the Citizens Committee had to give way to the development of units for middle- and upper-income families. There is no evidence that Negroes will find difficulty in obtaining units on the rebuilt site, if they can afford the rents; eight of the first two hundred tenants of Lafayette Park–University City were Negro. But the problem of decent housing for the former residents remains unsolved.

If future urban redevelopment projects follow the Gratiot pattern of replacing slum dwellings with middle- and upper-income housing developments while the number of public housing units remains the same, as is the case in Detroit, what will happen to the former slum dweller? Will the core city be able to "redevelop" the slum dweller out of town to the suburbs? Will the palliative measures of "paint-up, fix-up" campaigns and neighborhood conservation programs suffice to make used housing available under non-slum conditions? As the displaced slum dweller seeks new shelter and penetrates new urban neighborhood boundaries, what pathologies of social tension will occur, with what resultant costs to the city? It is still too early to cast up the final accounts on the Gratiot project.

2
The Urban Renewal
of Corktown

A Neighborhood Challenges the Bulldozers

Introduction

Detroit's growth falls into three stages. The first or pre-automobile stage ended around 1900 with the city's 250,000 people concentrated within a twelve-square-mile semi-circle bounded by Grand Boulevard and the Detroit River. The second stage, halted by the depression of the thirties, was brought about by the industrial expansion that accompanied and followed World War I and the developing automobile industry. During this second stage, the population increased to 1,500,000 and spread well beyond the Grand Boulevard boundary. An additional 300,000 dwelling units were built to house this rapidly expanding population. Although a building code had been adopted in 1911 to insure the structural safety of dwellings, no zoning ordinance stood in the way of the developers and builders as they exercised ingenuity in cramming homes on lots and devoting land to profitable use. The result: thirty-foot lots with side yards too narrow to be driveways; a grid-iron pattern of narrow streets jammed with the parked cars of residents with no available off-street parking; and a variety of uses—residential, commercial, and industrial—distributed apparently at random. The housing units built during this stage made up over half of the city's housing inventory during the fifties.

The third growth stage, from 1940 to 1960, saw most of the remaining vacant land in the city filled. The population reached a peak of about 1,910,000 in the mid-fifties, but by 1960 it had declined to 1,670,144, 179,424 less than the 1950 total of 1,849,568. Meanwhile, in the surrounding suburbs, population growth continued at a rapid rate. In 1940 a zoning ordinance was passed, and in 1948 a master plan for the city was adopted. A zoning ordinance and a master plan are devices by which professional planners attempt to channel behavior and events in ways that will increase the probability of achieving certain social and economic values. Thus postwar growth took place within the framework of regulations designed to achieve a more rational use of available space.

It had taken a long time for professional city planning to become institutionalized in Detroit's governmental system. The city charter, adopted in 1918, provided for the appointment by the mayor of a nine-member Detroit City Plan Commission charged with preparing a comprehensive city plan for the physical development and improvement of the city. Although over the years commissioners had been appointed and had served out their terms, the commission had virtually no staff, a small budget, and, with the exception of arterial road construction and the location of public buildings, little effect upon the pattern of the city's development. Those capitalizing upon Detroit's booming growth during the 1920's were in no mood to tolerate interference from a city planning agency. The depression provided ample time for second thoughts. In 1938 the Plan Commission was called upon to draft a zoning ordinance, and with the adoption of the new law in 1940 and the beginning of work on a master plan that same year, the commission began to build a professional planning organization capable of playing a major role in future decisions.

By the time the Plan Commission had become established as the recognized official agency for physical planning, most of the vacant land had disappeared. In addition, a disturbing emigration of population and industry from the city had begun. Instead of finding raw land whose development they could guide toward desired goals, the planners were faced with the necessity of removing the objectionable land uses commonly referred to as slums and blight and replacing them with more desirable uses. In addition, in order to preserve as many as possible of the available dwelling units, it became necessary to take measures to conserve neighborhoods from deterioration and to encourage the upgrading of those that had begun to deteriorate.

The federal Housing Act of 1949 contained provisions designed to assist cities with slum clearance and redevelopment, and the law was broadened in 1954 to include assistance for the rehabilitation and conservation of neighborhoods. The 1954 revision reflected a shift in policy in federal aid to urban areas. Earlier legislation had been primarily concerned with slum clearance and providing housing on a project-by-project basis for low-income families. The 1954 act recognized the necessity for a broader view of what might be needed to maintain an urban system, and thus required from each locality requesting aid a

> . . . workable program (which shall include an official plan of action, as it exists from time to time, for effectively dealing with the problem of urban slums and blight within the community and for the establishment and preservation of a well-planned community with well-organized residential neighborhoods of decent homes and suitable living environment for adequate family life) for utilizing appropriate private and public resources to eliminate, and prevent the development or spread of, slums and urban blight, to encourage needed urban rehabilitation, to provide for the redevelopment of blighted, deteriorated, or slum areas, or to undertake such of the aforesaid activities or other feasible community activities as may be suitably employed to achieve the objectives of such a program . . . (Sect. 101 [c] [1]).

The requirement of the workable program was not the answer to a planner's prayer, for it meant broadening the planning process to include private developers, code enforcement, housing, community organization, and public-relations personnel. The 1954 law also gave official meaning to the words "urban renewal." They were used in the law to include both slum clearance and redevelopment, and neighborhood rehabilitation and conservation activities.

To be successful, urban renewal must be concerned with more than living quarters for urban populations. It must also attend to the maintenance of the tax base upon which the city is dependent for the financing of its services. As an economic system, the city must attract and hold industrial and commercial facilities within the city limits in order to provide employment for residents as well as a source of tax revenues. This case is an account of the decisions and events that led to the determination that seventy-five acres located inside the Grand Boulevard area, in a section of the downtown district known as Corktown, constituted a slum residential area that should be developed for industrial use.

The protagonists are the City Plan Commission and the residents of Corktown, and the significant action takes place in the decade from 1950 to 1960, amid the elaborate institutional structure and procedures that developed along with substantial federal participation in urban renewal.

The two major issues in this case were (1) whether or not Corktown was a slum, and (2) for what and for whom Corktown should be redeveloped. It may be helpful to keep the following questions in mind: When is a slum a slum? What are, or should be, the criteria for urban blight? If none can be universally agreed upon, whose opinion should be accepted? What is the purpose of the required public hearing? Who supplies the end-values towards which the planner aims his plans?

Early Planning for Corktown

A Public Housing Site. Corktown is in the old part of the city of Detroit, a part that was settled by 1900. One could quibble over the precise boundaries, but most would agree that it includes the area bounded by Michigan Avenue, Fourth, Fourteenth, and Fort Streets. The area was originally settled by Irish immigrants, many of whom came from county Cork and gave the neighborhood its name. Having been built prior to the advent of zoning ordinances and modern building regulations, the neighborhood consisted mostly of single-family frame dwellings with a liberal intermixing of commercial and industrial establishments. By the late 1930's, when the area first came up for consideration, most of the original residents and their families had left the neighborhood, and by the 1950's it was a rare resident who could trace his origins to the earlier Irish settlement. Nevertheless, sentiment dies hard. Indicative of this is the following letter which appeared in the March 6, 1938 edition of *The Detroit News* and was signed "Irish Dreamer":

> Hardly a week passes but what one reads in the newspapers about a big banquet or some other such celebration where the Detroit Irish, all formerly of Old Corktown, are most conspicuous among the prominent citizens present . . . they always tell the world, and proudly too, that they got their start in Old Corktown.

. . . I am often reminded of the words spoken a few years ago by one of our councilmen when an effort was made to clean up Hastings Street. "Hastings Street," he said, "is the stench in the city's nostrils." Some of these Corktown streets are even worse. Detroit is planning a Civic Center, why not set apart "a little bit of heaven" in old Corktown? Beautify the district. Plant trees, hedges, lay out lagoons, widen streets, and have a central building, like Tara's Hall or Blarney Castle.

"Irish Dreamer" was no doubt moved to write by the discussion that had begun over the possibility of locating a public housing project in Corktown. Carl L. Bradt, director of the Detroit Housing Commission, had begun a study of the site in the spring of 1938, and when he learned that the U.S. Housing Authority had earmarked funds for Detroit, he proceeded to seek local approval of the site so that construction could begin. His choice of Corktown was based upon the results of a survey showing that 19 percent of the area was vacant, 57 percent of the dwellings were substandard, and 83 percent of the dwellings were renter-occupied.

Opposition to the use of Corktown for public housing came from two local government officials. Henry Beyster, Department of Public Works commissioner, argued that many of the Detroiters who had moved to the outskirts and suburbs were getting tired of commuting to the downtown district, and he felt that ultimately there would be a need for a good residential district near the downtown area. Corktown was the most logical site for such a neighborhood, he maintained. City Planner Herbert L. Russell also opposed using the Corktown site for public housing, but for different reasons. He felt that part of the area would eventually be needed for commercial use, as the planned beautification and modernization of the waterfront along the Detroit River were realized. Part of the Corktown site would then provide valuable warehouse space. Other parts of the site contained fairly good homes, according to his own staff surveys, and with the waterfront improvement, he argued that this property would also be improved.

A further complication to the decision-making dilemma facing the mayor and the Detroit Common Council, who ultimately had to approve public housing sites, was a neighborhood opposition movement. A protest meeting was staged by a large group of residents (the newspapers reported five hundred) at one of the local schools. City officials, including Mayor Edward J. Jeffries, Jr., attended. The mayor pointed out the need to eliminate slum conditions, but at the same time affirmed his loyalty to Corktown, his birthplace. Other speakers who attempted to explain the advantages of the housing project were heckled, and the meeting ended with no action taken except the tabling of a resolution calling attention to slum conditions in the area.

As opposition continued to build up, Housing Director Bradt announced that the Housing Commission would continue studies of both the Corktown site and another site to the east of Woodward Avenue, the Gratiot site. Later in 1939, the Plan Commission, in answer to an inquiry, stated that it intended to zone Corktown for industrial or commercial use. The Housing Commission decided to drop both the Corktown and Gratiot sites from consideration for public housing and instead to choose a site north of Corktown, which was developed after World War II as the Jeffries public housing project. Corktown had survived the first assault.

Residential vs. Industrial Use: Master Plan Decisions. Between 1940, when the zoning ordinance was adopted, and 1948, when the master plan was approved, the Detroit City Plan Commission sprang to life. The skeleton staff that had functioned under the nine appointed commissioners was expanded from an authorized strength of eight to fifty-five, and the budget increased from $26,595 to $255,289. Since the legal basis for planning had been in existence since the adoption of the charter in 1918, this expansion reflected a substantial shift in local values concerning the role that professional planning should play in the city's future development. At the same time, working out a master plan for the city forced a consideration of what values were to prevail in making decisions on the allocation of land uses. How much land should be allocated for industrial use and how much for residential? What areas should be considered for redevelopment, and for what should they be redeveloped? These are value-loaded questions, and the professional planner involved in working out a master plan finds himself face to face with them. His expertise does not provide value-free answers. Thus, Detroit's first brush with professional city planning involved issues where the stakes were high and where personal bias, when reflected in values related to planning, counted a good deal.

In one way or another, Corktown always seemed destined to be caught in the planning web. There seemed little question among planners and other public officials that Corktown should be redeveloped; the issue was whether it should be redeveloped for residential or industrial use. This issue came to a head as work on the "future generalized land-use plan" progressed. This plan was the key to the whole, since it designated those areas which were to be devoted to residential, commercial, industrial, and other uses. Once adopted, it would take extraordinary effort to bring about changes. Now was the time to get in one's oar. Various interested groups began to make their views known to the Plan Commission. The commission hired a recognized planning consultant, Ladislas Segoe, to assist the staff with the development of the plan, and conferences were held on the staff level with industrial and other interested groups before the plans were submitted to the commission.

On August 2, 1945, the staff presented the industrial use plan to the commission. Representatives of the Greater Detroit Board of Commerce and other business groups were present at the meeting. Segoe explained that the plan was designed to provide maximum industrial land use and at the same time permit proper planning of "living space" for the city. He pointed out that the staff did not claim that the plan included enough land to take care of all likely future industrial developments. This information distressed some of his audience. Willis H. Hall, secretary-manager of the Board of Commerce, wanted to know why more land could not be made available for industry. He was told that large-scale industry was interested in large sites composed of hundreds of acres which could only be found outside the city limits. But this meeting did not resolve the issue. Willis Hall was to continue to press for allocation of more land for industrial use.

As part of the master plan studies, a consulting firm had been hired to conduct research and make physical plans for those areas designated as future slum-clearance sites. Corktown was one of the sites. Models and drawings were made, and in March 1944, the Plan Commission received a complete program for the area consisting of high-density apartments, terrace apartments, a shopping center and other public service facilities. The plan was for a model residential neighborhood. It was proposed that public financing be used for clearing the site and that the redevelopment be done by private investment. Both the staff and the commission endorsed the project, but Albert E. Cobo, then city treasurer, refused to go along with the financing proposals, advising the Plan Commission to stick to planning and leave financial matters to others. (As it turned out the consultants' plan for Corktown was analogous to what did eventually occur on another slum-clearance area, the Gratiot site.)

Although the consultants' plan was not adopted, the staff determination that Corktown should be put to high-density residential use did stand for awhile—but not for long. Early in 1945, the Pennsylvania Railroad petitioned the Plan Commission, sitting in its capacity as a zoning commission, to approve a zoning change for a part of Corktown from residential to industrial use. The commission noted that staff studies had indicated the preferred use to be high-density residential but postponed action on the petition. Later the same year, as the demand for greater allocation for industrial uses mounted, the petition was again reviewed, with the following reported in the commission's minutes:

> . . . It was pointed out that the property lies within the area designated in the future land-use plan as residential. However, at present the particular block in question is badly run down. Also Mr. Emery [George Emery, planning director] reported that the Detroit Real Estate Board had recommended that the area adjacent to the above property . . . be placed in the industrial category, and that at the last meeting with their [representative] they were rather indignant that this had not been done.

The commission faced the dilemma of choosing between staff recommendations that the Corktown area be classed residential and the demands of the two powerful private organizations, the Detroit Real Estate Board and the Greater Detroit Board of Commerce, that the area be devoted to industrial use.

On November 15, 1945, the Plan Commission held a special

meeting to vote on the requested zoning change. During the ensuing discussion, staff members pointed out that Corktown as a
whole was a borderline area, and that they were reluctant to see
any action taken on a spot-zoning change that might prejudice a
later decision covering the whole area. The commission decided
to consider only the particular block under contention, and after
lengthy discussion, it was decided to rezone the block for light
industry. The minutes note that "the secretary was instructed to
draft a communication to the Real Estate Board and Board of
Commerce calling attention to these allocations on the part of the
commission."

As work on the master plan proceeded, Corktown continued to
play an important role. As part of the master plan, a transportation plan was drafted and presented to the Plan Commission for
approval. The plan called for three future freight terminals, one
of which was to be located in the Corktown area. In the discussion
before the commission, City Planner George Emery explained that
light industry was intended for the area, but that the commission
had not made clear what its final decision would be. Willis Hall
testified that industry must be given room to grow in the city in
order to maintain an economic balance, and he recommended that
Corktown be included among from 3,000 to 4,000 additional acres
of industrial land. Father Clement Kern, of Most Holy Trinity
Roman Catholic Church in Corktown, led a small group of residents who inquired about the future disposition of the area. This
action was an inquiry and not an effort to pressure the commission into a decision. Since the commission was filled with indecision over Corktown, the residents received little satisfaction. The
commission was split between those who favored supporting staff
recommendations in spite of opposition from the Board of Commerce and the Real Estate Board and those who were reluctant to
go along with the staff in the face of opposition from organizations
supported by the major real-estate and business interests in the
city. The staff itself was split. While Director Emery had recommended industrial use for Corktown in the transportation plan,
another staff member, Donald Monson, persisted in recommending
residential use.

The Plan Commission staff had grown from thirteen in 1942 to sixty-nine in 1946. Although the professional members of the staff could be classified as "professional planners," these words imply an identity of training, skills, and values that did not exist among them. Collegiate backgrounds varied including engineering, art, architecture, sociology, etc. Some saw in planning a vehicle for carrying out social and political values, and others were more concerned with the engineering and economic aspects of land use. Some looked upon the Board of Commerce and the Real Estate Board as the reactionary outposts of a political minority, and these staff members felt obligated to act in what they considered to be the interest of the political majority. Other staff members attempted to maintain bureaucratic political neutrality. Most saw in the master plan effort an exciting opportunity to have a hand in the future development of one of the nation's major cities.

While the Plan Commission was adopting a transportation plan which allocated Corktown for industrial use, staff member Donald Monson was working on a master plan for slum clearance and redevelopment. By August 1947, Monson's redevelopment report was ready. In it he recommended that the Corktown site be returned to residential use. In stating his recommendation, he presented it as the best choice among a number of alternatives, as it would avoid reducing Detroit's participation in the federal housing program, which he claimed would bring "the opposition of all labor, Negro, and liberal groups in Detroit." The report continued:

> While Corktown could be entirely redeveloped for public housing should it be made available for residential use, the staff of the Housing Commission does not think this wise. Segregation by income groups on a rigid basis is not more desirable than by color. For the sake of a more balanced community life in the neighborhood, it is proposed that the unit be redeveloped partly by private capital. . . .

By the time these proposals were presented to the Plan Commission, the mayor had appointed Willis Hall to fill a vacancy on the commission, and Hall had been made chairman of the commission.

Monson's report was provocative for a number of reasons. In September 1946, the Plan Commission and the Housing Commission had held a joint meeting at which it was agreed that the Housing Commission would follow the master plan in designating sites for its housing projects. When the public housing program began in the thirties, the Plan Commission, without staff, zoning regulations, and master plan, was in no position to assist the Housing Commission, so the latter's staff made the initial designations, subject to Housing Commission and Common Council approval. In a sense, then, the Housing Commission held the initiative in the slum-clearance program through the selection of sites for projects. The agreement to follow the designations of the Plan Commission was a major step forward in achieving co-ordination between two city agencies and assuring that the housing program would fit in with over-all plans for the city.

The agreement was also recognition of the improvement in status of the Plan Commission staff in the city bureaucracy. At the time the Housing Commission agreed to follow the Plan Commission designations, the latter had designated Corktown for industrial use, but it was known among the Plan Commission staff that the Housing Commission staff considered Corktown a likely public housing site. Monson's wife worked for the Housing Commission. Her assignments included doing research on future sites. Both Monsons were considered to be strong advocates of public housing and opponents of segregated housing. Monson's recommendation that the Corktown site be changed back to residential use and be used in part for public housing not only challenged the Plan Commission's earlier decision that the use be industrial but also aroused the ire of those commission members who were opposed to public housing. Some of the commissioners felt that the staffs of the two agencies, Housing and Plan, were ganging up to undo a decision the two commissions had reached earlier.

The Plan Commission's response to the Monson recommendation for Corktown was to "instruct the staff to work with the Housing Commission, keeping in mind the attitude of this commission and the redevelopment program approved by this commission in order to avoid conflict." The decision may have seemed ambiguous, but the meaning was clear to those involved. It meant that the Plan Commission was not in a position to insist that no other use but industrial be considered for Corktown if the Housing Commission were to insist upon public housing for the site. The agreement that the two commissions would co-ordinate their activities was too recent and as yet untested to be jeopardized by an open conflict. A majority of the Plan commissioners, led by Chairman Hall, favored industrial use for Corktown and were suspicious of staff recommendations leading to public housing, whereas the minority, led by Commissioner Milton Selander, tended to support staff recommendations and defend the staff from the criticism leveled at it by some of the commissioners. As might be expected, personality and ideological differences were involved. If the Housing Commission had offered strong support for the industrial use decision, the Plan Commission would have been on firmer ground, but it appeared that the Housing Commission, prompted by its staff, might press for housing for Corktown. In the light of these circumstances, the Plan Commission's instructions to its staff make sense.

During 1948 the public housing site-selection controversy was temporarily quiescent. The Republicans had control of Congress, and the prospects for federal funds for housing projects were dim. Chairman Hall kept up his effort for industrial space in Corktown. Although the master plan called for industrial use, the zoning maps adopted in 1940 still classified much of the area as residential. Early in 1948, a report was rendered at the chairman's request on a proposed zoning change in the area. The report stated that although the zoning change amounted to spot zoning, it would expedite the plan for the motor freight terminal proposed for the area. The next step seemed to be the entire rezoning of the area. Commissioner Selander, who was eager to further the cause of slum clearance, proposed that "since the commission is anxious to provide for industrial land, the city might accomplish several goals by adopting a program whereby areas would be selected where there is presently blight housing, take them in condemnation, and hold them for industrial redevelopment." It was unanimously moved:

> That the staff be instructed to make a study of areas to be redeveloped for industrial purposes, selecting areas totaling approximately one hundred acres and determining the advantages and disadvantages of the city's condemning this land and holding it for sale at prevailing costs to private industry.

This approach to redevelopment, city condemnation of slum sites and resale of them to private developers, was being applied to a site east of Woodward, the Gratiot redevelopment site, but there the re-use was to continue to be residential. The Plan Commission limited the study area to a light industrial area, Corktown, and the conduct of the study became the responsibility of Donald Monson. In the spring of 1949, he reported to the commission that the Corktown area bore the same relationship to the central business district as did the Gratiot area and that developing Corktown for residential use would enable people to live close to their work in the downtown business area or in the industrial area west of the Corktown district. He argued that there were ample industrial sites in the adjacent area where industry anxious to move into Corktown could locate. He urged that an area west of Corktown be selected for industrial redevelopment. Monson's report delayed any immediate decision, and the study was referred back to the staff.

With the election of Harry S. Truman and a Democratic Congress in the fall of 1948, the Housing Commission initiated proceedings to obtain approval of several public housing sites in anticipation of favorable action on housing legislation which would make funds available for projects. The pressure for public housing was great. Detroit had not built any permanent public housing projects since the late 1930's. The Housing Commission staff recommended twelve sites, eight of which were on vacant land. Among the four slum sites was Corktown. The inclusion of Corktown, of course, was a violation of the earlier agreement of the Housing Commission to abide by the master plan designations in site selection. Chairman Hall was properly indignant over this action, and he led the Plan Commission in refusing to reverse its decision on Corktown or to submit it to restudy. But the vote was close.

It looked as if the Common Council would have to make the final decision, but a municipal election campaign was under way in the fall of 1949, and the council was in no mood to dispose of controversial issues that could be postponed. For the Housing and Plan Commissions and their staffs the stakes were high. One mayoralty candidate, George Edwards, was a supporter of liberal causes, including public housing. Candidate Albert E. Cobo was outspoken in his opposition to public housing and in his support for projects that would encourage industrial development. Since the mayor could remove members of both the Housing Commission and the Plan Commission without cause, the tenure of the commissioners would depend upon the outcome. Most of the staff members, with the exception of the directors of the two agencies, had the tenure protection of civil service regulations, but this would not protect them from a hostile mayor and commission, who could impose intolerable policies and reduced budget allocations.

Albert Cobo won the election, and the effects upon the two agencies were immediate. The Monsons resigned their positions. Housing Director James Inglis resigned and was replaced by Cobo appointee Harry J. Durbin. Through resignations, removals, and changes in attitude, significant changes took place on both the Housing Commission and the Plan Commission—changes which were soon translated into new policies. The Housing Commission recommended that the council delete the eight vacant sites from consideration for public housing, and that further study be made of the Corktown site. After further study, the Housing Commission voted to delete Corktown, and on May 2, 1950, the council took formal action to delete Corktown from the public housing program. Corktown was now firmly established as an industrial site. The master plan decision had held up.

Planning the West Side Industrial Project

First Steps. During 1950 and 1951, Detroit's redevelopment efforts were concentrated on the Gratiot project. Any doubts concerning the legality of public condemnation of slum sites for resale to private redevelopers were removed by the Michigan Supreme Court in December 1951, and the Housing and Home Finance Agency's formal approval of the Gratiot project in April 1952 was encouragement to proceed with additional projects. On June 12, 1952, the Plan Commission approved the Corktown area as one of four slum-clearance projects within the Grand Boulevard area.

Meanwhile, Councilmen Edward Connor and Louis Miriani were voicing concern over the exodus of business and industry from the city. A number of civic improvement projects were in the planning stage, and one was under way that would create a new Civic Center fronting on the Detroit River. Connor and Miriani complained in the press that the business firms dispossessed by these projects had no place to go and called upon the Plan Commission to come forward with some plan to help them out. By this time, Plan Director Emery had resigned, and Acting Director Armin Roemer reminded the council that the commission was not in the land-selling business. The Plan Commission did, however, inform the council that they were prepared to begin preliminary planning work on a portion of the Corktown redevelopment area and were applying to the HHFA for funds to carry out this work. At this time, the end of 1952, local officials were optimistic that with the assistance of the urban redevelopment grants available under the Housing Act of 1949, a major redevelopment program would soon be under way, of which Gratiot and Corktown were but the beginning. Although some delays had occurred in processing the grant application for the Gratiot project, it was felt that the experience gained there would speed action on Corktown.

Federal housing legislation required that each locality designate a single agency, known as the Local Public Agency, to deal with federal officials in the handling of grants for urban renewal. The council passed a resolution designating the Housing Commission as Detroit's Local Public Agency. The preparation of project plans and the other technical work required preparatory to submitting an application to the federal agency, however, were the responsibility of the Plan Commission. Although the Plan Commission staff did the technical planning, their work had to pass through the Housing Commission staff on its way to Washington. Under these conditions during the planning phase of a project, the uninitiated were often confused over who was responsible for what. Occasionally, even councilmen had difficulty keeping the roles of the two agencies straight.

The transfer of funds from the U.S. Treasury to local officials for use for a specific redevelopment project was no simple matter. The first step, in 1952, was a request to the Division of Slum Clearance and Urban Redevelopment of HHFA for preliminary approval for funds to permit the Local Public Agency to begin preliminary studies leading to information that would substantiate a formal application for funds for a specific project. In other words, the local agency asked the central agency for approval to gather the necessary information to prove to the central agency that the project the local agency had in mind did in fact qualify. In granting preliminary approval, the central agency did not agree that the proposed project would eventually qualify, but its action created a presumption that it would. Such a request (for a prior approval) for Corktown was forwarded by the Detroit Housing Commission for the Plan Commission to the Division of Slum Clearance and Urban Redevelopment in November 1952. This was the first formal step in the process of converting a part of Corktown into what was now inelegantly designated the West Side Industrial Project.

The letter of preliminary approval from HHFA did not arrive until April 22, 1953. The delay, which was considerable for what was considered to be a fairly routine procedure, was the result of difficulties the Housing Commission was having on the Gratiot site. The Housing Act of 1949 required that "decent, safe, and sanitary dwellings" be provided for all families dispossessed by demolition, and since the population of the Gratiot site was nearly 100 percent Negro, the Housing Commission was having trouble meeting these conditions. Criticism of the relocation process had been directed to HHFA officials by members of the Detroit Urban League. When federal urban redevelopment officials received the request for the preliminary planning grant for Corktown, they sent back to Housing Director Durbin an inquiry concerning the problem of relocating minority groups in the area. Durbin's assistant for slum clearance, W. Joseph Starrs, replied for Durbin that since the Corktown area contained proportionately fewer non-white families than the city as a whole, there would be no difficulty in finding satisfactory relocation quarters. Starrs took pains to point out that Corktown redevelopment would not involve the necessity for finding housing for a large number of Negro families. This apparently satisfied HHFA, for the letter approving the expenditure of $20,000 for the preliminary planning of the Corktown project arrived shortly thereafter.

By the time the letter of prior approval permitting work on

the preliminary planning had arrived, the Detroit City Plan Commission had a new director, Charles A. Blessing. Blessing, a professional city planner, had been a member of the Chicago city planning staff before accepting the position in Detroit. Because of the recent stormy past of the Plan Commission (the struggle over the designation of Corktown for industrial use was but one incident), the selection of a new director involved a good deal of pulling and hauling among the mayor, commission members and other city officials, as well as other individuals and groups in the community who felt that they had a stake in the type of leadership to be brought to the planning function. It also involved a clash of values over the role that planning should play in city government and the way in which planning activities should mesh with the work of other agencies, such as those dealing with housing, education, recreation, and public works. A second clash of values concerned the type of ideological orientation desired of the director. In the face of this complexity, a generalization is hazardous, but it appears that the dominant decision-makers saw as the goal of planning the maintenance of the city as a viable economic system capable of sustaining tax-supported services on a moderately high level and of providing the amenities for a predominantly middle-class population, and that they felt that this should be achieved with an aesthetic bias in favor of buildings of modern functional design and neighborhoods framed by green borders. This approach could be called an "economically sound, city beautiful" one. It was expected that Director Blessing shared these values and would help achieve them. Although Corktown was only one of a number of major projects under way at the time, the new director was eager to move as rapidly as possible on this first project to make land available for industrial use.

The Preliminary Plan. When the letter of prior approval arrived in April 1953, Detroit officials hoped that the planning phase could be completed soon, so that a formal contract with HHFA could be drawn up and work could begin. As it turned out, this planning stage was to take four and one-half years.

Two steps were required to obtain the grant. The first or preliminary planning step required the collection of data to prove

that the site was in fact blighted; agreement on the specific boundaries of the project; a complete redevelopment plan for the re-
use of the cite; cost estimates for clearing the area; and a relocation
plan for families living on the site. The Housing Commission was
responsible for the relocation plan, and the Plan Commission was
responsible for all other aspects of the preliminary planning. The
Common Council had to approve the preliminary plan before
sending it to Washington. Federal approval of the preliminary
plan permitted the second step, the completion of a final set of
plans to be filed with the application for a grant. (Subsequent
laws and regulations placed less emphasis on the first step and
concentrated on the second, but the extent of the review exercised
by HHFA and the amount of time the review consumed remained
key issues in the approval process.) HHFA approval of these documents culminated in a signed contract in which the federal government agreed to pay two-thirds of the net cost of the project.
For the Corktown project the first step took the most time, and
most of the substantive issues were resolved in accomplishing it.

The establishment of the project boundaries was a necessary
preliminary to detailed planning. The Corktown area included
more land than that required for the project, so it was necessary
to select a site within it. From April 1953 to January 1954, the
Plan Commission staff prepared data on existing land use, existing
and proposed trafficways, existing transit and truck routes, existing industries (classified by type and physical character), condition of housing structures, assessed valuations of residential and
non-residential property, and existing zoning. In addition, meetings were held with local industries and other groups in the neighborhood. By January 1954, the staff was ready to submit recommendations on boundaries to the Plan Commission.

Four possible project sites were proposed. The survey area
had been divided into three sites adjacent to each other, and a
fourth site had been marked out by combining parts of two of
the sites. Among the characteristics considered in evaluating sites
were cost of land acquisition, utility pattern, continuity with other
public improvements, amount of land to be gained through street
closures, the extent to which the area was cut up by thoroughfares, and the extent of the relocation problem. The fourth site

was arrived at by combining desirable elements (from the point of view of qualifying for slum-clearance funds) of two of the original sites. On this fourth site, the staff classified 65 percent of the housing bad, 25 percent poor and 10 percent fair. There were thirty-nine net acres involved (minus streets and alleys and other miscellaneous uses which brought the gross area to seventy-seven acres), of which twenty-two acres were residential and thirteen industrial. The Plan Commission accepted its staff recommendation that the fourth site be designated the project site, and the Housing Commission added its endorsement.

When the project area was submitted to the Common Council on February 5, 1954, the councilmen were reluctant to approve the site. Growing opposition from residents in the affected area was beginning to be felt, and the proposed site did not include any part of a skid row section which some councilmen thought should be included. As the councilmen discussed the proposal, it became evident that they did not have a very clear notion of precisely what area the Corktown project was intended to cover. Councilman William Rogell, former Detroit Tiger infielder, felt that it was time to clean up skid row, and he and other councilmen backed a proposal by Councilman Edward Connor that the Plan Commission study the feasibility of enlarging the Corktown project to include a section of skid row. This enlargement would require extending the eastern boundary of the proposed site across the John C. Lodge Expressway in order to link with the skid row district. The council decided to hold up any decision on the site until new studies had been completed.

During the discussion of the project area, Councilman Rogell had brought up another objection. He wondered whether some method could be devised whereby the residents of the area could receive the benefit of the higher property values which would result from rezoning the land for industrial use. He thought that it was unfair to condemn the property at a low value as slum housing and then resell it at a high price for industrial use. He suggested that the land first be rezoned as industrial and then sold without recourse to the federal program. From February to May, the decision was in abeyance while the Plan Commission staff held conferences with local groups and communicated with Washington. Federal redevelopment officials pointed out that skid row could not be included in the site, since it did not have the characteristics to qualify under existing laws and regulations. The "unrelated" individuals who composed a large portion of the skid row population did not constitute "families," and 52 percent of the population of an area had to be members of residential families if the area was to qualify as a project area. Detroit officials were also reminded that the purpose of the redevelopment legislation was to eliminate blighted housing, not to reclaim for industry an area already devoted to industrial use. On May 26, 1954, the council approved the project boundaries as initially proposed by the Plan Commission.

Approval of the project boundaries did not clear the way for a speedy submittal of the preliminary report. The site was selected on the presumption that the area was blighted, and the Plan Commission staff was convinced that it was. At a public hearing held in July, local residents contested the claim and moved the council to insist upon more documentation of the existence of blight. Meanwhile, the Housing Act of 1949 was in the process of being amended by Congress, and Detroit officials were notified that any action on Corktown would have to await final Congressional action. By the fall of 1954, it was apparent that the early optimism concerning the speed with which Corktown could be processed was unwarranted.

On September 28, 1954, the Plan Commission transmitted to the council the documentation of blighted conditions in the project area. Both federal and state law required that the existence of blight be established as a prior condition to redevelopment. Michigan law—the Rehabilitation of Blighted Areas Act (Public Act 344, 1945)—defined a blighted area as ". . . an area developed or undeveloped, improved or unimproved, characterized by obsolescence, physical deterioration of structures therein, improper division or arrangements of lots and ownerships and streets and other open spaces, mixed character and uses of the structures, or any other similar characteristics which endanger the health, safety, morals, or general welfare of the municipality. . . ." The Manual of Policies and Requirements of the HHFA listed the following as indicators of blight:

Dilapidation of structures and dwelling units (disrepair, damaged building members, inadequate original construction).

Inadequate dwelling facilities (lack of hot water in dwelling unit; shared toilet, bath, and kitchen; lack of central heating).

Overoccupancy of dwelling units.

Land use and coverage (overcrowding of buildings on land, lack of yard space, intrusion of non-residential uses).

Environmental influences (narrow, inconvenient, congested, or unsafe streets).

Evidence of economic deterioration (low rent, declining property values, absence of new construction).

Social blight (high morbidity and mortality rate).

The task of the Plan Commission staff was to show that, based upon these criteria, Corktown was indeed a blighted area.

Detroit's thirteen thousand residential blocks had been surveyed and rated according to the following factors: overcrowding, dilapidation, lack of sanitary facilities, income, monthly rentals, owner-occupancy and age of structures. Based upon the rating, blocks were classified as in need of either redevelopment (demolition and replacement) or conservation with some degree of improvement varying from very minor to major alterations. On the Corktown project site, nineteen of the twenty-one blocks fell into the redevelopment classification. The various redevelopment areas within the city were additionally evaluated to determine priorities for redevelopment. In this survey, blocks were given ratings according to condition of housing (rotting of building members, structures out of plumb, makeshift or deteriorated roofs, poor foundations, lack of central heating) and environmental conditions (overcrowding of land, poor outside housekeeping, commercial and/or industrial nuisances, traffic and/or lack of parking). Redevelopment areas were then placed in four categories of blight intensity to determine priority for treatment. The Corktown project area fell within the first priority.

Additional evidence of blight was submitted from data provided by other city agencies—Police Department, Fire Department, Board of Education, Department of Building and Safety Engineering and Department of Health. These data were presented to show that, compared with averages for the city as a

whole, the project area contained a higher rate of building violations, a higher school absenteeism and truancy rate, and a higher
rate of deaths from tuberculosis, other infections and parasitic
diseases, and violent and accidental causes. These data were vigorously challenged by local residents on the grounds that the reporting areas used, such as census tracts, police precincts, school
districts and health districts, did not precisely coincide with the
project area and were not a true measure of conditions within the
area. The evidence convinced the council that further study was
warranted, and the Housing Commission was authorized to apply
to HHFA for the necessary funds to continue studies of the project
area. On November 9, 1954, HHFA approved the request, and it
appeared that the Corktown project was finally picking up speed.

From the fall of 1954 to March of 1955, the Plan Commission
was engaged in completing its documentation of the preliminary
report to be sent to Washington. The difficulty that the Housing
Commission was experiencing in finding private developers for
the now available land in the Gratiot redevelopment site had
cooled some of the enthusiasm for redevelopment, but the staff
felt that the industrial re-use planned for Corktown would attract
buyers. The preparation of the industrial use plan for the redeveloped area, which had to be submitted as part of the preliminary
report, required numerous conferences with industrial groups and
a number of tentative plans, which were subsequently altered to
accommodate changes in parcel sizes and alterations in traffic patterns. Finally, on St. Patrick's Day, March 17, 1955, an appropriate
date on which to consider Corktown, the council approved the
studies of the Plan Commission and authorized the Housing Commission to submit to HHFA the preliminary plan of the West Side
Industrial Project.

Federal approval of the preliminary plan was not obtained
until January 10, 1956, nearly a year later. The first question raised
by Washington was whether the project area was, in fact, blighted.
Urban Renewal Director Hugh McCullum wrote to Housing Director Durbin that more persuasive evidence was needed to justify
clearance of the area. He went on to point out:

> Form H-672 indicates that a majority of structures and dwelling
> units are standard. . . .

While we recognize that the proposed change in land use is an important factor in your determination, it must be definitely established that the residential structures are not suitable for rehabilitation.

This letter was prompted by data supplied in the preliminary report that showed 657 standard structures and 435 substandard structures, but these data did not cover the precise area of the project site. HHFA recommended that a house-to-house survey be conducted of the actual project area and each dwelling unit classified. The Plan Commission staff did this, with the result that 78 percent (282) were classified as substandard and 22 percent (79) were classified as standard. Meanwhile, local residents had called upon Congressman Charles C. Diggs for support. In April, Diggs appeared at a joint meeting of Plan officials and members of the Corktown Home Owners' Association after which he contacted HHFA to inquire about the prospects of rehabilitating the Corktown area rather than redeveloping it. Congressman Diggs's interest may have alerted HHFA officials to a careful review of local data proving the need for redevelopment.

The industrial redevelopment plan also received careful scrutiny. HHFA informed local authorities that:

> In reviewing the proposed street design for the intended redevelopment of the project, it appears to us that the internal truck circulation is inadequate for an industrial development of this type. . . . Since this project is not serviced by rail facilities, all transportation in and out of the area will be mainly by trucks, so that the basic design should be one that facilitates ease of movement within the area and avoids . . . excessive truck movements.

This detailed review of their plans came as a surprise to local planners, who were having their first extensive experience with federal authorities. As might be expected, the federal action prompted feelings of irritation over interference in local matters, and several weeks of negotiation ensued before the proposals of the local planners were acceptable to HHFA officials. During this period, the staffs of both the local and central agencies were becoming familiar with the professional competencies of each other. The local staff felt that, as a result of this experience, they had impressed HHFA with their competence and that their plans would receive less detailed review in the future.

Also complicating the review process and adding to the delay was the application of the provisions of the Housing Act of 1954 to the Corktown project. The new law changed the application procedure for redevelopment grants by requiring that a "workable program" for urban renewal precede specific project requests. Although the Corktown project had been initiated under the Housing Act of 1949, the new provisions were nevertheless applicable, and the Plan Commission staff proceeded to prepare such a document. Fortunately, the master plan had included a master plan of redevelopment. In effect, Detroit had a "workable program" before the federal requirement was enacted, and it did not take long to put this into acceptable form to satisfy the new law. The workable program was ready for council action by April 1955, and its prompt approval by the council was followed by equally prompt approval by Washington in June. In spite of the speedy approval of the workable program, approval of the preliminary plan for Corktown was not accomplished until the following January.

The Civic Center and the Wholesalers. The difficulties and delays entailed in Washington's processing of Corktown became increasingly frustrating as city officials struggled to accommodate a group of wholesale firms which were about to be displaced by the construction of a convention hall and exhibits building as part of the downtown Civic Center. To those who looked upon the Corktown project as a step toward preventing industry from leaving the city, the plight of the wholesalers seemed to provide an opportunity to demonstrate the value of the project.

The Civic Center project was close to the heart of Mayor Cobo, as indeed it had been to those of his predecessors, Mayors Jeffries and VanAntwerp. The urge to leave one's imprint upon the community in the form of a massive civic improvement is common among public officials, and Mayor Cobo was no exception. A large convention hall and exhibits building located on the waterfront in the downtown area was to be his special contribution. (After his death, the hall was renamed Cobo Hall.) As the plans for this project progressed and construction drew near, B. H. Zendle, secretary of the Detroit Associated Wholesalers, sent a letter to the council in which he said that the Civic Center project would scatter a number of wholesalers located on the site to less convenient areas in the city and prompt some of them to leave the city. He pointed out the need for a central location for the wholesale business close to retail outlets, and he suggested that the skid row area be cleared of its blight and be made available to the dispossessed wholesalers. This letter, dated August 10, 1954, was turned over to the Plan Commission, and Director Blessing answered it, saying:

> During the past years we have carried on very intensive studies in the area of redevelopment, and we are certain those projects commonly known as the Corktown project and Skid Row project would warrant discussion with your group. . . .

He suggested that members of the Associated Wholesalers meet with members of the Plan Commission staff to discuss the matter. At the first meeting the wholesalers expressed little interest in Corktown, which was further removed from the central business district than was skid row. A month later, in October 1954, the wholesalers requested a second meeting, at which they did express an interest in the Corktown site; but they were concerned about whether a move from the Civic Center area could be co-ordinated with a move into Corktown. The Plan Commission staff hopefully replied that "we have concentrated on the Corktown project in order to provide accommodation for people such as yourselves." The planners told the wholesalers that land would probably be ready for constructon in Corktown late in 1955. It was decided to submit the matter to Mayor Cobo so that he could expedite the proceedings.

The mayor had appointed a Civic Center Development Committee composed of influential citizens to help promote the Civic Center projects. This committee was headed by Willis Hall. Hall had resigned from the Plan Commission as the result of his disagreement "on a matter of principle" with the mayor over a zoning change, but the mayor had promptly appointed him to head the Civic Center Development Committee. Hall's influence in civic affairs was not diminished by this. A meeting of Hall's committee with the wholesalers and the Housing and Plan Commission staffs was held early in 1955 in order to work out a co-ordinated eviction of the wholesalers from the Civic Center site and relocation to Corktown. Prior to the meeting, the attorney for the whole-salers had warned that his clients could not afford two moves and that they would move either to Corktown or out of the city. Their price tag for remaining in the city was land costing less than $25,000 an acre. The meeting produced no more than hopeful assurances from Housing Director Durbin that the Corktown land would be ready in time for the move. Soon after the meeting, the two city agencies along with Hall's committee and Mayor Cobo joined in urging the council to approve the clearance of a 7.5-acre site in the Corktown project area for the wholesalers. The plan was approved by the council and accepted by the wholesalers, and the local newspapers welcomed the outcome as proof that indus-try could be accommodated within the city through wise official action.

What appeared to be a solution to the wholesalers' problem and a demonstration of the value of redevelopment all in one package never materialized. While city officials and wholesalers were agreeing on a plan, federal officials were questioning the pre-liminary plan for Corktown. As 1955 drew to a close, all hope of co-ordinating the Civic Center evacuation with Corktown occu-pation ended, and the Civic Center Development Committee re-ported in January 1956 that it "would be inequitable to hold up the Civic Center development for two years pending redevelop-ment of Corktown." The mayor and the council concurred with this conclusion. The Civic Center, which was entirely a local proj-ect, could not wait out the time required for decisions under the federal-local redevelopment program. As time went on, Plan Com-mission staff members were less upset by this turn of events. They felt that the wholesalers had put up a strong front in an effort to get some cheap land from the city in an area strategically located for their purposes. When the time came to leave the Civic Center site, few if any actually left the central business district but instead found other quarters in the area. It was felt that their operations were such that they could not afford to leave that area. In any event, the construction of the Civic Center buildings was well under way long before the first condemnation suit was settled in Corktown.

The Relocation Plan. Following the approval of the preliminary plan for Corktown in January 1956, the Plan Commission and the Housing Commission proceeded to prepare the final plans for the project. This planning was largely a technical process culminating in detailed redevelopment, land acquisition, and financial and relocation plans. All of this was carried on under the scrutiny of federal authorities, although much of the work was a more minute coverage of work done in the preliminary planning. Of special interest to HHFA officials was the relocation plan.

The relocation plan and the carrying out of that plan were the responsibility of the Detroit Housing Commission. The relocation of families located on the project site had been a major problem in carrying out the Gratiot redevelopment project. Reverberations had been felt in Washington, and even though the Corktown site contained only a small number of Negro families, HHFA officials were determined to make sure that the relocation of Corktown families would be more obviously in accord with the statutory requirement that displaced families be housed in decent, safe, and sanitary quarters. The displacement of families from the Gratiot site had begun before relocation plans had been developed, and to many observers, there seemed to have been little relationship between the relocation plan, which had optimistically foreseen few problems, and actual practice. For Corktown, there was ample time to prepare a relocation plan well in advance of any need to move families, and the experience obtained at Gratiot was fresh in the memory of both local and federal officials. Planning reflected this experience.

In preparing the relocation plan, a 25 percent sample survey (908 families and 608 single persons, a total of 1,516 families and single persons) of residents of the project site was conducted in order to determine composition characteristics relevant to relocation. Among the findings were the following:

Relocation Residents	Number	Percent
White families and single persons	1,236	82
Non-white families and single persons	280	18
Home owners	108	7
Tenants	1,300	86
Subtenants	108	7

Single persons under 65	312	21
Single persons over 65	120	8
Two-person families (adults)	292	19
Two-person families (1 adult, 1 child)	20	1
Three- to five-person families	364	24
Six- to nine-person families	164	11
Over nine-person families	8	.5
No information	236	15.5

The relocation plan submitted by the Housing Commission pointed out that a Relocation Office had been authorized by the council and that such a unit was being set up as a part of the commission's organization. This new unit would be responsible for all relocation required within the city as well as within the Corktown project. In addition, a master relocation plan was to be prepared, and a Relocation Advisory Committee was to be appointed to advise on relocation activities. The plan went on to specify procedures that would be employed to avoid a recurrence of past difficulties. Housing accommodations of rehoused families would be inspected to determine whether or not they met the standards established by housing laws and regulations, and substandard relocations would be classified as temporary, with follow-up assured until relocation responsibility had been discharged. The plan also gave assurance that every effort would be made to avoid losing track of families and that procedures would be set up to attempt to trace those who did disappear, with the aid of records made available by the utility companies. A guarantee that each resident had received notice of his rights and the assistance available to him in finding rehousing was to be obtained by requiring a signed receipt for such documents, which were to be delivered to residents by a member of the staff. The plan contemplated that formal eviction notices would be required in only about 50 percent of the cases and court action to evict in 24 percent, since most of the residents would move voluntarily.

The relocation plan, prepared in December 1956, contemplated that relocation would begin by the summer of 1957. As it turned out, relocation for Corktown did not start until late in 1958, and by that time the Relocation Advisory Committee had been in operation for a year and the master relocation plan had been completed. The Relocation Advisory Committee included among its twenty members: four from the Housing Commission (three staff and one commissioner); a representative from the Plan Commission staff; and five members from other governmental agencies dealing with housing, welfare, and/or minority group problems. The remaining ten members were drawn from labor, real-estate, and other interested groups. Of special significance was the inclusion of William Price, director of community services, Detroit Urban League, an outspoken critic of the Gratiot relocation and a spokesman for Negro rights. Corktown was represented by Father Clement Kern, pastor of Most Holy Trinity Roman Catholic Church. The Relocation Advisory Committee was ready with its first report by August 1958.

The Relocation Advisory Committee report included ten recommendations. The gist of these were that ample notice to vacate should be given in writing to owners and tenants facing relocation; that court action should be used only as a last resort; that in case of hardship, the city should acquire property from owners who wished to sell prior to condemnation; that the scheduling of forced moves should be related to family and business planning; that the commission should notify those facing displacement of available relocation services at the time the condemnation appraisal contract was let; and that "every possible means shall be utilized to help those being displaced to raise their living standards." These recommendations did not conflict in any way with the provisions of the relocation plan for Corktown or with the master relocation plan that was ready by the summer of 1958. With the exception of the recommendation that in hardship cases the city purchase property prior to condemnation, the formal relocation plans embodied provisions establishing procedures comparable to those recommended by the advisory body.

Corktown Goes Down Swinging

Corktown's Community Organizations. While the final redevelopment and relocation plans for the Corktown site were being put in order during the summer of 1957, the residents of Corktown were losing their last battle in a struggle to prevent a part of their neighborhood from being converted into the West Side

Industrial Project. The doctrine of urban renewal is replete with references to the need for public support of renewal programs and the need to evoke the participation of renewal-area residents in renewal projects. The requirement that a public hearing be held prior to project approval is a guarantee that residents be heard, but it does not guarantee that they will be heeded. Some Corktown residents wanted not only to be heard but also to be heeded, and in order to accomplish this, they examined the doctrine of urban renewal and sought to employ it to protect their own neighborhood, while at the same time local officials were applying the doctrine to support the redevelopment of a part of the neighborhood for industrial use.

Foremost among the difficulties in the choice of Corktown as a redevelopment site was the refusal of some residents to consider it a slum. These residents considered the statistics gathered by the Plan Commission staff purporting to prove the existence of slum conditions irrelevant, inaccurate, or both. The refusal to accept the slum designation was coupled with an underlying suspicion that a conspiracy was under way to turn Corktown over to industrial developers. Moreover, Corktown was not composed of the indifferent, unorganized, depressed masses commonly associated with slum sites. The public hearings that had been held on the Gratiot site went virtually unattended by the nineteen hundred families affected by the project. But Corktown had social organization, and it was brought into play to protect the area.

By the 1950's, only a few Irish families remained scattered throughout the area that had been a close-knit Irish community at the turn of the century. Two groups made up the major share of the mid-century population, the Maltese and the Mexicans, who, it is estimated, together comprised from 60 to 65 percent of the population of Corktown. The non-whites, mainly Negroes, made up the next largest group, 18 percent, and the balance was composed of southern whites and of southern Europeans from at least ten countries. Although "Corktown" was no longer descriptive of the population, the neighborhood name continued to be used in the press and by public officials, and it continued to evoke emotional associations with its past history. The name did not hurt the cause of the contemporary occupants.

Despite these changes in ethnic composition, Corktown continued to display characteristics associated with the concept of a neighborhood. There were a number of organizations built around ethnic, religious, and economic interests, and these organizations gave community organization a pluralistic structure; but as the plans for redevelopment progressed, the desire to preserve the neighborhood provided a common bond among the various groups. Not all of the groups were equally sophisticated in the strategy and tactics of neighborhood pressure politics, and as the struggle over Corktown developed, one organization, the Corktown Home Owners' Association, Inc., led the fight for the neighborhood.

The Maltese were the largest group and the best organized from a social standpoint. They were fairly prosperous in comparison with the other residents, and many owned their own homes. Some were veterans of World War II, having served in either the Canadian or the United States armed forces. The Maltese had two organizations taking part in the controversy, the Maltese Benevolent Society and the Maltese Legion Auxiliary. While these two groups attended meetings with Plan Commission officials and had representatives at public hearings, the language barrier reduced their effectiveness. The Mexicans were also handicapped by language, but the Mexican-American Auxiliary did participate in meetings and hearings. Both the Mexicans and the Maltese looked to Most Holy Trinity Church for direction.

Father Clement Kern, pastor of Most Holy Trinity Church, was in a position of leadership which was easily the strongest of any individual in Corktown. He could converse with his parishioners in their own languages, and, of course, many of them turned to him for advice. The Mother Cabrini Clinic and the Casa Maria Settlement House were adjuncts of the church which sent representatives to meetings on the redevelopment project. It was evident that Father Kern's attitude would influence many Corktowners.

The head of the Corktown businessmen's group was a prominent citizen of the area and the community's undertaker. Although representing the small group of prosperous Corktowners, the businessmen's group did not appear to have real importance as a source of opposition to the city's plans. The Corktown Credit Union was also active in the area and had become a widely used depository for savings. The Credit Union had been organized with the aid of Councilman Edward Connor when he was head of the Citizens' Housing and Planning Committee, a private organization, with the thought in mind that the accumulated savings would be used to purchase new homes in a new community consisting of former residents. Apparently few except Connor took this plan seriously, but the Credit Union did provide a convenient banking service. Another neighborhood organization was the Corktown Co-operative, a venture in which many residents had invested. Many skid row expatriates worked for this organization, which bought used articles and sold the renovated merchandise at its four stores. These three organizations played no significant role in the controversy, but they indicate the amount and diversity of community organization that existed in Corktown.

In addition to Most Holy Trinity, there were two other churches serving Corktown. A Baptist church served the Negro population and took no part in the controversy. The rector of St. Peter's Episcopal Church during part of the controversy, Rev. John F. Mangrum, did take an active part in opposing the redevelopment. He was the only one of the three clerics to present a vigorous opposition, but Father Kern had by far the largest number of parishoners in the area. The following letter, which the Rev. Mangrum sent to the Plan Commission, is indicative of his attitude toward the project:

> It is very good of you to invite me to attend the meeting of the Plan Commission relative to the disposal of the people in Corktown—or should I say the buildings? The city government seems so much more interested in buildings than people!
>
> There are a few reservations that I would like to make. First, that attendance at your little tête-à-tête will in no wise constitute endorsement of your shop-worn city plan to me. I intend to fight it every inch of the way. . . .
>
> It is a fine thing for you to do to allow discussion of this, and to hear God's side in this matter—that is, the side of the people who live here. Sincere commendations to you for that. And please know that my firm opposition to all your shenanigans has nothing to do with the professional respect you must justly merit from all of us. Just know that I am certain the plan for Corktown is evil and bad, and must be beaten completely. The proposed "redevelopment" is not progress, is not just, and is at base a cruel, cruel proposal. I am certain of that.

Before his departure to a new assignment in Florida late in 1955—an exodus greeted with relief by members of the Plan Commission staff—Rev. Mangrum was to contribute many an eloquent caveat against the redevelopment project. But the most effective and persistent opposition came from the Corktown Home Owners' Association, led by its president, Miss Ethel Claes. The association was formed in 1951, but it was not until Miss Claes became president in 1953 that its opposition began to take effect. As this organization took over the leadership of the opposition to redevelopment, other community groups became less active. The diminished activity of these groups may have been due in part to the departure of Rev. Mangrum and the shift in Father Kern's position from questioning the redevelopment plan to attempting to help carry it out, but as the membership of the Home Owners' Association increased from two hundred to over a thousand, they were able to channel the energy for opposition through a single organization. Whether or not the association was representative of the majority of Corktowners can only be conjectured—the Plan Commission staff felt that it was not—but that it represented a large segment of the estimated eight thousand residents in the area cannot be denied.

The Opening Rounds. Aside from the concern expressed by Father Kern and a few residents of Corktown during the time of the master plan decisions, it was not until 1951 that residents became alert to, or at least responded to, the prospects in store for the area. As articles began to appear in the local press about Detroit's redevelopment program, residents began to direct inquiries to the Plan Commission and the Common Council. Finally, on January 15, 1951, a petition was forwarded to the council protesting the rezoning or condemnation of Corktown. The petition had been prepared by Ethel Claes and included the signatures of twelve hundred residents. As was the usual procedure when in receipt of such communications, the council forwarded it to the relevant agency for explanation, in this case the Plan Commission. The staff explained the matter as follows:

> . . . it is a misunderstanding on petitioners' part in that the federal loan is not for the purpose of condemning property, but for the purpose of conducting studies to determine whether or not a portion of

the 240 acres qualifies for redevelopment, and, if so, precisely which section should be so redeveloped.

This explanation satisfied the Plan commissioners, and the matter was referred back to the council accompanied by the following explanation from Plan Director Emery:

> Miss Claes has apparently seen some statements relative to studies of possible redevelopment in this area. . . .
> The section of this area which is occupied by the Claes Book Shop is characterized by much better housing and physical conditions and would be most unlikely to be included in the early stages of any redevelopment. . . .
> . . . under the circumstances it does not appear that there is any real basis for concern by Miss Claes in relation to her property for some time to come, and before any decision is made there will be hearings held and further opportunity for the property owners involved to adequately present their position.

This explanation satisfied the council, but it did not satisfy Miss Claes and her supporters, who could detect that these communications were carefully worded so as not to commit the Plan Commission against the redevelopment of all of Corktown while at the same time telling residents that it was still too early to object to decisions not as yet made.

When the Plan Commission made public its redevelopment priority schedule in the fall of 1952, in which Corktown redevelopment was listed as No. 2, the residents responded with a series of meetings during which they planned to carry out their own renewal program. *The Detroit News* for August 10, 1952 reported that:

> A move is under way to spruce up Old Corktown. Under the plan everyone in the area will be encouraged to join in a clean-up campaign.
> The Corktown Civic Improvement Committee named the Reverend John F. Mangrum . . . as its public-relations director.
> Along with Committee Chairman George F. Trombley, he suggested that the city set up a recreation center for men.
> The two also urged that representatives of organizations in Corktown make an inspection tour of the district soon, then hold a meeting to discuss plans for community clean-up and betterment.

The suggestion was also made that a Civic Development Foundation be organized for the purpose of paying out funds for home improvement. Corktown was thus displaying a willingness to carry out a neighborhood conservation and rehabilitation program on its own. Meanwhile, Miss Claes was preparing and sending off to HHFA another petition, which was promptly returned to her along with a copy of the Housing Act of 1949 and advice that the issue was a matter of local concern. With this rebuff from the federal bureaucracy, the Home Owners' Association realized their only hope lay in influencing the council.

The prior approval to proceed with preliminary planning had been received from Washington early in 1953, and during that year the Plan Commission staff was at work preparing preliminary plans and organizing data to aid in the selection of a specific project site. These activities did not, however, take place unnoticed or without constant reaction from residents. The *Detroit Times* of March 10, 1953 carried the following letter to the editor:

> Where will the people of Corktown go when their homes are condemned and they are told to get out? What will they be able to buy with the money they will receive? . . .
>
> It is unfortunate that we people of Corktown are located on such a desirable spot; . . .
>
> So—our neighbors covet our property—and under the guise of slum clearance the city would condemn our property FOR THE REAL PURPOSE OF SELLING IT TO INDUSTRY. . . .
>
> How right will it be when it is YOUR house and property which your fellow patriots will snatch for any reason, with carefully prearranged legality?
>
> Lawyers and Judges: Do not ride on the backs of these modern landgrabbers! Is there no spirit to fight for an ideal? . . .
>
> If people in industry wish to obtain this land, let them deal directly. Let's not be intimidated by a few politicians and city planners parading as specialists in city affairs. SPECIALISTS FOR WHOM, we ask?

In June of 1953, Rev. Mangrum appeared before a civic group, the Vortex Club, and reportedly charged the City Plan Commission with acting in an "un-American way." Following his speech, the club passed a resolution asking the city to answer the following allegations concerning Corktown redevelopment:

1. Expressways and river-front development make the property's

potential value extremely high. Yet the residents are asked to sell so private industry can purchase the property.

2. It is being declared a slum so the current property value will be held way down, paying property owners less than enough to buy homes elsewhere.

3. If Detroiters allow Corktown to be condemned in this way then other areas will be in the same danger.

4. It is un-American for a plan commission made up of members not elected but appointed, to take such action without a public hearing or possible referendum vote.

When contacted by the newsmen to respond to these charges, a member of the Plan staff was quoted to the effect that "the area is only being considered for condemnation and resale to private industry. It has not been designated a slum. There will be a public hearing after a survey of the area now under way is completed." These were far from being words of assurance that Corktown would be left intact, and they did nothing to allay the fears of the Corktown residents.

Local elections were to be held in November 1953, and as election day approached, some of the councilmen seemed sympathetic to the arguments put forth by the opponents of redevelopment. Councilman Rogell accused the city of taking advantage of residents by condemning property as slum residences and then selling it for industrial use. He was to persist in his argument that if the land were to be used for industrial purposes, it should be condemned as industrial property. As the election approached, other councilmen suggested that perhaps rezoning would solve the Corktown controversy, but for the most part the front-running candidates were noncommittal, and Corktown was not a major issue in the election. The Plan Commission did its best not to rock the boat. On the one hand it did not claim to be abandoning the Corktown project, but assurances were given that residents would have ample time to be heard, once the surveys and plans were developed.

The First Public Hearing. The Housing Act of 1949 required that before a local community adopted a redevelopment plan for an area, a public hearing must be held. Precisely what the hearing was supposed to accomplish was not clear from the legislation, but the hearing process has become a traditional part of our administrative culture. The timing of the hearing was of strategic importance to both the administrator and the persons being heard. To the administrator, in this case the Plan Commission, it would have been advantageous to postpone the hearing until all the data had been collected and the plans completed, in order to make an impressive showing. To the Corktowners, a timely hearing would have been one held early enough in the planning process to forestall their being presented with a *fait accompli*. The nature of American local government is such that regardless of ambiguity in federal requirements concerning a hearing, persistent pressure by local citizens upon their councilmen is the best method of forcing the hand of the administrator. This strategy is the one the Home Owners' Association proceeded to adopt.

The first public hearing on Corktown's redevelopment was held on July 22, 1954. The events directly leading to the hearing began in November 1953, with the preparation of a petition addressed to the council by the Home Owners' Association. As was described earlier, while these events were taking place, the Plan Commission approved a project site within the Corktown area, and the council, after some hesitation, accepted the site and approved further studies. While the project site included only a part of the Corktown area, some seventy-five gross acres out of about two hundred and fifty, the opposition to redevelopment was based upon the premise that redevelopment of any part of the area would hurt the whole area. The fact that the project site did not include the property of the leaders of the opposition movement did not deter them from their efforts.

On November 18, 1953, the Home Owners' Association submitted to the council a formal request for a joint hearing with the council and the Plan Commission so that "matters may be threshed out" concerning the possible rezoning of Corktown for light industrial use or condemnation for redevelopment. Before the request was sent, the Plan Commission had attempted to head off such a move by inviting Miss Claes to meet with members of the Plan Commission staff and have explained to her the plans for the area and the reasons behind them. The lawyer for the Home Owners' Association and Miss Claes listened to the planners, but both came away unconvinced and proceeded with the request for the hearing. The formal request was addressed to the council in the form of a seven-page, single-spaced letter, which presented thirty-one major reasons (so numbered) for keeping Corktown a residential area. It was signed by the officers of the association, and attached were several sheets containing the signatures of area residents. The following excerpts from the letter reveal the main arguments:

. . . it is clear that rezoning or condemnation of but a part of this Corktown area . . . will mean . . . the entire area . . . would depreciate to a level where the properties would be worth almost nothing, for the shadow of rezoning and of light industry would darken the sale prospects of the remaining property, and appraisals would be automatically and inevitably depressed.

. . . it is extremely dubious that light industry will want to come into this particular area, and . . . the admission of sporadic instances of light industry into the area merely confuses the owners, destroys morale, renders hope of property improvement impossible, and should not be permitted.

. . . this area is essentially one of home owners. Many of us having lived here for over thirty years and it would be impossible for us to find equivalent housing in an equivalent area. . . .

. . . it is an open, well-known, and notorious fact that condemnation has resulted in gross inequities. . . .

. . . in this area are many mature persons on old-age pension, which . . . suffices to keep the recipients off the welfare because their houses are paid for, but who would be unable to buy other houses with the proceeds of their present homes were they to suffer condemnation.

. . . much of the criticism leveled against our area arises from laxity or oversight of the city hygenic agencies, who do not show us a good example, . . . if these agencies did their part of the work a little more thoroughly, [the people in] the area would be encouraged to do theirs and the entire area would soon take on a very different aspect. . . .

Just as there are newer thoughts on the expressways, so there are newer thoughts on slum eradication; the Baltimore and New Orleans and Philadelphia plans show more modern methods of revivifying the patient other than by killing him. If the would-be improvers of our area are really motivated to get rid of a slum, then modernization, not annihilation, is indicated, at least it should be first tried, without running the city into debt.

It is sometimes heard that there is a dearth of industrial localities

for small businesses. Many sites are available, for example north of
Larned and east of Brush. There is no reason to rezone our area with
such a large field still available, and the council should resist the
special pressure groups that wish to seize this area.

. . . we ourselves have contacted the Board of Health, the Board
of Education, the police, and other social and governmental agencies for such data as [are] pertinent to a slum area, for example, child
delinquency, school absence, incidence of contagious diseases, incidence of sex [crimes] and other crimes, and we have not found such
data, and we declare that this area is not a slum and wish to bring
to light such data for or against such an appellation to show that it
is erroneous.

The new trend in housing policy of the government as stated by
Albert Cole . . . is to *sustain* residential investment through repair,
restoration and modernization. The houses in our area are sound, but
the older houses should . . . be revived and modernized rather than
torn down. . . . The burden is upon the Plan Commission to show
that the area is beyond reclamation. Examination of the area reveals that at the present moment considerable face-lifting is proceeding. . . .

From the point of view of the Plan Commission, the request
for a hearing came at an inopportune time. The council had not
as yet approved the project site, and the Plan Commission staff
was not eager for a public row that might result in some councilmen taking public stands that would make it difficult for them
to approve the commission's site at a later date. The professional
planners were especially dubious of the councilmen's ability to
resist the pressures of a public hearing and were therefore eager
to forestall the hearing until after site approval had been obtained.
The letter from the Home Owners' Association showed that there
was a good head of steam building up in the neighborhood, and
the public hearing could only result in an explosion.

Councilman Connor came to the rescue. Recognizing the explosive potentiality of the neighborhood situation, he proposed
letting off steam gradually, through a series of meetings between
Housing and Plan Commission staff members and groups of residents. Connor, with an academic background in the social sci-
ences at the University of Chicago, placed a high value upon the
informal meeting as a vehicle for achieving agreement among divergent points of view. The Plan Commission staff welcomed the

suggestion because it meant a postponement of the public hearing and afforded them an opportunity to sell their views to residents in the area. Connor's suggestion was formally adopted by the council, which authorized that the informal meetings be held, following which a public hearing would be scheduled.

Although the material recommending the selection of a specific project site had already been collected by the staff, the Plan Commission, following the adoption of Councilman Connor's suggestion for informal meetings, agreed to be guided by the results of these meetings in presenting materials to the council in support of the site. A number of meetings were scheduled during the spring of 1954, but the three key meetings were with Father Kern, the Home Owners' Association, and Rev. Mangrum.

The first of these meetings was held on April 26 and included Father Kern and representatives from the Casa Maria Settlement House and from Mother Cabrini Clinic. This was the Mexican and Maltese group. This meeting, as well as the others, was held in the offices of the Plan Commission staff, and minutes were kept for the commission's records. (In later years the staff became more sophisticated in the staging of "informal hearings" and met in places more convenient to residents and less forbiddingly replete with the formal trappings of bureaucracy.) After the Plan Commission staff had presented a review of the Corktown project, the meeting was opened to questions and discussion. Head City Planner Francis P. Bennett told the group, in answer to the charge that redevelopment was being promoted by selfish business interests, that the city was not primarily interested in providing more houses or more industry through its redevelopment program but that the primary interest was to eliminate blighted conditions. Rehabilitation of the neighborhood through repairing and fixing up houses could not do the job. Father Kern raised a question concerning the foreign-born residents who would be ineligible for public housing, but he was assured that decent, safe, and sanitary housing would be provided regardless of citizenship and that no new slums would be created.

As the meeting continued, the planners made progress. The Corktown leaders present seemed sold on redevelopment but concerned over how they could convince the people of the area that the project was a good idea. Father Kern pointed out that the general notion was that a conspiracy was afoot and that the city would have a hard time selling the project for industrial re-use once the land was cleared. He noted that in the forthcoming public hearing they could expect some "professional screamers" to object to any project. He felt that if they could sell Ethel Claes on the project, everything would then go smoothly. He suggested that the proper approach would be to present the project in the affirmative light of conquering future slums rather than in the negative light of eliminating existing blight. From Bennett's point of view, this meeting was a great success. It indicated that the leaders, at least, of the area's largest religious and ethnic groups were behind the project and willing to work with the planners to sell the project to the other residents.

The May 3 meeting with the Home Owners' Association was a different matter. Miss Claes led the questioning, and her rejoinders to the planners' answers gave her the opportunity to make her points. First the Home Owners' Association wanted to know why no hearings had been held on the selection of Corktown as an area for redevelopment. The association's representatives were told that "when you realize how early in the process we are, then you can see why it has been impossible to hold a public hearing." The planners were then quizzed about their reasons for selecting Corktown. They explained that the decision was based upon studies which indicated that the area was a slum. The slum contention hit a sore spot. The planners' data were challenged, and in answer to a direct question as to what the crime rate figures for the area were, the staff member's answer was that no figures were available "since the analysis was not completed."

The Home Owners' Association wanted to know why the city did not help to rehabilitate the area if they considered it substandard. The response was hardly calculated to soothe irritation, for Planner George Villican told the Home Owners, "It's the people's obligation to improve the area. They have had all these years to improve—but they didn't. It's not our problem. We merely study problems." This statement brought the angry retort from Ethel Claes that "you're influenced by the use [planned for the area] and the preconceived use is to be industrial, so you cannot conceive of rehabilitation." She tried to obtain a commitment that if the homes were put in good shape they would not be condemned, but the planners could do no more than hedge in their answer. Miss Claes left the meeting still unconvinced of the need for the redevelopment project and determined to disprove the slum allegation.

The meeting on May 10 with Rev. Mangrum was equally unsuccessful from the Plan Commission staff's point of view. The tenor of the meeting is apparent from the following exchange, as reported in the minutes:

MANGRUM: You can talk all you want to about finding houses for the people, you will not find them, and not find neighborhoods to put them in. You should hear the phone calls I get, people say your damned so and so down there, we don't want them up here with us . . . it is going to be an awful upset . . . on the people who get kicked out. . . .

BENNETT: I think in connection with the human side of it, that fundamentally that's our approach too. . . . Basically the whole movement for redevelopment is inspired to eliminate slum conditions, not for economic reasons.

MANGRUM: You come out here the day they tear down the people's houses and watch their faces and tell me that. And five years from now we will go and look at those people who have been relocated and see if they're happy then. . . . they will be torn out. I'll bet they won't be better off.

You don't have to live with them. You don't have to go down there. You don't have to watch, to talk, to explain. Statistics to you—that's all.

The informal meetings did not change the mind of anybody who felt strongly one way or the other about the controversy, nor did they cool down the controversy to any great extent. The fact that some members of the Plan Commission staff seemed to rub their audiences the wrong way may have added some heat to the situation. The meetings did reveal that Father Kern was prepared to assist the project by minimizing the fears of residents, and although his influence was greatest among the least vocal and politically least sophisticated groups in the area, they were numerically important.

While the Plan Commission staff was holding its informal meetings during the early part of 1954, the Home Owners' Association and Rev. Mangrum continued to promote their cause through efforts to refurbish the neighborhood and through publicity designed to rally support from the rest of the city. The prolific pen of Rev. Mangrum kept up a steady flow of criticism of city officials for their treatment of Corktown. His letter to the editor of the *Detroit Free Press,* which appeared in the February 11, 1954 edition, reflects the intensity of his feelings. The letter said in part:

> I read with pain that the Common Council gave informal approval to clearing part of Corktown.
>
> Such was not always the wish and will of many council members.
>
> Last fall, Mr. Miriani came to Corktown to tell the home owners' group that he did not want to see families dispossessed. Blanch Wise stood before several hundred neighbors to say it should not be done. Mr. Kronk indicated he would not want to see people put out of their homes. Mr. Connor said the city plan was conserving neighborhoods rather than destroying them. . . .
>
> The tragedy is that nobody in the whole city cares what happens.
>
> The pain, loneliness, and confusion of the frightened Americans in Corktown is soul-rending to those of us who have watched their heroic struggles to get an American chance to preserve their homes against forced usurpation.
>
> I write this, not just as a citizen, but as a priest of the Episcopal Church.
>
> Destroy families, tear up homes and supplant them with questionable business development and the wrath of God will fall on our city. . . .

The Home Owners' Association joined forces with Rev. Mangrum, and together they arranged a neighborhood meeting to be held at St. Peter's Episcopal Church on April 20, 1954. The letter distributed to residents notifying them of the meeting warned them that:

> Your property is in danger of condemnation, and you will suffer a great loss as the result.
>
> The reasons given by officials for attempting to condemn are:
>
> (1) You are in a slum, and your property is in poor shape.
>
> (2) That you are in a slum with a lot of sickness and tuberculosis, high infection diseases, high infant death, and high rate of violent crimes in the area.
>
> THIS IS ALL WRONG, and each of us must show the true facts. Therefore:
>
> (1) As to the condition of your property: Are you ready to fix it up so as to obtain the approval of the Building Department?

(2) As to area condition: Will you sign an affidavit that you have no such sickness and know of no crimes of violence nor criminals in Corktown?

The results of the meeting were gratifying to its sponsors. Three physicians signed affidavits testifying to low disease rates in the area. Posters were prepared showing improvements that had been made in homes and depicting "typical" homes in the neighborhood. As a result of these efforts, the Home Owners' Association submitted another petition to the council just prior to the public hearing, which had finally been set for July 22. The petition, submitted on July 16, notified the council:

> We . . . inform this honorable council that we took the statements [concerning slum conditions] to heart, and we have canvassed practically the entire area in person. To this present petition attached are affidavits showing that the families do not have TB, do not have social diseases, that there is no substantial child delinquency, that crimes involving violence and involving inhabitants of this area are unknown, that the usual statements as to infantile and old-age mortality are not true. . . .
>
> As to overcrowding or substandard housing, if this is all the reason for condemning . . . then obviously such a reason is totally inadequate . . . overcrowding can readily be stopped . . . the entire area offers and would gladly bring their houses up to date. . . . The entire area gives the council its solemn assurance on these matters. There are new houses and new buildings in this area. There is much modernization and improvement in evidence.

The long-awaited public hearing was held in the council chambers from 4:00 P.M. to 5:45 P.M. on July 22, 1954. One observer reported the attendance as "the largest turnout in my recollection," but regardless of the accuracy of this report, the chambers were, in fact, crowded to capacity with between four hundred and five hundred residents of Corktown. The Plan Commission opened the hearing with a presentation of statistics gathered in its various surveys and studies to establish that Corktown was indeed a blighted area in need of redevelopment. These statistics included data on the number of substandard dwellings, diversity of land uses in the area, infant mortality rates and the like. No matter how delicately these data were presented, to the assembled residents the planners' facts and figures added up to the allegation that Corktown was a slum.

When it came their turn to be heard, the twelve speakers chosen to present the case for Corktown rebutted the planners' data and maintained that Corktown was not a slum. Robert D. Day told the council:

> I live in as nice a home as almost anyone in the room. I wouldn't be able to replace it or even make a down payment on a new home with the price I would realize in a condemnation case. We take as much pride in our neighborhood as any other in the city. . . .
>
> Leave us alone for a time. Don't tamper with the west side like you did with the east side. You are not real-estate men. Just stick to your business.

Mrs. Anella Wright declared, "What we have there in Corktown is a small United Nations. Every race is represented and they are God-fearing people." A speaker for the Maltese group assured the council that "I raised my family in respectability, and they could not be products of a slum. The city's master plan was a master mistake. All we need is a little help in improving our property." "We object to being called a slum," one resident asserted, adding, "We are not slummy people." The last speaker was Ethel Claes. She alleged that the Plan Commission's figures were inaccurate and misleading because the reporting areas for the crime, school, and health statistics used by the commission did not coincide with the area under consideration. She called attention to the affidavits concerning health and crime conditions in the area that the Home Owners' Association had submitted to the council and reminded them of the home improvements currently being carried on by residents. "This is real life, not dead old statistics," she concluded.

As the exchanges became more heated, Council President Louis Miriani took control of the hearing and moved it to a close. First he criticized the Plan Commission for its presentation, telling them, "I have yet to see any information which would indicate this is a slum area." The council then approved a motion to authorize the Plan Commission to present a fully documented report on blight in Corktown. Other action taken to soothe the residents was a resolution that the council would personally tour the area, and another public hearing was ordered for a future date to be determined later. (Apparently the personal tour never took place, although at least two councilmen did visit the area.)

The Corktowners left the hearing feeling that they were finally making some headway in their battle. An editorial in the *Detroit Free Press* (July 24, 1954) confirmed their optimism. The editorial appraised the hearing in these words:

> The way in which residents of Corktown descended in their righteous wrath upon Common Council Thursday . . . suggests that the councilmen are going to be very wary about approving such an undertaking.
>
> . . . it is yet to be proven that the Corktown section is a slum area and that the rezoning and land acquisition are justified. . . .
>
> The manner in which 450 Corktown residents . . . fiercely defended their right to continue living in their present homes was most impressive.
>
> It is doubtful if an area whose people exhibit such civic pride and community spirit could possibly be a slum . . . age alone does not mean blight or slum conditions.
>
> In light of the Gratiot-Orleans project, the city should be cautious about embarking on a similar enterprise on the west side. . . .
>
> If there is money available for rehabilitation the city does not have to go as far west as Corktown to find an appropriate project. They can find it in skid row, an area which needs renovation if any place in Detroit does.
>
> Cleaning up skid row will not eliminate a community of decent citizens who take pride in their homes, and who, through their schools and churches, have roots well planted. . . .

The Council Acts. By October, the Plan Commission had completed its task of compiling additional evidence of blight in the project area. Acting upon the new evidence, the council approved an application to HHFA for additional funds to continue the planning for the Corktown project and, the following March (1955), approved forwarding the preliminary project report to Washington for approval. Meanwhile, Miss Claes had gotten in touch with her congressman, Charles C. Diggs, a Democrat representing Michigan's Sixteenth Congressional District. Diggs had been critical of the relocation of Negro families from the Gratiot redevelopment site, so he was not unfamiliar with redevelopment problems. A Negro, he took a strong stand on public issues affecting his race, and although the number of Negroes on the Corktown project site was not large, Diggs could be expected to show an interest in relocation plans being made for them. On April 15,

1955, Congressman Diggs along with his aides and Miss Claes met with the Plan Commission to discuss the project.

At this meeting, Miss Claes continued in her efforts to disprove the evidence of the Plan Commission on slum conditions. She was told to forward her documents to the regional office of the Urban Renewal Administration. (She did, and they were returned with the advice that they be brought to the attention of local officials.) Congressman Diggs's questions showed his concern over relocation. He wanted to know where the people from the Gratiot site had been relocated, whether the Gratiot residents had improved their lot, and he inquired as to what assurances there were that industry would move into the site if it were available. The planners' evidence of slum conditions and assurances that relocation plans had been carefully developed and that the site would attract industry apparently did not satisfy the congressman, for he proceeded to write to HHFA and request a re-examination of the evidence of blight. The response of HHFA, noted earlier, was to request a further documentation of blight and an examination of the possibility of rehabilitating rather than redeveloping the area. This turn of events was welcomed by Miss Claes, who volunteered the services of the Home Owners' Association to assist in carrying out the rehabilitation study.

HHFA's suggestion that Corktown be considered for a rehabilitation project was made possible by the Housing Act of 1954, which amended the 1949 Act and authorized federal grants for rehabilitation and conservation projects as well as for redevelopment. The intention of this amendment was best described in the "Detailed Summary of the Housing Act of 1954," prepared by HHFA:

> A rehabilitation or conservation project . . . includes the restoration and renewal of a blighted, deteriorated, or deteriorating area by:
> (1) carrying out plans for a program of voluntary repair and rehabilitation of buildings and improvements in accordance with the urban renewal plan;
> (2) acquisition of real property and demolition or removal of buildings and improvements where necessary to eliminate unhealthful, unsanitary, or unsafe conditions, lessen density, eliminate obsolete or other detrimental uses, or to otherwise remove or prevent the spread of blight or deterioration, or to provide land for needed public facilities;

(3) installation, construction, or reconstruction of streets, utilities, parks, playgrounds, and other improvements necessary for carrying out in the area the urban renewal objectives in accordance with the urban renewal plan; and

(4) the disposition of any property acquired in the urban renewal area at its fair value for uses in accordance with the urban renewal plan.

By June 24, 1955, the Plan Commission staff had completed a review of the feasibility of a rehabilitation project for Corktown and concluded that:

The area is divided into two sub-areas, sub-area I being the most logical for rehabilitation. The cost to remove only the industries in sub-area II seems so prohibitive that it can hardly be considered for future residential use. However, it must be stressed that if only area I were rehabilitated it would be completely surrounded by non-residential uses and even after the investment would still represent a minimum level of housing desirability.

Meanwhile, the council met on June 16, 1955, and took the necessary formal action to declare the project site a blighted area and therefore eligible for federal funds. This action occurred while Miss Claes was out of town, and she was understandably upset upon hearing the news. In a letter to the *Detroit Times* on July 18, she accused the council of meeting in private in order to declare Corktown a slum and of evading holding an open hearing at which the evidence of the Home Owners' Association could be brought out in the open for comparison with that of the Plan Commission.

The council's action prompted the religious leaders, Father Kern and Rev. Mangrum, to make a plea for some arrangement whereby the residents of the area could continue to live as a community. At a meeting held in Mayor Cobo's office on June 27, they conceded that the area should be cleared but suggested that it be redeveloped for residential use. Mayor Cobo pointed out that the land was needed by wholesalers who were going to be forced to move to make way for the convention hall project, and he added that the Corktown site was an ideal location for them. The mayor then suggested that the possibility of providing apartments along nearby Michigan Avenue be considered. The Plan Commission staff member attending this meeting discouraged this suggestion by pointing out that the master plan called for industry in the Michigan Avenue area. The mayor, nevertheless, ordered the Plan Commission to consider changing the master plan to allow housing along Michigan Avenue, and the meeting was adjourned. A month later, the mayor received a communication signed by Housing Director Durbin and Plan Director Blessing which said in part:

> As requested . . . we are submitting . . . our comment relative to the possibility of a "private development" in the immediate vicinity of the West Side Project [Corktown]. . . .
>
> We wish to advise . . . that the future generalized land-use plan indicates that the most desirable and logical re-use of the land surrounding the above project is for uses other than residential. . . . we feel therefore that it would be improper and unwise to relocate the residents in an area which is not intended for residential use.
>
> We realize fully that the ethnic and social relationships found in the West Side Project are strong. However, experience with the relocation in the Gratiot area and in the so-called Temporary War Housing indicate that the families displaced tended to disperse throughout the city rather than congregate in a neighborhood where the physical and social environment was similar to the one they left.

For those intent on keeping redevelopment out of Corktown, 1955 had been a bad year. The possibility of a rehabilitation project for the whole area had been rejected by local officials, and the rehousing of area residents in a nearby project had also been rejected. Rev. Mangrum was given a new assignment by his church —some felt because of his active opposition to redevelopment—and his leadership was lost to the neighborhood. In January 1956, HHFA approved the preliminary plans for the Corktown project, and it appeared that all that remained to be done was the mopping up of details. But Ethel Claes and her Home Owners' Association were still not through fighting.

Corktown's Last Stand.   After the beginning of 1956, it became apparent that Corktown could expect no outside help in its efforts to fend off redevelopment. But the Home Owners' Association continued to carry on a campaign of self-help. The association participated in "clean-up, fix-up" campaigns and won a letter of commendation from the Junior Chamber of Commerce for its efforts. It also participated in the neighborhood conservation program that was being conducted by the Plan Commission. This was a program designed to educate and motivate neighborhood groups into taking steps to improve their neighborhoods. The Corktown Home Owners' Association was an eager participant, and a number of its members attended a banquet that was held to honor neighborhood groups cooperating with the program. The association members came equipped with posters showing the results that they had brought about in their area. The Plan Commission staff was not overjoyed by this zeal. The Home Owners' Association claimed that their posters had been deliberately hidden by the planners in order to avoid embarrassment. Undaunted, the Home Owners' Association sought aid from city departments to obtain better garbage and trash collection, and it vigilantly opposed zoning changes and illegal conversions in violation of the building code and zoning ordinances. The organization even arranged with the local Boy Scout council to assist in organizing troops in the neighborhood. In effect, through the leadership of Ethel Claes, the Home Owners' Association had taken those steps widely publicized by city planners, social workers, and civic betterment groups as the necessary steps to conserving neighborhoods, but it appeared that the association's neighborhood was located in the wrong place.

The Common Council set June 28, 1957 as the date for the formal public hearing required by the Housing Act. Although three years had gone by since the last public hearing, interest still ran high. The residents were better organized than they had been at the first hearing, and although they did not turn out in as large numbers, their arguments were more polished and sophisticated. After a number of speakers had been heard, Ethel Claes was given the opportunity to have the final word. Among her arguments were these, taken from a mimeographed copy of her speech:

> The public must be disabused that Corktown and skid row are one. In Corktown everybody works hard; there is no panhandling, and no street loafers, and there is no drink problem. . . .
> . . . Corktown and the project area is NO SLUM. . . .
> 1. We have found that for the past five years at least, there is less . . . crime [in Corktown] than in many other parts of Detroit.
> 2. Regarding public health matters: Actual inquiry shows there has

been no outbreak of epidemic diseases like polio or diphtheria.
. . . Our area has a low V.D. rate; there are no houses of assig-
nation. . . .

3. As to child behavior: There is less vandalism of schools in this
area . . . and the money damage figures at the Board of Education show this. *What better test of child conduct is there?*

It is well known that in the last three years a great improvement
has been made in the condition of houses in Corktown. We have held
competitions for the best improvements, and a great amount of work
has been done on the properties. . . .

A check will show that the houses that offend the eye or lack
improvements are, for the most part, owned by absentee landlords;
and here lies the key to this part of the problem. *The offenders derive an income from Corktown, but live elsewhere. . . .*

This association offers . . . to lay before the council the undertaking of each owner to bring his property up to code within a stipulated period. This action . . . can save the area, can save the city
a lot of money, and its inhabitants a lot of grief. . . .

When Miss Claes had finished, a speaker arose to support the
redevelopment. It was Willis Hall, member of the Greater Detroit
Board of Commerce and former member of the Plan Commission.
The residents greeted him with boos and cat-calls, but Hall stood
and presented the arguments he had advanced so often in the past
that the project was necessary to the economic future of Detroit
in order to prevent light industry and warehouses from leaving
the city. The hearing ended with residents declaring that "the
homes in the neighborhood are no more blighted than those where
the councilmen live. . . . Our homes are being rebuilt from the
inside out, and given time the exteriors will be improved."

The two public hearings were very much alike in terms of the
arguments and facts presented. The residents were still unconvinced that Corktown, including the project site, was a slum, and
the planners felt that they had ample proof that the project site
was blighted. The council adjourned the hearing with the announcement that a decision would be made within two weeks,
and on July 10, the decision was made. By unanimous vote, the
council decided that the Corktown site should be condemned for
redevelopment under the provisions of the Housing Act. It further decided that appraisals should be made on the basis of the
value of similar homes in other parts of the city and that the

appraisals were to be made available to owners prior to court action.

The *Detroit Free Press,* which had lauded the earlier efforts of the Corktowners in defense of their neighborhood, now applauded the council for its courage:

> It takes an appreciable amount of fortitude to make a decision which might run contrary to tradition and sentimentality. . . . Progress is not without sacrifices. But it is of paramount importance that Detroit, its vacant land gone, fully utilize existing space to strengthen its industrial structure . . . (July 11, 1957).

Redevelopment Begins. The second public hearing was one of the last remaining barriers to the execution of a contract with HHFA. With the hearing out of the way and the ironing out of some legal problems dealing with the appraisal procedures to be employed, a formal contract was executed on November 26, 1957, between HHFA and the City of Detroit for carrying out the West Side Industrial Project. The contract provided for a federal contribution of $3,580,000 and a local contribution of $1,790,000. These amounts were based upon estimates that the total cost of acquiring, clearing, and preparing the site would come to a little over $7,000,000 and that the revenue from the sale of the sites would be somewhat over $2,000,000. (The governmental contributions covered only the net cost.)

The signing of the contract cleared the way for the Housing Commission to proceed with land acquisition and relocation of site residents. In October 1958, eleven months after the signing, a condemnation jury announced its awards covering one hundred and ten parcels of the project site. The awards totaled $1,859,284, for which the city acquired thirteen business sites, nineteen multiple dwellings, sixty single- and two-family dwellings and eighteen vacant lots. Most of the awards were negotiated in advance by the Detroit corporation counsel's office, and only four property owners contested the condemnation. By March 1959, only thirty of the one hundred and forty families living in the first area planned for clearance remained on the site.

The Housing Commission had learned from its experience in relocating residents from the Gratiot site and was following the procedures set forth in the relocation plan submitted to HHFA and endorsed by the commission's Relocation Advisory Committee. The relocation director, Homer Saunders, set up offices on the site and proceeded to work through community leaders, notably Fathern Kern, in paving the way for the necessary move. The orientation of the relocation program was reflected in Saunders' reference to it as a "public-relations job." But there was more than public relations involved in easing the task of moving residents from the Corktown site. The small percentage of Negroes (18 percent) for whom housing had to be found, an additional supply of public housing units (not available during the Gratiot relocation), and a substantial increase in the supply of private rental units available to low-income families made the Corktown relocation task much less difficult than the Gratiot one. In addition, aids to relocation had been provided by the Housing Act of 1954 and subsequent amendments. Section 221 provided assistance to displaced families in the form of forty-year FHA mortgages of 100 percent of the appraised value of homes for amounts up to $10,000, and, in addition, relocation payments of up to $100 for an individual or family unit were authorized to cover moving expenses. (Few of the displaced Corktowners were planning to make use of the Section 221 housing provisions.)

In spite of what might be considered optimum conditions under which to carrying out relocation, it is not difficult to find "human interest" stories which illustrate that, for some at least, urban redevelopment does hurt. The following excerpt is from an article on relocation by Allan Blanchard in *The Detroit News* of March 14, 1959:

> Some residents who have been only recent inhabitants of the area left with no qualms at all, having not been around long enough to feel and love the tradition of Corktown.
>
> But there were others, like Mrs. Eliza Tilburg, 82, who, when moved from her rented home on Howard, near Tenth, just went around the corner to another old home, 1606 Porter. This also is in the path of the city's plan for a new industrial area, but she hopes to stay there as long as possible.
>
> She has lived in Corktown for almost sixty years. Her first husband Fred Sutton, took her there as a bride. He died in Corktown, as also did her second husband, Tilburg.

Her daughter grew up and went to school there. And now, even though many old friends are gone and the city has offered to find her a better place, she cannot bear to leave.

"It is my home," she explained, "I would be lost elsewhere."

Or John Saliba, 59, the Maltese barber who has been cutting hair in Corktown since the mid-twenties.

"I go in July," said the barber, "only because there is no more hair around here to cut."

As the land was cleared and readied for re-use, it was offered for sale to private developers. The permissible land uses were light industry and truck terminals; warehousing and wholesale establishments; office and printing trades; and 1.3 acres for a commercial center including a hotel or motel, cafeteria, meeting rooms, and small shops to service those who would work in the area. By the end of 1960, 12 percent of the project site had been sold and new buildings had begun to appear. The Housing Commission, responsible for the sale of the land, claimed that buyers were on hand for additional properties as the land became available for sale and predicted that the completed project would put $31,000,000 worth of new projects on the tax rolls, "replacing worthless residential and commercial slum properties."

Concluding Comments

The early history of the Corktown project was a part of efforts to develop a master plan for the city. Local policy-making had reached a point where the need for planning was finally acknowledged and the organizational structure for carrying it out was set up. With the development of the master plan, planning ceased to be an academic question and became a matter of decision-making on the future use to which specific plots of land would be devoted. The conflict between City Planner Monson, who wanted Corktown zoned for residential use, and Commissioner Hall, who held out for industrial use, demonstrated what happens once planning gets down to cases. What is especially worthy of note, however, is not that this was a typical conflict between an employee of a board of commerce fighting for industrial sites and a planner fighting for some form of integrated (economically and racially) housing, but that there were no technical or scientific criteria by which decisions on land use could be made and the conflict thereby avoided. Lacking such criteria, the settlement between Hall and Monson was made on the basis of political power. Mayor Cobo's election settled it in favor of Willis Hall. If Cobo had lost the election and Monson's position had won, it would still have been a political settlement, although one suspects that professional planners would have hailed this outcome as a victory of professional planning over politics. The master plan was an expression of prevailing social and economic values, and an examination of how crucial master plan decisions were reached reveals the power distribution in the community at that particular time.

During the master plan discussions, it was generally accepted that Corktown was a blighted area and should be redeveloped. Ten years later the residents were still protesting that their neighborhood was not a slum. Probably most people have an image that is evoked by the word "slum," and most would agree that slums are something to be rid of. When the condition of housing and of other physical accoutrements is bad enough, it does not take sophisticated techniques to identify it; eyes, ears, and nose suffice. But as one moves from the patently obvious slum neighborhood to the "poor neighborhood," the need for more precise methods becomes apparent. Here again scientific criteria for making a determination that an area was or was not a slum were lacking. When various indicators such as crime, morbidity and mortality rates, school absenteeism and other such data were cited, the Corktowners could point to the fact that their area did not have the poorest rating in the city and compared favorably with other areas that were not being considered for redevelopment. That many Corktowners were poor, no one would deny; but that in itself could hardly be considered a justification for redevelopment.

Perhaps the most convincing evidence that Corktown should be redeveloped was the physical condition and appearance of the dwellings and the diversity of uses, i.e., commercial and industrial intermixed with residential; but these conditions were not spread uniformly throughout the area. The tactic employed by the planners was to select a project site that encompassed an area which included the worst conditions, in terms of current criteria of blight, in order to present the best possible case for qualifying for federal funds. This amounted to selecting a 75-acre site from among the 250 acres that made up the neighborhood. The planners, in their arguments, emphasized that they were only concerned with the project site, but the neighborhood groups were defending the neighborhood as a whole. Members of the Plan Commission staff and the Housing Commission staff admitted privately that some of the blocks near the project site were in good condition. A Housing Commission staff member said that he expected the surrounding area to deteriorate once the redevelopment project was completed, and then all of Corktown could be condemned and put to industrial use. This raises the queston whether the planner has an obligation to consider the whole neighborhood, rather than just the project site, if redevelopment will result in spreading blight; or, in other words, whether redevelopment is justifiable as a means of making future redevelopment projects in the area more feasible.

Turning to neighborhood resistance to redevelopment, the Corktown case suggests a number of pertinent questions. When should a neighborhood be heard concerning its future? Was the proper time for a full-dress hearing when the master plan was being developed? When redevelopment was first being considered and before preliminary commitments with HHFA had been made? Before the planners had completed documentation of blight? Or should the hearing have been delayed until plans had been completed and local officials were confident that the project would meet federal approval? Was the purpose of the hearing to give notice to residents of a *fait accompli* or to provide residents with an opportunity to present evidence in rebuttal to that presented by the bureaucracy? Was the hearing merely a ritual preserved to afford the neighborhood groups a chance to let off steam? It is evident from the Corktown case that there was no clear policy on either the proper time for a hearing or the purpose the hearing was to serve, other than meeting a federal requirement. To the professional staff, the public hearings were a "damned nuisance." Since they were held before the council, and the councilmen were considered unpredictable, any number of embarrassing situations could arise for the planners as they defended their decisions before a hostile audience. Members of the local bureaucracy point to the Corktown project as a case where the public hearings only resulted in delaying the project, the council usually concluding after each hearing that more study was necessary. The hearings did not influence the decisions of the planners, nor did they, in the long run, deter the councilmen from following the recommendations of the planners. Neither did the hearings cool off or change the minds of those in the neighborhood opposed to redevelopment. If the part played by the hearings in this case indicates the prevailing role of the public hearing, then the hearing would appear to be more of a procedural ritual than a substantive remedy for those in the path of urban redevelopment projects.

In some respects the reaction of the Corktown neighborhood to redevelopment challenged the ideology and doctrine that was associated with urban renewal. It has become increasingly popular for city planning departments to hire sociologists and those trained in community organization skills for the purpose of assisting neighborhoods in the organization of programs of self-help which would lead to the conservation of neighborhoods through clean-up and fix-up campaigns. In fact, Detroit's neighborhood conservation program received the special attention of HHFA in the form of a grant for a pilot study, which culminated in a slick 260-page publication describing the elaborate mechanism that had been developed by city agencies for working with neighborhood groups (*Neighborhood Conservation—A Pilot Study,* by Maurice Frank Parkins, Detroit City Plan Commission in cooperation with Housing and Home Finance Agency, 1958). The Corktown Home Owners' Association and other organized groups in the area said that they were willing to cooperate with any official effort at conservation or rehabilitation, but they received little or no assistance from local public agencies. (In their clean-up efforts they discovered that some of the vacant lots in serious need of attention belonged to the city.) It would appear that the sociologist's role in Corktown was not to assist in organizing the neighborhood for conservation purposes but rather to help convince the residents that they should recognize the need for redevelopment and cooperate with such a project. Should this be the social scientist's role in the planning agency? Is he the advance "con" man who either talks the neighborhood into submitting to redevelopment or urges the owner to invest in costly home repairs, according to the dictates of current public policy? Is he the "hidden persuader" for the planner?

Members of the bureaucracy argued that Miss Claes and Rev. Mangrum did not really represent the neighborhood, that they were troublemakers; if they could have been persuaded to drop their opposition, things would have progressed more rapidly. The role of Father Kern is pointed to as an example of responsible leadership. It does not imply that the leadership of Father Kern was not responsible, to suggest that the leadership of Miss Claes and Rev. Mangrum was also responsible to the values they held. The roles played by Miss Claes and Rev. Mangrum were typical of conflicts of this sort rather than unique occurrences. How representative any one of the three leaders was cannot, of course, be determined, but then "representative-ness" seldom can be put to a test. If the Corktown project could have been put to a vote, what would have been the proper constituency? The project site? The Corktown neighborhood? The city of Detroit? Or the whole metropolis?

The role of the two clerics in this case shows that men dedicated to humanitarian values can arrive at opposite conclusions concerning the extent to which redevelopment serves those values. What seemed to weigh most heavily with Rev. Mangrum was that the purpose of the project was to make land available for industrial use.

A number of questions could be raised concerning the role of HHFA, but of special note is the detailed review that was exercised over local plans and the leisurely pace with which this review took place. Presumably, more recent legislation will speed the review process and place more finality in local decision-making, but there is still sufficient remaining federal discretion to permit extensive central review, if desired. Timely action from the point of view of Washington may appear as needless delay to a local jurisdiction. If Washington had acted sooner, perhaps the Civic Center wholesalers could have moved into Corktown when they were forced to move by civic projects. Is a project strung out in time as long as this one was more expensive in energy in the long run than one that is pushed through more expeditiously? Should there be a "statute of limitations" upon the length of time to be consumed by any one step in the planning and review process?

The Common Council plays a strategic role in decision-making. Even if federal legislation did not require local council action, there are ample state and local provisions that require the council's approval of urban renewal projects, and this approval must be had at various stages as projects move from preliminary planning to the condemnation stage. It can postpone action by waiting for more studies, and it holds over a project a potential veto which can be withheld until the final step is ready to be taken, i.e., the signing of a contract for a federal grant. As long as this veto is available, those groups having access to the council can hope to influence the decision. Did this have the effect of prolonging the controversy? Should the council be forced to commit itself at an earlier stage for or against the project per se and retain approval authority only to the extent of assuring that the project was carried out as intended? It would seem that the interests of Corktown residents would have been better served if a decision with some semblance of finality had been forthcoming at an earlier stage than it did in this case.

As metropolitan systems expand, as they are destined to do, the demand for space for residential and industrial developments in the core city will have to be met, at least in part, from redeveloped areas. As this takes place in organized neighborhoods, such as Corktown, many of the earlier assumptions relating redevelopment to slum clearance will be subject to challenge. There is, however, a strong temptation to let the desirable ends of redevelopment justify the means for achieving those ends.

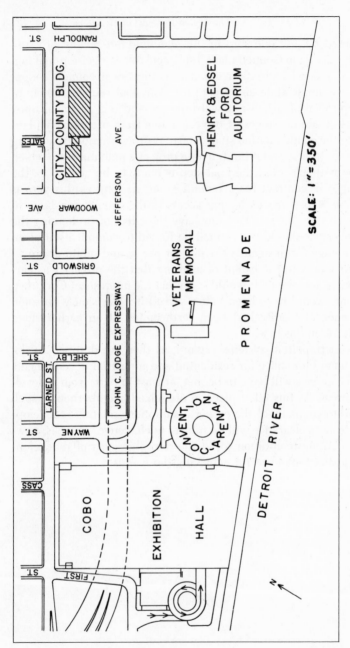

2. Detroit's Civic Center

Courtesy Graphic Arts Section, State University of Iowa

3
Detroit's City-County Building

An Exercise in City-County Cooperation

Introduction

On September 23, 1955, local city and county dignitaries and a large crowd gathered in downtown Detroit to dedicate the new City-County Building. The building, occupying two city blocks, was composed of two distinct but interconnected units which provided offices and courtrooms for most administrative and judicial officials of the city of Detroit and Wayne County. Yet neither the city nor the county held title to the building. Instead, the legal owner of the structure and the land on which it rested was the Detroit-Wayne Joint Building Authority, which was also responsible for the maintenance, repair, and administrative operation of the building. This case deals with the creation of the Detroit-Wayne Joint Building Authority and the construction of the City-County Building.

From the date of completion of Detroit's old City Hall in 1871 there had been a precedent for joint occupancy of a public building by the city of Detroit and Wayne County. Wayne County leased space in the old City Hall until expansion of both city and county activities necessitated the construction of a separate County Building, which was completed in 1902. Public attention was again centered on the space needs of the city and county late in the 1920's, when the Detroit electorate turned down a $20,000,000 bond issue for a city-county building by a vote of 148,251 to 221,000. The motive force behind the presentation of this issue to the voters was Mayor John C. Lodge, to whom "civic consciousness" and "pride in the community" dictated that the city and

---

*This case, in somewhat revised form, will appear in the Inter-University Case Program series.

county should have an "ample building" as the seat of government (*Detroit News,* October 28, 1928). In locating the proposed building, Mayor Lodge chose a site at the foot of Woodward Avenue, along the river waterfront, in a proposed civic center development. While the mayor's views did not carry with the electorate, they expressed the future political consensus that underlay the eventual construction of the City-County Building.

During the next sixteen years, there were two more unsuccessful attempts to gain voter approval for construction of a public office building that would house both city and county offices. The first was in April 1937, when city voters were asked in two purely advisory referenda whether they favored (1) the construction of a new administration building to house city and county offices, or (2) the purchase of an existing downtown office building. The city electorate disliked both propositions by approximately two-to-one majorities. In November 1944 the entire electorate of Wayne County (including the city of Detroit) was asked to approve a $7,000,000 general obligation bond issue to finance the construction of a city-county building under county auspices. The proposition was defeated 150,920 to 216,157.

In the face of thrice-demonstrated voter opposition, the city and county refused to drop the idea of a city-county building. It was only by means of the most complete cooperation in a novel venture that the city and county were able to transfer the city-county building from the arena of political discussion to a site in downtown Detroit.

Early Planning

The Joint Study Committee. The end of World War II found the Detroit City Plan Commission planning for the eventual construction of a city-county building as part of a civic center master plan. The master plan set the boundaries, general character and layout of the center, and specified the buildings to be included. The civic center (subsequently enlarged) was to occupy a strip of land along the river front in the heart of downtown Detroit. The plan called for a "veterans' memorial" group of three buildings (a veterans' service building, a convention hall, and a civic auditorium) to be located between Jefferson Avenue and the river front; a waterfront plaza and large expanses of landscaped area; and a bank of city-county, state, and federal office buildings. These three office buildings were to line the north side of Jefferson and face the veterans' memorial group across Jefferson. The three office structures were to be similarly proportioned and equal in height.

The civic center master plan followed closely a treatment of the civic center site rendered by Suren Pilafian, noted architect, in September 1945. Pilafian had been retained by the City Plan Commission for this purpose starting in 1944. The structures in Pilafin's rendering were designed with clean, simple lines. The exteriors of the veterans' memorial buildings were to be finished in marble, while the office structures were designed to be functional and non-ornamental. The specific design of these structures, however, was not incorporated into the master plan, which achieved official status in March 1946 when the Detroit Common Council unanimously adopted it.

The city moved ahead rapidly. While condemnation proceedings on the site for the veterans' service building were begun, a Joint Study Committee on the need for additional office space for city and county agencies was at work.

The Joint Study Committee was established in January 1946 by unanimously adopted resolutions of the Wayne County Board of Supervisors and the Detroit Common Council. Representing the county on the committee were Jacob Sumeracki, popularly elected chairman of the county's chief fiscal body, the County Board of Auditors; Leroy C. Smith, executive officer of the Wayne County Road Commission; and Jesse Ziegler, supervisor (elected head) of Livonia Township. Ziegler was later elected chairman of the County Board of Supervisors. Detroit's representatives were Albert E. Cobo, popularly elected city treasurer; George Emery, director of the Detroit City Plan Commission; and Charles G. Oakman, city councilman and formerly city controller. Oakman and Cobo, by virtue of their city positions, were also members of the County Board of Supervisors, a body numerically dominated by the Detroit delegation (which included all of Detroit's elected officials plus several appointed administrative officials). This broadly representative committee comprehended the diverse interests of elected and appointed officials and legislative and executive bodies in the governmental structure of both the city and the county. Each of its members was a respected, forceful, and influential person in his own bailiwick.

As the Joint Study Committee set to work on the city-county building, local leaders sought to obtain commitments from federal and state officials on the construction of federal and state office buildings in the civic center. These efforts quickly came to naught, and local attention focused on the proposed city-county building.

The committee's investigations were carried on during the spring and summer of 1946. Much of the work on these preliminary surveys (e.g., a study of the space requirements of all city and county agencies) was done by the City Plan Commission staff. Late in 1946 the committee reported its findings. In *The City-County Building*, a fourteen-page brochure which the Plan Commission prepared and published in July 1947 as an outgrowth of the committee's report, the committee's view was summarized:

> The proposed city-county building is undoubtedly among the most urgently needed of all projects now being considered in Wayne County. Considered from any of a dozen angles, the proposal is logical, sensible, and sound. Indeed, no valid argument can be raised against it.

Noting that county and city offices were in thirty-one different buildings and that city and county rental costs were nearly $375,000 annually, the committee recommended that action be taken as soon as possible on the construction of a city-county building and proposed the purchase of a two-block site bounded by Jefferson and Woodward Avenues and Larned and Randolph Streets. The Detroit Common Council and the Wayne County Board of Supervisors unanimously adopted the committee's recommendations.

The Referendum. Acting on the premise that there was no doubt about the eventual construction of the building, on June 22, 1947, the Detroit Common Council appropriated $1,000,000 toward the purchase of the site and authorized condemnation proceedings against properties in the two-block area. At the same time the council indicated its intention to pay $1,000,000 annually until approximately 60 percent of the cost of the building had accumulated. The following month, for its part in financing the joint facility, the Board of Supervisors voted to place before the county electorate three referenda on the joint building. The first proposition would authorize the county to acquire land and erect a building in conjunction with the city. The second proposition, on which only property owners were eligible to vote, requested authority to issue $8,000,000 in general obligation bonds (bonds pledging the full faith and credit of the county). On these two issues only a simple majority was necessary for passage. The third proposal asked approval of an increase of one-half mill in the property-tax rate for five years.

The tax increase was necessary to assure prospective bond purchasers that the county would have the funds available to pay off the principal and interest on the bonds. It had not been necessary to secure voter approval of a similar issue in the 1944 election because the county was not then taxing up to the limit legally permissible under state constitutional and statutory provisions. By 1947, however, the county was taxing at its legal limit. The state constitution provided that the limit could be exceeded only by a vote of the electorate. More importantly, a two-thirds majority was required.

Forewarned by prior defeats at the polls, city and county officials launched a vigorous selling campaign on the three propositions. The Detroit City Plan Commission prepared the fourteen-page brochure titled *The City-County Building: A Report Answering the Questions Frequently Raised Concerning the Office Building Projected by the County of Wayne and City of Detroit.* It emphasized that a new joint facility would be convenient to the public, result in greater efficiency in both city and county government, and promote long-run economy. News releases favorable to the proposals were prepared. Endorsements from prominent public officials and private persons were sought, obtained, and released to the press.

At the November 1947 election a substantial majority voted in favor of the project, but the failure of the third proposition to secure a two-thirds majority defeated the entire scheme. The votes on the propositions were:

Proposal	Votes For	Votes Against	Percent-age For	Percentage Required for Passage
Site and construction	266,332	134,515	66.4	50.0
Issuance of bonds	140,033	101,218	58.2	50.0
Increase in tax rate	219,030	159,076	57.9	66.7

The substantial majorities by which voters endorsed all three propositions encouraged sponsors of the building project. One statement characteristic of this post-election outlook was, "We will explore every legal byway to make the building a reality." Among the alternatives mentioned were:

1. to resubmit the third proposition to the voters, hoping for a two-thirds majority;
2. to seek a change in the state constitution so that a simple majority in favor of a millage increase would carry the proposition, and then resubmit the proposition;
3. to enter into a lease-purchase agreement whereby a private firm would construct the building, and the city and county would join in leasing the building space and eventually obtain title to the building;
4. to attempt to finance construction of the building by the issuance of revenue bonds.

The Detroit-Wayne Joint Building Authority

Establishment of the Authority. The fourth alternative, issuance of revenue bonds, was the "legal byway" that local officials decided to press for. By the revenue bond method, which appears to have first come up in a discussion between Councilman Oakman and Treasurer Cobo, both principal and interest on the bonds had to be paid exclusively from the earnings of the enterprise which the bonds had been issued to finance. Local officials proposed that the revenue to pay off the principal and interest be obtained from annual charges to the city and county according to the amount of space they occupied in the proposed building. This procedure would require state legislative authorization. It was also believed to be desirable, if not mandatory, that both the city and county avoid direct responsibility for floating the revenue bonds because of possible legal and financial complications. Some years later Charles Oakman stated the problem faced by local officials:

> The people had given us a mandate to proceed on the building, they just didn't like the method [increasing taxes]. We had to come up with a method or excuse for getting around the constitutional fifteen-mill limitation without perpetrating a fraud on the taxpayer, of course. That's where the Building Authority came in.

Detroit and Wayne County officials were fortunate in one respect. The state legislature would not normally have met until January 1949, but Governor Kim Sigler called a special session in January 1948. Since the governor determined the legislature's agenda at special sessions, local officials asked Sigler to submit to the legislature a proposal permitting any city that was a county seat to join with the county in creating a joint building authority empowered to issue revenue bonds. Although Sigler was at first reluctant to comply because the local officials had approached him at the last minute, he was finally persuaded to add the legislation to the agenda; but he informed Detroit and Wayne County officials that they were on their own in getting it through the legislature.

In presenting their case before the legislature, the Detroit-area officials were aided by local officials from other cities and counties who appreciated the potential usefulness of the law in their own jurisdictions. The bill cleared both houses of the legislature without major incident, and on May 10, Governor Sigler signed Act 31 of the Public Acts of 1948. Oakman recalls the legislative stage as one in which "we simply had to explain that we weren't starting any dangerous precedent. It was more a matter of explanation and education than anything else." By later amendment the act extended the use of this method of financing a building to any city, village, or township, acting alone or jointly with other units. Of the fourteen sections in Act 31, the following (as amended) set forth the basis, purpose, organization, powers, and financing method of the Joint Building Authority:

> Section 1. Any county, city, village or township may incorporate, as provided in this act, an authority for the purpose of acquiring,

furnishing, equipping, owning, improving, enlarging, operating and/ or maintaining a building or buildings and the necessary site or sites therefor, for the use of the county, city, village, or township.

Section 5a. Any joint building authority of any county and a city or village shall be directed and governed by a board of commissioners of three members, one to be elected by the board of supervisors of the county, one to be elected by the legislative body of the city, and one to be elected by the joint action of the board of supervisors of the county and the legislative body of the city, and if the said legislative bodies are unable to agree upon a choice for the third members within sixty days of the election of the first member, then the said third member shall be appointed by the governor. Said commissioners shall serve for six-year terms. Said board of commissioners shall designate one of their number as chairman and one as secretary, and shall adopt bylaws and rules of procedure and provide therein for regular meetings.

Section 7. Such authority shall be a body corporate with power to sue and be sued in any court of this state. It shall possess all the powers necessary to carry out the purpose of its incorporation and those incident thereto. The enumeration of any powers in this act shall not be construed as a limitation upon such general powers.

Section 8. The authority and any incorporating unit or units shall have power to enter into a contract or contracts whereby the authority will acquire property contemplated by the terms of this act and lease the same to the incorporating unit or units for a period not to exceed forty years. The consideration specified in such contract for such use shall be subject to increase by the authority if necessary in order to provide funds to meet its obligations.

Section 11. For the purpose of acquiring, improving and/or enlarging any such building or buildings and the necessary site or sites therefor, and furnishing and equipping the same, the authority may issue self-liquidating revenue bonds in accordance with and subject to the provisions of Act No. 94 of the Public Acts of 1933, as now or hereafter amended: *Provided,* That such bonds shall be payable solely from the revenues of such property, which revenues shall be deemed to include payments made under any lease or other contract for use of such property: *And provided further,* That no such bonds shall be issued unless the property whose revenues are pledged has been leased by the authority for a period extending beyond the last maturing of the bonds. For the purpose of Section 33 of said act, the limits of the authority shall be deemed to coincide with those of the county creating or joining in the creation thereof. If a sufficient referendum petition shall be filed as provided in said section requesting a referendum upon the question of the issuance of revenue bonds by the authority, then such question may be submitted by the commission of the authority at any general or special election to be held in the county.

Section 11, quoted above, refers to "the provisions of Act No. 94 [the Revenue Bond Act] of the Public Acts of 1933." Act 94 is the basic legislation governing the issuance of revenue bonds by any public corporation in the state of Michigan. Two important provisions of the act specify that (1) revenue bonds are not subject to state debt limitations and (2) the issuance of revenue bonds is not subject to a vote of the people unless 10 percent of the registered voters petition for a referendum within thirty days after the revenue bonds are authorized.

The legal basis for a joint building authority was now established. Detroit and Wayne County officials lost no time in drafting the articles of incorporation. A draft was completed late in May, and by early July identical articles had passed the procedural legislative stages of the County Board of Supervisors and the Detroit Common Council. They were given final approval by these bodies on July 9 and July 14, 1948, respectively.

A significant event preceded these July actions. On June 24, 1948 the Detroit Council appropriated $628,000 which, with the $1,000,000 appropriated a year earlier, satisfied court-awarded judgments in the condemnation suits against properties in the two-block site. The council's action was a firm commitment to construct the building even though the voters had defeated the proposal a few months before. When the site was purchased local newspapers reported the estimated total cost of the building at $12,000,000.

The Detroit-Wayne Joint Building Authority became more than a paper organization late in July 1948 when the two governing bodies appointed the authority members for six-year terms. The Detroit Common Council selected one of its own members, Councilman Charles G. Oakman, to represent Detroit. The County Board of Supervisors appointed Jesse Ziegler, Livonia Township supervisor and a member of the Board of Supervisors since 1922. Detroit Treasurer Albert E. Cobo was selected as the joint appointee of the two bodies. These appointments were unanimous actions on the part of each governing body. The prominent status of all three appointees, as well as their previous membership on the Joint Study Committee in 1946, indicated the apparently high priority that governing officials attached to the Joint Building Authority and its *raison d'être*, building a building.

Cobo's appointment was especially noteworthy. Formerly a top financial executive for the Burroughs Adding Machine Corporation, Cobo was loaned to the city during the depression of the 1930's to help straighten out its finances. His success in this venture was warmly received by the voters, who proceeded to elect him city treasurer for seven consecutive two-year terms. During that time he won respect and a modest degree of prominence for his sound methods of administration. It was no surprise then, that when the three authority members met for the first time on August 17, 1948, the other two members elected Cobo chairman of the Detroit-Wayne Joint Building Authority.

The Interim Agreement.   The first and most pressing problem facing the authority was to conclude identical interim agreements with the city and the county under which the latter two jurisdictions could properly appropriate funds to the authority. The authority could then use these funds for numerous preliminary projects, such as engineering studies, architectural and design plans, construction drawings, and bid specifications. No fewer than five drafts of an interim agreement were discussed, pored over, and revised by city and county officials.

The crucial problem was the extent to which the city and the county could commit themselves to pay future rental costs. These costs would cover operation and maintenance of the building as well as principal and interest on bonds issued. The county and city were reluctant to enter into a contractual commitment that might at some future date force them to reduce other city and county expenditures in order to meet their commitment without exceeding the legal tax limits. On the other hand, an ironclad guarantee that the building would be rented for a specified amount was necessary to assure buyers for the bonds. The immediate interests of the authority prevailed, despite the possibility of future financial strain on the city and/or the county. After further study of space requirements and construction costs, the three parties—the Building Authority, the Common Council, and the Board of Supervisors—approved the interim agreement in January 1949.

Under the interim agreement the city agreed to pay to the

authority $450,000 and the county $350,000 annually to cover the principal and interest on the bonds. (The city's share was less than half the $1,000,000 figure specified in its 1947 resolution of intention.) These annual payments, or "advance rentals," were to start immediately and were to be drawn upon by the authority to finance the expenses of initiating the project. For these annual payments the authority estimated that it could provide a building with about 1,000,000 square feet of gross space, or nearly 700,000 square feet of usable space. This space was estimated as sufficient to house all city and county offices, with the exception of the few whose functions were deemed inappropriate for being housed in a centralized administrative building, e.g., county sheriff, police and fire departments. Based on the annual advance rental payments, the city planned to occupy about 56 percent of the building, the county 44 percent. The space specifications in the interim agreement were flexible, in that the authority was not legally committed to construct the building to meet the specified dimensions.

All work done for the authority in preparing the interim agreement was performed by city and county personnel. The authority per se had no employees and never did employ anyone until the building was very near completion. Over the next six years, hundreds of man hours of county and city employees' time were spent performing important as well as routine tasks that could have been technically called "authority" jobs. For example, the authority members met at least once a month and frequently more often. The committee clerk of the County Board of Supervisors served as clerk to the authority, keeping all records and performing all necessary clerical and stenographic services until the building was completed and occupied in 1955. The clerk's minutes usually listed the following persons in attendance at the authority meetings (in addition to the three governing members):

Paul T. Dwyer—corporation counsel, city of Detroit
John G. Dunn—assistant corporation counsel, city of Detroit
William C. Larson—accountant, controller's office, city of Detroit
George R. Thompson—city engineer, city of Detroit
Edward P. Riehl—deputy controller, city of Detroit
Philip J. McHugh—assistant prosecuting attorney, Wayne County

John D. Hayes, administrative assistant, Board of Auditors, Wayne
County
Wilsie E. Davey, county accountant, Wayne County
S. B. Chadman, committee clerk, Board of Supervisors, Wayne County
C. F. Freiburger, assistant committee clerk and legislative agent,
Board of Supervisors, Wayne County

These representatives did not attend to make their presence known
or to defend their units' prerogatives. Usually one or more of them
had responsibility for reporting on some problem that would assist
or guide the authority members in determining some course of
action—reviewing bids for construction contracts, estimating and
allocating space, deciding between manual and automatically operated elevators. The cooperation and efforts of a group which
had no direct obligation to the authority was crucial to the development of the interim agreement.

The Test Case. One other issue of primary importance still
confronted the authority. Was it legal? Or was Public Act 31 an
illegal method, a subterfuge for circumventing the will of the people as it had been expressed in the vote on the third proposition?
Before any investor would purchase bonds that the authority
hoped to sell, all doubts about the legal status of the authority had
to be settled. A court decision was especially necessary to assure
the bona fide character of bonds secured only by the income from
the rental of building space to the county and city. Attorneys of
the bond counsels retained by the authority urged a test case.

In March 1949 one Edward A. Walinske, acting as a citizen
and taxpayer, brought suit in Wayne County Circuit Court against
the Detroit-Wayne Joint Building Authority. Walinske was an
assistant to the corporation counsel of the city of Detroit. Walinske's side of the case was developed by the city's legal staff and
the authority's defense was drafted by the same staff in cooperation with the legal staff of the prosecuting attorney of Wayne
County. Plaintiff Walinske claimed as follows (*Walinske* v. *Detroit-Wayne Joint Building Authority*, 325 Mich. 574–5, 39 N.W.
2d 73):

(1) Plaintiff contends that a vote of the electorate is required
by the constitution, the state statutes, and the charter of the city of
Detroit to authorize the proposed construction and issuance of bonds.
He claims that the city and county, by entering into a lease bind-

ing them for a long term of years to pay a rental sufficiently large to pay the operational cost of the contemplated building, the interest on the revenue bonds as it becomes due, and also the principal of the bonds as it becomes due over the period of the lease, and the fact that the lease and the bonds are to be for the same term and when the bonds are retired the authority must convey the building to the city and the county, is in effect a contract to pay the cost of the building.

(2) He further claims that the proposed bonds to be issued by the authority are in fact full faith and credit bonds of the city and county and subject to their bond debt limitations. He admits that the bonds are to be issued by the authority, and that the city and county do not pledge their credit to pay the interest and principal directly, but that they do so indirectly by agreeing to pay rent to the authority sufficient to pay such interest and principal over a long period of years.

(3) He further claims that this is an illegal method circumventing the law and constitutional provisions, as the city and county are attempting to do indirectly what they could not do directly.

On May 5 a judge of the Wayne County Circuit Court upheld the authority and dismissed the suit. The plaintiff then appealed to the Michigan Supreme Court where, on September 9, 1949, the authority was upheld in all points challenged by Walinske. In its key passages the Supreme Court's opinion read as follows (*ibid.*, 579, 581):

The authority, not the city and county, is to pay for and erect the proposed building, and is to be the sole obligor on the proposed revenue bonds. The city and county will not pledge their full faith and credit, but they merely agree to pay over a term of years a reasonable annual rental for an absolute necessity the same as they would for any other services. It is true that a prudent investor in the revenue bonds will be attracted by the fact that the city and county agree to pay sufficient rent so as to pay the bonds and interest, that the moral risk of the lessors is the very best, and that a quasi-municipal corporation like the authority is the obligor on the bonds. The method is new, but is being adopted by municipal corporations, under enabling acts, to provide for much-needed facilities which they otherwise could not have without raising the tax rates they could charge or because of bond debt limitations. Inasmuch as the bonds proposed to be issued by the authority are not faith and credit obligations of its incorporators, they need not be voted on by the electorate, nor are they subject to the debt limitations of the municipalities.

There is no fraud in reaching a desired end by legal means even though other means to that end would be illegal.

All other contentions . . . [of the plaintiff] have been considered and are without merit and warrant no further discussion.

Perhaps the most interesting part of the court's decision was the candid recognition that this "new" method was being used to provide "much-needed facilities" outside of tax and debt limitations. The court was clearly not disposed to question the motives of state and/or local actions.

With doubts about the legal status of the Joint Building Authority favorably resolved by the fall of 1949, a joint office facility for the city and the county was no longer a proposal but an operational project. The three members of the authority looked for an early start and rapid completion of the City-County Building. Discussions on the design, size, cost, and financing of the building had gotten well under way while the test case was being pressed. In November, one month after the court decision, Albert Cobo was elected mayor of Detroit, from which post he could be expected to command top-level support for the Joint Building Authority. Nonetheless, over five years were to elapse before the first agency moved into the nearly completed building.

Planning and Construction

Size, Cost, and Design. During the early months of the existence of the authority there was considerable discussion of the interior and exterior character of the building the authority proposed to build. With Cobo taking the lead, consensus was reached among the three members that the City-County Building should be a major component of the developing Civic Center and that architecturally the structure should be designed to harmonize with the remainder of the center. The authority set out to construct a monumental, ornamental-type building.

One corollary question entered the discussions on the design of the structure. Were judicial officials also to be housed in the City-County Building? The initial response of the three members on the authority was not to provide for judicial quarters. Their thinking was guided by two considerations. First, since the high-ceilinged courtrooms (about forty would be needed) would require a great deal of space, especially in comparison with conventional office space for other elected and administrative officials, they might force the building to a height that would be incongruous with the rest of the Civic Center buildings. Second, there was some discussion of modifying the Civic Center plans to provide for a courts building near the eastern end of the center to house the forty-odd popularly elected local judicial officials.

The authority was soon compelled to revise its thinking on the exclusion of the judiciary from the City-County Building. The chief cause of this revision was Judge Ira W. Jayne, senior presiding judge of the Wayne County Circuit Court bench. Judge Jayne made a strong case for housing the judges of the eighteen circuit courts and five probate courts as well as four circuit court commissioners in the City-County Building by citing the cramped, inconvenient, and deplorable quarters in which the several county judges were currently housed; but the fact that Act 31 was to be tried in the first instance before the Wayne County Circuit Court undoubtedly gave added weight to his views. The authority, with some reluctance, decided to provide space for the county judges, as well as for nine city judicial officers. All the courtrooms were located in a twenty-story tower or court unit of the proposed building. A "link" unit, or series of passageways, connected the tower section to the thirteen-story office unit.

With the inclusion of the judiciary, the building which the authority members talked of in late 1948 was a structure of approximately 1,250,000 square feet. The cost was estimated at $14,000,000, since current construction costs were about $11.00 per square foot. The net usable space in such a building would be about 900,00 square feet. This was approximately the amount of space requested by all county and city agencies in a survey of their estimated space requirements as reported to the authority in January 1949. Before concluding the interim rental agreement the authority reduced the gross space requirements to about 1,000,000 square feet (700,000 net) by eliminating thousands of square feet requested for storage space. The authority also took note of rising construction costs, now $12.00 per square foot. It estimated that the funds already paid by the city and county as advance rentals would make it unnecessary to borrow more than $10,000,000.

At the authority's February 1949 meeting representatives of

the Building Owners and Managers Association of Detroit appeared. They endorsed the construction of a central municipal office building, but expressed concern about the size and design of the contemplated structure. The association's representatives felt that a tower-type structure such as the proposed twenty-story court unit was out of keeping with the proposed design of other buildings in the Civic Center, namely, lower and smaller. They also opposed the erection of a building that would contain more floor space than was "actually needed." The implication was that a building of 700,000 square feet (net) was too large. At this time the city and county (including the judiciary) occupied 597,000 net square feet of floor space, of which nearly 150,000 was leased in downtown private buildings. The authority took note of the association's objections but deferred any action on them until after the legal status of the authority was settled.

Immediately after the Supreme Court decision in September 1949, the authority started the process of selecting an architectural firm. After nation-wide advertising and specifically inviting nationally prominent firms to consider the job, the authority narrowed the field to three firms. At its February 10 meeting the authority selected Harley, Ellington and Day, Inc., a leading Detroit firm, and a formal contract was executed the following month. The architects informed the authority that current estimates of building costs were running between $15.00 and $17.00 per square foot, or a total building cost of from $15,000,000 to $17,000,000 for a building of 1,000,000 square feet (gross). Because of the higher cost figures the authority directed the architects to reduce the planned size of the building to 950,000 square feet (gross). As to design, the firm was directed to prepare plans and present scale models of structures that would harmonize with the civic center master plan.

Two different designs and accompanying models were ready by July 1950. The authority referred these designs and models to the Detroit Common Council, the Wayne County Board of Supervisors, the Detroit City Plan Commission, and the elected judicial officers, requesting that these bodies submit their preferences to the Building Authority. Consensus was quickly obtained, and the architects were told to go ahead with detailed preliminary drawings.

On August 24, 1950, the architects presented a complete set of preliminary drawings for a building of 945,000 square feet (gross). The startling part of their presentation was an estimate, supported by comparative cost figures, that the structure would cost $19,975,-000, or in excess of $20.00 per square foot. Rising construction costs accounted for the bulk of the increase, but a substantial part ($2,000,000–$3,000,000) of it was the result of the decision to face the entire building with marble. Confronted with this high figure, the authority promptly decided to reduce further the size of the building. Two alternatives were open. (1) The judges and their courtrooms could be eliminated, restricting the structure to legislative, executive, and administration uses. Excluding the courts would also restore the structure to a continuously uniform height consistent with Pilafin's original concept of the building. (2) A portion of the eastern end of the building could be lopped off, reducing the office unit section.

The judiciary, led by Judge Jayne, again carried the day. The easterly 120 feet of the office unit (six window-bays) were eliminated, reducing the total size by 208,000 square feet and the cost by about $4,500,000. The building would now have 737,000 square feet (gross), with 508,000 square feet of usable floor space. The amount of usable floor space was 89,000 square feet (14.9 percent) less than the 597,000 square feet which the city and county occupied in early 1949. The eastern end of the office unit was to be faced with brick making it possible to extend the office unit at some future date to its originally contemplated size.

The loss of over 20 percent of the building's gross square footage was, in a sense, the price of retaining the ornamental character which the authority wanted the building to have. The exterior and interior design of the structure, as finally settled upon in August 1950, promised a lush building. During the next two years additional customized appointments were decided upon, so that by the time the building was completed it surpassed the generous plans made in 1950. For a description we turn to selected portions of a memorandum prepared by the authority for the building dedication ceremonies.

> The exterior of the building is faced with white Vermont marble on three sides. . . .
> One hundred and twenty-seven caissons of steel and concrete

ranging from four to seven feet in diameter carry the weight of the great superstructure down 125 feet deep to solid rock. . . .

The building is custom-built in every detail, complete with partitions; venetian blinds; vaults; sculpturing; landscaping; underground sprinkling system; thirty-six courtrooms equipped with benches, jury boxes, pews, clerks' and reporters' desks; restaurant; off-street loading facilities; a great, two-story high auditorium without post or pillar to obstruct the vision—plus a thousand and one more extraordinary details. The building is entirely air-conditioned. . . .

. . . .

Our new seat of local government boasts twenty-eight different kinds of marble As previously stated, white Vermont marble was used principally for the exterior. Italian travertine was used mainly for the walls and floors of the public corridors; thus their maintenance is a relatively simple matter. The first floor lobby and corridor on the thirteenth floor of the office section have walls of beautiful Italian Loredo Chiaro marble. As further evidence of the diversity in the type of marble selected, one might point out that the "Norwegian Rose" marble used in one of the courts comes from a quarry 150 miles north of the Arctic Circle. In all, a total of 295 railroad carloads of marble were used.

. . . .

Perhaps the most spectacular feature of the building is the auditorium which is the meeting room for both the Common Council formal sessions and all meetings of the County Board of Supervisors. This room, located in the office unit, is lighted from the north by a great thermopane panorama window twenty-five feet high and ninety-three feet long. The room is designed in amphitheater form so that it can be used for official meetings and hearings, and will comfortably accommodate five hundred persons. Special attention was given to acoustics and visibility.

In view of the features indicated above, it is understandable that this building has been described as . . . the most outstanding of its type in a decade of unusual construction projects.

Clearly the City-County Building was to be more than a mere office building. No precise figure can be given to the additional cost necessary to make the building serve more than its functional purpose. Estimates have ranged between $2,000,000 and $6,000,000.

Probably as significant as the estimated amount of added cost is the fact that the Joint Building Authority decided to incur the additional expense to make the structure a major component of the Civic Center. The built-in co-ordination of overlapping membership between the authority and the other two units, especially the city, unquestionably served to foster a decision that was in keeping with city plans. Despite possible consequences for the county's financial condition, the County Board of Supervisors and the county member on the authority did not object to the monetary cost of the decision.

There are a number of possible explanations for the absence of objections from the county. First, at the time the decision was made the added costs were an indeterminable amount. Second, whatever additional costs were incurred would be spread out over a long period, rather than "peaking" with disastrous impact on the county budget. Third, a majority of the members of the Wayne County Board of Supervisors represent the city of Detroit, and, provided they sided unanimously in favor of the city, they could have defeated any objections raised from out-county (non-Detroit) supervisors. Fourth, final authority for making the decision on the building rested with the Building Authority, a quasi-independent body on which Detroit officials occupied two out of the three posts.

But perhaps the most important reason for building the City-County Building as a major component of the Civic Center was Mayor Cobo's strong personal attachment to the Civic Center as one of "his" most important city projects. Between 1945 and 1958 public capital expenditures on the Civic Center (including the City-County Building) and related facilities totaled over $100,000,000. The City-County Building proved to be the second largest public "investment" item in the Civic Center, the largest being the massive (2,500,000 square feet), elaborate, and costly ($54,000,000) Cobo Exhibition Hall and Convention Arena. About $6,000,000 of the cost of this structure was contributed by businessmen and industrialists. Private expenditures on new banking, office, utility, and transportation-related buildings in the area came to $100,000,000. It is problematical whether these private expenditures would have come about without the Civic Center public "investment" program, that was designed to stimulate private investment in the deteriorating downtown area and bring about a revitalization of the heart of Detroit. The City-County Building was an early and integral part of Mayor Cobo's Civic Center program.

In mid-1950 it seemed that the first step toward realizing the mayor's aim was well under way. The August 1950 reduction in the size of the building had brought its cost within bounds. The minutes of the September 1950 meeting of the authority noted the estimated *total* cost of the building (i.e., including the cost of site acquisition, demolition, and architectural designs) to be $17,131,000. This estimate was still highly tentative, pending numerous decisions on the internal and external appointments of the structure, such as air conditioning and automatic elevators. On October 2, the authority authorized the architects to proceed with detailed drawings and specifications for bids on construction of the building. But the domestic effects of the recently initiated Korean conflict were about to play havoc with the authority's plans.

The Steel Shortage. At their August 1950 meeting the authority members had speculated on the effect that the war would have on the availability of steel and other building materials, as well as its effect on building costs generally. The impact of the war on the thinking of authority members was further reflected in a discussion at their December meeting when they explored the advantages of making the basement of the building into a bomb shelter, at a cost of $750,000. This idea was dropped when it appeared unlikely that federal funds would be available for that purpose.

While the war had not gone unnoticed by the authority members, they were not prepared for the "freeze order," issued on January 13, 1951 by the newly created National Production Authority of the Department of Commerce. The order banned the construction of office buildings during the national emergency to conserve vital war material. The Building Authority promptly initiated a request to the NPA to start construction on the City-County Building. City officials did the staff work to complete the "Application for Authority to Commence Construction." The authority approved the application and forwarded it to the NPA on March 9.

The authority had some reason to expect federal officials to look favorably on this request. In February the authority had received a letter from the Housing and Home Finance Agency notifying local officials that their request for federal planning funds had been approved and that a $450,000 loan was available to help complete the detailed plans, blueprints, and specifications for the building. The letter, which came one full year after the authority's request for a two-year, $450,000 loan to pay the costs of preliminary studies and plans for the City-County Building was submitted, stated that the loan had been granted on the grounds that the building "merits essential civilian requirements and fits into national defense needs."

It soon became apparent, however, that HHFA and NPA differed, for a while at least, on their notions of national defense needs. On May 4, 1951 the authority received a letter from the NPA denying the request for a construction permit. That refusal was shortlived, however. During the months of February, March, and April, Detroit and Wayne County officials had been active in soliciting assistance from Michigan's Congressional delegation to relax federal building controls applying to the City-County Building. Letters, telegrams, and informal contacts were initiated by local officials to all U.S. senators and representatives from Michigan. In addition, one meeting specifically on the City-County Building's construction-permit problems was held locally and was attended by all six Detroit-area members of the House of Representatives. Whatever pressures were mobilized, either singly or in concert with public and private builders in other parts of the country, they proved to be irresistible. On May 3, 1951 the NPA amended its freeze order to permit construction to start on any facility if actual site clearance had started prior to January 13, 1951. This amendment amounted to a go-ahead on the City-County Building even though the NPA's construction-permit denial was received on May 4. A letter from NPA on June 7 officiallly cancelled the denial.

The authority could now proceed with construction if it could secure steel and other critical materials. NPA's June letter constituted only a "permit to shop" and in no way represented a priority or a defense order for steel supplies. Early in the summer of 1951, the authority drafted and forwarded a request to NPA for an allocation of steel. It based its request for steel priorities on (1) the utility of the building as a civil defense control and communication center, (2) the potential use of the building as a downtown bomb shelter, and (3) the relief that the building would bring to the critical problem of inadequate space for local government, military, and defense agencies in the Detroit area. The NPA turned down this request in November 1951. The federal agency was anticipating an acute steel shortage and could offer no guarantee as to when steel supplies would be available for civilian needs.

In fact, the Korean emergency had already made steel not only scarce but also expensive. In early July 1951 the authority received bids and let contracts for the construction of the substructure and steel frame for the building. Revised projections based on the higher cost level in these bids put the estimated total cost of the building at $20,000,000, an increase of nearly $3,000,000 in one year.

Actual construction began on July 11, 1951, when formal ground-breaking ceremonies were held. Ground-breaking forced the authority to repay the $125,000 advance on the federal loan which it had received only three months before. The repayment was made in August and terminated the authority's brief contacts with federal officials on planning loan funds.

Other federal contacts were in the making, for NPA's refusal to give the authority a priority on steel endangered progress on construction. Mayor and Building Authority Chairman Cobo, along with a small delegation of elected and appointed local officials, went to Washington in December to seek assurances and time-tables on the availability of steel for expressways and other major public works, including the City-County Building. Cobo followed up the personal-visit approach with frequent phone calls to various federal officials in an attempt to prod them into action. Oak-man recalls that on at least one occasion Cobo talked directly with President Truman, who commited himself to the mayor to the extent of saying, "If you are still stuck a few months from now, let me know."

Federal response to local pressures came the following March. The NPA notified local officials that it would grant allocations of steel for non-military uses over the six-month period from June to December 1952 in sufficient quantity to permit construction to proceed on the City-County Building. The actual amount subsequently allocated was four thousand tons, most of it going for the building's steel skeleton. With this assurance as to the availability of steel, in mid-1952 the Building Authority advertised for bids to complete the superstructure of the building.

Financing. The problem of obtaining steel to get the building started had been met, but it left in its wake another problem: paying for the completion of the building. As cost estimates had skyrocketed, the authority members had evidenced concern over the size of the bond issue that would be necessary. Obviously, a larger bond issue would require larger annual rental payments to pay interest costs and retire the principal on the bonds. This was an unpleasant prospect for authority members, who were anxious to keep annual charges as low as possible in order to reduce the possible dislocating effect on county and city budgets. Where in 1949 a $10,000,000 or $12,000,000 bond issue had been mentioned, by mid-1952 it appeared that a much larger issue would be necessary. By that time Detroit had advanced (counting the donation of the site at about $1,600,000) nearly $6,600,000 and Wayne County $1,250,000. With estimates on total cost running between $24,000,000 and $26,000,000, from $16,000,000 to $18,000,000 remained to be raised through bond financing or other means. This figure was reduced in the late summer and fall of 1952 when Detroit and Wayne County contributed $1,500,000 and $750,000, respectively, out of their current budgets. Sums contributed by the city and county as advance rentals now totaled slightly over $10,000,000.

Firm and final cost estimates were finally available in October 1952, when bids were received from general contractors for completing the building. The low bid, by a Detroit firm, was $16,870,-000, bringing the total cost of the building to $26,087,565. This latter figure was $6,000,000 higher than the total cost estimate made only fifteen months earlier, and $9,000,000 higher than that made in July 1950, just after the outbreak of the Korean conflict. Deducting advance rentals, almost $16,000,000 remained to be raised.

The authority prepared to seek bond financing. It first sought the formal assent of the Common Council and Board of Supervisors to issue not more than $16,500,000 in revenue bonds. The $16,500,000 was merely a ceiling figure, the hope being that a lesser amount would actually be required. This amount was approved by both bodies, although the issuance of the bonds was in no way contingent on such approval. (All contracts, costs, bond ordinance, and other major actions were referred to both the City Council and the Board of Supervisors. Of this procedure Oakman says, "We could have gone on alone and almost disregarded them if we had wanted. Instead, we took everyone into our confidence. We saw ourselves, the authority, as merely a creature of the city and county.") At the same time the council and the board also ratified a final rental agreement with the authority.

The rental agreement was the contractual basis and security upon which the authority could issue its revenue bonds. The apportionment of rental charges was based on the final space allocations which had been made early in 1952. The city was to occupy 53 percent of the net usable space, the county 47 percent. The percentages varied from those set in the interim rental agreement of January 1949, which had allocated 56 percent of the space to the city and 44 percent to the county. As costs spiraled and the building shrank, agencies had to be eliminated as prospective tenants and new tentative determinations had to be made. By September 1950 the central administrative offices of five city agencies (Housing, Parks and Recreation, Traffic Engineering, Water, and Welfare) had been squeezed out.

The chief reason for the progressive reduction in the city's share of the building space was apparent to most observers on the local scene. The county was operating in a position of present and continuing financial stringency. County officials argued that they could not participate in the joint venture unless all county departments could be housed in one place. With limited funds, they argued, the county could not afford the expense of paying the operating and maintenance costs on two separate buildings. Authority Members Cobo and Oakman, mayor and councilman, respectively, from Detroit, deferred to the county in this respect. As the building size was reduced, the prospective occupants eliminated were, with minor exceptions, city agencies. Ironically, the county still maintains the old County Building, which houses three county agencies and the City Traffic Violation Bureau, and in 1959 the county also paid $184,000 in rentals to house county offices at nine different locations, although five of these were social welfare field offices. Nevertheless, the county's argument was persuasive at the time and offered a handy rationale for dropping city agencies.

According to the percentages set in the final rental agreement, the city would pay $583,000, and the county $517,000, of the total $1,100,000 annual payment to cover interest and principal on bonds totaling $16,500,000. If only $13,500,000 in bonds were issued, the rental agreement called for an annual payment of $900,000— $477,000 from the city, $423,000 from the county. Annual operating costs would be over and above these figures. An additional provision in the forty-year lease-contract was that the city and county were to recover the advance payments they had made out of rentals coming due after the bonds were retired.

After completing the above arrangements, the authority, on November 6, 1952, adopted a bond ordinance authorizing the issuance of not more than $16,500,000 in revenue bonds. The thirty-day waiting period during which 10 percent of the registered voters of Wayne County could have petitioned for a referendum passed without incident. (The anomaly of the referendum provision in Michigan revenue-bond statutes is apparent in this case. Petitions bearing about 135,000 signatures of registered voters would have had to have been filed in thirty days to cause a referendum on this bond issue. Practically speaking, it would be impossible to obtain the signatures within the short time allowed.) The authority then applied to the Michigan Municipal Finance Commission for that agency's approval of the proposed bond issue. The assent of this state agency, required by Michigan statutes before any local unit can offer bonds for sale, came on December 3, 1952. The authority then prepared and distributed a forty-page bond prospectus in anticipation of the sale of bonds on January 7, 1953.

Rather than issue the full $16,500,000 legally authorized, the authority offered only $13,500,000 for sale, holding the remainder of the issue in reserve. This decision was based on the expectation that during the time it would take to complete the building the city and the county would continue making advance payments and perhaps avoid issuing the additional authorized bonds.

There had been some doubts as to whether the Joint Building

Authority's revenue bonds would be favorably received on the New York bond market since they were not an ordinary type of state or local bond issue. These doubts were dispelled when the bonds were given an "A" rating by Standard and Poors and three bond houses bid on the bond issue. The low bid on the thirty-year serial bonds was accepted at an average net interest rate of 2.9916 percent. At this rate the total interest cost over the life of the bonds would be about $7,670,000. Like all state and local bonds, the interest on the authority's bonds was exempt from federal income tax, a feature which undoubtedly added to their attractiveness. The last of the bonds were scheduled for retirement in 1982. Present (1961) predictions are that because of the sound financial condition of the authority, the call feature, inserted in the bonds to permit their retirement prior to their due date at a specified premium price, will be taken advantage of in order to pay off all the bonds by 1976.

With the bonds successfully sold, the authority executed the contract with the general contractor at its January 1953 meeting. Barring delays beyond his control, the contractor estimated that the structure could be completed in two and one-half years. During this time both the city and the county continued to make advance payments credited as advance rentals. These additional contributions, totaling about $500,000 from the city and nearly $2,000,000 from the county, made the sale of additional bonds unnecessary. The total advance rentals credited to the city of Detroit amounted to more than $8,600,000, to the county nearly $4,000,000. These two figures provide a rough quantitative measure of (1) the fiscal capacity of the two governmental units, and (2) the greater commitment and higher priority that the City-County Building carried with the city, chiefly via Mayor Cobo.

The building neared completion in January 1955, and, appropriately, the City Plan Commission was the first agency to move in. The Wayne County Road Commission managed to get all of its administrative personnel housed in the new building at the price of moving three county and two city agencies out. Thirty-six judicial officials, each with his own high-ceilinged courtroom, were comfortably ensconced in the tower section of the building. When all the tenants were installed, the building housed slightly more than three thousand of the twenty-two thousand city and seven thousand county employees. During its first year the building cost the Joint Building Authority $1,820,000—$920,000 for principal and interest on bonds and $900,000 for building maintenance and operation. The city and county were billed $964,600 and $855,400 respectively. The City-County Building was in business.

Concluding Comments

The history of cooperation between the city and the county in the use of building space and the compelling logic of locating a joint governmental office building in the downtown Civic Center paved the way for both political and "expert" (city planners') support of the City-County Building. The building also shared in the general support which Detroit business and industry gave to the Civic Center project. When this consensus was reinforced by the limited voter sanction received in the 1947 referendum, the building had secured stature as a necessary and desirable project. But limits on local taxing powers and voter disapproval of a tax increase conspired to prevent its realization. In order to circumvent these barriers, local political leaders chose a technique which showed their willingness to go outside the normal system of local policy formation by seeking certification of the project at other levels of government and in the courts.

The technique was the special authority device and the revenue-bond method of financing. The smoothness with which these unorthodox arrangements were made and put to use would have been impossible without the high degree of cooperation that oiled the city-county partnership. City-county agreement enabled the authority to make the best use of its quasi-autonomous status. To the extent that the authority was independent of the two local governing units it had a fair measure of discretion in making decisons about the size, etc., of the building. To the extent that the dual allegiance of its members made it dependent on the city and the county, the authority was able to capitalize on local officials' strong desires for the building. When forces beyond the authority's control (the steel shortage and the rise in building costs) created construction and financing problems, the city and county were quick to reinforce the authority's efforts. In order to obtain steel the city and county mobilized pressure without regard to party lines—Cobo and Oakman (officially non-partisan) were Republicans, while Detroit-area legislators and congressmen and President Truman were Democrats. As costs shot up and it appeared that a large revenue-bond debt might unduly tax the county's and city's financial capacity (for each added dollar borrowed, interest cost was fifty cents), the city and county paid substantial sums as advance rentals. The political consensus that underlay these actions was such that all actions of the two governing bodies (the Detroit Common Council and the Wayne County Board of Supervisors) with regard to the Joint Building Authority were unanimous in favor of the authority. The City-County Building stands as a monument to that unanimity.

4
Water for Southwestern Wayne County

An Exercise in City-County Competition

Introduction

Water is a key resource in the development of a metropolis. Although the basic demands of the human organism can be satisfied with a quart or so a day, the daily per capita consumption of the urban American is over 150 gallons, and the rate is increasing. An industrial economy imposes heavy demands upon water, and so does an urban sanitation system that permits millions of people to live in close proximity under healthy conditions. Household technology has added thirsty appliances, such as the automatic washer and garbage disposer. Cultural values aggravate the demand by placing a high value on cleanliness, resulting in frequent showers and baths, and an equally high value on green grass. The latter is especially significant in urban areas, such as Detroit, where most families live in single residences and where suburban migration brings with it a demand for larger lots, which are converted into greenswards as a badge of pride in home ownership and a symbol of middle-class status. To those involved in water supply, this has a special significance, since the peak demands for water occur during prolonged summer dry spells when millions of anxious citizens seek to moisten the roots of their withering grass with their lawn sprinklers.

A primary consideration in urban water supply is the physical location of water resources in relation to the population to be served. Like the other Great Lakes cities, the Detroit metropolitan area is in an extremely favorable location. Bounded on the east by Lake St. Clair and the Detroit River, through which the waters of Lake Huron flow to Lake Erie, the Detroit metropolis is within easy reach of a surface fresh-water supply far in excess of any forseeable demand. Until recently, ground water was also in abundant supply in the area, and many of the satellite cities were able to meet their needs through community wells. In view of this abundance, it is easy to understand the annoyance and frustration that result when residents are ordered to restrict the use of water for lawn sprinkling or when pressure drops too low to permit toilets to be flushed. After years of uninhibited water use, in the summer of 1952, the residents of Detroit and surrounding jurisdictions who received their water from Detroit were asked to restrict their use of water. This was the first indication of a "water crisis."

The principal supplier of water to the metropolitan area is the Detroit Department of Water Supply. This city agency had been supplying other jurisdictions since the latter part of the nineteenth century, and by 1954 it was serving about forty units of government. The post-World War II building boom and the industrial expansion necessitated by the Korean conflict had extended the Detroit water system to the point where the management felt it necessary to restrict use during the summer months in order to maintain adequate pressure throughout the system. In August 1954 the Detroit Water Department took a step which laid the groundwork for a city-county controversy that lasted until December 1959. In itself the controversy is not extraordinary, but it is an extraordinary illustration of a metropolitan system in the process of developing one of the necessary resources for survival and growth, water.

But why all the controversy? The need for water is universally conceded. Why not set up a single water agency, metropolitan in scope, and have done with it? This, in fact, was suggested in a report on the area's water needs which was published in 1924. The end result of the city-county water controversy may very well be a metropolitan water authority, but, as this case will show, the development of major service facilities that transcend normal political boundaries is not a simple matter. As the core city diminishes in importance in the face of surrounding metropolitan growth, its agencies, such as the Detroit Department of Water Supply, face a relative loss of influence and prestige, as competing agencies are organized to service the new populations. If new interjurisdictional agencies are to be formed to service the metropolitan population, should they be built around the core-city agencies, or should county agencies, with their broader jurisdictional scope, provide the basis for the supra-agencies? This is a case study of a struggle by a core-city agency, the Detroit Department of Water Supply, to maintain its position as the dominant bureaucracy for the provision of water throughout the metropolitan area.

The Decision to Build a Wayne County Water System

The Lenhardt Policy. On July 27, 1954, the Detroit Department of Water Supply pumped 695.8 million gallons of water. This was over 100 million gallons beyond the 584 m.g.d. (million gallons daily) rated capacity of the system, and 35 million gallons beyond the 660 m.g.d. which was considered a safe capacity for filtering water under favorable summer conditions. In spite of this maximum effort, Detroiters were restricted in their use of water for lawn sprinkling, and in some of the suburbs receiving water from Detroit, low pressures reduced the supply to a trickle. The first public evidence of a water shortage had come in 1952, when restrictions were imposed upon lawn sprinkling. As the summers continued hot and dry and the young lawns of new subdivisions turned brown and crisp, the water crisis became more evident and more annoying. By the summer of 1954, citizens and local officials turned to the management of the Detroit Department of Water Supply for some explanation of the cause of the shortage and what was being done about it.

The Department of Water Supply was created in 1853 by state legislation passed at the request of the Detroit Common Council. Earlier experience with private ownership of the water system had proven unsatisfactory, and from 1836 on, water supply was the responsibility of the municipality. The city charter, adopted in 1918, provided for a four-member Board of Water Commissioners "which shall have charge of the Department of Water Supply." Commissioners were to be appointed by the mayor for four-year terms, and a qualification for appointment was residence in the city. The charter charged the board with the duty of supplying the city with a sufficient quantity of pure and wholesome water "to be taken from the Detroit River or such other sources as may be deemed expedient." The board had the authority to construct the various works necessary to a water system and the power to fix water rates. The charter also provided that: "the board may sell and deliver water outside the corporate limits of the City of Detroit in such amount and within such limitations as may be prescribed by law and may extend its water works as required to render such service."

The department's first major works, Water Works Park Pumping Station, was put into service in 1876, and this plant, with its additions, continued as the sole plant for the city and its various customers until 1935, when the second installation, Springwells Pumping Station, was put into service. The Springwells plant ended a shortage that had existed since 1927 and provided a water surplus sufficient to absorb the increased demand brought about by World War II and the postwar building boom. By 1952, demand had caught up with this supply, but at the same time that restrictions were being imposed and complaints about the water shortage mounted, a third plant, Northeast Pumping Station, was under construction. This plant would bring added water supplies to the area, with partial operation beginning in 1955 and full operation the next year.

The construction of Northeast Station completed a master plan for system expansion that had been adopted by the Board of Water Commissioners in 1924. The reports of the engineers who proposed the 1924 plan were published by the Water Board in a volume entitled *Reports on Additional Water Supply for Detroit and Environs.* The engineers viewed the Detroit area as a rapidly growing industrial complex and recommended that the water system be developed to keep abreast with it. "As to population for which provision should at this time be made in planning works for the future, your commission estimates that 3,400,000 people will reside within an area of about 300 square miles, including the present city, at some time between 1950 and 1960, who will be dependent upon the Detroit Water System." The population estimate was a little over-optimistic. By 1955, the department was, in fact, servicing an area of about 305 square miles with an estimated population of 2,850,000, but the predicted maximum day demand of 676 m.g.d. was remarkably close to the 695.8 million gallons pumped on July 27, 1954.

The master plan called for the Springwells and Northeast plants, both of which were located so as best to serve parts of the metropolitan area. The master plan aimed at providing water service not only to the city of Detroit but to the metropolis as a whole, regardless of political jurisdiction. In his report as a member of the commission, George H. Fenkell, the superintendent and general manager of the Water Board, pointed out that:

> In addition to Detroit proper and its immediately adjacent territory, there lies beyond the city a considerable area, having an eastern and northern boundary to include Port Huron and Pontiac, and a western and southern boundary of Ypsilanti and Monroe, which must be taken into consideration in any comprehensive plan for a water supply for a Greater Detroit. Such an area, as herein considered, includes roughly 1,665 square miles and will contain by 1950–1960, it is estimated, about 1,000,000 additional population to the 3,400,000 within the city proper.

Fenkell envisaged an eventual expansion of the system to include this larger area. The 1924 consultants cannot be accused of taking a narrow or conservative view of the area's prospects and needs.

It was within the framework of this broad, regional orientation for planning the Detroit water system's development that General Manager L. G. Lenhardt approached the task of doing something about the water crisis in the summer of 1954. In a four-page single-spaced letter, dated August 11, 1954, to the Detroit Common Council, he provided an explanation for the water crisis, told what the immediate prospects were for relieving it, and stated what further action should be taken to meet future water demands. The letter said in part:

> Since the end of World War II about 500,000 people have been added to the connected load of this department, with no increase in production facilities. Such regulation of use as has been imposed since 1952 is largely due to the some twenty hours of the year, less than one-quarter of 1 percent of the total, that peak loads occur. No essential use has been curtailed and even lawn sprinkling has been unrestricted within the city limits four days per week.

. . . .

> The story of supply to the suburbs is clouded in history. The

1853 report states that there were supplies beyond the city to both the east and the west some time before 1851. It seems probable that service between the city and the Water Works Park plant started about the time that plant started operation, and it is known that at least three suburbs, probably more, were supplied prior to 1892. In 1904 thirteen suburbs were listed as being supplied. Despite annexations of previously supplied suburbs, the areas supplied without the city limits grew steadily until the onset of World War II, when about 14 percent of the water pumped was supplied beyond the city limits.

. . . .

At the present time the department serves forty units of government, the Wayne County General Hospital, the Detroit House of Correction, and the Wayne County Training School.

. . . .

The two primary producing plants of the Department of Water Supply are the Water Works Park and the Springwells plants, with total rated capacities of 584 m.g.d. based on the filter plants. During favorable summer water conditions 660 m.g.d. can safely be filtered.

. . . .

At 660 m.g.d., with a maximum hour of 40 million gallons or less, we can satisfactorily balance pressures around the city limits and safely refill reservoirs during off-peak hours. When we pump 695.8 million gallons, as on July 27, 1954, there will be soft points of pressures at some spots at the limits, although on that day generally pressures within the city were satisfactory. Further, with such high deliveries we are gambling with reservoir refill although in this case it was completed on time.

. . . .

The Northeast Station cannot be fully completed until 1956. . . . When fully completed this will give total plant capacity of 885 m.g.d. under favorable conditions. . . . To ensure fullest possible delivery through the tunnel system, even at low lake levels, it will be necessary to install a raw-water booster station at Water Works Park. . . . With boosting we can supply 1,050 m.g.d. through the tunnel system, which would supply approximately 3,800,000 people with 276 gallons per capita per day, as against the maximum daily demand to date of 253 gallons per capita. The raw-water booster station should be ready by June 1957.

To take full advantage of the capacity of the boosted tunnel system will necessitate a fourth plant to be located at about the city's periphery in the northwest section. . . . It is felt that with the fourth plant this is as far as Detroit should go. It is profitable and economical for both Detroit and the suburbs to expand thus far, as it would utilize the very large investments this city has in its intake and tunnel system. To go farther will necessitate other intakes and other sources of supply. Studies indicate that eventually we should not supply out-county territory below approximately Van Born Road and westerly of, say, the line of Southfield Road south of the city of Dearborn.

The county of Wayne must undertake construction of facilities in the areas in southwesterly Wayne County thus roughly delineated. This plant would have its intake in Lake Erie and be a complete plant with filter, pumping stations, transmission mains, and reservoirs. It should be planned large enough to take care of parts of Monroe and Washtenaw counties and possibly of capacity to ultimately supply about 1,500,000 population. Thus the metropolitan area will have water plant capacity for about 5,500,000 population, which will be close to the ultimate population.

The two crucial points in the Lenhardt letter were (1) that the Department of Water Supply should plan no further expansions beyond that which would utilize the boosted raw-water supply available from the intake and tunnel system, an estimated 1,050 m.g.d., and (2) that Wayne County should immediately prepare to construct its own water works to service the southwestern part of the county. The Common Council did not challenge these conclusions, but on August 17, it passed a resolution directing the Water Board to supply it with answers to a number of questions including: "a report as to what is necessary to service the people and industry of the city of Detroit proper, and when we will be in a position to do it; what must be done by our present customers at the present level; what their needs are, and what it would take to service them adequately; a forecast of the future needs, and what it is necessary to do to supply such needs; what our present customers are doing to help themselves, and what it is necessary for them to do."

The formal reply to the council resolution was dated January 10, 1955, and was submitted by the Water Board and signed by General Manager Lenhardt. The covering letter summarized "what seem to us to be the salient features and conclusions of the report" as follows:

1. No new suburban territory should be serviced at the present time other than that which we now serve or which has been under negotiation.
2. It is not practicable to discontinue service to any suburban area now serviced until other means of supply are available. This would take at least ten years in many cases.

3. The economy of the entire area is so bound together that water supply is essential throughout the area, if Detroit, the core of the area, is to continue to prosper.

4. The capacity of the Water Works Park, Springwells, and North-east Stations plants will be absorbed by 1960 at present rate of growth, even with usage being regulated during peak summer demand. At that time 3,200,000 will be served and about 31 per-cent of the water pumped will go to the suburbs.

5. A fourth plant must be built on the west side which must be in operation by 1960 or service will suffer. This will utilize full capac-ity of our intake and tunnel system which can supply an ultimate 3,500,000–3,750,000 population, with suitable regulations as to usage during summer peaks. (Expansion of Springwells Station was later substituted for a new Northwest plant.)

6. The capacity of the intake and tunnel system should govern the amount of service to the suburbs. This makes for greatest econ-omy to both Detroit and suburbs.

7. A complete plant must be built and operated by others to serve the southern and westerly areas of Wayne County. It should be in service well before 1970, and the county so notified. Adjustments of suburban areas served can be agreed upon before that time.

8. Completely unregulated usage would require expenditures of at least a presently estimated $150,000,000 for facilities in addition to those previously proposed and would necessitate rate increases of at least 60 percent. Construction could not be completed for about ten years, during which time restrictions would be neces-sary. In our opinion this is not practicable and is uneconomical.

9. After completion of both the proposed Northwest Station and the Wayne County plant it may be possible to develop the necessary facilities to allow unregulated lawn sprinkling within the cor-porate limits. Until that time it will be necessary to continue regu-lation of lawn sprinkling. However, upon full completion of the Northeast Station next year, regulations may be relaxed to allow sprinkling on all days from 9 P.M. to 9 A.M.

The preoccupation with restrictions on lawn sprinkling was evident throughout the report. The Detroit councilmen wanted to know what the water-supply situation would be if all restrictions on water use were lifted for city residents and supplies to the suburbs were cut off. The report pointed out that many of the suburbs were so inextricably tied in with the Detroit system that it would be virtually impossible to detach them from it, and that all suburbs then being served had long-term investments and commitments dependent upon the Detroit supply. The report did not suggest any retreat from the then current suburban links, with the exception of some communities in western Wayne County that could be tied into a county system and were necessary to make the county system economically feasible. As to unrestricted lawn sprinkling, the report had this to say: "Unrestricted lawn sprinkling comes to a peak of about twenty to thirty hours a year, spread over the summer months, based on past experience. However, these unrestricted uses would cause large plant expenditures for facilities which would be idle 95 percent or more of the time."

As to future expansion of the Detroit system, the report reiterated the position stated by Lenhardt the previous August, to the effect that the system should be developed to the capacity of its intake and tunnel system; "however, we do not feel it incumbent upon the city of Detroit to go beyond this point and construct new intakes, tunnel systems, and plants to take care of demands in areas which are not remotely contiguous to our borders." Population data were cited to show that although the Detroit population served by the system was expected to increase by only about 45,000 from 1954 to 1970, the suburban population served was expected to show a 700,000 increase, so that by 1970 the distribution would be 2,000,000 Detroiters and 1,500,000 suburbanites. Obviously, any plant expansion would benefit the suburbs to a greater degree than the city. "It is evident, therefore, that well before 1970 it will be necessary for some other agency, perhaps a metropolitan authority, to provide additional complete water works with their own intakes for the southerly and westerly areas of Wayne County, and perhaps also by that time for the northerly portions of this metropolitan area."

The Lenhardt policy was clear. The Detroit water system was approaching its maximum development, and additional water supplies for suburban areas would have to be developed through some agency other than the Department of Water Supply. The mayor, Common Council, county officials, and other responsible community leaders apparently considered this a prudent policy, since all went about the task of making provisions for an additional water system to absorb the growing demands that could no longer be met by the Detroit system.

Wayne County Government. In order to put the relationship between Wayne County and the city of Detroit in sharper perspective, a brief look at certain demographic characteristics of the county and its governmental organization is necessary. The county has a land area of 623 square miles, with Detroit occupying 140 square miles of the northeastern section. Detroit's northern boundary, Eight Mile Road, is also the county line which separates Wayne from its northern neighbors, Oakland and Macomb counties. The northeastern and central sections of Wayne County are the most densely populated areas. This part of the county includes Detroit and the satellite cities immediately adjacent to it. The western and southwestern sections of the county contain the only remaining farms and open lands. Detroit, with the largest share of the county population, has historically been the dominant factor in county affairs. But by the late 1950's, the population trend was running against the big city.[1] Detroit's 1,900,000 population was still the largest single segment of the total county population of 2,800,000, but the Detroit population was estimated to have increased only 3.3 percent during the interval from 1950 to 1957, while the out-county population (outside the corporate boundaries of Detroit) had grown by 55 percent during this same period. By 1957, the county contained, in addition to Detroit, ten cities of over 20,000 population (Dearborn led with 118,000) and five townships, each with populations of over 20,000. The area of most rapid growth was, of course, the western and southwestern sections of the county where land was still available for large subdivisions.

Viewed on an organization chart, Wayne County government is a hodgepodge of elective officials (fifty-eight, including twenty-one judges) and appointive boards and commissions (thirteen boards and commissions with a total of fifty-six members) employing over seven thousand personnel and spending over $80,000,000 annually. The basic structure is that prescribed by state law for all counties, but through the usual devices of legislation applicable to only certain population classifications and of permissive legisla-

[1] The population data used in the case are the estimates in use at the time the events in the case took place. The 1960 census revealed them to be optimistic for Detroit, which was, in fact, losing population, whereas the out-county increase for the decade was close to 60 percent.

tion, the state legislature has provided routes by which the county has been able to take on an increasing number of functions answering the service demands of an urban population. Over the years, attempts have been made to provide home rule for the county, but these attempts have been frustrated by a rural-dominated state legislature. Although this structure is a nightmare to one with a passion for clear-cut lines of authority and responsibility, it does manage to function as the vehicle for providing a wide range of public services through a bureaucracy composed of a mixture of holdovers from an earlier, pre-merit-system service (the merit system was adopted in 1942 and is still in the process of development) and a new generation of professionally oriented personnel.

The three county agencies that played a part in this case are also the three most important units of the county. The governing body of the county is the Board of Supervisors, whose membership totals 111 and consists of the township supervisor from each of the county's townships and representatives from each of the cities, prorated on the basis of population. Detroit's delegation to the board is composed of the mayor, the Common Council, and certain other city officials designated by the charter (e.g., the chairman of the Water Board), and the additional number required to make up the city's quota is supplied by appointments prorated among the mayor and councilmen. The result of this selection pattern is a form of functional representation, since the appointments traditionally go to representatives of major interests in the city, such as the Board of Commerce, labor groups, etc. Detroit's population edge is reflected in the number of representatives allocated to the city, but the Detroit delegation cannot be depended upon to vote as a solid block against out-county supervisors. The crisscross of interests involved in most major issues is too complex to permit such a simple basis for choosing sides. This was certainly the case in the water controversy.

Detroit councilmen play a major role on the Board of Supervisors. Heading the largest delegation to the board and representing the jurisdiction providing the major share of the county's revenue, this is to be expected. The board has both policy-making and administrative authority. Policy-making decisions are reflected in the budget allocations to various agencies and the approval of new programs, while administrative control is exercised to some extent through the power to appoint members to the various boards and commissions. As with other large legislative bodies, the principal vehicle for the exercise of influence is the committee structure, and the Detroit councilmen will be found holding key assignments to key committees. The most important committee is the Ways and Means Committee, through which all matters involving money must clear before being considered by the board. There are twenty-one other standing committees, of which the Capital Improvements Program Committee, headed by Detroit Councilman James Lincoln, was of special importance in this case. The chairmanship of the Wayne County Board of Supervisors during most of the water controversy was another Detroit councilman, Edward Connor.

The County Board of Auditors, consisting of three members elected for three-year staggered terms, is as close as the county comes to having a central administrative agency. The auditors function as a central fiscal office, having under their direction a Budget and Finance Division, which prepares the annual budget for submittal to the Board of Supervisors. Without a single executive responsible for the direction of county operations, the budget is not the instrument of central administrative control that it would be in a strong mayor or strong governor system, but it does provide an integrating influence in an otherwise unintegrated system. When the county was faced with the necessity for planning its own water system, the Capital Improvement Program Committee of the Board of Supervisors turned to County Budget Director Alfred M. Pelham for the staff assistance necessary to draft a program.

The Board of Wayne County Road Commissioners is the third agency that commands our attention. The board consists of three commissioners appointed by the Board of Supervisors for staggered terms of six years. The executive head of the agency, appointed by the commission, has the title of county highway engineer. The Road Commission is an excellent demonstration of how a well-led administrative bureaucracy operating in a service vacuum can extend its operations and influence by providing needed services. Perhaps this could happen only amid the relative disorganization of county government, but by the late 1950's, the Road

Commission was not only responsible for the county road system under its Highway Division, but, in addition, was developing and maintaining a county park and parkway system and operating an airport, a water-supply system, and a sewage-disposal system. In terms of annual budget, the Road Commission is by far the most important county agency, and in terms of services provided, the agency most in evidence to a large segment of the county population.

The Road Commission is probably the most autonomous of the county administrative agencies. This autonomy is partially due to the fact that the bulk of its funds are obtained from gas- and weight-tax reimbursements from the state (approximately $17,000,000 from state funds out of a total budget of $23,000,000 for fiscal 1958–59), while the sewage-disposal and water systems are financed from users' fees. Only the parks and airport functions received appropriations from the Board of Supervisors in fiscal 1958–59, and the total was under $3,000,000. With this degree of income independence, the Road Commission is less vulnerable to the usual annual appropriation control exercised by legislative bodies than are agencies dependent upon general fund appropriations. With the help of considerable financial independence from the usual channels of local political control, the Road Commission leadership has taken advantage of its capacity to provide much needed services throughout the county in order to build the political support necessary to protect the autonomy of the agency. No doubt, at any given time, the Board of Supervisors would contain a number of out-county representatives who felt indebted to the Road Commission for services rendered to their constituency or who were anticipating such services. This existing or anticipated indebtedness does not imply graft or illegality of any sort. The politically strategic distribution of services is a standard practice of sophisticated bureaucracies, and even if the services had been distributed at random, the agency would still have won friends and influence, since the services they provided were needed. Roads, water, and sewers are the most keenly felt community needs of an expanding urban population as well as the key factors in the development of an area.

With a strong demand for its services, the resources for serving this demand, and a leadership sensitive to its capacity to exercise influence through the agency's programs, the Road Commission had the ingredients for developing a sturdy bureaucratic unit that could withstand assaults upon it both from within the county, on the part of central fiscal and personnel agencies, and from without.

The Millage Campaign.   Although Lenhardt's recommendation that Wayne County develop its own water system was not formally presented to the Detroit Common Council until January 1955, county officials had been notified of this position the previous August and immediately began making plans to get the project under way. The first problem was finance. The county's power to tax and borrow was limited by law, and the financing of a project as expensive as the contemplated water works would require special voter approval. The Board of Supervisors, through its Capital Improvements Program Committee, called in County Budget Director Pelham to work with the committee in drafting a long-range capital improvements program, including a method for financing it. Pelham was ready with his report by January 1955. Speed was necessary, since voter approval would be required, and it was hoped that this approval could be obtained at the regular spring election, due to be held on April 4.

The capital improvements program unveiled in January contained a number of projects, such as a hospital addition, a jail annex, and a new juvenile detention home, but by far the most important part of the program was a plan to spend $50,000,000 to develop a county water system which would include an intake and filtration plant as well as transmission lines. The proposed financing would require voter approval of three propositions which would authorize the county (1) to increase the fifteen-mill limit on taxation by three-quarters of a mill for fifteen years, (2) to spend the three-quarters of a mill, plus an additional one-quarter of a mill from current revenue, for capital improvements for ten years, and (3) to issue $26,000,000 in faith and credit bonds. The tax moneys spent for the development of the water system would be returned to the county from users' fees. The program was approved by the Board of Supervisors, which took the necessary action to submit the three propositions to the voters in April.

The most noteworthy aspect of the campaign for the adoption of the three propositions that would make it possible for the county to construct its own water system was the extent of agreement among top leadership in the community that the project was necessary and desirable. Increasing voter resistance to self-inflicted tax hikes through lifting of millage ceilings created some concern, so a careful campaign was carried out to develop voter support. It had to be a selling campaign, since there was no active opposition to the program being voiced by any individuals or groups of importance against whom an assault could be launched. Detroit's supervisors, led by Mayor Cobo and the nine councilmen, actively supported the proposals, and the Greater Detroit Board of Commerce, through its Water Study Committee, organized a Water for Wayne County Committee, consisting of "a cross section of top-echelon Detroit life," to help sell the program to the voters. Raymond Hodgson, vice president of the National Bank of Detroit, headed this committee, and one of his published statements represented his committee's position: "Everyone in Detroit and Wayne County must be told that the water-supply crisis is very real. We have reached a point now where a ceiling has been placed on further industrial and residential growth." The rare phenomenon of the Board of Commerce supplying leadership in a campaign to raise taxes made this a unique campaign, to say the least, and the board's bedfellows included labor leaders, the three major newspapers, and all those of any importance in city-county politics. Pelham played the role of the public servant available to supply the necessary facts and figures to support the proposals, but he, along with other county officials, was happy to see the "citizens" carrying the campaign ball.

During the campaign for the proposals there was no public questioning of the basic elements of the Lenhardt policy, nor were any counterproposals debated as alternatives to the county water system. A rare event had taken place: a genuine consensus among community leaders representing diverse interests on what was required in order to promote the general interest of the metropolitan community, and a backing up of that consensus with political action to win popular support for the program.

Because the financial plan submitted to the voters included

three separate elements—taxing, spending, and borrowing—three separate propositions had to be voted on. Yet the three were part of an integrated financial program, and if the taxing proposition were to fail while the spending and borrowing propositions passed, the program would be unworkable. Part of the selling job in the campaign was not only to convince voters of the need for a county water system, but also of the necessity for voting affirmatively on all three propositions. All three propositions were approved at the election held on April 4, but whereas the proposition authorizing borrowing passed with a two-to-one margin, the proposition authorizing the millage increase narrowly passed. The fears of county officials were almost realized, but not quite.

By April 5, 1955, it looked as if the major obstacle to the construction of a county water system had been overcome, and none too soon. The summer months brought a recurrence of the water shortages experienced the previous summer, and the shortage was especially acute in the area serviced by the Wayne County Metropolitan Water Supply System. This system was begun in 1942 in order to bring Detroit water to outlying suburban areas. At that time, the Water Board had no authority to build mains beyond the Detroit city limit, so the Road Commission undertook to build and maintain this out-county transmission system. It served one of the most rapidly growing sections of the whole metropolitan area. Over nine thousand new homes had been built in the service area since the previous summer, and average daily water consumption had jumped from 20.5 m.g.d. to 27.5 m.g.d. for this period. Throughout the summer, the Road Commission's executive head, County Highway Engineer Leroy C. Smith, conducted a running battle with Lenhardt and the Water Board in an attempt to get more water for the county system. The shortage of water necessitated restrictions on lawn sprinkling in the county's service area and a ban on new housing construction in two of its townships. The Water Board refused to furnish additional water, and Lenhardt criticized the county system as being inadequate—lacking in storage and distribution facilities. The Board of Supervisors responded to this crisis by approving the construction of additional transmission facilities, and by the end of 1955, an agreement was reached with the Water Board to provide the necessary water for the new transmission lines. By the time this agreement was reached, Lenhardt had retired and had been succeeded by Gerald J. Remus. Building restrictions were eased, and it appeared that the county system could manage to get along until its own supply facilities were completed. There was no hint during the summer of 1955 that an additional county supply was not needed.

The Hazen-Sawyer Report. There was never any question over which county agency would be responsible for the construction and operation of the proposed water works. The Road Commission was already in the water business with its distribution system, and it was the logical agency to run an expanded operation. Early in 1955, the Road Commission contracted with the engineering firm of Hazen and Sawyer to investigate the "expansion of the Wayne County Metropolitan Water Supply System to serve the Wayne County area south and west of Detroit." By the end of the year, the investigation was completed, and a final report was submitted to the Road Commission. This report provided county officials with basic data for their decision-making.

The Hazen-Sawyer report accepted as a starting point the conclusions of the Lenhardt policy to the effect that the Detroit water system was approaching its ultimate capacity, based on its present raw-water supply, and that the county must develop an independent source of supply before 1970. In determining the water requirements for the area to be serviced by the county system, the key variables employed were population growth and average daily per capita water consumption. It was estimated that by the year 2000 the service area would include a population of 800,000 in the county, and if communities in adjoining Washtenaw and Monroe counties were included, the population of the service area would be about 1,000,000 and ultimately 1,500,000. The required capacity of a water-supply system is calculated on the basis of maximum daily requirements rather than average daily requirements. It was estimated that peak daily demand would reach 200 percent of average daily demand. Thus it would require a supply of about 280 m.g.d. to handle the maximum day demand of the population in the county by the year 2000, and 450 m.g.d. if the adjoining county areas were included. (Peak hourly demand was calculated at 300 percent of average daily demand, but this could be handled by storage facilities.) The report recommended that the intake and raw-water conduit under the river be built with a full capacity for 450 m.g.d. "The extra cost of providing large capacity is relatively small, and the job should be done once for all time."

In evaluating sources of supply, the report considered the Great Lakes–Detroit River system from Lake Huron to Lake Erie. Lake Huron's sparkling blue water had always held a strong psychological appeal as a source of water for the Detroit area. In the 1921 study, it was considered as a source for Detroit that could be used without filtration or treatment, but the high cost of transmission, including pumping costs, made this uneconomical. The Hazen-Sawyer report noted that the high cost of transmission was still an obstacle and that the water would now require treatment, which would add to the cost. The St. Clair River and Lake St. Clair were also considered as unlikely sources because of (1) distance and (2) water quality, which was not significantly different from that available at more convenient sites. The most intensive consideration was given to the nearest sources, the Detroit River and western Lake Erie.

The Detroit River did not have Lake Huron's psychological appeal. Bordered by big cities and factories, its banks punctured by drains constantly pouring the effluence of man and industry into its waters, the Detroit River did not appear to the casual observer to be a likely source of water for human consumption. Its thirty-one miles connect Lake St. Clair on the north with Lake Erie to the south. "An outstanding and indeed fortunate characteristic of the Detroit River from a water-supply standpoint is its relatively uniform, steady flow, generally of the 'streamlined' type, with little cross-flow of water from one side of the river to the other. The persistent streamlining throughout most of the river has been demonstrated many times by the appearance of silt streaks after dredging operations in Lake St. Clair, by float studies, and by bacteriological and chemical analyses proving the tendency of polluted water to hug the shores." With these words, the report pointed to a condition that the casual observer would not detect, and it was this characteristic of streamlined flow, i.e., the tendency of shore water to hug the banks of the river, that led the engineers to their recommendation of an intake site in the lower (south of Detroit) Detroit River.

The Hazen-Sawyer report described in detail the flow characteristics of the river and evaluated the quality of the water according to a number of established criteria to determine its suitability as a raw-water supply. "Characterization of the lower Detroit River as the 'sewer for metropolitan Detroit' is not warranted. The Trenton Channel does serve this purpose, but the quality of the main flow of the river is affected to only a slight degree." The streamlined characteristic of the flow was dramatically demonstrated by the finding that "the water in the center of the river is generally at least 150 times better than the water along the shore." Some pollution does reach midstream, but in diluted form. "No one will dispute the value of a pure source of water when it can be obtained at reasonable cost. However, where coagulation, sedimentation, filtration, and chlorination are required in any event, within limits, the exact degree of pollution has little effect upon the quality of the finished product." The report gave these conclusions:

1. Above Fighting Island South Light, the mid-river water is occasionally subject to diluted bacterial and industrial pollution, with concentration increasing slightly towards the south.
2. The mid-river water and the Lake Erie water near Point aux Peaux are equal bacterially.
3. Lake Erie water is subject to more frequent and intense taste-and-odor and turbidity-removal problems than Detroit River water.
4. The quality of Detroit River water is well within accepted standards, and without question a safe and satisfactory water supply for Wayne County could be obtained at several points along the Detroit River, from Fighting Island South Light northward.
5. The problems of treating western Lake Erie water and the long distance through which the water would have to be transmitted eliminate Lake Erie as an economical source of supply for Wayne County.

A number of intake sites were considered, but two in the Detroit River were considered to be the best alternatives. The Fort Wayne project placed the intake in United States waters about midstream, opposite Fort Wayne in Detroit; the Grassy Island project located the intake further south and in Canadian waters.

The estimated cost of the Fort Wayne project was $56,690,000, and the Grassy Island project $50,860,000. The reason for the choice of the Grassy Island project is summarized in these words:

> In the Fort Wayne project the intake would be located above the Detroit sewage-treatment plant and the Rouge River. While this location has definite psychological value, the investigation has shown that the water quality in the center of the river at Grassy Island is substantially the same as at Fort Wayne, and would not insure better water quality. In these circumstances, the extra cost of going to Fort Wayne is not warranted, and the less costly Grassy Island project is selected as the best for Wayne County.

In reporting their recommendations that Wayne County proceed to construct in the lower Detroit River an independent water system with a 450 m.g.d. capacity intake and an ultimate capacity to service a population of 1,500,000, the engineers, Richard Hazen and Alfred W. Sawyer, included two important hedges that were to receive a good deal of attention. One dealt with pollution:

> While the water in the middle of the Detroit River is remarkably free of shore pollution and Lake Erie water is good, it must be recognized that no water supply from the Detroit River or Lake Erie will remain satisfactory unless upstream sewage and industrial waste pollution is controlled by adequate collection and treatment works. We anticipate that the pollution control activity will continue in the Great Lakes–Detroit River area and that disposal facilities will be added as necessary. These steps must be taken to protect existing water supplies and bathing beaches whether or not a new water works intake is built.

The other hedge dealt with the scope of their investigation:

> Analysis of the water needs of the entire Detroit metropolitan area and determination of how they could best be met are beyond the scope of this investigation. It is recognized that solutions other than a lower Detroit River intake are available, such as greater utilization of the Detroit water works for the southern and western part of Wayne County, and construction of a new supply from Lake St. Clair or Lake Huron to serve the area north of Detroit. While such a plan has not been studied in any detail, it is evident that the necessary water transmission capacity over long distances would be expensive, and the cost to Wayne County would be at least as much as an independent county supply from Belle Isle.

With the Hazen-Sawyer report in hand and the necessary voter approval for the financing of the water system, county officials proceeded to draft detailed plans for submission to the Board of Supervisors. By the summer of 1956, County Highway Engineer Leroy Smith was ready to present to the Board of Supervisors plans calling for an intake at the Grassy Island site and a filtration plant in Allen Park. The capacities were those recommended in the report, 450 m.g.d. for the intake and 150 m.g.d. for the filtration plant. As county officials proceeded through the necessary steps to obtain formal approval of plans for carrying out an agreed-upon policy, they were surprised to find the policy challenged by the agency that had first insisted upon it, the Detroit Department of Water Supply.

The Battle Is Joined

The Remus Policy. On December 22, 1955, L. G. Lenhardt retired. He had been superintendent and general manager of the Detroit Department of Water Supply since 1938. It had been generally assumed that he would be succeeded by the assistant superintendent and general manager, Leo V. Garrity, but the Water Board bypassed Garrity and chose instead Gerald Remus, the head of Water Works Park Station. The decision not to appoint Garrity might have indicated that the board was becoming restive with the type of administrative leadership exercised by Lenhardt. Garrity, Lenhardt's assistant for fifteen years, was closely identified with his superior's policies. The public reason given by the board for bypassing Garrity was that they wanted a younger man. Garrity was fifty-six and Remus forty-seven. Some years later, Remus told a reporter that when he was interviewed by the Water Board members in the summer of 1955, he was asked what he thought of the proposed independent county water system. He told the board that to permit the county to get into the water business would result in the decline of the Detroit Department of Water Supply. He was quoted as saying, "If I were general manager I'd buy out the county's water system." At the time, Remus thought that this response had killed his chance for the top position, but apparently the board liked the attitude expressed by this response and perhaps the substance of it as well. In any event, in September 1955, it was announced that Remus would be acting superintendent during Lenhardt's absence prior to his formal retirement date, after which Remus was appointed superintendent and general manager. Although Mayor Albert Cobo's role in this major personnel change is not known, it can be inferred from his behavior in other instances involving major changes in top positions that his approval was necessary for this appointment to take place.

When he learned that he was not to get the appointment as general manager, Garrity resigned from the Water Department. The reaction of the Road Commission's Leroy Smith was immediate and public. "We were shocked to learn that Garrity had resigned from the city under such conditions, but we gained, for it made him a free agent," he was quoted as saying. Smith said that he would try to hire Garrity. Garrity must have welcomed this response, perhaps with some surprise, since less than three weeks before, he, Garrity, had charged that the county's water troubles were its own fault and had questioned what the county had done to improve its own internal distribution system. Detroit Councilman James Lincoln, who was also chairman of the County Board of Supervisors' Capital Improvements Program Committee, expressed the ambivalent feeling forced upon him by this dual role: "As a member of council I'm sad to see Garrity leave city government, but, as a member of the county government, I'm happy there's a chance he may be with us here." Garrity declined the county's offers and instead set up shop as a consulting engineer.

In turning over the leadership of the Water Department to Remus, the Water Board was making not only a major personnel decision but also a major policy decision, since Remus' concept of the role of the Detroit Water Department in the metropolis was different from Lenhardt's. Lenhardt had based his policy upon the premise that the Department of Water Supply, as an agency of the city of Detroit, would have fulfilled its maximum growth with the complete utilization of the capacity of its raw-water intake, which was more than sufficient to supply the needs of the city. Remus, on the other hand, considered the department as the core agency for supplying water for the whole metropolis. For Lenhardt, the independent county water system was necessary to meet the growing demand for water in southern and western Wayne County, but for Remus, an independent county water-supply system would create a competing bureaucracy furnishing water in the metropolitan area which could seriously limit the future growth of the Detroit Department of Water Supply. Once the county intake and filtration plant were finished, the county water bureaucracy would be in a strong position to compete with the Detroit Department of Water Supply. By June 1956, Remus had convinced the Water Board and the mayor that the Detroit Department of Water Supply could adequately take care of the county's water needs until 1980 and that it was unnecessary to build a separate county intake and filtration plant at this time. Remus had also found a sympathetic audience at the Detroit Board of Commerce.

The first signs of a reversal of the Lenhardt policy came early in June. At a meeting of the County Board of Supervisors, Mayor Cobo proposed that the county water project be delayed pending study of the possibility of developing a Lake Huron source. He was supported by Willis Hall, secretary-manager of the Board of Commerce and one of the appointed members to the Board of Supervisors. At the same time, the Capital Improvements Program Committee of the Board of Supervisors received an offer from the Water Board to "furnish all Wayne County water needs." The supervisors did not accept the Cobo proposal as grounds for delaying the county project, and some thought it was merely a desperate effort to cause delay. The Capital Improvements Program Committee forwarded the Detroit offer to furnish water to the Road Commission for examination, but the committee proceeded to examine the detailed plans for the county water works. It soon became clear, however, that the change in policy represented by Remus' claim that the city could adequately furnish the needed water for Wayne County could not be disregarded or brushed aside as a mere tactical maneuver on the part of a brash new agency head.

From the beginning of June until mid-September, an intensive struggle was waged between those supporting a county water works and those who now opposed it. The issues were complex, involving raw-water tunnel capacities, safe capacities for filter

beds, projected per capita water consumption, projected population growth and industrial growth, accounting procedures for determining water costs, and the extent of pollution of raw-water
supplies. These are difficult issues to reduce to simple terms that
can be easily understood, and in the effort to win public support
some issues were oversimplified and distorted.

Although the Detroit offer to furnish all of Wayne County's
water was made to the Capital Improvements Program Committee
on June 7, a detailed report on how the offer could be put into
effect was not forthcoming until June 22. This report, bearing
Remus' name and entitled "Proposed System Expansion Program,"
was sent to the Road Commission in response to a request from
Leroy Smith to the Water Board "for the grand plan of the Detroit Water Board for furnishing all the water needs of Wayne
County. . . . with the complete engineering data supporting it."
The Remus report was more like a manifesto than a dispassionate
engineering report, and although it included a number of conclusions, the data supporting them were sparse.

The gist of the report was that the Detroit water system, with
its raw-water tunnel system approaching capacity and three pumping stations in operation, was nearing the completion of the master
plan begun in 1924. A new master plan was now in order to meet
future needs. The basic premise of the Remus policy was stated:
"One water system for the Detroit metropolitan area would be
the most efficient and would furnish water at the lowest unit cost
because production in large quantities has definite economic advantages." The report asserted that the pressurization of the raw-
water tunnel system would result in added capacity at the enlarged Springwells plant and at the new Northeast plant, and that
this added capacity would permit the city not only to meet the
demands of current customers through 1970 but also would create a water surplus that could be used by additional customers.
Another intake would eventually be needed, and the report suggested that its most economical location would be on the St. Clair
River, north of Detroit, near Marine City. A decision on this new
intake, the report went on to say, could be postponed until 1966,
at which time demand could be better calculated.

The Wayne County problem was dealt with in these two paragraphs:

The Wayne County Road Commission could get their purified water requirements from the Springwells Pumping Station when this station's enlargement program is complete in 1959. A portion of the water that would normally be pumped from Springwells Pumping Station to the northwest area would be supplied from Northeast Pumping Station. The cost for facilities to redirect this load would be approximately $6,000,000.

The transmission mains required to transmit water to the southwest Wayne County area should be paid for by Wayne County from the $50,000,000 Water System Improvement Fund they have authorized, provided Wayne County wants this water. Mains supplying water in Wayne County now extend generally to all areas where deficiencies exist, and this system would have to be supplemented with more mains, clear-water storage, and repumping equipment.

The appendix to the report included some key statistics. The tunnel capacity of the Detroit system was given as 1,330 m.g.d.; the filtering capacity of the three plants (with contemplated expansions) was given as 1,335 m.g.d., and the maximum day demand for 1970 for Detroit, the suburbs then served by the system, plus an additional service area north of Detroit and the "Wayne County plant load," was estimated to be 1,257.5 m.g.d. This metropolitan area maximum day demand was well within the maximum 1970 capacity which Remus reported for the system.

The Garrity-Mosher Reply. The Remus report was a direct formal challenge to the need for a Wayne County water works, but it did not deter the Capital Improvements Program Committee from approving both the start of condemnation proceedings to acquire sites for the works and the purchase of a site for the shore shaft of the water intake. At the committee's meetings in late June and early July at which these decisions were made, the Remus proposal was hotly debated, but Leroy Smith was able to convince the committee that delay in acquiring the sites would cost the county additional money for land acquisition. Meanwhile, the Road Commission had hired a firm of consulting engineers to review and evaluate the Remus proposal for them. The consultants were Leo V. Garrity and L. W. Mosher. Garrity, former assistant general manager of the Detroit Water Department, was thus given the opportunity to review the proposal of the man who held the position that many people felt Garrity should have obtained. By the end of July, Garrity and Mosher had completed their analysis of the Remus proposal and submitted their findings to the Road Commission. On August 23, Leroy Smith sent a formal analysis of the Remus proposal to the Capital Improvements Program Committee. This analysis incorporated the findings of Garrity and Mosher and is quoted at length:

> At the request of your Capital Improvements Committee, at a meeting held on June 7, 1956, this office agreed to examine the new offer of the city of Detroit to "furnish all Wayne County water needs." This offer is, of course, diametrically opposed to the previous stand of the Detroit Board of Water Commissioners, which board precipitated the development of a plan for a proposed new source of water supply for a major part of Wayne County by informing the county that Detroit would not be in a position to supply sufficient water to the rapidly growing suburban area south and west of Detroit. This action by Detroit is well documented, consequently we make no further reference thereto.
>
> .   .   .   .
>
> The Detroit report lists the pressurized tunnel capacity as 1,330 m.g.d. and the ultimate filtering capacity of the enlarged three stations as 1,335 m.g.d. This filtration rate is equivalent to a rate of about 200,000,000 gallons per acre per day, which exceeds recommended design rates.
>
> .   .   .   .
>
> The tunnel system must supply the maximum day requirements for finished water plus an allowance for wash water and other wastage; therefore, the net available quantity for delivery to the system must be less than the 1,330 m.g.d. quoted. It is estimated that this net quantity would be not more than 1,231 m.g.d. If filtration rates were reduced to more nearly reflect recognized engineering practice the net should be reduced to about 1,068 m.g.d. For this analysis we will use the higher net rate of 1,231 m.g.d.
>
> The simple addition of the theoretical maximum day capacities of three large stations would not necessarily reflect the maximum quantity that could be delivered to a metropolitan area on any given peak day. Volume and locations of demands vary from hour to hour and day to day and it becomes impossible to maintain maximum theoretical rates from all stations on any given day. A liberal allowance of 95 percent of theoretical maximum would reduce the 1,231 m.g.d. rate to a rate of 1,170 m.g.d. available to consumers over the metropolitan area. Again this rate is based on excessive filtration rates.
>
> The population estimates on the proposed metropolitan area for 1960, 1970, and 1980 given in the Detroit report appear to be in error by

including parts of Wayne County twice. The corrected populations would be less than shown in the report. Estimates of maximum day demands for some of the suburbs likewise appear to be in error.

After correcting the population estimates and applying the proper maximum day per capita rates, we find that for the year 1970 the maximum day demand for the proposed expanded metropolitan area would be 1,315 million gallons while the net available for distribution would be 1,170 million gallons, showing a deficiency of 145 million gallons. The estimated requirement for the Wayne County service area as indicated in the Hazen-Sawyer report for the year 1970 is 146 m.g.d.

. . . .

. . . We estimate that the cost of water to Wayne County at Springwells, based on the ten-cent rate, will average about 80 percent more than the cost of producing water from the proposed new county facility.

. . . .

CONCLUSIONS

After a thorough analysis of the Detroit report we can only conclude as follows:

1. It is our opinion that the Detroit report overrates the safe and prudent capacities of their three stations when all proposed expansions have been completed.

2. Their long-range promises regarding future expansion of facilities are nebulous and are entirely without official sanction at this time.

3. Certainly by 1970, and probably at an earlier date, under the Detroit plan, there would be a shortage of water for the metropolitan area, and we can foresee the necessity of again asking the electorate of Wayne County to approve funds for the construction of a complete new facility to alleviate the shortage.

4. If the county should pay the proposed Detroit rates for all its water needs, rates to county customers would have to be increased approximately 30 percent over those now in effect.

5. The entire metropolitan area would be dependent upon a less reliable and inadequate water-supply system. A second and even third intake are highly desirable as a safety factor.

. . . .

In view of the foregoing, this office can only recommend that the county plan as originally conceived, to provide the southern and western parts of Wayne County with a complete new water-supply facility, be carried out without delay.

In his letter accompanying the June 22 report, Remus had suggested an "intermediate approach" whereby the county would take water that was in excess of Detroit's immediate needs from the Springwells plant and postpone building its own works until the Springwells supply was needed by the Detroit system in about 1970. But Smith's report to the Capital Improvements Program Committee did not leave any room for "intermediate approaches." His attitude toward the Detroit Department of Water Supply and the Detroit Common Council was reflected in the following sentence from a letter he sent to Remus on July 23: "We can see no firm assurance that future administrations, either in your department or the city council, will carry out all necessary expansions to augment the supply of water as the demand increases." Smith had no confidence in the promises coming from the department, and the accuracy of the department's estimate of its capacity to provide water to the county, he felt, had now been effectively challenged.

The employment of Garrity to review the Remus plan was a provocative decision. It could be justified on the grounds that Garrity had intimate knowledge of the Detroit water system, and since the Remus report was thin in engineering details supporting its claims, only one familiar with the system could judge it. On the other hand, as Lenhardt's assistant, Garrity was associated with the Lenhardt policy, and Remus supporters claimed he could not be considered an objective critic of a policy designed to reverse the Lenhardt policy. Add to this the suspicion that a personal animosity might exist between two men who had vied for the same position, and it is obvious why Smith's letter to the committee, based upon the Garrity-Mosher report, did not lay the controversy to rest.

By the end of August, county officials had regained their poise, which had been so suddenly disturbed by the announcement of the Remus policy early in June. The Garrity-Mosher report provided the technical data for challenging the capacity of the Detroit water works to do the job Remus claimed for it, and this same report, plus the efforts of the county's own fiscal expert, Alfred Pelham, presented a financial analysis of the Remus plan which showed that even if Detroit could provide the water, the cost would be substantially higher than it would be if the county were to proceed with its own plant. These analyses proved convincing to the Capital Improvements Program Committee, and on August

28, they voted to proceed with the county water project. The Remus proposal was considered to be "impractical and far too expensive." Approval by the committee implied approval by the full Board of Supervisors, since the board had agreed to abide by the committee's decision.

The City Loses a Round. City officials were not yet ready to give up the struggle. City Controller John H. Witherspoon led the fight for Mayor Cobo. As controller, Witherspoon was the chief fiscal officer for the city, but Mayor Cobo also used him as his chief deputy for the general administration of city affairs. He was as close as anyone came to being the mayor's stand-in. Council President Louis Miriani was also a strong supporter of the Remus proposal, and, as council president, he was acting mayor during Cobo's absences from the city. The president of the Board of Water Commissioners, Oscar A. Wagner, gave his new general manager, Remus, strong public support. With the exception of Remus, each of these city officials leading the battle for the Remus plan was ex officio a member of the Wayne County Board of Supervisors.

On September 10, a hearing was held before the Detroit Common Council to "air views" on the controversy. This could hardly have been for the benefit of the councilmen, since they had been well exposed to the views of all parties, especially Councilman James Lincoln, who was chairman of the county's Capital Improvements Program Committee. This formal staging for the presentation of arguments did provide another public platform from which views could be proclaimed, with good coverage guaranteed by the local news media. Since the Board of Supervisors had not yet taken the formal action necessary for proceeding with the county project, supporters of the Remus plan were hopeful that the hearing would build up public support for their position and force the board to reverse the decision of the Capital Improvements Program Committee.

At the hearing, Pelham presented the county's position. The launching of the Wayne County water project was one of Pelham's last major concerns before his imminent retirement. His presentation was well prepared and carefully documented. He reviewed the reasons for the initiation of the county project and pointed to the general agreement with the Lenhardt policy that culminated in the voters' approval of the county works. He cited the Hazen-Sawyer report as the basis for the location of the intake and design of the works and noted that Hazen and Sawyer were the same consultants employed by the city. Finally, he discussed the financing of the county plan, stating that, under it, users' fees would pay back the entire cost of the system in twenty-five years, whereas if the county were to purchase all of its water from Detroit, it would take one hundred years to pay for the transmission system alone at current water rates. He took pains to point out that city taxpayers would not be subsidizing the county system.

Witherspoon, Wagner, and Remus presented the case for the Water Department. They conceded that the Water Department had urged the county to build its own system but maintained that they "were in error both in fact and in judgment. We admit that and feel that we should now proceed in a more satisfactory manner." Remus repeated his contention that the county could get the water it needed from the Springwells expansion, which would be completed by 1959, well ahead of the scheduled county plant. The debate was becoming heated. The city maintained that the proposed county plant would be substandard because it was designed to operate at the filtration rate of 160 million gallons per acre per day, whereas Detroit operated at the rate of 200 million gallons per acre per day. (Actually, Detroit's newest plant, Northeast Station, was designed for a normal operating rate of 160 million gallons per acre per day, although the higher, 200-million-gallon rate was permissible under health standards for short periods.) But the council setting was, apparently, no place to quibble over details. This is evident from the statement of one of the city's key supporters, Henry F. Vaughn.

Henry Vaughn, Doctor of Public Health, and dean of the School of Public Health at the University of Michigan, had, at one time, been commissioner of health for the city of Detroit. His position and background gave authority to his statements on health and sanitation. He was "shocked" at the proposal to draw water from a downriver intake. He was quoted in *The Detroit News* as saying: "Engineers may tell you filth in the water can be sterilized and cleaned, but I'm choosy about the dirt I eat or drink. All the county will be doing is purifying sewage."

Dean Vaughn was not the first to suggest the health theme as a counterargument to the downriver intake. Remus had hinted to Smith in his letter of June 22, in which he had suggested an "intermediate approach," that "time certainly would help you resolve some of the complications involved with an intake in foreign water and the Sarnia contamination problem." After the Vaughn testimony, however, the health theme began to play a more important role. It will be recalled that the Hazen-Sawyer report had anticipated a negative "psychological" reaction to locating the intake below the Detroit sewage-treatment plant, but their detailed studies had revealed that the river's flow characteristics, particularly its "streamlined" flow, prevented shore contamination from penetrating mid-stream to any dangerous degree. Presumably, Dean Vaughn had read the Hazen-Sawyer report and grasped its significance, but if he had any evidence to disprove it, he did not make such evidence public. In fact, in all of the discussion over the health question, there is no evidence to challenge the Hazen-Sawyer conclusions concerning flow characteristics.

The council hearing did not solve anything, nor did the council make any decision as a result of the hearing. Two days later, on September 12, Remus sent a report to the Ways and Means Committee of the Board of Supervisors answering the Smith analysis (based on the Garrity-Mosher report) of his original proposal and reiterating the city's offer to supply all of the county's water needs. Section 3 of this document dealt with some of Smith's objections to the Detroit proposal. Remus again asserted that the tunnel capacity of the Detroit system was 1,330 m.g.d., but the various points raised by Smith concerning percentage of maximum capacity available at any given time were not dealt with. It was stated that the filtration rate of 200 million gallons per day per acre "is a sound and reliable figure," although the authority Remus cited for this gave the normal operating rate as 160 million gallons per acre per day. Rate figures were cited to show that county water rates would not cover fixed charges on the project and that these charges would have to be paid from tax funds, forcing Detroiters to pay for a water system they could not use.

The following paragraph indicates the tone of this section:

> The Wayne County Road Commission's criticism of the Detroit sys-
> tem should be ignored since it is not documented to any great extent.
> It indicates lack of understanding of the Detroit proposal; it estab-
> lished that very little study was done by Mr. Kunzie [*sic;* Albert
> Kunze, county water engineer] of the Detroit proposal, and this is
> understandable since he is not an authority (through lack of experi-
> ence) on either the Detroit tunnel system, filtration rates, future De-
> troit planning, or water systems.

The fourth section of Remus' report contained a number of
"general statements" and "concluding statements." The object of
these was to question the wisdom of locating an intake in the
downriver area because of the danger of pollution and to suggest
that since Detroit was already in the water business, it was in a
better position to take care of the needs of the whole area. A close
look at one paragraph leads one to question the care with which
this document was prepared. One of the concluding statements
said:

> The county consulting engineers establish that raw water on the
> Michigan side of the international border is less favorable than water
> on the Canadian side for an intake. Industrial activity on the Canadian
> shores, particularly at Sarnia, is ever increasing. Sarnia wastes have
> many times seriously affected Detroit's raw water. Is it reasonable
> and wise, considering all factors of this type, to construct "another
> intake" in this downriver location?

As a matter of fact, the Hazen-Sawyer report gave preference to
two sites for an intake. The Fort Wayne site would have put the
intake in American waters, and the Grassy Island site located it in
Canadian waters. Both sites were acceptable as a water source.
The choice of the Grassy Island site was based on its proximity
to the proposed filtration plant and not because Canadian waters
were cleaner than American waters. The reference to Sarnia wastes
in this report is even more puzzling, in view of the fact that Sarnia,
at the head of the St. Clair River, was much closer to the Detroit
water system's intake than the proposed downriver intake. Com-
pounding the confusion, Remus enclosed with this September document his June 22 proposal, which included a plan for another
intake near Marine City on the St. Clair River. A Marine City

intake would be directly below the Sarnia source of pollution. The tone and logic of this report convinced some county officials that Remus was not interested in facts; his primary objective, they felt, was to prevent the county from setting up a competing water system.

The day after the Remus document was submitted to it, the Ways and Means Committee of the Wayne County Board of Supervisors, the board's most powerful committee, voted eleven to six to proceed with the county water plan. Ordinarily, this action would have been the end of the issue, with formal adoption by the full board following as a matter of routine. But Witherspoon and Miriani were determined to continue their fight against the county plan before the full board. They were saved from this effort by a ruling by Bond Counsel John Nunneley that the proceeds from the bond sale authorized by the voters had to be used for a complete water system including an intake and filtration plant. If the money were not spent for this purpose, he ruled, the $26,000,000 bond issue would be invalidated. The ruling came three days before the Board of Supervisors was due to meet and vote on the issue.

The September 17 meeting of the Board of Supervisors turned out to be a routine affair. The decision of the bond counsel had weakened the city's position, which had rested on the assumption that the proceeds from the bonds could be diverted to building only those works necessary to tie in with the Detroit system, and both Witherspoon and Miriani announced in advance of the meeting that they would now vote for the county plan. When the formal vote was taken, Water Board President Oscar Wagner was the only supervisor to cast a negative vote. Prior to the meeting, he had sent a letter to each of the supervisors warning them that since Detroit would have to supply water to the county during the six or seven years it took to build the plant and since this load would be summarily cut off when the plant was completed, "it would only seem fair and equitable that the county be assessed its full and fair share for the capital investment necessary to provide this interim service and to amortize our investment over this period, which would require a considerable increase in water rates to Wayne County for this period." This threat went unheeded. The Board of Supervisors cleared the way for the Road Commission

to proceed, and in October they received the necessary approval
from the Canadian government to construct the intake in Canadian
waters and the approval of the Michigan Department of Health
to locate the intake at the downriver site. As plans proceeded to
the construction stage, the Road Commission hired Leo Garrity in
February 1957 to superintend the construction of the intake tunnel. The county water works was beginning to take shape.

The National Sanitation Foundation Report. On March 28,
1957, the board of trustees of the National Sanitation Foundation
submitted a "Report on the Water Supply for the Six-County Metropolitan Area [of] Southeastern Michigan" to the Inter-County
Supervisors' Committee. The publication of this report reopened
public debate on the need for a county water works. This was not
accidental. The report was the result of a rather complicated strategy that was carried out largely through the Greater Detroit Board
of Commerce. It would be difficult to identify all those who had
a hand in the strategic and tactical decisions involved in this maneuver, but Gerald E. Warren, secretary of the Water Study Committee of the Board of Commerce, was the key person in carrying
out the decisions. As a full-time staff employee of the board, he
had available the vast resources of the board itself. These resources
included not only the capacity to raise money for desired studies
or other purposes but also the network of influence that existed
by the very nature of the membership of the board, which included
the major businessmen in the community.

The National Sanitation Foundation report was made at the
behest of the Inter-County Supervisors' Committee. This committee consisted of members representing the boards of supervisors of
the six counties that make up southeastern Michigan—Macomb,
Monroe, Oakland, St. Clair, Washtenaw, and Wayne counties. Detroit Councilman Edward Connor had been one of the organizers
of the Inter-County group and was chairman of the committee at
the time these events took place. He was also chairman of the
Wayne County Board of Supervisors during this period. As chairman of the newly formed Inter-County Supervisors' Committee,
Connor was eager to get some projects under way under the auspices of this group in order to demonstrate to the community the

usefulness of intercounty cooperation and also to bind the group together. Both Connor and Miriani were at this time weighing their chances to succeed Mayor Cobo, and whereas Miriani could use his position as president of the Detroit Common Council (a position won by polling the most votes in the councilmanic election) to gain attention as a civic political leader, Connor had to rely upon his county and inter-county role to establish his claim for leadership. Detroit's non-partisan elections encourage this type of behavior: to succeed in politics without benefit of the party label requires that the candidate attract attention to himself. From Connor's point of view, the Inter-County Supervisors' Committee was ripe for a project.

"National Sanitation Foundation" sounds like the title of an official governmental agency, but it was a non-governmental voluntary foundation with headquarters at the School of Public Health of the University of Michigan. The president of the foundation was Henry Vaughn, also dean of the School of Public Health and former Detroit health commissioner. The close relationship between the foundation and the Detroit Board of Commerce during this period is reflected in the list of foundation trustees for 1957, which included Harvey J. Campbell, executive vice president of the Board of Commerce, and Simon D. Den Uyl, vice president of the Board of Commerce. Other Detroit businessmen, including Walker L. Cisler, president of the Detroit Edison Company, were among the foundation's trustees, along with Detroit Health Commissioner Joseph G. Molner. It would not be unfair to say that the foundation's board of trustees consisted, for the most part, of men whose primary interest was the Detroit metropolitan area, although the word "National" in the foundation's name might not lead one to assume this.

It will be recalled that the Board of Commerce participated in the county's campaign to obtain voter approval for financing the county water works. Who changed whose mind and when is not known for sure, but some time before the Remus policy was made public in June 1956, doubts about the wisdom of the county plan began to spread. The Lenhardt policy had stimulated efforts in Oakland and Macomb counties to develop a water system independent from Detroit's. These two counties had formed a Southeastern Michigan Water Authority, which was studying a Lake Huron source of supply. With the approval of the Wayne County water works financing in 1955 and the development of the Southeastern Michigan Water Authority, it began to look as if a number of independent water systems would come into being. It seemed reasonable that, before these separate systems were built, a study be made of the water situation for the whole metropolitan region. Since the Inter-County Supervisors' Committee was the one agency whose constituency encompassed all of the area involved, it was the logical choice for sponsor of such a study. Thus Gerald Warren found in Edward Connor a responsive audience to the proposal that the Inter-County Supervisors' Committee hire the National Sanitation Foundation to conduct a study of water, sewage, and drainage problems in the six-county area, with first priority given to water. Early in 1956, the Inter-County Supervisors' Committee asked the National Sanitation Foundation to undertake such a survey. The money for the survey was provided by businessmen who, in the words of the foundation's covering letter to its report, "are interested in the solution of these critical problems on a truly metropolitan basis."

The foundation did not itself conduct the study but acted as a middleman for hiring consultants and staff to do the work. Heading the staff was a three-man Board of Consultants, consisting of Louis E. Ayres, of Ann Arbor, Richard Hazen, of New York City, and Abel Wolman, of Baltimore. All were recognized consultants. Ayers was especially familiar with the Detroit system, and Hazen was one of the two consultants who had prepared the Hazen-Sawyer report for the county. A technical advisory board was set up to assist the consultants, with Gerald Warren as its secretary, and both Remus and Albert Kunze, the county's water engineer, as members. This advisory board included among its members representatives from business and industry as well as from the various political jurisdictions in the six-county area. This structure was designed to absorb some of the shock resulting from the clash of interests, as proponents of a single metropolitan water system under the Detroit Water Board met head on supporters of a different approach. After all, the National Sanitation Foundation was not a detached research organization vis-à-vis the Detroit–Wayne

County water controversy (its president, Henry Vaughn, testified against the county intake before the final report of the foundation was submitted), and the fact that the survey was staffed with consultants and advisory committee members who were already involved in the controversy assured that the underlying issue would be a political one: what jurisdiction or jurisdictions should provide water for whom.

The drafting of the final report provoked some preliminary clashes, particularly from Wayne County officials who felt that the plan for the county water works was not getting fair treatment. The final wording of the report reflects the tension under which it was written. Both Detroit and Wayne County officials could quote from it, and did, to support contrary conclusions.

The report specified an area to be served by a central water system. This service area included Wayne, Oakland, and Macomb counties. Population estimates for this service area predicted an increase from 2,879,000 in 1955 to 6,000,000 by 2000. The 1970 population was estimated at 4,218,000. The maximum daily water demands were estimated as follows: 1955, 696 m.g.d.; 1960, 885 m.g.d.; 1970, 1,254 m.g.d.; 1980, 1,593 m.g.d.; and 2000, 2,100 m.g.d. The critical finding was the capacity of the Detroit system to meet this demand. "The safe working capacity of the Detroit water system, with the completion of the raw-water booster station and the additions now planned at Springwells, will be 1,115 million gallons per day, with its present single source. With later additions at Northeast Station, the available capacity would reach 1,275 million gallons per day. An ultimate capacity of about 1,375 million gallons per day could be made available if it proves practicable to take full advantage of the raw-water tunnel capacity." These data supported the Remus claim that Detroit had the capacity to provide water for the whole area through 1970 without an additional intake; they contradicted the county's claim that the maximum day water demand in 1970 would be 1,315 m.g.d. and that Detroit's capacity would be only 1,170 m.g.d. The foundation's conclusions on the capacity of the Detroit system were based upon engineering data concerning the pressurized raw-water tunnel capacity and anticipated expansion in the various plants to process the additional supplies of raw water. In calculating this capacity, the consultants used a filtration rate of 200 million gallons per acre per day.

The estimates of water demand used in the report were based upon population estimates obtained from the Detroit Metropolitan Regional Planning Commission and upon estimated projected per capita consumption rates. The per capita maximum daily consumption rate used by the foundation report for the area to be served by the Wayne County water works for 1970 was slightly lower than that used in the Hazen-Sawyer report, 277 gallons daily compared with 300 gallons daily, but since different population estimates were also used for this service area, the maximum day demand for 1970 was substantially the same in both reports, 155 m.g.d. (National Sanitation Foundation) and 146 m.g.d. (Hazen-Sawyer).

The Detroit system was considered adequate, with certain expansions, through 1970. The report's conclusions concerning a new source are summarized as follows:

> . . . the water demands in the Detroit service area are presently approaching the capacity of the Detroit water system. Additions to Springwells and Northeast plants could take care of demands until 1970. Expansion of the Water Works Park Station, if found economical, would take care of needs until 1973. By that time additional raw-water capacity will be needed. This capacity may be provided in several ways, such as a new supply from Lake Huron, a new supply from the lower Detroit River, a supply taken from some location in between the above sources, or a combination of these.
>
> It is our judgment that a raw-water quality is available at each of the potential intake locations which would be within accepted national standards. With orthodox water treatment, a safe and satisfactory water supply may be obtained at any one of the intakes either along the Detroit River or from Lake Huron.
>
> It is doubtful whether any variation in water treatment practices would be so significant at any one of the sites as to affect materially the economics of the choice of one site or another. In comparing sources, however, the cost of maintaining a satisfactory raw-water supply in the lower Detroit River may be of significant economic importance and should be considered.
>
> The Board of Consultants records its judgment that, other things being equal, an intake site is preferred which would be upstream from the Detroit area rather than downstream. Since the population of the service area may double in the next forty or fifty years and amount

to over 6,000,000 persons by the year 2000, an intake location above the major sources of pollution would be preferred.

These conclusions reflect the internal pulling and hauling that occurred over the preparation of the report. In the face of the Michigan Health Department's approval of a county intake in the lower river, along with the findings of the earlier Hazen-Sawyer report concerning pollution, which the foundation's report did not contradict, it would have been difficult for the consultants to find the lower river unsafe as a source of supply without substantial new evidence. By declaring the river source safe but at the same time expressing a preference for a site north of Detroit because of potential future pollution, the report provided arguments and quotable passages that could be used by both sides.

The report proposed four alternative programs and provided cost estimates for each. Plan A called for expansion of Northeast Station, expansion of Water Works Park Station, and a new supply from Lake Huron for a total cost of $142,000,000. (The expansion of the capacity of Springwells Station from 340 m.g.d. to 540 m.g.d. and the construction of a booster pumping station to increase the capacity of the whole system were already under way and would be completed regardless of other developments. Their completion would give the Detroit system a capacity of 1,115 m.g.d.) Plan B substituted a new supply from either Lake St. Clair or the upper Detroit River for the Lake Huron supply and was estimated to cost $125,000,000. Plan C also called for the full development of the Detroit system included in A and B and added as a new source the Wayne County project, but with construction postponed for ten years. The cost of this plan was estimated at $114,000,000. Plan D called for immediate construction of the Wayne County project, expansion of Northeast Station, and expansion of the Wayne County plant. Under this plan, the Water Works Park expansion would be dropped. The fourth plan was the least costly, $105,000,000.

Each of the four plans would produce 1,625 m.g.d., or enough water to take care of demand beyond 1980. To increase capacity beyond this amount, Plan A would require a new intake and a fifty-three-mile pipeline from Lake Huron, whereas each of the other three plans provided room for expansion without adding new intakes. It was estimated that it would require $73,000,000 to build the Lake Huron works with a 225 m.g.d. capacity. The largest single item in the cost was a fifty-three-mile, ninety-inch pipeline which would cost close to $30,000,000. "To double the first installment should cost less than $73,000,000 because some of the facilities could be increased easily. However, much of the cost is in the intake pipe and long transmission main, which would have to be duplicated." Operating cost of the Lake Huron project was also higher than the other projects, $39.00 per million gallons compared with $31.00 for the Wayne County project.

In weighing these four alternatives in the body of the report, much attention was given to raw-water quality. Some of the statements make the conclusions quoted above appear even more enigmatic. "It is doubtful whether any variations in water-treatment practices would be so significant at any one of the sites as to affect materially the economics of the choice of one site or another. In comparing sources, however, the cost of maintaining a satisfactory raw-water supply in the lower Detroit River may be of significant economic importance and should be considered." After pointing to a possible population increase of as much as 50 percent by the year 2000, the report stated that at least two-thirds of this population would be located north of the Wayne County intake and implied that this could be a serious pollution hazard but added, "Prompt steps should be taken by treatment to prevent the effects of substantial increases of pollution in all of these areas, regardless of the ultimate choice of a new intake site. Such steps must be taken because they are neither unreasonable nor burdensome." (The fact that such steps could be required to protect the public health was not mentioned, nor was mention made of industrial waste and pollution. Perhaps the latter was assumed, but the constant reference to population increase and sewage created the impression that stream pollution was primarily the result of disposal of human waste.)

The final paragraph from the section of the report dealing with water quality is worth quoting in full:

> If the differential in cost between an intake development at a northern site and one at a southern location is not too great, a site above the populated area would be preferred. These considerations

of raw-water quality, however, cannot be realistically considered wholly independently of the direction of growth of the population, the plans for sewage treatment therefor, and the centers of gravity for ultimate water distribution and service. When all of these considerations are tested against the economics of each of the programs, it is our view that consideration of water quality alone will not be dominantly significant in a final decision.

A number of pages of the report dealt with comparative costs of the four plans. As shown earlier, the over-all cost of Plan A was the highest and that of Plan D the lowest. The report, however, frequently mentioned that for the immediate future, Plan D would be most expensive, since it called for the immediate construction of a major facility, whereas the other plans postponed this investment. In the words of the report: "The principal advantage of the first three plans over Plan D is the saving in water costs during the first years until a major new source of supply is necessary. This saving is indicated by the accumulated cost of $18,255,000 for Plans A, B, and C in 1971, compared with $27,474,000 for Plan D in 1970. In later years, the relatively small additional investment lowers the unit costs under Plan D substantially." These sentences also provided both city and county officials with support for opposite conclusions.

The recommendations concerning the administration of the area water system were the most provocative part of the report. They were stated in the first section of the report as part of the "Principal Facts and Conclusions":

> The planning and design of the water service of a great metropolitan area should be under central direction if the best interests of all users are to be served. The city of Detroit might be the central agency. The construction and administration might well be handled by a metropolitan district, as was visualized in the planning of the 1920's, or by a district encompassing the six-county area, outside the limits of Detroit.

. . . .

> The board recognizes also the desire of Wayne, Macomb, and Oakland counties and all the suburban municipalities to obtain the water supplies necessary to encourage the development of their industrial and residential areas. At the same time, the board believes that the results obtained by separate water supplies will not be as satisfactory as those possible through an extension of the present

Detroit system into a truly integrated system operation for the entire metropolitan area. Realization of such a system will depend upon satisfactory financial arrangements and assurances that new facilities will be built as necessary to provide a reasonable margin of capacity over water demands.

On March 29, 1957, the National Sanitation Foundation presented its report to the Inter-County Supervisors' Committee. The presentation was made by one of the consultants, Abel Wolman, and an observer from the Road Commission reported that Wolman "didn't present the report; he sold it." Wolman emphasized the need for a single water system. He told the committee that individual development of water systems by a number of communities would be a costly operation, and he urged that construction of the county plant be delayed and that the county build mains to link with the Detroit system and purchase their water from Detroit. Remus "listened with enthusiasm" and was reported as saying that "this is exactly what we have been trying to tell everybody. It establishes the fact that we can do the job and do it the cheapest, and that we're willing to do it." Connor was on the spot. The Wayne County Board of Supervisors, of which he was chairman, had already approved the county water works after a stiff fight, and now, as chairman of the Inter-county Supervisors' Committee, he was in receipt of a report that recommended that the county works be delayed. His response to the report was to suggest that the whole problem needed more study but that a decision should be made soon in the interest of the people of western Wayne County who wanted water. The report had succeeded in reopening the issue of the need for the county works.

Conflict over the Intake Bids. The spring and summer of 1957 saw the city-county water controversy develop to a new pitch of intensity, helped along by the local elections due to be held in November. Some of the actors had changed. The head of the Road Commission, Leroy Smith, had retired and had been succeeded by Joseph W. Gross. In September, Mayor Cobo died, and Council President Louis Miriani, by virtue of his position, became mayor. In November, Miriani won an easy election victory and became mayor in his own right. During this same period, Connor decided not to oppose Miriani in the primary race for mayor and instead ran again for the council. Miriani continued to support Remus and oppose the county works, whereas Connor attempted to play a mediating role but on crucial votes sided with the county. Probably both men felt that their behavior regarding the water controversy would have some effect upon their political futures. The Board of Commerce warmly applauded Miriani's stand but considered Connor to have "voted against the city." Both were successful at the polls at the end of the year, but Miriani had won the bigger prize, and Connor had seen the council presidency, the reward to the councilman who had polled the most votes, won by Councilwoman Mary Beck. But since Miss Beck had voted with Connor for the county plan, Connor could hardly blame his lesser popularity on the position he took in the water controversy during the pre-election summer months of 1957.

By reopening the issue of the need for the county works, the National Sanitation Foundation report also reawakened public debate on the subject. Both sides to the controversy sought an audience for their views. The means employed for conducting this "public debate" were typical of local controversies. One such method was to have public officials representing both sides appear at a public gathering to present their views. The annual regional meeting of the Michigan Municipal League in April provided such a forum. The audience was certain to be attentive, since it consisted of mayors, city managers, councilmen, and other city officials from the service area of the proposed Wayne County system. The debate was over which system, Detroit's or Wayne County's, could produce water for the area at the cheaper rate. The protagonists were Kunze, the County Road Commission's water engineer, and Remus, the Detroit Water Department's general manager. Both cited the National Sanitation Foundation report as evidence in support of their arguments. Kunze pointed out that of the alternative plans cited in the report, the Wayne County plan was the least expensive and would thus result in lower rates. Remus denied this and considered it a "joke" that Wayne County could produce water more cheaply than the Detroit Water Board, in view of the superior experience of the latter. Remus then developed what had earlier been and was to continue to be one of his most frequently used arguments—pollution in the lower Detroit River. "The county intake site is downriver from the Fox Creek and Conner Creek drainage outlets into the river, and suburbanites would be drinking water which had run off from the east-side streets." (Detroit's worst slums were on the east side.) He further pointed out that if the county works were built, the city of Detroit would "be left holding the bag with an unneeded addition on our hands." (This was a reference to the Springwells addition, a $35,000,000 project begun in 1956 as an alternative to the fourth plant Lenhardt had said was needed in his 1954 report.) The ensuing discussion was heated, and while the audience was well entertained, nothing new in the way of facts seems to have been presented.

In June, quotations from Remus began to appear in the Detroit newspapers warning that if the county works were built it would mean higher water rates for all Wayne County residents. June brought an increase in tempo for a very good reason. The county had not yet begun construction on the intake, but the time was approaching when bids were to be opened and contracts signed. The most opportune time to defeat the county plan would be before actual construction had begun. An argument that now began to assume more prominence was that the city had contracts running until 1982 with some of the areas to be serviced by the county works, and the city intended to hold the county to the contract terms. As arguments began to pile up, the council decided to hold another hearing on the controversy. It took place on July 2. Again star protagonists were pitted against each other, this time Remus and Lenhardt, but a three-hour session did not bring the parties any closer to an agreement. As the summer wore on, Connor began to take a more definite stand in support of proceeding with the county works without delay. Miriani continued to support the Detroit system and a Lake Huron intake. The hearing ritual had been no more productive of settlement than the public debate before the Municipal League.

In August, it was announced that a group of taxpayers had organized a Wayne County Water Users' Committee to oppose plans for building the county intake. This group had a close identification with the Board of Commerce's Water, Sewage, and Drainage Committee. On the Executive Committee of the Water Users'

Committee were John Wilt, chairman of the Board of Commerce's counterpart committee, and Gerald Warren, of the board's staff. Some of the letters sent out under the letterhead of the Board of Commerce's committee contained key points that were identical with statements sent out under the Water Users' Committee letterhead. This similarity was, of course, noted and pointed out by county officials who came under the fire of the Water Users' Committee. As the time when the Board of Supervisors would have to act on the intake bids drew near, the Water Users' Committee went into action with news releases, letters to taxpayers, and other promotional activities designed to build opposition to the county works.

Early in September, Detroit's auditor general, David Addy, released a report on the Wayne County plan that was critical of the size of the project (too large for demand), the operating cost estimates (too low) and the voter-approved plan for financing the works (costs had to be shared by those deriving no benefit). He recommended that the authority to construct the water plant be rescinded. Meanwhile, County Highway Engineer Joseph Gross announced that the Road Commission was accepting bids for the construction of the intake. On September 11, a dramatic move was made by the Remus forces. A suit was filed in Wayne County Circuit Court (Michigan court of general jurisdiction) asking that the Wayne County Road Commission be enjoined from executing contracts for the construction of the intake. The suit was brought by Anthony Maiullo as a taxpayer and bondholder. He claimed that if the county works were built, Detroit and suburban water-users of the Detroit system would be placed in the position of subsidizing a competitor, since 85 percent of the $50,000,000 project would be paid for by Wayne County citizens who would derive no benefit from the system and, in addition would face higher water rates because of loss of revenue to the new competing system. According to one newspaper account of the suit, Maiullo charged that the issues had been improperly submitted to the voters—the impropriety being that a strenuous campaign had been conducted "under the ruse of a water crisis."

It was apparent from the allegations in the suit and the comments made to reporters that Maiullo had been working in close collaboration with Remus. The press soon confirmed this. (The most complete report of the Maiullo, Miriani, and Remus collaboration appeared in the *Detroit Free Press* of October 6, 1957.) Maiullo told a *Free Press* reporter that he had been brought into the picture at the instigation of Remus. Remus told him that the Water Board wanted to keep the Wayne County business for the city. Maiullo arranged a luncheon at the Detroit Yacht Club where he and Remus were joined by Miriani. At the luncheon, Maiullo offered to file suit to restrain the county, and Miriani told him to go ahead. Remus was not certain whether he had first contacted Maiullo, or Maiullo had first contacted him. "It just developed out of a series of conversations. I don't know who suggested that we lay it before Miriani. Miriani is a great friend of Maiullo." Remus said that his acquaintance with Maiullo stemmed from an earlier time when Maiullo, an attorney representing a group of land investors, had prevailed upon the Water Board to build a water pipeline to property in Madison Heights which Maiullo and his associates owned. Maiullo acknowledged that Remus aided him in drawing the bill of complaint at a Sunday work session in Maiullo's office, and he further acknowledged that he had received help from the Detroit corporation counsel's office. Although this was a taxpayer's suit, city officials were deeply involved with it. In response to the suit, the court issued a temporary injunction.

On the date the suit was filed, September 11, the Road Commission opened the bids on the intake and tunnel and found that they were $800,000 under the engineering estimates. The county had forty-five days in which to act upon the bids, until October 26. County officials urged that the bids be approved before the deadline in order to take advantage of the low price. City officials, opposed to the county works, were determined to delay action on the bids beyond that date and create an indefinite postponement. Thus the fate of the downriver intake depended upon what took place in the forty-five-day period.

Remus urged that the city formally intervene and join Maiullo in his suit to restrain the county. The argument of Remus, at this time quoted most frequently, was that the county works would result in an annual loss of $1,000,000 from water revenues to the Detroit system and require higher rates for the remaining users.

Finally, on September 24, over the objections of Councilmen Connor and Lincoln and Councilwoman Beck, the majority of the council voted to order the Detroit corporation counsel to intervene in support of the Maiullo suit on the grounds that the county distribution system would overlap a service area for which Detroit had contracts to provide water until 1982. In a news release the Water Users' Committee hailed this vote as "significant. It was the first vote that has been won by our side. . . . Three council members, Connor, Beck, and Lincoln, are caught in a crosscurrent of responsibility as they also serve as chairmen of key county committees. They have voted against the city thus far." While the council was deciding to join the suit, the Wayne County Board of Supervisors decided to take up on October 8 the question of approval of contracts amounting to $11,097,000 for construction of the intake and tunnel and various other related works.

October 8, then, appeared to be the day for the crucial decision. In a dramatic move, the Water Board offered to buy out the Wayne County water system, "in order to eliminate the middleman in suburban water transactions." The Road Commission's reply to the offer was immediate and terse. In rejecting it, they said it was "inadequate, inoperative, too costly, and showed no method of financing needed expansions nor schedule of expansion construction. . . ." County officials considered this offer at this time as another tactic employed by Remus and the board to delay action on the intake contracts.

Since its organization the Water Users' Committee had been busy. A release dated September 18 contained the following optimistic statements:

> Our committee activity has produced amazing results. Every type of citizen organization has shown an interest. Neighborhood organizations, trade associations, businessmen, union people, and just plain citizens are willing to do their part in arousing citizen interest in opposition to a project that would draw drinking water from the lower Detroit River.

As the October 8 meeting approached, the committee intensified its activities. It described its own efforts in a statement issued on or about October 4, which said in part:

Immediate action in opposition to the proposed county water plant is urged on city, township, and village officials in the latest move of the Wayne County Water Users' Committee, leader in the fight to abandon the tax-supported project.

Oliver D. Marcks, chairman of the committee, in a formal letter to 250 elected officials, urged this action to fortify the supervisors with "grass-roots citizen support" against the pressures being brought to bear on them by agents of the Wayne County Road Commission who want the plant built.

The letter from Marcks, dated October 4, 1957, and sent to mayors, councilmen, and township supervisors across the county, summarized the arguments that had been used against the county plan:

It is respectfully suggested that your financial experts be asked to get you the figures on how much it will cost your citizens in taxes if the Wayne County Water Plant is built. That information can be quickly translated into how much it will cost each individual home owner. All taxpayers in Wayne County will be taxed to build a plant to serve an area that has less than 4 percent of the assessed valuation in the county.

You should be alerted to these facts:

1. Competent engineers have verified the fact that the intake below Detroit's sewage-treatment plant is not needed. The county's own engineer concurred in these findings as a member of the National Sanitation Foundation board of consultants. These distinguished engineers recommended that the area under dispute continue to be supplied from the central system.

2. The Detroit Board of Water Commissioners has offered to build the facilities needed to provide water in the area for all time. These facilities would be paid out of water revenues and *not out of the tax dollars of the people you represent.*

3. It has been conservatively estimated that it will cost county tax- payers in the neighborhood of $240,000,000 to build a storm sewer system which would protect the downriver intake from upstream pollution.

4. The central system has a $35,000,000 expansion at the Spring- wells Pumping Station under way which will be completed in eighteen months. This investment must be paid for by water users. If there is a competing system, it means that those who remain in the central system will have to pay this investment off in higher water rates. At the same time they will be taxed to duplicate a com- peting system to serve the same area.

5. An estimated $150,000,000 sewer expansion is needed in out-

county Wayne. County tax dollars could better be used for desperately needed sewers rather than [for a] duplicate . . . water system that is not needed.

As elected representatives of taxpayers you have a vital stake in this matter. Protests will be effective only if registered by local units of government. Fortify your representative on the Board of Supervisors with a strong resolution opposing construction of the downriver intake. This action is needed because of the tremendous pressure being brought on the supervisors by representatives of the Wayne County Road Commission.

Next vote of the supervisors on this question will be held at 12:00 noon on Tuesday, October 8, 13th floor, City-County Building. We will be pleased to answer any questions you may have in regard to this matter.

Substantially the same letter was sent to its members by the Board of Commerce and was signed by John Wilt, chairman of the Water, Sewage, and Drainage Committee.

Although the litigation had not been completed by October 8, the Board of Supervisors was asked to vote to accept or reject the contractors' bids pending the outcome of the litigation. When the vote was taken, the tally found fifty-two voting to accept the bids and thirty-seven voting to reject them. Since a majority vote of the membership, which then totaled one hundred and nine, was required in order to approve contracts, the supporters of the county works were three votes shy; but this did not end the matter. It was decided that a motion to reconsider the action on the contracts would be in order at a later date, October 25, and if the necessary majority votes could be rounded up for the motion to reconsider, then the county project would still have life. It became evident that the controversy would continue until the October 25 deadline. The Detroit councilmen who had been supporting the county (Connor, Beck, and Lincoln) voted for the contracts, and the remaining councilmen, led by Mayor Miriani, voted against approval. The *Detroit News* editorial on October 10 took the three to task for supporting the county, and referred to the Road Commission as a "public works empire." On October 14, the *News* continued its attack on the county works in its editorial column. The Board of Supervisors was criticized for being neither representative of, nor responsible to, county residents.

The period from October 8 to October 25 was one of intense

activity. Both sides knew that the October 25 vote could be decisive for their cause, and elaborate maneuvering went on to line
up support. Much of this occurred behind the scenes and can only
be established by hearsay, but what did appear on the surface was
an elaborate effort to end the controversy through some sort of
compromise. From time to time, various compromise plans had
been suggested, and attempts had been made to get city and county
officials to sit down together and work out a solution. None of
these efforts had produced evidence of a willingness to compromise on either side, but the October 8 vote of the Supervisors
came as a surprise to some county officials who felt that when the
crucial votes were taken they would win without difficulty. Now
they were not so certain. Another blow to the county position came
on October 16, when Bond Counsel John Nunneley declared that
the county could build its own distribution system to connect with
the Detroit water system immediately and the intake, if needed,
could be built later. If not needed, the bonds for financing it would
simply not be issued. Miriani and Witherspoon, who had withdrawn opposition to the county plan a year earlier because of the
bond counsel's ruling that the intake and complete works were
necessary to validate the bond issue, welcomed the new interpretation as a basis for working out a settlement with the county which
would postpone construction of the intake.

On October 18, at a joint meeting which included Miriani, the
Detroit councilmen, City Controller Witherspoon and the County
Road Commission, it was decided to appoint a "summit committee" of six members, consisting of Miriani, Connor, Witherspoon,
Charles Edgecomb, chairman of the Wayne County Board of Auditors (an elective post), George Shaffer, president of the Water
Board, and William Kreger, chairman of the County Road Commission. In forming this committee, it was announced that the issue
would be moved up to a policy-making level and removed from
the hands of engineers and technicians who in past meetings had
demonstrated a lack of ability to reach agreement. The summit
committee met the following day, and the newspapers reported
that a compromise was near. At the meeting, Miriani stated his
position to be that the county should build a distribution system
for the west and southwest area and delay building the intake. He

did not ask that the intake be abandoned but that it be built when needed, or, he suggested, perhaps the county would decide to join in the construction of a Lake Huron source.

With the Board of Supervisors' vote only three days away, the top-level committee met again on October 22. At this meeting, Road Commissioner Kreger told Mayor Miriani that there was fear in the out-county area that Detroit would not be able to supply all of the needs of Oakland, Macomb, and Wayne counties. This argument angered the mayor, and he blamed Garrity and Lenhardt for creating doubts about the Detroit system. (At this time, Lenhardt was a private consultant, and Garrity was in the employ of the Road Commission as a water engineer.) Miriani complained that the former Water Department heads had been banqueted and honored on their retirement from city service and now they were criticizing the agency "and telling us that the water system they used to work for is lousy." In spite of this outburst, some progress was made. Connor proposed that the Board of Supervisors make the Water Board the county's agent for supplying water instead of the Road Commission. The $50,000,000 expansion money would still be spent on system expansion in Wayne County, and water rates and other issues would be settled by a contract. The committee ended its session by drawing up a list of key questions for which Kreger and Shaffer were assigned to obtain answers. The questions were: Where would the gate linking the two systems be located and who would pay for it? If the city or county were the supplier, how much water would be available, when, and at what out-county locations? What would the rates be if (1) the city furnished water, or (2) the county furnished it? What were Detroit's plans for Oakland and Macomb counties' water needs and would they affect the supply to Wayne County? What size transmission lines would Detroit provide to serve Wayne County in the present and in the future? The basic questions were the same ones that persisted throughout the controversy—Detroit's capacity to furnish the water and the cost of furnishing it.

At the October 22 meeting, five possible solutions to the controversy were agreed upon: (1) The county should proceed with its own plan. (2) Detroit should take over the entire job. (3) Detroit should buy the county system and operate it. (4) The county should proceed with the transmission lines but delay the intake. (5) The Water Board should be made the agent of the county to build and operate the system. Although some of the differences among the alternatives were small, agreement upon what alternatives were available did represent some progress. At this point, it looked as if the county would defer construction of the intake and build only the transmission lines. This course was implied in a statement by Kreger that "I think we would agree to delaying the intake, but not abandoning it, as soon as we decide how, when, and where the city-county system can be tied together."

At a meeting held the following day, however, the possibility of agreement diminished. Although confined to his bed with the flu, Miriani was not silent. Both *The Detroit News* and the *Detroit Free Press* ran stories of his criticism of Lenhardt and Garrity, who, he was reported as saying, were at the bottom of the county's insistence upon building its own system. He was quoted as saying, "The only reason there's a water fight between the city and county is because these two want to build a new water empire to keep themselves on the public payroll." Road Commissioner Kreger offered to compromise by holding up construction of the intake, provided the city would agree to a definite future construction date for the water works. The Water Board's Shaffer said that the city attorney had advised him that it would be impossible to set a future construction date. He cited the contracts which tied the city to covering suburban customers until 1982. Now it was Kreger's turn to protest: "I thought we were here to compromise. You're not compromising—you haven't budged an inch." Kreger made it clear that the county was not prepared to postpone its water works indefinitely. As it turned out, this was a crucial meeting. If the city could have made a firm commitment on a construction date for the county works, perhaps agreement to defer the intake could have been reached; but the city's refusal to set a firm construction date did nothing to allay the fears of out-county officials who doubted the capacity of the Detroit system to provide the needed water. County officials pointed to this action as evidence that the Water Board was not willing to make a firm commitment on the construction of the works needed for the county but that the Water Board was attempting to scuttle permanently the construction of the downriver intake and filtration plant.

On October 24, Circuit Court Judge Wade H. McCree dismissed the Maiullo suit and ruled that bids on the water system could be accepted by the county. The next day, the twenty-fifth, the Board of Supervisors voted to reconsider the acceptance of the bids for the water intake and tunnel. The vote to reconsider carried with the necessary fifty-five-vote majority, and the board proceeded to approve the contracts by the same vote. Thirty-seven votes were cast in opposition. Miriani was at home with the flu, but his vote would not have affected the outcome. Ecorse's Mayor William W. Voisine left a hospital bed to cast his vote in favor of the county project. His vote did count, since with it supporters of the county works were able to get just enough votes for the needed majority. The three Detroit councilmen who had consistently supported the county project, Connor, Beck, and Lincoln, backed it again with their votes. The vote reconfirmed what had been demonstrated in the past: that although the Detroit supervisors were the largest delegation on the board, they did not vote as a bloc. The splitting of the Detroit vote plus the overwhelming out-county support was sufficient to carry the day for the county project. Witherspoon and other supporters of the Water Board took the vote as a defeat for the development of a single metropolitan water system, but Connor and Kreger claimed that integration of the two systems could still take place.

The Settlement

Preliminaries to Agreement. The Board of Supervisors' action in approving the intake and tunnel contracts settled the question of whether or not there would be an intake in the lower Detroit River. The city did succeed in obtaining a one-week injunction from the Michigan Supreme Court that restrained the county from proceeding with construction, but on November 7, the Supreme Court lifted the temporary injunction. Although Maiullo and the city continued to press the litigation claiming that construction of the county works would result in a breach of the contracts which the city had with other jurisdictions for the supply of water, and that the city would lose money at the rate of $1,000,000 a year from the date when the county works went into operation until the expiration date of the contracts in 1982, the lifting of the temporary injunction cleared the way for the signing of contracts and the start on construction. Remus did not give up easily. As late as February 1958, he announced that the Detroit intake tunnel had been inspected and found in excellent condition and that with boosting and the decline in water demand resulting from the economic recession, the city would be able to take care of the county through 1970. "Is it too late," he asked, "even at this eleventh hour, for them to re-appraise their program and save the tax money collected for the unnecessary construction?" County Highway Engineer Joseph Gross's response to this publicly posed question was that it was too late. By the spring of 1958, the construction of the intake and tunnel were well underway.

Compared with the two previous years, 1958 was a period of calm in the water controversy. As construction of the intake and tunnel proceeded, public discussion over whether it should be built died out, but efforts to combine the two systems continued. Some of the pressure was off. The elections were over, and the intake issue was settled. It might appear that the Road Commission had won a clear victory, but this was not the case. The voters had approved financing the water system through income from tax revenue and from the sale of a $26,000,000 bond issue. The bonds had not yet been sold. Construction of the intake and tunnel was being financed by funds already available, but before the plant that would process and pump the water could be built, the bonds would have to be sold. Before the bonds could be released for sale, the county had to obtain an opinion from a bond counsel that the issue was valid and not subject to challenge in court. Such an opinion could not be obtained until the litigation begun by Anthony Maiullo and the city had been settled. In the spring of 1958, the case had again reached the Michigan Supreme Court, which remanded it to the Circuit Court for the taking of additional testimony. The case was to languish there until the controversy was finally settled.

Late in July, the Water Board made a formal offer to the County Road Commission to buy out the county water system. The offer was referred to the Board of Supervisors for consideration, thus coming to rest in the Capital Improvements Program Committee still headed by Detroit Councilman Lincoln. Under this offer, Remus agreed to complete the county water works to be used for peak and emergency use and to go to Lake Huron for an additional supply. Lincoln insisted that the county works should be completed before any other source should be developed. But in spite of these differences, serious thought was now being given to ways for combining the two systems.

Then still another technical report by consultants was added to the already substantial pile. This one, "On the Progressive Development of the Wayne County Water System," was prepared for the County Road Commission by Mosher Associates. This firm included L. W. Mosher, who along with Leo Garrity had prepared for the Road Commission an analysis of Remus' first report on an expanded system. This latest document differed from all earlier reports in predicting a larger population through the year 2000 than had been projected in any of the earlier reports. Its projected maximum day demands were, therefore, higher than those included in any of the previous reports. It reported that the service area of the Wayne County water plant would have a maximum day demand of 140 million gallons in 1965 and 239 million gallons in 1975. For the same service area, the 1970 maximum day demand had been predicted at 146 million gallons by the Hazen-Sawyer report and at 155 million gallons by the National Sanitation Foundation. The Mosher report went on to show that the full capacity of the Wayne County intake would be needed by 2000 to service the southern and western part of the county and adjoining parts of Monroe and Washtenaw counties. This report, unlike the others, included detailed land-use projections for the service area. One could conclude from it that there was a need for the Wayne County plant even though those areas receiving water under contract from Detroit were to continue to receive water from that source, i.e., the county plant was not dependent upon former Detroit business.

The Sale of the Wayne County Water System. By the beginning of 1959, the county's capital improvements program had begun to feel the pinch caused by the inability to market the $26,000,000 in bonds. Although the water works was the largest single item, other projects were also dependent upon the proceeds. Lincoln urged the county prosecutor's office to attempt to press the litigation in order to get a decision, but apparently the issues were complex enough to warrant extensive delay in the process of obtaining the testimony requested by the Michigan Supreme Court. It was no secret that the delay was to the tactical advantage of the city, since the county could not be assured of being able to finish its water works without the bond money. There was even a chance for an indefinite stalemate to develop. If the current suit were to be settled, it would be possible to start a new litigation on other issues, which would again delay the sale of the bonds. With this as a possibility, it became apparent to a few of those close to the controversy that such a stalemated battle between the Road Commission and the Water Board would not be in the public interest. During April and May, efforts to bring about a settlement were renewed and intensified. These efforts bore fruit, and on August 3, 1959, the city and county entered into a formal agreement that terminated the controversy.

The agreement opened with a number of statements of mutual understanding between the two parties, among which were included these two paragraphs:

WHEREAS, it is agreed and determined by both the city and the county that certain areas in southern and western Wayne County are in urgent need of water facilities or further and additional facilities and that for the preservation of the health, safety, and welfare of the entire county of Wayne, such further and additional water facilities should be acquired and constructed at the earliest possible moment.

WHEREAS, it is agreed and determined by both the city and the county that the best interests of each will be more adequately and properly served, and the extensions and improvements to provide water service vitally necessary to the public health, safety, and welfare will be realized at an earlier time and more economically if the management and operation of the county system were integrated with the management and operation of the city system, so that both systems will be under the direction and management of the Board of Water Commissioners of the city; . . . .

The agreement proper consisted of sixteen numbered paragraphs from which the following was taken:

1. The county and the city shall enter or cause to be filed with the appropriate courts a stipulation or stipulations dismissing the appeal from the decree of the Circuit Court for the county of Wayne. . . . [This was the suit brought by Maiullo and the city.]

2. The county shall, forthwith, upon the execution hereof and the cessation of said litigation, cause the General Obligation Bond Issue . . . to be issued and marketed. The county shall, as expeditiously as is practicable after the execution hereof, complete the intake and raw-water tunnel and construct the balance of the capital improvement program water facilities, including the proposed Allen Park pumping plant and the purification, filtration, and storage facilities appurtenant thereto, and, as funds become available, contract for the construction of transmission facilities . . . . The County Board of Road Commissioners shall retain jurisdiction over the construction of the said facilities, and shall perform all things necessary to be done to the satisfactory completion thereof.

3. The county hereby leases the Wayne County Metropolitan Water Supply System . . . to the city commencing December 1, 1960, provided the city as a condition precedent to such commencement delivers to the county the initial payment of four million dollars; . . . . It is further understood and agreed that those portions of the said system . . . shall be delivered over to the city as soon as each portion thereof is completed. The term of this lease shall be until December 1, 1991. . . .

. . . .

5. The city hereby agrees to pay for the lease of the demised premises certain specific rentals at the times and in the amounts set forth. . . . [By 1991 the total rental would equal $54,200,000.]

. . . .

7. It is further understood and agreed that the city is in substantial agreement with the reports of the engineering consultants of the county as to population estimates of future growth in Wayne County and the engineering concepts for the expansion of the Wayne County Metropolitan Water Supply System, and the projected estimates of the city and the county as to timing of the expansion, the construction needed, and the amount of expenditure to be made are close to identical. . . .

8. . . . during the term of this lease, the Detroit Water Board will build transmission mains to supply water to any governmental unit located in that portion of Wayne County lying to the south and west of the city of Detroit, which requests said construction; provided, however, said governmental unit has submitted its application . . . to the Sewage Disposal and Water Supply Committee of the Board of Supervisors or such other committee as may be designated by the Board of Supervisors and received approval. . . .

9. The city agrees to keep the Wayne County Supply System in good operating condition and to make such replacements and repairs as are from time to time needed. The city further agrees to operate the filtration and pumping facilities as an operating unit and not a stand-by plant, and that it will operate same in accordance with the best practices and will increase the size of the plant when future conditions so demand.

10. It is further understood and agreed that the city shall charge for the water . . . just and equitable water rates. The rates shall bear a reasonable relationship to costs. The books and records of the water department of the city shall be open for examination and inspection by the county, and at the county's election an independent audit may from time to time be had. . . . The city shall file with the county a schedule of rates, and thereafter shall consult with the appropriate committee of the Wayne County Board of Supervisors relative to any proposed change in said rates which may be applicable to any unit of government lying within the County System. At the request of any such unit within the County System the said supervisors' committee shall hold hearings as to the reasonableness of said rates. The city, the county, and any unit of government lying within the county system may apply to the Circuit Court for the county of Wayne for a determination as to the reasonableness of any water rate, anything to the contrary notwithstanding.

11. . . . the county shall appoint a representative to sit with the Board of Water Commissioners of the city. Said representative shall attend the meetings of said board and shall participate in the meetings, except that he shall not be permitted, unless and until there has been a change in the charter of the city of Detroit, to vote. The city pledges its support to efforts to secure an amendment to its charter to provide for the appointment of non-resident member of the Board of Water Commissioners.

12. The county shall assign and transfer to the city its water supply contracts. . . . The revenues derived thereafter under said contracts and from the operation of the County System shall belong to and become revenues of the city. . . .

13. . . . the employees of the county and/or the Wayne County Road Commission now having work assignments with the operation of the county system may at the employee's election remain as county employees, with full county rights, and they will work for the Detroit Department of Water Supply by contractual agreement. Such employees will be under the supervision of the Board of Water Commissioners, and will be assigned to function as an integral part of the Board's organization, and with the work standards and practices characteristic of the department's operations. . . . [They are also given the option to become city employees.]

. . . .

15. In consideration of the mutual promises of the parties hereto and the undertakings of the city here made and the payment of the sum set forth . . . , the city shall have the right and option at the end of the term of this agreement or any extension thereof to purchase the Wayne County Metropolitan Water Supply System and upon the tender of one dollar ($1.00) the county agrees to deliver forthwith a proper conveyance of said system to the city.

The lease-sale agreement thus gave the Water Board the authority to operate the county water system and integrate it with the Detroit system, but at the same time it guaranteed that the construction of the county intake, water plant, and transmission lines to service southern and western Wayne County would be completed, and it placed the authority for this construction in the County Road Commission. The Road Commission was left in a position to make certain that the hotly contested water works would be completed. Water rates, another major point of contention, were to be set by the Water Board, but with a system of review established that could result in the local courts making the final determination as to their reasonableness. The agreement was lauded by public officials from both the city and the county, and the Board of Commerce welcomed it with the following article by John Wilt, chairman of the Water, Sewage, and Drainage Committee, in the board's weekly publication *The Detroiter* for August 3, 1959:

> Farseeing public officials have cleared the way to a truly metropolitan water system for the Detroit area, centrally administered and assured of an adequate supply from diverse sources. . . .
> The action, strongly urged over the years by the Greater Detroit Board of Commerce, means more water to the suburbs and at an earlier date. It means development of areas handicapped in the past by uncertainty as to water supply. It means the long-sought Lake Huron supply is nearer realization.
>
> .   .   .   .
>
> The water situation, confused in recent years, has been clarified through sound thinking on the part of city and county leaders. Mayor Louis Miriani provided staunch backing for the Detroit Water Department in its efforts to develop an area system. County Auditor Charles Edgecomb played an essential role in bringing together the proper parties at the critical moment. Councilman James Lincoln, head of the county's Capital Improvements Program Committee, worked long and hard to bring together the many pieces of the water

puzzle. Joseph Gross, county highway engineer, and John Jacoby, general counsel for the Road Commission, carefully protected the interests of the out-county residents and came up with an agreement that will be highly beneficial.

Gerald Remus, Detroit's Water Department general manager, and his staff, had the vision to recognize their system's potentiality and the courage to fight for it. The people of the Detroit metropolitan area will benefit over the years from this cooperative effort which will bring solution to the long-standing water-supply problem.

It would be extremely difficult to point to any one person as the key individual in working out the lease-sale agreement. The Board of Commerce tactfully spread the credits among those who held formal positions of responsibility for the settlement. A good deal of negotiation was necessary in order to arrive at a final agreement, and much of this was conducted privately and informally. Alfred Pelham, by then retired from his position as county budget director but still acting as a consultant on the county capital improvements program, worked on preliminary drafts of the final document and was consulted by Lincoln, who acted as principal negotiator for the county. As soon as the formal approval of the document had been obtained from the Detroit Common Council and the Wayne County Board of Supervisors—both bodies approved it with virtually no opposition—the bonds were released for sale. (By then Maiullo's suit had been dropped.) By the first week in November 1959, the Road Commission had run out of available funds to continue construction of the water works, but that same week funds from the bond sale became available. The completion of the county water works had become a certainty.

Concluding Comments

A perennial question that plagues a governmental system in which major public services must be provided by a bureaucracy equipped with technical knowledge and skill is the relative weight to give to the information and recommendations of the bureaucracy in arriving at a policy decision. The formal structure for local policy-making, which in this case included the mayor, Common Council, and Water Board for the city, and the Board of Supervisors and Road Commission for the county, is designed to provide channels through which the technical information and recommendations of the bureaucracy can be filtered and cast into a policy form that reflects a variety of values. But in this case these bodies did not always function in this way. When Lenhardt announced that the Detroit water system had about reached its capacity and advised Wayne County to build its own, there was no serious debate over whether his facts were correct or whether the conclusions he reached, which certainly had widespread policy implications, were warranted. The Water Board and the Detroit Common Council accepted his reports and conclusions as did the Wayne County Board of Supervisors and the Road Commission. The period before any formal action had been taken to add another system to the metropolitan area would seem to have been the proper time to re-evaluate the water-supply problem and explore alternative methods for meeting needs, but this the policy-making bodies did not do. No evidence could be found that Lenhardt's executive staff disagreed with his conclusions. (At the time that Lenhardt was submitting his recommendations, Remus was a member of his executive staff and number-four man in the departmental hierarchy, but no record could be found of his objecting to the Lenhardt policy at that time.) There was no hint within the Detroit water bureaucracy that other policy solutions should have been sought, and the County Road Commission was not reluctant to take on a new activity. The manner and speed with which the Lenhardt policy became public policy was noteworthy in view of later events.

When the Remus policy was announced, the Board of Water Commissioners was made up of the same men who had been in office when the Lenhardt policy had been supported. The same mayor held office, and the same councilmen sat in the council. The policy-making personnel had not changed, but direction of the bureaucracy had. The basic difference between the Remus policy and the Lenhardt policy was not a matter of different judgments concerning the capacity of the Detroit system to provide water to south and southwestern Wayne County, although on this point they certainly did disagree. The fundamental difference between the two policies was the role they envisioned for the Detroit Department of Water Supply. Lenhardt repeatedly stated that he felt that the Detroit water agency should not expand beyond that point permitted by the full utilization of the single intake. Since this was sufficient for Detroit's needs, any additional construction would benefit the suburbs, not Detroit, and therefore should not be constructed by a Detroit agency. Lenhardt had suggested setting up a metropolitan water agency, of which the Detroit agency would be a part, to take care of the whole area's problems. Remus based his policy on the premise that the Detroit Department of Water Supply should become the metropolitan water-supply agency. He saw the Lenhardt policy as leading to a competing water system in Wayne County and possibly another competitor serving Oakland and Macomb counties. If these developments were to take place, then the Detroit Water Department was approaching its maximum growth and might even lose customers when competing systems were completed. The Remus policy was aimed at forestalling competitors and establishing the Detroit Water Department as the metropolitan water agency. Thus the essential differences between the Lenhardt and Remus policies were not differences that could be resolved by the application of water-works engineering criteria.

When faced with these two alternative policies, the policy-making agencies of both the city and the county were forced to apply values different from those supplied by the bureaucracy and by the various expert consultants on water supply in order to resolve the controversy. The initiation of the basic policy debate concerning the organization of water-supply services for the metropolitan area arose from a change of command within one bureaucracy. Once the policy issue was joined, the two bureaucracies played a major role in the ensuing conflict. From this perspective, the controversy is a case study of urban power politics. Traditional party politics played no part. Detroit's elections are non-partisan and Wayne County's partisan (the Democrats most often win county posts), but the major organized effort to influence outcomes in this controversy stemmed from the Detroit Water Department and the County Road Commission.

Of the members of the two bureaucracies, Remus played the most conspicuous political role. Without the support and encouragement of the Water Board and Mayors Cobo and Miriani, he could not have functioned as he did, but these officials who held offices of formal political responsibility gave to their career water executive free rein to conduct an active campaign in support of his policies. Remus received a big assist from the Board of Commerce's Gerald Warren, and with a sympathetic press, especially *The Detroit News*, Remus was able to obtain the widespread attention for his arguments that is so important where local issues are involved. The Road Commission staff played a less conspicuous but nonetheless active political role. Whereas Remus might be classified a newcomer to local bureaucratic politics, Leroy Smith was an established professional, and so were many of his top staff. They did not enjoy the same favorable attention in the press as did Remus and did not have the gratuitous assistance of a citizens' Water Users' Committee. Nevertheless, when the crucial issues came to a vote in the Board of Supervisors, the Road Commission was able to obtain the necessary votes to win approval of the water plant in 1956 and, even more important, to win approval for the construction contracts in 1957, after a campaign which saw Remus and his supporters employ all of the influence they could marshal to defeat the Road Commission in the Board of Supervisors. In this, the most naked test of strength in the whole controversy, one where the outcome could be counted in votes, the Road Commission bureaucracy won.

In their struggle, both bureaucracies made use of consultants and experts with special studies and reports to support their positions. The initial county report by Hazen and Sawyer was prepared before the controversy developed, but none of the succeeding studies and reports could ignore the controversy. Consultant Richard Hazen became a key figure, since he had co-authored the report upon which the county was basing its plans, and the National Sanitation Foundation succeeded in hiring him for their study for the Inter-County Supervisors' Committee. Because the bureaucracies and their supporters used these reports for tactical purposes, the results were often distorted or thrown out of balance by quoting out of context and by omitting qualifying statements. But while political biases exaggerated differences between technical consultants, they did not create them.

A key issue in all of the studies was projected water demand. In order to arrive at demand, per capita water use had to be estimated, and this estimate depended upon such variables as future land use and population growth. To project both population and land-use development over a ten- to forty-year period involved a number of estimates based on hypothesized events, and it was not unlikely that two sets of equally qualified experts would disagree on some of the variables involved. In spite of this apparent latitude, the consultants were close to agreement on 1970 maximum day per capita demand regardless of whether they were employed by the county or by the National Sanitation Foundation. The various reports did use different population estimates, but this was because each used the latest projection available at the time of the report.

Another key issue on which the consultants agreed was the pollution in the Detroit River. The two major reports, the Hazen-Sawyer report and National Sanitation Foundation report, agreed that the downriver intake site was safe. Both reports pointed to the necessity of taking steps to guarantee that the river supply would continue to be protected from pollution. The National Sanitation Foundation report pointed out that much of the future population expansion would occur north of Detroit, i.e., north of the Detroit intake at the head of the Detroit River. This would seem to guarantee that pollution would be kept under control, since the same report recommended that the Detroit system drawing from this intake be developed as the central unit in a metropolitan water system.

On one significant point the experts did disagree—the capacity of the Detroit system to meet all of the water needs of southwestern Wayne County and for how long. Without recapitulating the points of differences (in area, population, and demand data) in the various relevant reports, it is sufficient here to point out that Garrity and Mosher and Mosher Associates reported that Detroit did not have the capacity, and the National Sanitation Foundation said that with certain expansions Detroit did have the capacity through 1970.

None of the reports satisfied the expectations of those who hoped that a solution to the policy question would be forthcoming from a group of experts whose recommendations would carry enough weight to bring about a "non-political" solution that all could accept without embarrassment. This road to settlement is a typical expectation in our political culture, and the results of this case are also probably typical. A comparison of the Hazen-Sawyer and National Sanitation Foundation studies points up the different uses of technical consultants in arriving at policy decisions.

The Hazen-Sawyer assignment was not to explore broad policy alternatives; rather, it was the outgrowth of a policy decision that a Wayne County plant would be constructed. The report provided recommendations concerning its location and size in order to meet the demand which the study determined would exist in a given service area, and finally it provided a cost analysis of alternative solutions. This might be termed the classic role of the expert in American administration. The policy-maker weighs the alternatives thus provided by the expert and makes his choice.

The National Sanitation Foundation report had a much broader scope. Without the restraint of predetermined policies, it in effect had to deal with broad policy choices. Should a Wayne County water works be built? What alternatives to the county works should be considered? What role should the Detroit system play in the over-all metropolitan water system? Is a single water system for the whole metropolitan area preferable to several separate systems? Even though these questions were discussed in terms of daily per capita water consumption and maximum day demands, the alternative choices could not be reduced to the language of water supply. There were too many other variables, such as the difficulty involved in setting up a service agency that overlaps a number of political boundaries, to name but one, that had to be taken into consideration in making such policy choices. This was borne out in the course of events. The National Sanitation Foundation report did not turn out to be a persuasive document that deterred the Board of Supervisors from approving the construction of the county intake, although it was used to support the arguments of those already on record for a single system. It did not resolve the controversy, and it would be difficult to determine whether it aided in the ultimate solution or whether it delayed that solution.

In the final analysis a political settlement of the controversy was made. The elected officials in city and county government worked out an agreement that was acceptable to the community and to the two bureaucracies. The final agreement could be considered a victory for both sides. The county got its water works, and the residents in southwestern Wayne County were assured of a water supply and the means to deliver it. The Road Commission retained the authority to supervise the construction of the water system included in the capital improvements program and thus could be assured that the water system would be completed so as to satisfy the designed capacity recommended by the county consultants. Remus got control over the operation of the Wayne County water system, but with the following strings attached: he had to abandon his ace in the hole, litigation that could hold up the bond issue; he had to operate the downriver plant, which would be built under the supervision of the Road Commission; the county water rate structure would be subject to special scrutiny, including possible judicial setting of standards of reasonableness; and, of course, rent would have to be paid on the lease. With the bonds sold and the proceeds on hand, the county would have little to lose if the city were to fail to live up to its side of the agreement, since completion of the county works could proceed in any event.

Only time will tell whether or not the Detroit Department of Water Supply will be transformed into a metropolitan water agency, but the odds are in its favor. With the absorption of the Wayne County system, its only close rival will have been eliminated. The settlement of the Wayne County water controversy opened the way for the metamorphosis of the Detroit Water Department from city to metropolitan status.

5
The Case of
the Missing Port

The Metropolis Welcomes the St. Lawrence Seaway

Introduction

With the spring thaw of 1959 came the annual opening of the Great Lakes shipping season, but there was a difference that year. The St. Lawrence Seaway had finally been completed, and large ocean-going vessels were poised to penetrate the hitherto inaccessible waters of the Great Lakes. A seaway, consisting of a system of locks, canals, and channels which would open the Great Lakes to navigation by deep-draft ocean-going ships, had been discussed, debated, and fought over since 1895. The influence of the railroads, allied with that of the politically powerful eastern seaboard states, was successful in blocking the necessary treaty arrangements with Canada which would permit construction of the project. By the early 1950's, however, it appeared that Canada was prepared to proceed with an all-Canadian seaway. This prospect, combined with a demand from American industry for access to newly discovered sources of high-grade iron ore in Canada, brought about the political change of heart that resulted in Congressional approval, in 1954, of a joint American-Canadian project.

A look at a map of the Great Lakes–North Atlantic region will show why the lure of a seaway had been so persistent over the years. The early settlers had used the St. Lawrence River, which links Lake Ontario on the southwest with the Gulf of St. Lawrence and the Atlantic Ocean on the northeast, as an access route to the Great Lakes region that extends some 1,100 miles from the eastern end of Lake Ontario to the western end of Lake Superior. For canoes, the waterfalls and rapids along the route were a nuisance but not an insurmountable barrier. As heavier, deeper-draft vessels came into use, the natural barriers of this waterway system

—rapids and falls in the St. Marys, St. Lawrence, and Niagara rivers, which isolated Ontario and Superior from the other lakes—imposed restrictions which resulted in a number of separate water transportation systems dependent upon land transportation for connection with other parts of the Great Lakes–St. Lawrence system. But these barriers were nibbled away over the years. In 1833, Canada built a canal to bypass Niagara Falls and link Lakes Erie and Ontario. This canal was replaced in 1932 by the Welland Canal. The Soo Locks opened Lake Superior in 1854. Also over the years, the Canadian government constructed and then improved a system of canals and locks along the St. Lawrence. By the time the seaway agreement was reached in 1954, small ocean-going vessels could travel the 2,200 miles from the Atlantic Ocean to Duluth, Minnesota.

The typical pre-seaway, lake-ocean ship, limited in size by the St. Lawrence locks and channels, was about 258 feet long with a 41-foot beam and a cargo capacity of 2,500 tons. The 14-foot depth of the channel restricted cargoes to 1,300 tons. The opening of the seaway in April 1959 provided passage for vessels with a maximum draft of 25.5 feet, a maximum length of 715 feet, and a maximum width of 75 feet. Ships with cargoes of 7,500 tons could now traverse the route from the Atlantic to the mid-western hinterlands of the United States and Canada.

The history of the Detroit metropolis is directly related to its strategic geographic location on the Detroit River, the strait connecting the upper and lower Great Lakes. The opening of the Erie Canal in 1828 started a flow of goods and passengers which resulted in the expansion of Great Lakes shipping and the growth of such port cities as Buffalo, Cleveland, Toledo, Detroit, Milwaukee, and Chicago. By the middle of the nineteenth century, the Soo Locks had opened Lake Superior to inter-lake shipping, and the five Great Lakes became part of a single water transportation system. Iron ore, limestone, lumber, and grain flowed east, and manufactured goods, coal, and people traveled west. In terms of number of vessels, Great Lakes shipping reached its peak in the 1880's, when over 2,000 ships, many still propelled by sail, were in service. By the 1950's, the number had decreased to a little over 700 vessels, but most of these were the long (from 600 to 700 feet), low-slung "lakers" with the distinctive dachshund-like silhouette, capable of carrying from 18,000 to 24,000 tons when fully loaded. This shipping supplied the raw materials for heavy industry in the Detroit region and provided for the movement of finished products, such as automobiles. Although at an earlier period passenger service and general cargo shipping had been a significant part of Great Lakes commerce, this type of shipping had virtually disappeared by the 1950's.

As the 1959 shipping season progressed and large ocean-going ships began to appear in the Detroit River, an embarrassing situation developed. There were not enough terminal facilities to handle the ocean-going vessels loaded with general cargo for delivery or pick up at the Port of Detroit. In reviewing this situation at the close of the 1959 shipping season, a Waterfront Development Committee appointed by Detroit's mayor, Louis Miriani, had this to report:

> . . . a total of three berths for large ocean-going vessels or six berths for smaller vessels was available during 1959. . . . Based on U.S. Customs figures of entries of overseas vessels at the Port of Detroit in 1959, there have been numerous days on which from four to seven overseas vessels entered the port. This does not include various vessels engaged in domestic and Canadian commerce which created an additional load on the port facilities.
>
> No comprehensive statistics have been found as to the total number of ships delayed because of lack of berths or as to the aggregate length of delays encountered. However, it is evident from published articles and pictures in the press, figures as to ship entries, the unanimity of opinion of shipping agents and ship operators, and the personal observations of the committee, that numerous and lengthy delays were encountered in 1959. As an illustration, a written submission by a shipping agent operating in Detroit details numerous instances of delay in the handling of shipments at Detroit, with substantial increases in cost and dissatisfaction among the ship operators.

For a city and region that had traditionally taken advantage of the benefits provided by the Great Lakes water transportation system and had supported and fought for the St. Lawrence Seaway, this first season's experience was disappointing. Why was the Port of Detroit unprepared for the seaway opening? This case deals with that question. The events covered in the case took place in the period from 1955 through 1959, that is, from the time of the certain knowledge that the seaway would be built through its first season of operation. Two basic themes run through the case. One is the issue of whether port development should be undertaken by government or whether it should be left to private enterprise. For many port cities, this would be an anachronistic controversy, the decision in favor of public facilities having been reached years ago, but for Detroit this was a contemporary controversy. The second theme is the issue of what type of agency should be responsible for port development. Should it be subject to county control, or should it have autonomy to tax, borrow, and construct revenue-producing facilities? This, then, is a case involving the adjustment of a metropolis to the change in its physical and economic environment brought about by the engineering activities that culminated in the conversion of the Great Lakes into a part of the ocean-going transportation system.

The Early Years

Establishing the Port Commission. The establishment of the Port of Detroit was authorized by Wayne County voters at a special election held on November 7, 1933. The enabling legislation under which it was created, the Michigan Port Districts Act (Act 234, Public Acts of 1925, as amended), had originally provided for establishment of an agency independent of local political control, with broad powers, including the power to levy taxes (not more than two mills and not to exceed $500,000 in annual revenue) and the power to build, own, and operate port facilities. Under the original act, the Port Commission would consist of three commissioners appointed by the governor for staggered three-year terms. No serious effort to establish a Port District under the act was undertaken until 1932. It then appeared that an agreement on a seaway treaty between the United States and Canada was in the offing. When Wayne County officials reviewed the enabling legislation, they concluded that it gave the Port Commission too much autonomy, and in the interest of "county home rule" they succeeded in having the law amended by the state legislature. Since the enabling law favored the establishment of port districts coterminous with the county boundaries in which they were organized, the Wayne County Board of Supervisors proceeded to recommend to the legislature that the act be amended to make the

Port Commission subordinate to the Board of Supervisors. Specifically, it was recommended that (1) the Board of Supervisors
determine the amount of money to be raised and spent by the Port
Commission, including authorization of bond issues and other borrowing; (2) the commission be subject to the budgetary control
of the board through the submission of an annual budget; and
(3) the number of commissioners be increased from three to five.
These recommendations were adopted by the legislature as amendments to the original enabling act. When the Wayne County voters
approved the establishment of a Port District and Port Commission, they were not approving the organization of an independent
port agency. On the contrary, they had only approved setting up
another agency of county government.

The voters had created a Port of Detroit District coterminous
with the boundaries of Wayne County; i.e., the Port District included all territory within the county boundaries, whether or not
it was organized or incorporated as a separate political jurisdiction. In the Port District's thirty-two miles of deep-water frontage
(twenty-two miles on the Detroit River and ten miles on the two
banks of the River Rouge) were the ten miles along the Detroit
River that were within the city of Detroit. Thus the city of Detroit
was included as a part of the Port District along with other jurisdictions within the county. This was a novel arrangement. Ordinarily, county agencies did not operate in Detroit but served only
those areas outside the city. The Port of Detroit Commission, although appointed by the governor (this was later changed to provide for appointment by the Wayne County Board of Supervisors),
was dependent upon the County Board of Supervisors for funds
for personnel and program. Because the word "Detroit" was used
to identify the port and was part of the commission's official title,
many people assumed that the Port Commission was a city agency
and that "the Port of Detroit" referred to a city-wide rather than
a county-wide area.

The first port commissioners were appointed by the governor
in 1933. The establishment of the commission was hailed as a step
in the direction of preparing the metropolitan area for the anticipated seaway, but hopes were dampened the following year when
Congress failed to approve the project. During the depression years
of the 1930's and the war and postwar years of the 1940's, the Port

Commission never had more than a skeleton staff, and its program, which consisted primarily of promoting the port and certain improvements in the river channel, was of necessity minimal. The annual appropriations provided by the Board of Supervisors during the 1940's were small, averaging around $15,000 annually, but even these small amounts were more than the Port Commission was able to spend. During these years, about one-third of the annual appropriations went unspent.

In 1951, the Port Commission submitted a request to the Board of Supervisors for $80,000 for a survey of the Port District to serve as a base for a master plan for the port. The power to develop a port master plan was one power that the commission did have. The County Board of Auditors, a three-man elected board under which the County Budget and Finance Division was located and through which budget requests had to clear, recommended to the Ways and Means Committee, the Board of Supervisors' most powerful committee, that the Port Commission get together with the Detroit City Plan Commission and the Detroit Metropolitan Area Regional Planning Commission and reach agreement on what plans and surveys would be needed in order to prepare for the seaway. The Ways and Means Committee took this advice and requested that the three agencies meet.

Max McCray, port director under the commission, followed through with this request, but with some reluctance. All three agencies could claim an interest in port planning. The Detroit City Plan Commission considered the city waterfront as part of its proper jurisdiction. The Regional Planning Commission, which included within its scope not only Wayne County but also the adjoining counties in the metropolitan area—Oakland, Macomb, and Monroe counties and part of Washtenaw County, considered waterfront planning as its proper concern. Since the Port Commission had jurisdiction over the Port District, it considered its interest in port planning to be the paramount one. To have to sit with the other planning agencies as if all three had equal responsibilities for port planning was considered by the Port Commission to be in contradiction to the purpose of setting up the Port District. This view was expressed in a minority report filed by the Port Commission following its meeting with the other two planning agen-

cies. The majority report recommended that the county appropriate $50,000 to the Regional Planning Commission for the purpose
of conducting a port economic study. In its minority report, the
Port Commission objected to the economic study, on the ground
that it would still leave the area without a master plan of port
development, and to the designation of the Regional Planning
Commission as the agency to carry out the study, because "the
Port of Detroit Commission alone among all local agencies is qualified by objective, by experience, and by law to determine and
remedy the needs of the port and its district."

The jurisdictional dispute between the Port Commission and
the other planning agencies was settled by contracting with the
New York engineering firm of Knappen, Tippets, Abbett, and Mc-
Carthy to conduct a port economic survey of the Detroit region.
For the county, the contracting agents were the Board of Auditors,
the Regional Planning Commission, and the Port Commission; the
Detroit City Plan Commission was represented along with the
county agencies on the study-advisory committee. The survey results were submitted in December 1952, and the two-volume report, hereinafter referred to as the KTAM report, provided a comprehensive analysis of the port's needs and potentialities.

The KTAM Report. Because it provided the first over-all
analysis of the Port of Detroit in terms of its economic function in
the region, its physical layout, and its organization, including the
Port Commission, and projected the future influence of the St.
Lawrence Seaway upon the port, the KTAM report must be reviewed in some detail. No attempt will be made to cite the elaborate economic data assembled to demonstrate the extent to which
the Detroit economy was dependent upon water commerce. It is
sufficient here to note that these data were never in dispute, and
they were summarized in the report as follows:

> The Port of Detroit is a basic part of and essential to the over-all econ-
> omy of the Detroit region and, in a large measure, to that of the state
> of Michigan. The port not only contributes considerable direct and
> indirect income to the community each year but is one of the primary
> reasons for the development in the Detroit region of many of the
> area's basic industries, particularly those relying heavily on deep-
> water navigation for the low-cost transport of their bulk raw materi-

als. Among these are the steel, pulp and paper, cement, chemicals, oil refining, and ship building and repair industries. It is estimated that in 1950 port activities contributed at least $15,000,000 in "new" income directly to the community and that the indirect community benefits stimulated by the circulation of money approximated $30,-000,000. It is estimated further that the direct savings in transportation costs to local businesses and industries through the use of low-cost water transportation are currently in excess of $34,000,000 per year. Moreover, the port-based industries in the Detroit region contribute an aggregate of at least $200,000,000 annually in the form of payrolls and the purchase of local services and supplies.

One set of findings and recommendations dealt with waterfront planning and zoning regulations:

> There is a growing scarcity of industrial and terminal sites on deep-water channels in the Detroit region. Unless steps are taken to alleviate this situation, the lack of attractive waterfront sites for industry will act increasingly in the future as a deterrent to further industrial development and expansion in this region. This situation is particularly acute along the city of Detroit frontage on the Detroit River, where no industrial acreage of any consequence remains undeveloped and where 60 percent of the frontage is not now used for marine purposes. Moreover, the River Rouge and, to a somewhat lesser extent, the Detroit River below the city of Detroit no longer offer the extensive undeveloped tracts of land on deep-water channels which were available in those areas ten or fifteen years ago.

This condition was attributed to failure in the past to plan waterfront land use, and the report recommended that the Port Commission "take more active steps in the zoning of waterfront areas on a regional basis to the end that these areas will be preserved for or returned to marine use." To carry this out, the report recommended that the Port Commission be given "the power to establish and regulate, in cooperation with city and regional planning commissions and zoning authorities, zoning of the waterfront and the properties adjacent thereto within the Port District."

The findings and recommendations that had the most direct bearing upon future events were those dealing with cargo terminal facilities, their current adequacy, and the effect that seaway traffic would have upon them. The report noted that most of the tonnage handled at the Port of Detroit consisted of bulk cargo—coal, iron ore, limestone, sand and gravel, petroleum and petroleum products. This cargo required specialized handling facilities, which were provided at the private terminals, in many cases owned by the user, that lined the waterfront. The report asserted (and later reports were to concur in this conclusion) that bulk cargo would continue to provide the overwhelming majority (over 90 percent) of the tonnage passing through the port and that this tonnage could be adequately handled by private terminal facilities, which could be expected to be expanded to meet future demands. The seaway, which would permit ships of deeper draft to enter the port, would create a need for channel deepening to accommodate ocean-going bulk cargo ships, and it was suggested that the time might come when the Port Commission would find it "necessary and desirable to use public funds for the purchase of land for the construction of industrial bulk marine terminals, in order to attract certain industries." No such need then existed, according to the report. During the ensuing controversy over port terminal facilities, bulk cargo facilities were not involved.

The KTAM survey did find the Detroit port facilities deficient for the handling of general cargo. Certain specialized types of general cargo, such as assembled automobiles, were being taken care of through specialized terminal facilities, but the port was found to have neither the terminal facilities to handle potential "domestic" general cargo (general cargo coming from points in the Great Lakes area) nor the facilities for handling the increase in "foreign" general cargo that would come with the opening of the seaway. Most of the overseas cargo would fall in the general cargo classification, such as miscellaneous packaged cargo, often requiring special handling in loading and unloading and undercover storage. The report noted that the port's tonnage of domestic general cargo had declined 96 percent since 1929 because of high labor and operating costs, mounting terminal costs, excessive delays, and intensification of railroad and truck competition. The solution recommended for the domestic trade was promotion of "the use of some type of *container*, whether it be a freight car, a truck trailer, or a detachable trailer-box, to provide land-water transport from consignor to consignee without intermediate individual handling of the item contents of the container." The Port Commission "should act as the initiator and co-ordinator by bringing together, for the common good, local shippers and consignees, the trade unions concerned, and the steamship companies and, if necessary, by aiding in the establishment of the terminals required."

"It is in the movement of general cargo commerce that the completion of the seaway will open the greatest opportunity to the Port of Detroit." The report then estimated that "a year after seaway operations commence, [there will be] an increase in the port's direct overseas trade [from about 50,000 tons a year] to about 300,000 tons per year. This is expected to increase to 750,000 to 1,000,000 tons annually within the succeeding five years, provided suitable marine facilities and services are developed at the port." The report went on to say:

> The port's seaway traffic could be handled either by the expansion of existing terminals or by the progressive development of new ones. The Detroit Harbor Terminals [a private terminal], with a relatively small expansion of property now owned by that company, could probably handle Detroit's seaway traffic for the first year or two after the seaway opens, provided the owners make the necessary improvements. These would give time for the initiation of a new terminal development program . . . which could be financed as either a private or a public project and could consist in either a very major expansion of the Detroit Harbor Terminals or in the development of a new terminal elsewhere on the waterfront.

Three methods for financing port improvements were cited in the report: (1) development by private enterprise using private capital, (2) development by private enterprise with the assistance of public funds, and (3) development as a public enterprise using public funds. Although preferring the first two methods in that order of preference, it was conceded that the third method might have to be considered for the financing of terminals for overseas export-import general cargo traffic. In view of the ensuing controversy, the following excerpts from the report are especially important:

> In general, public port authorities have not been able to construct, or acquire, and operate public terminal facilities on the basis of their own credit and income earned from their own operations. Normally a port authority's bonds based solely on marine terminal revenues are not considered to be a good investment and are not marketable at reasonable interest rates. Port authority bonds, therefore, are usually supported in some other manner in addition to or other than port terminal revenues. In general there are three ways in which this is done. The first is by the issuance of general obligation bonds secured by

the port agency's power to levy and collect taxes within its district. . . .

The second . . . is the issuance of "revenue" bonds secured by the revenues of the port agency but backed by the faith and credit of the local city, county, or state. . . .

The third . . . is by turning over to that agency a strong revenue-producing public facility, such as a toll bridge or tunnel, which can be used as a credit base for future port revenue bonds.

. . . it is to be noted that the support of either public funds or public credit has been necessary in every known case of major port improvement by central port administrations in this country, during the last decade or more. In some cases this support is not obvious but, on investigation, some sort of subsidy can be discovered. Moreover, because of the growing intensity of competition between ports in this country, the trend toward the direct or indirect subsidy is forcing competing ports more and more to similar devices.

The estimate of port needs and methods of financing them led to this cautious conclusion: "It may be necessary, if the projected St. Lawrence Seaway is developed, for the commission to undertake or sponsor a progressive program of general cargo terminal development to serve the Detroit region's and Michigan's overseas export-import trade, if private enterprise cannot be persuaded to undertake this work."

The KTAM survey included within its scope examination of the organization and powers of the Port Commission. During the 1952 state legislative session, Wayne County officials had succeeded in having the Port Districts Act amended to authorize the appointment of port commissioners by the Board of Supervisors. With this accomplished, the Port Commission came under the complete control of the county. The recommendations of the KTAM report were aimed, on the one hand, at giving the Port Commission additional powers so as to give it "full authority within its district in all matters concerning navigable waterways, navigational improvements, and related waterfront structures and facilities," subject, of course, to the general authority of the federal government; but on the other hand, the report conceded that these powers had to be exercised "in cooperation with city and regional planning commissions and zoning authorities" and "subject to budgetary controls." How the Port Commission could develop a degree of freedom to act on its own, while at the same time obligated to clear all substantive zoning decisions with the affected local jurisdiction (which, in most cases, would be the city of Detroit), and with all of its decisions involving money subject to the budgetary control of the County Board of Auditors and the ultimate control of the County Board of Supervisors, was not made clear. In spite of the apparent contradiction in these recommendations, a careful reading of the KTAM report reveals that the consultants were convinced that a successful port agency must have the power to regulate waterfront activities, including both construction and traffic; the power to construct docks and other facilities; and the power to have access to its own "rents, fees, charges, and other revenues from the operation of the Port District to pay operating, maintenance, depreciation, and such other costs and expenses as may devolve upon the Port Commission in connection with Port District business." The degree of autonomy to be granted the port agency was to continue to be a key issue.

Finally, the consultants dealt with the staffing of the Port Commission. They found the current staff, consisting of two people, the director and his secretary, insufficient and recommended that it be expanded "first in the field of port traffic and promotion, then in waterfront zoning, and finally in the planning and, if necessary, the prosecution of actual marine improvements." It recommended that the budget be increased to $40,000 to permit the hiring of a transportation analyst and someone to handle port promotional activities.

In summary, the port economic survey of 1952 showed the economic benefits the Detroit region derived from its port and recommended the expansion of port facilities in order to exploit estimated future benefits. It found that the port terminal facilities for handling bulk cargo, which accounted for and would continue to account for the largest share of the tonnage handled, were adequate and would probably continue to be so. The one deficiency in terminal facilities was found to be in the capacity to handle general cargo. Domestic general cargo traffic, the consultants concluded, could best be taken care of by the development and use of special container-ships, with appropriate terminal facilities being provided by the private shipping interests. Terminal facilities for general cargo in the overseas trade were currently available through private terminals. But it was projected that the most important consequence of the St. Lawrence Seaway would be an immediate increase in overseas two-way general cargo commerce from around 50,000 tons to 300,000 tons annually, with a gradual increase to about 1,000,000 tons annually. The Port of Detroit did not have adequate terminal facilities for this overseas trade, and although the consultants recommended that the private terminal operators be given an opportunity to provide the needed facilities, they made it clear that no other port in recent years had been able to develop general cargo terminals without some form of public subsidy or public port construction.

Reaction to the KTAM Report. The KTAM report did not evoke any strong reactions. Some might quarrel with its hedging over the need for public port developments, but the thorough documentation of its interpretations and conclusions provided a valuable factual base for policy-making. Until the construction of the seaway was assured, the only immediate action suggested by the report was increasing the staff and the powers of the Port Commission, and even in these two areas, the Board of Supervisors did not appear to be in any hurry for action. Late in 1953, the Detroit–Windsor Tunnel Authority, the agency operating the toll tunnel under the Detroit River between Detroit and Windsor, Canada, offered to sell the tunnel to the Port Commission for $18,000,000. It was estimated that the tunnel would net the commission some $40,000,000 by 1990, at which time it would become the property of the city of Detroit. Such a revenue-producing facility, if owned by the Port Commission, could be used as the basis for selling revenue bonds as suggested in the KTAM report.

In January 1954, the Board of Supervisors approved submitting to the state legislature a request that the board be given the authority to approve the purchase of the tunnel by the Port Commission. Willis Hall, secretary-manager of the Greater Detroit Board of Commerce and member of the Board of Supervisors as an appointee of one of the Detroit councilmen, agreed that the Port Commission's activities should be expanded but warned against its becoming an independent bureaucracy. The enabling act died in committee in the state legislature. The Port Commission seemed uncertain whether or not ownership of the tunnel would be a good thing for the port agency but did protest the lack of powers. The commission chairman was quoted as saying: "We have come to the conclusion that our present statute gives us inadequate powers to complete a port the way it should be developed." Port Director Max McCray echoed this view when he resigned in May 1954, stating that the commission was powerless to act.

The port director's resignation plus the progress in Congress of the seaway issue, which at last made that project a certainty, activated the Board of Supervisors in the summer of 1954 to take a more serious view of the status of the port agency. City of Detroit Controller John Witherspoon, ex officio member of the Board of Supervisors, urged that a standing committee be organized to deal directly with the Port Commission. This was a significant proposal. Because of its large size (it varies with population changes but was 109 in 1958) and mixed legislative and administrative functions, the Board of Supervisors conducted most of its affairs through standing committees. Major activities, such as highways and health, had separate standing committees, and the actions of the substantive standing committees ultimately had to clear through the Ways and Means Committee. To set up a standing committee for an activity was to recognize its importance. Witherspoon's proposal was adopted, and he was appointed the first chairman of the Port Committee of the Board of Supervisors.

Meanwhile, the Port Commission had decided to request the powers it considered necessary to carry out its responsibilities. These included the powers that had been recommended in the consultants' report and, in addition, fiscal autonomy, which would permit the commission to raise revenue and budget its expenditures independent of the County Board of Auditors and the Board of Supervisors. The Port Commission's request was a bold bid for the type of autonomy that would permit the commission to become a major operating agency with the authority to regulate port activities through zoning and licensing, as well as authority to construct and operate port facilities, including terminals, dockside railroads, roads, bridges, tunnels, and other structures deemed necessary. As the search was then under way for a new port director, the commissioners felt it would aid in recruitment if the agency's powers were broadened. The commission's request, which was included in a report to a county reorganization committee, apparently never reached the stage of serious consideration by the Board of Supervisors; but early in 1955, the board did approve a request to the legislature that the Port District be given the power to draw up a master plan, to regulate construction and maintenance of port structures, to recommend waterfront rezoning, and to acquire and operate certain facilities such as piers and warehouses. When passed, these changes did not weaken the board's control over the Port Commission, nor did they give the commission more room to maneuver at its own discretion, since fiscal independence was not granted.

The Short Career of Sterling St. John, Jr., as Port Director

The St. John Policy. By June of 1955, the Port of Detroit Commission had hired a new port director, Sterling St. John, Jr. He was not the first choice. The position had first been offered to Robert Wylie, former director of the Port of San Francisco and a retired U.S. Army brigadier general, but he declined, he said, because the $15,000 salary was too small. St. John, at forty-six, had a variety of port experience, including port consultant work for San Francisco and Los Angeles, and he had recently conducted a port economic survey for the Port of Buffalo. The Greater Detroit Board of Commerce welcomed the new director with a banquet; public officials hailed his arrival as the beginning of a new era in port development; and the *Detroit Free Press* reported that "the new man . . . is a quiet, likeable fellow who gives an impression of considerable energy and good common sense." St. John's most quoted remark during this reception glow was: "We have four years to prepare for the big ships."

Prior to St. John's arrival, during the spring of 1955, while the state legislature was considering the proposed changes in the powers of the Port Commission, spokesmen for the Detroit Board of Commerce began to raise objections to public development of port facilities. The Board of Commerce had supported efforts to obtain approval for the St. Lawrence Seaway. Detroit business and industrial leaders, members, of course, of the Board of Commerce, also were directors of the Great Lakes–St. Lawrence Association, an organization devoted to promoting seaway development. But with seaway construction under way, the Board of Commerce, through memoranda, conferences, and other communication devices, was opposing any increase in the powers of the Port Commission and cautioning against the development of public port facilities.

In March, the Port and St. Lawrence Seaway Committee of the Board of Commerce sponsored a meeting of industrialists and businessmen to discuss the future of the port. At this meeting, Gerald Warren, the board's staff man assigned to port affairs, said that port development should emphasize bulk cargo facilities, and he warned against being stampeded into building a multimillion-dollar general cargo terminal. This meeting was followed by a board-sponsored bus tour of dock facilities, on April 7, to show how well equipped the private terminals were to meet the increased shipping expected to follow the seaway opening. A staff memorandum prepared by Warren and released that same day contained the following position statement: "We are opposed to the creation of an autonomous governmental authority that has the power to tax, condemn land, and drive private terminal operators out of business with a tax-free facility when in the foreseeable future private terminal operators will be fully equipped to service this business." This position was elaborated upon in the newspaper accounts of the bus tour. Port Commissioner David Lowe, who was also president of Detroit Marine Terminals, Inc., one of the port's two major general cargo facilities, was quoted in *The Detroit News* of April 8 as having told the touring businessmen that:

> We maintain that the private docks, with an expansion program of $25,000,000, can take care of all the traffic that will come in through here until about 1970. It would be extremely costly for the government to move in and try to establish a port.

Lowe estimated that it would cost the government $100,000,000 to get "the kind of capacity we have." In the same news account, Gerald Warren was quoted as having said:

> The plain fact of the matter is that terminal operators are starving for business today, and they will continue to starve until someone gets

out and promotes the use of the St. Lawrence Seaway to the shipper.

Every one has looked to the government to meet the seaway development. We feel that the Port Commission should be a promotion agency to sell shippers on using the seaway, and we also feel the Port Commission should not go into the construction of public facilities in competition with private facilities.

The Board of Commerce was to stick to this position, staked out early in 1955, that private facilities could be developed to meet the seaway demand and that the Port Commission should function primarily as a promotion agency. *The Detroit News,* in an April 12 editorial, questioned this position:

. . . aggressive development of a port necessitates some degree of public participation, since only a public authority will invest in facilities for commerce aspired to but still to be developed.

When the new port director arrived on the scene in June 1955, he was thus faced with a brewing controversy over whether, in fact, additional port facilities were needed and whether future development should be through public or private investment.

One of Sterling St. John's first acts was to establish a port development policy. On July 11, 1955, a six-point policy was approved by the Port Commission.

1. The Port of Detroit Commission has a primary obligation and duty to determine the requirements of the Port of Detroit for waterfront facilities and supporting services necessary to meet the demands created by the seaway and deepening of the connecting channels. The Knappen report [KTAM report] will be used as a benchmark in this determination.
2. The Port of Detroit Commission will make these standards known as soon as they are determined.
3. The Port of Detroit Commission thereafter will encourage private enterprise to construct the necessary facilities and to establish the supporting services.
4. If, by 1957, private enterprise demonstrates that it cannot carry the financial burden alone, but will need public assistance, the Port of Detroit Commission will work for a year on specific problems of this nature.
5. If, by 1958, it is certain that private enterprise will not, alone or with the assistance of the Port of Detroit Commission, develop all of the facilities and services deemed necessary, then the commission will proceed to acquire, erect, or establish them to be ready by 1960.

6. The Port of Detroit Commission is determined that the shippers, the steamship lines, and the land carriers shall have adequate facilities, without congestion and with the best service at the lowest cost in the country. The commission expects private enterprise to take advantage of their opportunities and the commission will help them; but the commission will not let the users of the port down, in any case.

This policy was in line with the recommendations of the KTAM report and gave the private terminal operators first crack at port development. It was a wait-and-see policy, and it was greeted with a wait-and-see attitude.

In September, the Port Commission office was moved from the County Building Annex, an old store and office building, to new quarters in the recently finished Veterans' Memorial Building, overlooking the Detroit River. A summer inspection cruise of port facilities left the commissioners "content that private harbor operators rather than government can best provide any facilities needed here when the St. Lawrence Seaway becomes a reality." But although the surface was calm, some county officials were becoming impatient with the new director's wait-and-see policy. One commissioner, John Basso, the nominee of County Auditor Charles Edgecomb, voted against the permanent hiring of St. John when the matter was raised at the end of the port director's six-month probationary period. He was overruled by his fellow commissioners. Basso, a lawyer and member of a family active in county politics, could be expected to have close ties with influential members of the Board of Supervisors and other county officials. His brother was deputy county budget director and later became budget director. Basso's opposition to St. John thus carried some political significance.

January 1956 found Sterling St. John in trouble with County Auditor Edgecomb. As part of an expanded port promotion program, the director had proposed and been granted authority to hire a public-relations man. In a "secret" memorandum to his commissioners, the port director complained that political pressure was being put upon him to hire a local person, while he preferred to hire outside of Wayne County in order to avoid any political taint. The contents of the memorandum became known to County Auditor Edgecomb, and he took this as an opportunity to display publicly his indignation over any hint that politics could play a role in the county's hiring system. Apparently the memorandum had included disparaging statements concerning politicians, and Edgecomb cited these statements as an affront to himself, fellow county auditors, and all members of the Board of Supervisors. With a merit system only a little over ten years old, county officials were still sensitive to hints of political influence in hiring.

Hard on the heels of this incident, during the last week in January, the port director presented his program for the coming year. County officials greeted the program with varying degrees of disenchantment. Edgecomb was "completely disappointed"; County Budget Director Alfred Pelham found the report too general and a "rehash of old data," with no specific plans for action; and Detroit Councilman Edward Connor, also chairman of the County Board of Supervisors, was indignant over the lack of progress that was indicated. The program was meager. It called for additional studies to inventory current facilities and future needs, the preparation of a waterfront zoning ordinance, and a publicity and education campaign. Additional staff were requested to carry out the program. Since the reaction to St. John's memorandum on political influence had come the day before the program report was released, it is difficult to determine whether the program report was being criticized on its merits or because of irritation stirred up by the memorandum, but in any event Sterling St. John was in trouble with county politicians. He did, however, have the support of a majority of his commissioners, who complained in a ten-page statement that the county budget director and the county auditors had cut their budget request from $140,000 to $90,000. Support was also forthcoming from the Lakes Overseas Agents Association, composed of Detroit representatives of overseas lines, who gave St. John a vote of confidence and asserted that he was hampered by lack of staff.

A week later, Connor, chairman of the Board of Supervisors, held a "peace conference" attended by the Port Commission and its director, influential supervisors, Pelham, and others. This meeting ended with everyone shaking hands and agreeing to "work together for a finer port." The Board of Commerce's Willis Hall attended this meeting as a member of the Board of Supervisors'

Port Committee. He had not joined in the criticism of St. John, and he did assist in the hand-shaking resolution of the controversy.

But the era of good feeling did not last long. A month later Port Director St. John and Commissioner Lowe, the private terminal executive, publicly supported a bill that would revise the state tax laws so as to exempt from local personal-property taxation products in a warehouse or dock facility in transit to another state. It was variously estimated that this would cost the city of Detroit from $500,000 to $1,500,000 a year in lost tax revenue. Detroit's mayor, Albert Cobo, all nine councilmen and eighty-three members of the County Board of Supervisors joined in criticizing the port director for his support of this bill. To St. John, the bill made sense, since it would encourage shipping through the Port of Detroit by eliminating the tax on goods temporarily stored there. The state legislature and the governor agreed with the port director, for the bill was passed and signed, but local officials were not pleased by the port director's continued support for the legislation.

The Detroit News Panel Report. The Detroit News was impatient with the progress towards port development. The *News* had been a vigorous supporter of the seaway and was now backing immediate port development to take advantage of it. During April 1956, the *News* engaged a panel of five port experts to review local port facilities and report on their findings. The panel was composed of Harry C. Brockel, municipal port director, Milwaukee; Bernard J. Caughlin, general manager, Los Angeles Harbor Department; Ernest B. Griffith, general manager, Toronto Harbor Commissioners; N. T. Koomans, director of port authorities, Rotterdam, The Netherlands; Captain T. L. Lewis, assistant general manager, New Orleans Dock Board; and G. H. Pouder, executive vice president, Baltimore Association of Commerce. The panel's report appeared in the *News* in four installments between April 24 and 30 and was reprinted in a single document, *The Port of Detroit*, from which the following quotations were taken.

The panel noted that the Port of Detroit was "typical of an unplanned, essentially industrial waterfront" which had developed without the aid of planning and regulation to get the maximum benefit from waterfront uses. It then focused upon the immediate problem, which was considered to be "the challenge of making the transition from a traditional lake port to a combined lake and ocean port, with facilities and services adequate for a diversified and growing foreign commerce."

To pinpoint the problem, the panel recognizes that the Port of Detroit is fairly well equipped to accommodate present and prospective bulk cargo movements, including essential raw materials moving in bulk.

. . . .

It is apparent that the principal deficiency in the physical facilities of the Port of Detroit is in the field of general cargo terminals to accommodate the industry and consumers of Michigan.

It is also apparent that the principal area of community disagreement, and, in fact, a rather considerable controversy, revolves around the questions as to what steps shall be taken to correct Detroit's present deficiency in general cargo terminals, and whose responsibility it is to correct that deficiency.

. . . .

The panel is unable to agree with local interests who contend that the port is presently well equipped and is functioning efficiently in the field of overseas general cargo accommodation.

. . . .

The handling of high-value general cargo is the most lucrative of all port operations. This is the type of cargo for which ports everywhere most vigorously compete. It is this class of cargo which stimulates regular shipping services by modern vessels. It is this class of cargo which generates community income through the well-paid services of stevedores, longshoremen, terminal operators, warehousing, customs brokers, freight forwarders, steamship agents, ship chandlers, ship repair services and other specialists.

. . . .

In a word, it is cargo which creates prestige and profit for the port and encourages maximum development of ship services to a wide range of international ports. It is job opportunity to the community to a remarkable degree and a trade incentive of the highest order.

. . . .

Unless this community has the assurance, within the year, that private enterprise will fill this serious gap, the Detroit Port Commission should be empowered to proceed with the expedited planning and development of adequate port terminal facilities to accommodate the prospective cargo and vessel requirements of the port.

. . . .

The powers, prestige, and resources of government in practically all areas of the world have been dedicated to the development of strong and efficient port gateways, because of the obvious public interest involved and because of the favorable, economically stimulating effect of intelligent port development upon the commerce of a city, a region, or a nation.

Having pointed to the need for general cargo facilities and the responsibility of government for developing these facilities, the panel proceeded to evaluate the Port of Detroit Commission.

At the root of the Detroit port problem is the apparent lack of public acceptance of the Port of Detroit Commission.

. . . .

It would appear to the panel that this lack of acceptance, particularly with other units of government, is primarily due to the Port Commission's having continually reached out for added powers, without having solidly established itself by performance or having utilized the limited authority available to it. It also appears to the panel that it is only within very recent time that an effort has been made by the commission along the lines of professional port development and planning. In any case, the net result is a totally static condition in the Port of Detroit.

The panel recommended that the budget of the Port Commission be increased to permit the hiring of additional professional staff, that the Board of Supervisors grant to the commission the authority to use the permissive tax levy available under the enabling act, that the commission be authorized to issue revenue bonds, and that the power to appoint commissioners be taken from the Board of Supervisors and made a responsibility of the governor and/or mayor. These recommendations were designed to give the port authority more autonomy.

The panel report carefully refrained from pointing to individuals or groups in the community, but the *News* editorial on April 24, the day the first installment appeared, was less restrained:

These findings [of the panel] suggest, to us at least, that the Board of Commerce could do no greater service to the community than to get out of the port planning picture.

This is not the board which, over the years and under Harvey Campbell, fought magnificently for the seaway and for countless other great civic causes.

. . . .

Our present port plight reveals the board in another and incredibly meaner role. In the name of private enterprise, it would protect the immediate advantage of a handful of its members, to the vast ultimate damage of the whole community of free enterprisers in an expanding port situation.

. . . .

We suggest then that the board abandon its maneuver of fronting for the interests of a few at the expense of the many. The whole case for private enterprise is stultified by so nearsighted a view.

We suggest that it call off its spokesman ("eager and uninformed," in the happy phrase of one of our panel group), who talks up the port's future on the one hand and talks it down on the other.

We suggest the board confine itself to its natural role of providing trade data for its clients and drumming up new industry and commerce in the port area. We suggest it leave port development to others of more vision and larger faith.

The *News* panel devotes a large middle section of its report to the Port Commission. The commission is conspicuously the weakest of all local agencies of government. And this, we believe, is in large part by design.

When more than one influential figure in our port situation has said that a weak commission and enfeebled port direction are perfectly suited to his purposes and convenience, the commission is hobbled from the start.

The editorial proceeded to recommend that "figures of such stature as instantly to command the community's faith" be appointed to the commission.

The panel report provided ammunition for those who felt that the Port Commission was dragging its feet. City Controller Witherspoon, chairman of the Board of Supervisors' Port Committee, attacked the commission's decision to give private enterprise until 1958 to provide facilities, and Detroit Councilman Louis Miriani, serving as acting mayor during Mayor Cobo's absence on vacation, backed Witherspoon and added criticism of the commission's efforts to reduce warehouse taxes. From his vacation retreat, Mayor Cobo announced that the panel report demanded action and that he would get action when he returned to Detroit. Even Sterling St. John found use for the report in support of adding some staff positions to his agency's roster, and he submitted a request for them to a joint meeting of the Port Commission and the Board of Supervisors' Port Committee on May 7.

But before this meeting, a significant event occurred. The Board of Supervisors voted forty-five to thirty-seven to appoint Troy H. Browning, president of a steamship company, to succeed Ferris Fitch on the Port Commission. Browning, nominated by Detroit Councilman Miriani, had the support of the powerful Detroit delegation to the Board of Supervisors, and Fitch, who had decided to permit himself to be nominated in order to oppose Browning before the board, was, in effect, forcing a vote on the commission's policy and its director. Browning was an active critic of both, and his appointment meant that a severe challenge was in store for both the policy and the director.

The Last Days of Sterling St. John. At the May 7 joint meeting of the Port Commission and the Board of Supervisors' Port Committee, Port Director St. John presented a supplementary request for additional staff personnel. Evidently he had not cleared this with his commissioners, since they appeared surprised by it. Even Commissioner Lowe, who was considered to be a St. John supporter, was critical of the director for not having first cleared the matter with the commissioners. Both Connor and Miriani pointed to this as added evidence of St. John's incompetence as an administrator. Connor commented that he "would make a good second man" but was not up to the director's role. Miriani was quoted, "We will never get anywhere as long as this St. John is around." The Port Committee pressed the commission for specific plans and gave the commission a deadline of ninety days in which to produce specific plans for new docks, berths, sheds, and warehouses. Commenting on the lack of these facilities, the *News* panel had said: "It is almost incredible . . . to find such minuscule and inadequate facilities in a large center of population, in a world trade center of the first magnitude, and in a community which prides itself on being a port of consequence." At this joint meeting it was decided to call upon N. R. Danielian, president of the Great Lakes–St. Lawrence Association, to provide some guidance on suggested steps for a port development program.

Danielian was quick to react to this request. In a memorandum dated May 8, 1956, the day after the meeting, he outlined specific steps for a port development program with the end objective to "route the largest possible amount of tonnage through the Port of

Detroit." The following summary of the steps and timetable appeared at the end of the memorandum:

1. Approval of new facility requirements by September 1, 1956.
    Related activities leading to this decision:
    (a) Re-evaluation of traffic estimates.
    (b) Inventory of private facilities.
    (c) Conversion of traffic estimates to facility requirements.
2. Approval of method of financing by January 1, 1957.
    Related activities leading to this decision:
    (a) Examination of *firm* plans of private operators to expand their facilities.
    (b) Exploration of the law and procedures necessary to select the most advantageous type of financing.
3. Approval of site for new facilities by January 1, 1957.
    Related activities leading to this decision:
    (a) Confidential survey of sites.
    (b) Preparation of legal steps necessary for acquisition.
4. Start of construction of facilities by September 1, 1957.
    Related activities leading to this:
    (a) Preparation of detailed designs.
    (b) Condemnation and land acquisition January–August 1957.
    (c) Financing—sale of bonds and attendant activities, January–August 1957.
    (d) Letting of contracts for construction.

The Danielian memorandum provided the precise, step-by-step program that the Port Commission and its director had not been able to produce, and it was formally adopted by the Port Commission and the Board of Supervisors' Port Committee as the timetable for port development. The commission and the Board of Supervisors formally requested the Great Lakes–St. Lawrence Association to carry out the necessary survey work for the first step, i.e., determining facility requirements based upon a re-evaluation of traffic estimates and available private facilities. These decisions were reached by the middle of May, and Danielian promised to have his report ready in September.

For Port Director Sterling St. John matters were rapidly coming to a head. By turning to an outside agency, the Great Lakes–St. Lawrence Association, for help in outlining a program, the Board of Supervisors had made it clear that they had no confidence in the Port Commission staff. In fact, the manner in which the board's Port Committee had taken over the port issue demonstrated their lack of confidence in the Port Commission. Although he had made his peace with his commissioners for bypassing them in the development of his report on additional staff needs, St. John could anticipate a radical change in the commission on July 1, the date when Troy Browning's appointment would become effective. Of the five commissioners, Fitch was St. John's most ardent supporter, but St. John had, in addition, the support of Alvan Macauley, vice president of the National Bank of Detroit, who had served on the Port Commission since it was first established in 1933, and of David Lowe. Commissioner John Basso was the most openly opposed to St. John, but Henry Sullivan, an assistant to the president of the Detroit Edison Company, was considered to be lukewarm toward the port director. Just prior to the June 27 meeting of the commission, Fitch's last, Lowe announced that he too would retire from the commission at that meeting, and Troy Browning let it be known that he would resign from the commission if St. John were not fired. Browning promised that his first act as a commissioner would be to submit a resolution for St. John's discharge.

The June 27 meeting of the Port Commission brought to an end another period in the port's history. It was the last meeting for Commissioner Fitch, who over the years had met frustration in his attempt to obtain for the port agency the Detroit-Windsor tunnel. He had felt that with a revenue-producing source the Port District would have been able to develop some fiscal autonomy, which would have permitted the undertaking of additional projects, such as port promotion. Commissioner Fitch had also believed that private terminal facilities were adequate and would be for some time, and that no haste was required in building public terminal facilities. Retiring Commissioner Lowe shared this latter opinion. He had an optimistic view of the expansion programs planned by private terminal owners such as himself. He had been and continued to be a ready source for quotations concerning such plans. (For example, on May 4, 1956, he was quoted in *The Detroit News* as having said that the private terminal operators were ready to expand facilities so that by 1959 they could handle fourteen large ocean-going ships simultaneously.) This was also the last meeting for Sterling St. John, who turned in his resignation "to save the commission further embarrassment in its work. I want the commission to have a free hand to develop the Port of Detroit as it sees fit." Commissioner Basso's reaction was: "Now we will choose a director who is aggressive and decisive and has the confidence of the commission."

Sterling St. John's tenure as director of the Port of Detroit had lasted about thirteen months. Two weeks after his resignation, he had this to say, as quoted in the *Detroit Times* (July 13, 1956):

> When I resigned two weeks ago someone called my position untenable. I agree, the position of executive director is untenable for anyone under present conditions, no matter who fills the job, or how much they pay him, or how able a politician he may be. This is because the Port Commission does not have powers commensurate with its responsibilities. There are too many bosses to tell the commissioners whom they can employ and how much they can pay. They are all port experts, and there are scores of them. A new man will have peace for a while, but then someone will object to something and the sharpshooting will start all over again.

A New Port Director Arrives—and Departs

A New Policy. The brevity and turbulence of Sterling St. John's career as port director did not deter applicants for the vacated post. In July the Civil Service Commission increased the pay range for the position to a starting salary of $17,500 and a maximum salary of $20,860, making it the fourth highest paid position in the county classified service. By August 1, eleven applications were on hand. Again the position was offered to Robert Wylie, who again, after some hesitation, turned it down. By August 9, some eighteen hours after he had been called to come to Detroit for an interview, the port director at Olympia, Washington, Carlis J. Stettin, was offered and accepted appointment as director of the Port of Detroit, effective September 16, 1956. The Port Commission, with the aid of the Civil Service Commission, had wasted little time in filling the position.

By September 1956, the Port Commission had changed complexion. Troy Browning, an active advocate of public port development, was now chairman. Robert Holmes, a Teamsters Union official, had been appointed by the Board of Supervisors to succeed David Lowe, and he, too, supported public port development. For the first time in its history, the Port Commission was composed of individuals prepared to support an aggressive program of port development. The commission also had the support of two of the city's three major daily newspapers. *The Detroit News,* bolstered by its panel report, was a persistent advocate of speeding the construction of port facilities, and so was the *Detroit Times,* with somewhat less enthusiasm and space. The *Detroit Free Press* had in the past and continued to find the arguments of the Board of Commerce in favor of private port development more convincing.

The ninety-day deadline that the Board of Supervisors' Port Committee had given the Port Commission on May 6 to come up with specific plans was lost in the shuffle of resignations and personnel changes. But true to its promise, in September the Great Lakes–St. Lawrence Association delivered a report on seaway traffic potential and an inventory of existing port facilities. This report carried great weight because the organization that produced it carried weight. The secretary of the association was the Board of Commerce's Gerald E. Warren, and included among the association's directors were Mayor Cobo and prominent Detroit businessmen. The association's estimates of seaway traffic were derived by a method somewhat different from that used by the KTAM consultants; nevertheless, the predicted seaway traffic of 300,000 to 340,000 tons for the Port of Detroit by 1959, with the amount rising to around 1,000,000 tons annually by 1965, was almost identical with the KTAM projections for overseas general cargo commerce. The association's findings concerning the adequacy of existing facilities were summarized and evaluated in the January 1960 report of the mayor's Waterfront Development Committee:

The Great Lakes–St. Lawrence Association evaluated the annual capacity of the Detroit installations for general cargo as follows, taking into account their age, design, water depth, efficiency under normal working hours and conditions, and other characteristics:

	Tons
Detroit Harbor Terminals, Inc.	96,000
Detroit Marine Terminals, Inc.	60,000
Great Lakes Engineering Works	25,000
Nicholson Terminal and Dock Company	25,000
TOTAL FOR EXISTING TERMINALS	206,000

The figures on capacity given above have been criticized by the local port operators, who assert that they have actually handled substantially larger tonnages than shown and that the capacity of their facilities should be given a higher rating. It is recognized that a determination of this kind is necessarily a judgment figure and not subject to precise mathematical calculation. However, in the view of the committee, the report of the Great Lakes–St. Lawrence Association represents a competent and carefully prepared study and the findings are entitled to weight. They are also supported generally by the report of the panel of national and international port experts who reviewed the port facilities of Detroit in April 1956.

The association thus found existing facilities to be inadequate to handle the anticipated seaway tonnage but more than adequate to handle general cargo available up to the opening of the seaway in 1959. That additional facilities would be needed was, of course, obvious, but the association's report did not make specific recommendations concerning whether additional facilities should be made under private or public auspices. It did, however, recommend that first priority be given to the provision of a four-berth terminal summarized in the Waterfront Development Committee report as consisting of:

> . . . two open-pier berths, each 500 feet long, and two additional 500-foot berths, each supported by 60,000 square feet of transit shed area. . . . This type of terminal . . . , with adequate equipment could handle 84,000 tons per season through each transit berth and 96,000 tons per season through each open-pier berth—for a total terminal capacity of 360,000 tons per seaway season.

As the Port of Detroit's new director, Carlis J. Stettin, took over the reins in the fall of 1956, he had the support of a commission dedicated to take action, and he had in hand a report from a respected agency spelling out a need for action. At forty-seven, Stettin had had a number of years experience in shipping and port operations. At Olympia, Washington, he had been the director of a public port agency with some degree of political autonomy and with revenue-producing facilities. He was not greeted with the same amount of banqueting and civic enthusiasm that had accompanied Sterling St. John's arrival, and the Board of Commerce was especially cool.

Soon after the Great Lakes–St. Lawrence Association report had been submitted, Port Commission Chairman Browning and Port Director Stettin issued public statements that the commission should proceed to build the general cargo terminal facilities that the association's report said would be required. Stettin was for immediate action. "We are being surveyed and reported into a coma," he said, and went on to point out that the four-berth terminal facility recommended by the association would be too risky an investment for private terminal owners. By November 1, Stettin had had his first clash with the Board of Commerce's Gerald Warren. Warren had criticized Stettin's public port stand, and Stettin's reaction was to threaten to resign. The Port Commission backed its new director, and Browning, himself a member of the Board of Commerce, criticized Warren as one of the hired help of the board who "make very big shots of themselves by fighting any type of program."

In contrast to Port Director St. John, who had been slow to produce specific plans for port development, Port Director Stettin disclosed, on November 19, an elaborate seventy-million-dollar, twenty-year port development program. The first stage called for construction of facilities to handle fifteen ships and would cost $27,000,000. Details of design and location as well as financing were vague, but, as one official put it, it was "good to have a port director who is not a defeatist." Fiscal officers pointed out that it would take faith and credit bonds and an additional tax to pay for such a program, all of which would require the approval of the Board of Supervisors and the county voters. Willis Hall, as manager of the Board of Commerce and as a supervisor, objected to the program, but by March 1957, the Board of Supervisors had approved an additional appropriation of $91,000 to the Port Commission for the purpose of conducting a port survey that would result in a master plan with a step-by-step program for development.

The appropriation was less than that requested by the Port Commission and $26,000 less than the amount approved by the County Board of Auditors. As it turned out, the appropriation was more than adequate, since the port agency continued to demonstrate a chronic inability to spend appropriated funds, using only $32,000 for the survey. In returning the surplus some time later (December 1958), the Port Commission explained:

> The Board of Supervisors appropriated so much money for a certain number of consulting positions to supplement the commission staff, and the per consultant allotment was not sufficient to hire the necessary consultants to do the project, so none were hired at all.

In the Board of Commerce's weekly publication, *The Detroiter* (May 27, 1957), Stettin outlined how he planned to use the additional funds:

> In the very near future, the commission will hire engineering, legal, financial, and real-estate counsel to prepare specific proposals which, it is planned, will be taken to the voters of Wayne County this fall. This will be done with full confidence that our enlightened electorate will approve it. It has been the goal of the commission to provide five berths for the larger ocean vessels by the time the first one arrives in the spring of 1959.

During the summer of 1957, a local firm of consulting engineers was hired to develop detailed plans for the first stage of the program. By the beginning of September, the Port Commission was ready to present a plan to the Board of Supervisors and the public. At a joint meeting attended by the board's Port Committee, its Ways and Means Committee, and the Port Commission, the port plan was unveiled. It called for berthing facilities to handle four large ocean-going ships and three transit sheds with a total capacity of 162,000 square feet of covered storage space on a thirty-two-acre site which included Riverside Park, a city park. With some modifications, this was the type of facility recommended by the Great Lakes–St. Lawrence Association report. The project cost was estimated to be $13,500,000, which would be raised through faith and credit bonds. The terminal would be built and operated by the Port of Detroit. Pointing to the planning and consultation that had gone into the proposal, Stettin said, "It is this or nothing. . . . All of the experts agree that this is it."

Willis Hall, member of both the Port Committee and the Ways and Means Committee, raised numerous objections. He claimed that the law required that the port authority finance its projects from its own revenue, not through faith and credit bonds, and he objected to a part of the plan that called for office space for the Port Commission and additional office space for rental. Detroit councilmen, especially William Rogell, objected to taking Riverside Park, and Hall also questioned the legality of converting the park to port use. It soon became evident to Stettin and his supporters on the Port Commission that the plan would never reach the voters in its present form.

A Port Proposal Goes to the Voters.   To become operational, the port plan had to go through these steps: approval by the Board of Supervisors' Port Committee; approval by the board's Ways and Means Committee; three-fifths majority approval by the Board of Supervisors (since the plan required authority to issue faith and credit bonds); and finally, voter approval of the bond issue and additional tax to pay for the port expansion. The first step, approval by the Port Committee, was accomplished on September 11, but not without cost. The program was reduced to two berths and one transit shed, the office building space was reduced, and Riverside Park was eliminated as part of the site. These changes cut the cost to $9,500,000. Detroit's councilmen, Miriani and Connor, both of whom a year earlier had been critical of St. John's lack of concrete progress in port development, supported the reduction. Councilman Rogell was pleased to have the Riverside Park site preserved, but Willis Hall could take the credit for successfully whittling down the proposal.

If this was a blow to Carlis Stettin, who a week earlier had labeled the plan "this or nothing," he contained his disappointment and went along with the reduced program. On September 12, the Ways and Means Committee, which included key members of the Port Committee, endorsed the decision of the Port Committee and sent the reduced program before the full Board of Supervisors, where it received unanimous approval on September 16. Two propositions would be submitted to county voters. The first would authorize issuance of $9,500,000 in faith and credit bonds to pay for land acquisition and port construction. Voting on this proposition would be limited to property owners, and it would take a three-fifths majority of those voting on the proposition to approve it. The second proposition authorized a tax increase of sixteen cents per thousand dollars of assessed valuation for sixteen years to pay off the bonds and required only a simple majority for approval.

The unanimous approval by the Board of Supervisors of the port proposals on September 16, the deadline for approving proposals for a special election, gave the Port Commission and supporters of the port program seven weeks in which to build voter support. Since it was not a general election year, the voter could concentrate upon the few issues before him, but it had the possible disadvantage of attracting only a light vote. The port commissioners and Port Director Stettin immediately went to work to marshal support. *The Detroit News* was a powerful ally, devoting generous amounts of space to news items, special features, and editorials intended to build interest in the port issue and support for it. Endorsements were obtained from major interest groups. Organized labor supported the port proposals, and so did the board of governors of the Propeller Club of Detroit. The latter was considered especially significant because its members were engaged in Great Lakes shipping rather than foreign overseas shipping, and thus they would derive no direct personal benefit from an installation designed to serve the overseas general cargo trade. Another significant endorsement came from the Riverside Development Division of the mayor's Detroit Tomorrow Committee. The committee included industrialists and business and labor leaders, with the Riverfront Development Division chaired by Thomas Reid, director of civic affairs for the Ford Motor Company. By the middle of October, no significant opposition had appeared, but the Board of Commerce had not yet been officially heard from.

On October 16, the Board of Commerce sent a letter to its members informing them that the board of directors had voted not to support the Port Commission's proposal because it conflicted with the board's policy on business and government. The letter noted that Thomas Reid had opposed this decision, arguing that "good work had been done by reducing the original $13,500,000 proposal to $9,500,000—the minimum for any public port development," but the plea of the Ford executive did not succeed in winning over the directors. The policy with which the port proposal was in conflict stated that when government engaged in competition with private business or business-type enterprises, capital costs, interest, taxes, and other operating costs should be included in the charges for the service, and any loss should be carried in the budget in a manner "so that the taxpaying public will be fully informed of the inability of government to operate the enterprise on a self-supporting basis."

The action of the directors of the Board of Commerce was no surprise, but it had been hoped that they would stay out of the port issue. Although Willis Hall had consistently opposed public port development and had succeeded in reducing the size of the project from four to two berths, he had gone along with his fellow supervisors in their unanimous approval of the motion to submit the proposals to the voters. The fact that Hall and the board's port specialist, Gerald Warren, opposed public development did not necessarily mean that the directors would go along with their staff. The board had been a long-time supporter of the seaway, and many of its members anticipated economic benefits to the community and their own businesses when the seaway opened. Three of the port commissioners, Browning, Macauley, and Henry Sullivan, were Board of Commerce members but not directors.

Browning objected to the directors' decision, contending that it did not represent the membership of the Board of Commerce but was the result of the influence of staff members Hall and Warren. This line of argument was taken up by supporters of the port proposal. It was even suggested that the directors themselves did not support their own decision, since it was claimed that eight of the twenty-four were absent, and of the sixteen present when the vote was taken some were silent and noncommittal. But when *The Detroit News* conducted a telephone poll of the directors, they found that a majority of them did support the decision. The following comments were quoted as typical reasons given for the stand: "We may need these facilities at some future date, but not yet; private enterprise can take care of our needs for some time;

existing private terminals are operating at less than capacity; the proposal is socialism." The directors were not seeking to avoid responsibility for their decision.

The upshot of Browning's assault on the board's opposition and Hall's role in it was a televised debate between them held a week before the election. This was not the debate Browning had wanted. He had proposed meeting the board's president, Ross Roy, an advertising executive, in a debate on the issue, but Roy had declined in favor of Willis Hall, who was eager for the opportunity. Browning felt that the proper level of debate should be on the non-staff level, i.e., port commissioner vs. Board of Commerce director, and he took Roy's refusal as another indication that the decision had been Hall's and did not represent the board's membership. Browning ended up having to face Hall. As might be expected when two strong personalities, each convinced of the righteousness of his own cause and convinced of the selfish interest of his opponent, meet in verbal battle, the debate provided excellent entertainment. Hall was a much more skilled debater than Browning, but each succeeded in irritating the other to the extent that a heated argument continued after the program ended. The consensus seemed to be that the debate demonstrated only that Troy Browning and Willis Hall disliked each other and that Hall was the better debater. While the debate was not an adequate vehicle for exploring the issues—the adequacy of port facilities, the tonnage to be expected from the seaway, the economic benefits to the community to be derived from overseas general cargo trade, and the economics of financing port development through private development, revenue bonds, or faith and credit bonds, it may have moved some uncommitted persons to take sides on the port question, and it certainly attracted attention to it.

As election day neared, the port supporters received two assists. At a meeting of the board of directors of the Great Lakes–St. Lawrence Association held in Detroit on October 25, one of the port commissioners, Henry Sullivan, asked the association's president, Danielian, if he felt that the port proposal was in line with the recommendations made in the association's report of the previous year. Danielian replied that the project was in line with the report's technical recommendations and that nothing had happened since the report was filed to change the opinion expressed in it that additional facilities were required for the seaway trade. A few days later, on October 30, the executive board of the Detroit Tomorrow Committee endorsed the port proposal. This endorsement was a significant counter to the disapproval expressed by the Board of Commerce, since the committee contained leaders from big business and industry as well as labor. The Detroit Tomorrow Committee represented top community leadership, and its endorsement could be expected to carry weight.

In presenting its case for a public general cargo terminal, the Port Commission stressed the following points. The KTAM report and the Great Lakes–St. Lawrence Association report had both predicted that overseas general cargo tonnage would increase to around 300,000 tons annually with the opening of the seaway and continue upward to about 1,000,000 tons annually. Additional facilities would be needed to handle this cargo, and these facilities would not be provided through private development. William P. Young, president of Detroit Harbor Terminals, Inc., a private terminal currently handling most of the port's overseas general cargo, concurred with this view. He acknowledged that nationally most port facilities were controlled by public agencies, and he did not oppose the proposed development. Young said that without a guarantee of tonnage- and dollar-volume of business he was in no position to develop the needed facility. The Port Commission emphasized that port expansions planned or under way at sister lake ports such as Chicago, Cleveland, Toledo, and Buffalo were all being financed by government. Finally, the commission stressed the economic benefits to be derived from an expanded overseas general cargo trade. An often quoted figure was a U.S. Department of Commerce estimate that a port area derived a direct economic benefit of $12.50 for every ton of cargo handled, and the KTAM report had said that indirect economic benefits were twice the dollar value of the direct benefits. Based on these estimates, the additional seaway tonnage would bring economic benefits to the community far in excess of the cost to taxpayers, about eighty cents a year for the average home owner, for construction of the terminal. Informed community leaders in government, business, industry, and labor agreed with these points.

Opposition to the port proposal was centered in Willis Hall. The Federated Civic Associations of Northwest Detroit also formally opposed the port, but they had no spokesman like Hall, whose position they adopted. It was evident that Hall did not represent Detroit business in general in this controversy, nor did he represent all members of the Board of Commerce. Since the board's members were not polled, it cannot be ascertained how they stood. But while it was easier to identify those he did not represent than to identify those he did, port supporters generally assumed that the traditional foes of the seaway, the railroads, were behind Hall.

Hall contended that there was no need for a public facility—the tonnage estimates were overoptimistic, and private facilities could be expanded to accommodate any additional business that did develop. Furthermore, he maintained that if a public facility were to be built, it should be financed by revenue bonds, so that those who benefited from the facility would pay for it. He complained that the port proposal had been hastily planned and rushed through the Port Committee and the Board of Supervisors without proper time for study. On a number of occasions, he accused *The Detroit News* of sponsoring the port development as a "pet project," and he asserted that businessmen and political officials were being pressured by the *News* to give their support. He criticized Troy Browning, a ship owner, for serving on the Port Commission, since Browning had a personal interest in port development, and he claimed that Stettin and the Port Commission were engaged in empire building; the Port Commission and its director should confine themselves to promoting trade for the port. Hall's views were given extraordinarily good newspaper coverage not only in the *Free Press*, which was sympathetic with them, but also in the *News*, so that the public was well exposed to arguments on both sides of the controversy.

The special election on the port proposal was held on Tuesday, November 5, 1957. Although the port issue had been before the public but seven weeks, it had received prominent attention in the local news media. The dramatic overtones of the Browning-Hall conflict had been played up and could be expected to attract attention. The total number of votes cast on the proposition to increase taxes, open to all voters, was 286,516. For comparison, a year later, in a general gubernatorial election, 806,376 votes were cast in Wayne County. On the bonding proposition, voting on which was limited to property owners, 237,017 votes were cast. Thus 82 percent of the total number who went to the polls were property owners. It required a three-fifths majority to approve the bonding proposition. The vote was 139,681 for the bonds and 97,336 against, or a little more than 1 percent under the necessary 60 percent. An additional 2,500 favorable votes would have carried the bond issue. The tax proposal, which required a simple majority vote to carry, was defeated; 130,516 for the tax to 156,000 against it. This vote was not so close, with 54 percent voting against the tax increase. A closer analysis of the vote revealed some interesting differences. The out-county vote (outside the city of Detroit) had been light (28,357 on the bond proposition), but it had been negative compared with the city vote, which taken by itself would have barely approved the bond proposition. It was evident that the suburbs were less enthusiastic over the port proposal than were the core-city voters, but a majority of both city and out-county voters had turned down the increase in tax millage, without which the bond approval would have had little meaning.

The port director and the commissioners were disappointed but not disheartened. Chairman Browning placed blame for the defeat on Willis Hall and the Board of Commerce but pointed to the narrow margin of defeat on the bond issue as an encouraging sign. Stettin and the commissioners felt that they had not "sold" the out-county people as effectively as they should have, but that that would be remedied in the next campaign. The commission did not take the vote as a sign that it should abandon plans for a public port. Board of Commerce President Ross Roy interpreted the results as public agreement with the board that port development should be financed by the users and not by the taxpayers.

A Second Port Proposal Goes to the Voters. During the first few months of 1958, a number of key personnel changes took place among those involved in the port issue. Late in February, Troy Browning resigned from the Port Commission because of "heavy business commitments." Willis Hall and others had criticized

Browning, a steamship owner, for serving on the commission because of a conflict of interest between the commission's jurisdiction
and Commissioner Browning's business. Hall had supported a bill,
introduced by Republican state legislators, which would prohibit
anyone with a business interest that could benefit from port development from serving on the Port Commission. The legislation
was worded in broad terms, and critics pointed out that it would
prevent almost any local businessman or labor official from serving. The bill died in committee, but it did serve to embarrass
Browning and put him in a defensive position. In addition, having
been chairman of the commission during its unsuccessful campaign in which he himself had become an issue, Browning may
have felt that his resignation would help the commission by removing himself as a point of contention. There is no question that
the time and energy he had devoted to his Port Commission responsibilities had intruded upon his private business life.

A few weeks after Browning's resignation, the new commission
chairman, Henry Sullivan, announced that he would retire. There
may have been public port supporters who welcomed the Browning resignation because he had become a "controversial figure";
but Sullivan, a Detroit Edison Company executive, was highly regarded among top-echelon community leaders, and his departure
could not be neutralized by imputations of conflict of interest. His
appointment to the commission had been greeted with the observation that it was the type of appointment that would raise the prestige of the commission, and his resignation raised eyebrows, particularly since it occurred during a period when Sullivan was at
odds with other commissioners over Stettin's personnel policies.
Stettin had recommended, with the commission's approval, that
the position of port relations executive, the euphemism for public-
relations officer, be abolished and a new position of administrative
assistant to the director be established. Stettin gave as his reason
that since there was no port to publicize, a publicist was not needed
on the staff. The abolishment of the public-relations post was a
sensitive move, since the position was one that Sterling St. John
had fought to have established, and he had then tangled with
County Auditor Edgecomb over the appointment, which eventually went, as Edgecomb had insisted, to a local publicist. In

requesting that the commission reconsider the move to abolish the position, Sullivan related that this decision "has raised a lot of hell in town" and that he had never before been so pressed by members of the Board of Supervisors over a decision that, he felt, might ruin the commission's program. But the commissioners, led by Basso and Holmes, supported Stettin. Sullivan resigned.

Browning and Sullivan, each in a different way, had been strong members of the commission. The two new commissioners were Thomas Lane, an engineer and president of his own industrial scale firm, and Harry Meisner, an attorney and ex-naval officer. Upon their appointment, both stated that they were in favor of public port development. Neither of the two new commissioners had experience in port matters and community planning comparable to their predecessors, nor did they have comparably established community leadership roles. Commissioners Basso and Holmes assumed the leadership of the newly composed commission.

Important personnel changes were also taking place in the Board of Supervisors' Port Committee. Detroit's new mayor, Louis Miriani, had picked a new city controller. Former City Controller John Witherspoon, who had been chairman of the Board of Supervisors' Port Committee, lost his seat on the board, and the Port Committee chairmanship went to Detroit Councilman William Patrick. In all, seven new members were appointed to the Port Committee by the chairman of the Board of Supervisors, Terry L. Troutt, an out-county supervisor. In making his selections, Troutt deliberately chose members favorable to a public port. Out-county supervisors whose jurisdictions had voted against the port proposals were replaced by supervisors from areas that had supported it. Miriani asked to serve on the committee so that the influence of Detroit could be concentrated in support of port development. The one outright opponent of a public port remaining on the committee was Willis Hall. According to Troutt, Hall was permitted to remain in order to have the opportunity to suggest alternative proposals, or, as Troutt put it, "to put up or shut up."

The changes in the Port Commission and the Board of Supervisors' Port Committee balanced each other, for, if the Port Commission was weakened by the loss of Browning and Sullivan, the Port Committee had been strengthened with proponents of a public port, including Detroit's mayor. At the time that the Port Committee was being reorganized to strengthen its support of the Port Commission, Stettin was involved in the elimination of the public-relations position, a move that annoyed a number of the supervisors. Stettin's success in accomplishing his staff change was evidence that his recommendations carried weight with both the commission and the board, but it did not improve his popularity among many supervisors, including Miriani, who was perturbed by Sullivan's resignation. The situation was fluid, and Stettin's balance was precarious.

By May (1958), serious attention began to be given to the formulation of another port proposal to be submitted to the voters in the November election. It was generally assumed that last year's proposal would be used, but, at the commission's request, Stettin took the proposal back to the consultants to see if the cost could be cut. Meanwhile, with the opening of the Great Lakes shipping season and with the seaway now but one year away, steady pressure was applied through speeches and special feature stories, particularly in *The Detroit News*, to point out that Detroit was lagging behind other Great Lakes ports in preparing for the seaway. Typical was a speech by the administrator of the federal government's St. Lawrence Seaway Development Corporation, Lewis Castle, before the Economic Club of Detroit, a weekly luncheon group that included top-echelon community leadership from all major areas of interest. Castle encouraged the use of public funds for port development and maintained that he could cite no large-scale successful private development. Willis Hall or others with his views were usually on hand on these occasions to challenge such statements or question their applicability to Detroit.

Late in May, William Young, president of Detroit Harbor Terminals, Inc., proposed, in a letter addressed to the chairman of the Port Commission, that the commission purchase 1,030 feet of river frontage adjacent to the terminal and lease it to his firm for fifty years. The estimated cost of the land acquisition was $850,000, and the letter suggested that the purchase be financed by the sale of revenue bonds secured by the rent from the lease. Detroit Harbor Terminals would pay the cost of improvements, which would be made over a period of time. Young estimated that current facilities were adequate to handle general cargo through 1959 and that the expanded facilities would provide berths for five ships up to five hundred feet in length. The *Free Press* greeted this move as the answer to the area's port needs.

Young's timing was excellent, since it arrived before the commission had approved a firm proposal. In deference to the strong role that the Board of Supervisors' Port Committee would play in the process of obtaining the necessary approvals for submitting a new proposal to the voters, Stettin had proposed that they meet jointly with the Port Commission. A joint meeting was held on June 4. Miriani made it clear that he was going to play a dominant role. He felt that the causes of last year's defeat were the lack of a documented case from the commission on the need for the project and lack of time to sell it to the voters. At his urging, it was agreed that a concrete plan should be ready for the joint committee by July 1. Stettin was also instructed to prepare an evaluation of the Young offer. A few days after this meeting, Stettin appeared on a local radio interview program and said that the Port Commission should be given more autonomy. He was careful not to offend the supervisors by his remarks, but his experience with the joint committee was ample evidence of the problem he faced in being held responsible by both the Port Commission and the Port Committee.

As the July 1 deadline approached, William Young prodded Stettin for an answer to the Detroit Harbor Terminals proposal. Stettin countered that there were a number of technical and legal points to be considered, but he promised that the Young offer would not be ignored. What Stettin sought were specific details and firm plans concerning what the firm intended to do with the property. The river frontage involved was the same frontage the commission planned to develop for its own terminal. On June 26, some of the details of the Detroit Harbor Terminals offer became known when a vice president of that firm appeared before the Port Commission and outlined his plans. He told the commissioners that Detroit Harbor Terminals would develop at first only 400 feet of dockage, which would increase the firm's capacity to three berths for 500-foot ships, and that "adequate transit sheds" would be constructed. The balance of the river frontage would be developed later as needed. The commission withheld any immediate evaluation of this proposal, but a few days later, on July 1, its own new proposal was made public.

A major change in the Port Commission's new plan was reduction in cost to $7,100,000, over $2,000,000 less than the previous proposal. The plans called for a general cargo terminal with berths for two ocean-going ships along a 1,080-foot wharf, two transit sheds with 114,000 square feet, plus the necessary heavy lift and other shore-side cargo handling facilities, on a twenty-seven-acre site. The whole was to be financed through the issuance of general obligation faith and credit bonds paid for by a special tax of eleven cents per thousand dollars of assessed valuation per year for seventeen years. The reduced cost resulted from changes in design which called for less expensive bulkheading and a reduction in the amount of office space. The economic recession then in progress had resulted in additional savings in cost of materials and over-all construction costs. If anything, the reduced cost created some embarrassment, since it exposed the commission to the charge that the previous year's plan was extravagant or carelessly formulated.

When it met on July 9, the Board of Supervisors' Port Committee did not take action on the commission's new proposal but requested a more detailed evaluation of the Young proposal prior to its July 31 meeting, so that the commission project could be compared with it. By mid-July, the commission was ready with its evaluation of the Young offer. The commission's main objections to the Young plan were that (1) it did not guarantee enough development to meet the expected tonnage; (2) the first stage, four-hundred-foot dock expansion, would provide space for only one additional large ocean-going vessel; (3) the site requested, nine acres, was too shallow to provide full development of the river frontage (the Young plan called for all of the river frontage in the commission's plan but less land for storage, transportation, and other dockside facilities); (4) the Young plan would not give the Port Commission the control over rates and terminal practices necessary to protect the public interest of the community at large; and (5) the plan was based on the false premise that general cargo tonnage would increase but gradually with the opening of the seaway. In short, the Port Commission found the Young plan inadequate and recommended that its own plan be approved for submission to the voters. Young, of course, disputed these conclusions, and he was joined by David Lowe, terminal operator and former port commissioner.

When the Port Committee met on July 31, the controversy had already reached major proportions. The six railroads serving the metropolitan area had sent to Port Committee Chairman Patrick a joint letter in which they stated their opposition to "any program which would favor a select few at the expense of all of the taxpayers," and "in addition, our opposition . . . is based . . . on our understandable desire to avoid any further competitive disadvantage in our own battle for tonnage." The Port Committee failed to clear the proposal at this meeting. Dearborn's Mayor Orville Hubbard, whose appointment to the Port Committee had been based upon his previous support of the public port, now changed his position and sided with Willis Hall in urging adoption of the Young proposal. At Hall's urging, the committee decided to postpone action until its August 11 meeting. Many of the port commissioners and supervisors were becoming convinced that the Young proposal was no more than a delaying tactic designed to keep the issue in the air until it was too late to include it on the November ballot.

Another postponement occurred on August 11, when the Port Committee decided to wait one more week in order to obtain a legal opinion on the Board of Supervisors' right to withhold issuance of the bonds, if approved, until needed. Finally, on August 18, the Port Committee approved the Port Commission's proposal for submission to the voters, but in a form that would give the Board of Supervisors the authority to determine when the bonds would be issued. Port Committee approval could be attributed largely to the efforts of Mayor Miriani, who caucused with the Detroit members of the Port Committee and instructed them to vote for the port proposal. He made it clear that he wanted the issue placed before the voters so that a decision could be reached and hinted that if the plan again failed, the city of Detroit might proceed with its own port development program. Only Hubbard and Hall voted against the plan in the Port Committee.

Time was passing. The Port Committee had taken nearly two

months to approve the port proposal. The attempt to have more time in which to promote the plan with the voters was being successfully frustrated. The Ways and Means Committee passed along the port proposal to the Board of Supervisors where the matter was voted on at a special meeting held on September 4. Only eighty-five of the one hundred and nine supervisors were present, and approval of the port proposal, since it included faith and credit bonding, required a three-fifths majority, or sixty-six affirmative votes. Ordinarily, the supervisors approved committee-adopted proposals with little opposition, but twenty-four negative votes were marshalled against the proposal through the efforts of Hubbard and Hall. Three Detroit council members, Blanche Parent Wise, Del Smith, and William Rogell, voted against the Port Commission's proposal, and so did five of their appointees, including, of course, Willis Hall, an appointee of Smith. The remaining sixteen negative votes had come from out-county supervisors. With only sixty-one affirmative votes, the motion to submit the port plan to the voters was defeated, but the majority did succeed in having it sent back to the Port Committee for reconsideration. Alternative proposals, the first to be submitted formally, were also defeated. Willis Hall proposed a bond issue of $2,500,000 to acquire land to be leased for private port development, and Mayor Miriani proposed a $4,800,000 bond issue to finance the construction of dockage and utilities, with the remaining terminal facilities to be financed by revenue bonds. Neither of these came close to passage.

On September 9, the Port Committee again approved the Port Commission's plan. By now tempers were short. Further debate was out of the question. When the Board of Supervisors met on September 15, only two members were absent. The vote in favor of submitting the commission's port plan to the voters was eighty-five to twenty-two. The opposition had not been able to gain any votes through the delay, but they had kept the issue in doubt an additional eleven days. As it turned out, the Port Commission did not gain much of a time advantage over the previous year. In 1957 the supervisors had approved the port proposal on September 16, and in 1958, with a head start, the county political system had ground out a decision on September 15. This year, 1958, it had required the efforts of Mayor Miriani and the Detroit delegation to the Board of Supervisors, along with strong out-county support, to get the plan before the voters.

The 1958 campaign for a public general cargo terminal for the Port of Detroit differed from that of the previous year in many respects. To begin with, 1958 was a general election year with races for governor, U.S. senator, congressmen, and the state legislature demanding attention. Now both private general cargo terminal operators were opposed, whereas the year before, Young, who now had a plan of his own, had not opposed the public facility. The opposition to the public port was still led by the Board of Commerce, but although the number of public opponents of the port proposal had not increased to any significant degree, the number of public supporters of the plan had shrunk. As opponents took pains to point out, this year, endorsements had not been received from the Propeller Club or from the Riverfront Development Division of the Detroit Tomorrow Committee. Organized labor did renew its backing. *The Detroit News* continued its indefatigable support, but there was no single member of the Port Commission comparable to Troy Browning who could dramatize the cause with energetic and enthusiastic campaigning.

Early in October, at a time when good strategy called for a solid front in support of the proposal, one of the commissioners, Alvan Macauley, announced his resignation from the Port Commission as of October 15. He gave as his reason the pressure of his private affairs. An executive of the area's largest bank, the National Bank of Detroit, Macauley was the senior member of the commission in years of service, having served on it since 1933. Observed in the midst of many stormy commission meetings over the years, Macauley had earned a reputation for being even-tempered and having a moderating influence. In contrast, Carlis Stettin had the reputation of being a strong-willed man who wanted to run his organization as he saw fit and who pursued his goals with determination. His goal was a public port facility run by the port director. In the world of shipping with which he was associated, the position of port director carried with it authority and prestige, but a port director without a port was like a captain without a ship. When alternative proposals were suggested, such as the Young plan or a reduced bond issue which would permit land acquisition but not completion of terminal facilities, Stettin brushed them aside and used all the influence that he could muster to hold the commission to a policy of at least a minimum cargo terminal facility owned and controlled by the port agency. Stettin's apparently uncompromising stand, in the face of the pressure being brought to bear against it by the Board of Commerce and with the concomitant personality conflicts which arose, brought about Macauley's resignation. This, however, did not become public knowledge: Macauley was too responsible a citizen to permit his personal reaction to the situation to become an issue. His resignation left the commission without a representative from a major business or industry.

With Macauley gone, Holmes and Basso became the senior Port commissioners, with Basso now chairman. These two commissioners, along with Stettin and his staff, led the campaign for the port proposal. It was a difficult campaign to wage. The Young proposal that Detroit Harbor Terminals be permitted to lease land from the port agency and to construct terminal facilities raised complex questions concerning anticipated general cargo tonnage when the seaway was opened and the capacity of existing facilities to handle the increase. No new studies of the quality of the KTAM and Great Lakes–St. Lawrence Association reports had been conducted to introduce any new facts, and both these reports were quoted by both sides in support of various points. The Citizens Research Council of Michigan, a private research organization most of whose directors were members of the Board of Commerce, issued a report, reproduced and distributed by the Board of Commerce, that questioned the tonnage estimates of the two earlier studies and maintained that private terminals could handle the expected cargo. A frequent argument was that the toll structure of the seaway would be such that it would discourage traffic and cut down on tonnage. Adding to the confusion was a contention by Willis Hall that the description of the land sought for the port, as written in the ballot proposal, did not coincide with the legal description of the land sought and that approval of the proposal would not permit the commission to acquire the amount of river frontage claimed. The county legal staff conceded the error in wording but gave assurance that it would not affect acquisition of the intended site. Again the *Detroit Free Press* was the best source of arguments against the proposal and *The Detroit News* the best source of arguments for the proposal. Considering that this was a general election, all three major papers devoted an extraordinary amount of space to the port issue.

The voters defeated the two port propositions on November 4. The proposition authorizing the $7,000,000 bond issue was defeated 152,140 to 241,496. Since the proposition required a three-fifths majority for approval, a three-fifths majority vote against it was a decisive defeat. The defeat of the proposition authorizing the tax increase to pay for the bonds was no less decisive. On this issue, 137,868 had voted for the tax, and 339,791, or 71 percent, had voted against it. At this same election, 806,376 Wayne County voters had voted for governor; about half this number had voted on the bond proposal, which was limited to property owners, and close to 60 percent had voted on the tax proposal. There was no possible way in which these results could be interpreted as a victory for the Port Commission. They were taken as a victory by the staff of the Board of Commerce, who privately credited Willis Hall with having defeated singlehandedly *The Detroit News,* the *Detroit Times,* the Board of Supervisors, the Port Commission, and those supporting a public port.

The Seaway Comes and the Port Director Goes. With no prospect in sight for voter approval of a port project and with no revenue source that would permit the issuance of revenue bonds without voter approval, the Port Commission had reached an impasse. The newest commissioner, Kenneth Dahlka, who had been appointed to finish Macauley's term, held the view that the commission's policy should consist of port promotion, and he and Commissioner Lane joined forces in an attempt to reduce the budget of the agency. The other three commissioners supported Stettin's objections to such a reduction, but the issue was revived in December when a supervisor from Mayor Hubbard's Dearborn domain proposed that the county withdraw financial support from the port agency. Although many considered this a grandstand tactic, the argument that the voters had rejected a public port operation in favor of private development could not be ignored. The Board of Supervisors' Port Committee, however, recommended that the agency be continued with a budget of about $140,000. This amount was less than the amount budgeted for each of the previous two years, but it was still more money than the agency had ever succeeded in spending in a single fiscal year. While the budgetary future of the agency was being debated, two of Stettin's staff members resigned, and he was left with an assistant, a port trade representative and clerical staff. Under these circumstances, the Port Commission budget was very generous.

Willis Hall's pressure against Stettin continued to be unrelenting, but following the second referendum, Hall was joined by others who tended to associate the plight of the port with the personality of Stettin. At the Board of Supervisors' Port Committee meeting in February 1959, Committee Chairman Patrick told the port commissioners that they should "work in a cooperative spirit with the Board of Commerce." When Commission Chairman Basso said that the commissioners had met with the board's Port Committee and that the latter had not been cooperative, Willis Hall complained that the reason for this was that the port director had been running around condemning business in the community. At this point, Miriani interjected his wonder over whether or not the commission had the necessary leadership, since it continued to lose issues. His reference was to Stettin. It may not have been evident at the time, but in retrospect it appears that it was not to be long before the Port of Detroit would again be without a director.

The opening of the shipping season was duly celebrated in recognition of the significance of the now operating St. Lawrence Seaway, which converted the Great Lakes ports into sea ports. The following quotation is taken from the May 7, 1959, edition of *The Detroit News:*

> Simon D. Den Uyl, new president of the Greater Detroit Board of Commerce, and Harvey Campbell, executive vice president, stood on the bridge of the cargo ship "Santa Regina" as they headed a welcome to Detroit's first American-flag ocean freighter that was a mockery. The big ship flying the Stars and Stripes had no place to dock for cargo, but it halted to receive five plaques noting the advance of the ocean-going American merchant marine into the Great Lakes.

The reporter noted that Willis Hall was not present on the bridge, and Commissioner Holmes was quoted as saying, "One thing we can say to the voters is, 'We told you so.'"

The physical presence of the large ocean-going cargo vessels brought home with convincing reality the fact that the St. Lawrence Seaway was no longer a topic for debate but a going concern. The "big ships" were in the Detroit River. Only three at any one time could be berthed in the Port of Detroit for taking on or discharging general cargo, and some with cargoes destined for Detroit had to discharge it at other ports. Those who had fought the port proposals claimed that the traffic jam of ships waiting for berths was a problem of scheduling, not of dock facilities, and at the same time terminal operators promised to expand their facilities to absorb the now obvious additional tonnage. The Port Commission announced that it was considering a west-side dock plan, and a few weeks later it announced that it was considering an east-side dock plan. It was rumored that Carlis Stettin was looking for a new job. Finally, in May, Mayor Miriani announced that he intended to appoint a committee consisting of top executives from Detroit city government and leaders from the community. By June, the mayor's forty-man Waterfront Development Committee was under way with the immediate charge to determine: "What kind of facilities we must build, where, and how quickly it should be accomplished."

Carlis Stettin's last local clash came over appointments to the Waterfront Development Committee. The mayor had requested that the commission be represented, and the commissioners took this to mean one of them. Stettin maintained that the port director should be considered a member of the commission and sit on the mayor's committee. Miriani, who said he did not want Stettin on his committee, settled the issue by appointing Commission Chairman Basso to the committee. This appointment was a blow to Stettin. Since Detroit city executives were on the committee, it meant that port matters would be considered by heads of agencies that did not have jurisdiction over the port. At the Port Commission meeting on August 5, 1959, Carlis Stettin announced his resignation as director of the Port of Detroit, effective August 21. He had accepted a position with the Port of New York Authority.

Stettin said that he had decided to leave because of the failure of the community to recognize the need for additional port facilities. Before he accepted the position, he said, he had been led to believe that the community wanted to develop a public port. "I tried to sell a plan for port development twice," he told the *News*, "and the only plan we have today is a plan of confusion." He blamed much of the port's failure to develop upon the activities of Willis Hall. Hall, in his turn, greeted the resignation with pleasure and was quoted as saying, "This is the best news the Port of Detroit has had since the opening of the St. Lawrence Seaway. I wish him luck, and I am glad to see him go." Mayor Miriani's quoted remarks were in a similar vein. He blamed the two ballot defeats on lack of leadership from the port director and added: "My experience with him proved to me that he was unable to get the feel of public service that career executives of the city have been able to do. Unfortunately he was unable to draw forces together. He was never able to get cohesive support." Commission Chairman Basso was loyal to his director. He commented that Stettin's departure "will be a tremendous loss to the community." Under the heading "No Regret," the *Detroit Times* for August 8 editorialized on the resignation: "The criticism of Stettin must be that he was too unbending, too singular of purpose because of both his personal nature and his training as a technician in port work," and added that supporters of the public port plan "did so in spite of Stettin, not because of him."

Stettin's departure gave rise to suggestions for changes in the organization of the port function. A *Free Press* editorial recommended that the Port Commission be abolished, and one member of the County Board of Auditors and two port commissioners suggested that the port function be turned over to the city of Detroit. The latter suggestion was based on the assumption that most of the desirable sites for port development were within the city limits and out-county voters had demonstrated a lack of interest in supporting port development. Nothing came of any of these suggestions, except that it was decided not to appoint a new port director until after the mayor's Waterfront Development Committee had reported and a future port policy had been determined. By the end of 1959, the Port Commission staff consisted of a former newspaper reporter who had been Stettin's administrative assistant and was now acting port director and two clerical workers. The seaway had arrived, but the Port of Detroit Commission had been reduced to its pre-seaway dimensions.

Aftermath. As the first seaway shipping season entered its final months, *The Detroit News* summarized its view of the port situation in an editorial on September 12, 1959, entitled "Still Waiting for Docks—Lead Frittered Away":

> . . . the costly delays the Port of Detroit has repeatedly inflicted on ship operators this summer bear witness to our woeful inability to provide the speedy service ships and shippers must have if our port is to realize its natural potential.
>
> Detroit started out in the new seaway era ahead of its competitors. It needed no costly dredging to make most of its waterfront accessible. Ships need no tugs to dock on the Detroit River, nor must they thread their way through ticklish bridges and channels to come alongside. It had two private terminals, going concerns, to handle existing business while preparations were made to accommodate the increase sure to come.
>
> That lead has been thrown away. The preparations were not made. Detroit entered the seaway age no better able to reap its bounty than it was the day the first shovel dug in to commence it. While other ports spent and worked to make by hand what nature gave Detroit, we have squabbled year after year over a synthetic issue: public vs. private development. "Let the users pay!" the cry has been. "Don't put this crushing (fifty-five cents a year on the average home) burden on the taxpayer!"
>
> We bow to no one in our regard for doing the work of the world under private auspices, where private interests are able and willing. . . . But in port development, as in many other fields, private endeavor has proved inadequate.
>
> No port worthy of the name runs wholly on private steam, as we are told Detroit can. The nature of the business requires heavy investment, with no gilt-edge guarantee of immediate profit, such as our local dock operators have demanded before they will expand. What private capital has been unwilling to do, public agencies have done—elsewhere. . . .
>
> We have been told almost yearly that forward-looking private dock operators are about to build what is needed (even as they have said, in the next breath, that no more is needed). Some of the new facilities now promised for the 1960 shipping season were first talked up in 1955. The record gives no assurance that next year will be any different from last year, or the year before. . . .

. . . .

The years ahead will confirm Detroit's potential as a port, either in business here—if we invest to accommodate it—or in business elsewhere that Detroit could have won, but didn't.

But the *Detroit Free Press* sized up the situation in an editorial on September 30, under this title "Our Port Needs Met—It's a Win for Taxpayers" saying:

> The bureaucratic empire builders who have had their eye on Detroit's port facilities—and the taxpayer's wallet—have been given the answer by private enterprise to the question of expanding the city's dock facilities in terms which should silence them for a long time.
>
> Mayor Miriani revealed Monday that an $8,000,000 port facility expansion program is under way financed entirely by private capital.
>
> . . . .
>
> This expansion was done, as private interests promised that it would be, without putting a heavy arm upon the taxpayer.
>
> It seems to be a complete justification of the position taken by the Greater Detroit Board of Commerce which strongly opposed two successive efforts to win public approval of bond issues to finance development under the jurisdiction of the Port of Detroit Authority.

A more objective appraisal of the situation became available when the mayor's Waterfront Development Committee issued its report on January 28, 1960. The committee found, as had the previous surveys, that the port facilities for handling bulk cargo were adequate, but "the immediate and basic question for decision relates to the adequacy of the facilities . . . to handle the actual and potential commerce in general cargo, particularly in relation to the greatly expanded opportunities for trade available through the opening of the seaway." After reviewing all available data on tonnage handled during the 1959 season, the committee concluded that the overseas traffic totaled over 300,000 tons. "This lends credence to the estimates in the report of Knappen-Tippets-Abbett-McCarthy made in 1952 and [that] of the Great Lakes–St. Lawrence Association made in 1956 that shortly after the seaway was developed, and assuming adequate port facilities and modern equipment, the Port of Detroit overseas traffic would increase to 300,000 tons and would aggregate 1,000,000 tons or more within five or six years thereafter." Comparing tonnage with available facilities, the committee concluded:

On the basis of our study and the consideration of all the facts submitted, it is the conclusion of the Waterfront Committee that the facilities at the Port of Detroit for handling overseas general cargo were inadequate in 1959 and that unless expanded promptly and substantially will become increasingly inadequate under the pressure of the burgeoning seaway traffic.

The committee noted that Detroit Harbor Terminals proposed to increase its dock by 993 feet in order to accommodate four large ocean-going vessels, double its 1959 capacity, and that Detroit Marine Terminals proposed an 800-foot dock extension that would permit three large ships to dock at this facility. "Upon completion, these projects will provide at least four additional berths for large ocean-going vessels and related transit shed and other facilities. Thus, in 1960 at least seven large vessels can berth simultaneously at these two terminals for loading and unloading, as compared with three large vessels in 1959." It should be noted, however, that Detroit Marine Terminals is located on the River Rouge, which has a twenty-one-foot channel, compared to the seaway standard of twenty-seven feet, and the maneuvering of large ships in the Rouge requires the aid of a tug. (These limitations do not apply to Detroit Harbor Terminals, located on the Detroit River.) The committee concluded that "the present port facilities when expanded by these sizable additional facilities should be reasonably adequate to handle overseas commerce anticipated at the Port of Detroit for the immediate future."

Based upon its findings, the committee made the following recommendation:

If for any reason the port operators fail to fulfill fully their commitments to construct the additional facilities as described, the city of Detroit should take immediate action to obtain through purchase or condemnation suitable sites for port development and lease such sites on a competitive basis for development and operation as public ports by private interests. This has been done very successfully by several of our sister cities on the Great Lakes and permits the creation of necessary facilities with a very modest utilization of public funds. The personnel and experience of the Port of Detroit Commission may be useful to the city in such a program of this kind.

The effect on the over-all economy of Detroit in the growth from 134,626 tons of general cargo in 1958 to 331,484 tons in 1959 and to a potential of a million tons or more in the future is too important to be left to chance. The general welfare of the city is the one vital consideration that must govern.

The city of Detroit must be prepared to act quickly and adequately if the terminal operators fail to meet the challenge of expanding seaway development. Detroit can no longer afford to fall behind the timetable of seaway port needs.

The Waterfront Development Committee has faith in the terminal operators but an alternative course of action must be readied so that the great growth in economic values through increased employment and buying power that will come from an expanding Port of Detroit will most assuredly be realized for the common good of our community and its citizens.

Although not all of the expected private terminal improvements had been completed by 1961, enough had been accomplished to give encouragement to those who claimed that private development could accomplish the task, but not enough had been accomplished to quiet those who claimed that the ultimate potential of the port could not be achieved without a public general cargo terminal. In January 1962 the port development issue was reopened in a surprising fashion when the Port Commission rehired Carlis Stettin as port director. Stettin was to have a second chance to guide the port's development, but the passage of time had neither solved all the outstanding issues nor established a community consensus that would make his task simple.

Concluding Comments

The two major controversial issues running through this case were (1) whether government should engage in port development through the construction of terminal facilities, and (2) what place the port function should have in the governmental structure of the metropolis. Turning first to the public vs. private port theme, it would be difficult to cast this in terms of the traditional ideological struggle of private enterprise arrayed against supporters of public projects. Rather than ideological attachment, expectation of economic benefits to be derived from port operations was the basis for choosing sides in this controversy. By water, northern European ports are as near or nearer to Detroit than to the East Coast ports of New York and Baltimore, and the direct water route to Detroit is shorter than the combined water and rail routes via East Coast ports for all of the major European ports. The railroads, therefore, were opposed to public port development that might result in a more favorable rate advantage for the water carriers. The economic interests of the private terminal operators were obviously involved: a public port would provide competition and influence the rate structure. Prior to the opening of the seaway, the terminal operators could point to unused general cargo capacity. These were economic stakes that welcomed any support that could be derived from an ideological argument against public ports per se. The closest to an ideological stand was that taken by the directors of the Board of Commerce, but the directors justified it on the economic ground that the public port terminal would not raise sufficient revenue to be self-financing.

Support for public port facilities was also based upon economic rather than ideological grounds. A noteworthy aspect of the 1957 campaign for the public port terminal was the degree of consensus among business, industrial, civic, and labor leaders that the economic benefits which the community could expect from the overseas general cargo trade warranted an expenditure of public funds to provide the facilities to exploit this trade. But whereas the opponents of the public port could point to the specific costs involved in providing it, the supporters could point only to estimates of future benefits, which, when reduced to an estimated savings of a few cents per pound of coffee, could be made to appear a ridiculously insignificant gain from a multimillion-dollar investment. If the votes on the port issue were taken as a guide, then it could be concluded that the supporters of the public port did not succeed in convincing the electorate that the economic benefits to the community outweighed the direct cost to the taxpayer.

The second theme, the structuring of the port function, was less obvious but no less significant. The establishment of the Port District as coterminous with the boundary of Wayne County recognized the metropolitan nature of the port function, i.e., that the Port of Detroit involved more than the city of Detroit; but the subordination of the port agency to the County Board of Supervisors nullified any advantage that the super-jurisdiction might have implied. One reason for depriving the port agency of independence was that the agency was a potential power threat to both city and county government. If the port agency were to develop revenue-producing port facilities and to exercise the power to tax, it would give rise to a rival bureaucracy with major operating functions and fiscal independence. In discussing this possibility, public officials would cite the Port of New York Authority as a type of independent bureaucracy to be avoided.

That the port agency would not get out of hand was well assured as it was woven into the web of county government. The enabling legislation was amended to transfer the power to appoint port commissioners from the governor to the Board of Supervisors. The Port Commission budget had to clear the budget office under the independently elected County Board of Auditors. The Board of Supervisors established a standing Port Committee to oversee the work of the commission, and budget requests had to clear this committee as well as the Ways and Means Committee of the Board of Supervisors. Detroit councilmen sat on both of these committees. On the Board of Supervisors were not only elected officials from the county's various cities and townships but also appointed members representing major community interests, such as the Greater Detroit Board of Commerce. This structural maze, composed of varied economic interests and political influence, was sufficient to prevent any independent action by the port agency. The case raises a serious question whether under this structure an agency dealing with vital economic interests, as a port agency inevitably must, is capable of any action whatsoever. It could be argued that the port agency was designed to be impotent.

The port agency itself was an imperfect administrative instrument. A good case for the commission form of organization can be made, since the county does not have a single responsible executive to whom an appointive port director could be held accountable for his use of the broad policy-making and rule-making powers granted him by the enabling laws, powers that are not ordinarily accepted as appropriate for a single executive. But locating the power in a commission is not an unmixed blessing. Appointment by the Board of Supervisors meant that the commissioner had survived the complex political clearances imposed by the various power blocs represented among the supervisors. It can be questioned whether this process is conducive to the selection of outstanding citizens to an unpaid, time-consuming position. In addition, while personal loyalty to a President, governor, or mayor often motivates an appointee to undertake a difficult assignment, a plural body such as the Board of Supervisors cannot command such personal allegiance. Finding qualified but detached commissioners is another problem posed by the commission structure. Three commissioners—Lowe, a private terminal owner, Browning, owner of a steamship company, and Holmes, a Teamsters Union official—had direct interests that would be affected by port developments, and it would be difficult to find any business or labor leader in the community whose interests would not be affected by the economic consequences of port development. So far, local governments have not developed clear-cut conflict-of-interest laws and regulations for service on local boards and commissions. If and when they do, however, it will be necessary to face the fact that the metropolitan economy is a complex system of interrelated parts, and that to find citizens who are qualified by knowledge and experience to serve on planning, housing, port commissions and the like but who do not have some stake in the outcome of the decisions of these bodies will be an impossible task.

The two port directors, Sterling St. John and Carlis Stettin, had much in common. Both were professionals in port management and development; both were from outside of Detroit and Wayne County and were not familiar with the local political scene; both were the Port Commission's second choice for the position, which does not reflect upon their ability but did provide a rationalization for those who would maintain that the port problem stemmed from failure to hire the right man for port director; both came with the feeling that they understood the policy of the Port Commission and that with the help of the Port Commission it could be carried out; and both resigned with expressions of failure and frustration. There was one significant difference. St. John had come to carry out a policy that would encourage private development, and Stettin had come to promote and build a public port facility.

Both St. John and Stettin walked into a local power struggle and were battered by it. The constant pressure under which each of the port directors worked exposed the raw side of their per-

sonalities, but no normal, self-respecting person could be expected
to absorb the criticism that each received without being provoked
to respond to it. A popular local myth was that neither St. John
nor Stettin had the proper personality or executive skill for the
port directorship—the right man could have solved the port problem. This, of course, was nonsense. The proponents of a public
port development were no more likely to be talked out of their
position by Sterling St. John than Willis Hall was likely to be
charmed out of his stand by the warm smiles of Carlis Stettin.
The port directors won the support of the side they favored, but
they did not change the balance of power to any significant degree.
The public port proponents were powerful enough to force the
resignation of St. John, hire a director who favored a public port,
and twice place a public port proposal on the ballot, but they
were not powerful enough to win popular support for the proposals. The two port directors were the victims of a power equilibrium.

It would be easy to exaggerate the influence of Willis Hall if
defeat of the two port proposals is taken as the criterion of his
influence. The odds were in Hall's favor. In 1957 and 1958 the
Detroit metropolis was experiencing an economic recession. Many
school districts in the area were seeking tax increases which required voter approval, and many were being defeated. The need
for voter approval of two propositions—one for bonding authority,
limited to property owners and requiring a three-fifths majority,
and the other for a tax increase, open to all voters and needing
only a simple majority—added another complication for the not
too perceptive voter. The issue itself was not something that
could be easily explained. To the casual observer, the Detroit
River with its 113 piers, wharves, and docks and the River Rouge
with its 42 terminals at which ships were constantly being un-
loaded or loaded gave an appearance of a busy, well-equipped
port. That these facilities were designed for bulk-loaded lake vessels and were not at all useful for the ocean-going general cargo
vessel was not readily observable. In view of the existing dock
facilities, a request for a multimillion-dollar investment to provide
terminal facilities that would accommodate only two large ocean-
going vessels at a time may have appeared to be extravagant, especially when private terminal operators were claiming that they

could handle all the cargo. These circumstances aided Hall's campaign to defeat the public port proposals, but he and his staff were skilled tacticians at exploiting gratuitous advantages.

The Detroit metropolis entered the seaway era still in contention over how it should accommodate itself to its new seaport status. The power equilibrium that on the one hand prevented the construction of the public port facilities and kept the port agency in a weak position in the governmental structure, on the other hand kept alive the demand for more adequate port facilities and a port agency with the authority and status to carry out a vigorous port development program. A change in this balance will depend upon the actual consequences brought about by the seaway. As the mayor's Waterfront Development Committee stated, failure on the part of the private terminals to keep up with tonnage demands would result in new efforts for public financing of port facilities. These efforts would probably take the form of public acquisition of land and leasing to private developers. This is something less than the public general cargo terminal for which Carlis Stettin had fought. Meanwhile, the Port Commission, with its name changed at its own request to Detroit–Wayne County Port Commission, was relegated to a state of limbo to await a shift in the equilibrium.

6
Detroit's Metropolitan Airport

The Fourteen-year Struggle over an Airport Site

Introduction

Detroit faced the postwar air age with a prewar airport system. The city's sole facility for commercial passenger flights was City Airport, a tiny (253 acres) patch of land just a few minutes by car from downtown Detroit, but capable of handling, at best, lumbering two-engined DC-3's. A second airport, built and operated by the Wayne County Road Commission, was located some eighteen miles west of the city, and its prewar use had been limited to handling a local air division of the Michigan National Guard plus private and company planes. Both airports had been constructed in 1930. By 1945, City Airport was completely surrounded by built-up areas, and an added obstacle, which also served as a landmark, was a three-hundred-foot-high gas storage tank near the edge of the field. County Airport, however, was still beyond the reach of suburban expansion and was surrounded by open fields, farms, and a scattering of homes.

A third airport made its appearance soon after World War II began, when the federal government built Willow Run Airport, just eight air miles west of County Airport, to serve the Willow Run (Ford) bomber plant. The Willow Run field was much larger than the county field (1,986 acres vs. the county field's 640 acres), with runways almost twice as long as the county's. At the same time, a four-lane limited-access highway was built from Detroit's western boundary to the Ford bomber plant in order to give Detroit-area workers easier access to the plant. Since the expressway traversed the northern edge of County Airport, it afforded more direct access to the county port and brought it twelve road miles closer to Detroit than the Willow Run Airport. Although the expressway was

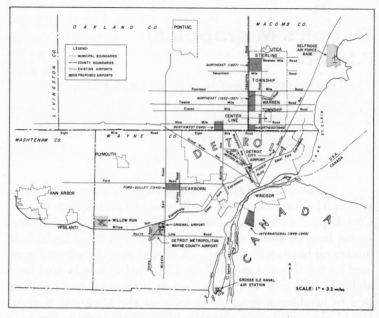

3. Existing and Proposed Airports in the Detroit Metropolitan Area

Courtesy Graphic Arts Section, State University of Iowa
Adapted from AAA map

financed almost entirely by federal funds, a major participant in setting the route and building the highway was the Wayne County Road Commission, the county unit which operated County Airport.

This was not the first advantage the Road Commission had obtained for its airport from the federal government. During the thirties it had received the most advanced air navigational equipment from the U.S. Department of Commerce. Less stringent flying restrictions were imposed at the county field than at City Airport. A grant from the Public Works Administration to the commission covered 45 percent of the cost of a new combined passenger terminal and administration building, which was completed in 1938. On July 1, 1941, the U.S. Army Air Force leased the field from the county "for the duration of the national emergency." The airport was used as a jumping-off base for American bombers being ferried to England under terms of the Lend-Lease Act. The Army extended the airport's runways to 5,500 feet to handle the larger aircraft.

Meanwhile the obsolescence of City Airport was becoming painfully apparent. It could not accommodate the four-engine planes expected in postwar domestic passenger service, and the cost of expansion was prohibitive because residential and industrial development had engulfed the field before the start of the war. Realizing that the airlines would have to find a new base of operations in the postwar era, both the city and the county prepared to meet the challenge.

After briefly considering a site northwest of Detroit, Detroit's mayor, Edward J. Jeffries, Jr., had settled on a site to the northeast, in Warren Township, for a new city airport. A long and complex legal battle ensued between the city and opponents of the airport, namely, property owners and the local school district in Warren Township. The issue reached the Michigan Supreme Court, which upheld the city of Detroit in its claimed right to condemn and acquire property outside its jurisdiction for use as an airport. Finally, in May 1945, the city won its condemnation suit, but it was a pyrrhic victory: the one-square-mile site was too small. Furthermore, other parties had mobilized strong pressure in favor of alternative sites. Important among these "other parties" was County Highway Engineer Leroy C. Smith and the three-member County Road Commission.

While county road commissions have traditionally enjoyed a fair measure of operating autonomy within the sprawling structure of Michigan county government, the Wayne County Road Commission's autonomy had been enhanced by the scope of its activities. It is a multi-purpose, multimillion-dollar operation. Besides building and maintaining county surface roads, its chief and ostensible function, the Road Commission has, over the years, been given responsibility for expressways, parkways, parks, golf courses, County Airport, and water-supply and sewage-disposal facilities for numerous suburban areas. In 1959 Road Commission expenditures totaled about $65,000,000 when all of its many operating and construction fund accounts are included. A large part of these expenses are paid by (1) state grants for road purposes outside county budgetary channels, and (2) flexible financing arrangements (such as issuance of revenue bonds), which the state has empowered the commission to use. State law thus provides the commission with a substantial degree of financial independence. A final source of Road Commission autonomy was the tenure and personality of its chief executive officer, County Highway Engineer Leroy Smith.

Leroy Smith was county highway engineer from 1918 through 1956, when he retired. During his nearly forty years in local and state politics, Smith earned a number of epithets from those with whom he or his organization clashed. Ruthless, scheming bull-headed, and cantankerous were a few of the adjectives applied to him by his foes. Smith's friends and associates were more likely to describe him as persistent, firm, strong-willed, astute, and dexterous. These opinions circulated largely behind the scenes, for Smith's name was not widely known outside the circle of those familiar with county affairs. Although he was quoted from time to time in the daily press, he consciously shunned the public limelight, particularly in the later years of his political life. By virtue of his long contacts and shared professional interests with the politically important county road commissions in the other counties around the state, Smith could make his presence felt in the state legislature. A year before Smith retired from his $23,000-a-year post, the *Detroit Times* (October 23, 1955) said of him:

> Besides becoming a power in Wayne County, state capital veterans have unlimited respect for Smith. They declare he can get more out of the legislature in a five-minute telephone conversation than experienced lobbyists can win in five weeks of wining and dining.

According to many, Smith was "unbeatable."

During the early forties Smith had toyed with alternative solutions to the airport problem, at one point proposing that the county build a large new airport in the northwestern part of the metropolitan area. But by early 1944 Smith had dropped these plans and instead proposed expanding the existing County Airport by from one to four square miles. The expansion plans were ambitious. They called for 10,000-foot runways in three directions, expanded terminal facilities, and other related structures. The boundaries of the expanded airport would be Middle Belt, North

Line, and Vining Roads, and the Wabash Railroad, which parallels the south side of the Willow Run Expressway. The Road Commission forwarded these plans to the Board of Supervisors in August 1944 and they were approved in September. Condemnation proceedings against nearly three square miles of property around the existing airport began and funds for land purchases were appropriated. Smith's comment on the plans was: "Such enlargements of Wayne County Airport, together with certain improvements, would be the most economical method of providing an airport for metropolitan Detroit with all of the facilities postwar aviation activities will require." Leroy Smith's hat was in the ring. He had set his course.

Smith's decision marked the beginning of a fourteen-year battle to convert an out-of-the-way county field into Detroit's major metropolitan airport. In the struggle against opposition from many organized local quarters as well as from the city of Detroit and the airlines themselves, Smith marshalled political support on the state and federal levels. By 1958 Smith's opponents had pressed for five different alternatives to the county port, while Smith could look back on a record of unwavering loyalty to the choice he made in 1944.

The Northwest Site

The City Backs the Northwest Site. While Smith was laying his plans for the county port and Jeffries was embroiled in litigation over the northeast site, favorable sentiment had been developing in the press and in the business community for building an airport at the southwest edge of Windsor, Canada, just across the Detroit River. This site, only six miles and twelve minutes' driving time from downtown Detroit, seemed preferable to the northeast site chosen by the mayor. The Michigan Aero Club, which more or less represented the interests of the airlines, aircraft manufacturing firms, and private plane owners, came out for the international site in December 1943, at the same time recommending the creation of a metropolitan Detroit airport authority "to plan, initiate and carry through a comprehensive multi-airport plan, assuming responsibility for locating, engineering, and financing of airports and landing fields found to be necessary for the Detroit area."

Six months later Samuel M. Dean, chairman of the Civic Affairs Committee of the Engineering Society of Detroit and a top executive of the Detroit Edison Company, urged Mayor Jeffries and the chairmen of the boards of supervisors of Wayne, Macomb, and Oakland counties to send representatives to a conference involving federal, state, and local units to study the Detroit area's airport needs. Although Mayor Jeffries opposed the "metropolitan approach," he did send a representative to the meeting, which was held on July 26, 1944. All units were represented, and the consensus was that the several local units should join with the Michigan Aeronautics Commission in developing a regional airport plan. The state commission had some $80,000 available to finance a study of the region's airport needs, and local matching funds would be required. The quasi-official agency that grew out of this meeting became known as the Detroit Metropolitan Aviation Planning Authority. In January 1945 the Michigan Aeronautics Commission and the Aviation Planning Authority, with Samuel Dean as its chairman, contracted with the St. Louis airport consulting firm of Horner and Shifrin for a $75,000 study of Detroit-area airport needs. It was at this point that the Greater Detroit Board of Commerce decided to take a hand in Detroit's airport situation.

Early in 1945 Donald S. Kiskadden, vice president and general manager of the Buhl Land Company and a member of the Aviation Committee of the Board of Commerce, contacted Glenn Richards, Detroit's public works commissioner. Richards' department administered City Airport, and Richards himself had announced preliminary runway and building plans for the northeast site in February 1945. Kiskadden told Richards that he and other Aviation Committee members believed that the city was wrong in seeking the northeast site but had been unable to secure an appointment with Jeffries. He then asked Richards' assistance in gaining access to the mayor, explaining: "We've sold the people on a northwest airport—we'll *give* the city an airport site in the Eight Mile–Wyoming area." At Richards' suggestion Jeffries consented to talk with the committee. When he heard the details of the committee's offer Jeffries confided to Richards, "I'm in a tough spot. How can

I turn them down? Publicly I'll have to go along with it. We'll withdraw from the northeast site."

Public announcement of the northwest site came on June 1, 1945, when Mayor Jeffries outlined the substance of the offer made to the city by the Aviation Committee of the Board of Commerce. The board had secured options on 704 acres of land near Eight Mile and Wyoming Roads and had offered to purchase and give the land to the city provided the city would (1) drop the northeast site and (2) condemn and purchase two square miles of surrounding property. Jeffries' letter to the council recommended acceptance of the offer and initiation of condemnation proceedings against the site. The mayor had abandoned the northeast site and was now supporting a plan that would provide Detroit with a three-square-mile northwest airport.

Support for the northwest site came quickly from spokesmen and engineers for the major airlines, which were waiting with baited breath for some action that would provide a sizable and serviceable airport for the postwar period. They rejected the northeast site as being too small and criticized County Airport as being too far from downtown Detroit. Jeffries referred specifically to the airlines' expressed view in his letter to the council recommending condemnation proceedings against the northwest site:

> Apparently all the airline experts agree that the Dequindre [northeast] site is not large enough, . . . would cost considerably more to expand, and would cause some inconvenience to residents in the area.
>
> The Wayne County Airport is too far removed.

The council set June 11 as the date for a public hearing on the northwest site. The hearing was conducted on schedule, with the mayor and the Board of Commerce calling for speedy action and Samuel Dean of the Aviation Planning Authority and H. S. Shifrin of the consulting firm urging the council to postpone their decision for six weeks, until the final report of the regional airport survey was completed and published. The Horner-Shifrin firm disclosed that in its preliminary findings the northwest site had not ranked high. Engineers and technical advisors from the airlines, however, testified strongly in favor of the northwest site. Caught between experts, the Common Council was divided on the issue.

Informal polls showed a three-to-three split, with two council members hospitalized (they also were split) and one away in military service. Powerful pressures were mobilized in an attempt to break the deadlock in favor of the northwest site. Ernest R. Breech, chairman of the Board of Commerce's Aviation Committee, told the council in a blunt letter:

> We want an airport. We want it large enough to be adequate for years to come. . . .
>   . . . We have made our offer. We feel that we now are deserving, along with the other citizens of Detroit, of a ready response—one way or the other.

In a rare page-one editorial, the politically influential *Detroit News* exclaimed: "Wake Up, Councilmen!" The *News* criticized the council's "do-nothing," "stupid, bungling, stumbling policy" and called for immediate favorable action on the northwest site. The councilmen opposing the northwest site held firm, contending that the city should wait for the final results of the Horner-Shifrin study since the preliminary findings of that study were unfavorable to the northwest site. They also charged that there was no guarantee that the Board of Commerce could act on its offer since funds to buy the land on which it had the option had not yet been collected. Finally, they argued that the value of the land, about $750,000, was only a small percentage of the estimated $25,000,000 cost of the airport. The council deadlock was broken on June 19, when Councilman George Edwards returned to Detroit on a three-day emergency leave from his military post in Texas and voted for condemnation of the northwest site.

The council's action on the northwest site prompted immediate protests from local civic and neighborhood associations in the vicinity of the proposed site. As the city and suburbanites girded for battle over the airport, the long-awaited Horner-Shifrin report finally appeared. It was released on July 12, 1945.

The Horner-Shifrin Report. The 173-page Horner-Shifrin report, entitled *Airport Plan, Detroit Metropolitan Region,* considered existing airports and sites for future fields to serve the air-space needs of the Detroit region projected to 1960. It made recommendations on forty-five airports and possible airport sites within a radius of forty miles from downtown Detroit and pointed to the need for co-ordinated airport and air-space use plans that would best accommodate both scheduled and non-scheduled air movements. To accomplish this co-ordination the report recommended creation of a metropolitan aviation authority, to be given responsibility for developing and implementing a master plan of airports in the region.

The central concern of the study and all who awaited its completion was: Where should Detroit's *major* passenger terminal be located? The consultants focused their attention on four possibilities: the existing County Airport site, the international site in Windsor, the northwest site, and a site south of Ford Road and west of Gulley Road in Dearborn Township. Their investigations of the four sites produced the following information:

Airport Site	Distance from Center of Gravity of Air Users* (miles)	Travel Time from Center of Gravity of Air Users* (minutes)	Estimated Cost of Development (dollars)
Ford-Gulley	14.0	27	$17,900,000
International	9.1	18	16,700,000
Northwest	12.7	32	20,650,000
Wayne County	18.8	29	16,375,000

*West Grand Boulevard and Second Avenue (location of the General Motors Building and the Fisher Building)

The consultants strongly favored the international site (p. 133):

> From practically every consideration entering into a desirable regional airport plan, that plan in which the international site is used and developed as an international airport is very nearly an ideal solution for the Detroit region.
>
> This major airport involves a cost only slightly greater than that at the Wayne County site, which is the lowest of all.

But they immediately proceeded to write off this "ideal" site because "it is not feasible at this time to adopt this site and proceed directly to its development [as a result of] the international complications which must be overcome." The conditions under which a Detroit-owned airport could be located on foreign soil would require much negotiation. Furthermore, any formal agreement on ownership, operation, customs, immigration, etc., would need the approval of the city of Detroit, the state of Michigan, the U.S. Congress, the Dominion of Canada, the Ontario provincial government, and the city of Windsor. The Horner-Shifrin report urged that action be taken "at once to render feasible the ultimate development of the international airport."

In the meantime, the report recommended, a new airport should be developed on United States soil at the Ford-Gulley location (which was near the site of the Ford Airport, located in Dearborn, an airport built in the 1920's by Henry Ford and closed in 1946, a year after the Horner-Shifrin report was released, when the Ford Motor Company moved its fleet of planes to Wayne County Airport). The advantages of the Ford-Gulley site were (1) its proximity in distance and travel time and (2) the parks and parkways surrounding it, which could serve as buffer zones around the airfield. The consultants concluded that "the Ford–Gulley Road site should have a definite preference over the Wayne County site and consequently over the remaining sites on the United States side of the region." Other material in the Horner-Shifrin report made it clear that the consultants ranked County Airport only slightly behind the Ford-Gulley site. Nevertheless, the consultants recommended that the County Airport not be expanded as planned by Leroy Smith. The report relegated the county field to the status of a "minor airport." According to Public Works Commissioner Glenn Richards, who was to ally himself with Smith on the side of the County Airport, the recommendation of the Ford-Gulley site was a compromise solution: "The experts [Horner-Shifrin] liked the Wayne County Airport but there was tremendous pressure against its selection. . . . The experts didn't want to slap the Board of Commerce too hard [by picking County Airport]."

The report was highly critical of the northwest site. This site "had the least to offer" as a location for the area's major air terminal. First, it was farthest in travel time from downtown Detroit. Second, it had an undesirable air-traffic pattern. The high-grade residential character of the northwest area would generate demands on air space for private and other non-scheduled flying use. Conflict between scheduled and non-scheduled air movements could and should be avoided by locating the area's major air terminal in the south or southwest part of the metropolitan area. Over 85 percent of the scheduled air movements entered or departed from Detroit in easterly, southerly, or westerly directions. A south or southwest location for the airport would minimize flights over population concentrations. Third, it was the most costly of the four sites considered (largely because of inadequate drainage in the vicinity of the site). In addition, it was thought that such an airport would depreciate surrounding high-grade residential property and "cast a large shadow" over the future residential development in the northwest area. The consultants gave a firm recommendation against the development of the northwest site.

Reactions to the Report. The immediate effect of the Horner-Shifrin report was to compound the confusion and controversy. The Board of Commerce found its northwest site sharply criticized and downgraded by the experts. The Road Commission and Leroy Smith were faced with a recommendation that the county field not be expanded. Finally, an entirely new site was injected into the unsettled situation.

Various official and unofficial agencies reacted to the study recommendations. At its July 19 meeting the Detroit Metropolitan Aviation Planning Authority accepted the Horner-Shifrin report for study and forwarded a copy of it to the Civil Aeronautics Administration for that agency's review and comments. The Planning Authority also dropped the northwest site from its list of acceptable sites and indicated that only three sites would be considered—the international site, the Ford-Gulley site, and Wayne County Airport. The Board of Commerce and Mayor Jeffries continued to support the northwest site. At a July 20 luncheon sponsored by the board, Harry Pack, chairman of a special engineering committee of the airlines serving Detroit, addressed a group of 250 businessmen. He vigorously criticized the report in general and the Ford-Gulley site in particular, argued that the northwest site was the most desirable because it was nearest to the center of the metropolitan area, and pointed out that the airlines wanted the northwest site. Mayor Jeffries reportedly endorsed Pack's stand at the meeting, telling the group that the northwest site was "an ideal location for an airport and the city will back the Board of Commerce in support of it." After the luncheon meeting the Board of Commerce stepped up its fund-raising activity. It had already raised about $360,000 and had extended its options on the land to November 1.

Debate continued to center on the northwest site for the remainder of July and all of August. The Ford-Gulley site was lost in the shuffle. Early in September the Board of Commerce submitted to the mayor and council official documents covering its offer and trust agreement with the city. The matter was again in the lap of the council, with the recollection that that body had voted in June to start condemnation proceedings on the northwest site by a bare four-to-three majority. Would the council officially accept the land and the trust agreement in the face of adverse recommendations on the northwest site by the consultants? An informal poll showed three for acceptance, three opposed, and two undecided. The ninth councilman and former tie-breaker (Edwards) was still in military service. The council set September 18 as the day it would vote on the offer. The offer was rejected when the council deadlocked four-to-four. A spokesman for the Board of Commerce did not express concern over the outcome. "These are just dilatory tactics. We can bring back the man [Edwards] who broke the tie before."

The grounds on which the four councilmen who cast negative votes were against the Board of Commerce offer are worthy of note. Despite all the ammunition against the northwest site provided by the Horner-Shifrin report, a new reason was offered for opposing the northwest site. As one councilman put it, "We have an airport at our back door—Wayne County's." The other three councilmen applauded the point. One commented, "It will take only a year and a half to complete development and expansion of Wayne County Airport. The northwest site will require more than five years." Whatever behind-the-scenes discussions had taken place among the councilmen after the release of the Horner-Shifrin report, it was clear that a near majority of the council looked favorably on County Airport as the area's major terminal. Mayor Jeffries and Donald Kiskadden responded with criticisms of County Airport, and the airlines sought to dissuade city officials on the county field both publicly and privately.

The shift in the debate from the northwest site to the county field was not an idle or tangential development. A northwest airport would take from three to five years to complete. In the meantime the airlines would need a base of operations larger than the tiny City Airport. To alleviate the immediate crisis, Councilman Eugene VanAntwerp, who had voted for the northwest site in June (on condemnation) and again in September (on acceptance of the offer), introduced a resolution requesting the Wayne County Road Commission to prepare the county field "with the greatest possible speed for the reception of aircraft as the *interim major airport* for the city of Detroit" (italics added). His resolution was introduced on October 2 and the eight councilmen present passed it unanimously on October 9.

One week after passing the VanAntwerp resolution the Common Council handed the northwest site a potential setback. By a five-to-three vote the council rescinded its action of June 19 initiating condemnation proceedings against the northwest property. The four earlier opponents of the northwest site were joined by VanAntwerp. VanAntwerp explained his reversal on the northwest site as follows:

> I never have been very strong for the northwest site, but I voted for the condemnation resolution last June in order to get some machinery, at least, in operation for the acquiring of a major airport for the city. Since the council would not agree to accept the land gift for the northwest site, I voted for the resolution to rescind because I am not in favor of acquiring by condemnation land which could have been accepted as a gift.

The northwest site was saved from extinction by Mayor Jeffries' veto of the rescinding resolution.

While the city was stalemated over the northwest site, the Wayne County Board of Supervisors was not hamstrung on the county port. Taking their cue from the council's October 9 resolution favoring county airport expansion, the fifty-nine members of the board voted unanimously to direct the Road Commission to speed the expansion of the county field. The resolution, passed on October 23, ordered the Road Commission ". . . to proceed without delay to prepare plans, study and negotiate financing, and . . . make all necessary arrangements [in order to] improve, develop, and expand the Wayne County Airport facilities so that [the airport] will be available for use by the airlines as *the major metropolitan airport terminal* for intrastate, interstate, and international transport as soon as possible" (italics added). There was no "interim" designation in the county resolution. Leroy Smith had won his first local endorsement of the county airport as "the major metropolitan airport terminal."

The Board of Commerce's options on the northwest properties were due to expire at the end of October. As the end of the month approached, board members moved to allay fears that the board was backing out. Kiskadden, in a letter to Mayor Jeffries on October 26, announced that the board was reviewing its options "because we still believe that the greatest good can be accomplished for all the people of Detroit by the selection of the northwest site."

As Kiskadden's letter reached the mayor, another letter was in final draft stage in Chicago, Illinois. This three-and-one-half-page letter, dated October 29, 1945, was from George W. Vest, regional administrator for the Third (north-central) Region of the Civil Aeronautics Administration, in response to the Aviation Planning Authority's request for the CAA's views on the Horner-Shifrin report. Vest concurred with the consultants' views ruling out the international airport as not feasible in the immediate future, but he disagreed with the favorable recommendation on the Ford-Gulley site. An airport at that location would be only three miles from the Ford Airport in Dearborn and four and one-half miles from the county field. The new airport would "seriously interfere" with operations at these two existing airports, and "it is therefore our opinion that the Ford-Gulley site is not acceptable as the terminal airport." On the northwest site, Vest agreed completely with the findings of the Horner-Shifrin report that such an airport would be "very undesirable" and would lead to "perpetual conflict" and "air congestion" between scheduled and non-scheduled flights. "We, therefore, are of the opinion that the terminal airport should not be located at the Eight Mile–Wyoming site. . . ." Moving on to County Airport, Vest said:

> The other remaining master site receiving consideration is that of Wayne County Airport. It is our belief that this field should be developed as the major terminal for the Detroit region. The greater percentage of scheduled aircraft arriving and departing from Detroit

comes from the southerly portions. Therefore, by locating the major terminal in the south of the concentrated population areas and reserving the northerly sections for personal flying, we will achieve an automatic traffic separation between scheduled and non-scheduled flying. We feel there is no practical way to accomplish the desired segregation except by location of the facilities involved.

Vest concluded by saying that ". . . the Wayne County Airport is the most desirable site at this time for the major terminal in the Detroit region" and that ". . . the master airport plan for the Detroit region with Wayne County Airport . . . as the major passenger port is approved by the Civil Aeronautics Administration." Leroy Smith had a second and most important official designation of his airport as the major air terminal for the metropolitan area.

Vest's letter, which was released to the public after the meeting of the Aviation Planning Authority on November 13, gave a new and potent weapon to backers of County Airport. In addition to the weight of official blessing, the CAA endorsement of County Airport carried financial implications. There was every expectation that a continuing federal-aid-to-airports program would be approved by Congress in its 1946 session. (Such a program was enacted at that session and provided for federal grants on a fifty-fifty matching basis.) The thought that the federal government might not lend its financial support to an airport other than Wayne County was enough to sober the thinking of any sensible local official.

CAA support of Smith's County Airport was not a matter of sheer luck. Smith had actively sought designation of County Airport as the major air terminal from CAA officials through correspondence and personal contacts. He had journeyed to the CAA's Chicago office on a number of occasions and had also pressed his case before CAA officials in Washington, where he had many long-standing contacts from previous experience on both highway and aviation matters.

The events related above have, for the most part, been matters of public record. Below the threshold of the public record were many maneuverings, some of which are indicated in the following letter, dated November 30, 1945, from Donald Kiskadden to Leroy Smith, and reproduced in full:

Dear Roy:

In talking to Bill Mara [William A. Mara, member of the Aviation Committee of the Board of Commerce and director of advertising and public relations, Bendix Aviation Corporation] this morning, he said that he had talked to you and that you were under the impression that some of the members of the Airport [*sic*] Committee, and particularly one Kiskadden, had accused you of "double-crossing" them. Mr. Cochran of Giffels & Vallet had told me the same thing some time ago, but I wasn't particularly disturbed until I heard it again the second time this morning.

Now to get the records straight, let me say that I have never accused you of any "double-crossing" in regard to this airport situation, nor have I heard any member of our committee at any time even intimate such a thing. In fact the only reference I can remember that I have ever made about you was that at least at one time I was sure you felt the northwest site was the best available major site for metropolitan Detroit. I was always careful to add that of course Mr. Smith couldn't say that officially as long as the county had their interest in the Wayne County Airport.

As far as Wayne County Airport is concerned, I and the rest of our committee have always felt that it should be developed and enlarged—that eventually Detroit will need at least three fairly sizable airports, Wayne on the west, [the] northwest [airport] for the central location, and in the future a major airport on the far east side of the metropolitan area. We have felt that just because certain residents of Palmer Woods, Sherwood Forest, Huntington Woods, and Pleasant Ridge object to the northwest location that we shouldn't abandon our efforts to get a centrally located major airport which would serve not only the people of Detroit, but many of those in Oakland and Macomb counties who are properly considered a part of our metropolitan area. At the same time we recognize that Wayne County Airport has an important place in the picture and that it should be enlarged and developed and must be used as Detroit's major airport until a more centrally located one can be built. Our only objection to Wayne is that we sincerely believe that it should not be Detroit's permanent major airport.

It is unthinkable that two peaceful old gents like you and me should have any misunderstanding, let alone quarrel over airport locations or anything else. That is the only reason for writing this letter, of which there will be only one copy, which will go into my files.

In the confusion and jostling for position that had followed the release of the Horner-Shifrin report, the county had come out on top. The Common Council had not only backed away from the northwest site, it had endorsed a resolution favoring the county airport. In a backhanded way the report resulted in the CAA's conferring its seal of approval on the county port, and the Ford-Gulley site, which the report had recommended for immediate development, was all but forgotten.

The airport site endorsed by the Board of Commerce had been defeated, but the board's opposition to the county field was undiminished. The board's principal spokesmen on airport matters during the coming thirteen years of controversy, Donald S. Kiskadden and William A. Mara, were already in the forefront. Mara, who had been Detroit's first airport commissioner in the 1920's, was soon to succeed Ernest Breech as chairman of the Aviation Committee of the Board of Commerce. With the exception of the two-and-one-half-year tenure (December 1950–July 1953) of George N. Monroe III, the Aviation Committee chairmanship was held by either Mara or Kiskadden until 1958, when the airport controversy ended. The defeat of the northwest site set the stage for a countermove engineered by Mara and Kiskadden and designed to drain Leroy Smith's victory on the northwest site of its meaning.

The Airlines Choose Willow Run.   An indication of the weight given to the CAA opinion came on December 6, 1945, when spokesmen for the airlines indicated their intention to serve Detroit from County Airport. The next day Leroy Smith announced that work would begin on the expansion of County Airport. The airport, Smith said, would be available to the airlines on January 15, when the Army Air Force expected to close out its operations and return the field to the county. The expansion would not interfere with air movements on the existing runways since an entirely new runway system would be built on the newly acquired property adjacent to the existing field.

On December 28, two days before the federal government made a formal public announcement that Willow Run was to be put up for sale or lease as surplus war property, *Detroit News* Aviation Writer James Sweinhart informed Donald Kiskadden of the government's forthcoming action, of which Swinehart had learned from the Washington bureau of the *News*. Kiskadden, an alumnus of the University of Michigan Law School, immediately called Alexander G. Ruthven, president of the University of Michigan. As Kiskadden recalls the conversation:

> I told him that here was an opportunity to expand the facilities of their engineering school and serve a public need at the same time. I explained that the university could get the field, hangars, facilities, and so forth for a wind tunnel and almost any other kind of major scientific projects they wanted. They could then lease the field to the airlines. I then asked if we could set up an appointment with his vice presidents, business manager, and engineering deans to discuss the university's purchasing the field. He agreed and Jim Sweinhart, Bill Mara, and I went out to Ann Arbor and did some convincing. They investigated the matter in some detail and finally agreed to purchase the airport after Detroit turned it down.

Detroit and Wayne County, as units of local government, had priority in acquiring surplus federal property, but neither was expected to exercise it in this case. The university, as an educational institution, would be entitled to acquire the property on much more favorable financial terms than would the commercial airlines.

On January 9, 1946, the airlines announced that they were not going to move to the county field after all and that by March they hoped to be operating out of Willow Run Airport. Robert Averill, regional vice president of Capital Airlines and chairman of the Airlines Negotiating Committee, stressed that the proposed move to Willow Run would be a temporary expedient—until Detroit provided more adequate and centrally located facilities. Averill listed several reasons for the airlines' decision to avoid County Airport—inadequate and poor conditions of the runways, only partial wind coverage, inadequate clearance on the runways, absence of hangars capable of handling four-engine planes, and lack of passenger facilities. Averill acknowledged that the airlines' move to Willow Run would create passenger inconveniences—a long trip to the airport (thirty-three miles from downtown) and makeshift terminal facilities. He added: "It is unthinkable that the three million people in the metropolitan area should be required to suffer the expense and inconvenience of such great distances for one day longer than is necessary to provide the centrally located northwest passenger terminal." Apparently the airlines interest in the northwest site had waned only slightly.

One week after the airlines' announcement the Detroit Common Council considered and rejected its priority to purchase Willow Run. The Road Commission expressed no interest in Willow Run, since Smith found the airport's high maintenance costs and distance from downtown Detroit objectionable. The way was clear for the university and the airlines.

The public announcement of the entrance of the University of Michigan onto the airport scene was made on February 15. The university agreed to purchase the airport and related facilities for one dollar ($1.00) and announced its intention to set up an aeronautical research center there. In acquiring Willow Run the university agreed to certain terms insisted upon by the federal government. There were three important ones: (1) The university agreed to maintain the runways and other facilities in good and serviceable condition. (2) The federal government was granted unrestricted possession of the airport during any national emergency declared by the President. (3) Federal aircraft could use the landing facilities without charge. In addition, the federal government retained ownership of a twenty-three-acre parcel of land plus barracks and storage buildings on the east side of the airfield.

Meanwhile Capital Airlines formed a corporation to lease and operate the flight facilities of the airport from the university. The terminal corporation, officially known as the Airlines National Terminal Service Company (ANTSCO), agreed to assume full maintenance costs for the airport and reportedly agreed to pay "a substantial yearly rental." Just what these costs and the rental charge were was not disclosed, since the university, by virtue of its constitutional and quasi-autonomous status within Michigan state government, can withhold the details of its financial operations. Nonetheless, the financial attractiveness of the arrangement was apparent. The university acquired extensive research facilities at nominal cost, while the airlines avoided paying whatever price the government would have negotiated with them had they sought to buy the airport themselves.

Immediately after the university officially took possession of the $21,000,000 airport on June 3, the contract with ANTSCO was signed. On June 15, 1946, Capital Airlines flew the first scheduled flight into the airport.

The airlines' intention to use Willow Run as a temporary expedient eased the crisis on the airport issue, but it did not deter the city of Detroit from continuing its attempts to do something about a major airport. Now seemed an appropriate time to act on the "ideal solution" suggested in the Horner-Shifrin report—the international site. On February 12, Councilman VanAntwerp introduced a resolution officially designating the proposed international airport as Detroit's major air terminal. VanAntwerp's resolution received firm support from the Board of Commerce. But Glenn Richards, who had been working actively on behalf of County Airport within the city administration, had reached the mayor's ear. One day after the introducing of VanAntwerp's resolution, Jeffries elaborated seven reasons for opposing the international site as Detroit's major airport:

> First, it does not seem that this location is sufficiently superior to that of the present County Airport to be attractive enough so that we should take Detroit capital and develop a Canadian enterprise.
> Second, it seems poor public relations to advertise throughout the world that the Detroit Municipal Airport is located in Windsor, Canada.
> Third, the ramifications of an international site are multitudinous. It would be subject to the whims and fancies of the parliament of Canada and the State Department of the United States.
> Fourth, all contemplated growth of metropolitan Detroit would be away from the contemplated international site.
> Fifth, the building of the Lodge and Crosstown [Ford] Expressways brings the County Airport considerably closer in travel time to every section of the city.
> Sixth, the county has owned and operated an airport for more than fifteen years. We have a sizable investment in it. It is being expanded expeditiously. Are we, the people of Detroit, who make up 85 percent of Wayne County, to abandon this project?
> Seventh, as you know, I favored the northwest site which your body turned down. I feel very strongly that the second-best location is the Wayne County site, and I think we should do everything to expedite the building of a first-class airport at that location (Journal of the Common Council, City of Detroit, 1946, p. 346).

The mayor was now clearly in favor of County Airport.

The VanAntwerp resolution failed to pass by a three-to-five vote at the March 5 council meeting. Jeffries' firm stand and the defeat of the resolution marked a turning point for County Airport. One week later, on March 12, Councilman William Rogell introduced, and the council passed by a seven-to-one vote, a resolution "that this Common Council hereby designates the Wayne County Airport as the major airport for the Detroit area and it shall be known as Detroit-Wayne Major Airport."

There was no "interim" designation in the March 12 resolution. Leroy Smith now had three official endorsements—the Detroit Common Council, the County Board of Supervisors, and the Civil Aeronautics Administration—of County Airport as the metropolitan area's major airport. Following the council's resolution the County Board of Supervisors changed the official name of the county airport to Detroit-Wayne Major Airport. For Leroy Smith this was not a negligible plus, but it was small consolation for the airlines' reversal of their plans to move to the county field.

Smith Fights Back. During the summer of 1946 one airline, Capital, operated four-engine craft regularly from Willow Run. The other seven airlines flew two-engine craft out of City Airport, but they were actively negotiating with the University of Michigan and ANTSCO to use Willow Run. Despite the airlines' stated aversion to the county field, there was a fleeting chance that they might be attracted to it before committing themselves to Willow Run. Characteristically, Leroy Smith and his associates moved with dispatch.

On May 13, President Truman signed the Airport Act of 1946. The act authorized a system of federal grants to local units on a fifty-fifty matching basis. Smith immediately proposed a $15,-000,000 expansion program for Detroit-Wayne Major. He recommended that the County Board of Supervisors request a $5,000,000 federal appropriation and a $2,500,000 state appropriation. Local matching funds of $2,500,000 would come from a proposed bond issue of $7,500,000. The $5,000,000 in excess of local matching requirements would be used on expansion projects not eligible for federal aid, e.g., a new terminal building. Resolutions requesting the state and federal funds passed the Board of Supervisors and were forwarded to state and federal officials. The Detroit Common Council also passed resolutions supporting the county's requests. Early in July the Board of Supervisors approved the submission of the $7,500,000 airport bond issue to the voters at the forthcoming November elections.

Smith's efforts to forestall the airlines' move to Willow Run met with some initial success. In mid-July American Airlines, which handled nearly one-third of all passenger traffic to and from Detroit, announced that it planned to locate at Detroit-Wayne Major rather than at Willow Run. The six other airlines continued negotiations with the University of Michigan and ANTSCO, and late in August they announced an agreement whereby they would move to Willow Run in October. In September American Airlines announced that it too was moving to Willow Run. The announcement came after three weeks of intensive negotiation between American and Road Commission officials. The chief stumbling blocks to agreement were the reportedly high fees and charges that the Road Commission demanded.

American's decision was a blow to Smith's hopes of winning the November bond issue. The pressure was off. With all the airlines accommodated at Willow Run, the immediate need for an enlarged County Airport diminished and with it, presumably, the will of the voters to approve the bond issue. Despite support for the bond issue from Mayor Jeffries, Councilmen VanAntwerp and Charles E. Dorais, and Ernest Breech, now chief executive of the Ford Motor Company, it was defeated by a five-to-four margin at the polls.

Undaunted, Smith redoubled his efforts to secure funds from the CAA for his expansion program. Late in November he journeyed to Washington for informal discussions with CAA officials. On February 6, 1947, the CAA announced its intention to allocate $1,600,000 for Wayne Major out of federal funds becoming available in fiscal 1947–48. The "grant offer," as it was called, required that an equal amount of state and/or local funds be raised. Despite a rebuff at the polls a few months earlier, it appeared that Smith might have more than $3,000,000 to begin his expansion program if he could raise matching funds. But as a result of the economy drive in the first session of the Republican-controlled Eightieth Congress, the federal grant offer was revised downward drastically. The CAA announced that it would allocate only $550,000 to Wayne Major.

Contenting himself with the smaller amount, Smith sought the necessary matching funds. He also needed authorization from the state for the Road Commission to receive and spend the federal funds. Smith's influence in the state legislature stood him in good stead on his twofold mission. The federal grant offer had been extended in February, when the biennial session of the legislature was already under way. Requests for a state appropriation of $500,000 and authorizing legislation were dropped in the legislative hopper. By the end of the session the legislature had given the Road Commission authority to receive the federal funds and had appropriated $275,000 in matching funds. This sum combined with a similar amount appropriated by the County Board of Supervisors matched the revised grant offer of $550,000. With $1,100,000 in his pocket Leroy Smith announced (or re-announced) in September 1947 a long-range expansion program. (Technically speaking, Smith's program was not an expansion of the existing county airport. The runways and buildings on the original site would not be used as integral parts of the new airport. Instead, an entirely new system of runways would be built on the land acquired south and west of the existing field.) The expansion program was designed, he said, "to lure the airlines away from Willow Run."

Although the scheduled commercial airlines were firmly situated at Willow Run by 1947, Wayne Major was not idle. The Air National Guard was still quartered at the field, which also became a center of brisk air freight traffic, with three regularly operating air freight lines. In addition, several corporate (e.g., Ford Motor Company, Great Lakes Steel Corporation, and Wyandotte Chemicals Corporation) and private aircraft were based at the airport.

Federal agencies were also present. Since the U.S. Customs and Immigration Service had designated Wayne Major as a port of entry into the United States in 1946, flights entering the United States from Canada were cleared at the airport by U.S. Customs and Immigration officers. The port-of-entry designation was expected to yield a future advantage: when international air travel was inaugurated from Detroit, Wayne Major would be the logical base for these flights. The CAA was also well ensconced at Wayne Major, for that agency had selected the county field as headquarters for several of its operations in Michigan. CAA units leasing space and facilities at Wayne Major included the Air Route Traffic Control Center, Detroit Communications Station, Communications Maintenance Department, Airways Maintenance Department, Aviation Safety District Office, and the Bureau of Safety Investigation. Air commerce and its varied ancillary activities functioned without difficulty at the "old" County Airport as work started on the land to the south and west, where the "new" Detroit-Wayne Major Airport was to be built.

Eight air miles to the west the passenger airlines were operating smoothly at Willow Run. 1947 was their first full year of operation at Willow Run. The year proved to be a modest success despite some passenger resistance to the fifty-minute ride from downtown Detroit. Total passenger traffic for the year was 722,000. About two hundred flights were scheduled from the airport daily. An instrument landing system was completed and in operation by the end of 1947. Some improvements had been made in the converted hangar which served as a passenger terminal building: a passenger lobby and waiting room had been partitioned off, and a restaurant, cafeteria, and other facilities were soon opened. But the gleaming new ticket counters stood in sharp contrast to the dark, cavernous ceilings of the hangar and its rusty exposed girders and noticeable drafts circulated through the massive structure. The airport looked like the "temporary expedient" which the airlines had declared it to be when they decided to move into it in order to avoid the county field. But the grubbing, grading, paving and other construction under way a few miles to the east were a constant reminder that Leroy Smith had not changed his mind on where he thought the airlines should make their permanent home.

The International Site

The Detroit Metropolitan Aviation Authority. The fall of 1947 found Smith's efforts on behalf of Wayne Major only partially rewarded. In the more than two years since the filing of the Horner-Shifrin report in July 1945, County Airport had received three endorsements as the area's major air terminal. The three were from the Wayne County Board of Supervisors (October 23, 1945), the Civil Aeronautics Administration (October 29, 1945), and the De

troit Common Council (March 12, 1946). The Michigan Aeronautics Commission had also gone on record as favoring improvement
of the county field. During the same period threats to the airport's
"major" status posed by proposed airports were defeated. Both the
northeast and northwest sites had been ruled out. An abortive
threat from the international site had been fended off in February
1946. Equally important, work was now in progress to expand the
county field into a major airport. But in spite of these victories, the
airlines were not at Detroit-Wayne Major; they were at Willow
Run, thanks to a bit of maneuvering by Donald Kiskadden and
William Mara.

Curiously, Smith and Kiskadden now shared the same opinion
about one aspect of the airport situation—they both saw the location of the airlines at Willow Run as a temporary situation. When
a new close-in or centrally located airport became available, the
airlines were expected to move. Smith and Kiskadden differed
widely, of course, as to where such an airport would be located.
Nevertheless, the desire to relocate the airlines set the stage for
another major clash over airports and another challenge to Leroy
Smith and Detroit-Wayne Major.

The seeds of this battle were planted in the same two-year
period during which Smith had secured his victories. The Horner-
Shifrin report had recommended the creation of a metropolitan
aviation authority. The legal basis for creating a metropolitan
aviation authority was Section 134 of the Michigan Aeronautics
Code, which permitted any two or more political subdivisions of
the state to conclude a joint agreement creating a special authority
which could exercise powers vested in any single political subdivision by the Aeronautics Code. Membership on the governing
board of such a body, as well as its powers, financing, etc., were
to be spelled out in the joint agreement between the local units.
An incidental provision also permitted the state to be a party to
the joint agreement. Accordingly, late in 1945, Samuel Dean, chairman of the Detroit Metropolitan Aviation Planning Authority, proposed that the five units represented on the Planning Authority
(the city of Detroit, Wayne, Macomb, and Oakland counties, and
the Michigan Aeronautics Commission) seriously consider the
creation of a metropolitan authority by concluding a joint agree-

ment. Leroy Smith and Glenn Richards both expressed skepticism of Dean's proposals, and lengthy negotiations preceded the consensus that was finally reached in the fall of 1946, when the joint body, the Detroit Metropolitan Aviation Authority (DMAA) was created.

The composition and powers of DMAA were indicative of the direction in which political currents ran during the months of negotiation. Its governing body consisted of eight voting members of which the boards of supervisors of Wayne, Macomb, and Oakland counties each appointed one, the city of Detroit appointed two, and the Michigan Aeronautics Commission appointed two. The eighth member was selected by the Wayne County Road Commission. Each voting member also had an alternate coming from the same constituent unit. The agreement provided that of Detroit's two representatives, one was to be a councilman and one an administrative official. When appointments to the DMAA were announced, it occasioned little surprise that Glenn Richards was named as Detroit's administrative official and Leroy Smith was selected to represent the Road Commission. Councilman Eugene VanAntwerp, who had been on several sides of the airport question, represented the Detroit Common Council. VanAntwerp was elected chairman of the DMAA at its first meeting in January 1947. Cass S. Hough, an industrialist from Plymouth, in western Wayne County, was selected as an alternate for one of the two representatives named by the Michigan Aeronautics Commission. Hough was currently the chairman of the Aeronautics Commission and was soon to become an arch foe of Leroy Smith's aims for Detroit-Wayne Major. Glenn Richards' alternate to the DMAA was Colonel C. V. Burnett. Except for active duty in World War II, Burnett managed City Airport from 1934 to 1957. At the time of his appointment as an alternate to the DMAA, Burnett headed the Aviation Division in Richards' department.

Under the joint agreement the DMAA was granted the power "to create, adopt, and establish a master plan for the . . . development and operation of airports within or without the territorial limits of the signatories." Before this master plan became final and binding, the joint agreement required that the plan be ratified by the governing bodies of the five constituent units and that it be submitted to the Civil Aeronautics Administration and the Michigan Aeronautics Commission for their consideration and approval. The DMAA was an airport planning body, and not a particularly strong one at that. Ironically, in naming the new agency the Detroit Metropolitan Aviation Authority, the word "planning" was dropped from the title of its predecessor.

The Board of Commerce had misgivings about the DMAA. An unnamed spokesman for the board's Aviation Committee saw the long arm of Leroy Smith behind concessions made on representation and powers and called the DMAA joint agreement "a smokescreen to foist off the Detroit-Wayne Major Airport on the people of Detroit as the city's principal passenger terminal." But despite its lack of power and its representational and political disabilities, the DMAA attempted to make its own independent contribution to resolving Detroit's airport problem. It hired a staff director, Eugene Fryhoff, in November 1947. By the spring of 1948 Fryhoff had recruited three professional aides and had started a master plan study of airports in the Detroit region. Despite inadequate financial support and lack of encouragement from Glenn Richards, who became chairman when VanAntwerp resigned the post upon winning the mayoralty election in November 1947, Fryhoff expected to complete the master plan study by the fall of 1948.

The DMAA Staff Report. While the DMAA's master plan study was in progress, renewed interest in the international airport site was triggered by the mayor of Windsor, Ontario. In June of 1948 the mayor proposed joint discussions leading to the construction of such an airport. These overtures elicited favorable responses from Mayor VanAntwerp, the Detroit Board of Commerce, *The Detroit News,* and the airlines. In September 1948, shortly after joint discussions began, a first draft of the DMAA master plan study was completed and circulated among DMAA members. Although the draft was purportedly for review and discussion by DMAA members, the newspapers obtained copies of the sixty-two-page report and gave it prominent coverage.

The DMAA staff report, titled *Airports for the Detroit Region: A Master Airport Plan,* concluded that (1) Detroit is predominantly a short-haul city (average passenger trip of 371 miles), indicating the need for close-in airport facilities, (2) increased air traffic will require two major airports by 1960, and (3) both air freight and international flights will constitute a significant proportion of Detroit's air traffic and should be planned for accordingly. It therefore recommended that

(1) the international airport serve as Detroit's major passenger terminal, and that steps toward site acquisition and construction be taken *immediately,*

(2) Wayne Major be expanded as planned, but that it serve as the major air freight terminal and as a secondary passenger terminal serving the western parts of the metropolitan area, and

(3) Willow Run be consigned exclusively to military use.

A final major recommendation was that "a properly constituted airport authority should be established with the necessary legal powers to plan, finance, construct, own, and operate airports in the Detroit region," because "efficient and economical administration of airports in the region cannot be accomplished under existing conditions where each airport is under the control of a separate and distinct governing body." The staff report declared the DMAA inadequate to the tasks of metropolitan airport development.

The DMAA staff report, like the Horner-Shifrin report three years earlier, favored the international site. While this site was as theoretical in 1948 as it had been in 1945, the old County Airport of 1945 was now Detroit-Wayne Major Airport, and the expansion plans which Smith had first announced late in 1944 were now on their way to realization. The County Airport, which the Horner-Shifrin report had relegated to "minor" status, was endorsed in the DMAA report as a major airport (albeit primarily for freight) which should continue its expansion program.

A rebuttal to the DMAA staff report appeared early in October when the Road Commission released a sixteen-page report ambitiously titled, *The Airport Problem of Metropolitan Detroit: Past, Present, and Future.* This report pointed to the advantages of using Detroit-Wayne Major, called the passenger and revenue projections used by the DMAA staff to support the need for, and fiscal feasability of, the international airport "extremely optimistic," and cited the practical obstacles to locating a United States airport on foreign soil. One of these obstacles was that, in the opinion of the general counsel of the CAA, federal aid could not be granted the international airport because of its location on foreign soil. Complications concerning the application of state and federal taxes, the employment of American as opposed to Canadian workers, and customs and immigration arrangements were also cited. The report concluded with a recommendation "that the enlargement of Detroit-Wayne Major Airport . . . be continued as originally outlined," and that the DMAA staff study be placed "on file for future reference when and if present facilities in the Detroit metropolitan area which are already built and being expanded become saturated and inadequate." In a rare lapse, Leroy Smith had announced his strategy—to kill the staff report by placing it on file.

The clashes at the October 25 DMAA meeting were sharp and heated. When the smoke of the battle cleared, Leroy Smith had suffered a major defeat but salvaged a partial victory. Over objections from Smith and Richards, the body voted to print and distribute the report. The concession gained by Smith was a deferral of the DMAA's official endorsement of the staff report's recommendations. This action was delayed, according to the frontispiece in the published report, "until interested persons and officials have an opportunity to express themselves after reviewing the report."

During the next three months support for the international airport snowballed. Endorsements seem to come from every quarter, as the Michigan Aeronautics Commission and newly-elected Democratic Governor G. Mennen Williams officially endorsed the site, and Republican U.S. Senator Homer Ferguson announced his support of it. At the local level the three metropolitan daily papers gave it editorial support, and several Detroit associations, including the Detroit Board of Commerce, the Detroit Real Estate Board, the Detroit Hotel Association, and the Aircraft Owners and Pilots Association, passed resolutions urging favorable action on the Canadian site. Walter Reuther, president of the United Auto Workers, added his support. The airlines' endorsement was the most fervent: in January 1949 they petitioned the CAA to cut off federal aid to Wayne Major.

Amid the many endorsements of the international site, only Smith and Richards had expressed opposition. Richards' position was anomalous. As public works commissioner and DMAA representative (and chairman) he was presumably the spokesman on aviation matters for the VanAntwerp administration. VanAntwerp had recorded his firm support of the international site, but Richards said (*The Detroit News,* January 24) that the Canadian site was "impractical, unnecessary, and financially unsound at the present time," adding, however, that he would "certainly follow the instructions of the city" if formal actions were taken to investigate and develop the site. The council was scheduled to consider the mayor's request for funds to finance an engineering study of the site on February 2.

One day before the scheduled council meeting Leroy Smith came out in favor of the international airport. His support was conditional—provided that construction of the international airport would not stop the expansion and completion of Wayne Major as the area's "interim major air terminal." Some years later Cass Hough, testifying before a Congressional committee, described the deal offered by Smith:

> We had a more or less verbal understanding, a tacit agreement, if you will, with Mr. Smith and the votes he was able to muster on the authority that if we would strike from the report the inference that Wayne County Airport would never amount to very much, he would be willing to go along and help us develop the international site. . . . I do not need to tell you on the committee that trades are made all the time . . . in this case it was a definite trade.

According to Hough, the trade went awry:

> Mr. Smith did not keep his word. Mr. Smith is even quoted in the paper—and I am sure the paper quoted him accurately—not more than three weeks after Mr. Smith promised his support for helping get the international airport at Windsor—he is quoted in the papers as saying that he "scoffed at the probability of an international airport ever serving Detroit in Windsor"—to show you the way agreements are honored (*Federal Role in Aviation,* Hearings before a Subcommittee of the Committee on Government Operations, House of Representatives, 84th Congress, 2nd Session, p. 641; hereafter cited as *Federal Role in Aviation*).

On February 2 the council voted funds for a study of the proposed site. The DMAA, which also met on February 2, unanimously adopted the formerly disputed staff report and forwarded it to the CAA for review and comment. Implicit in the DMAA action was tacit consent to the further expansion of Wayne Major.

The DMAA's unanimity disintegrated one month later. At the March 2 meeting some board members criticized the authority's staff director, Eugene Fryhoff, for his "premature" and "unauthorized" submission of a master plan for the new airport to the CAA accompanied by a request for a public hearing before CAA regional officials. On March 30, 1949, a majority of the board voted, with Hough leading the dissenters, to disassociate itself from any responsibility for calling the CAA hearing on the master plan. Proponents of the international port remembered that when the CAA had commented on the Horner-Shifrin report, the federal agency had dismissed the consultants' recommendation and had come out in favor of Wayne Major.

The CAA Gives an Opinion.   The CAA hearing was held in Chicago on April 13. DMAA staff members were there, along with private citizens and public officials from Detroit and Windsor speaking in favor of the Canadian site, and officials from the Road Commission and the University of Michigan, who were allied in their opposition to the international airport. University representatives pointed out that Willow Run had been provided without cost to city, county, or state taxpayers and urged its continuation as Detroit's major air terminal.

The CAA did not make its findings and recommendations known until several weeks after the Chicago hearing. Meanwhile *The Detroit News* and the Board of Commerce kept the airport issue near the center of local attention and noted with concern Glenn Richards' persistent reluctance and/or outright opposition to the Canadian site. On June 1, Richards tendered his resignation from the DMAA to the Detroit Common Council, and the council accepted it unanimously. Richards recalls a discussion with a leading councilman:

> He [the councilman] told me that I was right and that he would like to be able to back me. But, he said, the trouble was that it was such a hot issue. I told him that if he and the other councilmen would feel better, I would get out of the picture. That's what I did. It satisfied a lot of critics and made it easier for the mayor and council.

The death knell on the international site was sounded on July 11, 1949. A letter of that date from George W. Vest, CAA regional administrator, presented the findings and recommendations of the CAA regional office based on the April 13 public hearing. The gist of the seven-page, single-spaced letter was that the site was acceptable from an air-traffic standpoint and that the DMAA should explore arrangements for making the airport feasible, *but* that a second major airport was not needed or justified by passenger projections. The CAA official recommended "that actual physical development of this [international] site be deferred until such time as careful estimates indicate its need" and "that the construction and improvement of Wayne Major Airport be continued."

The CAA's crucial dissent from the DMAA report, the basis on which the CAA challenged the need for a second major air terminal, was on passenger projections for the Detroit area. The DMAA estimated 2,200,000 passengers in 1955, 3,000,000 in 1960. The CAA, echoing the Road Commission's opinion of these figures as expressed in the commission's October 1948 report, *The Airport Problem of Metropolitan Detroit*, termed these estimates "optimistic." The CAA estimated 1,100,000 passengers for 1955. Actually, there were 2,160,003 air passengers in and out of Detroit in 1955. They were easily handled at one airport (Willow Run) because of the increased size of passenger aircraft and other technological developments. The CAA, in its 1949 letter, had arrived at the right conclusion, but for the wrong reason.

There were loud protests on the local scene against Vest's second letter, as there had been against his first (October 29, 1945). D. W. Rentzel, CAA administrator in Washington, extended the opportunity for an appeal, or possibly just an olive branch. He was quoted as saying that the report (letter) was only a recommendation. "While the report is important, it is by no means conclusive. If the people of the Detroit area, through their local units of government, show us they want this international airport, they can have it. The whole matter is automatically subject to review at the Washington level."

The international airport hung on, chiefly through the persistent efforts of the airlines, for the remainder of 1949 and all of 1950. The interest of Detroit officialdom in the port waned considerably, partly because of the reported demand by Canadian officials that the airport be built with all-Canadian materials and all-Canadian labor. The site was officially and ignominiously dropped on March 15, 1951, following a meeting of airline officials and representatives of the U.S. State Department and Commerce Department. A report had been received from Canadian authorities that all but assured the Dominion government's refusal to cooperate on the international site. The ostensible reason was that the site failed to fit the Dominion's master plan for airports.

There the international airport rested. The site which the DMAA staff report had favored and which the Horner-Shifrin report had called "ideal" was a dead letter. The net effect of both reports had been to elicit CAA support of Wayne Major. For Leroy Smith, another major challenge to Detroit-Wayne Major had been surmounted. The county's airport was still the metropolitan area's *major* air terminal in name, if not in use, and the DMAA report had endorsed the continued expansion of its facilities. While debate continued over what it should be, the county field was, in fact, being transformed into a modern airport.

Wayne Major Continues Its Improvement Program. The sharp local clashes over the international airport obscured unpublicized stratagems unfolding at the state level before the Michigan Aeronautics Commission. The maneuvering centered around Leroy Smith's efforts to secure additional federal grants for the continued development of Wayne Major. The first federal grant for the fiscal year 1947–48 was $550,000. An application for a larger grant was filed late in 1947 for the fiscal year starting July 1, 1948. On July 2, 1948, the CAA announced an allocation of $1,000,000 to Wayne Major. This was shortly after passage of Act 32 of 1948, the "anti-channeling" act, which introduced a third party, the state, into Smith's financial dealings with the federal government.

According to the federal Airport Act of 1946, a state could choose to make itself an intermediary between the local unit and the federal government, or it could permit direct national-local allocations. In 1948 the Michigan legislature decided to stop direct national-local channeling in Michigan. The anti-channeling act sought to give a state body, the Michigan Aeronautics Commission, a voice in the distribution of federal funds for airport development to local units. To accomplish this, three sections were added to the Aeronautics Code. These sections (1) authorized every political subdivision to accept federal grants for airport development, but (2) prohibited the submission of grant requests to the CAA without the prior approval of the Michigan Aeronautics Commission, and (3) made the state commission the agent for every local unit in accepting, receiving, accounting for, and disbursing any federal funds granted to Michigan local units under the Airport Act. Henceforth, the Michigan Aeronautics Commission would presumably occupy an authoritative role in Detroit's airport problems via the all-important medium of controlling the flow of federal funds.

The composition of the eight-member commission was not altogether reassuring for Smith and Wayne Major. Two of the five commissioners who had been appointed by the governor were Cass Hough and William M. Joy, both members of the Detroit Board of Commerce who shared the board's views on airport policy. But among the remaining three members, who held seats on the commission by virtue of their other state administrative positions, was the popularly elected state highway commissioner, Charles M. Ziegler. Ziegler and Smith were close friends who shared a professional interest—highways.

Late in the summer of 1948 Smith came before the Michigan Aeronautics Commission to seek approval for receipt of the $1,000,000 allocation for Wayne Major which the CAA had announced in early July for fiscal 1948–49. At the same time he filed applications for several projects totaling another $1,000,000 for fiscal 1949–50. He ran headlong into Hough's vehement opposition. Smith's requests came at the early stages of the developing controversy over the international site and pitted Hough against Smith on both the state and local levels.

Smith obtained the federal moneys. How he accomplished the feat can best be told in words of his arch foe, Cass Hough. Hough's views were officially recorded at the Congressional hearings in 1956, nearly eight years after the dispute. Hough stopped short of accusing the Road Commission of duplicity or "hoodwinking" the state body, but he did allege that the Road Commission permitted members of the state unit to think that federal funds were being used for the "improvement of an existing airport rather than the building of a new airport." As the modern airport which Smith was building next to the original County Airport site took shape and was put into operation, the county's original, aging facilities fell into disuse. It became clear that "expansion" of the original County Airport actually meant replacement of it by its newer neighbor. "All of a sudden we woke up . . . to an aeronautical monstrosity," Hough said (*Federal Role in Aviation*, p. 648).

Another of Hough's contentions was more damaging. He charged that the Road Commission had used the presence of the Air National Guard at the county field as justification for seeking "improvement" moneys. Federal grants, of course, were to promote civil aviation. The presence of military planes at an airport could never be used (officially, at least) as a basis for securing funds. Hough's testimony on this point was as follows:

> During the nearly five years I served as chairman of the Aeronautics Commission, the Wayne County Road Commission made any number of appearances before the Michigan Aeronautics Commission asking for funds, and in every single case the main thing they hung their case on was a request for money to improve the airport because the Air National Guard was at the airport. I think that is very significant. Here is a division of government which has a white elephant on its hands—and it would have been a much whiter elephant and bigger one if the Air National Guard was not operating out of the airport—coming to the Michigan Aeronautics Commission asking for funds predicated mainly on the fact that the National Guard needed longer runways, better taxiways, and all things they needed because they were going to get jets, and so forth. . . . It's a ridiculous position (*Federal Role in Aviation*, p. 640).

Why, under these circumstances, did the Aeronautics Commission approve federal funds for Wayne Major? Here Hough drew a distinction between "allocating" federal funds and "channeling" them. The former term he applied to the exercise of discretion in the distribution of funds; by the latter term he meant the mere ratifying of CAA decisions on where (to what airports) the federal money would go. Hough claimed that the Michigan Aeronautics Commission had been simply a channeling agency in the case of Wayne Major:

The Wayne County Road Commission put the Michigan Aeronautics Commission in a very tough position, which they are adept at doing. They put us in the position that if we said "no" in the channeling of federal funds into Wayne County Airport, we were denying federal funds to the state of Michigan. Funds would presumably go to waste, and no use would be made of the funds, and they might just as well be in Michigan (*Federal Role in Aviation*, p. 643).

According to Hough, Leroy Smith had accomplished an "end run" around the Aeronautics Commission to the CAA. This was the bitter pill that the Aeronautics Commission had to swallow. The Road Commission's vagueness about the nature of Wayne Major's "expansion" program and its references to the presence of the Air National Guard were useful in promoting the commission's acceptance of this "very tough position." Smith's arguments for the county field may not have won the state body over (Hough claimed that the Aeronautics Commission had never endorsed Wayne Major, either formally or informally, as the terminal airport for the metropolitan area), but they were successful enough to keep the Aeronautics Commission from withholding approval of grants to Wayne Major. If Act 32 of 1948 was intended to insulate local units from direct national-local contacts by inserting the Michigan Aeronautics Commission as an intermediary, then the act clearly failed of its purpose in the case of the Wayne County Road Commission.

Following Hough at the Congressional hearing was Brigadier General Lester J. Maitland, who became executive director of the Michigan Aeronautics Commission in March 1949. Regarding the presence of the National Guard as a justification for Wayne Major's expansion, Maitland acknowledged that "it could have happened previous to the time I took over." But after he took charge, Maitland testified, "We have never given a dime toward military development of any sort, including the National Guard." What was Maitland's position on the development of Wayne Major as the Detroit area's terminal airport? Maitland testified that Governor Williams asked him to study and report on the Detroit airport situation. After making a "very, very thorough study" in which he "went through all the reports, all the investigations," Maitland stated that he "concurred wholeheartedly" with the development of Detroit-Wayne Major.

Leroy Smith had a new-found ally in the person of the executive officer of the Michigan Aeronautics Commission. His other ally, the CAA, had not forsaken him by any means. In May 1949, shortly before Vest's letter squelching the international airport, the CAA announced approval of Smith's request for a $1,000,000 grant to Wayne Major for the fiscal year 1949–50. State and local matching funds of $450,000 and $550,000 respectively were approved by the state legislature and County Board of Supervisors. With a $2,000,000 kitty assured, Smith announced, in June 1949, plans for a "big push" on the expansion program. The plans included completion of the major runway pattern, installation of an instrument landing system, and construction of a control tower and first stage of a passenger terminal to serve the new runways. Smith called this a "final bid" to attract the airlines from Willow Run. He predicted that the expansion would be completed in 1952 and that the airlines would move to Wayne Major shortly thereafter.

Another event during the summer of 1949 solidified the Road Commission's position on Wayne Major. On August 24 Governor Williams announced that he had appointed John P. McElroy, personnel and public-relations director of the Wayne County Road Commission, to a four-year term on the Michigan Aeronautics Commission. McElroy had wide experience on the state capitol scene, where he was a registered legislative representative (lobbyist) for the Road Commission. He had regularly presented the commission's programs and proposals to committees and individual members of the legislature. In accepting the non-compensated state post, McElroy retained his $7,500-a-year post with the Road Commission. The irony of McElroy's appointment was that he replaced William Joy, whose term on the Aeronautics Commission had expired. Some members of the Board of Commerce saw Leroy Smith as the prime mover behind the appointment, but McElroy, a long-time Democrat and native of Ireland, ascribed his appointment to Lieutenant Governor John W. Connolly, whom McElroy had backed for the state post and whose father, Democratic Circuit Court Judge William F. Connolly, had been a close (and politically valuable) friend of McElroy's.

McElroy's appointment was a tremendous boost for the Road Commission's cause. Up to 1950 Wayne Major had secured two federal grants totaling almost $1,600,000. In 1950 the commission approved the receipt of federal funds for six separate projects at Wayne Major. These grants, amounting to over $1,360,000, exceeded the original federal grant offer, extended in May 1949, for fiscal 1949–50 by $360,000. The state provided matching funds of $450,000. In 1951 four federal aid projects at Wayne Major were approved by the commission. The federal sums involved were approximately $500,000, the state, $100,000. The federal, state, and local funds invested in Wayne Major in these two years totaled nearly $4,750,000. McElroy's presence on the commission was not the single nor, perhaps, the primary factor in securing the grants. But his presence combined with Joy's and Hough's departure (Hough was not reappointed when his term expired at the end of 1950) eliminated any stumbling blocks at the state level.

Personnel changes on the Michigan Aeronautics Commission, together with substantial federal, state, and local funds for Wayne Major and the death of the international site left Smith and the Road Commission well situated by the end of 1949. Wayne Major's position was further consolidated in the spring of 1950, when the state legislature authorized local units to pass and enforce airport zoning legislation. Road Commission personnel soon completed an ordinance to zone the area around Wayne Major. In August 1951 the Wayne County Board of Supervisors passed the airport zoning ordinance, which placed restrictions on approximately 350 square miles of territory around the airport, controlling land use and height, bulk, and use of structures within a ten-mile radius from the center of the airport. The area was now zoned for development as a major airport. But Road Commission officials were still dissatisfied since there was no immediate prospect that airlines would be operating from the county airport even though the field was a beehive of construction activity.

Leroy Smith made his "big push" for the transfer of the airlines in 1950 and 1951. Reportedly, American Airlines led a negotiating committee for discussing with the Road Commission the arrangements under which the airlines might shift from Willow Run to Wayne Major. The negotiations proved fruitless, and on October 4, 1951 the airlines announced that they had signed a ten-year lease with the University of Michigan. The lease, which was to run from

1952 to 1962, contained a clause permitting the airlines to rene-
gotiate or terminate the lease after three years, in 1955. The clause
was designed to keep the airlines flexible after 1955 and perhaps
to encourage action by local officials on a more convenient site.
By the time the airlines signed the ten-year lease the city of
Detroit had, in fact, settled on "a more convenient site," located
northeast of Detroit.

The city's efforts to secure land for a northeast air terminal
began in 1951 and terminated in 1958. As challenges to Wayne
Major, these efforts reached their peak in the three-year period
from 1952 to 1955.

The Northeast Site

The Detroit Aviation Commission Proposal. The groundwork
for the city's challenge to Wayne Major was laid by the Detroit
Common Council in October 1949, two months after John Mc-
Elroy's appointment in August, when the council approved an
ordinance creating a three-man Aviation Commission. The new
agency was empowered to "plan, construct, improve, and operate
airports . . . within the territorial limits of the city and within or
without the state of Michigan." It was also to "represent the city
in all aviation matters affecting the city." As airport spokesman
for the city, the commission replaced Glenn Richards, who was
silenced by his resignation from the DMAA in June 1949. The
new agency was also a replacement for the DMAA, which had
failed miserably in its attempt to put across the international site.
The tenuous political status of that agency, the deep cleavages
within it over the international site, and Richards' resignation combined to paralyze the unit; it became a paper agency. By creating
the new Aviation Commission, Detroit, implicitly at least, was
adopting a go-it-alone approach after dismal results via the metropolitan approach.

Out-going Mayor VanAntwerp made the appointments to the
new commission in December 1949. All three appointees were flying enthusiasts, business executives, and members of the Detroit
Board of Commerce. One of the three appointees was William
Joy, ex-member of the Michigan Aeronautics Commission. Ac-

cording to standard procedure under the city charter, the council had no say in the appointments, and incoming Mayor Albert E. Cobo indicated that he would make no changes in the personnel of the commision. When the new Aviation Commission met in January 1950, one of its first actions was to appoint Colonel C. V. Burnett, manager of the Detroit City Airport, as the commission's director. Burnett continued in his post as airport manager, but now, as the director of a commission with quasi-departmental rank, he was in a position to speak and act with more authority on airport problems.

The Aviation Commission came onto the scene as the proposed international airport was fading. Although some effort was made on behalf of that ill-fated project, the commission spent several months probing for likely directions in which to move. By 1950 the northern parts of the metropolitan area in Macomb and Oakland counties were experiencing rapid population growth. Industry had also decentralized into these environs. General Motors and Chrysler had plants and engineering centers in the northern suburbs, and the Korean conflict was to bring a further influx of defense facilities into the area. Postwar expansion had brought a shift in the metropolitan area's population and industry.

Given the population and industrial concentrations in the northeast area and the long distances from there to either Willow Run or Wayne Major, a proposal to build a northeast terminal seemed to have commanding logic. First, a northeast site was more centrally located with respect to population in the metropolitan area. Second, such a site would permit split operations at the northeast site and at Willow Run or Wayne Major, depending on which of the two western airports was used. Split operations would make air travel more convenient for residents and businessmen in the northeast, who sometimes had ninety-minute drives to reach Willow Run, a surface-travel time that frequently exceeded the time spent aloft to reach their destinations. Third, increases in passenger traffic and air movements would overload Willow Run and/or Wayne Major in the next five or ten years and require a second major airport for the metropolitan area. The gist of this reasoning was that two major metropolitan airports, one in the northeast and one in the southwest, were necessary; but the question of which of the rival southwestern facilities should be retained was left unanswered. The Detroit Aviation Commission and the Detroit Board of Commerce came to view a major northeast air terminal as indispensable, and they were intent on obtaining a northeast site before suburban population growth engulfed all available land close to Detroit's city limits.

Since federal funds would be needed to finance a northeast site, city officials contacted the CAA. C. V. Burnett wrote to George W. Vest, the CAA regional administrator, in August 1951. Burnett sought a commitment from Vest promising federal aid for developing a two-and-one-half-square-mile site at Eleven Mile and Dequindre Roads, just three miles north of the other Warren Township site, on which the city had given up its court-determined option in 1945. Extensive informal discussions followed Burnett's letter, and Detroit district CAA officials inspected the site at least once. On February 4, 1952 Vest replied in a letter that was encouraging but noncommittal. Vest noted that the site had "definite possibilities" and that "there appears to be no insurmountable objection or difficulty which would preclude consideration of this site for a second terminal airport." He promised federal aid provided that (1) "the need for another major airport has actually developed at the time the request is made," (2) studies show the site can be satisfactorily developed "without undue effect on the surrounding areas," and (3) the "policies of the Civil Aeronautics Administration in effect at that time do not preclude such an allocation."

Vest's reply appeared to be sufficient encouragement for Detroit officials. On the recommendation of the Aviation Commission, Mayor Cobo endorsed the project and recommended a $3,000,000 bond issue for site acquisition in his 1952–53 budget. The balance of the financing for the $16,000,000 airport was to come from the sale of City Airport ($5,000,000) and from federal grants ($8,000,000). Cobo also recommended that the council authorize condemnation proceedings against the site and appropriate funds for an engineering survey. Before the council acted on the mayor's recommendations, Burnett received another letter from a CAA official, Merle W. Hemphill, acting director of the CAA's Office of Airports in Washington. Hemphill observed:

The location is strategic with reference to population, industrial centers, and terrain. It balances the airport pattern with reference to existing airports, providing the proposed airport supplants the present Detroit City Airport.

We wish you success in this undertaking and you can rest assured that we will assist the city of Detroit to the fullest extent possible.

Did Hemphill's letter constitute federal approval of the northeast site? Burnett, the Aviation Commission, and Mayor Cobo interpreted it so. They pressed the council for quick action.

Despite Council President Louis Miriani's inclination to back the county port, the council acted favorably on the northeast airport requests in April 1952. In the same month the council passed an ordinance reconstituting the Detroit Aviation Commission, expanding its membership to five, and permitting Mayor Cobo to fill all five posts with new appointees. Cobo named the new commission members in August. He retained two of the former commissioners (including Joy) but named one of the three new members, William Packer, Sr., to the chairmanship of the commission. The Detroit Board of Commerce and its Aviation Committee, of which Packer was a member, gave their formal endorsement to the northeast airport project. Detroit went ahead with condemnation proceedings.

Detroit's moves to locate the northeast airport in Warren Township provoked intense opposition from township residents and officials as well as from other suburban residents and officials in the general vicinity. In a letter to the editor appearing in *The Detroit News* (September 5), Mayor James L. Eisele of Suburban Center Line objected to a *News* editorial which had called the northeast airport a "Perfect Site for an Airport." Eisele wrote: "We in this proposed airport area—and there are thousands of us—believe that the lives, limbs, and property of our men, women, and children should be placed ahead of the convenience of a handful of executives of some of the large corporations who are locating in this area. They don't need an airport at their doorsteps." Eisele's allusion to "large corporations" and "executives" pointed up one suburban explanation of why Detroit was seeking a northeast airport.

Suburban protests reached the Chicago offices of the CAA in

such proportions that Vest discussed the subject at length in letters to the Aviation Commission on August 21 and September 4. Vest warned the city "to be certain that [your] action is within the public interest" and suggested that "it might be desirable to set up a public hearing at which time all interested parties could be heard and their views considered before final action is taken by the city." In the earlier of his two letters (August 21) Vest said, "In view of these developments [suburban protests], we do not feel that this airport site should be approved at this time," but by September 4 Vest backtracked and gave the site "technical approval." Vest noted that two additional steps were required "prior to final approval." The first was favorable action on the northeast airport by the Michigan Aeronautics Commission, to which the city had applied for approval of the northeast site as qualifying for federal aid. The second was an expression by the Detroit Common Council that another airport for the Detroit area was needed and that in acquiring and developing the Eleven Mile Road site the council was "acting in the public interest."

Acting on Vest's suggestions, on October 8 the council held a public hearing to consider the northeast airport. The council considered the site survey and preliminary master plan for the airport, which had just been completed by an airport consulting firm. (Copies of this 122-page document, the Smith-Hinchman-Gryllis report, also went to the Michigan Aeronautics Commission and to CAA officials in Chicago and Washington.) In the course of the meeting a suggestion was made that approval of the airport be delayed so that suburban officials and residents could be notified and invited to raise their objections before the council. This was dismissed as unnecessary, and the council proceeded to give formal approval to the site, finding, as suggested by the CAA letter, that the airport was necessary, that the site was satisfactory, and that its acquisition was in the public interest.

The Michigan Aeronautics Commission Acts. Following council approval of the northeast airport, Burnett and Packer appeared at the October meeting of the Michigan Aeronautics Commission to request that body's approval of the airport. Five Warren Township leaders and two state representatives from the suburban area attended the meeting and argued against Detroit's request. The commission gave the suburbanites a partial victory by granting their request for a public hearing on the airport. The hearing was set for November 7.

Three weeks before the hearing the Detroit Metropolitan Area Regional Planning Commission completed and released a staff study on air traffic and airport sites undertaken at the request of Detroit officials. The study revealed that 64 percent of all passenger traffic and 70 percent of all cargo traffic emanating from Detroit originated north and east of Grand River Avenue. From this finding the study concluded that a northeast airport was an "obvious necessity." The study reported that there were only four suitable sites for a northeast airport and that the Warren Township site was the closest one to Detroit. The report then presented a set of data on population distribution that seemed to confirm the need and desirability of a northeast airport:

Radial Distance (in miles) from the Airport	Population around Wayne County Airport	Population around Proposed Northeast Airport
5.0	71,800	146,345
7.5	206,650	570,215
10.0	426,250	1,051,415
12.5	615,350	2,204,020

The conclusion drawn from these data was that the northeast airport was more centrally located in relation to population (and presumably airline passengers) than Wayne Major. The data provided more ammunition for the critics of Wayne Major and solidified support within city quarters for the northeast site. "A northeast airport would better serve the population of the metropolitan area," became a stock argument with proponents of the northeast airport.

Warren Township area residents continued to oppose being "served" and vented their wrath in official resolutions, public statements by community leaders, and mass meetings. On November 7, the day set for the public hearing, a seventy-five-car motorcade from Warren Township descended on the state capitol. Over two hundred suburban residents, civic leaders, and public officials took their case against the airport before the Michigan Aeronautics Commission.

The day-long public hearing was a climactic affair. Burnett, Packer, Kiskadden, and Mara presented Detroit's case for the airport. The city's case rested on two major points: (1) centrality of the airport, as shown by the Regional Planning Commission study, and (2) *future* need, as indicated by passenger projections to 1960 contained in the Smith-Hinchman-Gryllis report. Burnett contended that since the proximity of Willow Run and Wayne Major to each other prevented simultaneous air movements under instrument landing conditions, substantial increases in air traffic would require another major airport. Detroit representatives acknowledged that a northeast airport was not an immediate necessity. But they contended that if a suitable site was to be assured for future use, the site had to be obtained now, before suburban population growth engulfed this "ideal" site.

Suburban opponents of the northeast site challenged both the present and future need for such an airport, pointing to the expansion of Wayne Major as fulfilling metropolitan airport needs. They charged that the proposed airport would endanger the lives of school children and other inhabitants; create a public nuisance, since noise might interfere with the educational development of children in surrounding schools; cause a substantial loss of valuations from the tax rolls; and reduce private property values in the vicinity of the airport. The suburbanites also complained about Detroit's overbearing attitude toward Warren Township and its residents, especially its failure to consult with township officials or to invite them to a public hearing. The case against the northeast airport was concluded by filing with the Michigan Aeronautics Commission resolutions of opposition from twelve Oakland County and eighteen Macomb County local units of government.

The Aeronautics Commission deferred action on the northeast airport for three weeks. In this interim Commission Director Maitland sought an opinion from the state attorney general on the discretion available to the commission to pass on applications for federal aid, i.e., Detroit's request. In an opinion dated November 24, the attorney general stated:

No standards to govern the determination of the commission are set by the act, which gives in effect to the commission the power of life and death over applications by political subdivisions for federal aid in connection with airports. And since the approval or disapproval of the application by the commission is a condition precedent to the power of the municipality to submit the application for aid to the federal government, it would appear that the commission is not obligated to give any reasons for its approval or disapproval of the application or to take into consideration any particular state of facts in making a determination.

The commission, in other words, had unlimited discretion in passing on Detroit's request.

The Aeronautics Commission met in closed sessions on November 25 and 26. With the eight commission members during the informal and formal sessions over the two-day period was William C. Knoepfle, chief of the Airports Division for the CAA's Third Region. Near the end of the second day of "thorough informal discussion," according to the official minutes of the commission, Commissioner McElroy moved "that the application for approval by the Detroit Aviation Commission for the construction of a major airport in Warren Township, Macomb County, be denied." By a four-to-two vote, with two commissioners abstaining, McElroy's motion carried. The commission then approved two recommendations drafted by Maitland and directed to the Detroit Aviation Commission. The recommendations were (1) that Detroit seek a suitable northeast site for the location of an "executive-type" airport to replace Detroit City Airport, and (2) "that the Detroit Aviation Commission wholeheartedly and actively support the completion of the Detroit-Wayne Major Airport."

The response of Detroit officials to the commission's actions was immediate and sharp. Mayor Cobo charged that Maitland had encouraged the city to proceed with plans for a northeast airport. On this basis he (Cobo) had put a $3,000,000 bond issue in his budget, but now Maitland had turned against the site. Maitland replied that "the commission's procedure was completely legal, completely legitimate, and the vote wasn't even close. Besides," he added, "there isn't a thing the city can do about it."

A different tack was taken by Aviation Commission Chairman Packer. In *The Detroit News* of November 28, 1952 he questioned the motives of John McElroy and McElroy's dual status on the Aeronautics Commission and the Wayne County Road Commission. Packer said, "I would like to know if John P. McElroy, a Wayne County Road Commission employee and a member of the State Aeronautics Commission, is interested in advancing aviation in the Detroit area or in advancing the County Road Commission airport?" Two days later he was quoted as saying, "McElroy is the lieutenant of the Wayne County Road Commission—the owners and operators of the Wayne County Airport— . . . [whose] aim is to kill any federal money for any airport besides Wayne County." He added that McElroy "lobbied the state board unmercifully to beat Detroit's request." When asked what Detroit's next step would be, Packer said:

> Our first consideration will be to ask Governor Williams to stop John P. McElroy from voting on the issue. I intend to ask the governor how McElroy can sit as prosecutor and judge on our request for approval of the site in Warren Township. I understand that McElroy made the motion to deny approval of our request and that he lobbied the rest of the commission into supporting his stand.

Willis Hall, secretary-manager of the Detroit Board of Commerce, seconded Packer's challenge to McElroy's status on the commission, and other proponents of the northeast site either called on McElroy to resign or called for the governor to remove him.

Governor Williams refused to be drawn into the controversy. McElroy commented, "I will not refrain from voting on any question concerning aeronautics in Michigan. Our recommendations [in denying the northeast site] have saved the Detroit taxpayers an unnecessary expenditure of $10,000,000 and saved another $10,000,000 of federal funds."

Mayor Cobo received official notice of the commission's action in a letter from Maitland. Maitland offered three reasons for the denial of Detroit's request. First, the need for a major northeast airport had not been proved. Maitland cited comparative statistics indicating that the number of passengers projected for Detroit in 1960 could be handled at one terminal airport. He also cited the opinion of the CAA official present at the closed sessions that Wayne Major and Willow Run could serve Detroit's needs for the foreseeable future. Second, the commercial airlines had not expressed interest in a northeast airport. Third, the northern part of the metropolitan area should be reserved for private flying. This last point, which had appeared before in the Horner-Shifrin report and in CAA letters, prompted Maitland to invite Detroit to submit a request for an executive-type northeast airport designed to handle private non-scheduled flying.

Taking this cue, the Detroit Aviation Commission scaled down runway lengths, cost estimates, etc., for the Warren Township site and submitted its plans for an "executive-type" airport to the Aeronautics Commission in January 1953. The airport site, however, was still the original two and one-half square miles. Packer and Burnett were candid about Detroit's intentions. The city planned to build an executive-type airport now but to expand the runways to eight thousand or ten thousand feet as the need for a major airport arose. The Michigan Aeronautics Commission appeared ready to approve Detroit's revised request despite McElroy's continued opposition. The commission, however, never acted on Detroit's scaled-down plans. Suburban opposition to the airport was not only intense; it was also sustained. Under the leadership of Warren Township officials the resourceful suburbanites took the offensive. They carried their case to the state legislature.

Legislative Maneuvers. The legislature was currently in session and had under consideration a bill that could stymie Detroit's attempt to locate the northeast airport in Warren Township. The bill was introduced in the House of Representatives by the state legislator from Warren Township. It required that before any city could establish a *new* airport in a township with a population of more than thirty-five thousand, the city had to secure the approval of the county board of supervisors in the affected county. Warren Township was the only township in Michigan whose 1950 population exceeded thirty-five thousand, and the Macomb County Board of Supervisors had already recorded by a large majority its opposition to an airport in Warren Township.

The bill cleared the house with little difficulty, partly because of the personal popularity and key leadership position of Warren's legislator, Howard Carroll. Reportedly, Wayne County Road

Commission personnel were active in behind-the-scenes efforts to pass the restrictive bill. Fifteen of Wayne County's twenty-seven representatives voted for the legislation, five voted against it, and five did not vote.

The course of the bill through the Michigan Senate was more complicated, involving two public hearings by a senate committee that held life and death powers over the bill. At a critical juncture a six-member citizen delegation from Warren journeyed to the state capitol for an entire week of legislative sessions. Members of the delegation approached each of the thirty-two senators personally and furnished them with literature showing the number of homes and schools that would be uprooted or endangered by locating the airport in the township. According to newspaper reports, they entertained various senators, particularly the seven members of the key senate committee, at dinner meetings, where they explained their opposition to the airport. The efforts of the Warren delegation appeared to have the desired effect on the senate committee. An informal poll held before the delegation's visit showed two members of the committee for the restrictive legislation, four against, and one undecided; after the visit, two members previously opposed to the bill indicated that they favored it, as did the one member who had been undecided.

The activity of these Warren Township citizens did not occur without some raised eyebrows. One senator, who refused to be quoted, said, "they wined us and dined us; how can working people leave their jobs to come down here on an obviously expensive lobby junket without some considerable financial help?" Warren Township Superintendent of Schools Paul K. Cousino, one of the township's most active delegates, warmly contests the notion that the bill was "wined and dined" through the senate ("I took only one senator out to lunch"). He and other suburban participants acknowledge that the township government paid for the expenses of the Lansing trip as well as those of subsequent trips to Kansas City and Washington, D.C., where Cousino also testified against the northeast airport.

Late in April the senate committee voted to report the controversial bill to the entire senate, where it subsequently passed by a wide margin. One of the senators voting against the bill opposed it (1) as a piece of special legislation and (2) on the manner in which its passage was secured. On the latter point the senator, who was not from the Detroit metropolitan area, was quoted as saying:

> The battle against the Northeast Airport project is being led by the Wayne County Road Commission. They're afraid a northeast site will upset their grandiose plans. We've been lobbied on this bill with arguments that reach the point of utter absurdity. It's an insult to our intelligence.

The restrictive legislation became law on May 4 when it was signed by Governor Williams. Practically speaking, Detroit was now foreclosed from establishing a *new* airport in Warren Township. The law, however, did not apply to the expansion of *existing* airports. (This exclusion and the township population figure were incorporated by the sponsors of the legislation as concessions to allay opposition from other Michigan cities whose airport plans, including expansions, would otherwise have been put in the hands of township-dominated boards of supervisors.) If Detroit wanted a northeast airport in Warren Township, it would have to purchase an existing airport and expand it. Interestingly enough, there was an existing privately-owned airport at Fourteen Mile and Dequindre Roads, less than a mile north of the northern boundary of the site at Eleven Mile and Dequindre. But again the resourceful suburbanites were in control. A prominent Warren citizen obtained a one-year option on the airport during the progress of the restrictive legislation through the legislature. For the time being Detroit was effectively stymied on the northeast airport.

The conflict and recriminations over the northeast airport had accentuated city-county differences. In June 1953 the Board of Commerce attempted to pour oil on troubled waters. Aviation Committee Chairman William Mara called a "unity" meeting between principals from the Road Commission and Detroit Aviation Commission. Mara hoped to negotiate a compromise whereby Wayne Major would be completed and the northeast airport site would be acquired. More fission than fusion resulted from the meeting, and its tenor is indicated by the use of the word "liar" in some of the less heated verbal exchanges. The meeting quickly disbanded. Leroy Smith reportedly expressed his adamant private opinion that "not a dime will be spent on the construction of a northeast airport until Detroit-Wayne Major is completed and the airlines are located there!"

Cobo's New Strategy. Leroy Smith had cause to be adamant in his opposition to a northeast air terminal, especially one that qualified for federal aid. Because of the Korean emergency, Congressional appropriations for federal airport grants were cut to a trickle in the fiscal years 1951–52 and 1952–53. But worse was yet to come. The first session of the Eighty-third Congress, following the economy proposals of newly elected President Eisenhower, appropriated no funds for the federal airport grants program in fiscal 1953–54.

The cutbacks in federal grants were reflected on the local scene: Wayne Major received only $350,000 in fiscal 1951–52, $150,000 in fiscal 1952–53, and nothing, of course, in fiscal 1953–54. The Road Commission's annual report for 1953, published early in 1954, noted that "expansion work has been curtailed" because of the reductions in federal moneys. The same report summarized construction progress on the new airport: "To date, the drainage system, water main, four runways including the instrument landing system runway, the cargo building, the first stage of the terminal building and taxiways and aprons to both buildings and the runway lighting system . . . have been completed."

The slowdown on Wayne Major's expansion program was offset, however, in April 1954, when Pan American Airlines inaugurated international air travel from the Detroit area using Wayne Major. Six flights weekly departed on through flights to Europe. Pan American selected Wayne Major because its longer runway (7,900 feet) permitted longer non-stop flights and because the airport had been designated a port of entry. The first regularly scheduled commercial air carrier was now operating from Wayne Major.

One month after Pan American's choice of Wayne Major, another threat from the northeast airport developed. When the option held by a Warren citizen on the private airport in the township had expired in February, a Detroit industrialist who was also a member of the Board of Commerce had immediately purchased the airport, ostensibly for his own business purposes. The strategy behind this move was publicly revealed in May when the businessman offered to sell the airport to the city of Detroit. The Detroit Aviation Commission and Mayor Cobo both recommended that the Common Council purchase the field and institute condemnation proceedings against the two square miles of property lying south of the private field. This would give the city of Detroit a northeast airport site between Twelve and Fourteen Mile Roads in Warren Township. The council acted favorably on the recommendations, but a few days before, Warren Township had filed a suit to condemn the existing airport property for use as a township park.

The issue between Detroit and Warren Township was now posed in the form of two condemnation suits—Warren's suit against the airport and Detroit's suit against the adjacent two square miles. It appeared that Detroit's claim to a northeast airport site would be settled by the courts rather than by the legislative and administrative processes which had previously thwarted the city. At the juncture, however, a shift in Mayor Cobo's attitude on the northeast site became evident.

The first indication of a modification in Cobo's position came in the summer of 1954 when Detroit asked for a delay in the condemnation trials. A second and more significant turn came in August, when Leroy Smith, finding that federal funds were drying up, proposed a referendum on the issuance of county bonds to finance the completion of Wayne Major and Cobo came out in support of Smith's plans. Cobo said, "I see no conflict between this plan and our proposal to build a northeast airport" but he avoided any explicit statement regarding priorities between the two projects— whether Wayne Major should be completed before or after a northeast site was acquired. Cobo could not state a priority that accorded Wayne Major equal or preferred status over the northeast airport without undercutting the Detroit Aviation Commission and the Board of Commerce, both of which were pulling out all the stops in the battle with Warren Township over the airport site. The board was sponsoring large advertisements in Warren Township weekly newspapers under the title, "Citizens for the Northeast Airport." It had also hired a youthful and personable public-relations man, who frequented the service club and civic association meetings in Warren in order to present in a calm and polished fashion the assets which the airport would bring to the township. The township countered with its own speakers and a "strategy group." In contrast to the efforts of the board, Cobo's advocacy of the northeast site was restrained.

What were the reasons for Cobo's policy shift? Cobo may have entertained some doubt or second thoughts on the feasibility of obtaining the Warren Township site. The two condemnation suits might be long and expensive, and the outcome of either might be unfavorable to Detroit. Even if they were favorable, Michigan condemnation law prohibited condemnation of public street right-of-way. The roads and streets in the proposed airport site were under the jurisdiction of the Macomb County Road Commission. Unless this commission cooperated, and it was doubtful that it would, acquisition of the Warren site might be delayed months, years, or indefinitely. Even if this problem were eventually re-solved, the area might by that time be built up, since Michigan condemnation law provides that a condemning jurisdiction obtains no interest in the property under suit until public necessity and just compensation are determined by a condemnation jury. This regulation permitted residential construction to proceed apace on the land that Detroit was proposing to take by condemnation. By 1954 the unyielding vehemence of suburban opposition may have convinced Cobo that the suburbs would do their best to maximize these obstacles to the northeast airport.

If Cobo harbored doubts about the northeast site, what may have induced him to support the completion of Wayne Major? First, civic prestige. By 1954 Wayne Major was newer, larger, and more modern than Willow Run, and it was twelve road miles closer to Detroit. Both the distance and the barn-like atmosphere of the Willow Run terminal seemed to be never-ending sources of dis-pleasure and ridicule for Detroit public officials. Second, financial considerations. Detroit had a substantial investment in Wayne Major's development since city taxpayers paid roughly two-thirds of all the county's tax revenue. Nearly $4,000,000 in local moneys had been spent on Wayne Major's development from 1947 to 1954. Third, broad policy strategy. With the Road Commission as an ally, a wide variety of benefits might accrue to Cobo and his administration, such as assistance in securing passage of Cobo-supported legislation in the state legislature and allocation of county road funds to repair and maintain the major traffic arteries in Detroit and to construct and maintain the expressway system being built in Detroit. Fourth, political aspirations. Cobo had his eye on the governorship. He was Detroit's non-partisan mayor, but it was generally known that he was a Republican, despite his inactivity in organized party affairs, and that to win state office he would need all the suburban support he could muster. If Cobo could maintain popularity on his home grounds, fellow Republican Leroy Smith might cultivate Republican support for Cobo in the rural out-state counties where Cobo was unknown but where Smith had numerous contacts through the uniformly Republican county road commissions. (Cobo won the Republican nomination for governor in 1956 but lost the election by a large plurality to incumbent Democrat G. Mennen Williams.)

Whatever the reasons, the northeast airport suffered from a decided lack of mayoral push in 1954 and 1955, and Cobo veered toward a viewpoint favorable to Leroy Smith's cause. From Smith's standpoint one thing seemed assured. Cobo would not press hard and quickly for the northeast site but would only do enough to keep the Board of Commerce happy. The northeast airport would remain quiescent while Smith made his "final push" to get the airlines to Wayne Major.

Smith's "Final Push" Begins.   Despite announced support from Cobo, Smith's proposal for an $8,000,000 bond issue failed to strike the usually responsive note with other county officials. The county was entering a period of severe financial stringency and a bond issue referendum did not seem politic at this time. Worse yet, Wayne Major had received a federal grant of only $80,000 for the current fiscal year (1954–55). The hardest blow came when Wayne Major received no federal funds for fiscal 1955–56 despite a $60,-000,000 appropriation by Congress in 1955.

The snag this time was the CAA itself. The federal agency was disturbed by the fact that although it had allocated substantial sums to Wayne Major, few direct benefits had yet been conferred on civil aviation. From 1947 to 1955 the CAA had spent $3,989,559 on Wayne Major's development. This sum was just under 50 percent of all federal funds allocated to the entire state of Michigan during that time period. According to the records of the Michigan Aeronautics Commission, state and county matching moneys spent on Wayne Major in the same period were, respectively, $1,098,860 and $3,933,716. In sum, just over $9,000,000 had been spent on the development of Wayne Major. Now the CAA was asking for results. The director of airports for the CAA, Herbert Howell, told Smith that before more federal funds could be allocated to Wayne Major, "a definite arrangement would have to be made for the transfer of a substantial segment of Detroit's airline activity to the Wayne Major Airport."

Concerted efforts to secure "a definite arrangement" began early in 1955. They marked the re-entrance of Glenn Richards into the airport controversy, from which he had withdrawn in 1949, and also revealed the degree to which Cobo had gravitated to Leroy Smith's corner.

Richards' return to the scene started by happenstance on a skiing excursion to northern Michigan late in 1954. Richards recalls the incident and succeeding events as follows:

> I happened to see Jack Tompkins [district sales manager], of American Airlines, at the lodge and we got started talking about the airport controversy. I told him he should be ashamed and he asked why. I told him the airlines were in the wrong for causing passengers the inconvenience of going the extra 14 [*sic*] miles to Willow Run. Those miles add up in tremendous costs. He agreed and indicated American felt that it might be time to do something about it. He said they would talk it over with C. R. Smith [the airline's president].
>
> I told him all the airlines should try to do something about it, but he said that Leroy Smith was so bullheaded the airlines found it hard to deal with him. He said the county's offer was not attractive enough to make the airlines switch from Willow, where they were doing fine financially. He said that if I were appointed to head a negotiating committee, maybe something could be worked out.
>
> Several weeks later I was with the mayor and several councilmen on a trip to Philadelphia for a conference. I told them about my meeting with Tompkins and indicated that I would like to get back into the airport picture again. I told them I had stayed out from 1949. I asked what they had accomplished during these five years. I told them nothing. They didn't get the international or the northeast airports, and Detroit-Wayne Major still wasn't built up. Passengers still

had to go all the way to Willow Run. That's all your Airport Commission has done, and that's not much of anything, I told them.

I suggested that I thought I could sell Detroit-Wayne Major, but that to do it I would have to be appointed airport co-ordinator, or a step above the Aviation Commission and the County Road Commission. The mayor agreed and so did the Board of Supervisors and the Road Commission. They set me up as the co-ordinator for the city and county. I went right to work.

Shortly after Richards' designation as airport co-ordinator, identical confidential letters were sent out to the presidents of the seven major airlines serving Detroit (American, Capital, Delta, Eastern, Northwest, Trans World, and United). The letters, dated February 9, 1955, were signed by Cobo, by Detroit Councilman Edward Connor (who was also chairman of the County Board of Supervisors) and by Michael J. O'Brien, chairman of the Road Commission. The tenor of the letters was "now is the time to move." Among the points made were: Richards had been authorized to act on behalf of all parties; completion of expressways puts the county field within twenty minutes of downtown; runways, taxiways, and aprons at Wayne Major were near completion; and expansion of the ultra-modern terminal building and control tower was under consideration. The letters concluded by inviting each airline to designate a representative to negotiate with Richards.

The "final push" for the transfer of the airlines was under way and Leroy Smith appeared to be playing a subordinate role. Subsequent events showed, however, that Smith remained in the eye of the storm until his retirement on December 31, 1956. These events also marked the intrusion of an entirely new question into the airport situation: where to locate United States military aircraft based in the metropolitan area. On the fulcrum of this issue Detroit's long-standing airport problem was finally settled, but the conflict now expanded to the national scene, with the executive branch and the U.S. House of Representatives becoming the scene of several encounters.

The Wayne-Willow Controversy

Enter the Military. The thrust from the northeast airport had been blunted, and Glenn Richards was bidding for the airlines' transfer to Wayne Major, when on March 1, 1955 the U.S. Navy approached the Road Commission. The Navy wanted to transfer its Air Reserve squadron currently based at Grosse Ile Naval Air Station to Wayne Major. Grosse Ile's four-thousand-foot runways could not handle the Navy's jets, whereas Wayne Major's long, wide runways were ideal for such craft. The Navy would base sixty jets at the airport and conduct about 32,000 air operations a year. Leroy Smith responded to the Navy's inquiry with an emphatic No. He suggested that the Navy base its craft at Willow Run, where runways were also adequate to accommodate jets.

If Smith expected to attract the commercial airlines he would have to avoid military use of Wayne Major. Three years earlier the President's Airport Commission (Doolittle Commission) had strongly urged that civil and military operations be segregated. Following this recommendation and their own preferences, the private airlines did their best to avoid operations at airports where military craft were based. Twenty jets from the Michigan Air National Guard were based at Wayne Major, and annual military air movements totaled about 20,000, compared with about 110,000 civil air movements. Basing the Navy Reserve squadron at Wayne Major would brand the airport with the "military" stigma and reduce the prospects for the transfer of the airlines. On the other hand, if the Navy Reserve and National Guard squadrons could be steered to Willow Run, they might force the airlines out of that location in short order.

A third military air unit introduced further complications. On March 3, the U.S. Air Force notified the University of Michigan that it planned to use the government-owned facilities on the eastern edge of Willow Run as headquarters for an Air Force Reserve fighter-bomber squadron. The squadron would conduct about 20,000 operations annually. University officials were stunned by the Air Force's intentions. For nearly a year the university had been seeking a lease from the federal government for these very properties for use in its expanding research program, much of which was done under contract for the Department of Defense. University officials immediately took their problem to Congressman George Meader of Michigan's Second District, which included Ann Arbor, where the university was located. Meader's home was in Ann Arbor and he was an alumnus of the university's law school. There were no doubts as to where his loyalties lay.

Robert Miller, president of ANTSCO, also contacted Meader. Miller expressed concern over the Air Force's intention to base military jets at the busy commercial terminal. His objections were on grounds of safety, traffic congestion, and air-space use. He suggested that the military planes be based at Wayne Major since the Air National Guard was there and since Pan American operated only three or four passenger flights a week from Wayne Major, compared with the 320 a *day* handled at Willow Run. Miller observed, "It appears to us that this is all a part of a pattern to force the airlines to Wayne Major Airport." Meader apparently agreed, for in the March 18 issue of his regular newsletter to constituents, an issue devoted entirely to a review of the airport situation, he said: "Smith knows that only the airlines can bail him out of debt at Wayne Major and is using every means at his command to see that they are forced out of Willow Run. And worse yet, he is attempting to use the Navy and the Air Force as pawns in his game." In Washington Meader took the problem directly to Secretary of the Air Force Harold Talbott, who promised to review the matter and report back but never did.

Meader's action was met by efforts of Detroit and Wayne County officials to exert compensatory influence. On March 29 a letter was dispatched to Secretary of Defense Charles E. Wilson. Like the letter of February 9 to the airline presidents, this letter was on Board of Supervisors' stationery and was signed by Cobo, Connor, and O'Brien. The initials of the dictator of the letter, however, were LCS—Leroy C. Smith. The letter asked Wilson to intervene and settle the dispute by assigning the Navy and Air Force Reserve units to Willow Run. Several points were made: the long-intended plan to develop Wayne Major as the metropolitan area's air terminal; endorsement of the plan by the CAA and local governing bodies; the reluctance of the airlines to use Wayne Major because of the "subsidy" which the airlines' financial arrangements at Willow Run gave them; and finally, the economy and efficiency to be gained by using Willow Run for all military aircraft. The letter to Wilson concluded on a confidant note: "If this military situation could be cleared up by using Willow Run

Airport, we are sure that we could soon reach an agreeable contract with the airlines to move to the Detroit-Wayne Major Airport, which is recognized by all as one of the finest locations for commercial airlines services in the country."

Wilson did not intervene personally to settle this local conflict that had now reached the top echelons of the executive branch of the federal government. Instead he referred the issue to the President's Air Co-ordinating Committee. This committee and its subsidiary Panel on Airport Use are federal interdepartmental co-ordinating bodies which hear and recommend settlements of inter-agency disputes on aviation matters. The Airport Use Panel set June dates for hearings in Detroit on the question of where best to locate the military aircraft.

The Cobo-Connor-O'Brien letter to Wilson spurred Meader to action again. On April 13 he delivered a speech on the floor of the House of Representatives in which he upbraided Smith and criticized as unnecessary, extravagant, and improvident the expenditure of federal funds on Wayne Major. He concluded with an allusion to one possible national-level sanction that could be employed against Smith: "It is my hope that the Appropriations Committee will give a good, long, hard look at this latest development in the scheming of Leroy Smith to drive the commercial airlines out of Willow Run to bail him out of his improvident expenditures at Detroit-Wayne Major Airport" (*Congressional Record*, April 13, 1955, p. 4392).

As these skirmishes opened at the federal level, the Detroit Board of Commerce attempted to reinvigorate the northeast site. The board's Aviation Committee issued a one-page "Statement of Position on Detroit Area Airports," which concluded as follows: "Mayor Cobo and Wayne County officials have invited representatives of the airlines to consider moving from Willow Run Airport to Wayne County Airport. We believe that even if this move were to be accomplished it would only be a minor improvement. The essential need is for the more centrally located northeast airport."

The "Final Push" Continues. With simultaneous attacks coming from both the federal and local levels, it appeared that Smith

and his associates would be sternly tested. Wayne Major proponents took the offensive. In mid-April Glenn Richards surprised
many observers by seeking to revive the long-dormant Detroit
Metropolitan Aviation Authority. While the DMAA had been
noted chiefly for its connection with the international site, its controversial staff report of September 1948 had recommended that
the airlines be shifted from Willow Run, that commercial passenger service be instituted at Wayne Major (as a secondary terminal), and that Willow Run be assigned the role of a military
airport. Richards' efforts at reviving the DMAA were designed to
mount additional pressure on the airlines to transfer to Wayne
Major. Richards proposed that a DMAA meeting be held on May 3.
At the April 20 meeting of the Michigan Aeronautics Commission
the proposed meeting of the DMAA came up for discussion. Since
the Aeronautics Commission was entitled to representation on the
metropolitan body, two representatives were designated to attend
the May 3 meeting. The two were Maitland and McElroy, and the
position they were to take was forecast in a resolution passed
unanimously at the April 20 meeting of the Aeronautics Commission:

> WHEREAS, the Civil Aeronautics Administration originally chose this
> location [Wayne Major] as the most desirable site for a major airline
> terminal to serve the Detroit metropolitan area, and
>
> WHEREAS, the Michigan Aeronautics Commission has approved the
> construction of the Detroit Wayne Major Airport through its approval
> of projects and authorization of state funds throughout the past years
> for improvements to the Detroit Wayne Major Airport, and
>
> WHEREAS, the City of Detroit, the Wayne County Board of Super-
> visors and the board of Wayne County road commissioners by reso-
> lution favor the Detroit-Wayne Major Airport as the scheduled air-
> line terminal for the Detroit area, and
>
> WHEREAS, the time and distance saved by the traveling public using
> the scheduled airlines would be materially reduced, resulting in great
> savings,
>
> NOW THEREFORE BE IT RESOLVED that the Michigan Aeronautics
> Commission go on record as favoring the transfer of all scheduled
> airline operations from the Willow Run Airport to the Detroit-Wayne
> Major Airport as soon as practicable.

The meeting of the DMAA called by Richards for May 3 convened as scheduled. Richards opened the meeting by outlining what he thought the DMAA should do: review and update previous airport surveys and designate the major airport from which the airlines should serve the metropolitan area. Without much hesitation he added, "I think Wayne County Airport is the logical designation." Since the northeast airport was back in the picture, Richards offered an observation on that project: it should be a general-purpose private airfield. C. V. Burnett, who was present at the meeting to represent the interests of the Detroit Aviation Commission, immediately challenged these remarks. Burnett took exception not only to Richards' ideas on airports but also to Richards' right to represent the city of Detroit on the DMAA. Burnett contended that Richards' resignation from the DMAA in 1949 and the subsequent creation of the Detroit Aviation Commission made the commission or its delegate (Burnett) the official city representative on the DMAA. After much discussion over who represented what, the meeting broke up in an impasse.

A few days later Detroit's city attorney ruled that neither Richards nor Burnett was entitled to represent the city on the DMAA —the position was vacant. The next question was, who should be appointed? As prescribed by the joint agreement creating the DMAA, the appointment of an administrative official was to be made by the Common Council. The council, however, asked Cobo to indicate his choice, Richards or Burnett. The mayor picked Richards. At the same time Cobo made his first public statement on priorities between the county field and the proposed northeast site. He said, "It has been my understanding that the members of the Aviation Commission have been in agreement with a policy of moving [the airlines at Willow Run] to the Wayne County Airport first and then acquiring land for the northeast airport."

Richards, with Cobo's reaffirmed support, stepped up efforts to induce the airlines to move. A conference was set for May 24 between the airlines and county officials. The day before this conference the board of directors of the Detroit Board of Commerce adopted the Statement of Position on Detroit Area Airports previously approved by its Aviation Committee. This action had a chilling effect on the conference the following day. With the northeast airport still a real possibility, the airlines rejected overtures to induce their transfer to Wayne Major. In fact, they took steps in the opposite direction by announcing a program of capital improvements at Willow Run, including complete remodeling of the terminal building. Glenn Richards recalls the events around the May 24 meeting as follows:

> The whole thing was a dodge by the airlines to stay at Willow Run, where they were making tremendous profits. It was just something too good for them. They didn't want to move and give up their gold mine. I told them flatly that there wasn't going to be a northeast airport before Detroit-Wayne Major was completed. They knew it. But the whole northeast airport provided a good smokescreen and excuse for them to stay at Willow Run. The Board of Commerce helped them out. It promised the airlines that the northeast airport would be built. I told the airlines it was a lot of hooey.
>
> Before the May 24 meeting we had talked individually with the airlines. I thought I had convinced American. We were going to give them the best rates possible at Detroit-Wayne Major. Afterwards it was a question of going to each airline and talking business.

When or if the airlines would move was heavily dependent on where the Air Force and Navy Reserve squadrons would locate. A decision on basing the military craft was expected to come from the hearings, findings, and recommendations of the Airport Use Panel of the President's Air Co-ordinating Committee. As the date of the hearings approached, the County Board of Supervisors and the Detroit Common Council passed identical resolutions endorsing the proposed transfer of the airlines and calling on the Defense Department to locate all military flying activities at Willow Run.

Congressman Meader's Amendment.   Richards' efforts during April and May to break down the airlines' resistance to moving to Wayne Major had not been successful; but neither had Congressman Meader's attempt in late April to make such a move difficult, if not impossible.

On April 27, the U.S. House of Representatives had under consideration a bill to amend the National Defense Facilities Act of 1950. The bill authorized for three years the expenditure of up to $250,000,000 for training centers and other facilities for the Army, Navy, and Air Force Reserve units. Meader offered an amendment to the policy-statement section of the bill. The amendment, which was aimed directly at the Wayne-Willow controversy, proposed adding the following policy guideline for the military to follow in locating Reserve facilities:

The minimizing of interference with commercial civil airline traffic by locating Reserve flight training operations, insofar as possible, at airports which do not handle heavy commercial scheduled airline traffic.

Enactment of this policy would practically compel the Navy and Air Force Reserve units to locate at Wayne Major.

In support of his amendment Meader reviewed his case for basing all military craft at Wayne Major, with the airlines remaining at Willow Run. He made four main points: (1) the satisfactory present location of the airlines, (2) the presence of the Air National Guard at Wayne Major, (3) the recommendation of the Doolittle Commission regarding segregation of military and civilian air operations, and (4) the estimated $20,000,000 needed to equip Wayne Major to handle all commercial airline traffic. Sprinkled liberally through Meader's discussion of his proposed amendment were caustic references to Smith, McElroy, and the Road Commission. The Michigan representative summarized his position:

My amendment proposes going one step further in announcing Congressional policy—that is to say that where facilities which are suitable are available in a particular area, there should be as little interference as possible with commercial airline operations. In this instance it would require the basing of the jet-training operation of the Navy and Army, together with that of the Air National Guard, at a perfectly suitable airport, namely, Wayne Major, and would avoid interference with the busy commercial operations at Willow Run (*Congressional Record*, April 27, 1955, p. 5163).

Meader's amendment had one flaw: the point in the legislative process at which it was offered. The policy statement offered by Meader had not been considered by an armed services subcommittee during hearings on the defense facilities bill. Meader recognized this flaw but expressed the hope that the subcommittee chairman and floor manager of the bill, Democrat Overton Brooks of Louisiana, would accept the amendment. But Brooks objected to it:

I feel that I must reluctantly oppose the gentleman's amendment while at the same time expressing sincere hope that the military departments will examine very carefully the principle which is contained in the amendment.

I should not want to accept an amendment of this type until the committee has had an opportunity to consider it in all its various ramifications. With that in mind I hope the gentleman will withdraw his amendment at this time (*Congressional Record*, April 27, 1955, p. 5163).

After some parliamentary maneuvering Meader's amendment was brought to a voice vote. It was rejected. On a slim procedural ground Leroy Smith's forces narrowly escaped a major setback.

Smith and his associates quickly recognized the need to maintain contact with Congress. They sought and gained varying degrees of support from Senator Patrick McNamara, who was a Detroit councilman from 1951 to 1954, and five of the six Detroit-Wayne County congressmen. All these legislators were Democrats, although geography appeared to be of greater significance than partisan considerations in subsequent events.

In objecting to Meader's amendment, Representative Brooks referred the policy issue to the military departments to "examine very carefully." This the military did through the medium of the Airport Use Panel. Thus the outcome of Meader's efforts on the national scene, like those of Richards on the local scene, came to rest in the lap of the Airport Use Panel.

The Airport Use Panel Hearing.   The stakes were high and clearly defined as the Airport Use Panel began hearings on June 22 at the Veterans' Memorial Building in downtown Detroit. The problem facing the panel was succinctly stated in the memorandum subsequently issued containing the panel's recommendations: "*Problem:* Determine in the best interests of the public the most feasible civil-military utilization of the airports, existing and proposed, in the Detroit, Michigan area" (Airport Use Panel Memorandum No. 8-55). Paul Morris, the panel chairman from the CAA, prefaced the hearings with a statement setting down the procedure and ground rules by which the panel operated:

I should like to emphasize that the Airport Use Panel conducts its hearings solely for the purpose of collecting "facts." We are not

a legal body, we have no power to subpena witnesses, and consequently, must rely, in large measure, upon those who participate in
our hearings to voluntarily give us the technical data and information we need. Supplementing the information which will be presented
during this hearing with data available to us in Washington, we will
objectively consider all information so collected and prepare a report
of our *Recommendations*, copies of which will be made available to
those concerned with this matter.

We are aware, of course, that our *Recommendations* in this case,
as in most cases involving divergent technical, economic, and political
views, may not be universally popular. You may be sure, however,
that "we will write them the way we see them," and that all sides of
this issue will receive, to the best of our ability, fair and impartial
consideration by the panel.

For your information, the Airport Use Panel is part of, and is responsible to, the Air Co-ordinating Committee (ACC) which reports
directly to the President. The ACC was established by interdepartmental agreement in 1945 and formalized by Presidential Order in
1946, to co-ordinate aviation policies and programs, both domestic
and international, involving more than one federal agency. By its
terms of reference, decisions of the Airport Use Panel, when unanimous, become the final decisions of the ACC. In the absence of
unanimous agreement by the panel, problems may then be referred
to the ACC, and failing to reach unanimous agreement in that body,
presented to the President for final resolution. Implementation of
panel decisions is the responsibility of the federal agency or agencies
having primary statutory authority.

The five other panel members, besides Morris from the CAA,
represented the following federal agencies: Civil Aeronautics
Board, Department of Defense (Secretary's Office), Army, Navy,
and Air Force. The witnesses before the panel included local officials, elected and appointed; elected federal officials or their representatives; state officials; representatives of chambers of commerce; labor union leaders; and airline representatives. Also
present were representatives from the CAA regional and district
field offices and spokesmen for the Reserve units, the precipitators
of the current controversy. Those favoring transfer of the airlines
were Cobo and Edward Connor (backstopped by Richards and
McElroy), Maitland, Representative John Lesinski, Senator Patrick McNamara, and union leaders from the Wayne County CIO
and the Teamsters Union Joint Council No. 43; opposing the

transfer were Robert J. Wilson (Capital Airlines vice president and designated spokesman for all the airlines), Representative George Meader, University of Michigan officials, representatives from chambers of commerce in Ann Arbor and Ypsilanti, and elected officials from Ypsilanti, Ann Arbor, and some townships in Washtenaw County. William Mara represented the Detroit Board of Commerce at the hearings. Significantly, no members of the Detroit Aviation Commission were present. Cobo had let it be known that they would not be welcome to speak at the panel hearings since he, Cobo, would present Detroit's position on airports.

Cobo assumed the leading role in arguing for the transfer of the airlines. His formal statement was thirty-six pages long. Connor, although elected as a Detroit councilman, spoke wearing his other hat as chairman of the County Board of Supervisors. His presentation paralleled and elaborated Cobo's. Cobo emphasized the official endorsements given Wayne Major, the size and modernity of the airport, and its convenience for Detroit air passengers. He also argued that Willow Run was constructed as a defense facility, inferring from this that the original intent was to use it as a military airport, an intent best implemented, according to Cobo, by assigning all the military air units to Willow Run. Both Cobo and Connor charged that the airlines enjoyed a "subsidy" or "free ride" at Willow Run and pointed to the extra road miles traveled to reach Willow Run when Wayne Major was passed on the journey. Connor charged that the location of the airlines at Willow Run instead of at Wayne Major forced Detroit air passengers to travel an estimated 23,590,796 miles per year unnecessarily. This figure was derived by multiplying the number of air passengers in 1954 times 12.3 miles, the difference in the distances of the two terminals from downtown Detroit. Using ten cents as an average per-mile cost figure, Connor estimated that airline users would save more than $2,250,000 annually if the airlines moved to Wayne Major.

At the hearings Cobo's position on Wayne Major and the northeast airport was in line with his earlier statement—move the airlines to Wayne Major and then secure the land for the northeast. To give the northeast airport a priority equal to or higher than Wayne Major's would reduce the airlines' willingness to move to the latter airport and to assume part of the costs of completing the airport. These costs, to be financed about equally from public and private (airline) outlays, were estimated variously at from $15,000,000 to $30,000,000. Cobo made public at the hearings a letter from the Road Commission which promised support for a northeast airport after Wayne Major was completed.

Representative Meader appeared in the capacity of a congressman acting as an advocate at bar before a group of federal administrative officials. Meader contended that Detroit-Wayne Major was better suited for military jet planes because its runways were newer, heavier, and wider. It would be unwise, he said, to force the airlines and taxpayers to spend $20,000,000 or $30,000,000 to complete the county's airport when the airlines had declared themselves in favor of a northeast terminal. An added cost of transfer, he argued, was the severe economic loss it would inflict on the University of Michigan. Furthermore, basing the jet squadrons at Willow Run would result in incalculable losses in property values around the airport. University officials and local government and chamber of commerce representatives supported and elaborated Meader's comments. University officials stated that if the airlines moved, the university would be financially unable to meet the terms under which it purchased the airport, namely, to maintain it in good and serviceable condition.

Representatives from the three military units spoke before the panel. The Air Force stated its preference for Willow Run; the Navy preferred Wayne Major, as did the Michigan Air National Guard, which had invested $2,500,000 in the county port.

In brief but significant testimony, CAA officials from Detroit (district office) and Kansas City (regional office) did not express preferences for, or opposition to, any proposals for locating or relocating the airlines or the military aircraft. It appeared that technical aeronautical problems such as air-space use, air-space congestion, and air-traffic control were not critical to a decision on where the various aircraft should be based.

Perhaps the most interesting testimony at the hearing was that presented by Robert Wilson of Capital Airlines on behalf of the airlines. Wilson reaffirmed the intention of the air carriers to remain at Willow Run and countered the two chief points made against Willow Run by Cobo and Connor—the proximity and subsidy arguments. On the former, Wilson said:

In the present case, there can be no doubt that there will be benefit to the passengers, for the Wayne County Airport is nearer [Detroit] and some time will be saved. Against this is the cost to the taxpayers and the airlines. In order to make Wayne County suitable for a commercial operation, it will, in our opinion, cost between $20,000,000 and $30,000,000. In our opinion, after serious consideration, we do not believe that the benefit to the passengers in this particular case is sufficient to warrant the expenditure by the taxpayers of Wayne County and the airlines. There is a further factor that must be considered from the economic standpoint. The people of Detroit want an airport in the northeast part of the city. We feel there is merit in the desire, and even though we do not like a split operation in a city, we feel there should be another airport serving Detroit. We further feel that instead of expending additional moneys on Wayne County Airport, with so little additional benefit to the passengers, that any moneys which the taxpayers and the airlines are called upon to pay should be expended on the northeast site.

Wilson's arguments for the northeast airport were seconded by William Mara, who urged favorable consideration of this site. The prospect of a northeast airport still loomed as a deterrent to the Wayne Major move.

Wilson denied that the airlines were "riding some kind of gravy train at the expense of the taxpayer, in their operation of Willow Run." He cited figures showing that ANTSCO lost money from 1946 through 1953 but that it had earned a profit in 1954. ANTSCO, however, was merely the airlines' agent for operating the terminal and landing field, so these figures were not significant. ANTSCO enabled the airlines to maintain and operate the field at a minimal cost. In addition, since ANTSCO was not obligated for amortization costs of the terminal and landing field, it paid the university only nominal rent. Willow Run was unquestionably favorable financially for the airlines. Exactly how favorable it was and who else was benefited or disadvantaged by the arrangement were precisely the points at which opinions diverged. After hearing testimony for two days, the Airport Use Panel was confronted with the issue of whether the arrangement was in the public interest and should continue. The panel's decision was not expected for three or four months.

At the panel hearings, Mayor Cobo had attempted to span the conflict between the Road Commission and the Aviation Commission by supporting the projects of both units. Cobo's failure to bridge the gulf separating the two projects and the two commissions was apparent to most participants and observers. One active participant saw fit to call this to Cobo's attention. Harvey Campbell, executive vice president of the Detroit Board of Commerce, wrote a confidential letter to the mayor on June 23, 1955, one day after Cobo's appearance before the federal panel. Campbell's letter illustrates the close support given the city by the Board of Commerce on the northeast airport and also provides a short summary of the strategy and conflict surrounding that project. The letter is reproduced in its entirety.

Dear Al:

You made an excellent presentation before the Airport Panel yesterday morning and I hastened to congratulate you upon it. However, there was no time for me to call your attention to a loophole in your testimony. I am not going to jump into this fight personally if I can keep out of it, but I want to express myself confidentially to you. It seems to me you are caught in the middle between a couple of commissions one of [which] is giving you double-talk.

You read the letter from the Wayne County Road Commission which said, in effect, "that after the Wayne County cause had been composed exactly as they want it and after a demand has been proved for another airport, they would go along with you in your efforts to acquire *a* northeast airport." The letter didn't promise that they would help you acquire *the* northeast airport now being prepared for court by Bert Sogge [city condemnation attorney].

Before you go to the expense of proceeding with the condemnation I would suggest that you ask Leroy Smith of the Road Commission and John McElroy of the Michigan Aeronautics Commission to tell you to your face that they are willing to go on the witness stand in the condemnation case of the Warren property now under consideration and promise you that they will testify that it is necessary. They have told our committee, honestly and flatly, that they don't believe we will ever get that specific airport and that they will not recommend it. They do recommend going out three more miles to Sterling Township. Commissioner Glenn Richards has expressed his personal opinion that the city of Detroit will lose its suit.

My apprehension is not because of an apparent demand for another airport immediately. But you and I have agreed and I have acted under your instructions, practically, in attempting to pursue a near-in northeast airport so that we could acquire the property now and cinch it for later, even ten years from now. Otherwise, if we wait until Wayne's demands are satisfied and the airlines are probably shoved out of Willow Run, we'll have no chance to get any kind of a property this side of Rochester. Every year's delay means another three miles distance.

Regardless of the controversy between Wayne and Willow Run, I hope to see you achieve the condemnation of the Warren property and not deviate a whit from the purpose outlined in your office when we met with Don Kiskadden and a few others, many months ago. You, frankly, are now in the position of having two public officials working at odds. Commissioner Burnett is being paid to acquire the northeast airport as specifically directed by you. Commissioner Richards is working with the Wayne County Road Commission to keep Bud [Burnett] from succeding, and to thwart your purpose. As the feller said, "That's one helluva way to run a railroad."

Please get Bert Sogge on the job and tell him where to look for his interference.

Good luck!

Campbell's letter and its pointed remarks on Cobo's airport policy remained confidential until 1957, when a clash between Cobo and the Aviation Commission prompted Campbell to send a copy of the letter to the board of directors of the Board of Commerce.

The split on airport policy broke out in public one month after the panel hearings in Detroit. The Detroit Aviation Commission wrote Mayor Cobo charging that Glenn Richards had belittled plans for a northeast airport while the commission had remained silent at the mayor's request. Seldom one to accept a taint of criticism with grace, Cobo shot back, "Nobody is ever asked to remain silent in my administration." He then expressed surprise over the displeasure of the commission and reiterated his statement of priorities: "It has been my understanding that the members of the commission have been in agreement with a policy of moving to Detroit-Wayne Major first and then acquiring land for the northeast airport." Cobo acknowledged that Richards may have been "over-pressing" his support of the county airport but added, "I've heard nobody else complaining that this was the case." Richards had a few comments of his own:

> The Detroit Aviation Commission is in disagreement with everyone else in the area. All other official groups favor using the Detroit-Wayne Major Airport now, with the proposed northeast field to follow. I have never belittled the northeast airport, but I have always said the county airport is the best in the nation.

The Airport Use Panel Report. As maneuvering proceeded at the local level, the Airport Use Panel was having its difficulties with "the Detroit case," which the panel, in its 1955 annual report, recognized as "the most controversial and diversified case ever undertaken by the panel." On August 2, six weeks after the hearings, a letter to Leonard Jurden, CAA regional administrator in Kansas City, left the Washington office of the CAA. The letter asked, on behalf of the Airport Use Panel, for a study of the air-traffic control problems resulting from four hypothetical situations involving the use of Willow Run and Wayne Major. The four situations distributed the airport users as follows:

(1) at Willow Run: air carriers, Air Force Reserve
    at Wayne Major: Air National Guard, Navy Reserve
(2) at Willow Run: Navy Reserve, Air Force Reserve, Air National Guard
    at Wayne Major: air carriers
(3) at Willow Run: Navy Reserve, Air Force Reserve
    at Wayne Major: air carriers, Air National Guard
(4) at Willow Run: air carriers, Navy Reserve, Air Force Reserve
    at Wayne Major: Air National Guard

Two situations located the airlines at Willow Run; two placed them at Wayne Major. But in all four situations, some military craft were based at Willow Run. The Air Force, which had stated its preference for Willow Run at the hearings, was the only airport user assigned to the airport it preferred in all four situations.

From Jurden's office in Kansas City the study request was immediately relayed to the CAA tower chiefs at Detroit City, Wayne Major, and Willow Run airports. The tower chiefs were given until August 19, and on August 17 the traffic control study was dispatched to Kansas City. In a covering letter the Detroit district chief summarized the opinion of the committee that performed the traffic control analysis: ". . . it is the opinion of this committee that insofar as air-traffic control is concerned, it does not make any appreciable difference as to how the additional [i.e., military] operations are distributed . . ." (*Federal Role in Aviation,* p. 1406). A two-page statement summarizing the results of the study was equally noncommittal. No opinions were expressed in favor of any of the four alternatives outlined. Local CAA operating personnel were not taking sides on how to solve the military-civilian conflict.

The traffic control study remained at the CAA regional office in Kansas City for about two weeks. During this time it was reviewed and revised, and when it was forwarded to Washington on September 2, it had lost its non-preferential character. In commenting on situation (2) (air carriers at Wayne Major, all military craft at Willow Run), the revised report stated:

> Although this action would require the relocation of the terminal radar equipment . . . and rearrangement of the present airway route structure, we believe that this move will greatly increase the efficiency of operations in the Detroit terminal area. For one thing, terminal radar located at Wayne Major will have a greater utilitarian range, in that it would be centrally located and able to afford surveillance over a greater portion of the entire terminal area.

The reference to the location and surveillance of radar in the terminal area resulted from the different location of the terminal buildings and control towers at the two airports. At Willow Run the terminal and tower were located at the extreme westerly edge of the airport, while at Wayne Major they were located near the center of the airfield. Why this particular feature should be mentioned as an advantage by regional officials and not by the Detroit district personnel actually controlling the air movements is open to speculation. In any case, CAA regional personnel favored situation (2) in their report to Washington.

On November 4, 1955 the Airport Use Panel released its findings and recommendations. The twenty-one-page report (Airport Use Panel Memorandum No. 8-55) gave the Smith-Richards-Cobo-Connor forces a complete victory. The first two recommendations were:

1. That the Detroit-Wayne Major Airport be developed and utilized as the major civil air terminal serving the Detroit area.
2. That the scheduled air carriers now using the Willow Run Airport transfer their operations to the Detroit-Wayne Major Airport as soon as adequate facilities can be made available to serve their needs.

The net effect of further recommendations was to achieve full segregation of scheduled civil and military air operations between the two airports. Detroit-Wayne Major would be used exclusively for civilian flights, dominated by the scheduled commercial airlines. The Air Force Reserve, the Navy Reserve, and eventually the Air National Guard were to locate at Willow Run with some non-scheduled civil operations. The panel's final recommendation repeated a proposal that by now had become a commonplace in every review of Detroit's air problems: "That consideration be given to the establishment of a single metropolitan airport authority to administer the civil airports in the Detroit area." Since the panel members agreed unanimously to the recommendations, they were construed as binding on all federal agencies with no appeal permitted.

The Airport Use Panel based its recommendation for the transfer of the airlines primarily on the greater public convenience served by the airlines locating at Wayne Major, i.e., the twelve-mile advantage enjoyed by the county airport: "There is no reasonable justification . . . to impose upon the majority of the public the burden of traveling some twenty-four extra ground miles in a round trip to the Willow Run Airport when, in doing so, the Detroit-Wayne Major Airport is passed en route." The panel acknowledged that additional costs to the taxpayers and to the airlines would be involved if the airlines moved, but it was skeptical of the $20,000,000 to $30,000,000 estimate offered at the hearing as the cost of the transfer. The report observed: "In arriving at the exact costs of transferring the carriers to Detroit-Wayne Major Airport . . . the possibility that certain profits may have been realized by ANTSCO in its operation at the Willow Run Airport should not be overlooked." Earlier in the report, the panel had examined this possibility:

In simple terms, the university received from the federal government, without charge, a ready-made, multimillion-dollar airport with all necessary facilities. The airport was then leased to ANTSCO, which collects all revenues from the airport and its concessions, and in turn, pays the costs of its maintenance and operation. Inasmuch as the airport was originally received without cost, however, there is no initial capital investment to be amortized. The scheduled air carriers are charged landing fees by ANTSCO, but since ANTSCO is composed of the same air carriers, they, in effect, pay these fees to themselves. When the landing charges are balanced against the revenues received from concessions and other sources, it appears entirely possible for the carriers to use the Willow Run Airport free; in fact, if the revenues are sufficiently great, the carriers stand to make a profit by doing so. Regardless of its redeeming features as a successful business enterprise, the panel has been unable to ascertain that any substantial benefit has accrued to the public as a result of this arrangement.

The implication was that since the airlines had enjoyed such a favorable financial situation at Willow Run for nearly ten years, the costs of making the move to Wayne Major should not prove burdensome or objectionable.

On the other hand, the panel expressed doubts that the financial attractiveness of the Willow Run arrangement was sufficient to enable ANTSCO to finance major runway and building improvements without benefit of federal aid. The panel assumed (incorrectly) that Willow Run could not qualify for federal aid because ANTSCO was a private concern. (Despite the legality of federal grants to Willow Run, only two small grants totaling $174,-000 had been awarded to Willow Run, and applications for them had been submitted to the Aeronautics Commission by the University of Michigan, not by ANTSCO.)

Besides accessibility, the Airport Use Panel saw several other advantages in the county airport: (1) Its runways were wider, newer, longer, and of heavier design. (2) Its approaches were free of obstructions. (3) A new terminal then under construction would be functional and time-saving. (4) Instrument flying operations could be handled more efficiently when the new, centrally located terminal building was completed. Why these advantages accrued more to the benefit of the commercial airlines than to military aircraft was traceable to "public convenience" and the "public interest."

Indeed, the panel summarized its orientation in this statement (p. 17): "Viewing this matter from the standpoint of public interest, the panel is unable to find any compelling reason for the air carriers' remaining at the Willow Run Airport." The burden of proof was on the airlines: unless they could justify remaining at Willow Run (and they clearly had not, so far as the panel was concerned), the presumption was that they should and would move to Detroit-Wayne Major.

The transfer of the airlines was one side of the coin. The other side was the use of Willow Run by the military. The Navy and Air Force Reserve squadrons could be based at Willow Run in the existing unused facilities owned by the federal government and in the space to be vacated by the transfer of the airlines. To duplicate these facilities at Wayne Major would require an outlay of $5,000,000 and would delay occupancy until construction was completed. Military expenditures would be smaller and facilities would be available sooner if military aircraft were located at Willow Run. Thus, the question, "Whither the airlines?" also involved questions of timing and of who should be compelled to shoulder additional costs, the commercial airlines or the U.S. Department of Defense. The commercial airlines "lost."

The entrance of the military onto the scene of the airport controversy had moved the focus away from possible sites for a new airport to the airports in existence. The opponents of Wayne Major had to abandon the promotion of an alternative site and concentrate instead on defending Willow Run as a base for commercial flights. The unorthodoxy of the airlines' financial arrangements and Willow Run's inconvenience for the passenger public made this defense difficult. The added expense which the Defense Department (and ultimately the taxpayers) would have had to incur in order to reserve Willow Run for commercial use introduced an additional argument for transferring the airlines to Wayne Major, an argument which undoubtedly weighed heavily with the Airport Use Panel. Later, when the Airport Use Panel's recommendations came under heavy fire from Congressman Meader, the composition of the panel became a point at issue. Of the six members sitting on the panel, four were from military agencies.

The Airport Use Panel's recommendations gave the Wayne Major forces a decisive victory. Only an unprecedented reversal of the panel's decision by the President of the United States or some unforeseen outflanking move would prevent the airlines from moving to Detroit-Wayne Major.

The County Airport Wins

American Airlines Decides to Move. Following the release of

the Airport Use Panel's memorandum, Mayor Cobo made two public pronouncements on the airport situation. He first assured the
airlines that they would get a "square deal" if they accepted the
panel's recommendations and moved to Wayne Major. At the
same time he ordered a speed-up on land acquisition for the northeast airport in Warren Township. Shortly thereafter the Detroit
Aviation Commission filed a request with the Michigan Aeronautics Commission for approval of an executive-type airport in Warren Township.

If Cobo and county officials expected immediate acquiescence
to the Airport Use Panel's recommendations, either from the airlines or from other quarters, they were quickly forced to revise
their thinking. Sharp criticisms of the recommendations came
from Representative Meader, but the airlines themselves proved to
be the major stumbling block.

The airlines met with Richards and County Road Commission
personnel on November 17. Six of the seven airlines attending
the meeting indicated their disapproval of the panel's report. The
six, Capital, Delta, Eastern, Northwest, Trans World, and United,
declared their intention to remain at Willow Run and later formalized their position in letters to Smith and Cobo on December 29, in which they declared that they had decided "once and
for all" against moving to Detroit-Wayne Major. These abortive
negotiations disclosed firm estimates of the public and private
costs for equipping Wayne Major for use by all the airlines. The
figure presented to the airlines by city and county officials was
$28,260,000.

The seventh airline present at these discussions, American Airlines, expressed a definite interest in moving to Wayne Major
if agreement could be reached on rates. American, the area's (and
the nation's) largest passenger carrier, had originally been reluctant to use Willow Run, and, with its large-scale operations, it
found Willow Run's limited terminal accommodations more unsatisfactory than did the other airlines. Subsequent discussions
with American led to a public announcement by the airline on
January 17, 1956 that it intended to transfer to Detroit-Wayne
Major. This was a blow to Capital Airlines' Wilson and the Board
of Commerce's Kiskadden and Mara, the three who had led the

fight to keep the airlines at Willow Run. With the airline that handled one-third of all passenger traffic at Willow Run moving to Wayne Major, it was questionable whether the other airlines could remain competitive if they did not also move.

American's announcement was sufficient evidence to the CAA that a "substantial segment" of Detroit's airline activity would be located at Wayne Major. On February 9 the CAA announced an allocation of $975,000 to Wayne Major for fiscal 1956–57. The allocation was tentative. A final grant agreement would be concluded only after American signed contracts with the county and after local matching funds were assured. The obverse of the CAA's allocation to Wayne Major was its refusal to allocate funds to the University of Michigan for Willow Run.

CAA's refusal of the university's request for a grant of $86,000 was explained by Herbert H. Howell, director of the Office of Airports, at a Congressional hearing a few months later. Howell was questioned closely by Congresswoman Martha W. Griffiths, representative from Michigan's Seventeenth District—northwestern Detroit and northwestern Wayne County. (Mrs. Griffiths, the lone Detroit-area Democrat opposed to the airlines' transfer, was, like Meader, a graduate of the University of Michigan Law School.) Howell explained that he was responsible for denying funds to Willow Run because of a questionable clause in ANTSCO's lease with the university. The clause, in Howell's opinion, appeared to make ANTSCO responsible for all improvements at the airport. Howell acknowledged that the clause was subject to varying interpretations but indicated his firm intent to withhold funds from Willow Run until the ambiguity in the lease was erased to his satisfaction. He admitted, however, (1) that his decision reversed an earlier opinion by a CAA regional attorney holding that federal grants to Willow Run were legal, (2) that the questionable clause in ANTSCO's lease had been called to his attention by the Wayne County Road Commission, (3) that the CAA had not contacted or consulted with the airlines regarding their preferences, and (4) that he was withholding money, in Mrs. Griffiths words, "from an airport where two million people were landing and taking off annually." After these admissions the following exchange occurred between the congresswoman and the CAA official:

Mrs. Griffiths: Are you using your office to force the airlines into Wayne Major?

Mr. Howell: Indeed we are not. . . .

Mrs. Griffiths: You don't consider that [grant] a reward for [American's] moving there?

Mr. Howell: No, indeed (*Federal Role in Aviation*, p. 775).

Howell's statements notwithstanding, it was evident that the CAA was using its discretion to encourage, if not force the transfer of the airlines. Although the transfer seemed about to start, the opposition to Wayne Major and to Leroy Smith did not diminish. If anything, it took on new strength and vehemence.

The Northeast Site Is Revived. In the early months of 1956, challenges to Wayne Major came from four sources: (1) city officials, (2) the press, (3) the Detroit Board of Commerce, and (4) Congressman Meader. These attacks peaked during the months from January to April, although the last thrust, in the form of a Congressional investigation, came in mid-July. Perhaps at no time in the long struggle over Detroit's airport problems was a more concentrated public assault made on the county airport and on Leroy Smith.

Mayor Cobo had ordered an acceleration of land acquisition efforts on the northeast site after the Airport Use Panel report. Detroit prepared to battle Warren Township in the courts on the two condemnation suits held in abeyance since June 1954. Warren Township's suit to condemn the seventy-four-acre, Detroit-owned airport was set for trial on January 24, 1956. The trial began on schedule and was concluded on February 2, when the condemnation jury returned a verdict denying the township's claim. The denial was based on (1) the township's failure to prove the desirability and necessity of using the area as a park, and (2) the fact that Detroit purchased the airport prior to the commencement of Warren's suit. (There are no explicit provisions in Michigan law providing for the condemnation of one public corporation's property by another public corporation.)

Detroit officials greeted the verdict jubilantly. They prepared to press their condemnation suit against the two-square-mile site, but their plans received a jolt within the next ten days. On February 12, Warren Township Superintendent of Schools Paul Cousino announced that the Warren Consolidated School District had purchased a five-acre parcel in the center of the proposed airport site for "use as an elementary-school site once this airport menace has disappeared." Township Supervisor Arthur J. Miller revealed simultaneously that the township had purchased a sixty-six-acre farm also in the approximate center of the proposed airport. The farm, according to Miller, was to be used as a park, but he was candid about the township's strategy: "We're not kidding anyone, we bought the land for two reasons—the park and to stop Detroit." Recalling the condemnation suit that had terminated ten days earlier, Miller said, "We now have a chance for a return engagement with Detroit in court. Only this time the shoe will be on the other foot—with Detroit trying to condemn land we own." (The township paid $235,000 for the farm, or about $3,500 per acre; Detroit had paid only $1,350 per acre for the seventy-four-acre Warren airport.) The money to pay for the property came from a special recreation bond issue of $300,000 that had been passed by the township voters a few months earlier.

Title to the property purchased by the township (and by the school district) was clouded by Detroit's long-standing condemnation suit filed against all the property in the proposed site. This suit could provide the basis for challenging the suburban unit's claim to the properties. That possibility was reduced on April 9, 1956 when Macomb County Circuit Court Judge James E. Spier dismissed Detroit's suit for lack of progress. Reflecting on the court action some time later, Cousino observed, "Detroit lost on a technicality. We didn't really have a clear title to the property until their suit was dismissed." Cousino also believes ". . . that we could not have won without the battle that was going on between the big political figures from the Wayne County Road Commission and the Detroit Aviation Commission. If Cobo had *really* wanted the airport we couldn't have stopped them. Our only chance was to delay, confuse, and retreat like 'Swamp Fox' Marion in the Revolutionary War and hope that in time we would wear them down. We did it, but we were fortunate." Supervisor Miller, however, feels that the decisive factors in Warren Township's victory were the political, legal, and fiscal defenses that the resourceful suburbanites called upon in their fight against the airport.

At any rate, by the time spring arrived baseball diamonds, playground equipment, etc., were in place and in use on the "park" property which the township had obtained in February. Baseballs rather than airplanes were zooming around the proposed airport site. The only threat to the township's title to the property lay in the possibility that Detroit might obtain reinstatement of its original suit in the Macomb County Circuit Court.

Meanwhile the Detroit-Warren controversy had become the subject of sharp public debate. It began with a series of feature articles appearing in the *Detroit Free Press* between February 3 and February 15. The series coincided with the announcement of the CAA grant to Wayne Major (February 6) and with the land-purchase actions in Warren Township (February 12). The several multi-columned articles, which were later reprinted in an eight-page, newspaper-size brochure and given wide mail circulation among members of the business community, were written by Jean Pearson, aviatrix and aviation writer for the *Free Press*. She left no doubt as to what she considered to be the right solution for Detroit's airport problem: leave the airlines at Willow Run and build the northeast airport as the area's second major air terminal.

According to Miss Pearson, Wayne Major was "a 'make-do' airport . . . a rehash of an airport begun in 1928." The "make-do" character of Wayne Major was traced to alleged faulty planning and snail's-pace construction, and $19,000,000 was cited as the amount of public funds necessary to complete the airport while expenditures by the airlines would be over and above this amount. In addition, according to Miss Pearson, operating expenses at Wayne Major were excessive, especially when compared with those at City Airport. The profit-and-loss statements of the two airports between fiscal 1950–51 and fiscal 1954–55 showed that Wayne Major had incurred total net losses of $222,194, while City Airport had made a net profit of over twice that amount. Miss Pearson also noted that in contract discussions with the airlines, the Road Commission had insisted on clauses permitting frequent review and provision for upward revisions in rates if revenues failed to meet costs. (Wayne Major's development was to be financed partially by revenue bonds, which had to be paid off from the airport's operating revenue.) The airlines wanted rates which were fixed for relatively long periods of time. Miss Pearson called the county proposal "the blank-check deal." The obvious implication was that Wayne Major was an inefficient airport inefficiently managed. The *Free Press* series, coming as it did just after the condemnation jury gave the city a victory on its claim to the northeast site, was a well-timed prelude to Congressman Meader's attacks on Wayne Major on the national level.

Congressman Meader Intervenes. Following the *Free Press* articles, Congressman Meader launched a frontal attack. Speaking on the floor of the House of Representatives on February 23, Meader leveled charges against the Airport Use Panel, the CAA, policy-making by the executive branch, Wayne Major Airport, and Leroy Smith.

Meader fired his biggest gun first. He called for a Congressional investigation of the use of federal funds to expand Wayne Major. The use of $4,000,000 in federal funds to build up Wayne Major "only six air miles from a perfectly adequate airport [Willow Run] was "an unconscionable waste of public funds." Meader criticized the CAA for continuing to grant funds "to a white elephant which, rather than easing the congested air traffic in the Detroit area, actually has complicated it." Instead of spending $28,000,000 more on Wayne Major, Meader urged that the funds be used to develop the northeast airport, far removed from Wayne-Willow air-traffic patterns and more strategically located to balance airline service in the metropolitan area.

Meader disclosed that he had formally requested a Congressional investigation in a letter to Congressman Robert H. Mollohan (Dem., W. Va.), chairman of the Legal and Monetary Affairs Subcommittee of the House Government Operations Committee. Meader was the ranking minority member of Mollohan's subcommittee. In the letter to Mollohan, Meader suggested that the subcommittee ". . . explore the administration of the airport-aid program by the Civil Aeronautics Administration in its entirety, taking as an example the present and prospective expenditure of federal funds at Detroit-Wayne Major Airport, with a view to determining whether or not those moneys are being expended efficiently and economically in the interest of civil aviation and its future development in the United States." Interspersed through Meader's letter to Mollohan and his remarks in the *Record* were caustic references to the Road Commission, Leroy Smith, and John McElroy. But the chief objects of Meader's wrath were the Airport Use Panel and policy-making by the executive branch of government.

Meader termed the Airport Use Panel a "stacked deck" and "kangaroo court" and its hearings a "fraud, sham, and blunder." Prima facie evidence of the panel's bias, according to Meader, was the predominance of the military on the panel and the refusal of the panel to consider additional cost to the taxpayers and the airlines for equipping Wayne Major. Meader linked military domination of the panel and its parent body, the Air Co-ordinating Committee, to broader issues—the non-statutory base of the Air Co-ordinating Committee and the focus of policy-making in the field of aviation:

> As I told you, this Air Co-ordinating Committee has no statutory standing, being created by executive order, but it is presumed to bind the executive branch of the government. Let me tell you that I have come to learn that the executive branch of the government has come to have a lot more to say about the future of aviation in this country than the Congress does.
>
> What did that panel report? It reported exactly what it knew it was going to report before it went out there. It was going to give the military anything they wanted, and it was going to back up the CAA in its mistaken program of underwriting this huge expansion program to build one airport right on top of another one (*Congressional Record*, February 23, 1956, pp. 3276–7).

The Michigan congressman had a more immediate reason for being exercised over the role of the Airport Use Panel and the military. On February 9 a Navy captain in the Office of the Chief of Naval Operations wrote to University of Michigan officials asking, in rather blunt terms, when the university planned to provide space for the Navy jet squadron, as the Airport Use Panel had recommended. The Navy letter was followed by one of February 13 from J. W. Johnson, a CAA official who was also secretary of the Airport Use Panel, to Harlan Hatcher, president of the university. Johnson reminded Hatcher of the panel's recommendations and asked for a statement of the university's position. Moreover, Johnson asked that the university help to implement the panel's recommendation by not extending ANTSCO's lease at Willow Run. Such an action would, of course, force the airlines to move post haste. (Copies of Johnson's letter were sent—possibly for strategic as well as perfunctory reasons—to Mayor Cobo, Councilman Connor, Governor Williams, and the Michigan Aeronautics Commission.) Hatcher, in his reply to Johnson several days later, refused to consider such a precipitous action as refusing extension of the lease. He also refused to accept the Navy squadron at Willow Run. Meader termed Johnson's letter "a masterpiece of federal bureaucratic arrogance and impertinence" and contended that the panel was "way out of bounds" in trying to pressure the university.

In his concluding remarks Congressman Meader returned to the broad issue of policy-making in the field of aviation:

> It is not the role of the executive to make policy; it is not the role of some high-powered so-called experts to advise the executive on how to make aviation policy. . . .
>
> It is for Congress to do that job. It is my hope that the inquiry of the Legal and Monetary Affairs Subcommittee will provide a fund of factual information which will enable the appropriate legislative committees and the Congress to discharge its constitutional function in determining policy in the field of aviation. It is my hope that the committee's inquiry will also disclose the extent to which military thinking is influencing national aviation development (*Congressional Record*, February 23, 1956, p. 3280).

Meader's assault and the prospect of a full-scale investigation posed a threat from the last bastion for blocking the transfer of the airlines. If Meader could obtain the investigation and prove that Wayne Major was "a horrible mistake," Congress might intervene to prevent further expansion of Wayne Major. But neither Leroy Smith nor Mayor Cobo seemed perturbed. "That's the way people are," said Smith. "They play the game, they lose, and then they don't like the umpire's decision. I'm in favor of an investigation." Cobo seconded the motion: "What does he [Meader] contend—that all these experts are wrong and that he alone is right? I would welcome an investigation," he jibed. "Maybe then we can examine Willow Run's books and find out exactly what the airlines are paying" (*The Detroit News*, February 24, 1956).

One week after Meader's speech on the House floor, Congressman Mollohan announced that his subcommittee would hold hearings on the administration of federal airport grants and on the Wayne-Willow controversy. Mollohan stated that the subcommittee wanted to know if the CAA had been using the $250,000,000 appropriated since 1946 to build airports for the "horse-and-buggy era" of propeller aircraft or for the coming jet age. Mollohan set the hearings for July in Washington.

Smith, Cobo, *et al.* took Meader's attack more seriously than their public statements let on. The Wayne Major forces aided a Detroit congressman in replying to Meader's charges. On March 13 Representative John Lesinski of Michigan's Sixteenth District (which covered southwestern Wayne County, including Wayne Major) spoke to the House on the Wayne-Willow controversy. Lesinski's main theme was that "because of the influence of politics, our national defense is suffering for the lack of facilities." This statement referred to the Navy's inability to secure space at Willow Run. The chief culprits, Lesinski charged, were Capital Airlines and the University of Michigan:

> The collusion between Capital Airlines and the University of Michigan to hold up a matter which will benefit a metropolitan area of 4,000,000 people is an affront to a community that pays into the national treasury above-average taxes. Of course, you can see why Capital Airlines is acting as it is. We, as taxpayers, have built Willow Run. And we, as taxpayers, are continuing to pay the larger portion for the airlines' use of Willow Run. Imagine the airlines presently paying only $38,000[1] for the use of Willow Run, whereas they should be paying out approximately $2,000,000 annually for an air terminal which would be comparable to the one at San Francisco.

Lesinski concluded:

> It is a shame that we of Detroit have to put up with a disgraceful-looking air terminal to serve our area. What we have is a converted hangar that could more properly and readily be used by the military for storage and repair of aircraft. We in Detroit need and should have a proper air-passenger terminal that we could be proud of and

[1] Lesinski did not indicate the source of this figure. When ANTSCO released its rental figures four months later, it was revealed that ANTSCO's rent varied from year to year and that its fiscal 1955–56 rent was estimated at $68,000.

not have to put up with such a disgrace to the community as we now have because of the whims of one individual.

The presently scheduled hearing before the Government Operations [Mollohan] Committee will have no effect on the problem. If action is not taken to implement the recommendations of the President's Airport Use Panel, I have prepared and am going to introduce a House resolution to investigate the whole procedure at Willow Run and to force ANSCO [ANTSCO] and the University of Michigan to reveal their books so that we, the American people, can see what is going on behind the scenes (*Congressional Record,* March 13, 1956, pp. 4625–6).

Lesinski's speech, with its references to "the whims of one individual" and elsewhere to "one congressman [who] can say for 4,000,000 people what airport they are to be served from," served as the lively starter for a long and prickly debate between Lesinski and Meader. It began with some initial sparring, in which Lesinski accused Meader of "fighting for ANTSCO" and Meader retaliated with several pointed and taunting references to Lesinski's come-lately interest in the airport controversy and to recent briefings given Lesinski by John McElroy and Glenn Richards. After further exchanges, Meader disclosed that he had written letters to the chairmen of the Michigan House and Senate appropriations committees suggesting that the Michigan legislature withhold further appropriations from Wayne Major until the Congressional investigation of the airport aid program was completed. The chairmen of these two committees were, like Meader, Republicans, and they had both been elected from state legislative districts within Meader's Congressional district. Congressman John Dingell, Democrat from Michigan's Fifteenth District (wholly within Detroit's limits) asked if Meader would object to having his request expanded to include withholding the expenditure of any state funds at Willow Run. Meader replied:

The gentleman's colleague, Mr. Leroy Smith, very effectively took care of that by coming down here and going before the CAA to oppose a very modest request of $86,500 for Willow Run when Wayne Major was asking for over $1,000,000; but his representatives took it up with the officials in the Civil Aeronautics Administration and urged them not to give any money to Willow Run, and they did not give any. Talk about somebody talking to an official of the government, it seems to me that the people at Wayne Major Airport—

I do not know who is doing it, but I know some of them have been down here, and their efforts to see members of Congress and also members of the Civil Aeronautics Administration and the Under Secretary of Commerce have been very successful in getting the major part of federal airport aid funds and in getting action they wanted.

In response to another question from Dingell, Meader centered again on his favorite targets, the Airport Use Panel and the CAA:

They [the panel] had kicked this question around in the Department of Defense and come up with a firm position on it, even though there had been some disagreements along the line. So it was Department of Defense policy that the request of the Air Force to go into Willow Run be granted. As far as the CAA is concerned, they have been sucked in on this deal by Leroy Smith as long as ten years ago when he came down here and got a commitment to develop Wayne Major Airport.

The debate concluded with Dingell trying to secure an admission from Meader that the economic and financial interests in Meader's district "overwhelm his respect for the good judgment of the Airport Use Panel" and Meader claiming that the "tremendous waste of tax funds" outweighed the interests of his constituency.

The exchanges ended on this personal note. The debates emphasized the extent and depth of Meader's involvement and pointed up the access enjoyed by Wayne Major proponents in Washington and the use they had made of it. The real test would come when the Mollohan subcommittee hearing began in July. In the interim the controversy continued unabated at the state and local levels.

Funds and Planes for Wayne Major. Maneuvers began at the state level when the Michigan Aeronautics Commission met on March 8. The minutes of that meeting record the following:

IT WAS MOVED by Commissioner McElroy and supported by Commissioner [F. Joseph] Flaugh that the following resolution be adopted by the commission:

NOW, THEREFORE, BE IT RESOLVED by the Michigan Aeronautics Commission that the findings and recommendations of the Airport Use Panel, as contained in its report of November 4, 1955, be heartily approved and endorsed, and

BE IT FURTHER RESOLVED that until such time as an additional airport facility, suitable for air-carrier operations, is deemed necessary for public need and convenience within the Detroit metropolitan area, the Michigan Aeronautics Commission endorses the continued development and expansion of the Detroit Wayne Major Airport facilities as Detroit's major air terminal. Motion carried.

The resolution put the state body squarely and explicitly behind Wayne Major and was an implicit slap at Detroit's continued efforts on the northeast site in Warren Township. The Aeronautics Commission's action was a harbinger of intense activity in the state legislature.

The Wayne County Road Commission had requested a state appropriation of $487,500. This amount, when combined with an equal amount of county funds, was intended to match the $975,000 allocation which the CAA had made upon hearing that American Airlines had decided to move. The chairman of the Michigan House Aeronautics Committee, taking up Congressman Meader's theme, suggested that the state halt the allocation of grants to Detroit area airports until the "state of confusion caused by political jockeying" had cleared away. The state legislator, an out-state Republican, contended that there were many unanswered questions which "apparently will continue to be unanswered so long as the supply of funds continues" (*The Detroit News,* March 15, 1956). A few days later, on March 21, Mayor Cobo journeyed to Lansing in an attempt to clear up the "state of confusion" and answer questions at a meeting of the senate Appropriations Committee. Cobo acknowledged, "You have been unusually kind to Detroit over the years, and Detroit appreciates it very much." But the activity of airline representatives, who had been working to block the passage of state matching funds for Wayne Major, combined with Meader's letters and the statements of the Aeronautics Committee chairman, secured a delay in senate action on the airport appropriation bill. The delay was to permit a hearing on "all the issues" before the senate Appropriations Committee.

At the hearing, which was held on March 27, Mayor Cobo clashed with Robert J. Wilson of Capital Airlines. Wilson contended that it would cost $28,000,000 to move the airlines to Wayne Major. Cobo claimed that $13,000,000 was a more accurate figure. The difference between the two figures stemmed from the inclu-

sion or exclusion of private expenditures by the airlines. In a cava-
lier interpretation of prior events, Cobo told the senate committee,
"We didn't ask the airlines to come in. It was a federal panel
which made the suggestion" (*The Detroit News,* March 28, 1956).

The Michigan Senate eliminated all state funds for Wayne
Major in the appropriation bill. The full amount was restored in
the house, and after considerable maneuvering in conference committees, Detroit-Wayne Major emerged with a $242,000 appropria-
tion, half of the original request. The appropriation represented
a partial but significant victory for Smith, McElroy, *et al.*

A member of the Board of Commerce gave his explanation of
Smith's continuing success in a debate held at a Detroit Economic
Club luncheon on April 9 (the same day on which the Macomb
County Circuit Court dismissed Detroit's condemnation suit on
the northeast site). The principals in the debate were Glenn Richards and William A. Mara. The following remarks by Mara, taken
from a transcript of the debate which was later inserted in the
hearings of the Mollohan subcommittee (*Federal Role in Aviation,*
pp. 592–3), are quoted for both their content and their candor:

> Now, if Detroit is to avoid becoming a whistle-stop town in a jet
> age, our public officials will have to do a sudden right-about-face
> and show a great deal more wisdom in their airport planning than
> they have shown so far. And if the taxpayer is to escape a terrible
> licking by having $30,000,000 of his tax money spent foolishly, these
> same public officials will have to substitute reason for the brand of
> confusion which has been their trademark whenever they have dealt
> in airport matters. (Applause)
>
> I think actually that the subject assigned to today's talk is per-
> haps the best illustration of the confusion that surrounds the Detroit
> airport problem. Look at the subject on your announcement. It says,
> "Which should be Detroit's major airport?" Now, Mr. Richards, and
> some of our other thoughtless officials are again guilty of horse-and-
> buggy thinking when they call Wayne our major airport and relegate
> the northeast site to the subordinate role. They just aren't facing the
> facts. The simple fact is that no one airport can properly serve the
> needs of the Detroit metropolitan area. No one airport can do it.
>
> Now, I hesitate to get into personalities (laughter), but the issue
> is such that it cannot be separated from personalities.
>
> There are two reasons, I think, for the illogical and apparently
> senseless position which our city and county officials are taking. One
> is that so much money has already been spent and is planned to be

spent on Wayne County Airport that they are willing to throw in another $30,000,000 to rescue the white elephant. The other reason is where the personalities come in. It is a compelling one, but it is . . . difficult to understand unless you have lived with this problem.

Here it is. Wayne Airport is the brainchild of Leroy Smith, our Wayne County highway engineer and a man who is considered by many to be the most able politician in these parts, and I am one who thinks he is a very able politician. When Leroy Smith began Wayne Airport years ago, some called it "Smith's Folly" because of its off-center location far southwest of the city at that time. This rankled the old gentleman and made him more and more determined to force the adoption of this location as Detroit's major airport. It has become an obsession with him, and I am sure that he views this airport as his monument. At any rate, he has been eminently successful in blocking all other attempts to solve our airport problem.

He maintains John P. McElroy, who is in this room today [and] who is a registered lobbyist and Leroy Smith's assistant, as a member of the State [Aeronautics] Commission at Lansing. It is Mr.˙ McElroy's job to get funds for Wayne Airport and to kill funds for any other airport which threatens Wayne. Mr. McElroy does not operate for the common good, but only for what Mr. Smith considers to be the common good. Mr. Smith is also the brains who plans all the present airport campaign moves. He thinks up the words which Mr. Richards uses, and Mr. Smith has used Mr. Richards in the past to block airport progress. Mr. Smith works effectively in the background, where he pulls the strings which move the actors about the stage.

I have tried earnestly to work with Mr. Smith on various airport projects. I invited him to be present at meetings of the Board of Commerce Aviation Committee. In one of my last conversations with him I asked him, in the presence of the committee, if he would support and work for the northeast airport. He replied definitely that he would not do so until such time as Wayne County Airport had been completed and the airlines had moved there.

Mayor Cobo can straighten out the Detroit airport mess if he decides to do so. He can cope with Mr. Leroy Smith successfully if he chooses. In my opinion, Mr. Cobo has been our most able mayor. He is a dedicated man and his integrity is unquestioned. He has named a Detroit Aviation Commission with capable men like Packer, [C. J.] Reese, [Harold R.] Boyer, Joy, [Warren] Carroll, and Burnett, who understand our aviation problems. They want to see northeast developed, and have so recommended, but the mayor, instead, seems to listen to Leroy Smith, who wants another $30,000,000 to fully develop his Wayne County monument.

We urge the mayor to listen to his Aviation Commission instead of Mr. Smith. The mayor has the whip hand because Detroit pays the bulk of Wayne County's taxes. He can force the successful completion of northeast and save taxpayers $30,000,000 if he will assume the leadership of which he is so capable.

A determined mayor and a determined citizenry can take us out of the whistle-stop category and give us the jet-age airports to which our town is entitled. (Applause)

Mara's perception of Cobo's power to force a settlement favorable to the northeast site may have been exaggerated, but he had put his finger on a key relationship at the local level—the Smith-Cobo alliance.

In the discussion and question period which followed Mara's speech, Robert Wilson of Capital Airlines was asked if the airlines would move to Wayne Major "if the management [of the airport] was placed in the hands of an authority entirely removed from politician [*sic*] influence?" Wilson's reply, which formally denied the presence of "personal" and "political" considerations, served to confirm their presence intertwined with the broad substantive policy issues:

> . . . I would be very impertinent to say as to what the management . . . should be. I don't think we would move anyway. It wouldn't make any difference. There are no personalities in this— this is a business judgment, as far as we are concerned. (At this point one individual laughed.)
>
> That was a dirty laugh. (Laughter) Oh, McElroy. Well, you being a registered lobbyist, I can understand that. (Laughter) (*Federal Role in Aviation*, p. 595)

Wilson, the moving force among the airlines officials for holding the airlines at Willow Run, apparently had the same low esteem for McElroy and Smith as did Mara and Kiskadden.

Two months after the Detroit Economic Club debate, the question of whether it was advisable for the airlines to move to Wayne Major became academic. After six months of negotiations American Airlines and Road Commission officials reached agreement on the terms and rates under which American would move. Formal contracts were signed on June 21. The contractual guarantee that one-third of Detroit's air passengers would use Wayne Major Airport was not just another victory for Smith; it was the capstone of Smith's long battle to make Wayne Major Airport a major passenger terminal.

Under the terms of the agreement, American contracted to lease hangar and cargo facilities from the county for a period of twenty-five years. These facilities, plus expanded terminal space, would be financed by revenue bonds issued by the county, the income from the lease-contract with American serving as security for the bonds. The cost of the new facilities was put at $8,000,000. An estimated additional $4,750,000 would be taken from public funds to finance airport improvements, e.g., longer runways and taxi strips, to handle increased operations at the airport. These facilities were scheduled for completion by January 1, 1958, at which time American would inaugurate regular domestic air-carrier service from Wayne Major. Rates charged American could be revised only at the end of each five years. It was generally conceded that American received a "good deal" on the terms by which it agreed to use Wayne Major.

American's signing triggered the CAA into action again. On July 2 the CAA announced that it was allocating $1,000,000 to Wayne Major for fiscal 1956–57, to be used to extend the northeast-southwest instrument runway to 10,500 feet. This allocation was in addition to the $975,000 allocation for 1956–57 which the CAA had announced five months earlier. Thus, as the county approached the Mollohan subcommittee hearings, it had fended off an attempt to eliminate state matching funds, salvaging half of the amount initially requested, then consummated a contract with American Airlines, which in turn provoked a new—and large—CAA grant offer. Leroy Smith entered the hearings with the American contract plus nearly $2,000,000 in CAA allocations in his pocket.

Congress Hears the Case. The Mollohan subcommittee hearings opened in Washington, D.C., in the early summer of 1956. During the first three weeks the subcommittee's investigation centered on civil aviation policies in general (e.g., the number of federal agencies dealing with aeronautical matters, the most desirable air navigation system, and military influence on civil aeronautics policies and practices). Congressman Meader was equally active a participant during this first phase as he was during the subsequent Wayne-Willow phase, since he had introduced a bill

(H.R. 11065) to create a commission on the reorganization of aviation agencies. The purpose of this bill, as Meader bluntly stated it, was "to clean up the mess in the executive branch of the government and the numerous and conflicting agencies controlling aviation."

The conflict over the federal government's aviation policies and programs was the setting for dramatizing Detroit's airport problems in sworn testimony, when on July 16 the subcommittee turned its attention to the Wayne-Willow controversy. For four days, July 16, 17, 18, and 20, seventeen witnesses from private and public life testified on "the Detroit case," and their testimony filled over three hundred pages of published transcript. (The supplementary documents, exhibits, etc., that comprised the appendices of the printed hearings filled an even larger number of pages.) Nevertheless the hearings were anticlimactic. American was moving to Wayne Major, with the likelihood that some or all of the other airlines would follow. The hearings were the last gasp of the foes of Detroit-Wayne Major Airport.

The chief issues were (1) whether the airlines should move to Wayne Major, and (2) what was the status of the northeast site. The role which the CAA had played in bringing about the existing situation was another point at issue which assumed increasing importance as the hearing wore on.

On the issue of Willow Run vs. Wayne Major, the arguments centered on technical and financial comparisons of the two airports. McElroy, spokesman for the Road Commission, raised doubts about Willow Run's seven-inch-thick concrete runways: "They are not in a good state of repair at the present time, I am informed." Wayne Major's runways varied in thickness from eleven to twenty-three inches. Robert Miller, president of ANTSCO, cited a statement in a memorandum prepared by a University of Michigan professor of soil mechanics: "The relatively thin concrete pavement at Willow Run has no limiting capacity within the range of present or contemplated wheel loads." A firm of airport consulting engineers, however, prepared a $4,500,000 expansion program for Willow Run in which it stated: "It is anticipated that by 1960 the runways will be approaching the end of their life expectancy." The

CAA said that Wayne Major's runways could be used for simultaneous instrument operations while those at Willow Run could not, and furnished data comparing the length and strength of the two airports' runways:

	Wayne Major		Willow Run
Longest Runway	7,900	(feet)	7,335
Runway Strength*	500,000	(pounds)	150,000

The superiority of Wayne Major's runways figured heavily in the list of seven reasons cited by Herbert Howell, director of CAA's Office of Airports, in support of the airlines' transfer to Wayne Major:

> One, a more efficient airport layout which has the terminal building in the center of the airport, resulting in shorter taxi distances to and from the runways. Two, longer runways. Three, stronger runways. Four, instrument runway separation adequate for instrument landings on the ILS [instrument landing system] runway with simultaneous IFR [instrument flight rules] takeoffs on the parallel runways. Five, a more adequate terminal building, not a converted hangar. Six, better air-traffic control capabilities. Seven, greater convenience to the public, through more rapid access; 12.3 miles or at least 13 minutes driving time for each of the 2,000,000 annual passengers arriving and departing from Detroit. Eight, increased passenger volume, particularly for short trips, due to decreased ground time to and from the airport (*Federal Role in Aviation*, p. 820).

Howell stated that these advantages made the airlines' shift to Wayne Major desirable, despite the cost of the transfer.

Just how much the transfer would cost was another bone of contention. The County Road Commission estimated the cost of transferring all the airlines to Wayne Major at $11,000,000 in public funds and $16,000,000 in private (airline) funds (a total of $27,000,000, which was $1,000,000 less than the estimate presented to the airlines by city and county officials less than a year earlier). But Howell set the "net" cost of the move to Wayne Major at only $4,500,000. Howell arrived at this figure by starting with $15,000,-000 as the total cost of outfitting Wayne Major to handle all the airlines. This figure was far below the $27,000,000 estimate given

*The maximum per-wheel load capable of being handled by the major (longest) runway.

by the Road Commission. The discrepancy, Howell indicated, arose because the overzealous local officials had "requested facilities from us [the CAA] that we do not consider necessary. . . ." From the $15,000,000 figure Howell subtracted $10,500,000 which would be "saved" by using Willow Run for the military aircraft—$6,000,000 by the Navy and Air Force and $4,500,000 by the airlines, which could dispense with their projected expansion program at Willow Run.

The airlines cited increased operating costs as another argument against transfer to Wayne Major. Robert J. Wilson, vice-president of Capital Airlines, estimated that annual operating costs would be $237,000 more for Capital at Wayne Major than at Willow Run, and $750,000 more for the six airlines currently planning to stay at Willow Run. (Capital was second only to American in air-carrier operations at Willow Run, carrying about 25 percent of all passenger traffic.) These figures give a rough approximation of the airlines' "good deal" at Willow Run.

The financial details and actual transactions between the University of Michigan and ANTSCO tend to be a muddle compounded by ambiguous public reports, such as ANTSCO's intent to pay "a substantial yearly rental"; public announcements of prospective allocation of federal funds for airport development, to be matched by the university, which when the expenditures were made were less than initially might have been implied; and the habit of the University of Michigan to exercise its "constitutional immunity" by playing its financial cards close to its chest. The only public airing of the actual amounts of money involved was at the Congressional hearing (*Federal Role in Aviation*, p. 760), where it was revealed that prior to 1952 ANTSCO had paid the university no rent, and that from fiscal 1952–53 through fiscal 1955–56 the university had received $172,672 in rents from ANTSCO. (The 1955–56 rental of $68,000 was an estimate.) During this same period the university had given about $66,000, the state of Michigan $64,000, and the federal government $150,000 for projects at the airport which, of course, would benefit the users.

Support for the northeast airport came from Wilson, speaking for the airlines (except American) and from William Joy, still a member of the Detroit Aviation Commission. Joy, who was present in Washington without the blessings of Mayor Cobo, spoke first as a private citizen, second on behalf of William Mara, and third on behalf of the Aviation Committee of the Detroit Board of Commerce. Mayor Cobo's representative at the hearings, City Controller John Witherspoon, omitted any reference to the much-discussed northeast site until he was questioned about it by Congressman Meader. Witherspoon reiterated Cobo's priorities—move the airlines to Wayne Major first—and emphasized that Joy, who had testified earlier, did not speak as a representative of the city of Detroit. Mayor Cobo was still firmly on Leroy Smith's side.

Superintendent of Schools Paul Cousino and Township Supervisor Arthur Miller argued Warren Township's case against the northeast airport. In a carefully prepared thirty-minute presentation complete with maps and charts, Cousino sought to demolish the vestiges of Detroit's pretensions to a Warren Township site. (Detroit was then seeking reinstatement of its original suit in the Macomb County Circuit Court.) Cousino promised that his community would "continue the fight against the establishment of a proposed northeast airport in every quarter in our own community, in the city of Detroit, in the legislature of Michigan, before the State Aeronautics Commission and the CAA, and in the courts of our land." Cousino begged the Congressional committee not to complicate Detroit's airport problem further by intervening since, he said, "the solution to our problem lies back in Michigan."

The most revealing testimony on the status of the northeast airport came directly from CAA officials. Howell explained that the CAA's current National Airport Plan provided for a new airport at an undetermined northeastern site. The new airport, however, was for private and business flying. It was explicitly not "a possible passenger terminal for Detroit to accommodate the major airlines in the long hauls." Robert Gale, deputy director of the CAA's Office of Air Traffic Control, armed with maps of air-traffic patterns in the Detroit area, described the complications in traffic control that would result from a new northeast airport. He summarized his highly technical presentation by saying, "The northeast airport, from a traffic control standpoint, would give us the worst headache that we could have in the Detroit area." In response to questioning by the subcommittee counsel, Jerome Plapinger, Gale indicated that a northeast airport would not create unsafe or hazardous conditions but would mean more delay and more complicated procedures for handling aircraft over the metropolitan area. Plapinger asked Gale if Detroit authorities had been informed of these findings. Gale replied:

> No; for this reason, we have never in the Office of [Air] Traffic Control or in our field facilities been requested to make a study of the northeast airport site. As a matter of fact we have never been given a site to study in that area. This presentation was made on the basis of actual newspaper clippings out of Detroit papers that indicated there were considerations for an airport in that area. As an illustration, we have no idea of what the planners who have been planning this airport have as to their runway configuration or precisely where it is located. This particular study on the proposed Warren airport was made for this hearing (*Federal Role in Aviation*, p. 839).

Plapinger asked, "Are you just going to keep this information to yourself or are you going to volunteer it to the Detroit officials?" "They will get it," was the reply.

Detroit officials did not wait for official receipt of the information. With this direct challenge to the northeast site coming from Washington, Cobo reversed himself on representation of the Detroit Aviation Commission. Commission Director Burnett collected what files, letters, and information he could assemble and boarded a plane for Washington the following day. He appeared before the subcommittee on the last day of the hearings.

Burnett's presentation showed his hasty preparation. He was without copies of official resolutions showing specific and bona fide actions to obtain the northeast site. More importantly, he was indefinite as to dates and names of CAA personnel with whom he had held informal discussions on such items as air-traffic patterns, runway alignments, etc. Nonetheless he claimed that "after consultation with the Civil Aeronautics Administration, we proceeded with plans" adding, "we have spent hundreds of thousands of dollars" (*Federal Role in Aviation*, p. 913). Under sympathetic questioning by Congressman Meader, Burnett levied heavy criticism against the CAA for encouraging Detroit on the northeast site and then cutting the ground from under the city.

As proof of the CAA's reversal, Burnett produced the "technical approval" letter received from Regional Director George Vest in September 1952. Furthermore, Burnett argued, the CAA had been appraised of Detroit's intentions on the northeast airport through the Smith-Hinchman-Gryllis master plan and engineering survey completed late in 1952 and forwarded to CAA regional and Washington offices. Burnett went on to relate the following episode:

> It is rather difficult, Mr. Congressman, to understand an incident which happened yesterday when I was trying to dig into the back files for such information as I was able to bring.
>
> I asked the controller at the Detroit City Airport, who was an employee of the Civil Aeronautics Administration, to come to my office and give me figures on our movements for 1955 and 1956 to date. Those figures I have.
>
> Then I asked him if he knew of any Navy cautionary area in our immediate neighborhood and if he would give me any information he had on it.
>
> He didn't know about it but he got a map which showed it.
>
> In the course of the conversation he was interrupted by a telephone call, and when he came back from that telephone call he advised me he would not be able to talk with me any more.
>
> I asked him what the reason was.
>
> He said, "I just can't talk to you any more."
>
> He indicated that he had been advised, possibly by some higher authority, not to.
>
> I think that this should be noted by the committee. It is rather peculiar that printed information cannot be discussed between an airport manager or a director of aviation and a member of the Civil Aeronautics Administration family (*Federal Role in Aviation*, p. 917).

The CAA hierarchy was apparently attempting to forestall the embarrassing situation which would have arisen if Burnett had secured information in Detroit that conflicted with or modified the positions taken by CAA personnel at the Washington hearings.

Both Gale and Howell were present during Burnett's testimony. When they came before the subcommittee, Meader subjected them to extensive questioning. Gale modified his earlier testimony by explaining that a northeast airport would not create an "impossible" traffic headache—merely delays in air movements from other airports, particularly Selfridge Air Force Base. He admitted that he had conducted the traffic control study only one week before the hearings began and specifically in anticipation of probable questions that would arise on the northeast airport. He denied ever having seen or known of the Smith-Hinchman-Gryllis report on the northeast airport. Howell, on the other hand, not only knew of the report but had a copy of it in his office files. Howell pointed out that the CAA had attached no importance to the northeast airport plan after the approval of the site by Michigan Aeronautics Commission—stipulated in Vest's "technical approval" letter as a precondition of "final approval"—was denied in November 1952. Howell continued:

> I am not intimately familiar with the northeast site. I have heard of it. I have not carefully reviewed all of the files on the matter. I am aware that our files contain a copy of the report to which Mr. Burnett referred. I am not aware that the CAA has ever approved, disapproved, or taken any action on the report (*Federal Role in Aviation*, pp. 930–31).

The Detroit Aviation Commission, its energies sapped in battling the suburbs and in attempting to find out where it stood with the mayor, had not impressed CAA personnel with its aims and its seriousness on the northeast airport.

Congressman Meader sought from Howell an evaluation of the CAA's handling of the northeast airport. Citing "Mr. Gale's testimony that as far as traffic control was concerned they did not know there was a northeast site, and yet you had information in your files indicating that the Detroit authorities were going ahead with that site," Meader asked if there wasn't a lack of co-ordination and of flow of information between the CAA's Office of Airports and its Office of Air Traffic Control. Howell replied simply that "throughout our organization we try to effect the greatest amount of necessary co-ordination in all of the decisions we make." Meader pursued the point and Howell reserved judgment because, as he said, "I do not know the degree of co-ordination that took place here. The correspondence I have reviewed, to me indicates that there was co-ordination." Not satisfied, Meader said bluntly, "What I am asking you is, Is this a horrible example of inefficiency in the CAA, or is it a run-of-the-mine case?" Howell responded "I cannot concur in calling it 'a horrible example.' It may be a typical

1952 example; I do not know. The 1952 decisions are more than four years old now, and that, in this industry, is a long time ago" (*Federal Role in Aviation,* p. 933).

Having failed to pin Howell down to an admission of CAA mismanagement on the northeast airport, Meader sought to make a similar charge stick on CAA's role in the Wayne-Willow controversy. In response to attempts to secure an admission that if the CAA could start from scratch it would never approve the development of Wayne Major, Howell and other CAA officials stoutly maintained the integrity of the decision to develop Wayne Major. They defended Wayne Major's runway alignments (flight paths extended from the instrument runways at the two airports intersected only nineteen miles from the airports) and other features which Meader had attacked. CAA officials avoided any admission that Wayne Major would be laid out much differently if, in Meader's words, "you had it to do all over again."

Howell summed up the CAA's views on its role in solving airport problems, both in Detroit and elsewhere:

> The CAA is aware of the many and varied interests represented at Detroit's airports. It has been mentioned before that, under our system of airport ownership in the United States, we leave the initiative for providing airport facilities up to the local community. Where conflicting interests are involved in local airport development, prudent administration of federal funds sometimes forces us to make decisions that might not be agreed to by all of the interests concerned. In this connection, we feel that a single local governmental unit should own or control, and operate, all of the public airports in a single area. Hence, we subscribe to the recommendation of the Airport Use Panel that consideration be given to the establishment of a single metropolitan airport authority to administer the civil airports in the Detroit area (*Federal Role in Aviation,* p. 770).

After the hearings had concluded, the Mollohan subcommittee convened to write and approve a report, which was released on July 27, 1956. A few of the committee's recommendations were indirectly related to the Detroit situation. One recommendation called for an end to military predominance on the Air Co-ordinating Committee and its subsidiary panels. Another recommendation proposed a clarification of the Air Co-ordinating Committee's role in the determination of aviation policy. But there was no recommendation that the CAA alter its federal aid policies as they applied generally across the nation or specifically to particular airports. Neither the Mollohan subcommittee, nor the House of Representatives, nor the U.S. Congress would act to prevent the transfer of the airlines to Wayne Major.

The Northeast Site Fades and a Metropolitan Airport Is Launched. After the Washington hearings the Detroit Aviation Commission continued in its efforts to secure the Warren Township site. The persistent obstacles faced by the commission—legal problems, township opposition, Smith-Richards opposition, and CAA opposition—were formidable, and progress was slow. In February 1957 Cobo became exasperated with the continued delay and openly expressed to the commission his displeasure with its failure to achieve results. Commission Member William Packer replied, "You can help if you'll start with Richards and McElroy," whom Packer accused of "knifing" the northeast airport from their positions with the Detroit Metropolitan Aviation Authority and the Michigan Aeronautics Commission. This open clash between Cobo and the Aviation Commission solidified the stalemate on the northeast site (and prompted Harvey Campbell to release to the board of directors of the Board of Commerce the contents of his confidential letter written on June 23, 1955 [see p. 363]).

The stalemate was broken on April 9, 1957, when a Macomb County Circuit Court judge refused to reinstate Detroit's original condemnation suit of 1954 against the two square miles around the Detroit-owned airport. Detroit's efforts to locate an airport in Warren Township were doomed for all time.

The Aviation Commission's concession of defeat on the Warren site was not acknowledged publicly until August 16, 1957, at which time Packer and McElroy disclosed simultaneously that negotiations were in process for the purchase of a four-square-mile site, bounded by Seventeen Mile, Dequindre, Nineteen Mile and Mound Roads, in Sterling Township. Cheap land and a larger area were the chief reported advantages of this location. Exactly how closely Packer and McElroy had cooperated was revealed on September 10, three days before a scheduled meeting of the Michigan Aeronautics Commission. A spokesman for the state body acknowledged that three days hence it would consider Detroit's request for approval of the Sterling Township site. The Detroit Aviation Commission's general plans for the site were for a *major terminal* airport. With Packer and McElroy in agreement, it appeared that the five-year stalemate on a northeast airport would be broken.

A handful of Sterling Township residents were on hand at the Michigan Aeronautics Commission meeting on September 13. The commission politely heard their brief and unorganized protests and then proceeded to approve unanimously Detroit's request for a northeast airport. The Macomb County Board of Supervisors and the school board of the city of Utica, on the northern border of Sterling Township, voted approval of the proposed airport. Packer, recalling these local endorsements, gave much of the credit to McElroy who "helped us tremendously on the Sterling Township site." Favorable responses were also forthcoming from the CAA officials who were consulted informally.

These events in the fall of 1957 appeared to mark a breakthrough for the Aviation Commission. The rocks upon which it had previously run aground—state approval and cohesive local opposition—were gone. In their place, however, came a new obstacle, when in November the city found itself with a new chief executive. A few weeks before the November election Mayor Cobo died of a heart attack. Louis Miriani, as council president, succeeded to the mayor's office and won a four-year term in his own right at the subsequent election.

Miriani brought to City Hall a new policy in dealing with suburban communities. His policy, which might be called a "cooperative" or "metropolitan" approach, boded ill for the proposed northeast airport. In January 1958 he denied the Aviation Commission's request for an $85,000 appropriation for an engineering survey of the Sterling site. Detroit's depleted treasury, a result of the impact of the 1957–58 recession, was the stated reason. But as Miriani's long-range policy aims emerged, it became apparent that the building of a northeast air terminal under Detroit's aegis was not among them. On June 20, 1958 three members of the Aviation Commission—Packer, Joy, and T. Melville Rinehart (a later appointee)—resigned, saying that business and personal interests prevented them from serving any longer. A few days later, Mayor Miriani filled the vacant seats on the Aviation Commission and told the reconstituted commission to abandon the idea of locating a new airport in Sterling Township. On September 28, 1958, the commission passed a resolution affirming that "Detroit Metropolitan Wayne County Airport [the name was changed in 1957] be designated as the major air terminal for commercial-type operations for the city of Detroit."

The resolution was largely a belated recognition of a *fait accompli*. After the Congressional hearings, while the northeast airport was dying a slow death, Detroit-Wayne Major was expanding at a steady rate.

When the mid-1956 Mollohan subcommittee hearings closed, the fiscal year 1956–57 had just begun. During that fiscal year, close to $7,700,000 was programmed for Wayne Major's development, followed by $3,660,000 in fiscal 1957–58. The total amount allocated during these two years ($11,360,000) exceeds by well over $2,000,000 the total of slightly over $9,000,000 spent on the airport during the entire preceding period (nine years) of its development. Adding to the 1947–58 total of $20,360,000 the $7,000,-000 spent from 1958 to 1961, the grand total so far invested in Detroit Metropolitan Wayne Major Airport is just under $27,400,000.

While all funds spent on Wayne Major prior to 1956 ($9,000,-000) were from tax sources, the bulk of post-1956 funds came from revenue bonds. Of the $18,360,000 spent between 1956 and 1961, approximately $11,925,000 came from revenue bonds issued on the security of the leases with American, Delta, and Northwest airlines (the latter two agreed to move a few months after American signed). The remaining $6,435,000 came from tax sources, with the federal government providing slightly over $4,000,000 and the county[1] and the state sharing the remainder.

The $18,000,000 poured into Detroit Wayne Major during 1956–61 financed enlargement of the airport from 2,300 acres to 3,200 acres, lengthening of the main (northeast-southwest) runway to 10,500 feet, and construction of taxi strips and of terminal

[1] Part ($840,000) of the county's share was an advance from the county general fund which is being repaid at about $200,000 per annum out of operating surpluses.

and hangar facilities to accommodate American, Delta, and Northwest airlines' passenger traffic. American, Northwest, and Delta moved to Detroit Wayne Major in late 1958. Capital (now merged with United), Eastern, Trans World, and United, carrying slightly more than half of the area's airline passenger traffic, held out at Willow Run until 1961. In October of that year, they signed lease agreements with the county which provide for their transfer some time in 1964. The capital cost of providing facilities (terminal, hangar, cargo, etc.) for the four airlines is estimated at between $18,000,000 and $21,000,000. This cost unlike the $18,360,000 cost of transferring American, Delta, and Northwest, is to be financed almost exclusively by revenue bonds. If no tax source is tapped to reduce the size of the projected bond issue, the larger revenue bond issue required to finance the new facilities will doubtless be reflected in higher rental charges paid to the county by the four late-comers. The minimum $18,000,000 estimate for transferring these airlines together with the $18,360,000 spent during 1956–61 to accommodate American, Delta, and Northwest puts the estimated total cost of transferring all the airlines to approximately $36,000,000. Adding to this figure the pre-1956 investments of about $9,000,000 gives a total of $45,000,000, the estimated gross cost of locating the commercial airlines at Detroit Metropolitan Wayne County Airport.

Between the initial and final phase of the airlines' move to Detroit Metropolitan attention turned once again to the metropolitan region's need for a second major airport. In November 1959, the consulting firm of Landrum and Brown of Cincinnati, Ohio, completed and published a master plan of air transportation requirements for the metropolitan area during 1960–1975. The consultants recommended that a second major airport be planned for development during the 1970 to 1975 period. This new airport should be located near Pontiac or, pending a change in military requirements for Selfridge Air Force Base, in the northeast section of the metropolitan area. When they came to the matter of assigning responsibility, however, the consultants were studiously indefinite, saying that counties and cities in the area "should approve the recommended program with such amendments as are necessary," and that "continued steps should be taken to combine the efforts

of the individual cities and counties as their mutual interests indicate." Conceivably the fourteen-year struggle over the development
of Detroit Metropolitan Wayne County Airport is but a prolog to
another one of similar duration.

Concluding Comments

Detroit "solved" its airport problem through heavy investment
in a single airport situated beside an expressway that will eventually connect to all parts of the metropolitan area. This solution
was arrived at by a long and complex struggle, in which the most
prominent and persistent protagonists were the Wayne County
Road Commission on the one hand, and on the other, the Detroit
Board of Commerce, with its allies, the Detroit Aviation Commission, the University of Michigan, and the airlines (even though
the support of the airlines as a group was weakened by American
Airlines' readiness to defect). Caught in the crossfire between the
Road Commission and the Board of Commerce were the mayors
of the city of Detroit—Jeffries, VanAntwerp, and Cobo. The constituency of the Detroit mayor compelled him to acknowledge the
interests of the Detroit Board of Commerce. But the impact of
the activities and resources of the Wayne County Road Commission on Detroit also compelled him to recognize pressures from
this source. Only after conclusive settlement of the issue in 1956–
57 did a Detroit mayor (Miriani) secure freedom of action on airport matters. The elected head of the largest and wealthiest jurisdiction in the metropolis had less power to play a decisive part in
the settlement of Detroit's airport problems than did an agency of
the county bureaucracy or the local spokesman for the city's business interests.

The multiplicity and strength of the independent local participants in Detroit's airport controversy might have raised the possibility that no resolution would be effected. The Detroit Board
of Commerce and the city of Detroit could not obtain a northeast
airport site in the face of the veto power held by the Wayne County
Road Commission, Warren Township, the state legislature, and
the CAA. On the other hand, the Road Commission could not, on
its own and without federal funds, develop Wayne Major Airport.

The availability of federal funds, however, interposed an external and authoritative agent for forcing a decision. Whichever agency or organization could mobilize support at the state and national level could bring about a solution compatible with its own goals.

In winning and holding federal support the Road Commission had several natural advantages. Prior contacts with federal officials on shared professional interests and similar functional goals gave the commission easier access to the source of funds. The fact that the Road Commission had an airport to begin with, not just a proposal for a site, meant that construction time would be shorter and snags fewer. As more expressways cut travel time to the airport from various points in the metropolis, the once far-removed County Airport became more and more accessible. As suburban expansion pushed potential alternative sites farther and farther away from the core city, alternative sites became less accessible (the northeast site proposed in 1944 was at Eight Mile Road; the northeast site proposed in 1958 was at Seventeen Mile Road). Once the flow of federal moneys to County Airport had begun, the Road Commission needed only to hold off the opposition while the county field was gradually being transformed into a major airport. Time was on the Road Commission's side.

The same advantages worked for the Road Commission in its dealings with the opposition. While the commission had a single existing facility to promote, the opposition, starting from scratch, spasmodically supported shifting sites that provoked opposition from groups other than the Road Commission. The Road Commission's ready-to-hand staff and extensive contacts in federal, state, and local government were operational resources which the opposition could not match. Smith assigned aides to investigate and develop the opposition's case for discussion in closed strategy sessions. As one member of these sessions said, "We were right about what the opposition would do 95 percent of the time." The Road Commission, by capitalizing on its extensive resources to blunt the offensive thrusts of the opposition, made its own defensive position more certain. The longer it held off the opposition and the bigger Wayne Major grew, the more the opposition had to retrench. By 1950, the opposition had been forced to abandon its efforts to assign Wayne Major to "minor airport" or even "major freight terminal" status—thus the last-ditch campaign for a second major passenger terminal. While the opposition, lacking a site to begin with, became entangled in the preliminaries of obtaining one, Smith and federal money made a major airport.

The power of a federal agency to resolve a metropolitan conflict through allocation of federal funds to one or another of the local governmental units in the metropolis raises the question whether this power should be curtailed by a Congressional policy requiring that metropolitan airports be under the jurisdiction of a single metropolitan agency or authority. A single agency undoubtedly would have effected a resolution of Detroit's airport problems sooner. Whether its resolution would have been a "better" or "worse" one than the resolution accomplished in fact is a moot point. Assuming that a metropolitan authority would have sought a "rational" solution, a look at the major questions that must be answered if such a solution is to be found will indicate the inherent difficulty of this approach.

(1) What are the locational criteria for an airport? Time in minutes or miles from downtown? The number of people within given radii surrounding the airport? Relationship to surface transportation facilities?

(2) What are the technical and safety requirements affecting the selection of an airport site? Should commercial operations be separated from private aircraft movements and/or from military aircraft operations? What is the optimum relationship between an airport and its immediate vicinity?

(3) Assuming that the specifications of an "ideal" airport have been agreed upon, to what extent can they be modified to fit the exigencies—physical, financial, etc.—of a given situation? To what extent should prior financial commitments (such as the existing investment which Wayne County Airport represented) constrain current decisions?

These questions were all major issues in the Detroit airport controversy. The biases and "selfish" interests apparent in the divergent answers given by many of the conflicting participants obscured the fact that the lack of "rational" criteria for judging would have produced disagreement anyway. The vehemence and persistence of disagreement which marked the Detroit airport controversy might be absent from the metropolitan authority's decision-making process, but the results of the process would hardly be free from attack. The net gain would be speed.

What might speed cost? In the case of Detroit, a metropolitan authority would probably have supported a northeast airport as well as Wayne Major. At present, the cost of constructing and operating a second airport could severely disrupt the city's and/or the county's current tenuous financial position. In addition, technological developments in weapons systems may eventually make Selfridge Air Force Base, like Willow Run, a piece of surplus federal property which could provide the metropolis with a northeast airport at greatly reduced cost. Who is to say that the costs incurred by the prolonged conflict over airports in the Detroit metropolis are greater than those that would have resulted from the unintended but eminently possible mistakes made by a single authoritative body?

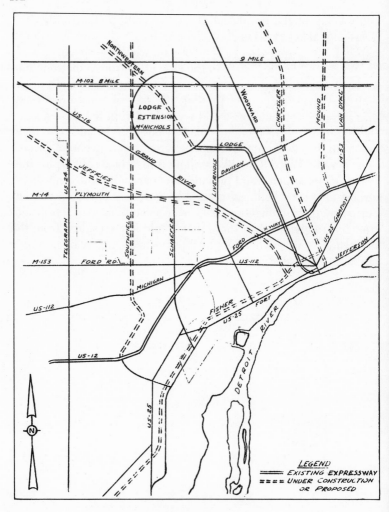

4. The Detroit Expressway System

Courtesy Detroit Department of Streets and Traffic

7
The Extension of
the Lodge Expressway

Expressway Strategy in the Motor City

Introduction

Of the many factors that have affected the twentieth-century urbanization of America, the automobile is one of the most significant. The depression of the 1930's postponed the mass ownership of automobiles that was made possible by the development, in Detroit, of low-cost mass-production techniques, but the prosperity that followed World War II provided the mass market with the income to satisfy the urge to own and drive automobiles. With mass ownership came mass liberation from fixed lines of public transportation, and core cities lost a major advantage for maintaining a captive population. Subdividers, real-estate developers, retail merchants, commercial establishments, and industry took advantage of a more mobile population. The core city continues to provide a centralized place of work for many, while the suburbs provide a decentralized living space. But the automobile creates demands as well as benefits. When in use it must have room to move with some speed and some degree of safety. It needs space, if it is to provide the demanded mobility. The effectiveness of the automobile is limited by the road system available to it.

A benchmark study in the field of traffic research was conducted in the Detroit metropolitan area in the early 1950's. The study was jointly sponsored and financed by the Michigan State Highway Department, the Wayne County Road Commission, the City of Detroit and the Bureau of Public Roads (U.S. Department of Commerce), with a budget of three-quarters of a million dollars. After three years of study, it was reported (Part II of the Report of the Detroit Metropolitan Area Traffic Study [1957]) that: "It seems hard to believe, but the expected 76 percent increase in vehicle miles traveled by 1980 would just about require doubling the present 1,600 miles of major through streets! To double the investment in major streets is frightening. The amount of estimated future traffic is intimidating. Nevertheless these are the coming problems which must be met forcefully and with foresight." The report went on to state that an alternative to doubling the existing 1,600 miles of arterial road system would be to build a 250-mile expressway system,[1] which would provide "the same amount of capacity with a better quality of service." This expressway system plus 118 miles of connecting arterial routes could accommodate the 4,400,000 persons and 1,555,000 vehicles expected in the metropolitan area by 1980.

Although a few miles of expressway were then in use and some construction in progress, it was evident from the report that this program would have to be accelerated and expanded if future needs were to be met. At the then estimated cost of $7,500,000 per mile (actual cost by 1960 had risen to $10,000,000 per mile), the 218 miles of new expressways recommended by the study would cost nearly $1,500,000,000.

This case deals with the events and decisions that occurred in the process of reaching agreement to extend the John C. Lodge Expressway three and one-half miles. Although this extension is but a small segment of the metropolitan expressway system, it is a vital link in the system. The Lodge Expressway extended from the Civic Center, the core of downtown Detroit, to within three and one-half miles of the city's northern border, Eight Mile Road. At its northern terminus, the Lodge Expressway connected with

---

[1] In classifying road systems the report used the following definitions, which are the definitions understood for these terms throughout this case.

Local Roads. These are neighborhood streets which are primarily designed to serve land use and to move vehicles from destination points to the second or arterial system. *The Arterial Street System.* This system of grade thoroughfares collects traffic from local roads and delivers it to express routes or serves short portions of all trips. These routes, because of their historical development, also serve abutting land uses and provide direct access to such land. *The Expressway System.* This completely separate system is designed solely to move vehicles freely and rapidly. It provides no direct access to abutting land and serves only intermediate portions of trips. It must be completely interconnected to provide free interchange between all parts of the area.

James Couzens Highway. Couzens was an eight-lane, divided, arterial road with a center mall eighty-four feet wide. At Eight Mile Road, Couzens connected with Northwestern Highway, a divided arterial road serving the southern and southwestern part of Oakland County. Couzens thus provided the rapidly growing suburban areas in south and southwest Oakland County access to the Detroit expressway system. Future plans called for expressway treatment of Northwestern Highway as part of a link with a state-wide expressway system serving the major urban areas as well as providing access to recreational areas in northern Michigan. The small mileage involved in the Couzens project was no measure of its significance in the development of a comprehensive expressway system.

The history of the Couzens project brings into focus a dilemma faced by core-city policy-makers. Is it better to provide easy access to the suburbs and facilitate the migration of middle- and upper-income families from the core city to outlying communities, or would it be better to let the traffic jams take their course and perhaps encourage the return of some of the population to redeveloped areas near the downtown central business district? Do expressways speed the demise of the core city, or do they bring economic benefits compensating for loss of property from the tax rolls as the result of construction? Often in the past, city expressways have been welcomed as a handy device for razing slums, since the beginnings of many urban expressway systems take place in the slum-infested center of the city. But as the routes push to the city boundaries and approach middle- and upper-income residential areas, the bureaucracy and elected officials face a more sophisticated and better-organized opposition than in a disorganized slum area. In penetrating the middle-class neighborhood, a more careful weighing of consequences takes place.

Planning and constructing the nation's major road system involves all levels of government and costs billions of dollars. Financing is complicated, involving federal, state, and local funds, most of which are derived from gasoline taxes paid by the users of the highways. As the chief administrator of federal and state highway funds within his jurisdiction, the state highway commissioner is in a position to play a major role in policy-making affecting urban areas. But though they pay but a small share of the bill for city expressway construction, city policy-makers are reluctant to give up decision-making prerogatives on construction occurring within the city limits, even when this is part of a larger expressway system. How to develop a state-wide expressway system that will at the same time tend to satisfy the values of each of the political jurisdictions through which it must pass was the problem faced by the state highway commissioner. The extension of the Lodge Expressway was newly-elected Commissioner Mackie's first major struggle with this problem.

Planning and Negotiating an Expressway System

The New Highway Commissioner Announces a Plan. Michigan and Mississippi are the only two states that elect a state highway commissioner. In the remainder of the states, he is appointed. The office of highway commissioner in Michigan has received special attention from a rural-dominated state legislature, which has sought to protect the office from being caught in the landslide of urban votes that fall elections are likely to evoke. Thus the highway commissioner in Michigan is elected at a spring election held in the odd years following a general election. He has a term of four years, while the governor and other elected state officers have two-year terms. In the spring election of 1957, a thirty-six-year-old civil engineer and registered surveyor from Flint, John C. Mackie, was elected highway commissioner on the Democratic ticket. It was the first time in over a dozen years that the Democrats had captured this post, although Democratic Governor G. Mennen Williams had been winning uninterrupted re-election since his initial victory in 1948. Mackie's nomination had come as a surprise to many, but his election was even a greater surprise to political observers who, in spite of recent Democratic successes in capturing state-wide offices, had conceded the highway post to the Republicans. Incumbent Commissioner Charles M. Ziegler had decided to retire, and the Republican candidate was Ziegler's deputy, George M. Foster. Not having to face the incumbent may have been a help to Mackie, but the other Democrats on the spring ballot also did well.

The Highway Department is a major agency of state government, and its control is a major political objective. Since most of its revenue is obtained from state gasoline taxes earmarked for its use and from federal grants for highway construction, the Highway Department is independent of the ordinary executive control exercised through the budget and relatively independent of legislative control (but not harassment) exercised through annual appropriations. With activities extending into each of the state's counties, the Highway Department has a ready vehicle for building a state-wide network of political influence.

Mackie's Republican predecessor, Charles Ziegler, who had held the office continuously since World War II, had developed close relationships with the rural county road commissions through policies such as turning over some state road-maintenance activities to counties on a contract basis. The Democrats criticized Ziegler for failing to develop a comprehensive highway plan for the state and for spending a disproportionate amount of the state's highway funds outside of the Detroit metropolitan area, which produced a large share of the gas-tax revenues. Ziegler could point to sixteen miles of expressway built or under construction within the city of Detroit which had been initiated under his administration. During his last term in office, Ziegler was involved in an elaborate set of maneuvers to frustrate the efforts of a state turnpike authority to construct a toll road from Toledo to Saginaw. Ziegler's tactic consisted of announcing plans for limited-access highway routes (freeways) paralleling or competing with the proposed turnpike route for traffic. Although other facts were also at work, Commissioner Ziegler played a major role in bringing about the demise of the turnpike project.

Mackie took office on July 1, 1957. During his campaign he had promised to develop a long-range plan for a state highway system, and he had promised that the Highway Department would no longer ignore the Detroit metropolitan area. The voters in the metropolitan area, especially Detroit and Wayne County, had responded by giving him the necessary plurality to overcome the rural support for his opponent. Mackie owed his election to the urban vote, and if he were to win future elections, he would have to retain this support. He was eager to demonstrate that this support was warranted. Two events that had occurred the previous year made it possible for him to move with remarkable speed. The first was the completion of the final report of the Detroit Metropolitan Area Traffic Study. This document, which provided a detailed plan for an expressway system based upon the best traffic research techniques then available, was a tremendous advantage to one eager to show results—to build roads. The second event was the passage by Congress of the Highway Act of 1956. This act continued the previous policy of providing 50 percent federal financial aid in the construction of the Primary Road System (arterial roads) but provided 90 percent federal aid for highways designated as part of the Interstate Highway System (connecting major metropolitan areas, cities, and industrial regions). As part of this program, $15,000,000,000 was to go for the construction of the Interstate System within and around cities, which would include five thousand miles of expressways in more than fifty metropolitan areas. With this legislation, Mackie would be able to obtain 90 percent federal aid for those parts of the metropolitan Detroit expressway system that could be designated part of the Interstate System.

Four months after taking office, Mackie announced a ten-year expressway plan for the Detroit metropolitan area. The occasion for the unveiling of the plan was a luncheon held on November 7, 1957, following the dedication of an interchange on the Lodge Expressway. The plan proposed the spending of $632,000,000 of federal and state funds in the metropolitan area over a ten-year period to construct eighty-one miles of new expressways—forty miles the first five years and the balance the following five years. Eight miles were classified as part of the Primary System, but the remaining seventy-three miles were classified as part of the Interstate System, eligible for 90 percent federal aid. Included in the first five-year plan was the extension of the Lodge Expressway to Eight Mile Road. In his speech presenting the plan, Mackie made it clear that he was aware of some of the obstacles to accomplishing the program:

> Now it is one thing to budget funds for urban expressways, but it is another thing to build them. I re-emphasize, the department is willing to make this $632 million in federal funds available for sorely needed state trunkline improvements in the metropolitan area, and

we have the engineering resources and know-how to build them, but the speed with which these budgeted funds are spent depends entirely on agreement by local affected communities on route location problems and on local cost participation as prescribed by law.

. . . .

The greatest single danger to the success of this program, as I see it, will be internal squabbles within communities themselves about location, or conflicts between neighboring communities which are unable to agree on route location.

The Tripartite Contract. Although the Mackie metropolitan plan included construction in Oakland and Macomb counties, the key to the system was the construction planned for Detroit and for Wayne County, in which Detroit is located. The first step in carrying out planned construction required formal agreements among the principal parties concerning specific projects to be built, allocation of costs, method of financing, and division of responsibility for engineering, construction, and right-of-way acquisition. Michigan law (Act 262 of the Public Acts of 1957) authorizes the state highway commissioner to contract with cities and with county road commissions for the purpose of formalizing these agreements. Michigan cities with a population over 50,000 are also required to pay 25 percent of the cost of state trunkline construction within the city, but county road commissions are permitted to assume all or part of the cities' share. To work out such details, a tripartite contract among the City of Detroit, the Wayne County Road Commission, and the State Highway Commissioner was necessary.

Contract negotiations were begun in mid-November 1957, and the contract was signed on May 20, 1958. The contract provided for the construction of four projects in the city of Detroit at an estimated cost of $300,000,000 and the expenditure of $1,000,000 for the planning of a fifth project. It was agreed that that portion of the cost not borne by the federal government would be shared by the three parties, with the state paying 75 percent, Detroit 12.5 percent and Wayne County 12.5 percent. The contract provided that the parties share in the cost of financing through a bond issue and assigned certain phases of the work to the city and the county. Although two of the four projects would be part of the Primary System and eligible for only 50 percent federal aid, the bulk of the mileage was in the remaining projects, which would qualify for 90 percent federal aid as part of the Interstate System. Assuming a total cost of $500,000,000 (this included $150,000,000 for the fifth project, which would only be planned under the contract) the combined city and county share of the cost would be under $20,000,000.

The negotiation of the tripartite contract involved some serious decision-making for the metropolitan area, and for this reason must be dealt with in some detail. When the new state highway commissioner sat down with city and county officials to work out a contract in November 1957, Detroit had about eighteen miles of expressway in operation. The Edsel B. Ford Expressway extended from the western border of the city to within a few miles of the eastern city boundary, and this remaining leg was under construction. The John C. Lodge Expressway, a north-south route serving the west side of the city, had reached its northern terminus at James Couzens Highway, but a short southern leg remained to be built that would pass under the Civic Center, then under construction. The interchange between the two expressways was about two miles north of the central business district. Another north-south expressway serving the east side of the city, the Walter P. Chrysler Expressway, was in the planning stage. Plans called for it to begin at the Civic Center and proceed north to the Ford Expressway. The Chrysler route passed through some of the city's worst slums, and its construction would assist urban redevelopment efforts which were under way to renew the downtown area.

There were other reasons for the Chrysler project (then referred to as the Oakland-Hastings Expressway). Planners saw it as the final segment of a "loop" formed by linking the Ford and Lodge expressways and surrounding the central business district with an expressway system. The mayor and councilmen were sensitive to the criticism of east-siders that the Lodge Expressway had been built first to service the wealthier sections of northwest Detroit and that the construction of the western part of the Ford Expressway had preceded the construction of the eastern half. Mayor Cobo had responded to this with a promise that the east side would get the next expressway to be built in the city; his successor, Louis Miriani, and Detroit's nine councilmen echoed this sentiment.

The principals in the contract negotiation were: John Mackie and his assistant for the Detroit area, Irving J. Rubin, for the state; Mayor Miriani and his commissioner of public works, Glenn C. Richards, for the city; and County Highway Engineer Joseph Gross for the Wayne County Road Commission. These representatives were, of course, supported by their own legal and technical advisors. At the outset, it was apparent that there was general agreement on three projects: the Chrysler Expressway to the Ford interchange, a Fisher Expressway, and a Southfield Highway project. The Fisher Expressway had been given first priority in the Detroit Metropolitan Area Traffic Study report. It would run from downtown Detroit southwest along a route near the Detroit River and connect with an expressway entering Michigan from Toledo, Ohio. This would provide the heavy industrial belt along the river with expressway service between Detroit and Toledo.

The Southfield Highway project had had an interesting history. Southfield Road was a north-south divided four-lane highway (for most of its length) on the western edge of Detroit that linked wealthy Birmingham in southern Oakland County with the Ford Motor Company complex in Dearborn. It was always considered a "belt-line" road, that is, one that provided intra-area circulation at the periphery but not a through route. In his effort to frustrate the building of a toll road, Commissioner Ziegler had succeeded in having Southfield designated part of the Interstate System, as a route which would link on the south with a Detroit-Toledo Expressway and on the north with Northwestern Highway. Northwestern would be made into an expressway and carry traffic northwest to route U.S.-23 near Fenton, Michigan. By connecting the Detroit-Toledo Expressway with the proposed Fisher project, Southfield's southern link with the Interstate route was broken, and Mackie requested that the Bureau of Public Roads shift the Interstate designation from the Southfield route to a location several miles to the west. Southfield, under the Mackie plan, would be developed into a limited-access superhighway connecting with Northwestern Highway on the north, which in turn would become an expressway from Eight Mile Road to Eleven Mile Road, where it would link with an east-west expressway.

The change in designation of Southfield from part of the Interstate System to the Primary System was a key factor in Mackie's over-all plan for the metropolitan area. It was made possible by an attorney general's ruling in October 1957 that a $25,000,000 bond issue approved during the Ziegler administration for the construction of an expressway along Northwestern Highway and extending to Fenton did not commit the new commissioner to this specific route. Instead of being used to develop Northwestern to Fenton, the bond funds were committed to converting the stretch of Northwestern between Eight Mile Road and Eleven Mile Road to an expressway, amid protests from landowners along the route proposed by Ziegler. The deletion of Southfield from the Interstate System created conditions appealing to city officials. It meant that Southfield could be developed on the existing right-of-way, whereas if it had been part of the Interstate System, construction standards would have required condemning a row of houses along the route that passed through one of Detroit's most desirable residential sections. The anticipated condemnation had already given rise to vigorous opposition from those living in and around the affected areas, and city officials were also concerned with the loss of tax revenue resulting from the removal of property from the tax roles and the lowering of property values in the area.

Another benefit from the change in Southfield's designation was that it permitted the designation of the northern extension of the Chrysler Expressway as part of the Interstate System. The southern leg of the Chrysler, i.e., the leg that ran from the downtown area to the Ford Expressway, had from the beginning carried the Interstate designation. But the Bureau of Public Roads would approve only one Interstate route running north from the city, and this designation had been given to the Southfield-Northwestern route. With the elimination of the Southfield-Northwestern route from the Interstate System, the way was clear to make the northern extension of the Chrysler a part of the Interstate System. From a traffic standpoint this made sense, since it would provide relief for Woodward Avenue, U.S.-10, through the metropolitan area and on northward towards Flint. This route was the most heavily traveled traffic corridor in the state. It was also an attractive plan because, like the southern leg of the Chrysler, this northern leg would provide a route serving the east side, and its construction would eliminate acres of urban blight.

Detroit officials had some reservations concerning the extension of the Chrysler Expressway north of the Ford interchange. Since this section would have to pass through Highland Park, an independent city completely surrounded by the city of Detroit, Detroit officials were reluctant to agree on this part of the project until the route through Highland Park was settled. But state highway negotiators were able to convince the city representatives that a commitment from Detroit to the project in the contract would make it easier eventually to settle on a route through Highland Park. Mackie wanted a commitment from Detroit on the Chrysler Expressway that would assure construction to the northern city limit. He was learning about the difficulties that can develop around expressways that end short of the city limits, as negotiations developed over the Lodge Expressway extension.

City officials would have been content to settle for a contract that provided for the construction of the three projects upon which there was general agreement: the Chrysler to the Ford, the Fisher, and the Southfield expressways. Mackie wanted a larger package, and the Wayne County Road Commission supported his view. The inclusion of the Chrysler extension was accepted by the city without too much objection. The real stumbling block was Mackie's insistence that the contract include a provision for the extension of the Lodge Expressway to link with either Southfield or preferably Northwestern. From Mackie's point of view, there could not be an integrated metropolitan expressway system with the northern terminus of the only existing north-south Detroit expressway three and one-half miles short of the city limit. If the Lodge Expressway were to become part of a metropolitan expressway system, it could not remain tied to a surface arterial road, James Couzens Highway, with a design capacity of fifty thousand vehicles per day and a current utilization rate of seventy thousand vehicles per day. Knowing the stormy history of earlier efforts for a Lodge extension, Mackie and his staff felt that their only chance to obtain a guarantee from Detroit officials for construction of the extension was to include this project as part of a package which included projects the city was eager to obtain.

There were a number of reasons why the Lodge Expressway ended where it did. One reason was that the city had wanted to preserve the Interstate designation for the Chrysler Expressway.

It was felt that if the Lodge went through to Northwestern at the city limits, this route would be classified as the north-south Interstate route, and the Chrysler would lose the 90 percent federal aid. The change in Southfield's designation eliminated this concern.

Another reason for allowing the Lodge to end where it did was that there was no easy place for it to go. Interestingly, and probably accidentally, the Lodge stopped at a socio-economic boundary within the city. The commercial and business establishments that had been built on Couzens Highway, for the most part since World War II, were of low elevation and modern design that blended well with the tree-lined boulevard with its shaded center mall. Few retail establishments had been built on Couzens, so there was very little over-the-curb customer business, but the streets did provide a prestige address for business firms. One small segment, less than one-half mile long, contained better than average ranch houses. It ran, for most of its route, through an area that ranks among the highest in the city in terms of value of homes, average income, and average rent charged. This economic range is the middle-class backbone of the city which tends to be attracted by the suburbs and which the city can ill afford to lose. There was no possible way of extending the Lodge Expressway without disturbing this community.

The reaction to any tampering with the Couzens area became evident in 1955 and 1956 when county and city traffic officials, anticipating the traffic jams likely to result when the Lodge was finally opened for its full length in 1957, began to suggest some action to extend the expressway. One plan suggested was that the Lodge be extended due west along an existing arterial route (Pilgrim or Puritan Avenues) to link with Southfield. This would have required extensive land acquisition and the razing of 750 or 800 homes. The Detroit Common Council's reaction to this proposal was a resolution passed on November 20, 1956 "opposing any further planning for the extension of the John Lodge Expressway to the proposed Southfield Expressway . . . until such time as the Common Council may by resolution direct other studies be made." Councilman James H. Lincoln, who lived one block from Pilgrim, went on record that he was "not for tearing out a large number of homes and businesses and taking much-needed assessed valuation from the tax rolls primarily so that the people of Oakland County can save two or three minutes getting to work and home again."

Early in 1957, the County Road Commission disclosed tentative plans for a $20,000,000 extension of the Lodge down the center mall of Couzens Highway. Three twelve-foot expressway lanes in each direction would occupy the eighty-four-foot center strip at surface level and dip under the major intersections. This plan was soon dubbed the "roller-coaster" plan and was greeted with strong objections from city planning and traffic officials. The conclusions of city officials concerning Couzens Highway were summarized in the Council Proceedings for July 16, 1957 as follows:

1. From a city planning standpoint, James Couzens Highway should be developed as a surface artery.
2. The development of James Couzens as a full expressway would result in the destruction of property values either by lack of vehicular access during and following the period of construction or by the direct condemnation of recently developed business frontage.
3. From a traffic engineering standpoint, a widening of James Couzens to five lanes in each direction with a modern flexible signal system would be adequate to handle the traffic entering and leaving the John Lodge Expressway.

The County Road Commission, which had the responsibility for the maintenance of Couzens, was thus at odds with city officials who complained that the county had dragged its heels on widening Couzens in order to build a case for an expressway.

There was a third reason why at least some city officials were reluctant to agree to an extension of the Lodge, and this reason involved the future construction of a Grand River Expressway. Grand River Avenue is a major arterial street running from the center of the downtown area almost due northwest to the city limits, from which it continues (as U.S.-16) as the direct route from Detroit to Lansing, Grand Rapids, and Muskegon. Grand River is a radial street which runs at an angle to the main grid street pattern of the city. Like James Couzens, it runs through middle- and upper-income residential neighborhoods along the northern part of its route through the city, but for a distance twice as long as does Couzens—about six or seven miles. It collects traffic from the fast-growing suburban areas west and northwest of the city and serves as the main artery of travel for many who work in the central business district, including many city officials who live in northwest Detroit. To some extent the Couzens-Lodge route serves the same area, but for many residents of the northwestern part of Detroit and of the metropolitan area, Grand River is the most direct route downtown. There was ample evidence that the traffic demand along Grand River justified expressway treatment, and the need had long been recognized. The Detroit Metropolitan Area Traffic Study had documented this need, but in spite of all the evidence, there had been reluctance among local political policy-makers to bring the Grand River Expressway question to the point of decision. This project would require finding a route that would be least damaging to the value of the commercial and retail properties lining the street, as well as the residential properties that cluster along it, in order to minimize opposition to the project. This was indeed a difficult, if not impossible, task, and one that both elected officials and career administrators, sensitive to public relations, were willing to postpone.

Some city officials, however, notably Public Works Commissioner Glenn Richards, did not want fear over the difficulties involved in the construction of a Grand River Expressway to bring about an indefinite postponement of this project, which they felt was sorely needed. The extension of the Lodge to a Northwestern Expressway, which in turn linked with a state-wide expressway system, might be used as an argument, Richards reasoned, for the indefinite postponement of the Grand River Expressway. It was evident that Mackie and his Highway Department colleagues were not in a hurry to undertake the Grand River project. Mackie was eager to build roads, to move dirt and pour concrete, and the Grand River project appeared to his staff to be one that could mire the department in years of bickering over possible routes with no construction taking place.

During the months of negotiation over the tripartite contract, it became evident that the relationships that existed among the three principals involved in the city's expressway projects had changed from previous years. Under Ziegler, city and county officials played the major role in the negotiations leading to construction contracts. They also got most of the publicity. Probably Detroit's mayor profited most by receiving credit for major construction projects. Mackie and his staff were determined to change this state of affairs. They made it clear from the outset of the negotiations that they were not a silent, acquiescing third party, but rather that they were determined to let it be known that expressways were state trunklines and that the state put up the largest share of the money and was also responsible for the administration of the federal funds. Although the county prepared the first draft of the contract, state personnel took over the responsibility for revising this and preparing successive drafts. Mackie, intent on constructing a metropolitan expressway system rather than individual expressways, continued to insist on a package approach.

In the spring of 1958, negotiations reached a climax. There was agreement upon the Chrysler (to Eight Mile Road), Fisher, and Southfield projects, but the city still objected to the inclusion of a Lodge extension. State revisions of the contract drafts continued to include the Lodge extension, but little discussion had been given to Grand River. It did not appear in the drafts. Finally, the state negotiators offered to change the description of the Lodge extension in the contract so as not to commit the parties to a particular route but to commit them only to some type of limited-access connection from the end of the Lodge to Northwestern. Negotiating in the absence of Mayor Miriani, Richards, representing the city, asked that the Grand River project be included in the package. Mackie's negotiators asked if the city would agree to the Lodge extension if the state would agree to include in the contract $1,000,000 for the planning of the Grand River Expressway until a route could be agreed upon, at which time the parties would draw up a construction contract. Richards agreed, and the negotiators proceeded to approve a final draft of the contract. In deference to those who feared a public reaction to the very mention of a Grand River Expressway, the contract referred to it as the Detroit-Muskegon Expressway, and it was later named the Jeffries Expressway. The negotiators having completed their work, the contract now required formal approval from the three governments involved. This was soon obtained from the state, by the State Administrative Board, consisting of the governor and other elected officials, and from Wayne County, by the County Road Commission and the County Board of Supervisors; but the necessary approval by the Detroit Common Council was not immediately forthcoming.

The contract provided for an administrative structure designed to give each of the three parties adequate say in the substantive decision-making that would have to take place in order to carry out the projects. An Administrative Committee, consisting of the state highway commissioner, the mayor of Detroit and the county highway engineer, or their designees, was charged with over-all policy-making, and all plans for specific projects had to be approved by this committee. In addition, an Engineering Committee with tripartite representation was responsible for detailed designs for specific projects. As it turned out, this structure was not considered by the Detroit councilmen as adequate protection for the city's interests.

Irving Rubin, Mackie's Detroit representative, was given the major role in seeing the contract through the council, and he was to continue to play a major role in subsequent events concerning the Lodge extension. Rubin, in his early thirties, had assisted Mackie in his election campaign, and after Mackie's election, Rubin left his business in Flint to take up the Detroit post for the State Highway Department. Rubin was not an engineer: he had majored in political science in college. Regardless of formal title, his job in Detroit was to see that a Mackie metropolitan expressway system plan was expedited and construction started as soon as possible. He had been one of the state's chief negotiators of the tripartite contract, and he had spent many hours since his arrival in Detroit getting to know the councilmen, city and county highway officials and newspapermen. Although they maintained a proper non-partisan pose in keeping with the Detroit non-partisan election system, all but three of the nine councilmen were considered to be Democrats (as was Mackie), and Rubin thought that this shared party affiliation would simplify his job.

The first objection that was raised by council members had been anticipated by Rubin and was easily adjusted. In the contract, the Lodge extension was described in such a way that it would be possible to accomplish it by an extension along Puritan or Pilgrim Avenues to Southfield. Richards and other city traffic and planning officials preferred this route, since it would avoid tampering with Couzens. But the council had already gone on record as opposed to such a route, and they were in no mood to change their position. Rubin assured them that an amendment to the contract eliminating such an alternative would be acceptable to the Highway Department. This change left Couzens Highway as the logical route for the extension.

With agreement reached on elimination of the Puritan and Pilgrim routes, it looked as if the council would be ready to approve the contract, but on the day a vote was to be taken, councilmen received a flood of complaints from residents along the Southfield route demanding a public hearing before the signing. Rubin attempted to persuade the council that to hold a hearing at this point would be premature, but he did not win his point. A public hearing was held on March 25, 1958. Over two hundred people attended the hearing, and it became apparent that part of the objection arose because of confusion over what treatment was planned for Southfield. Many of the objectors were still under the impression that Southfield would be an Interstate route and that construction would require an enlarged right-of-way, and therefore condemnation of much property. Highway engineers explained that Southfield would be treated as a superhighway under the Primary System and would require very little condemnation. The usual objections were voiced that superhighways create noise and dirt and depress property values, and these objections were met by assurances and counterarguments by the highway personnel. The hearing did not convince the council that they should withhold approval of the contract, and again it appeared as if the last hurdle had been passed.

The day after the hearing, as the council prepared to vote approval of the contract, Councilman Del Smith inquired whether the city was bound by the routes that were indicated in a map that accompanied the contract. The state's answer was that the maps were not part of the contract and therefore the routes indicated on them were not binding. But the question raised new doubts, so the Detroit corporation counsel was asked to render an opinion on the subject. Although the corporation counsel's Office had already gone over the contract numerous times and in great detail, on this last perusal they concluded, somewhat to their embarrassment, that a phrase in the first paragraph of the contract ("the board [county] and the city hereby consents to the designation of the projects as state trunkline highways") did, in fact, give the state highway commissioner the right to establish specific routes within the limits of the general route description provided in the contract. Moreover, the trunkline designation gave the commissioner discretion to make decisions concerning location of ramps and bridges and other vital design details. The corporation counsel concluded from this that his office would not approve the contract as to form unless an amendment were adopted which required the approval of all parties on route alignments, surveys, plans, and specifications before the acquisition of property or commencement of construction.

Apparently even the state highway personnel were not aware of the extent of the discretion permitted to them under this provision, but the amendment now proposed, if adopted, would have the effect of nullifying the contract as a "package" and would give the city the opportunity to veto all but the particular projects they considered to be in their self-interest. Rubin set to work assuaging the fears of the councilmen and assuring them that even though technically the commissioner had the right to make ex parte decisions, the decision-making structure set up by the contract gave all parties an opportunity to participate in crucial decisions. Besides, the highway commissioner was as sensitive to voter opinion in the city as were the councilmen, and he would not make decisions unpopular with the voters. His most practical argument was that the amendment would result in intolerable delays over each segment of each project as various protest groups sought to influence route location. But the councilmen were not easily swayed. To Mackie and Rubin this was an exasperating and frustrating situation. With the state willing to spend huge sums for expressways in the city for the first time in the history of Detroit, they expected a warm welcome rather than a fight from the council. The state officials were somewhat surprised to find that their strongest support came from two of the three Republicans on the council.

After a considerable amount of argument, debate, and attempts to influence opinions, an agreement was worked out and eventually accepted by both the city and the state. The county had remained on the sidelines, although supporting the position of the State Highway Department. The agreement provided that before condemnation or construction should begin on any portion of a project, the route location for that portion must become "established" by submitting the proposed location to the three parties, and failure of any party to disapprove within twenty-one days would automatically establish the route. With a veto power thus guaranteed, the council approved the tripartite contract on April 29. By May 20, 1958, all the formalities of approval of the amended tripartite contract had been accomplished, and Mackie was ready to proceed with his metropolitan expressway plan.

The First Plan

The Double-Deck Proposal. Soon after the tripartite contract was formally approved, a plan for the Lodge extension was unveiled. The speedy action on this one short leg of the expressway system made possible by the contract was evidence of the importance ascribed to it. Work on plans for the extension had begun on May 6, and by July 8, 1958, a plan calling for a double-deck expressway constructed on the center mall of James Couzens had received the approval of the various committees established by the tripartite contract and was informally presented to the Detroit Common Council.

Because of the earlier proposals to extend the Lodge along Couzens, when representatives of the state, city, and county sat down on May 6 to plan the Lodge extension, a number of alternative designs and treatments were at hand. What was sought was a plan that would provide the necessary capacity for present and anticipated traffic demand but would at the same time minimize any possible deleterious economic impact upon the Couzens area. Those working out the plans were well-qualified professionally to deal with technical questions of design and traffic engineering, and they were conscious of economic, social, and political values as well. The double-deck plan was the result of the careful weighing of multiple values in a rational decision-making process.

In arriving at the double-deck plan, alternative solutions were considered and discarded. These alternatives included: a rolling-grade expressway using the 204-foot right-of-way, coming to grade between intersections and dipping under them; a completely elevated expressway within the existing right-of-way; a one-way elevated expressway along an alley line and a one-way depressed section in the center mall; and an expressway that would leave Couzens at grade with intersections carried over or under it. The double-deck plan called for a one-way depressed section and a one-way elevated section directly above it with major cross streets at grade between the two levels. It would be constructed on the center mall and would require, in addition, one traffic lane from each side of the mall, reducing the remaining service drives to three lanes on each side of the double-deck. The double-deck expressway would have a capacity adequate to handle the anticipated 1980 traffic volume and these additional advantages: no property acquisition would be required; it would provide the least interference to traffic and business during construction—an important consideration since Couzens was a radial route with no parallel streets to which traffic could be detoured; it could be built in the shortest time; it would preserve existing twenty-foot margins between buildings and curb line; it would provide a twenty-foot margin between the expressway structure and service drives for additional trees and landscaping; three of the four existing lanes on each side of the mall would not be disturbed and construction would be confined to the center island; and since abutting structures would not be disturbed, they would remain to grace the street with their economic and aesthetic values and provide insulation between the highway and adjacent residential property.

Anticipating a public reaction to any treatment of Couzens and realizing that the unorthodox nature of the double-deck might add to it, the Highway Department hired Minoru Yamasaki, the nationally known and locally prominent architect, "to make sure that the proposed expressway preserves the existing highway as an attractive thoroughfare." Yamasaki prepared models and drawings which revealed a low-rising attractive structure of white concrete faced with sparkling quartz and surrounded by trees and shrubs threading its way through the center of James Couzens Highway. This was the final touch to a plan that had been care-

1. Proposed Double-Deck Expressway

Courtesy Michigan State Highway Department
Photo by Baltazar Korab

2. Proposed Cantilever Depressed Expressway

Courtesy Michigan State Highway Department

fully prepared in an attempt to satisfy as many divergent values and interests as possible, while at the same time accomplishing the construction of this vital link in an expressway system.

Approval by the Administrative Committee established by the tripartite contract assured state and county approval of the double-deck plan. It did not assure city approval. Having informally received the plan, the council sent it to the Detroit City Plan Commission for their recommendations. Although consisting of members appointed by the mayor, the Plan Commission could be expected to reflect the views of the professional planning staff, and based upon past experience, it would not be surprising to find that the city planners did not agree with the traffic planners. By July 23, the Plan Commission had completed its study and reported approval of the double-deck plan, but not without some reservations and not unanimously. The reservations were made part of its formal recommendation to the council:

> The major disadvantages of the proposal are its use of an elevated structure and its temporary removal of all center island landscaping. The commission holds firm to the belief that only depressed expressways preserve to the maximum the city's character and its land-use values, particularly residential values. Depressed design has been fully supported by the success and wide acceptance of the Lodge and Ford Expressways. It is with regret, therefore, that the City Plan Commission approves an elevated structure on James Couzens. It can do so, nevertheless, because the general design now proposed can meet the minimum requirements for retaining desirable qualities of the present thoroughfare if certain more detailed design conditions are met.

One commissioner, John Flaharty, would not go along with even this lukewarm endorsement, and he filed his own minority report. He argued that the double-deck design was a potential "source of deterioration of some of Detroit's outstanding commercial and residential property." He questioned the accuracy of the predicted need for an expressway, but conceding the need and the commitment to build under the tripartite contract, he proposed that only the depressed section be built for the time being and used as a reversible one-way expressway and the elevated section postponed until it became absolutely necessary. Many neighborhood civic associations, who considered Flaharty their representative on the Plan Commission, applauded and endorsed his stand.

Neighborhood Opposition. If the number of neighborhood civic associations is an indication of community organization, then the northwest section of Detroit is a well-organized community. Perhaps it would be more accurate to say that this section of the city consists of a number of well-organized communities. The Federated Civic Associations of Northwest Detroit, a confederation of neighborhood associations, had sixty member units, and since not all associations bother to pay dues and become members of the Federated, there were probably more than sixty in this section of the city. Bordering the little more than three-mile length of James Couzens were eight civic associations. In many cases the boundaries of a given association follow subdivision boundaries, and in other cases they follow "natural" boundaries such as those provided by major arterial thoroughfares or elementary-school districts. The usual organizational pattern is to incorporate the association as a non-profit corporation, with appropriate constitution and bylaws. Many associations are dormant for long periods, but they provide a structure around which the neighborhood can rally if the need arises.

The civic association plays an important role in local government, and both elected officials and the professional bureaucracy make use of and respond to the associations. If rezoning or a variance in a zoned use is up for consideration, the appropriate civic association can be expected to react by appearing at hearings and registering its desires with councilmen. They provide a useful link through which health, recreation, police, and other agencies can promote programs on the neighborhood level. In their zeal to protect the economic and ethnic homogeneity of a neighborhood, civic associations can play a disruptive role in the community.

The first reaction of an organization to the double-deck proposal came before the Plan Commission had announced its recommendations, and it came not from a neighborhood association but from a businessmen's group. On July 17, the James Couzens Business and Professional Men's Association held an emergency meeting to which representatives of the State Highway Department (Rubin), the city (Richards and Alger Malo, director, Department of Streets and Traffic), and the county (Oscar Gunderson, an engineer for the Road Commission) were invited. Anticipating that there would be need for a good deal of "communications" with various groups, the Highway Department had worked up a well-planned presentation, which Rubin presented to this group. The presentation, which consisted of charts and tables showing traffic volumes, street capacities, projected volumes, and drawings of different treatments for Couzens, including the double-deck as designed by Yamasaki, was aimed at convincing the audience that the highway planners had explored all feasible alternatives and that the double-deck plan was the only one that could provide the needed expressway and still preserve the desirable characteristics of Couzens. Rubin was a persuasive speaker, and his materials were simple, attractive, and as convincing as those skilled in the arts of persuasion could make them. Before the issue was settled, Rubin was to make this presentation many times to many different audiences. His audience on July 17 was not convinced. The businessmen's group feared that the beauty of the street would be destroyed by the elevated structure and that property values would decline as a result.

On July 31, 1958, the double-deck plan was formally presented to the Common Council, and the council proceeded to schedule a public hearing on the plan for August 14. By now the civic associations in the Couzens area had been alerted to the double-deck plan and were beginning to respond to it. The Federated Civic Associations of Northwest Detroit, in a press release, pointed out that while Detroit was spending millions of dollars to rehabilitate and redevelop blighted areas, it did not make sense to build an elevated structure that could result in the deterioration of high-value commercial and residential property. The federation endorsed the minority report of Plan Commissioner Flaharty. This was not surprising in view of the fact that Flaharty was a former president of the Federated, and his appointment to the Plan Commission had been in response to a demand that the civic associations have representation on the planning body.

Rubin and representatives of the city and county had been invited to appear before the Outer Drive–James Couzens Highway Improvement Association at a meeting held on August 7. This was precisely the sort of opportunity that Rubin was looking for—a chance to sell the double-deck plan to the people in the affected area before the public hearing was held. Haviland Reves, president of the association, had an intense interest in the fate of Couzens and in the activities of the association. His home was located near Couzens, but his personal stake in the developing controversy went deeper than his property interests in the area. Personally committed to his work with the association, he devoted a good deal of time to it. Reves chaired the meeting and led off with a lengthy opening statement which ended with an introduction of the speakers. A tape recording of the meeting reveals that during his introductory remarks Reves presented his own opposition to the double-deck plan and urged his audience to join the association's officers in carrying on the fight against it. Finally, Rubin got the stage.

Rubin began by assuring the audience that he was not there to sell them on a given plan but merely to present facts, so that if some wanted to oppose the double-deck plan, they could oppose it intelligently. He then gave the presentation that had been used with the businessmen's group. His audience of 250 heard him through, and there followed a question-and-answer period which also involved the city and county representatives. As usual at such meetings, questions frequently became speeches, and many were aimed at getting commitments and assurances that the speakers were powerless to provide even if they had been inclined to do so. Three hours after it began, the meeting adjourned with fifty people remaining in the audience. Rubin and his cohorts did not think that they had changed many minds, but they had performed their mission of presenting the facts.

In addition to the civic associations, two large churches—one Baptist and one Lutheran—abutted on James Couzens, and the highway passed through a large Roman Catholic parish. Although all three churches were opposed, to some degree, to the double-deck plan, the most active opposition came from Precious Blood Roman Catholic Church. The parish publication for Sunday, August 10, contained a notice urging parishioners to appear at the scheduled public hearing and oppose the project. It contained this caveat: "Our parish is a parish of fine homes . . . we don't want to ruin the work and labor of years which has gone into building the neighborhood." Throughout the ensuing controversy the Rt. Rev. Monsignor William Hermes of Precious Blood provided active opposition. The parish paper urged parishioners to protest, and the physical facilities of the parish were made available for rallies and strategy meetings. Assistance was given in the printing of form letters and obtaining signatures to petitions. Both Catholic and Protestant churches in the city had observed, within recent years, the effects of change in neighborhood composition upon older churches in the downtown area. The churches along James Couzens were new, and there was fear that the double-deck expressway might damage the neighborhood's stability.

The First Public Hearing. The August 14 public hearing was held on schedule at 10:00 A.M., and it attracted a full house. Five hundred persons jammed into the auditorium in the City-County Building for a session that was to last five hours. Since the public announcement of the double-deck plan, councilmen had been hearing from residents and businessmen in the Couzens area. The communications took a variety of forms, from phone calls and post cards to elaborate documents. In the latter category was a thirty-two-page statement prepared by Haviland Reves, president of the Outer Drive–James Couzens Highway Improvement Association, which detailed numerous objections to the double-deck plan and suggested a number of alternatives, the most exotic of which was a tunnel. A briefer statement was submitted by John R. Kohl, an owner of business property along Couzens, who was soon to take over the leadership of the fight against the expressway. He stated the problem in these words:

> Let us not lose sight of the fact that the only purpose of an express-
> way for the three-and-one-half-mile distance between the Lodge exit
> and Eight Mile Road is to save the motorist time. . . . Thus the
> question resolves itself to one of whether the city of Detroit should
> be forced by outside officials of the state to spend millions of dollars
> coming from the city, county, state, and federal taxes to build an
> expressway that might easily detract from the property value of
> existing property and thus reduce taxes to the city and would cer-
> tainly detract from the beauty of one of its most beautiful business
> streets, just to save motorists, most of whom would not even be resi-
> dents of Detroit using this particular stretch of road, a total time of
> from nine or ten minutes to a possible maximum of five minutes time.

In his letter Kohl suggested a number of steps that could be taken to increase the capacity of Couzens, such as widening and an underpass for the busiest intersection, without expressway treatment. Kohl also took issue with the projected traffic demand that was being used to justify the expressway. His arguments were sufficiently convincing to move Councilman Edward Connor to send Kohl's letter to City Public Works Commissioner Richards for comment. Richards conceded that the Kohl suggestions would increase the capacity of Couzens—city traffic engineers had made comparable proposals in anticipation of the opening of the Lodge Expressway—but he pointed out in his reply to Councilman Connor that the main reason for the expressway was not to save time but to prevent accidents. "The separation of the slow, local traffic from the fast, through traffic that wants to either get into or through our city is important from a safety standpoint. One of the big problems today is accidents caused by the mixing of these two types of traffic. Limited-access highways eliminate most of these accidents." The double-deck would not depreciate property values, Richards said in his letter, but rather would be designed to add to the beauty of the street. These same points were made by Richards in reply to letters sent directly to him by people in the Couzens area. By the time the public hearing convened on August 14, the council, highway officials, and area residents had been in communication with each other and were well aware of each other's views.

Mayor Louis Miriani opened the hearing with the equivocal statement that something had to be done on James Couzens and that the advice of the engineers should be heeded, but on the other hand, he noted that "no one is wedded to a particular plan." In view of the fact that city officials had already endorsed the double-deck plan through the various committees set up under the tripartite contract, the mayor's statement could be taken as a clue by the opponents of the plan that the city was not bound by this procedure. This was a hopeful sign.

The mayor was followed by city and county highway officials who documented the need for the expressway by citing traffic volumes and supported the double-deck plan as one that would not only protect property values along Couzens but would also add to its aesthetic appeal. Rubin then took over, giving the presentation which had by now become familiar to many in his audience. Rubin urbanely greeted his opponents by conceding that his biggest problem was their skill in bringing pressure to bear on public officials: "May I congratulate you on the campaign you have mounted against us," he said, "I wish you ill luck, but I do congratulate you." Architect Yamasaki was introduced, and he extolled the double-deck design, which he had embellished, as a "brilliant" solution. Everything that was presented verbally was supported by reports, drawings, models, photographs, and statistics, all of which were available to the councilmen.

The first speaker for the opposition was John Kohl. Although his residence was outside of Detroit, Kohl owned an office building on James Couzens from which he operated his business as divisional manager of Investors Diversified Services, Inc. Kohl was in his late thirties, a veteran of World War II, father of five children, and holder of a law degree, although he did not engage in practice. As a successful young businessman, with a substantial property holding (his two-story office building was worth about $100,000) on James Couzens, he could rightfully claim a personal interest in the future of the street, and he spoke also as the representative of the James Couzens Business and Professional Men's Association. Kohl spoke for sixty-five minutes. The points he had made in his letter to the councilmen were repeated and expanded. He also brought up additional objections to the double-deck: that dust from salt used to melt ice, as well as dirt, would blow off the elevated section and cause a nuisance; that maintenance cost would be high, since artificial lighting would be required at all times; and that ramps to and from the elevated section would block air and light to properties along the road. He pointed out that the completed sections of the Lodge Expressway had already developed traffic jams at the two interchanges, Ford-Lodge and Lodge-Davison. It would not make sense, he argued, to add to the volume on the Lodge as long as these interchange snarls occurred. He illustrated this point with an hourglass-shaped diagram, the narrow neck representing the Ford-Lodge interchange, which, he contended, placed an absolute restraint on the flow of traffic regardless of the capacity of the expressways linked by the interchange.

Kohl made a strong and impressive presentation. He was a persuasive speaker, and as the first speaker for his side, he was uninhibited by arguments that had already been stated. But Kohl's presentation put the next speaker, Haviland Reves, in a difficult position. When the hearing began, Reves would have been considered by most as the leader of the neighborhood opposition to the expressway. In fact, Councilwoman Blanche Parent Wise, chairman of the hearing, had asked Reves to arrange the order of speakers for the civic associations, and Reves had assigned Kohl to the first spot. With his forceful introduction, Kohl had literally taken over the leadership of the opposition. Because the length of Kohl's speech reduced Reves's time allotment to ten minutes, Reves had no opportunity to read his thirty-two-page brief. He did make the point that he estimated that the ten thousand home owners in the affected area would suffer a total depreciation of $80,000,000 in property valuation, which would in turn reduce the city's tax revenue. (These, of course, were estimates more easily stated than substantiated.) The tone of much of Reves's comment was indicated by the following quotes taken from the tape recording of the hearing: "I don't want to see huge trucks overhead nor hear them; we fear accidents on this elevated—why set up this man-killer?"

Reves was followed by representatives of other civic associations in opposition to the expressway. One suggested that the Couzens project be postponed until both the Grand River and the Chrysler expressways were completed. Another, from the Federated Civic Associations of Northwest Detroit, endorsed the minority report of Plan Commissioner Flaharty. No civic association appeared in support of the double-deck plan.

Following the civic associations' presentations, Rubin was given an opportunity to reply to points that had been made. He reminded Reves that the double-deck plan would move the through traffic seventy feet from the front of abutting structures, whereas currently and under any widening program, it would be only twenty feet away. Reves had also questioned a post-card survey that had been conducted by the Detroit Area Traffic Study, a traffic research organization maintained at Wayne State University through the financial assistance of the federal Bureau of Public Roads, the Michigan State Highway Department, Wayne County, and Detroit. The post-card survey consisted of handing a post card to drivers of all cars that could be served by a crew of nine men while the cars were waiting for the light to change in the northbound lane of James Couzens at the first intersection after leaving the Lodge Expressway between the hours of 2:00 and 5:00 P.M. on August 7. The card was worded as follows:

> The Highway Authorities have determined after considerable study that a combined elevated-depressed expressway constructed within the existing center island of James Couzens Highway is the most satisfactory method of extending the John C. Lodge Expressway.
>
> This survey is being conducted to determine what percentage of the motorists using this route favor the improvement as proposed.
>
> Do you favor this improvement?   Yes_____   No_____

Over five thousand cards were distributed in this manner. By the day of the hearing, 40 percent of the cards had been mailed in, and 83 percent of those returning the cards had checked "Yes." (Additional cards arrived after the hearing, but the pro-expressway percentage remained the same.)

Reves went to some length to show that the question was loaded, and he also questioned the sampling technique. Rubin explained that the percentage of cards returned was remarkably high, as was the percentage in favor of the improvement. This, he said, was the only way the users of Couzens could be heard, and no one could deny the randomness of the sample. (Checked against traffic counters placed at the intersection, 60 percent of the cars using the intersection received cards.) Point for point, Rubin proceeded to answer the contentions of the representatives of the civic associations, but there was no way in which he could provide a conclusive answer to the question that worried most people—what effect would the double-deck have upon Couzens and the surrounding area. In other American cities where elevated expressways had been built, construction had taken place in blighted areas with little regard given to the aesthetic impact of the structure. Kohl used these examples to demonstrate that elevated expressways were undesirable per se. Rubin cited no evidence where an elevated or double-deck construction had enhanced the beauty and/or the value of a street like Couzens, surrounded by middle- and upper-income residential areas. Photographs and models showing an attractively designed tree-lined structure were not as convincing as demonstrable proof.

Following Rubin's rebuttal, individuals were permitted to make statements limited to three minutes in length. By this time the hearing had been in session for over four hours. Nerves were frayed, and the statements were repetitious of what had preceded. As the proceedings came to an end, Councilman William Patrick suggested that a committee of real-estate appraisers be appointed to investigate the effect of a double-deck expressway on property values, since this seemed to be one of the key issues in the controversy. His colleagues agreed that this was a good idea and that it would be taken up at their formal meeting the next day. On this note the hearing was terminated.

The Council Decides to Wait.   Under the tripartite contract the Detroit Common Council had twenty-one days in which to make up its mind on a project. Since the double-deck plan had been formally presented to the council on July 31, August 21 was the deadline. Failure to take any action to disapprove by this time meant that the double-deck plan would automatically be approved. Since the double-deck plan had been informally presented to the council members on July 8, they had had considerably more than twenty-one days to consider the plan. Nevertheless, the public reaction to the double-deck plan was more than had been bargained for. This was evident from the vigorous opposition displayed at the hearing and the more than five thousand letters the councilmen had received. It was obvious that most of the letters were form letters and were part of a well-organized campaign. It was difficult to assess the political significance of the protest, but the councilmen did not feel that they could ignore it.

There were other reasons inhibiting a speedy decision. This was the first hard decision to be made under the tripartite contract. Some councilmen felt that they had been pressured into the package deal by Mackie and the Highway Department; the double-deck plan had acquired the reputation of being a pet project of Mackie's. The two women on the council, Mary Beck, considered a Democrat, and Blanche Parent Wise, considered a Republican, were the only members of the council who consistently supported both the need for an expressway along Couzens and the double-deck plan as the preferred treatment. The remaining seven councilmen were not so certain. Some doubted the wisdom of any expressway treatment for Couzens, and others preferred some treatment other than the double-deck. Mayor Miriani, serving his first full term as mayor, avoided taking any position, but he did provide a solution to the council's concern over the August 21 deadline. He suggested that in view of the controversy, further study should take place before a decision was made. Taking the mayor's suggestion, the council requested that the state highway commissioner grant a forty-day extension beyond the deadline. Mackie and the county were agreeable to this, and a favorable ruling from the state attorney general approved the extension under the contract terms. Although eager for a decision, Mackie had acted to prevent any accusation that he was using the contract to put an unreasonable time limit upon the council's deliberations. The mayor and the council hoped that the extra time would permit tempers to cool and produce a more reasonable climate for decision-making.

The forty-day extension made September 30 the new deadline. If during this period the council could come up with some substantial piece of objective evidence concerning the effects of an elevated expressway upon a neighborhood, they would be in a better position to make an independent decision regardless of the amount of pressure brought to bear against them during this same period of time. One such effort was a follow-up to the suggestion of Councilman Patrick that an independent appraisal be made.

Patrick's proposal was that a team of four real-estate appraisers be appointed by the council to determine: the extent of the area which would be directly affected by the expressway; the classification of commercial properties in the affected area; and the effect of the expressway upon the value of commercial and residential property in the area. Two of the four appraisers, he suggested, should be selected from outside Michigan and two from Detroit. These suggestions were put in a memorandum and submitted by the council, through the director of the city's Bureau of Real Estate, to the officers of the Michigan State Realty Association, which was then in session in Detroit, and to members of the Detroit Real Estate Board. Those groups concluded that such a comprehensive appraisal could not be prepared by the September 30 dead-line. At least ninety days, they maintained, would be necessary for such a study. In his report to the council of his efforts to arrange the study, the director of the Bureau of Real Estate made it clear that the membership of the state real-estate groups were not eager to take on the assignment:

> . . . the membership of this state association lacked experience in making a finding based on factual information. . . . such appraisal should be prepared by an appraiser who is familiar with a compara-ble problem in some section of the nation which would be similar to the matter now before your Honorable Body. . . .

This was not a very helpful suggestion, since there were no com-parable projects—at least it would be hard to reach agreement that they were comparable—and if outside appraisers could be found, their conclusions would be subject to challenge on the ground that as outsiders they did not understand local conditions.

In another attempt to obtain some insight into the question of property valuation, the council instructed Public Works Commis-sioner Richards to obtain from the Federal Housing Administra-tion their policy on mortgage applications in areas served by an expressway or areas planned for expressway construction. In re-sponse to this inquiry, the local Federal Housing Administration director wrote:

> The policy of the Detroit FHA Insuring Office has been not to accept any applications for processing located in a proposed right-of-way or within three hundred feet of same. This rule is applied until the expressway is completed, at which time a re-examination is made and any favorable or adverse effects on the resale value of adjoining residential properties are noted and then become a valua-tion matter. The only properties in the first block from the express-way which we find are adversely affected are those abutting or adja-cent to the expressway. Inasmuch as the expressways afford better transportation to and from places of employment, they add to mar-ketability.
>
> With reference to the proposed James Couzens elevated express-way, FHA applications would not be acceptable facing or adjoin-ing commercial properties which are typical of the highway. Other-wise, our usual expressway policy would apply.

This statement did not provide the clear-cut evidence the council sought. It became apparent that there was no scientific or even less sophisticated evidence of what impact the double-deck expressway would have upon property values, to say nothing of its possible effect upon other values, such as neighborhood stability.

Neighborhood Resistance Consolidates. While the councilmen were seeking some factual support to aid them in decision-making, neighborhood opposition to the double-deck plan continued to develop and to become better organized. Following the August 14 hearing, John Kohl emerged as the leader of the opposition forces. His ascendancy brought with it a shift in policy from the earlier period, when leadership had been less clearly defined and more or less assumed by Haviland Reves. Reves, a home owner in the Couzens area and president of a home owners' civic association, had organized opposition to the double-deck plan because he felt that the plan, as such, was not desirable. He did not deny the need for some form of expressway treatment for Couzens, and, in fact, had suggested alternatives to the double-deck plan. Kohl, on the other hand, had only a business interest in Couzens. His home was outside of the city. He represented the business and commercial establishments along James Couzens, and he took the position that no expressway whatsoever was needed. When the double-deck plan was first introduced, those who opposed it per se and those who opposed any expressway at all on Couzens formed a united opposition group, but as the controversy wore on, the difference between these two positions became more significant.

The shift in leadership to Kohl also represented a major shift in the tone and organizational quality of the opposition. Reves represented a type of community leadership often found in semi-dormant civic associations, where the president can use his organizational role, usually with the members' indifferent consent, to write letters to city officials protesting this and demanding that in the interest of the neighborhood. It is possible for one to become deeply involved emotionally in these activities, and since the policy-making mechanism of the civic association, although formally designed to make it possible to obtain a representative neighborhood viewpoint, seldom operates so as to achieve this, it is often difficult for the involved individual to distinguish between his own personal views and those he assumes to be the views of his neighborhood. But the free hand which neighborhood leaders have during periods of quiescence can be restricted rapidly when the neighborhood is confronted with some action that looms as a threat to basic neighborhood values. By early September, it had become evident that neighborhood opinion along James Couzens Highway, to the extent to which that opinion was expressed, was lining up behind the position taken by John Kohl—no expressway for Couzens. In the face of this, Reves continued to insist to his own civic association that simple widening of Couzens was "the most dangerous type [project] of all so far seriously proposed." But he found little, if any, support in his association, and on October 14, his resignation from the presidency of the Outer Drive–James Couzens Highway Improvement Association was accepted.

Neighborhood battles have their casualties. Haviland Reves was one. The final acceptance of his resignation (it was his fourth offer to resign, and he maintained that his resignation was not properly processed, so that in fact he did not resign but "was just pushed out") had been preceded by meetings held without Reves's knowledge and by attempts to have him agree to remain in his position in the association but to concede to the Kohl policy and to accept Kohl as the major spokesman for a united opposition to any expressway. These were conditions that Reves would not accept, even though his insistence that some expressway treatment for Couzens was necessary cost him the civic association presidency, which he valued, and created personal antagonism against him in his neighborhood. Reves's resignation, a lengthy document in which he detailed various acts which he considered to be unfair to him, revealed the extent of his emotional involvement and the hurt that he felt as his position of leadership disintegrated. Why Reves had to go is best explained by the following paragraph taken from a document prepared by Kohl entitled "To Divide Us Is to Conquer—Let's Stand United."

> It is MOST IMPORTANT that no interested persons or groups allow themselves to be drawn into any *discussion or vote* on WHICH KIND OF EXPRESSWAY you would prefer. *This position must be unalterable* so long as an X-way on James Couzens cannot serve the purpose for which X-ways are created.

Kohl brought more than a no-expressway policy as he took over the leadership role. He also brought energy and organizing talent.

Unlike Reves, who liked to prepare long letters, Kohl was economical in the use of the written word. Recognizing that the councilmen were more likely to heed the number of voters rather than the number of words, Kohl decided to organize as many people as possible. As the September 30 deadline approached, the neighborhood opposition was solidifying into a united front not only against the double-deck plan but also against any expressway on Couzens. If there were dissenters other than Haviland Reves, they remained silent. The irrepressible Reves, however, continued to write letters to the council and to highway officials, suggesting an alternative expressway treatment as a substitute for the double-deck plan.

Death for the Double-Deck. On Monday, September 22, Kohl again appeared before the council to protest approval of the double-deck plan. By now, the councilmen had felt the weight of the neighborhood campaign. Hundreds of letters, petitions with hundreds of names, phone calls, and telegrams were bombarding City Hall. In his appearance before the council, Kohl reminded the members that before Mackie became state highway commissioner, the city's own highway officials had recommended a simple widening of James Couzens, but after Mackie took over, Kohl contended, he had brought pressure to bear on the city for the Couzens project in order to have an access, via Northwestern and an expressway on Eleven Mile Road, to the finished leg of the Grand River Expressway between Farmington and Brighton. He also charged that commercial pressures were at work in support of the Couzens project. Although he did not reveal to the council what these pressures were, in his "Let's Stand United" document, prepared some time later, he did imply that officials of The J. L. Hudson Company's Northland Shopping Center had been involved in the state planning of the Couzens project prior to its public announcement. Kohl presented to the council his plan for Couzens: widening, a grade separation at Puritan, and synchronized traffic lights. This plan, he said, had the endorsement of four churches and seven home owners and business groups, including the Federated Civic Associations of Northwest Detroit.

The next day, Tuesday, September 23, at the urging of the mayor, the council decided to vote on the Couzens issue and dispose of the matter at its formal afternoon session. If the vote were to be taken, the double-deck plan was certain to lose. As yet there were only two council members (Beck and Wise) in favor of it, and Rubin had hopes that he might be able to swing some more votes by the time the issue came up on the thirtieth, the date when it had been generally assumed that the vote would be taken. When Rubin heard of this new turn of events, he rushed to the council chamber and urged that they reconsider their motion to vote that day. He reminded the members that they had scheduled a meeting for the twenty-fifth with Mackie and Yamasaki, at which time the architect was to present new sketches of the double-deck. Eugene VanAntwerp, who had made the motion to vote that day, was absent from the chambers when Rubin made his plea, and Mary Beck urged her colleagues to make a yield to courtesy decision and remove the vote from the agenda, which they did. When VanAntwerp learned what had happened, he was furious. Meeting Rubin in the hallway, he upbraided him for upsetting the procedure of a local legislative body and threatened to take the matter up with the governor. Rubin excused his action, pleading ignorance of the rules. The evening papers quoted Rubin as saying that the council posed a threat to the entire metropolitan expressway program by establishing the precedent of setting up the opinion of amateur traffic experts against the unanimous opinion of highway authorities. Statements like this one did not endear him to the councilmen.

The meeting with Yamasaki was held, as scheduled, on Thursday, September 25. Using colored sketches, he explained to the council that the double-deck plan would preserve the "serenity and quiet" on Couzens. He again pointed to its spatial advantages: it would rise only seventeen feet from grade, less than a two-story building; it would provide twenty-four feet on either side for landscaping; it would preserve the existing twenty-foot margin from the service-drive curb line to building fronts; and it would require a minimum amount of property acquisition. These points were not new, but they were being made by a reputable architect, known for his flair for attractive design, who would not be likely to be pleading for a structure that would turn out to be an eyesore. Yamasaki made it clear that he considered the double-deck plan superior to any other plan, and he warned: "If this project is built and done properly, you will be very happy many years from now. If you do something else, you will be very sorry later on."

On the day that Yamasaki was urging the council to approve the double-deck plan, John Kohl formed the Northwest Inter-Organizational Board. The board, of which Kohl was made chairman, was composed of representatives (three from each group) from eighteen civic associations, the James Couzens Business and Professional Men's Association, and six churches. This organization provided a central headquarters for keeping track of relevant events, receiving and distributing information, and co-ordinating the efforts of its member groups. Its basic platform was that no expressway was needed and that traffic problems could be solved by widening. A number of the civic associations affiliated with the board were located some distance from the Couzens area, but their numbers added weight to the organization. On the following day, Saturday, Kohl held a strategy meeting with representatives from the civic associations in the Couzens area and from the churches. A letter-writing campaign was planned, and a mass meeting was organized to be held the following day, Sunday, at the Precious Blood Church.

From the point of view of the promoters, the Sunday meeting was a roaring success. The basement, with a capacity of seven hundred, was soon filled, and an upstairs hall had to be used by about three hundred persons, who listened to the proceedings through loud-speakers. Kohl was the main speaker, and he rallied his forces against the "political trickery" of Mackie and Rubin, who were trying "to jam [an expressway] down our throats now." He urged his audience to swamp the mayor and council with letters and communications to prove that it would be political suicide to vote for the double-deck or any expressway for Couzens. Mimeographed form letters were available, addressed to each councilman and the mayor. All that was required were the signature and address of the sender. The wording of the form letters was identical with those sent out before the public hearing in August, with one notable exception. In August, the sender was "unequivocably and unalterably opposed to any type of elevated or double-deck ex-

pressway," but in September, he was "unalterably and unequivocably opposed to the double-deck or *any other* type of expressway"
for Couzens.

On Monday morning the mail and phone calls poured into City
Hall. By afternoon, *The Detroit News* was on the streets with a
full-page advertisement, designed by Kohl and paid for by his
organization, opposing a Couzens expressway. "A misuse of public
funds? Did you realize that your elected representatives are wast-
ing your property taxes?" These leads were supported by appropriate text to establish the points that made up the opposition's
arguments. This advertisement was the only vigorous support the
Couzens battlers could find printed in *The Detroit News*.

Although ordinarily the *News* would join in vigorous battle over
any issue that threatened devaluation of property and loss of tax
revenue to the city, in this controversy it remained detached. Bitter critics in the neighborhood attributed this to The J. L. Hudson
Company. Hudson's famed Northland Shopping Center was located less than a mile north of the James Couzens–Eight Mile Road
intersection, and it seemed to be an open secret that Hudson's
officials were in favor of an expressway along Couzens, which
would make the Northland Shopping Center more accessible. Since
The J. L. Hudson Company made generous use of *The Detroit
News* for advertising, critics inferred that the newspaper's attitude
had been influenced by one of its major advertisers. Whether or
not this was so, an accusation of "guilt by association" was not
extraordinary coming from an embattled group of people who
found it difficult to detect reason in any but their own position
and who were prone to suspect the motives of those who did not
support their point of view.

When the council met on September 30 to vote on the double-
deck plan, it seemed a foregone conclusion that it would fail. Kohl
and his lieutenants had succeeded in whipping up one of the most
overwhelming neighborhood protest movements in the city's history. Veteran politicians, such as Councilman Edward Carey, conceded that the pressure had been impressive, and another veteran,
Councilman Edward Connor, commented that although there was
terrific pressure against the expressway, he had received virtually
no communications in support of the double-deck plan. Before a

packed gallery of expressway opponents, the council prepared to vote. In view of the Kohl no-expressway position, Connor raised the question of the city's power under the contract to determine the type of expressway to be built, and Councilwoman Wise asked for a legal opinion on the binding nature of the contract. They were informed by an assistant corporation counsel that they were committed to a limited-access highway on James Couzens. The issue was not whether an expressway should be built, but what kind. It was pointed out, however, that the council could continue to reject alternative plans, presumably indefinitely, or until taken to court for breach of contract. With this advice, the council proceeded to vote, and the double-deck plan for James Couzens Highway was rejected seven to two. The two councilwomen, Beck and Wise, had stood up under the opposition and voted for the double-deck. Following the vote, Councilman William Rogell demanded that the state, county, and city engineers bring in alternative expressway plans for James Couzens. The council had defeated the double-deck plan, but it had not abandoned its commitment under the tripartite contract to approve an expressway for James Couzens.

The Second Plan

The Council Views the Couzens Controversy. Following the defeat of the double-deck plan, the committees established by the tripartite contract had to go back to work and develop a different expressway plan for Couzens. While this was being done during October and most of November, the Couzens issue was quiet. During this period each of the nine councilmen was interviewed concerning his views on the Couzens controversy. (An attempt was made to interview Mayor Miriani, but his secretary told the interviewer that the mayor was too busy to grant the interview.) The interviews were conducted by upperclassmen and graduate students at Wayne State University; assured that their responses would be held in confidence during the controversy, the councilmen gave candid answers to the questions put to them. The responses obtained in the interviews provide an interesting backdrop against which to observe the concluding stages of the controversy.

The councilmen were asked whether they considered themselves legally bound by the tripartite contract to provide some form of expressway treatment for Couzens, and all nine answered in the affirmative. In response to questions concerning the pressure brought to bear upon them by the people in the Couzens area, the councilmen conceded that the pressure had been great. Each reported that he had received thousands of protest letters. The arguments used by the protesters that most impressed the councilmen were that the expressway would lower property values; that there was no demonstrated need for an expressway; and that the double-deck was too much of an experiment to erect in a nice residential neighborhood. Six of the councilmen felt that the people were objecting to *any* type of expressway for Couzens, and only two thought that the opposition was aimed primarily at the double-deck treatment. One councilman said that the opposition had begun as anti-double-deck but had become anti-expressway. When asked if they felt that some of the opposition would be dropped when new alternatives were offered, six councilmen said that they thought the opposition would remain as strong, two felt it would substantially decrease and one felt it would lessen to some extent.

Because Kohl had concentrated arguments against the traffic engineering data used to justify the need for the expressway, the councilmen were asked whether they felt the data being used did establish the need for an expressway, and all nine responded that it did. Eight of the nine added that they felt that anticipated traffic demand formed the best basis for expressway planning; one councilman was not so sure but had no alternative to suggest.

A number of questions dealt with the double-deck plan that the council had turned down. The three basic advantages claimed for the double-deck treatment were cited (right-of-way would not have to be expanded; Couzens could continue to handle traffic during construction; and the center-island landscaping could be retained), and the councilmen were asked whether they agreed that these were advantages. Six agreed, two disagreed, and one felt that while these three factors might be reasons in favor of a double-deck, they had been overstated. On the other hand, the councilmen cited these disadvantages of the double-deck: its possible unattractiveness; neighborhood antipathy to it; and its high cost, compared with other treatments (the double-deck cost was estimated at $33,000,000 and the depressed expressway treatment at $28,000,000). Since cost did not figure much in the public debate, appearance and acceptability seem to have weighed most heavily with the councilmen. Opinion was split over the possible effect the double-deck would have had on property values: four thought that it would reduce property values; four thought that it would not affect property values, and one said that he did not know. The councilmen were asked if they agreed with the Engineering Committee's conclusion that the double-deck was the best possible solution from an engineering standpoint. Seven councilmen said that they did agree, and two said that they did not. When asked what alternative expressway treatments they would prefer, all but one, who was strongly in favor of a rolling-grade type, preferred to remain noncommittal.

One question evoked an immediate reaction in each interview, and the responses proved to be identical. When asked, "Do you think there is any solution which will, in the long run, satisfy all parties?" all nine councilmen answered "No."

The Cantilever Proposal. By November 20, 1958, the tripartite Engineering Committee had agreed upon an alternative expressway design for Couzens: a $28,000,000 depressed expressway to be constructed in the center of the Couzens right-of-way. The plan was tailored to the 204-foot right-of-way. In order to retain the service drives and twenty-foot, tree-lined set-back between curb line and building fronts, 108 feet of right-of-way were reserved for these purposes. The expressway would require 106 feet (three twelve-foot expressway lanes running in both directions separated by a ten-foot median strip with a twelve-foot refuge lane on each side of the expressway), which was ten feet more than the available right-of-way. This difficulty was taken care of in the plan by a five-foot overhang on either side of the expressway. That is, the surface service drive would overhang the expressway for five feet on either side. This plan was referred to as the cantilever plan. (In one of his many suggested treatments for Couzens, Haviland Reves had proposed a type of cantilever construction, and he hailed this new plan as one he had inspired.) In contrast to the double-deck, the cantilever plan would remove the landscaped center island and replace it with a fourteen-foot-deep cavity bearing traffic between perpendicular retaining walls. The plan also required condemnation of about $4,000,000 worth of property at four intersections to make room for ramp construction. It would require three years to construct, from six months to a year longer than the estimated construction time for the double-deck.

The tripartite Administrative Committee decided to submit the new plan to the Detroit Common Council on November 26. Glenn Richards, who had been designated by Mayor Miriani to represent him on the committee, dissented from this decision. The mayor's behavior during the double-deck controversy and his representative's reluctance to give active support to any plan before the Administrative Committee convinced Mackie that he would have to take some action to make it clear where responsibility for delay should be placed. On Monday, November 24, Mackie released a statement which said that Detroit officials had been mulling over various engineering designs for over six months and that it was high time for them to make a decision. Noting that there would be local opposition regardless of what type of treatment was decided upon, he warned the mayor: "Unless we get Detroit approval of some plan by the end of this month, I will be forced to scrap my publicly announced commitment to have the Lodge extension entirely under contract by 1960."

The red flag of "state interference" having been waved, Miriani retorted that Mackie's warning was "interfering with local government" and "usurping the city's responsibility, under state law, to review and act on the expressway plans." The next day, Tuesday the twenty-fifth, Miriani went before the council and requested more time so that everyone would have a chance to cool off. The council agreed and cancelled indefinitely a hearing that had been scheduled for the following day on the alternate plan. It was then decided to delay any action for at least ninety days, during which time City Plan Director Charles Blessing was instructed to hold meetings with people in the Couzens area to explain to them the new plan. The mayor and council responded to Mackie's call for action with a new three-month delay.

Mackie replied with a telegram addressed to the mayor:

Detroit city officials have had plans to extend the Lodge Expressway along Couzens before them for over two years—long before I became a highway commissioner. A vast majority of the citizens of the metropolitan area are impatiently awaiting the extension of its totally inadequate expressway system, and an end to its traffic jams and consequent economic loss through accidents and lack of mobility. These people deserve action. The State Highway Department and County Road Commission are intent upon seeing they get it . . . twenty-one days is plenty of time for various commission members to review plans and make recommendations, if they want to work at it. Judging from comments from some of your officials, they would prefer twenty-one months or perhaps twenty-one years. . . . In view of the continued inability of your city administration to agree on engineering proposals, I hereby withdraw my commitment to have this project entirely under contract by 1960. . . .

If, however, by submitting the proposals now I am antagonizing the council and endangering their favorable consideration, I would not be acting in the best interests of the motorists. Therefore out of courtesy to you and the council, I am willing to withhold submission of the two plans [double-deck and cantilever] to council while you implement your neighborhood campaign. The state will recommend, however, regardless of the outcome, that suitable engineering proposals for the extension of the Lodge be submitted March 2.

Mackie thus conceded to withhold submitting plans to the council until March 2, but he made it clear that responsibility for delay in the construction of the metropolitan expressway system rested with the mayor and council.

The Neighborhood Educational Campaign.   Following the instructions of the mayor and council, the City Plan Commission prepared to meet with the various groups in the Couzens area. The commission's carefully planned strategy is reflected in the following excerpts taken from the draft of the statements to be presented at various meetings:

The mayor and Common Council have directed the commission to hold these meetings in order that you may be fully informed of the various plans and proposals which have been developed to provide additional traffic capacity on James Couzens Highway. . . .

As you are undoubtedly aware, an agreement has been entered into by the City of Detroit, the Wayne County Road Commission, and the State Highway Department for the construction of an expressway on

James Couzens Highway . . . , and it is in the interest of resolving the manner in which this is to be accomplished that these meetings are held.

The commission is cognizant of the fact that any change in the character of the present James Couzens Highway is a matter of serious consideration. It is also aware of the serious traffic problem on this thoroughfare and that this traffic situation will become increasingly acute in the ensuing years. It is therefore its opinion that some change will have to be made in the traffic pattern on this thoroughfare in a form that will provide for a separation of the through moving traffic from that which is primarily of a local or service type.

. . . .

It is the hope of the City Plan Commission that from this presentation you will be fully informed on the several expressway proposals and after careful deliberation will advise the commission in writing of your preference to the designs presented. . . . If no report is received . . . , it will be assumed you have no preference as to the alternate proposals that were presented at this meeting.

The strategy was clear. The meetings were not to be debates over whether or not an expressway was needed, but rather, over what type of expressway should be constructed. The formal presentation at each meeting was made by a member of the commission staff and consisted of slides, charts, graphs, statistics, and the usual visual aids used with small groups. Although some of the older expressway plans for Couzens had been dusted off for presentation, the three alternatives that received serious attention were the double-deck, rolling-grade, and cantilever. Following the formal presentation, a question-and-answer period was held, during which Plan Commission members could be questioned; traffic experts were also on hand to handle technical questions concerning traffic volumes and expressway design.

John Kohl attended a number of the meetings and used the question-and-answer period to repeat the by now familiar points in his no-expressway argument. Another protagonist, Irving Rubin, did not attend these meetings. He had intended to do so but remained away on the urging of the planners, who felt that his presence, in itself, created controversy. When he did attend one meeting, Plan Commissioner Flaharty announced to the audience that Rubin was not there at the invitation of the Plan Commission. The audience at the meeting was the James Couzens Business and

Professional Men's Association, the group most actively opposed to an expressway. Rubin may have appeared at this meeting in order to demonstrate his willingness to face his toughest opposition, but after hearing Commissioner Flaharty's remark, he left. Rubin did not relish being left out. He did not consider this an exclusively city affair—not as long as the state was putting up 75 percent of the state-local share of the money, whereas the city was to pay only 12.5 percent.

The most significant result of the Plan Commission meetings was to establish that the issue was not whether to have an expressway but what type of expressway to have. By repeating this approach at meeting after meeting, it became apparent to many that the no-expressway position was a lost cause. Some groups began to give ground. Immediately after the Plan Commission presentation, the directors of the Maloney Park Civic Association, one of the groups in the Couzens area, passed a resolution that "if there is in reality an expressway to be built on the James Couzens Highway," they would go on record in favor of the cantilever plan.

There was still a hard core of opposition to any expressway. Following their meeting with the Plan Commission, the Outer Drive–James Couzens Highway Improvement Association was still "firmly and unalterably opposed to any form of expressway on James Couzens Highway." This was the organization that had been headed by Haviland Reves, and under its new president, Edward Chouinard, it was holding firm to the no-expressway position. The James Couzens Business and Professional Men's Association likewise was unmoved by its meeting with the planners and continued to endorse a no-expressway stand.

The meeting with Kohl's Northwest Inter-Organizational Board was cancelled. Before the meeting, which was scheduled to be held on January 26, 1959, Kohl sent letters to the board members telling them:

> I cannot urge too strongly the importance of every organization having their representatives at this meeting regardless of whether you may or may not have a scheduled meeting with the Plan Commission or even if your meeting has already been held. It appears more evident than ever that we are making progress in getting across our point that the purpose for which expressways are built cannot be

achieved by constructing an expressway on James Couzens at this time.

Therefore, it appears more important than ever that all organizations present a completely united front opposing any type of expressway and endorsing the surface improvements that we have continuously suggested. This is true whether the organization be religious, residential, or business; for united we cannot but win, but to divide ourselves and in any way endorse any type of expressway, even as a secondary alternative, is to play right into the hands of the highway commissioner.

Edmund Kuhlman, president of the Plan Commission, wrote to Kohl to cancel the scheduled meeting on the grounds that since the board had already made its decision, it would be a waste of time to meet with them. Kuhlman pointed out that the commission had met with two-thirds of the board's member organizations and had meetings scheduled with the remainder. Kohl objected to the cancellation, and so did some of the councilmen, who felt that the planners should meet with any involved group, regardless of its stand; but the commission held to its decision. The planners felt that the meeting with the Inter-Organizational Board would have been used by Kohl as another vehicle for expounding his no-expressway views.

While the Plan Commission was engaged in meeting with groups in the Couzens area, Rubin was at work attempting to marshal support for the expressway. "People who want expressways don't organize as opponents do," he told the Automobile Club of Michigan in a speech. The club came out in support of either the double-deck or the depressed treatment, urging that construction begin as soon as possible. Support was also forthcoming from the Michigan Society of Professional Engineers, which recommended the double-deck plan, the Carpenters' District Council, and the Wayne County AFL-CIO. The unions were for any type of expressway construction, hoping that the work itself would relieve the then serious unemployment in the area. Although this support did not result in the intense, persistent pressure that Kohl had been able to evoke from the neighborhood, it did demonstrate that not everyone was against an expressway on Couzens and that there was some articulate support for it in the community.

On January 6, Mackie went before the council to request approval of a $100,000,000 bond plan, which along with federal funds would provide for $300,000,000 worth of expressway construction. The plan included money for the Couzens project. A wary council inquired whether approval of the bond plan would commit them to a specific type of expressway on Couzens, but Mackie assured them that approval of the bond plan was only a commitment to build expressways, not a commitment to a particular route or type of construction. Three days later, the council approved the city's participation in the bond plan and, in effect, gave notice of their intent to approve an expressway for Couzens.

On February 19, 1959, the secretary of the Federated Civic Associations of Northwest Detroit sent a letter to the Plan Commission informing the commission that at the February meeting of the association's board of directors the following resolution "was unanimously passed":

> In view of the overwhelming number of member associations on record with the Federated Civic Associations of Northwest Detroit favoring the cantilever-type depressed expressway for James Couzens Highway, RESOLVED, that the board of directors of the Federated Civic Associations of Northwest Detroit recommend to the City Plan Commission the cantilever-type depressed expressway for James Couzens Highway.

A copy of the letter with the resolution was sent to the local newspaper. This action by the influential Federated dealt a mortal blow to Kohl's strategy of "united we stand."

The leaders of the civic associations located along Couzens were shocked by the Federated's action, and Chouinard, president of the Outer Drive–James Couzens Highway Improvement Association, questioned the Federated's poll. Although the facts about the poll were not immediately released, it later became known that not all of the Federated's sixty members were polled, only those twenty-six organizations that had shown an interest in participating in the Plan Commission's education campaign. Sixteen of the twenty-six replied to the query of whether they preferred the double-deck or the cantilever treatment for Couzens. The no-expressway choice was not given, although some nonetheless gave this response. Eleven of the responding associations said they preferred the depressed cantilever design, and no votes were cast for the double-deck. On this basis the board of directors passed its resolution. While nine of the twelve board members had been present at the meeting, their agreement was, as reported, unanimous. One of the absent board members was Victor Sarin, vice president of the Outer Drive–James Couzens Highway Improvement Association. (When questioned about his absence, he said, "I just forgot.") The no-expressway proponents pointed out that, of the eleven associations voting for an expressway in the Federated's poll, only one association was in the Couzens area. The other ten were twenty or more blocks away.

It was not surprising that this was the case, since the associations further removed would be the most likely to be influenced by considerations other than their own direct property interests. The Federated covered a large area, and when the Federated's influence had been useful to help defeat the double-deck plan, the no-expressway group had welcomed their support without questioning the possible interest of distant associations.

On February 20, the Plan Commission submitted to the council the responses that they had received. The tally showed: fourteen groups in favor of the cantilever depressed type, including two churches and the Federated Civic Associations of Northwest Detroit; one organization, the Detroit chapter of the Michigan Society of Professional Engineers, in favor of the double-deck; three groups not opposed to an expressway or no preference; and five groups opposed to any expressway. All of the groups opposed to any expressway bordered James Couzens and included the Northwest Inter-Organizational Board, the James Couzens Business and Professional Men's Association, and the Outer Drive–James Couzens Highway Improvement Association.

The Final Hearing and Council Decision.   As the neighborhood educational campaign drew to a close, the administrative machinery for approving an expressway design for Couzens, which had been stalled the previous November by the insistence of the mayor and council upon more time, was put into motion. By February 18, the cantilever depressed design had received the approval of the tripartite committees, and on February 23 it was formally presented to the council, which now had twenty-one days, or until March 17, to act on it. Councilman VanAntwerp was ready to act immediately and end "this civil war" as quickly as possible, but his colleagues decided that the neighborhood groups should have another chance to be heard. A public hearing was scheduled for February 27, and a final vote on the matter was scheduled for the council's formal session of Tuesday, March 3. The mayor announced that he would support the depressed design if at least seven councilmen would vote for it. This was about as much leadership as the mayor was willing to give on this issue; the vote of seven councilmen could override the mayor's veto. Mackie said that he still favored the double-deck design but that the cantilever depressed design was acceptable to him. He let it be known, however, that if the current alternative were turned down, the double-deck proposal could be revived.

Kohl observed these events with concern. He charged the Plan Commission with rigging the results of their educational campaign and criticized these results and the vote of the Federated as representing groups far removed from the Couzens area. He complained that the council's decision to expedite the hearing and vote would not leave time for careful consideration. By now the councilmen had become so accustomed to Kohl's reactions that only his silence could have surprised them. The crowning blow to Kohl's strategy was the council's decision to formulate ground rules for the forthcoming public hearing that would keep the hearing focused upon the issue at hand—the type of expressway for Couzens. The key rule was that "only organizations and individuals desiring to express their viewpoints and give information relevant to the type of expressway treatment which should be constructed on James Couzens Highway may participate in the hearing." If this rule were to stand, Kohl's position could not be voiced at the hearing.

The *Detroit Times* carried an editorial on February 26, the day before the hearing, criticizing the council for these ground rules. The editorial put its finger on a dilemma that faced Kohl and his no-expressway supporters with property on James Couzens when it noted that, whereas the double-deck plan required no property condemnation, the cantilever design under consideration would require condemnation of property worth several million dollars. If the no-expressway group were to be excluded from the hearing, it would mean that those with a direct property interest in the outcome could not be heard. The council relented and amended the rules as follows:

It is recognized that the organization most substantially and directly affected by these proceedings is the James Couzens Business and Professional Men's Association, which, the council has been informed, is opposed to any type of limited-access treatment to the street that nurtures its members' businesses and offices. This latter organization is an affiliate of the Northwest Inter-Organization Board, which group had been most prominent in its opposition to expressway treatment. Because of the direct and substantial interests of the foregoing groups and their past record of outstanding advocacy of the point of view they represent, it is hereby determined that the Northwest Inter-Organizational Board shall be made an exception to the general rules heretofore laid down and will be permitted the same time as other participating organizations to present its views.

Under the rules applicable to all other groups, Kohl's organization would receive ten minutes for its presentation.

This second public hearing on the Couzens issue was anti-climactic. Only 250 attended, compared with twice that number at the first. The audience was more restrained and to some extent seemed to be merely going through the motions. Rubin again opened the proceedings and was followed by representatives of various organizations. One new note was the appearance of speakers in favor of a Couzens expressway. These included the president of the Federated and the president of the Maloney Park Civic Association, as well as representatives of the Automobile Club of Michigan, the Michigan Society of Professional Engineers, and the Carpenters' District Council. Kohl had his say again. In two hours it was all over.

Kohl was not ready to give up. The council vote still had to be taken on Tuesday, and he and his supporters proceeded to organize another letter-writing and telephone campaign. By Monday morning, letters were again flowing into City Hall. Councilwoman Mary Beck permitted Rubin to examine the letters addressed to her; Rubin discovered that many of them appeared to have been signed by the same hand but with different names and addresses. This discovery impressed both Rubin and Miss Beck, but the newspapers, when informed about this, did not consider it very extraordinary. Miss Beck reported her discovery of apparently forged letters on a television interview program that night. The next day indignant members of the implicated civic associations accepted

Miss Beck's offer to show the letters to anyone who doubted her statements. Upon examining the letters, they conceded that some apparently had been signed by one person, but they contended that a call to the person whose name had been signed would reveal an opponent of the expressway. The incident of the "forged letters" had comic-opera overtones—nerves had become frazzled by the Couzens affair.

On Tuesday, March 3, 1959, the council, by a seven-to-two vote, approved the cantilever depressed expressway design for James Couzens Highway. Councilman William Rogell voted against the design because he preferred the rolling-grade design. Councilman Del Smith, who cast the other negative vote, thought that a simple widening would solve the problem. He was the only councilman to adopt the view that Kohl had been pressing. (It may have been that Smith felt politically less secure than his colleagues: of the nine successful candidates, he had polled the least number of votes in the last election, and it had taken a recount to establish his victory.) Mackie hailed the decision with the statement: "Now that the council has shown political courage and overcome stiff neighborhood pressures, we will get the job rolling." He politely ignored mention of the fact that the council had exceeded the March 2 deadline, which he had set during the previous November, by only one day. Within a week, the State Highway Department survey crews were aiming their transits down James Couzens Highway's tree-lined center mall.

Aftermath. On March 27, 1959, John R. Kohl, chairman of the Northwest Inter-Organizational Board, sent the following letter to the members:

The purpose of this letter is twofold.

The first is to thank you and the members of your organization for the many hours and the many other ways in which you helped the Northwest Inter-Organizational Board on the James Couzens Highway issue; and while at the present time it appears that we have lost our cause, I want to relay to all of you that the information I have received indicates that through our unity of action we waged one of the finest uphill fights last September in connection with the double-deck proposal that has ever been waged against such staggering odds within the city. We were almost as successful in February despite even greater odds. So again let me thank you most sincerely for your cooperation and support.

Now as to the second purpose of the letter, and this is one which I had hoped would not have to be included. During the last month of our fight, due to the unexpected sudden speed-up on the part of the state and council, our plans had to be changed as we worked of necessity, almost on a day-to-day basis.

There was little time in which to contact each organization in our board for individual approval of funds expended. Nonetheless, all moneys spent were entirely in good faith and the undersigned personally approved all such expenditures. Although the money was not in our possession at the time, it was believed we could readily raise it.

We now find a total of almost $750 in outstanding bills that still must be paid and I respectfully ask that your organization or institution make a request to the proper officials to voluntarily contribute $50 or such other amount as you may deem advisable so that we may liquidate this indebtedness as soon as possible.

I might add that our total expenditures from last summer have amounted to just under $10,000, of which the larger portion has gone for postage, a full-page newspaper ad, printing and envelopes, and during the last phase of the fight, a public-relations man. Otherwise, there were no fees paid to any individual for personal services. Thus, it would appear that a $50 assessment per organization would seem a very nominal amount, and I sincerely trust that your organization or institution will approve this expenditure.

Again thanks very much.

Concluding Comments

The approval of a design for the extension of the Lodge Expressway along James Couzens Highway was a major accomplishment for the State Highway Department. In terms of a metropolitan expressway system, it meant that a north-south expressway route was now available from the center of downtown Detroit to the northern city boundary. With this route assured, it was now possible to construct expressways north of Detroit linking suburban areas with the core city. If the Grand River Expressway project should bog down over route selection, the Lodge, extended along Couzens and Northwestern, would provide some expressway service to the populous suburban northwest area. This would furnish more time for resolving the anticipated problems involved in the Grand River project.

The Couzens controversy had accomplished some additional results for Mackie, Rubin, and the State Highway Department. It had demonstrated that Mackie was taking seriously his promise to construct a metropolitan expressway system; that the State Highway Department was no longer to be considered as primarily concerned with rural roads; that expressways were state trunklines and, therefore, the responsibility of the State Highway Department; and that the department intended to play a major role in decision-making concerning expressways as well as in financing them.

Mackie and Rubin learned some lessons from the Couzens experience. The strategy of a tripartite contract that included a number of projects, or package, had paid off. By including projects that Detroit had wanted very much, it had been possible to obtain a commitment for an expressway on Couzens, something city officials would have preferred to have postponed. By moving immediately on the Couzens project, Mackie was in a position to bring the maximum pressure to bear upon city officials with the argument that delay on Couzens would delay work on the other projects which were less objectionable from the city's point of view. This strategy, too, had paid off. Mackie's threats to withdraw funds from the metropolitan area for use elsewhere could not be ignored, and the council exceeded by only one day the time limit that Mackie had given them to come up with a decision. That the councilmen felt committed by the contract to approve some form of expressway on Couzens was evidenced by their responses during the November interviews and by their behavior. The months of negotiation that had gone into the tripartite contract had not been wasted.

But the contract strategy had not proved successful in every respect. Although the council had felt bound by the commitment to approve an expressway, they refused to remain bound by the twenty-one-day limit in which to consider particular routes and designs. Even though this placed them in the position of sole responsibility for delaying a project, they demonstrated that they were willing to accept this in return for more time to "deliberate." Mackie wisely conceded to these time extensions. Rubin, who had worked hard on the time-limit clause as a device for forestalling delays on the part of the council, was especially exasperated to see this technique fail. Both Rubin and Mackie learned that the council's reaction to too much pushing was stubborn refusal to move at all.

Even though the cantilever depressed design approved by the council would provide the expressway treatment the state had demanded for the anticipated traffic volumes, the defeat of the double-deck plan was an especially bitter pill for Irving Rubin. Some of the traffic engineers had been cool to this plan, but to Rubin it was the ideal answer to a sticky problem. It would preserve the unique characteristics of Couzens, even to the extent of the landscaped center margin; it would not require land acquisition, which he knew city officials wanted to avoid; and it could be built without too much disruption of a major traffic route, an advantage which would be seen and appreciated by motorists. In fact, the state was willing to pay the extra $5,000,000 that the double-deck plan would cost in order to obtain these values. With Yamasaki's sketches and models to demonstrate the aesthetic qualities of the project, Rubin though he had both the rational plan and the materials for selling it. Looking back over the events, Rubin concluded that his mistake had been in originally presenting only one plan, the double-deck. If he had approached the council with two or more plans, so designed that the virtues of the double-deck were obvious, he speculated, he might have had better success with the double-deck. Or he might have used as his first plan one that would not have been acceptable or that would have absorbed all the controversy before presenting the double-deck as the alternative. Rubin did not consider the defeat of the double-deck the result of any flaw in the plan itself, but rather the result of faulty tactics in presenting it.

For Mackie and Rubin this was their first full exposure to Detroit–Wayne County politics. Knowing that the majority of the councilmen were Democrats, they anticipated enthusiastic support for an expressway program aimed at serving the metropolitan area. But they were to learn that party affiliation had little or nothing to do with their relations with the councilmen on the Couzens issue. Their steadfast support came from the two women on the council, one a Republican and the other a Democrat.

The relevant politics concerning the Couzens issue arose from the factors involved in the substantive issue itself and how one felt about those factors. Party affiliation had no relationship to these variables, and therefore Mackie and Rubin could not use it to win support. The situation was nevertheless a political one, typical of politics in non-partisan Detroit, where the various values involved in substantive issues give rise to odd (from a partisan standpoint) groupings capable of exercising influence over the resulting decision-making. This was evident here. Detroit's three major daily newspapers either supported Mackie on the Couzens issue or else refrained from actively opposing him. Although they claim independence, it is rare, indeed, to find any of these papers (one of which, the *Detroit Times,* was purchased by *The Detroit News* in 1960) supporting a Democratic candidate or office-holder. Their support or non-involvement in the Couzens project could not be traced to partisan affection for Mackie. Nor were business interests opposed to the expressway. Not only would Hudson's Northland Shopping Center on the north end of Couzens become more accessible to Detroiters as the result of the Couzens Expressway, but also the downtown retail stores would become more accessible to suburbanites. The usual spokesmen for business interests, quick to oppose public expenditures that might result in higher taxes or a decrease in local tax revenue, were silent on the Couzens issue. Their silence did not hurt Mackie's cause, but it taught him some lessons about the complexities of urban politics.

The Couzens extension forced the council to decide on an issue that was, for them, extraordinarily difficult because the factors involved contained a number of unknowns, and the future of core cities may depend upon these unknowns. For some of the councilmen, the basic issue was the economic effect of a Couzens expressway. They were concerned not only with the loss of tax revenue due to the possible devaluation of property along the route, but also with the long-run effect of making the suburbs more accessible to those who work in the core city. "Why speed the exodus from the city of the middle- and upper-income families?" one of them asked in private. Particularly, he added, "Why do it at the expense of an already existing middle- and upper-income neighborhood in the city?" On the other hand, the councilmen conceded in the interviews that the data supplied to them by the various traffic studies did prove the need for an expressway on Couzens. In a sense, approval of the tripartite contract permitted the councilmen to have their cake and eat it. They approved a package expressway system but at the same time withheld the final approval of any particular route or design. When Rubin presented them with the double-deck plan for Couzens, they could not longer avoid the necessity of making a decision.

The November interviews made it clear that the council defeated the double-deck plan because of the neighborhood pressure organized against it. The interviews also showed that the councilmen were convinced that they would eventually have to approve some type of expressway for Couzens. Many of the councilmen were irritated by the tactics of both Rubin and Mackie, who, they felt, were pushing too hard for an early decision. Besides, they were not accustomed to having the state highway commissioner and his personal representative take such a direct interest in Detroit expressway decision-making. Caught between their own indecision and the pressures from the state highway people and from the neighborhood, the council welcomed the respite provided by the decision to postpone action while the Plan Commission met with neighborhood groups. This decision also provided time for some of the neighborhood opposition to die down. When the Plan Commission eventually reported a poll of civic groups with a majority favoring the cantilever plan, the council was provided with a rationalization for the decision which they had known for some time they would have to make. To the administrator eager to build highways, this delay was annoying and frustrating, but to the councilmen it was a necessary stage in the local decision-making process.

It is interesting to note the response of the councilmen when they were interviewed in November to the question: "In the long run, do you think the city will gain or lose by the development of expressways?" Seven said the city would gain, and two said that the city would lose. The two who said the city would lose were Rogell and Smith, the same two who voted against the depressed cantilever plan. The majority's response to this question is perhaps the best explanation of the council's final decision.

The key factor in the decision to build the depressed type of expressway was neighborhood opposition. If this opposition had not been so successfully organized at the time of the first public hearing in August 1958 and sustained until the council rejected the double-deck plan, the chances are good that the council would have approved the double-deck within the twenty-one-day period established by the contract. If defeat of the double-deck per se was the goal of the leaders of the neighborhood opposition, then their campaign could be rated a success; but this obviously was not their goal. The one neighborhood leader who did publicly take such a position, Haviland Reves, was deposed. If this is the case, then what precisely did the neighborhood opposition accomplish?

The most that Kohl's neighborhood opposition could claim toward their no-expressway goal was a six-month delay in the approval of an expressway design. By adopting the tactic that no expressway treatment whatever would be considered or debated, the organizations in the Couzens area placed the ultimate decision for the type of design in the hands of civic associations outside the immediate Couzens area. Thus the organizations in the Couzens area that stuck to their no-expressway guns never did function, at least publicly, to assess the values of the double-deck vs. the depressed design. What this opposition did accomplish was the effective elimination from rational, objective consideration of the double-deck plan. By the time the Plan Commission was sent to discuss alternative plans with neighborhood groups, the double-deck plan had already been turned down by the council and had become too controversial for serious consideration. The civic organizations which voted for the cantilever depressed plan could justify their choice on the ground that since the council had made it clear that some expressway treatment would be approved, and since the double-deck plan had aroused so much controversy among the Couzens-area organizations, approval of the depressed plan was a concession to those organizations holding out for no expressway.

Thus the vulnerability of Kohl's all-or-nothing strategy was that it left him and his supporters in the Northwest Inter-Organizational Board with no place to which to retreat. A no-compromise position was impossible to maintain through the frail organizational structure created by a coalition of neighborhood civic organizations, many of which, after winning the battle of the double-deck, began to lose interest in the whole controversy. As time wore on,

Kohl and his supporters could be pictured as unreasonable because they would not accept any compromise. It would have taken an extraordinary amount of organizational energy to hold together over time a large number of civic organizations committeed to a no-compromise policy on an issue which they did not feel would affect them directly. A hard-nosed bitter-end struggle requires stronger motivation than that displayed by the board's member associations outside the immediate Couzens area.

If the double-deck plan were, in fact, the best treatment for Couzens for the various reasons given when the tripartite Administrative Committee initially proposed it to the council, then it can be maintained that the effect of the neighborhood opposition was to bring about a decision in favor of an expressway design that was not the most desirable for either the neighborhood or the city. This was the conclusion reached by one of the most substantial property holders along James Couzens, Malcolm Leventen. Once convinced that some form of expressway would be approved, Leventen wanted to come out in favor of the double-deck treatment. As an architect, engineer, and general contractor who had been responsible for many of the attractive buildings that lined the highway, Leventen had the professional qualifications to evaluate the alternative plans and choose between them with an eye to the consequences of his choice upon his investments along the highway. He prepared a statement for presentation to the council, which included the following paragraph:

> I have taken the time to examine carefully the model which was built by Mr. Yamasaki, and the drawings which he had made showing the different possibilities of architectural treatment. I have been impressed by them. From my standpoint as an architect, an engineer, a builder, a resident of Detroit, and an owner of property on James Couzens, I urge the council to approve the double-deck plan. If the fully depressed plan is built and the double-deck junked, I feel that Detroit will have missed an opportunity to pioneer in a new type of highway construction. I sincerely believe that if the double-deck plan is constructed, James Couzens Highway will become the most famous street in the world, and property values on the street will rise substantially.

Leventen never did deliver his statement to the council, nor did he tender his drafted resignation from the executive committee of the James Couzens Business and Professional Men's Association. He decided to go along with the majority of his fellow businessmen. It is impossible to say what effect, if any, his open support of the double-deck plan would have had upon the decisions that mere made, but his silence is testimony to the extent to which Kohl and his supporters had succeeded in discouraging deviation from the no-expressway position even among substantial businessmen in the area.

Presumably, the public interest is best served when the decision-making process includes procedures whereby interested parties can be heard. From the point of view of a state-wide expressway system, a three-and-one-half-mile segment in Detroit is a small bit of a larger whole, and from the point of view of a Detroit expressway system, the interests of abutting owners are but a small part of the larger interests of the community as a whole. Should the smaller parts have an effective veto over the larger system's development? If not a veto power, certainly most would agree that the smaller segments of larger systems should have an opportunity to condition decisions affecting them, or to make known their preferences among sets of alternatives. Here, a number of mechanisms were employed to get at opinions of various groups: the post-card opinion poll of motorists on James Couzens; the public hearings before the council; and the Plan Commission's meetings with neighborhood groups. To what extent the hearing process functions as a therapeutic device for reducing local tensions created by any decision destined to upset the status quo and to what extent it functions to provide substantive guidance for the ultimate decision is difficult to determine, but that both functions are involved is evident in this case.

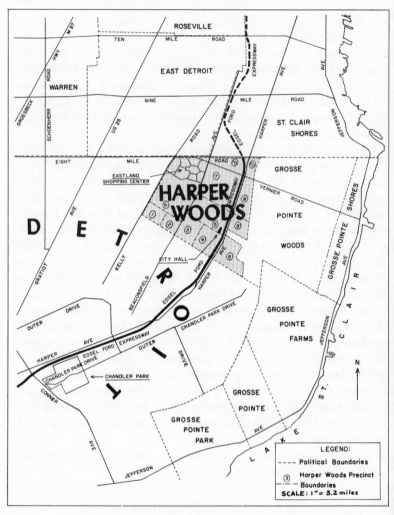

5. Harper Woods and Northeast Detroit Environs

Courtesy Graphic Arts Section, State University of Iowa
Adapted from AAA map

8
Harper Woods Versus the Ford Expressway

Crashing Suburban Gates

Introduction

To most people an expressway means progress, convenience, quicker access to work, perhaps more leisure time. But to a few people the coming of an expressway means demolition and loss of homes, business difficulties, inconvenience, and other unwelcome dislocations. To residents and property owners in and along the route of a proposed expressway, whether in the central city or a suburb, "progress" presents them with two courses of action. They may accept the plan to build an expressway and in so doing abandon their homes, businesses, and property; or they may protest against the proposed construction and attempt to alter their fate through political action. This case relates the trials and tribulations that the Detroit suburb of Harper Woods experienced as it found itself at the proposed eastern terminus of Detroit's major west-east expressway, the Edsel B. Ford, part of U.S. Interstate 94.

Like all routes designated "U.S." in the state of Michigan, the Ford Expressway was classified as a state trunkline. Under a 1944 tripartite agreement between the State Highway Department, the Wayne County Road Commission, and the city of Detroit, the State Highway Department was responsible for plans, specifications, and direct supervision of construction within the city of Detroit. All plans had to receive the approval of the County Road Commission (which had maintenance responsibilities for state trunklines) and the city of Detroit. By state statute the State Highway Department had to obtain the consent of the city's governing body before locating a new state trunkline within a home rule city.

*This case, in somewhat revised form, will appear in the Inter-University Case Program series.

A major item involved in local consent, and one frequently the subject of much intergovernmental negotiation, was the precise route of the trunkline.

On Detroit's northeastern boundary lay Gratiot Township. Since it was not an incorporated home rule city in 1944, its consent on route location was not required. Nevertheless, it was made a party and signatory to a tripartite agreement with the state and county that called for the expressway to be located approximately between Harper and Beaconsfield Avenues within the township (see map). Thus the township left a legacy of formal acceptance of the expressway when it incorporated as the home rule city of Harper Woods in 1951.

Harper Woods was and is predominantly a residential or dormitory suburb. The bulk of the residential structures in Harper Woods are one-story, ranch-style brick homes. Lot sizes range as high as 100 feet by 150 feet in the central part of the city, but the standard lot size is 50 feet by 100 feet. The median home value for Harper Woods according to the 1950 census was $9,393, slightly above the $8,966 median for the Detroit Standard Metropolitan Area. Similarly, average family income, according to 1957 locally estimated figures, was $7,800, compared with $7,100 for the Standard Metropolitan Area. Economically and socially, Harper Woods is on a plane with the adjoining suburbs to the north in Macomb County; it stands in marked contrast to the wealth and status of the nearby Grosse Pointe communities.

Harper Woods' population boom started in the late 1940's and reached its peak in the early 1950's. Its 1950 population was 9,148, compared with 858 in 1940. By 1955 Harper Woods' population was estimated at 17,000 by the Detroit Metropolitan Area Regional Planning Commission. The 1960 census counted 19,995 residents. Clearly the largest influx of new residents came during the time when the expressway controversy was at its peak, 1951–1955. Nonetheless, the influx in the years just preceding the controversy had been sufficiently large to overload the minimal services which the township was able to provide.

The biggest problems were roads and drains. Since none of the residential streets were paved, heavy rains turned some streets into quagmires and occasionally caused the open-ditch drain that traversed the community to overflow. Since under Michigan law roads and streets in unincorporated areas were under county juris-diction, the township could do little to improve its streets or pro-vide drainage for water run-off coming from the many new homes and other impervious surfaces in the community. The road and drainage situation became a major plank in the campaign for in-corporation waged by the Civic Action League (CAL), a political faction composed largely of newer township residents who wanted to get the area out of "the dust and mud of township government."

The CAL found another argument for incorporation in the sum-mer of 1950, when The J. L. Hudson Company, Detroit's largest downtown department store, announced its intention to build a multimillion-dollar regional shopping facility to be known as East-land Shopping Center on a 110-acre tract of land in the northwest part of the township. This commercial facility would provide the proposed city with an excellent tax base, and the CAL came out strongly in favor of Hudson's proposed venture.

Another aim of the CAL's drive for incorporation, more im-plicit than explicit, was to oust the "ins" who had long been in control of the township government. The "ins" were Democrats, whose organizational strength via the Gratiot Township (later Harper Woods) Democratic Club had been built on fertile ground. The bulk of the early residents who moved to Gratiot Township in the late 1930's and early 1940's were of blue-collar occupational status. There was also a goodly portion of blue-collar workers in the waves of new residents coming into the community in the late 1940's and early 1950's. The majority of these residents belonged to national minority groups and to labor unions, both of which were traditionally Democratic. With the exception of Dwight D. Eisenhower in 1956, no Republican national or state candidates have carried Harper Woods.

Responding to the CAL challenge, the Democrats contended that incorporation was premature and looked with a skeptical eye at the prospect of a major politico-economic force such as Hud-son's proposed shopping center intruding onto the local political scene. They claimed that the Civic Action League was an attempt by Republicans to take over township (and later city) affairs through a front group. Lawrence Gettlinger, president of the Democratic Club and an administrative assistant to United Auto Workers President Walter Reuther, went so far as to say that the CAL was "merely an auxiliary of the Republican Party" (*Harper Woods Herald,* October 17, 1951). Gettlinger's flat statement did not appear to be soundly based. The two prominent leaders of the CAL, L. Edwin Wenger and Joseph Grossel, were not officially tied to or active in the Republican party. This situation appeared to be the case with most of the rank and file members of the CAL, although two active CAL members were also active Republicans.

In spite of organized Democratic opposition, the CAL won its campaign for incorporation, but only by a slim margin, in February 1951. The Charter Commission, elected at the same time, had a Democratic majority, so that the charter drawn up was a compromise. It provided for a seven-member council elected at large on a partisan basis. Four councilmen were to be elected every two years, with the lowest vote-getter of the four serving a two-year term while the remaining three served for four years. The mayor was elected by the council from its own membership. There were no popularly elected administrative officers, boards, or commissions. Township employees were "blanketed in" under a civil service system established by the charter—a provision opposed by the CAL minority on the commission because of the large number of alleged Democrats employed by the township. Democratic commission members objected on principle to the council-manager form of government tacitly supported by the CAL, but they acceded to a provision permitting (but not requiring) appointment of a city manager. Despite the hybrid form of the charter and lack of all-out support from the Democratic Club, a favorable vote on the charter in October 1951 brought the city of Harper Woods into official existence.

Election of the first council at the same time as the vote on the charter stirred further controversy between the Democratic Club and the CAL. The CAL won four seats and the Democrats three. The CAL representatives were L. Edwin Wenger, founder and president of the CAL and an attorney with offices in Harper Woods and in downtown Detroit; Joseph Grossel, secretary of the CAL and co-owner of a small tool company in Warren, Michigan; Thomas Grula, a salesman for a marine motors firm; and Henry

Johnson, an employee of a Detroit brewery. The three Democratic Club councilmen were Harold Broquet, Harry Garman, and Mrs. Margaret Chalou, all of whom had been active but non-office-holding Democrats. Broquet was a maintenance supervisor for the Detroit Board of Education and wrote a column on local political affairs for a Harper Woods newspaper; Garman was a local insurance agent; and Mrs. Chalou was a housewife who later organized and became the first president of the Harper Woods Women's Democratic Club.

The four-member CAL majority elected Wenger as mayor, and guided by his firm hand and outspoken opinions, the majority acted with dispatch to remove all former township employees not covered by civil service and to enact an ordinance creating the position of city manager. Both measures were taken despite heated protests from the Democratic Club. A few months later the CAL-controlled council precipitated another fight with the Democrats when it proposed a charter amendment abolishing partisan council elections. The voters settled this issue at the November 1952 elections when they adopted the amendment, and Harper Woods officially had non-partisan elections.

The deep political division within the new city was both illustrated and sharpened by the active partisanship of the city's two weekly newspapers, the *Community News* and the *Harper Woods Herald*. The *News,* whose circulation was about half that of its competitor, supported the CAL and opposed the Democratic Club at every turn. The *Herald,* which printed Broquet's column and had held the city's advertising contract from township days, expounded Democratic Club views. Both the *Herald* and the *News* gave extensive coverage to conflict situations on the local scene; both were examples of "accurate" journalism in that their columns reflected the tension, excitement, and emotion gripping the community as the controversies over incorporation, drainage, and Eastland came to the fore.

The expressway issue, dropping as it did into an already overheated political atmosphere, accentuated the deep cleavages within the community. Harper Woods' four-year struggle opened early in 1952 and closed at the end of 1955. Before the last skirmish had been fought, the expressway issue had become tightly interwoven with the other highly controversial issues facing the new city as it sought to adjust to the demands placed on it by the metropolis.

The Expressway Approaches Harper Woods

Harper Woods Objects. By 1951 the route which the express-way would take through the city of Detroit had been decided, except for the last lap of its eastward journey. A decision on this part of the expressway through Detroit was in the offing as the Detroit Common Council met in January 1952.

The State Highway Department had outlined four alternative routes from the intersection of Harper and Conner Avenues to Detroit's eastern limits: (1) angling to the north so as to join and follow Kelly Road into the suburbs, (2) angling less sharply to the north so as to meet Beaconsfield Avenue and follow that street out of the city, (3) continuing to follow Harper Avenue to De-troit's eastern limits and presumably through the suburbs, and (4) following Chandler Park Drive and Outer Drive to the east-ern limits where the expressway would bend north and follow approximately the Grosse Pointe Woods–Harper Woods joint boundary line. These were general route designations running roughly parallel to, and possibly in the right-of-way of, the streets mentioned.

The Highway Department made clear its strong preference for the Harper Avenue route. The Detroit Common Council least preferred the Kelly Road and Chandler Park Drive routes. The former was undesirable because the expressway would remain in Detroit for a greater distance and would create problems of access to schools located along Kelly Road. The latter route was dis-tasteful because the expressway would bisect a large city park and also cut a swath through the finest residential area on the east side. Residents and local businessmen opposed all four alternatives and proposed a fifth route which called for heading the expressway due north from the Harper-Conner intersection to follow Schoenherr Road and link with Groesbeck Highway (M-97), an already estab-lished trunkline route to Mount Clemens and Port Huron, the expressway's ultimate destination. It was at this juncture that Harper Woods intervened.

In January 1952, Harper Woods' Mayor Wenger wrote to the Detroit Common Council in support of the M-97 route, one that would avoid Harper Woods completely. He also forwarded a resolution of the Harper Woods City Council that favored the M-97 route and opposed the Beaconsfield, Harper, and Chandler Park Drive routes. No mention was made of the route along Kelly Road, which was the western boundary of Harper Woods. The State Highway Department quickly rejected the M-97 route on the ground that this area was adequately served by Gratiot Avenue (U.S. 25). It urged Detroit to select the Harper route to best serve population concentrations and eliminate traffic bottlenecks that existed along Harper Avenue in Detroit's suburban environs.

Harper Avenue in Harper Woods, as in Detroit, was commercially developed. The predominantly small, one-story business structures were concentrated on the east side of the four-lane avenue and housed a great variety of locally-owned commercial uses, including drive-in restaurants, grocery stores, drug stores, bars, and gas stations. Harper Woods would not welcome the loss of some of its most valuable commercial property. On April 8, at Wenger's urging, the Harper Woods Council unanimously passed the following resolution:

> Resolved: That this resolution be adopted and sent to the Common Council of Detroit that Harper Woods is against having the Edsel Ford Expressway come through the city of Harper Woods and will not consent to it.

Wenger forwarded the resolution along with a letter to Charles M. Ziegler, the state highway commissioner. The letter read in part:

> . . . you are giving notice that you will have your way on the expressway route regardless of the hardships of the residents and businessmen of the Harper area.

> Since you are taking such an arbitrary stand on this expressway matter, you may expect an arbitrary stand to be taken by the people of Harper Woods when you bring the highway through the city, cutting it in half. Plans are being made in cooperation with east-side Detroit organizations to contest this matter in the courts.

Above and beyond his letter, Wenger threatened to sue the Highway Department and started a campaign to get signatures on petitions opposing the Harper route. On April 28 the Harper

Woods City Council officially "RESOLVED, that the council of the city of Harper Woods does hereby refuse to consent to any limited-access highway anywhere within the limits of Harper Woods." Copies of the resolution were forwarded to the State Highway Department and the cities of Detroit, St. Clair Shores, and East Detroit.

The Detroit Common Council was reluctant to settle with finality on the Harper or Beaconsfield routes, fearing that Harper Woods, by refusing to grant permission to extend the expressway through its jurisdiction, would force the expressway to dead-end at Detroit's eastern limits. This fear was short-lived, however, for the Detroit corporation counsel assured the Common Council that Harper Woods could not legally block the state from putting an expressway on Harper Avenue. In addition, Glenn Richards, Detroit's expressway co-ordinator and Department of Public Works commissioner, assured the council that no condemnation of private properties in Detroit along the Harper route would occur until Harper Woods' opposition was settled either in or out of court. Richards noted that since Harper Avenue was a county road and under the jurisdiction of the Wayne County Road Commission, the county—or the state, with the county's permission—could widen it or convert it to an expressway at the county's discretion. The long-standing cooperation and mutuality of interests between the State Highway Department and the Wayne County Road Commission virtually assured the Road Commission's support of the state agency in this matter. Its fears allayed, on April 29 the Detroit Common Council acted to eliminate the Kelly Road and Chandler Park Drive routes from further consideration. This narrowed the final choice, which the council did not make until nearly a year later, to either the Harper or the Beaconsfield route. Either one would put the expressway directly through Harper Woods.

So far as Harper Woods was concerned, Detroit had made up its mind. In five or six years, the Edsel Ford Expressway would be at Harper Woods' doorstep somewhere in the vicinity of Harper or Beaconsfield Avenues.

A Change of Heart. On May 20 state highway personnel, accompanied by Wayne County and Detroit highway administrators, met with Harper Woods officials. The chief engineer of the State

Highway Department presented alternative routes that the expressway might take through Harper Woods. There was still enough "play" in the lead end of the expressway route within Detroit's city limits for Harper Woods to set the route almost anywhere between Kelly Road and the city's eastern boundary.

In presenting alternative routes, state highway officials made two things clear. First, for Harper Woods the question was not whether there would be an expressway but rather where the expressway was to be located. On this point the state was prepared to recognize local preferences. Second, the state preferred a route closely following or in the Harper Avenue right-of-way. The state officials warned that the results of unyielding opposition by Harper Woods might be disastrous. Harper Woods' streets would be saturated with vehicles streaming off the expressway if it terminated at Harper Woods' southern limits. Furthermore, the state might make Harper Avenue into a limited-access surface highway even without the consent of the city. This would create great obstacles to the free movement of local traffic, police and fire vehicles, school children, etc., within the city and probably cause a severe drop in the value of commercial property along Harper. State and county personnel emphasized that this latter course of action could be imposed over any local opposition since Harper Avenue was a county road and completely subject to that jurisdiction's plans for it. The Wayne County Road Commission had already certified its willingness to permit the State Highway Department to convert Harper Avenue into such a highway.

No action was taken by the Harper Woods Council as a result of this May meeting, but further discussions were scheduled. Two more meetings followed, and on one occasion Wenger, Grossel, and Garman journeyed to Lansing to talk with state personnel there. One result of these meetings was to convince Wenger that Harper Woods could not avoid the expressway, that its coming was only a matter of time, and that good strategy dictated bargaining for the least offensive route possible. This changed attitude toward the expressway was shared and supported by the three other CAL councilmen and, lukewarmly, by Councilman Harold Broquet. Councilman Garman and Councilwoman Chalou were reluctant to capitulate to the state so soon.

Over the summer months, Mayor Wenger, hoping to find a

basis for compromise and rapid settlement of the issue, made a flurry of counterproposals to the State Highway Department. The unsettled situation on the location of the expressway was reportedly holding up proposed business construction and stifling the construction and sale of homes.

Late in June, Wenger proposed a plan for an elevated expressway along Harper. He believed that this would result in savings in construction cost, in fewer business properties being taken, and in reduced drainage problems. The Highway Department promised a report in July. When no report was forthcoming Wenger asked for another conference with state highway personnel. At this meeting, held in August, Wenger suggested a surface route along Harper Avenue with low retaining walls, service drives, and underpasses at major cross streets. Speaking for Detroit at this meeting, Glenn Richards stated that Detroit had no objection to a surface extension provided that it was a limited-access one. Highway Department personnel said that this plan was possible and promised details on it in four or five weeks. Wenger emphasized the necessity for settling the question immediately but stipulated that he would need time for the council to act on the route and to hold a public hearing on the question. The state did not respond until October, when they asked for a meeting with the Harper Woods Council.

The reasons for the state's delay on Wenger's proposals were never clear. One might have been the feeling of state highway personnel that the passage of time served to strengthen their bargaining position since the unsettled situation worked to Harper Wood's disadvantage. A second reason for the state's cautious approach may have been its desire not to overcommit itself. Pressing Harper Woods for a quick settlement might mean that the route selected would not conveniently connect with the route finally settled upon by Detroit. Although the Detroit Common Council had narrowed its choices to Beaconsfield or Harper, it might still reverse itself. The state would then be in the embarrassing position of having an approved route on Harper Avenue through Harper Woods but without an expressway to put there. Still a third reason may have been the reportedly slow, inept, or inefficient procedures by which the State Highway Department functioned at this time. Finally, it was rumored locally that the Highway Department did not want to force an unpopular route on Harper Woods or on any other locality until State Highway Commissioner Ziegler had been re-elected in the 1953 spring elections.

At the October meeting the differences between the state and the Harper Woods City Council—its controlling majority at least —were narrowed considerably as to both type of expressway and its route. Wenger's proposals led state personnel to assume that local consensus had been established on a route that would follow the Harper Avenue right-of-way. The state proposed a semi-depressed or "roller-coaster" expressway for this route. The roadbed would be depressed under crossovers at major intersections but would rise to surface level between the crossovers. This would permit some narrowing of the right-of-way and the saving of some residential and business properties from condemnation.

Nevertheless, some residential and business properties along the existing right-of-way of Harper would have to be condemned and demolished. The question was, which ones? On this point the state offered four alternatives: (1) take property only on the east side of Harper; (2) take property only on the west side of Harper; (3) take approximately the same amount of property on both sides of Harper; and (4) take property on the east side of Harper up to the City Hall and property on the west side of Harper north of the City Hall. CAL councilmen indicated that they were receptive to the "roller-coaster" idea and promised to study the four alternatives for taking property along Harper. Democratic council members were either noncommittal or expressed moderate protests against the whole idea of an expressway. Near the end of the meeting a state highway official mentioned that the state was still open to a discussion of the Beaconsfield route. The CAL councilmen strongly protested against any route requiring the demolition of a large number of homes. The Beaconsfield route would require the taking of approximately 450 residences, many of them less than five years old.

By November the CAL majority had narrowed its choices down to alternatives (2) and (4), the two alternatives which did the least damage to the more commercially developed side of Harper, the east side. Even Democratic members appeared to have "come around" on the expressway. The minutes of the November 6 council meeting noted: "Garman stated that he felt it was useless to fight the highway through Harper Woods. The other councilmen, except Chalou, felt that if the highway is to come, Harper Avenue is best." The council set November 26 as the date for a public hearing on the expressway route.

The Public Hearing. As the council's choice narrowed to Harper Avenue, complaints and protests grew among the businessmen and property owners along the avenue. The council's call for a public hearing stirred the Harper Avenue constituency to organize and to act. A moving force in organizing the Harper Avenue group was Anthony Vermeulen, partner in a large Detroit law firm and an owner of property on Harper. The group incorporated as the Harper Woods Residents and Taxpayers Association. Reginald Rivard, who was also active in the Democratic Club, served as secretary of the association. The association circulated petitions against the expressway and in a short time had nine hundred signatures. The petitions were presented to the council on the night of the public hearing. About five hundred persons attended the hearing. Numerous strong and lengthy protests against the expressway dominated the meeting, which lasted from 8:00 P.M. to 1:00 A.M. The minutes of the hearing record that "of all the people present only one person wanted the highway."

The protests of the expressway opponents fell into two general categories. First were the protests against an expressway per se. An expressway was a question mark or just a "big ditch" to many Harper Woods residents. Its primary and secondary effects on the small suburb or on cities generally were unclear at best, and it was easy to imagine the worst possible consequences. Some expressway opponents charged that an expressway dividing the city would give the community "civic schizophrenia," complicate police and fire protection, and generally insulate the shopping, school, and social facilities of one part of the city from the other part. They claimed that since Harper Woods was a home rule city, it could keep the expressway out forever if it wanted to. By withholding consent to the State Highway Department, the city could block that agency from condemning any property for the expressway. A further point of the opposition was that a decision at this time permitting the expressway was premature, since Detroit had not yet acted to set the final route within its limits. It would be six years or more before the expressway was completed in Detroit. This was plenty of time to sit tight and learn more about "The Thing."

The second category of protests was that directed specifically against the Harper route. Opponents pointed to the fact that this route would remove some of the most valuable property in the city from the tax rolls. Various estimates were given of the value of this property, some ranging as high as $12,000,000 market value or about $3,000,000 assessed value. The other anti-Harper argument was directed specifically at alternative (4). Opponents charged that leaving the commercial properties on the east side of Harper on a service drive along the expressway would depreciate the value of these properties and leave establishments there "dying on the vine."

Anti-expressway partisans had dominated the public hearing, and it was evident that feeling was running high on the expressway issue. Nevertheless, at the next council meeting the four CAL councilmen voted, over three negative Democratic votes, to initiate action on an ordinance permitting the state to locate a semi-depressed expressway along Harper Avenue following alternative (4). Wenger explained his (and his supporters') change of heart on the expressway as follows: "I started to lose my determination to fight the project after I learned that because Harper is a county road it could be widened to handle the expressway traffic without our permission." The reaction of the large anti-expressway contingent at the council meeting was noisy and bitter. Shouts of "unfair," "double-cross," and "recall" were numerous. After the tumult and shouting subsided, Wenger explained that the council majority was merely requesting that an ordinance be drawn up permitting the state to make preliminary surveys of the route. The ordinance, Wenger said, would have a clause delaying its effective date until after the spring elections, thus permitting opponents of the expressway plenty of time to petition for a referendum on the ordinance.

The Expressway Opponents Act.   Wenger's strategy went awry. The Residents and Taxpayers Association immediately circulated petitions, but not to force a referendum on the pending ordinance. Instead, the petitions were for a popularly initiated amendment to the city charter. The amendment would require a favorable vote of the people before any limited-access highway could pass through Harper Woods. Signatures equal to 25 percent of the voters at the last municipal election were necessary to initiate the amendment. About six hundred signatures were needed. Over a thousand were quickly obtained.

Meanwhile the CAL majority was preparing to act on the ordinance permitting the expressway. The ordinance was drafted and ready for action at the first council meeting of 1953, held on January 6. At the opening of that meeting Mayor Wenger and the other three CAL members were served with a temporary restraining order from Wayne County Circuit Court preventing them from acting on the proposed ordinance. A bill of complaint had been lodged against the four defendants charging them with "fraudulent, oppressive, and illegal" actions with an intent to "disenfranchise the people of Harper Woods." Behind this move, engineered by the Residents and Taxpayers Association, was the feeling that council action on the proposed ordinance might prejudice and possibly defeat the voters' will as it might be expressed in the vote on the initiated charter amendment.

The CAL defendants decided not to contest the court order chiefly because one of their number, Grossel, had decided not to vote for the ordinance on the ground that action was premature— Detroit had not yet set its route. Given the outburst of protests agains the expressway, the nominal council majority was content to let the issue ride until the forthcoming council election and the vote on the charter amendment. Since two CAL and two Democratic Club councilmen were up for re-election, the council election might provide a mandate for a future course of action on the expressway issue.

The charter amendment ran into snags during the following month when it was submitted to the governor for his approval, as required by Michigan law. Governor Williams vetoed the proposed amendment on the advice of the attorney general, who declared it invalid. His ruling was based on state statutes which provide that a city council must give its consent for a state highway to pass through the city. The amendment, the attorney general advised, would contravene state law by taking this consent power away from the council, the only place it was acknowledged to exist by state law. Despite the position taken by the governor and the attorney general, the Harper Woods City Council, taking advantage of the state law permitting an amendment to be submitted to the voters over the governor's veto by a two-thirds vote of the council, voted unanimously to place it on the ballot at the April election. Although the amendment was subsequently adopted by a vote of 2,213 to 940, its legality was questionable.

While the governor was taking action against the charter amendment, the Detroit Common Council was preparing another blow for the anti-expressway forces. In February it ended nearly three years of indecision by finally and officially designating Harper Avenue as the route the expressway would take to Detroit's eastern limits.

On the other side of the ledger, expressway opponents were cheered by the appearance of a new organization, the Save Our City (SOC) Committee, on the Harper Woods political scene. The SOC Committee was composed largely of Democratic Club members augmented by opponents of the expressway who had no prior political commitment. The SOC–Democratic Club alliance was ideally suited to advance the interests of both organizations. Harper Avenue businessmen would have been reluctant to contribute directly to the Democratic Club for its battle against the expressway. They could contribute to the SOC with no qualms since that group served their interests directly by opposing the expressway. With partisan elections dispensed with, courtesy of the CAL, Democratic Club candidates for council could run as Save Our City candidates in the primary and general election. They would enjoy the organizational support of the Democratic Club and the financing provided via the SOC Committee. If CAL wanted non-partisan elections, the Democratic Club was prepared to make the best of it.

Shortly after its formation in January 1953, the SOC Committee initiated its own publication, the *Save Our City News*, in order to carry its case to the community. The unique feature of this publication was its appearance weekly, from January 28 to

April 1, as a full-page paid advertisement in the *Harper Woods Herald*. It was relatively easy for extra copies of these pages to be run off as campaign literature. The *Save Our City News* was edited by Charles Francis, who was a Democratic Club member and an accountant with Federal Department Stores, a retail firm operating several stores in the Detroit area.

How well the SOC–Democratic Club alliance worked was revealed in the February primary, held because of the one independent running for council. The SOC put up a slate of four candidates. Broquet and Garman ran as incumbent councilmen. The other two SOC candidates were Victor Van Hulle, former Democratic township supervisor, and Martin Hogan, former CAL-appointed city clerk who had left the group because of its stand on the expressway issue and because of Wenger's methods, which Hogan considered high-handed. The CAL slate included the two incumbent councilmen, Grula and Johnson, plus John Boomgaard, an engineer for Chrysler Corporation, and Walter Thome, a Detroit high-school teacher. The primary results showed the strength of the SOC–Democratic alliance: SOC candidates polled between one thousand and twelve hundred votes, while the CAL slate garnered only about six hundred. Anti-expressway feeling was still running high.

Anti-Expressway Forces Move Ahead

The 1953 Election Campaign. The spring election campaign opened with the SOC clearly on the offensive. Its basic strategy was to exploit the expressway issue and anti-expressway sentiment to the fullest extent. While the SOC did not confine its attacks on the CAL to the expressway issue (some editions of the *Save Our City News* ran headlines such as "Reveal Water Bill Gouging" and "The People vs. Machine Rule"), the central argument of the SOC campaign was that the CAL was preparing to bring the expressway through Harper Woods and thereby "sell the city down the river." All of the arguments against the expressway that were lodged at the public hearing got thorough elaboration and skillful embellishment. The *Herald* supported the SOC cause, emphasizing the expressway during pre-election weeks as *the* issue at stake.

The SOC campaign received an assist of questionable value from an outside source three weeks before the election. On March 15 the Wayne County Bureau of Taxation informed Harper Woods officials that it was making an upward revision in assessed valuation on all land in Harper Woods. This upward revision was intended to equalize some of the disparities that existed between valuations of similar properties in different jurisdictions as well as of properties within the same jurisdiction. The county agency cited the example of commercial property along Harper Avenue at Detroit's eastern boundary assessed at $75.00 per front foot, while commercial property only a few feet away but within Harper Woods was assessed at only $20.00 per front foot. The County Bureau of Taxation proposed raising valuations along Harper to $100.00 per front foot as well as increasing other land values throughout the city. Democratic councilmen urged that the city reject the new valuations. Wenger opposed rejection on the grounds that the revised valuations were more equitable and that the net increase in taxes would be only $7.00 or $8.00 a year for the average home owner. Despite Wenger's explanation of the valuation changes, the incident seemed to hurt the CAL and help the SOC. SOC partisans must have received the valuation changes with some misgivings, however. The properties most directly affected by the valuation changes were those along Harper Avenue, the geographical hard core of SOC support.

In view of the primary returns, the CAL faced a formidable uphill fight. The central theme of the CAL campaign was "keep the rascals out." The CAL called attention to the accomplishments of its two-year administration, e.g., no tax increase, paving of streets, and the city-manager plan, but laid greater emphasis on the alleged "evils" of the "old despots," including gross inefficiency; incompetence; favoritism on assessed valuations; misleading the people on the expressway issue; the questionable integrity of SOC candidates; opposition to the Eastland Shopping Center; and opposition to incorporation, public improvements, the city-manager form of government, and "progress" in general. The *Community News,* which was the chief medium by which the CAL carried its case to the people, saw the election campaign as a struggle between the "sincere, honest, capable, self-sacrificing, and conscientious" CAL majority and the SOC "pirate crew." Stressing good government, democracy, public improvements, taxes, and the Hudson project as the "real issues," the *News* mentioned the expressway only as a secondary consideration. The CAL played the expressway issue down, except where some blame could be put on the old administration.

While the Democratic Club had formed a strong alliance locally through the medium of the SOC, the CAL found support from an outside source. On March 10 Deputy State Highway Commissioner George Foster came to Harper Woods to discuss and answer questions about the expressway at a public meeting. Also present were Leroy C. Smith, chief engineer for the Wayne County Road Commission, and Glenn Richards, Detroit Department of Public Works commissioner and expressway co-ordinator. A crowd of nearly one thousand persons jammed the Harper Woods High School gymnasium to hear these three generals of highway decision-making.

Foster, the chief speaker, was quoted by the *Community News* (March 12, 1953) as being blunt and to the point: "The expressway will go through despite any opposition. Neither the Harper Woods Council nor the voters have the legal power to stop or re-route the expressway from Harper Avenue." According to the *News* he commented further that the state did not like or want to use the "big stick" approach; that it preferred to cooperate with local units in locating expressways by mutual agreement; that the Harper route had been selected because the state understood that local officials wanted to save the large number of homes that would be eliminated if the Beaconsfield or some other route were followed. Foster mentioned that the expressway could help Harper Woods to solve its drainage problems. Since the state would need to construct a drainage system and pumping station to remove the storm water from the expressway, and since Harper Woods had under consideration the construction of a city-wide storm drainage system, the city and the state could join in the construction of one system rather than two separate ones, share the costs, and save money for both units.

Foster tossed a mild bombshell into the meeting when he disclosed that the state still considered valid the tripartite agreement of 1944 between the state, Wayne County, and Gratiot Township. There were doubts about the agreement's validity because the area had incorporated since the agreement was signed. Nevertheless, Foster reminded the audience that the state had this "gun behind the door" with which they might be able to cut through the center of the city, taking from four hundred to five hundred relatively new homes. Foster did not mention that a court test would be necessary to determine the validity of the agreement if it were challenged.

The timing of this meeting and the tenor of Foster's remarks were more than mere coincidences. The crucial city election was less than one month away. Foster's assurances that the expressway *will* go through, that the Harper route saves hundreds of homes, and that "local officials have already won many concessions from us," jibed neatly with the CAL campaign to retain its council majority. The *News* capitalized on these assurances. The *Herald*, accusing the *News* of a gross misrepresentation of what was actually said at the meeting, emphasized (1) that state officials admitted that they had to have the consent of a city before they could put an expressway through, (2) that the 1944 agreement was of doubtful validity, and (3) that the state would not force an expressway down a local unit's throat. The expressway issue was in the forefront as the voters went to the polls.

The Save Our City Committee Wins. The SOC slate swept the April 7 election, winning all four council seats. Votes for SOC candidates ranged from 1,700 to 1,850. CAL candidates polled from 1,250 to 1,450. The election of the four SOC members, plus incumbent Mrs. Chalou, gave the anti-expressway forces a five-to-two majority on the council.

For a local election the voter turnout was impressive and underscored the depth of community feeling on the expressway and on the personalities involved. Of the 6,923 registered voters, 3,227, or 46 percent, voted for local council candidates. Only a slightly smaller number, 3,148, voted on the popularly initiated charter amendment, which carried 2,208 to 940. An indication of the level of interest in the local issues was shown by the four hundred fewer votes cast for candidates for state-wide offices than for council candidates. The 46 percent voter turnout was considerably above the 25 percent turnout recorded for the whole of Wayne County at the election.

Anti-expressway sentiment was evident in the vote for state highway commissioner. Despite the substantial "Republicanization" of Harper Woods over the three gubernatorial elections from 1948 to 1952, Republican Charles Ziegler made only a modest gain between 1949 and 1953. Republican gubernatorial candidates had received 32.8 percent of the Harper Woods vote in 1948, 37.1 percent in 1950, and 41.4 percent in 1952. Ziegler received 30.9 percent in 1949 and 35.6 percent in 1953. Furthermore, Ziegler's percentage of the Harper Woods vote was lower than the percentages obtained in Harper Woods by all other Republican candidates for state offices in the 1953 election.

A precinct analysis of the voting at this and other elections permits additional observations (see Table 1).

Table 1

Percentages of the Harper Woods Vote Obtained by Civic Action League and Republican Candidates in 1953 and 1954

Precinct	Civic Action League, 1953	Republican State Highway Commissioner, 1953	Republican Gubernatorial Candidate, 1954
1	39.5	20.7	21.5
2	42.5	23.4	17.7
3	46.8	35.8	26.8
4	47.2	31.4	26.6
5	40.1	43.1	35.4
6	48.3	30.4	27.5
7	42.2	40.2	29.3
8	60.9	49.6	45.8
9	31.1	50.1	46.0
10	29.9	22.5	27.7

CAL candidates ran best in Precinct 8, followed by 6, 4, and 3. Their poorest showings were in Precincts 10 and 9, the northeast section of Harper Woods. This section was traditionally a Democratic stronghold; it was also the section most adversely affected if the expressway followed Harper Avenue.

The northeast area found itself in a peculiar and difficult position. If the expressway followed Harper Avenue, the northeast section would lose its major existing commercial tax base. The meager tax base that would remain would have to support the area's school taxes, which already ranged between twenty-five and thirty mills per $1,000 assessed valuation, as compared with city taxes of between six and fourteen mills. The addition of Eastland Shopping Center to the city's tax rolls would provide no relief to the northeast area's school-tax burden since by a quirk of school-district boundaries set in the early 1920's, the northeast area was included in the Grosse Pointe Community School District. Without Eastland Shopping Center taxes to offset the loss of Harper Avenue commercial taxes, the northeast area stood to be hit hard by the expressway. Had the average northeast-area voter fully grasped the financial impact which the CAL policy would have on the northeast area, the percentage of the vote garnered by the SOC in this area might have been even greater.

One anomaly is State Highway Commissioner Ziegler's comparative strength in Precinct 9 contrasted with the CAL's weakness there. The percentages reveal wide differences in CAL and Republican candidates' voting strength across the precincts. The variations suggest that there is little or no correlation between CAL and Republican voting in the Harper Woods precincts. Democratic charges linking the CAL to the Republican party are not substantiated so far as showing a common electoral base within the community is concerned. These data do not prove conclusively that no relationship existed; they merely indicate that given the available data, no relationship is established.

The expressway issue became the focal point of post-election comments. Harper Woods' new mayor, Harold Broquet, was quoted in *The Detroit News* (April 14, 1953) as saying:

> We don't think we need any expressway out here. The people have given us a mandate and we have five votes that will say no to the expressway every time it comes up. The people want us to fight the expressway and we intend to abide by the will of the people.

In the same news article Wenger was quoted as criticizing the opposition for "waiting for the traffic to be dumped on Harper, putting us in a position to beg the state for assistance." Anonymous comments from the State Highway Department indicated that the state expected to move ahead with plans for an expressway through Harper Woods in spite of the election results. The state was committed to putting an expressway through Harper Woods, and the Harper Woods administration was committed to keeping it out.

The Highway Department Is Rebuffed.   The appeal of the Democratic Club (SOC) in the 1953 election campaign had been mainly negative: it was against the expressway. After winning control of the council, the Democratic council majority discussed positive action on a project that might reinforce its anti-expressway plank. The project was a system of storm drains that would relieve the flooding of basements and roads which occurred with every heavy rainfall.

The new council majority's efforts to move ahead on the storm drainage system were hampered by administrative and financial problems. After the election all CAL-appointed officials, including the city manager, were dismissed, leaving an administrative vacuum. Co-ordinating responsibilities eventually gravitated to the fire chief, who was subsequently designated public works director and finally "city administrator." The Democratic administration was further plagued by a $100,000 deficit left by the CAL (and revealed only after the election). This shortage forced the Democrats to increase property taxes temporarily from six to fourteen mills. The CAL's financial legacy and the loose Democratic administrative structure were handicaps to progress on paving (no streets were paved in 1953), sidewalk construction, and, most importantly, the storm drainage system.

The Harper Woods Council ignored the State Highway Department's proposal to join with Harper Woods in construction of the drainage system in connection with the expressway. In May 1953 the council discussed drain plans with its newly rehired consulting engineer, the George Jerome Company. All alternatives with respect to the storm drainage system were based on the assumption that no expressway would come through the city. In fact, some plans were considered that would put a pumping station for the drainage system directly in the path of the expressway if it came along Harper.

In July 1953 the Highway Department wrote the Harper Woods Council requesting a meeting to discuss both drainage and expressway matters. The letter also asked Harper Woods officials not to consider major public improvements along Harper that would have to be removed or altered if and when an expressway were built there. The latter reference was aimed at both the storm drainage system and a suggestion by the council majority to build a new City Hall. The proposed location for the City Hall was directly abutting Harper Avenue. No meeting resulted from the state's request. The council majority held further discussions on the drain project throughout August with its engineer and with Grosse Pointe Woods. Early in September, the state wrote the council again, this time specifically requesting that Harper Woods delay its plans for the drainage system until state and city officials could confer on both expressway and drain matters. This second request, like the first, fell on deaf ears, and the council continued its discussions on drain plans and methods of financing.

By now the Highway Department was aware that it faced a group of determined and uncompromising local officials. The department sought to buttress its negotiating position as well as its legal case by requesting an opinion from the state attorney general on its jurisdiction over Harper Avenue. An opinion was forthcoming on November 20. It upheld on all points the authority of the Highway Department to "widen, depress, or elevate a limited-access road in the Harper Avenue right-of-way." Local opponents of the expressway contended that this opinion was meaningless since the state could not possibly put an expressway in the existing Harper Avenue right-of-way, which was about one hundred and twenty feet wide. A fully depressed expressway would require a right-of-way between two hundred and three hundred feet wide. The extra right-of-way, opponents pointed out, could be obtained only by condemnation, and local permission to condemn would have to be obtained.

Highway Department personnel decided to carry their case directly to the people of Harper Woods. They secured invitations to speak at home owners' groups and civic associations in Harper Woods. The memories of state officials are hazy about this part of their role in the controversy, and the files of correspondence indicating who talked to whom, where and when are no longer in existence. As nearly as can be established, there were at least a half-dozen instances in late 1953 and 1954 when state personnel talked to local groups in Harper Woods.

One significant inference can be drawn from the state's informal efforts to sell the expressway: the dubious formal (legal) grounds on which the state's case rested. The Highway Department clearly realized the practical impossibility of putting an expressway through on Harper Avenue without local consent to obtain additional right-of-way. Whether local participants realized this too is indeterminable; in any case, local leaders on both sides of the issue were already irrevocably committed.

In October 1953 Mayor Broquet both publicly and privately urged owners of vacant land along Harper to develop their properties as another way of blocking the expressway. The mayor's urgings may have had some positive effect, but the discussion and near action by the CAL to put the expressway on Harper appeared to have had a depressing effect on property sales and business development along Harper. The shaky property-value situation along Harper may have been one source of pressure for the review of assessments which took place in early 1954 and set off a controversy which clarified The J. L. Hudson Company's position on the expressway.

Hudson's Eastland and the Expressway. In August the Democratic majority had tried to move forward on a master storm drainage system in cooperation with Grosse Pointe Woods. Since The J. L. Hudson Company was also vitally interested in the drain project because of the proposed Eastland Center, a conference on the drain was held between officials from Grosse Pointe Woods, Harper Woods, and Hudson's. The *Herald* (August 19, 1953) reported that, according to Hudson officials, construction of the shopping center "definitely will begin in 1955." The same article also stated that "the expressway will have no bearing on shopping center plans." With a strong likelihood that the shopping center would become a reality, some members of the Democratic Club turned their attention to the Eastland Center property.

The issue of the Hudson property appears to have started at a council meeting late in November 1953. Democratic Club President Lawrence Gettlinger, speaking before the council, charged that tax favoritism had cost the city "$18,000 in taxes lost on the Hudson property alone by way of inequitable assessments" (*Herald,* December 2, 1953). At the next council meeting, the *Herald* reported, Gettlinger and Wenger tangled in a "long hassle" during which Wenger admitted that there were some inequitable assessments in the city. A representative of the Wayne County Bureau of Taxation was present, and he suggested that a committee of local citizens be appointed to discuss assessments with the bureau. The council appointed a six-man committee, chaired by Reginald Rivard, an active member of the Democratic Club who dealt in real estate, construction, and property management. He was a member of the city's three-man Tax Board of Review, which had final authority for setting assessed valuation, and also owned property on Harper Avenue. Of the committee members, only Boomgaard, who resigned before the committee reported, was identified with the CAL. This committee reported to the council on February 17, 1954.

In reviewing the assessments on various properties in Harper Woods, the committee recommended that the assessed valuation on the Eastland Center site be increased by $100,000, or about 30 percent. At the same time the committee recommended reduced valuations on several business properties along Harper Avenue. The council majority accepted these revised assessments and referred them to the Tax Board of Review for final approval pending any appeals by property owners. The expected political storm broke quickly.

Hudson's official response was a letter to the council from A. B. Perlin, Jr., Hudson's attorney and assistant to the treasurer. It read in part:

> Hudson's is willing to pay its fair share of taxes in the city. But it is not willing to be the excuse for non-payment of taxes by other people. This [the assessment increase] leaves us confused. We cannot put the pieces of the puzzle together. We are not angry with the council or the committee but the action leaves open the sound business question of whether or not we will be able to build on the property. It is very difficult for us to go ahead with plans until we can see the tax picture.

There is plenty of time for a review of the situation. We would not build the Eastland Center until next spring anyhow. We want to see how the Northland Center works out first. [Northland was another regional shopping center built by Hudson's in the northwestern part of the metropolitan area.]

. . . .

We do not think any policy could be worked out by the committee in the short time it studied the question. We were given just two days' notice to spend one evening with the committee. It is very unlikely that we would build pending a further study.

On the heels of this letter came various additional comments from other Hudson officials, including a request for a meeting with local officials to discuss tax problems, drainage, and the expressway. Whether these additional comments were as varied as the *Harper Woods Herald* and the *Community News* reported them is not subject to proof, but the two newspapers' reporting presents a study in contrasts. The *Herald* reported that the tax assessment would have no effect on Hudson's plans to build Eastland, and the *News* reported that Hudson's would not build Eastland unless it got a "fair" assessment.

Two weeks after the controversy broke Oscar Webber, president of Hudson's, spoke at the opening of Hudson's Northland Shopping Center in Southfield Township, Oakland County. He was quoted by the *News* as saying, "We still have hopes of building Eastland Center. But the people—I mean the officials of Harper Woods—don't seem to welcome us."

The question of whether Hudson's was or was not going to build Eastland took a further twist when the *Herald's* banner headline of March 17 read, "HUDSON'S GETS BUILDING PERMIT." The firm had obtained a building permit to put up a temporary frame structure which company officials said was intended to house building materials remaining after the completion of Northland. The *Herald* pointed to this action as additional proof that Hudson's was committed to building Eastland and that construction would start within a year.

The *Herald's* efforts to reassure the voters that the assessment question had not endangered Hudson's Eastland commitment were not entirely successful, and a movement to recall the four Democratic councilmen (Mrs. Chalou was not included) was well under way. The recall movement had started shortly after the first of March. While it was triggered by the Hudson property incident, it had all of the steam that a long succession of real or alleged grievances could muster.

Spadework and cultivation of the recall idea had been undertaken by the *News* early in January. A front-page editorial in the *News* on January 7 had asked whether the city could afford "ignorance and incompetence," "government by postponement," "bungling government" by "fumblers" until the spring elections in 1955, fifteen months hence, and had called attention to the fact that the people of Harper Woods had a weapon they could use "to rid themselves of the bunglers," namely, the recall. Another front-page editorial in the *News* (March 4) emphasized the assets which the Eastland Center would bring to Harper Woods, among other things "a tax reduction perhaps as high as 50 percent," and charged the Save Our City Committee with being "committed to keeping Hudson's out of Harper Woods." The editorial concluded:

> The people will have to decide whether they want the Hudson project or not. Under the present administration, THERE WILL BE NO HUDSON CENTER. If the people do not want to lose it, they should set about IMMEDIATELY to RECALL the present council majority.

The recall movement, which went under the name "United Recall Association," alleged violations of the city charter ranging from the city's purchase of insurance from an insurance firm represented by Councilman Garman to the appointment of a "city administrator" rather than a "city manager." Heading the recall movement was Peter Riegler, a Harper Woods resident who had not previously been very active politically, although he had been a dues-paying member of the CAL. The interesting as well as controversial aspect of Riegler's status was his place of employment: Riegler was manager of the west-side warehouse of The J. L. Hudson Company.

Democratic Club leaders denounced the recall movement as a smear campaign and roundly criticized Riegler and Hudson's for their relationship with it. Their comments were conveyed through the columns of the *Herald*. Thus, the same issues of the *Herald* that headlined Hudson's building permit and pointed to a new "era of cooperation" between the city and the firm also carried captions about Riegler reading: "Political Faction Led by Hudson Executive," and "Company Worker Manages Recall Petition Drive."

The prevailing uncertainty regarding Hudson's Eastland plans and Hudson's connection with the recall movement set the stage for a March 19 luncheon meeting between company and city officials. The meeting was held in the executive dining room of Hudson's downtown store, and its ostensible purpose was to discuss Hudson's interest in taxation and drainage. A joint statement summarizing the four-hour meeting was prepared and approved by all parties to the discussion. Parts of this statement, which appeared in the *News* but not in the *Herald,* read as follows (*News,* March 25, 1954):

> The Hudson representatives expressed extreme dissatisfaction with the tax treatment which Eastland property has received in Harper Woods, and explained to the committee the basis for that dissatisfaction.
>
> They stated that in view of this experience they will need concrete assurance that future tax treatment will be fair and non-discriminatory. It is their position that all property in the city should be assessed at the same percentage of value, and that their property has not been so treated recently.
>
> .   .   .   .
>
> The Eastland representatives declared an intention to appeal this year's increase but pointed out that a member of the [three-man] Tax Board of Review was also an active member of the committee which recommended the increase.
>
> .   .   .   .
>
> The J. L. Hudson Company wishes to go on record as stating that [it is] not sponsoring or supporting in any manner whatsoever the present recall movement in the city of Harper Woods, and that no circulators of recall petitions have been authorized by [it] to use its name in connection therewith.
>
> .   .   .   .
>
> The J. L. Hudson Company advised that [it does] not wish to enter into any controversy concerning the route of the Edsel Ford Expressway but [hopes] that plans can be determined at an early date.

Assistant to the Treasurer Perlin commented further on Riegler's status over and above the firm's official statement of disassociation. Perlin explained that Riegler was not a policy-making executive and that outside of working hours Riegler was a "free agent." Perlin said: "What he does on his own time is none of our busi-

ness. We didn't tell him to get into this thing and we are not telling
him to get out."

Hudson's interest in the expressway was not apparent from the
published statement. Mayor Broquet recalls:

> Hudson's told us that the expressway was absolutely necessary to the
> success of Eastland but told us that it couldn't come closer than a
> half-mile from the Center. To us that meant it had to go on Harper.
> Winter [Foster Winter, Hudson's treasurer] then asked us how come
> we wouldn't talk to the State Highway Department about the express-
> way and we told him it was because we could never get Ziegler to
> come to Harper Woods and talk to us straight, which we couldn't.
> We didn't want to hear any second- or third-level man. We wanted
> the head man to talk to. Then Winter said, "Gentlemen, I can set up
> a meeting with Mr. Ziegler for you in one day." We wondered how
> come he could do it so fast when we, the officials of an incorporated
> municipality of the state, had been trying for so long and couldn't.
> Anyway, he [Winter] picked up the phone and called Lansing and
> got Ziegler. He arranged a meeting for us with Ziegler in Lansing
> the following Friday. When Hogan and I went back to Harper Woods
> we were ready to meet and talk with Ziegler, but the other three
> council members and the rest of our group didn't want to, so we
> went along with the majority.

It appeared that if the SOC administration was jeopardizing the
construction of Eastland, it was more because of their expressway
policy than because of the assessment review. This became clear
when in April Hudson's appealed the $100,000 assessment increase
before the local Tax Board of Review, and the board halved the
increase. The retail firm was sufficiently satisfied to refrain from
appealing the remaining increase to the State Tax Commission but
nonetheless made no moves toward committing itself to build
Eastland.

The next issue of the *Community News* (March 25) reported
that a meeting between Harper Woods and state highway officials
had been arranged for March 26 by "a third party," but that the
meeting had been called off because of opposition within the Democratic Club ranks. Deputy Highway Commissioner Harry Coons,
the *News* added, had declined to answer when asked if Hudson's
was the "third party." When questioned further about Hudson's,
Coons pointed out that the State Highway Department had
widened Eight Mile Road ahead of schedule to accommodate

Northland Center and the increased traffic it drew. He added, "Hudson's has always been friendly to us."

The meeting with Hudson's and the maneuvering over meeting or not meeting with the Highway Department coincided with the circulation of recall petitions. The recall group had countered attacks against Riegler's involvement with similar charges against Charles Francis, former editor of the *Save Our City News,* who had become chairman of the Democratic Club. The CAL and the *Community News* pointed to Francis' employment as an accountant for Federal Department Stores, a large department-store chain which had recently started construction of Eastgate, a subregional shopping center, less than three miles from the proposed Eastland site. By the end of March the recall group had gathered 1,795 signatures, 297 more than they needed to force a vote. Despite this external threat and internal differences the council majority did not reschedule a meeting with state officials in place of the one set for March 26. The embattled majority held firm on its policy of giving no quarter and refusing to meet with state officials.

Affirmative actions were taken by the council on the drain project in May and June over the strenuous objections of Grossel and Wenger, who argued against acting on the drain before the expressway issue was settled. They proposed that the council write to Highway Department officials inviting them to a meeting in Harper Woods on the twin problems of the expressway and the storm drain. A motion to table this proposal indefinitely carried by a four-to-three vote, Democrat Victor Van Hulle voting with Wenger and Grossel against tabling. In voting for the tabling motion Councilman Hogan reportedly said, "There is no reason for contacting them. They know we meet the first and third Thursdays. If they want to, they can come down anytime" (*News,* June 24, 1954). At about this time Highway Department personnel were in Harper Woods but not in attendance at council meetings. State surveying crews were making preliminary surveys of the projected expressway route to the eastern edge of Detroit and along Harper Avenue a short way into Harper Woods.

The tabling motion made out of order any further discussion of inviting the state to a meeting on the expressway. Another blow to the pro-expressway forces came on June 25, when the Wayne

County Circuit Court ruled against the recall petition, killing the hopes of the SOC's opponents that a popular vote on the SOC policy could be held before the scheduled spring election. Councilman Wenger resigned a few days later in order to dramatize his and the CAL's dislike of Democratic policies on the expressway and the storm drain system. His resignation was greeted with unrestrained delight by Democrats and the *Herald.* The council named Charles Francis as Wenger's replacement. (Democrat Victor Van Hulle resigned shortly thereafter and Democrat Reginald Rivard was appointed to the vacant post.) Grossel remained as the lone CAL council member. Grossel was still able to call for discussion of the general subject of the expressway. On this point the following exchange between Grossel and Broquet reportedly took place at the July 1 council meeting (*News,* July 8, 1954):

> GROSSEL: We are jeopardizing people by not doing something. . . . They are surveying out here now. I read in *The Detroit News* that they expect to reach the Kingsville [Harper Woods] line by 1957 or 1958.
> The question isn't so much whether we can keep it out or not. The point is, what are you going to do with the autos? They will take our streets and use them to get to . . . the end of the expressway. We will be crying for relief from the traffic, but then it will be too late.
> BROQUET: We don't have to worry about it. We'll put up a stop light at the end of the expressway and traffic will back up into Detroit.

Despite the continued adamant anti-expressway position of the council majority, the presence of surveying crews and the real or supposed intention of the Highway Department to ignore local opposition made it more apparent that the council majority's policy of giving no quarter was being followed at considerable peril. Added pressure for a decision on the expressway came in late September, when Hudson's entered the picture again.

Renewed Pressure.   Hudson's had invited the entire council to a dinner meeting in the agreeable atmosphere of Northland's executive dining room. The basis for the evening's discussion was a letter dated September 29 (1954) from Foster Winter to the council. Winter's letter raised four issues that had to be "satisfactorily resolved" before Hudson's would begin construction of Eastland. The letter is reproduced in full:

Gentlemen:

For some time we have been giving careful consideration to the question of whether we should proceed with our tentative plans to construct a shopping center and branch store on our property located at Eight Mile Road and Kelly Road in Harper Woods. As you no doubt realize, a decision of this kind is of major importance and has many aspects which must be considered.

Within the past week we have reached the decision to proceed with the construction of this project provided a number of matters which are essential to the program can be satisfactorily resolved. Several of the matters are internal and involve such subjects as finance, engineering, tenant acceptance, etc., and are of no concern to you. There are, however, several other matters which require certain actions and decisions on your part. They are:

1. *Taxation.* Before we can proceed with any plan for this proposed shopping center we must have adequate assurance that this development is *really* wanted in Harper Woods both by the residents and by those who administer the city's business. We need some concrete assurance that this development will not be discriminated against in the matter of assessment for tax purposes. We want to make it clear that we do not expect or want any special favorable treatment accorded us, but we must be assured that *all* real property in Harper Woods is assessed on the same equitable basis.

2. *Expressway.* As you know, we own property on both the north and south sides of Vernier east of Beaconsfield. It is contemplated that some of this property would be included in the over-all plan being developed for Eastland Center. We have seen various maps of the proposed expressway routes through Harper Woods showing several different proposed expressway locations. I am sure you can understand it is essential to our planning that this matter of expressway location be determined forthwith so that our architects and engineers will have the benefit of knowing the final route determination. It seems to us that an expressway must be inevitable, and the sooner the location is settled, the better it would be for all concerned. We have no interest whatever in the choice of one route as opposed to any other so long as such location can be properly coordinated into our over-all traffic plan.

3. *Drainage.* We understand this subject is currently being given considerable attention, and while we do not have all of the details before us, we are encouraged to believe that action can be taken on this subject which will enable us to plan accordingly. We have been informed that whatever solution to the drainage problem is decided upon ought to be done in the light of the need for providing drainage for the expressway and thereby receiving the benefit of a contribution to the cost from the State Highway Department.

4. *Zoning.* Some of the property we own in this location has not yet been rezoned to permit its use as a shopping center or for com-

plementary uses. I refer specifically to a parcel abutting Kelly Road lying just to the south of the property which has already been zoned for shopping center use, the other parcel being a thirty-acre tract lying just to the east of Beaconsfield abutting Vernier Highway. We would also require the vacating of the plat of triangular-shaped property lying between Vernier, Eight Mile and Beaconsfield. We realize there are formal proceedings which would have to be undertaken in the zoning and platting matters, but we would like to have your reaction in advance concerning them.

We would appreciate it if you would discuss the matters we have enumerated here at your next meeting and hope that at that time you can take whatever action you deem appropriate. Let us reassure you that we would like to find a solution to these and other matters so that we can proceed vigorously with our plans in the hope that construction can be commenced during 1955.

Reporting on the dinner meeting, the *Herald* (October 6) noted the quandary in which the councilmen found themselves because company officials were reluctant to read specific meaning into the statements contained in the letter. The news article noted: "Councilmen said that their questions whether the letter amounted to an 'ultimatum' from the company met with a 'yes and no' answer from Winter." Hudson's was pushing, but it was difficult to say how hard.

At the October 7 council meeting the Democratic councilmen first discussed various possible interpretations of the Hudson letter, then heard remarks from the floor. Approximately 150 persons were in attendance, some with petitions asking the council to set the expressway route, others demanding that action be taken on the drainage system. An exceptionally heavy rain on October 3 had flooded most of the basements in Harper Woods and had forced the high school to close for two days because of flooding. The council refused to act on a motion by Grossel to set the route of the expressway. Grossel then charged that building the drain independent of the expressway would cost more and probably delay the construction of the drain as well. To the many drainage-conscious people present, Grossel's remarks appeared to strike home.

Despite increased cost and opposition from Hudson's, the council decided to go ahead with its plans for an independent drainage system. Later in October the council approved a resolution authorizing the Wayne County drain commissioner to take charge of constructing the drainage system. The council majority acted on the assumption, later proved false, that the cost of the drain could be financed on a "benefit" or "run-off" basis rather than on the basis of ad valorem assessments. The majority preferred the run-off basis of assessment because Eastland, with its extensive impervious parking-lot surfaces, would pay for a larger share of the drain on a run-off basis than on the basis of assessed valuation. To the SOC's consternation, the chief objectors to the benefit method of charging drain costs were not Hudson's officials but home owners on large lots in the central part of the city. Large lots meant more water run-off and, therefore, higher charges for the drain system. The drain assessment plan had backfired, and the beleaguered council now had discontent among the central-area voters to add to its problems.

Increasing internal and external pressures did not move the council to alter its course. After the council meeting of October 7, Mayor Broquet drafted a reply to Foster Winter's letter. The section relevant to the expressway indicated that Hudson's had objected to routes that would take the expressway by the doorstep of the proposed shopping center:

> The council has considered the expressway matter on many occasions and has come to the inescapable and irrevocable conclusion that a limited-access highway would be very detrimental to the interest of our community.

> You advised us at our recent conference that The J. L. Hudson Company could not build Eastland Center if a limited-access highway were placed along either Kelly Road or Beaconsfield Avenue.

> You can be certain that this council will not consent to a limited-access highway on either Kelly Road or Beaconsfield Avenue, or on any other street in the city of Harper Woods.

> It is the feeling of the council that a divided surface highway along Harper Avenue would adequately serve your needs and at the same time be beneficial to our community.

The council had decided to call Hudson's bluff by continuing to stand firm against any expressway through Harper Woods.

The last point in Broquet's letter was elaborated more fully when the mayor publicly proposed an eight-lane divided surface highway for Harper Avenue as a substitute for a depressed six-lane expressway. This proposal expressed Broquet's long-standing contention that existing surface streets in the northeast suburbs were sufficient, provided they were widened, to handle the traffic from the Ford Expressway if it stopped at Detroit's city limits. Highway personnel from the state, Wayne County, and Detroit cited statistics showing that each lane of the Ford Expressway could handle fifteen hundred cars per hour or peak loads of forty-five hundred vehicles per hour in each direction. Non-limited-access surface streets could handle only from five hundred to six hundred vehicles per lane per hour. Broquet countered these statistics by pointing to the several surface streets in the northeast area that could handle the dispersing traffic. Highway officials rebutted by pointing out that the traffic could not be evenly dispersed over the surface arteries. Nonetheless, Broquet's proposal for the eight-lane surface route was forwarded to the Wayne County Road Commission since Harper Avenue was under county jurisdiction. The Road Commission refused to place the matter on its agenda for consideration in the commission's 1955 widening program and declined to predict whether it would go on the commission's construction schedule at any future date. Chances for acceptance of Broquet's proposal looked dim.

The failure of the council to meet Hudson's request to set the expressway route "forthwith" and Hudson's failure to reply to Broquet's letter left the Eastland and expressway issues in mid-air. During October, November, and December the *News* played hard on the theme that Harper Woods was in danger of losing Eastland because of the "ostrich" attitude of the council majority. The *Herald* called Foster Winter in an attempt to determine the veracity of a headline in the *News* of December 9 that "Eastland Center Is Doomed" by the refusal of the council majority to pick an expressway route. Winter's response to the *Herald's* inquiry on whether construction of the shopping center would start in 1955 was a terse "No comment."

The SOC had come into office on the crest of anti-expressway sentiment. During its tenure it had kept the expressway out, but only at the cost of seeming to jeopardize the construction of a major tax-producing commercial facility and complicating the construction of much-needed storm drains. The question whether the state could legally force the expressway through Harper Woods was as unsettled in 1955 as it had been in 1953, but unabating pressures from the state, Hudson's, the CAL, the recall movement, and even the weather had worn down anti-expressway resistance in Harper Woods. By late 1954 the perils and possible costs of the anti-expressway policy had become more and more apparent. The SOC's anti-expressway policy was no longer the unmitigated asset it had been in 1953. In addition, the many new residents who had moved to Harper Woods since 1953 were uncommitted to the Democratic Club and/or to the SOC's anti-expressway policy. The SOC could expect a hard fight at the forthcoming elections.

The Tide Turns

The State Highway Commissioner Speaks. Shortly before the 1953 election Deputy State Highway Commissioner George Foster had come to Harper Woods to convince residents of the inevitability and the advantages of the expressway. As the 1955 election approached, Foster's chief, State Highway Commissioner Charles M. Ziegler, came to Harper Woods on a similar errand. On January 10 Ziegler and his new deputy, Carlos H. Weber, spoke to a gathering of about five hundred Harper Woods residents at a local hall. Detroit and Wayne County highway officials were also present at the meeting, which was sponsored by the Southeast Property Owners Association. The highway officials answered many questions about the proposed expressway and the state's willingness to cooperate on the drain. Newspaper accounts of the meeting reveal that state officials (1) predicted a traffic bottleneck and heavy use of local residential streets if the expressway stopped at Detroit's edge, (2) predicted a rise in property values if the expressway did come through, (3) offered no exact time schedule for construction but estimated that the right-of-way acquisition would start in about two years, (4) stated that the expressway would require no tax increase and only negligible direct costs to Harper Woods, (5) indicated that if a new administration offered a route on the west side of Harper the state would accept it, (6) indicated that the state would not be willing to take property on both sides of Harper because of the added expense, (7) rejected an eight-lane surface highway (Broquet's proposal) as well as a route west of Kelly Road completely bypassing the city, and (8) indicated their willingness to cooperate in a joint drainage system with the city.

To the direct question, "Could the state build without the city's consent?" Ziegler sidestepped, replying, "It was approved before Harper Woods became a city by the federal Bureau of Public Roads. But we would much rather sit down and work it out with the city officials."

The *Harper Woods Herald* and the *Community News* reported the meeting variously. The *News* (January 13, 1955) emphasized the state's willingness to cooperate on the drainage system, the raising of property values, and no tax increase. The *Herald* (January 12, 1955) stressed the state's "indefinite" answers on whether or not the state could put the expressway through over local opposition, when it might come through, and how much it would cost. Both newspapers printed "verbatim" accounts of the meeting which differed significantly from each other. For example, the first question asked was: "If the highway comes to the boundary [of Harper Woods] and there are no plans in Harper Woods, what would happen?"

The *News* quoted the response to this as:

There would be a *definite* bottleneck. It might correct itself to a *little* extent when drivers started leaving the expressway and using other streets. (italics added)

The *Herald* quoted the response as:

There would be a *slight* bottleneck. It *would* soon right itself to *some* extent because people would turn off the highway at other streets before they got here, but there would be a bottleneck. (italics added)

The *News* quoted Ziegler's responses to two questions:

Q. Have you found the council cooperative or evasive?
A. Before the election in 1953 we had many discussions with the council. Since, none. We have not taken the initiative. It was far enough ahead of us that we didn't have to. But we have read the papers.
Q. If a new administration proposed a route on the west side of Harper, would it be accepted?
A. Yes.

The *Herald* failed to quote these questions or responses but it did comment unfavorably about a "gag rule" in effect at the meeting under which no city officials or press representatives were allowed to ask questions. Broquet was then quoted as saying: "We heard all that was said tonight two years ago. I was interested in the questions they didn't answer. They never have answered whether or how they intend to try to force the highway through Harper Woods."

The 1955 Election Campaign. The primary election was scheduled for February 21. There were three slates and one independent in the race—the Democratic Club (which again adopted the Save Our City nomen), the Civic Action League, the newly formed Residents for Political Alliance, which took a stand in favor of Hudson's and the expressway, and Vernon McComb, the independent candidate. Despite the three slates there were only eleven candidates for the four council vacancies because candidates Grossel and Boomgaard were listed on both CAL and RPA slates. Running on the CAL slate, in addition to Grossel and Boomgaard, were Peter Riegler and Raymond Jasin, current president of the CAL. On the SOC slate were the three incumbent Democratic council members, Mrs. Margaret Chalou, Charles Francis, and Reginald Rivard, plus Bernard Rago. The CAL, the RPA, and McComb all contended that the expressway could not be stopped and that a route along Harper should be designated immediately. They also pledged cooperation with Hudson's and quick action on the drain project in conjunction with the expressway. All of them used statements made by state officials at the January public meeting as arguments in the campaign.

All participants looked to the primary as a warm-up and test of strength over the three important issues—expressway, drainage, and Eastland. The primary eliminated two RPA candidates (Matthew Makie and Leonard Preuett) and the independent (McComb) from the running. The results of the primary were:

Candidate	Votes	Candidate	Votes
Grossel (CAL-RPA)	1,463	Riegler (CAL)	900
Francis (SOC)	1,449	Jasin (CAL)	800
Chalou (SOC)	1,436	Makie (RPA)	666
Boomgaard (CAL-RPA)	1,403	Preuett (RPA)	627
Rivard (SOC)	1,397	McComb (Indep.)	586
Rago (SOC)	1,216		

The vote attested to the continued vigor of the SOC–Democratic Club alliance and the appeal of that administration's anti-expressway plank. At the same time the total votes cast for all anti-administration candidates exceeded the votes in support of the controlling majority—6,445 to 5,498. Every indicator pointed to a close vote at the final elections six weeks hence. But the incumbent majority had one circumstance in its favor. To retain control of the council it needed to capture only one of the four seats at stake, for Broquet, Garman, and Hogan did not come up for election until 1957.

The general election campaign began immediately after the primary and quickly reached an intense pitch, one that was sustained over the six weeks between the primary and the April 4 election date. The RPA and the independent candidate threw their support behind the four CAL candidates in a coalition move. The CAL came out with a ten-point platform in which Hudson's Eastland and the expressway were featured planks. The platform read as follows:

1. To cooperate with The J. L. Hudson Company in building their shopping center.
2. To decide the route of the Edsel Ford Expressway through our city immediately.
3. To place the route of the expressway on Harper Avenue and not in a residential area.
4. To request the state to cooperate in placing our main trunkline for the storm sewer in the expressway right-of-way to save future taxes for Harper Woods taxpayers.
5. To develop a park system for our future use.
6. To formulate a well-organized recreation program for our youth apart from politics.
7. To work towards the development of a youth center separate from the City Hall.
8. To obtain a workable master plan for the city's future welfare.
9. To reduce taxes for the general operation of government with an efficient administration.
10. NOT to spend large sums of taxpayers' money for a new City Hall nor any other public building until the highway issue is settled and a route determined.

The CAL candidates sought to exploit every possible angle and appeal for votes. They waged an aggressive campaign, complete with handbills, posters, and large newspaper ads (all in the *News*).

On election day they offered free rides to the polls, hired a sound truck to cruise about the city, as did the SOC, and had paid poll watchers and challengers at the voting booths. So extensive were the CAL's efforts that some persons, especially the opposition, wondered where the funds were coming from.

The *News* gave unremitting support to the CAL's campaign. Each week for the seven weeks preceding the election the *News* furnished the CAL with several hundred extra copies of the *News* for distribution to every household in Harper Woods. These pre-election editions had front-page editorials filled with critical and caustic remarks about the SOC majority and took added pokes in cartoons, one of which suggested that "selfish business interests" were the mainstay of the "Save Our Clique" group. The *News* gave extensive and favorable coverage to the campaign activities of CAL candidates, while its infrequent references to SOC candidates were invariably unfavorable. The *News* editorial just before the election struck chiefly at the "pocketbook" votes by citing alleged savings to voters if they elected the four CAL candidates. These "savings" were listed: $1,800,000 by linking the drainage system with the expressway; $200,000 by letting the state buy the site on which the old Township Hall was located for expressway right-of-way; and $1,000,000 resulting from the development of the Hudson property as a shopping center (paying $500,000 in taxes) rather than its conversion to residential use, requiring a $500,000 elementary school.

Faced with the activism and arguments of the CAL and the *News*, the SOC and the *Herald* were by no means languishing in the expectation of certain victory. Characteristic of an incumbent administration, however, was the generally defensive posture of the SOC and the *Herald*. In its March 2 and 9 issues the *Herald* focused its lead articles on the current flurry of activity surrounding the expressway route.

In mid-February Mayor Thomas Welsh of St. Clair Shores had proposed a four-city expressway conference between representatives of St. Clair Shores, Roseville, East Detroit, and Harper Woods. The purpose of the conference, as Welsh outlined it, was to arrive at a "united front" among the four suburbs on an acceptable route for the expressway. Such an agreement, Welsh contended, would strengthen the suburbs' hand in dealing with Detroit and the state on the route-location problem. Welsh charged that the state was following a policy of "picking off" the suburbs one by one on an expressway route and that unless the suburbs banded together they would all "hang" separately.

Mayor Broquet represented Harper Woods at the four-city conference. It was held in St. Clair Shores on March 4, and was marked by cordiality and a desire for cooperation among the representatives of the four suburbs. However, the diversity of interests among the suburbs was too great for a compromise agreement on what route the expressway should follow. Harper Woods' desire for the route to run west of Kelly Road would force the continuation of the expressway to pass through East Detroit, which wanted no part of the expressway under any circumstances. Conversely, a route along or just east of Beaconsfield Avenue proved acceptable to the three northerly communities but conflicted with Harper Woods' opposition to any expressway through its jurisdiction. Even if Harper Woods had acquiesced to having the expressway, no agreement with St. Clair Shores on route location would have been possible. If an expressway were to be forced on Harper Woods, the predominant sentiment there seemed in favor of a Harper Avenue route, where commercial rather than residential property would be taken. In a curious inversion of this position, Mayor Welsh insisted that if the expressway were to pass through St. Clair Shores, it must closely parallel Beaconsfield, taking residential property, rather than Harper, which was the city's major commercial street.

The intercity conference broke up on four notes of agreement: (1) St. Clair Shores agreed not to put Harper Woods in a pincers by approving an expressway route without consulting Harper Woods officials; (2) the representatives pledged their united support in opposition to the state-proposed route for the expressway, i.e., Harper Avenue; (3) they agreed to meet and consult further before taking action on expressway matters; and (4) they went on record as opposing an expressway route that would bisect any community. How such an ideal route could be found, given the truncated character of suburban boundaries, was not specified.

One way of viewing the *Herald's* emphasis on the joint highway conference was that it served to show anti-expressway partisans as well as the community at large that the incumbent administration was still active in protecting the community from the onslaught of "the big ditch."

The next two issues of the *Herald* shifted readers' attention to the drain problem. The March 16 issue conveyed a picture of an active council majority pressing for rapid progress to relieve flooding and health hazards. It noted that prospects were good for an early start on the project by Democrat Christopher Mulle, the county drain commissioner, to whom the council had given responsibility for the project by its resolution the preceding October. The article acknowledged Grossel's opinion that construction was not in the immediate offing but pointed out that Grossel and his former CAL associate (Wenger) had voted against the drain project each time it had come up. Delay in beginning construction was taken up again in the March 23 issue, which recounted the planning and financing problems to be solved as these were explained by the county drain commissioner.

The expressway returned to the limelight in the closing days of the campaign, when Mayor Broquet proposed locating the expressway along Kelly Road. At the St. Clair Shores expressway conference and in public statements before and after that meeting, Broquet had revived the Kelly route. This proposal contradicted the council's assurance to Hudson's in October that it would not consent to a Kelly or a Beaconsfield route; but it was consistent with Broquet's long-standing claim that he was not opposed to expressways per se but believed a Kelly-Beaconsfield route was the most logical one through the suburbs, one that was least likely to "chop up" the suburban communities (see map).

Rejections of Broquet's proposal were not long in coming. First, Detroit Common Council President Louis Miriani stated that Detroit would "never" reconsider its decision to locate the expressway along Harper Avenue. Second, an unidentified spokesman for Hudson's reiterated that firm's doubts about building Eastland if the expressway came out Kelly Road. Both of these rejections were reported in the *News* but not in the *Herald*. The third rejection came from State Highway Commissioner Ziegler, who returned to Harper Woods on March 24 to speak about the expressway before a group of five hundred people at a meeting sponsored jointly by four home owners' associations. The state flatly rejected the proposed Kelly route.

Both the *News* and the *Herald* reported the meeting. The *News* pointed to the readiness of state officials to cooperate in settling on an expressway route and to the state's willingness to join with the city in its drainage project. The *Herald* (March 30), claiming that "state and county highway authorities confirmed the contentions of the present city administration in the expressway controversy," centered attention on (1) the legal question mark over whether the state could put the expressway through without local consent and (2) rebuttals to free-wheeling CAL claims that state-local cooperation on the drain project would save anywhere from $500,000 to $1,800,000—the latter figure having appeared in a *News* editorial of March 31. The *Herald* article stated:

> Some five hundred persons heard a top county highway official state that no property could be condemned for an expressway right-of-way without the city's consent.
>
> State Highway Commissioner Charles M. Ziegler conceded that he does not know whether or not the project could go through without the city's consent.
>
> Deputy Commissioner Carlos H. Weber categorically stated that to his knowledge the state never has promised to pay $500,000 toward the city's drainage cost, as alleged by one political faction.

The campaign was over. The CAL's aggressive strategy appeared to be both deliberate and necessary in order to offset the organizational advantage enjoyed by the Democratic Club. The extreme claims, ominous warnings, caustic references, and devastating sarcasm in the columns of the *News* stood in sharp relief to the more subdued tones of the *Herald*. The Democratic Club members went to the polls with a fair degree of confidence in victory.

The Civic Action League Wins.   Most local observers predicted a heavy and close vote in the council election. Both predictions were correct. Of 8,151 registered voters, 4,374 voted. This 53 percent turnout was substantially above the 37 percent county-wide participation in the spring elections. All four CAL candidates

were elected and the CAL regained a four-to-three council majority. The margin of victory was slim, however, as only eighty-five
votes separated the lowest CAL candidate (Jasin) from the highest SOC candidate (Rivard). The vote totals were:

CAL		SOC	
Grossel	2,322	Rivard	2,059
Boomgaard	2,262	Francis	2,025
Riegler	2,161	Chalou	1,970
Jasin	2,144	Rago	1,966

The CAL candidates received 52.6 percent of all votes cast, up
from 42.1 percent in the 1953 election, and carried six of the city's
ten precincts. The CAL made percentage-point gains over its 1953
percentages in all but one precinct (see Table 2).

Table 2
*Percentage of the Vote Obtained by Civic Action League
in 1953 and 1955 Harper Woods Council Elections*

Precinct	1953 Election	1955 Election
1	39.5	53.5
2	42.5	49.6
3	46.8	62.3
4	47.2	55.4
5	40.1	56.4
6	48.3	67.1
7	42.2	43.6
8	60.9	52.3
9	31.1	39.0
10	29.9	31.5

The northeastern section remained the area of the greatest SOC
(Democratic Club) strength although the percentage majorities
gained in this less populated area did not yield sufficient votes to
offset CAL strength elsewhere in the city.

In post-mortems on the election, SOC leaders attributed their
loss to three factors: (1) failure to get across to the people the
SOC's alternate route for the expressway (Kelly Road), (2) opposition among home owners in the central section to the proposed
financing of the drain project on a benefit or water run-off basis,
and (3) failure to win the votes of the many new residents which

Harper Woods had acquired between 1953 and 1955. The SOC had faced a formidable task of selling the Kelly Road alternative to local voters in view of rejections of this route from the state, city of Detroit, and Hudson's. Furthermore, the SOC did not push the Kelly Road alternative until a few weeks before the election, when they sensed a slippage in anti-expressway sentiment. The more localized impact of the SOC's drain financing plans was evident from comparative precinct figures in the 1953 and 1955 elections. In the two central-area precincts, 5 and 6, the CAL's gains (sixteen and eighteen percentage points) outstripped those of any other precincts. These were the areas adversely affected by the SOC's drain financing plans. The CAL's loss (SOC's gain) in Precinct 8 also seems traceable to drain financing. Homes in this area were on small lots while the structures themselves were generally more expensive than those in the central section. Drain financing on a run-off basis, rather than on assessed valuation, was the much-preferred alternative of residents in this area. (Ironically, the issue over benefit financing proved to be academic since the state attorney general ruled a few months later that this method of financing this particular type of drain was invalid.) In other precincts where the CAL made substantial gains—1, 2, 3, 4, and 9—its success was partly the result of its ability to capture new residents in those areas, residents without prior local factional allegiances who held the balance of voting power in Harper Woods. As ex-mayor Broquet lamented later:

> There were always so many new people moving in you couldn't keep track—maybe eight or nine hundred more voters at each election. Whoever got to them first [CAL or Democratic Club], that's generally how they voted. Maybe that's one place where we fell down.

Grossel offered several reasons to explain the CAL victory:

> People were clamoring for answers—on the expressway, on the drain, on Hudson's because they might not build. The people had two years of indecision. We promised decisions, action, and something positive on the expressway, drain, and Hudson's. Our ten-point program helped tremendously. It did the trick. We had something concrete to give the people.
>
> Before [in the 1953 election] we didn't have anything concrete. The

expressway was new and unknown. A question mark. The people knew what they had and wanted to keep it. We lost. By 1955 they knew a little more about it [the expressway]. They weren't afraid. It was no longer just a ditch, a hazard. What's more we promised to put it in a specific place and save a lot of homes and save money on the drain as well.

The elections were like a pendulum. In 1951 the people wanted to try something new and we won on incorporation and the council. In 1953 the people reverted to the old township days. In 1955 they were ready to look ahead again and we were there with something positive.

Wenger added another reason: the *News'* all-out support of CAL:

Without them we couldn't have won. They were the best and only way we could get the facts to the people. They were a great example of responsible journalism!

Harper Woods Accepts the Expressway. On April 5, the day after the election, James B. Webber, executive vice president of The J. L. Hudson Company, announced that his firm would build Eastland Center, with the beginning of construction planned for the coming summer. (Ground was broken on August 11, and the $15,000,000, seventy-three-store shopping center opened in July 1957.) The Eastland question was settled, and the CAL intended to waste no time in dealing with the remaining issues.

The new majority interpreted their victory as a clear mandate on the expressway, Eastland, and drainage. After electing Joseph Grossel as mayor, the council, by a four-to-three vote, hired Robert J. McNutt as the new city manager starting May 6. CAL council members made it clear to McNutt that he was to place highest priorities on (1) determining the expressway route, (2) building the storm drain system, and (3) cooperating with Hudson's. McNutt, an energetic and ambitious person, did not have to be told twice. Given these mandates and assured of a majority support on the council, he set about to exercise a firm (many would say dictatorial) hand in guiding Harper Woods' municipal affairs.

McNutt was appointed at the council meeting of May 5. At the same meeting the council voted, again four-to-three, to request the State Highway Department to make preliminary surveys of the proposed Harper route of the expressway through the city.

The majority turned down a motion by the Democratic minority that a referendum vote be taken on the proposed route before the council gave final consent. This motion raised the question of the legality of the charter amendment adopted two years earlier which provided for a vote of the electorate before consent could be given to a limited-access highway. Shortly thereafter, the city attorney, relying on the state attorney general's ruling, held that the amendment was not binding. The Democratic council members continued to raise the charter amendment proviso until the final council vote was taken on the expressway. The majority overrode these objections to "violating the charter" on the aforementioned legal grounds and also on policy grounds. CAL members contended that a vote of the electorate was unnecessary and that it would entail the expense of a special election, use up valuable time, and delay the work on the drain system undertaken in conjunction with the expressway. Democratic opposition proved futile; surveys of the expressway route would start in June. Meanwhile the council passed a resolution warning property owners along the west side of Harper that any construction or improvements would be at the risk of the owner or builder.

Completion of the surveys and drafting of the detailed plans for the expressway, including entrance and exit ramps, vehicle and pedestrian crossovers, etc., were expected to take four months. In this interim Harper Woods officials were subjected to a sharp attack from Mayor Welsh of St. Clair Shores. Welsh charged that Harper Woods had reneged on its promise to consult with St. Clair Shores before deciding on the expressway route. The chief source of Welsh's displeasure came from Harper Woods' intention to put the expressway along Harper Avenue. Welsh still wanted the expressway along Beaconsfield Avenue in St. Clair Shores. Considering the effect of a Harper-route expressway through Harper Woods, Welsh observed: "If I lived in that sliver of Harper Woods that would be left on the east side of the expressway, I would petition for annexation to Grosse Pointe Woods. Then the rest of Harper Woods might as well petition for annexation to Detroit" (*News*, June 30, 1955).

Mayor Welsh's charge of bad faith and his affront to the territorial integrity of Harper Woods did not pass without comment.

Mayor Grossel denied that Harper Woods had any commitment to St. Clair Shores, adding: "We are going to cooperate to the best of our ability, but Harper Woods is not going to be the victim of a squeeze play between Detroit and St. Clair Shores" (*News,* June 30, 1955). The net effect of this sharp exchange was that each city went its own way in settling the expressway route. Co-ordination of inter-unit decisions on the expressway remained where it had always been, in the hands of state and county highway officials.

But Welsh's remarks about the "sliver" of Harper Woods east of Harper Avenue had touched a sensitive issue. Businessmen and residents in the northeast section of the city feared that the expressway would isolate them from the rest of the city. While residents west of the expressway in Precincts 7 and 10 would not be isolated from the rest of Harper Woods, the expressway would act as a barrier between them and the rest of their school district. In the southeast area the isolation issue had been reinforced by dissatisfaction over the proposed ad valorem method of drain assessment advanced by the CAL-controlled council. On August 17, the *Herald* reported that the Southeast Property Owners Association had discussed the possibility of seceding from Harper Woods and joining either Grosse Pointe Woods or Detroit. The *Herald* also reported that rumors were circulating to the effect that residents in the northeast were interested in joining with their southerly brethren, which would take the entire section east of Harper Avenue into Grosse Pointe Woods. In spite of a good deal of talk, no positive step was taken to initiate a secession and the proposal died.

State and county highway engineers presented detailed plans of the expressway through Harper Woods to the council on November 21. The plans called for a fully depressed roadbed with a major vehicular crossover at Vernier Road and lesser vehicular and pedestrian crossovers spotted frequently along the route. The route followed the west side of Harper, leaving the east side intact except in the southerly part of the city. The right-of-way would require the condemnation of fifty homes, forty developed business properties, and one hundred and twenty vacant parcels of land. The assessed valuation of business properties condemned and removed from the tax rolls was $600,000, residential properties, $400,000. The route above Vernier Road was given only a tentative designation pending negotiations between the state and St. Clair Shores on a final route in that jurisdiction. (The final determination of the route through St. Clair Shores put the expressway close to Beaconsfield Avenue and required the condemnation of six hundred homes.)

The council asked for several adjustments in the plans. The council wanted (1) a crossover in front of the proposed new City Hall in order to give fire and police vehicles direct access across the expressway, and (2) additional pedestrian crossovers. State personnel assured the council that their requests on these design features would be granted. (As a result of these concessions Harper Woods has more pedestrian and vehicular spans per mile [seven] across the Edsel Ford Expressway than any other municipality has across any expressway in the state of Michigan.) As the meeting concluded, the four CAL councilmen announced their intention to vote for the expressway substantially as presented.

There was some opposition from the minority councilmen and from a few persons attending the council meeting. Former Councilman Rivard and Mrs. Ruth Francis, widow of the late Councilman Charles Francis, both raised objections. Mrs. Francis read a lengthy statement listing several reasons why the expressway should not be approved. But the opposition was token, scattered, and mild. After a short time spent ironing out the differences with the state, the council set December 21 as the date for a public hearing and council vote on final plans for the expressway. The Harper Woods High School gymnasium was used in anticipation of a large turnout.

The hearing proved to be anticlimactic, with only about one hundred persons attending. Immediately after it the council convened in formal session and voted four-to-three (along strict factional lines) to commit itself irrevocably to the final plan for the expressway. On February 27, 1956 the Harper Woods City Council approved resolutions permitting the condemnation of properties for the route of the Edsel Ford Expressway. The route was settled and Harper Woods' struggle was over.

Harper Woods' opposition to the expressway had delayed its construction by about two years. The state found some consolation, however, when shortly after the Harper Woods settlement the U.S. Congress passed the Highway Act of 1956, which provided for 90 percent federal cost-sharing on the Interstate Highway System. The two-year delay resulted in the federal government paying $10,260,000 instead of $5,700,000 toward the cost of the Edsel Ford Expressway in Harper Woods. The difference is what the state and county "saved."

The Highway Act benefited Harper Woods as well. Harper Woods was scheduled to pay $11,385 (5 percent of the cost of overpasses) as its share of the cost of the expressway. Because of additional moneys available under the Highway Act, City Manager McNutt successfully renegotiated Harper Woods' agreement with the state. By a contract signed in May 1958, Harper Woods was relieved of all financial obligations concerning the expressway. Harper Woods got the Edsel Ford Expressway for nothing. The 1.8 miles of six-lane expressway, costing $11,400,000, was opened late in 1959, two years behind schedule.

Concluding Comments

Why did Harper Woods lose its battle against the expressway? Perhaps the most important reason was its lack of allies. Not one of the organizations whose support might have helped Harper Woods (the State Highway Department, the Wayne County Road Commission, the city of Detroit, the northern suburbs, and The J. L. Hudson Company) was inclined to take up the anti-expressway cause. The State Highway Department remained firm in its commitment to follow the Harper Avenue route. Despite its stated desire to "cooperate" with local units, the Highway Department actively participated in influencing local residents to favor the expressway and thus became an ally of the CAL. By refraining from pressing its questionable legal claim to putting the expressway through Harper Woods without that unit's consent, the Highway Department enhanced its political bargaining position. The Wayne County Road Commission, through its full-fledged cooperation with the state, further strengthened the state's hand. The city of Detroit, with its determination not to change the route from Harper Avenue, presented Harper Woods with a *fait accompli*. The suburbs to the north of Harper Woods adopted positions which eliminated the possibility of a suburban united front. The

J. L. Hudson Company supported pro-expressway pressures, primarily, perhaps, by refraining from building the shopping center which was to be a welcome asset to the community (in 1960 Eastland payed about one-third of Harper Woods' city and school-district taxes). With Hudson's on the side of the Highway Department and its allies, Harper Woods was faced with an external monolithic front determined to extend the expressway through Harper Woods on Harper Avenue.

At the same time that Harper Woods was confronted with unanimity externally, it was deeply split internally. The approach of the expressway did not weld Harper Woods into a single block of anti-expressway opinion. On the contrary, it exacerbated the rift in an already divided community. Harper Woods residents found themselves faced with two big unknowns: Could the state force the expressway through? and later, Would Eastland be lost if the expressway were successfully opposed? The CAL and the Democratic Club were quick to exploit the difference of opinion which this nebulous situation inevitably produced. As the expressway issue became more and more enmeshed with the other highly controversial issues (e.g., drainage, Hudson's Eastland, and paving) stirring Harper Woods, it became more firmly identified with the city's hardening political division.

In the long run, this hardening process tended to defeat the anti-expressway forces. The population of Harper Woods almost doubled between 1950 and 1955, and in April 1955 there were 8,151 registered voters in Harper Woods—only one thousand fewer than the total population of the city five years earlier. The number of votes cast in the 1955 election was about 25 percent more than the figure for the 1953 election. In Harper Woods' fairly evenly divided political situation, the balance of political power rested with the new voters, who had no prior commitments to either the Democratic Club or the CAL. The CAL had a psychological advantage by virtue of its being a faction of relatively new arrivals who were challenging the old regime. It also had the general trend toward non-partisanship in its favor. By capitalizing on its opportunity to mobilize the new entrants in support of CAL objectives, the CAL was able to gather enough votes to oust the Democratic majority and open the door to the expressway.

That the Democratic Club lost to the pro-expressway forces was partially the result of its lack of administrative skills, with which the city, county, and state were liberally endowed. The expressway issue and the other controversial issues bearing down on Harper Woods during the SOC's two-year tenure severely taxed the council's time, energies, abilities, and political skills. This situation put a premium on administrative skills; yet there was no full-time chief executive for a portion of the critical first year, nor was there a professional administrator who could step into the breach. The SOC lacked the administrative resources necessary to combat successfully the host of internal and external pressures upon it.

The conflict between Harper Woods and the state was marked by an absence of ideological arguments against state intervention, e.g., the destruction of home rule and local democracy by state intervention. These terms have a hollow ring in a satellite suburb of the metropolis in the 1950's—a suburb dependent on outside jurisdictions for providing places of employment for its residents as well as for the interjurisdictional cooperation necessary for handling many suburban problems. The expressway was therefore seen as a threat not to the community's functional autonomy but to its homogeneity, solidarity, and property values. The maintenance and enhancement of the community *qua* community has become a prime *raison d'être* of Harper Woods' existence as a unit of government.

9
The Twelve Towns
Relief Drains

A Case of Togetherness in Southeastern Oakland County

Introduction

That water seeks its own level is a fact revealed to school children through a simple laboratory demonstration. To be reminded of this fact by flooded basements and streets is a form of adult education that most householders would be willing to forego. Skill in the building of drains to dispose of storm waters and sanitary wastes is a condition precedent to the development of a healthy urban environment, and for centuries these skills have been known and practiced in various parts of the world. Bolstered by modern science and technology, sanitary engineering has reached the stage where it can design and construct, given the resources, a drainage system to meet the needs of any urban community. Thus it is easy to understand the disgust and exasperation of the suburban Oakland County resident who, in the mid-1950's, reported to the Michigan Department of Health that he found human excrement in the gutters in front of his home following a heavy rainstorm. He was more fortunate than his neighbors, who found it in their flooded basements. The solution to his and his neighbors' problem, he was told by health officials, was the construction of the Twelve Towns Relief Drains.

Oakland, one of the three counties making up the Detroit metropolis, is north of Wayne County and west of Macomb County. Both Wayne, which includes the city of Detroit, and Macomb have their eastern boundaries on the Great Lakes drainage system: the St. Clair River, Lake St. Clair, the Detroit River, and Lake Erie. Oakland is landlocked, and its natural drainage routes flow through Macomb and Wayne counties to the Great Lakes system.

Since 1940 suburban Oakland County has experienced rapid

517

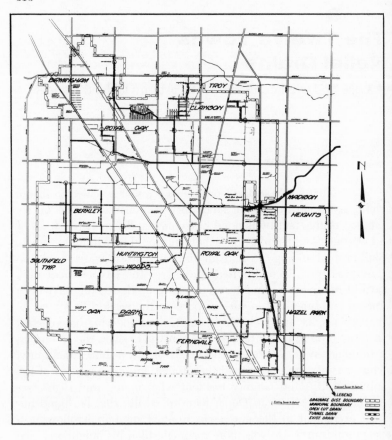

6. The Twelve Towns Relief Drains

Courtesy Michigan Department of Health

population growth. Its population of 254,068 in 1940 had grown to 396,000 by 1950 and reached 690,259 in 1960. Most of this growth took place in the southeastern corner of the county, adjacent to the city of Detroit. This corner of Oakland County was one of the first suburban areas to develop on Detroit's border. Traversed by Woodward Avenue, the major arterial road leading to downtown Detroit, and with commuter train and bus service available, this area provided the classic conditions for a "bedroom community" development, and its growth followed Woodward Avenue's northwestern course from the city. Status and income also followed the northwestern course of Woodward. East of the Woodward line, growth was less status-oriented, and here are to be found the more cross-sectional communities, such as Royal Oak, and those with a higher proportion of families with modest incomes, such as Troy, Madison Heights, and Hazel Park. By the early 1950's, the southeastern 10 percent of the county's 577-square-mile land area contained over half of the county population, and most of this population was concentrated in the 36-square-mile section making up the extreme southeastern corner of the county.

The terrain of southeastern Oakland County was not ideally suited for residential development. Much of the area was low-lying, and, with no natural waterways draining it, it served as a drainage basin for surrounding areas to the north and west. The resultant swamps were enough to discourage the Indians, whose trails bypassed the area, but as the city of Detroit grew and population spread to the suburbs, builders hauled in fill to convert swamps into building sites. Up to World War II, growth was gradual, and the Oakland County drain commissioner, an elected county official responsible for the construction and maintenance of drains, was able to piece together a system of drains, including open ditches, which was barely adequate for the population during the early 1940's and which became conspicuously inadequate as the postwar building boom developed. The thirty-six-square-mile area which made up this drainage system was referred to as the "Upper Red Run drainage basin." By 1950 it included all or part of twelve local political jurisdictions—nine cities and three townships.

By 1950, the drainage system for the Upper Red Run drainage basin consisted of two elements. A sanitary interceptor sewer was linked with the Detroit system, and Detroit was handling the area's sanitary sewage on a contract basis. The storm drain system consisted of trunk drains that had been constructed over the years for ten different but overlapping drainage districts. The storm drains had a common outlet at the upstream end of the Red Run Drainage Ditch, which flowed into the Clinton River, which in turn flowed into Lake St. Clair. The Red Run Ditch was the area's sole outlet to the Great Lakes system, and its development had had a stormy history. Originally a narrow twisting creek, Red Run had been converted by the U.S. Army Corps of Engineers, as part of a flood-control project, into a drainage ditch with a capacity to handle the storm run-off of the area. This had been accomplished only after years of controversy between Oakland and Macomb counties. Macomb County communities feared that the added load on Red Run and the Clinton River, both of which flowed through Macomb County on their way to Lake St. Clair, would increase flooding hazards in Macomb County. By 1950, however, the project had been completed, and Red Run was rated to have a capacity greater than that being utilized by the existing storm drain system in the Upper Red Run basin.

Neither the storm drain nor the sanitary system was adequate. The various communities within the system had combined sanitary and storm sewers. During dry periods the sanitary system was ordinarily adequate to handle its load, although the population increase was pushing it toward capacity operation, but when the storm run-off following a heavy rain was added to the system, the overflow was directed into the Red Run Ditch. This meant that raw sewage mixed with storm water was flowing into Red Run. Moreover, the storm drain system had not been sized for the capacity it now faced. The building up of vacant land had eliminated natural ponding areas, and the addition of roofs, driveways, sidewalks, and streets had added acres of impervious surfaces contributing to the storm run-off. As the storm drains became overloaded, forcing a backing up of water in the combined sanitary sewers, householders came face to face with the grim facts of poor drains and polluted basements.

This is a case study of the efforts of the communities in the Upper Red Run drainage basin to construct a system of relief drains that would eliminate periodic flooding of the area. It is a complex case. Basically, it involves the effort of a suburban population to adapt to certain conditions, brought about by climate, terrain, and population growth, through the available political institutions of city, township, county, and state government. The institutions were flexible enough to provide a mechanism for carrying out a project of multi-jurisdictional dimensions, but the distribution of costs and benefits to each jurisdiction provided ample ground for conflict. The struggle which preceded final agreement took nine years, from 1952 to 1961. Changes in state legislation and recourse to the courts had to take place before the Twelve Towns Relief Drains could become a reality.

Early Stages

Birth of Twelve Towns. In the fall of 1952, the U.S. Army Corps of Engineers surveyed the recently improved Red Run Ditch and notified Oakland County officials that it was now feasible to build a relief drain for the Upper Red Run drainage basin emptying into the ditch. Lying within the basin were all or most of the territory of the cities of Oak Park, Royal Oak, Berkley, Clawson, Ferndale, Huntington Woods, and Pleasant Ridge, plus portions of the cities of Birmingham and Hazel Park, and portions of Troy, Southfield, and Royal Oak townships. Geography and gravity bound these twelve communties together in a single drainage system with but a single outlet to a natural drainage system—Red Run Ditch, located in the eastern part of the basin. The natural gravity flow of surface water within the basin was from the northwest to the southeast, and existing drains followed gravity flow lines. Communities in the southern and eastern parts of the basin received drainage from their northerly and westerly neighbors, whether it flowed on the surface or underground. The drains of the various municipalities emptied into a system of county drains that had been constructed to serve particular areas regardless of municipal boundary lines. Thus the county drains carried the intermingled waters of several cities. If "relief" were provided to any part of this system, the whole system, that is several municipalities, would benefit. In such an integrated system, no one municipality could correct its drainage problems by itself without having some effect upon the rest of the system. In view of this, it became evident that if a relief system were to be built, it should be designed to serve the entire drainage basin.

Pressure to relieve the drainage problems of the area had been growing since World War II. As the building boom continued, each succeeding heavy rain brought complaints from residents with flooded streets and basements. The Michigan Department of Health began to take an interest in the matter when, as the sanitary interceptor became increasingly inadequate to handle heavy loads, raw sewage was diverted to Red Run. The state health commissioner notified the city managers in the affected area that unless something were done to relieve the flooding and prevent the discharge of raw sewage into Red Run, the Health Department would consider using its authority to withhold permits for sewer construction. Each of the cities in the drainage basin had the city-manager form of government, and the managers, eager to encourage their cities' growth, called upon the drain commissioner to take action to relieve the drainage problem. With the Corps of Engineers' approval for added flow to Red Run, the drain commissioner, prompted by pressure from the city managers and the Michigan Department of Health, prepared to act.

Under the then existing state drain legislation (subsequently revised as Act 40 of the Public Acts of 1956, Chapter XX, The Drain Code), intracounty drains, "necessary for the public health" where "the cost thereof is to be assessed wholly against public corporations," could be constructed when "two or more public corporations which will be subject to assessments to pay the cost thereof" petition the county drain commissioner requesting that the construction be undertaken. Since the drains for which relief was sought were county drains serving a number of public corporations, the various jurisdictions agreed to follow this provision of the drain law. By February 1953, each of the twelve jurisdictions—nine cities and three townships—had filed with the drain commissioner petitions requesting the construction of relief drains to serve the twelve-community area. The filing of these petitions marked the formal birth of the Twelve Towns Relief Drains project. As specified by the drain law, a Drainage Board responsible for the project was created consisting of the drain commissioner, the chairman of the County Board of Supervisors, and the chairman of the County Board of Auditors. Although the participating communities had no formal representation on this statutory board, committees were set up which included managers, councilmen, commissioners (some of the cities had city councils and some had city commissions), and township supervisors. These committees were outside the formal structure, however. The formal powers of the three-man Drainage Board were extensive, but support from the participating communities was necessary if the project were to get off the ground.

Following the formal organization of the Drainage Board for the Twelve Towns project, Drain Commissioner Ralph Main and his staff prepared preliminary plans for a system of relief drains designed to handle a five-year storm, i.e., the most severe storm that could be expected to occur in five years. The estimated cost of this system was $13,000,000. This was admittedly a minimal plan designed to hold down costs. It called for (1) small street openings to restrict the flow of storm water and force ponding in the streets, and (2) permanent disconnection of downspouts to relieve the load on the sewers. This plan was presented to the participating municipalities in the spring of 1953 and received a mixed reception. Several city managers and municipal representatives felt that it was inadequate. They insisted that Main's plan be submitted to a private engineering firm for review and that consideration be given to a ten-year storm design. This request annoyed Main, who was eager to get the project under construction and felt that calling upon a private firm for plans was a reflection upon the competence of his own office. Nevertheless, after some delay, the Drainage Board engaged the engineering firm of Hubbell, Roth and Clark, Inc., to check Main's plan and submit its own recommendations on what was required to provide adequate relief. The firm's report was submitted in June 1954.

The Hubbell, Roth and Clark report, which was based upon extensive study of the Twelve Town's drainage area, concluded that in order to obtain adequate relief, the system should be designed for a ten-year storm. To accomplish this, the report presented a tentative plan for a relief drain system consisting of three main branches which would converge at Red Run Ditch, and costing about $30,000,000. During the summer of 1954, the Main plan and the Hubbell, Roth and Clark plan were discussed and debated by the Twelve Towns communities. Proponents of Main's five-year storm plan argued that extra protection afforded by the ten-year plan was not worth the extra cost; they warned that the $30,000,000 cost would threaten the tax structure of many of the municipalities and cited the ponding of storm water in Oak Park's streets as a satisfactory solution to the heaviest storms. The mayors of Huntington Woods and Ferndale, however, were skeptical of the five-year design, and they expressed the feeling, shared by many others, that if the project were to be built, it should be sized to give long-term relief rather than temporary improvement. Some hope was expressed that a compromise solution could be worked out. No one was quarreling over the desirability of the larger system, but the cost was a major concern. Under existing legislation, financing would have to be done with twenty-year bonds, which meant high interest rates and a relatively short time for paying off the debt.

On October 22, 1954, a meeting of representatives from the Twelve Towns municipalities was held at the Northwood Inn in Berkley. Recent heavy rains had caused extensive flooding throughout the area. The preponderance of opinion at the meeting was that the ten-year design should be the basis for the relief system. Some communities were still hesitant. Hazel Park, which had been planning to build an independent system, was urged to stay in the Twelve Towns system, and Royal Oak Township and Clawson, both on the edges of the system, voiced reservations over costs and location of the drains. But the general tone of the meeting was that at last a mutual understanding had been reached that the Twelve Towns Relief Drains should be built and that the system should be adequate to handle a ten-year storm, which was considered to be the optimum economical size for a storm drain system. The reservations that were expressed by some municipalities were not considered to be insurmountable. In a spirit of cooperation, it was suggested and agreed that the municipalities would advance funds to the Drainage Board to pay for blueprints and other necessary expenses. The money would eventually be paid back to the communities when bonds were sold, but the contributions would relieve the Drainage Board of the necessity of borrowing from lending institutions. The commitment of funds was evidence of the desire of the contributing communities that the project be expedited.

Following the October 1954 meeting, the Drainage Board decided to expedite work on the preliminary design by dividing the project into three sections—a North Section, a Middle Section, and a South Section. Using the funds advanced by the municipalities, the board contracted with three different engineering firms, each firm taking one section, for the basic engineering data such as grades, pipe sizes, and approximate location of the relief lines. Preliminary estimates of cost were also requested. When the reports were completed in July and September of 1955, they did not provide firm cost estimates or final detailed plans. It seemed to be taken for granted that the system would cost about $30,000,000. Dividing the project into three parts caused some confusion by giving the impression that each of the three sections could be built as an independent system, and the Drainage Board had to explain repeatedly that the relief system required all three sections.

While the preliminary engineering studies were being conducted, the Twelve Towns issue did not remain dormant. The October 1954 meeting had left unsettled the question of allocating costs among the communities. New legislation had to be introduced that would permit the use of thirty-year faith and credit bonds to finance the project, and there was some jockeying over what areas were to be included within the project area, especially in Southfield Township.

By the time that the engineering reports were ready in September 1955, the enthusiasm for the Twelve Towns project that had been evident the previous October had begun to cool in some of the municipalities. The Drainage Board had hired Claude H. Stevens as its bond counsel and legal advisor. In examining the petitions establishing the board, Stevens, one of the area's most respected bond counselors and an expert in drain law, came across what he considered to be a legal defect in the resolutions passed by the various municipalities. Not wishing to jeopardize a later bond sale, he insisted that the whole procedure be done over in proper form. This request provoked grumbling over an additional delay in some of the cities; the necessity of processing new resolutions through councils and commissions provided an opportunity for those with doubts and objections to voice them. Three communities—the cities of Clawson and Berkley and Southfield Township—failed to pass a new resolution because of dissatisfaction over boundaries and/or cost allocations, but the nine other communities did file their petitions with the Drainage Board on October 26, 1955. Failure to file did not eliminate Clawson, Berkley, and Southfield from the project. The drain law required that "two or more" of the affected public corporations petition for an intracounty drain, and since all of Clawson and Berkley and part of Southfield were included in the drainage district for which relief was sought, they were equally bound by the process.

With the new petition in hand, the Drainage Board, on November 10, 1955, formally instituted the Twelve Towns Drainage District and the Twelve Towns Relief Drains project. The key paragraph in the board's resolution went as follows:

> That the City of Birmingham, City of Berkley, City of Clawson, City of Ferndale, City of Hazel Park, City of Huntington Woods, City of Oak Park, City of Pleasant Ridge, City of Royal Oak, Township of Royal Oak (including the territory conditionally incorporated as the City of Madison Heights), Township of Southfield (including the territory conditionally incorporated as the City of Southfield), and the Township of Troy (including the territory conditionally incorporated as the City of Troy) constitute as a whole contiguous territory which is served by the said existing county drains; and that it has become necessary for the public health to supplement said existing county drains by the construction of relief drains as set forth in said petition.

The resolution went on to state that the cost of the project would be assessed against the above-named communities plus the state of Michigan, on account of drainage to state highways, and Oakland County for the drainage of county highways.

The Twelve Towns jurisdictions were undergoing change at this time. Troy Township was on the verge of being and soon became wholly incorporated as the city of Troy. The incorporation of Madison Heights took eight square miles from Royal Oak Township, leaving the township with 424 acres. Southfield Township was in the process of being transformed into the city of Southfield

(26.6 square miles) and the village of Beverly Hills (4 square miles). Southfield's incorporation was not completed until 1958, whereas Troy and Madison Heights became cities in 1956. When the reshuffling was completed, of the original twelve jurisdictions, Troy and Southfield townships had been eliminated, and added were the cities of Troy, Southfield and Madison Heights, and the village of Beverly Hills. Twelve Towns thus grew to fourteen jurisdictions. The new jurisdictions did not simplify matters.

Boundary Problems. Having formally established the Twelve Towns Relief Drains project, the Drainage Board was next required by statute to hold a hearing:

> At such hearing, any public corporation to be assessed or any taxpayer thereof shall be entitled to be heard. After such hearing, the Drainage Board shall make a determination as to the sufficiency of the petition, the practicability of the drain, whether the drain should be constructed, and if so, the public corporations to be assessed, and shall issue its order accordingly, which order shall be known as the "final order of determination." Sect. 467, Chapter XX, Act 40 of the Public Acts of 1956. (The drain law of 1923 was revised in 1956. Citations are to the later act where the provisions are identical with the earlier law.)

Hearings were held on December 15, 1955 and January 17 and 27, 1956. That no formal objections to the project appear in the record obscures the fact that members of the Drainage Board, especially the drain commissioner and representatives from the municipalities, had put in weeks of negotiation to arrive at a plan acceptable to all concerned. The key issue, at this stage, was the amount of territory from each jurisdiction that would be included in the Twelve Towns Drainage District. The petition seeking the relief system specified ten existing county drainage districts for which relief was sought. These districts had been set up without regard for municipal boundaries, and it became evident that, depending upon where they were located, the relief drains would be capable of handling some areas outside of the ten districts. The Drainage Board was not bound by the original boundaries of the ten districts, which meant that additional area could be included. This latitude provided a margin for negotiation, assuming, of course, that the "outside" area under consideration was within the nat-

ural gravity limits of the drainage basin. Since the existing drainage district lines left parts of some cities outside a drain district,
it was advantageous to the cities to incorporate such excluded
areas into the Twelve Towns District. The costs for the relief drain
were to be assessed against each city as a whole, which meant
that those living in excluded areas would complain of paying for
benefits they did not receive. The Drainage Board granted added
territory to Hazel Park, Madison Heights, Royal Oak, Clawson,
and Oak Park but turned down the attempt by Troy Township
(later the city of Troy) to have a substantial amount of territory
added.

Troy, the northernmost jurisdiction in the Twelve Towns District, was the least developed and, based on the original ten drainage districts, had the smallest percentage of its total land area in
the Twelve Towns District. But with the population spread now
reaching Troy, developers were pressing to open new subdivisions.
Troy had neither sewers nor drains for urban development, and
Twelve Towns appeared to be an opportunity to get them. The
Drainage Board decided, however, that to include all of the area
requested by Troy would force them outside the natural drainage
basin, thus violating the logic of the system as well as adding substantially to the cost. Nevertheless, some added territory from Troy
was included.

Clawson, Troy's neighbor to the south, was closely observing
developments in Troy. From the beginning, Clawson had been
skeptical of Twelve Towns. It needed the drains but feared that
it would have to pay more than its share of the cost. Troy to the
north and a portion of Birmingham to the east drained through
Clawson. Unless Birmingham and Troy were adequately serviced
by Twelve Towns, Clawson could conceivably be part of Twelve
Towns but still be flooded by her neighbors.

Southfield Township straddled the natural dividing line of the
two basins draining southern Oakland County. The bulk of the
township, the middle and western sections, was in the River Rouge
drainage basin—a series of tributaries flowing into the River Rouge,
which in turn flowed into the Detroit River, south of Detroit. The
eastern edge of the township, about nineteen hundred acres, was
in the Upper Red Run section of the Clinton River drainage basin,

in other words, the Twelve Towns area. Drain Commissioner Main proposed that substantially all of the Southfield area be eliminated from Twelve Towns and drained into the Rouge basin. He estimated that this would save the Twelve Towns project $1,000,000. Since Southfield was a township at this time and therefore had limited taxing powers, it was considered expedient to keep its involvement in Twelve Towns to a minimum. This was agreeable to the cities bordering the Southfield area on the east and southeast, as long as assurance was forthcoming that the Southfield area would be drained. Otherwise the neighboring cities of Oak Park and Berkley would be flooded by the run-off from Southfield.

By the time the final hearing was held on January 27, boundary problems were solved, at least temporarily. Troy had reluctantly agreed, by formal council resolution passed on January 23, to go along with the Twelve Towns Plan and seek other solutions for the area left out of Twelve Towns. Clawson was apparently satisfied. Southfield Township, which later proved so obstreperous, raised no objections at the hearing. It appeared that only a negligible part of Southfield, 242 acres, would be involved. Representatives from Royal Oak Township and Madison Heights also appeared at the final hearing, but neither filed formal objection. But trouble was brewing over costs. There was growing feeling in Madison Heights that it would be cheaper for that city, through which Red Run flowed, to build an independent system draining into Red Run. Royal Oak Township, which now consisted of only 424 acres, populated for the most part by low-income Negro families, had begun to contemplate the cost in relation to the area's tax resources and wondered where the money would come from. As it turned out, silence at the hearing did not mean consent.

Following the hearing, the Drainage Board issued its "final order of determination." The order held that the petition requesting the project was sufficient "in all respects"; that the project was practical and should be constructed; and that the public corporations named in its November organizing resolution should be assessed the cost of the drains. The order amended the location and routes of the North Section and the Middle Section of the relief drain from those included in the petition. The final order of determination cleared the way for signing contracts for detailed construction plans, specifications, and estimates of cost. These contracts amounted to more than $1,000,000, and the board had had no authority to take on commitments of this size prior to the final order of determination. But the contracts were ready and waiting. They were awarded on January 30, 1956, with each of the three sections of the project awarded to a different firm.

By February 1956, it looked as if the Twelve Towns project was finally under way. The long negotiations that had culminated in the final order of determination seemed to have settled the demands of the municipalities over inclusion and exclusion of territory, although there were still rumblings in Troy that they wanted all in or all out, and Berkley was not happy over the exclusion of so much of Southfield. The next crisis would come when price tags were placed on each section and costs apportioned to each jurisdiction. In order to deal with the anticipated crisis and to expedite matters in general, the Drainage Board hired Ashton J. Berst to serve as co-ordinator for Twelve Towns. Berst, a civil engineer and retired city manager of Pleasant Ridge, one of the Twelve Towns cities, was familiar with the area, the project, the personalities, and the problems. The board also hired Charles H. Harmon, a tax consultant, to begin work on a formula for apportioning costs. In awarding the contracts, the board attempted to tie the contracting firms to a July 1 completion date, but although the firms balked at this, they did have their plans completed by August 9, 1956. By that time, however, the cities had succeeded in prying from the Drainage Board estimates of their shares in the cost apportionment.

Apportionment Problems

The Formula. During the early stages, the capacity of the Twelve Towns system and the areas to be served by it were the critical questions, but as the project moved toward the final plan stage, the question of apportionment of costs to the participating jurisdictions became paramount. Much of the support for the drain commissioner's five-year storm, $13,000,000 system was based upon an assumption that this would be about all that the communities were likely to be willing to buy. Heavy rains and serious flooding had created the pressure for the larger, more costly ten-year system, and the drain law was being revised to make it easier to finance the more expensive project. Nevertheless, each municipality was awaiting a special apportionment that would reveal the size of its bill.

The drain law (Sect. 468) gave to the Drainage Board the authority to establish the apportionment, stipulating that "in making the apportionments hereunder there shall be taken into consideration the benefits to accrue to each public corporation and also the extent to which each public corporation contributes to the conditions which make the drain necessary." This was a reasonable prescription, but it was difficult to apply. There were a number of relevant variables that could be taken into consideration in calculating contributions to the problem and determining benefits from the drain. Not all of the cities were equally built up. Those in the southeastern part of the Twelve Towns Drainage District had less vacant land than those in the western and northern part. The built-up areas contributed a greater run-off and at the same time were more costly through which to lay drains. Because of the terrain and the single outlet at Red Run Ditch, cities closest to Red Run would have drains much larger than the needed capacity of the single city in order to accommodate the water from a higher neighbor. (Madison Heights was the most extreme example of this.) One city, Huntington Woods (and a small part of Royal Oak), contained the Detroit Zoological Park and Rackham Golf Course, both owned by the city of Detroit. A final complication was the fact that within each of the jurisdictions there were parts of one or more of the existing ten drains that Twelve Towns would relieve, and these drains had been paid for or were still being paid for by special assessment districts within the various communities. These drains varied in age, some going back to the 1920's.

The apportionment formula that was finally adopted was based upon the following logic. The Twelve Towns Relief Drains were but part of a complete drainage system that consisted of the relief drains plus the existing drains within the original ten drainage districts. The cost of the total system was arrived at by adding the cost of Twelve Towns to the dollar value of the existing drains.

This latter figure was obtained by determining the cost of the original drains and increasing this to prices as of January 1, 1956. Certain adjustments were made to account for county at-large tax contributions to the system and losses to bond holders resulting from scavenger land sales. The original cost of the existing drains was thus appreciated to current value, on the theory that since the original drainage districts that built the drains had to continue to maintain them, the value did not depreciate. The figure thus arrived at was about $17,000,000. Having arrived at the total cost of the complete drainage system (the cost of the relief drains plus the cost of the existing drains), each municipality's share of the total was determined by the amount of area it had within the Twelve Towns District, calculated as a percentage of the total area. In calculating these percentages, acreage for Oakland County and the state of Michigan was included to take care of county and state highways. (At a later date, September 1957, Oakland County's acreage was increased to include the Detroit-owned zoo and golf course.) The area percentage for each unit of government was multiplied by the total cost of the system to determine each unit's share in the cost of the complete system, Twelve Towns plus the existing drains. In other words, the apportionment of cost was done on an area basis, on the theory that each acre of land in the Twelve Towns District contributed equally to the problem and would benefit equally from relief. The next step in the calculations was designed to give those municipalities which had paid for part of the existing system credit for this contribution. Tax Consultant Harmon determined for each unit of government the contributions by that unit, through at-large taxes or by citizens of the unit through special assessment districts, to existing drains appreciated to current costs. The dollar value of each municipality's contribution was subtracted from the municipality's share of the cost of the complete system; the remainder was the share of Twelve Towns apportioned to the municipality.

Using the August 1959 calculations and taking Berkley as an example, this was how the formula worked. Berkley's 1,622.6 acres (the entire city) was 6.6 percent of the Twelve Towns District (then 23,636 acres in all), which made Berkley's share of the total drainage system (then calculated at $64,090,179) $4,235,459. Berkley was credited with having made a $1,155,022 contribution to the existing drains, which left Berkley with a $3,080,437.65 bill for its share of Twelve Towns, or 6.5 percent of the total (then $47,-102,000) Twelve Towns cost.

The apportionment formula was the result of lengthy consideration and discussion of various possible methods. The decision to use the formula was made by the Drainage Board, which relied upon the advice of their Co-ordinator Berst, Tax Consultant Harmon, and Bond Counsel Stevens. Because of the possibility of legal challenge, the formula had to be one that would hold up in court, and at the same time it had to be acceptable to the majority of the participating municipalities. Consideration was given to various ways in which storm run-off might be measured in each community, but this would have involved extremely complicated computations which the board and its advisors considered less defensible than the use of area as a basis for apportionment determination. It could and would be argued that an acre of built-up land with roofs, streets, walks, and driveways contributed more run-off than an acre of vacant land, but it was considered fair to assume that eventually all land in the Twelve Towns District would become built-up to approximately the same degree. It was also recognized that actual construction costs would not be uniform throughout the District and that the cost of construction of a segment of the relief drain through any particular municipality might have little relationship to that municipality's apportionment. In some municipalities there would be very little construction. Nevertheless, the area-based formula had to stand or fall on the board's insistence that the Twelve Towns District was a single drainage system and that each municipality was inextricably dependent upon the construction of the total system.

During the spring and early summer of 1956, while the board was working out an apportionment formula and the engineering firms were working on plans and estimates, representatives from Oakland County and the Twelve Towns communities were instrumental in having the state drain law revised so as to facilitate the financing of the project. These revisions provided intracounty drainage districts with the authority to sell thirty-year bonds, to pledge the full faith and credit of the district for the payment of the debt, and to assess cities at large for the cost of drains. The revised law also provided that assessments made under it were exempt from any statutory or charter debt limitations of the public corporations involved and that taxes levied to pay the assessment were also exempt from statutory or charter tax limitations. These revisions were considered necessary to assure buyers for the bonds.

Pressure to get started with the project mounted. In the spring (1956), the Michigan Department of Health surveyed Red Run Ditch and found evidence of raw sewage and sewage sludge during dry-weather flow and declared that this constituted a nuisance and a hazard to health. This finding made it clear that a sanitary interceptor was as essential to the area's drainage problem as was Twelve Towns. On June 16 and 17, 1956, a Saturday and Sunday, a heavy rainstorm hit the area and caused serious flooding. Houses in Berkley had ground water coming from Southfield flowing in basement windows on one side and out the windows on the other side. Clawson, Royal Oak, Ferndale, Huntington Woods, and Oak Park reported flooded basements. Householders throughout the area complained bitterly as they proceeded to mop up the flood water and raw sewage that had invaded their homes. Berkley and Royal Oak city officials threatened Southfield with an injunction which would halt further building in the township until Southfield had installed adequate drains within its boundaries. All of the cities hardest hit by the storm turned to the Drainage Board and demanded that the Twelve Towns project be speeded up.

Now that an apportionment formula had been worked out and a financing method had received legal sanction, the next step was to establish costs for each municipality by applying the formula to the engineering estimates of cost. It had been hoped that these estimates would be ready by July 1, but Berst had to inform the cities that they would be delayed until August. This delay, on top of the storm, was too much. The cities insisted that the Drainage Board give them some idea of how much the project would cost each one of them. Since firm cost estimates were not available, the board was reluctant to do this, and Berst and Harmon objected that any premature estimates would result in future difficulties if the final engineering estimates proved to be higher. But the three men making up the Drainage Board were county political officials dependent upon the support of the voters and the Board of Supervisors. Pressure from the Twelve Towns area, which included about half of the county population and a majority of its major cities, could not be ignored. A meeting was called for July 12 to show how the apportionment formula apportioned costs on the basis of the two-year-old cost estimate of $30,000,000. In presenting these estimates, Harmon and Berst emphasized that they were unofficial approximations.

Objections and Revisions. Although the July 12 apportionment schedule was presented as merely an unofficial approximation, to the assembled representatives of the Twelve Towns communities, it was the first solid dollars-and-cents statement they had seen of what it would cost each community in relation to each other community. A variable in each community's share was the credit allowed for contributions to existing drains. This was the first time that these figures had been made public. The July 12 meeting was consumed in explaining the formula. The table presenting the data was detailed, with percentages carried out to the fourth place, and the immediate reaction seemed to be that the method of apportionment was satisfactory. But a few days later, after detailed study and comparisons had been undertaken by each of the municipalities, varied reactions were registered.

Oak Park immediately agreed on its share, considering it fair and equitable, but Clawson and Huntington Woods wanted more information before they would give their approval. The troublesome part of the formula was the credit assigned each municipality for existing drains, and Co-ordinator Berst was hard-pressed during meetings with municipal officials to explain this calculation. By July 19, Troy and Madison Heights had begun to voice strong objections. Madison Heights claimed that its share was too high and that its proximity to Red Run Ditch would permit it to build an independent system for less than its allocation in Twelve Towns. Madison Heights, with 5.4 percent of the Twelve Towns area, was apportioned 7.4 percent of the relief drains cost, whereas Ferndale, with 10.8 percent of the area, was apportioned 9.2 percent of the cost. These differences were due to the fact that older communities, such as Ferndale, received larger credits for existing drains than the newer cities, such as Madison Heights. Troy, another new city, had 4.2 percent of the Twelve Towns area and was apportioned 5.9 percent of the cost. Troy maintained that unless a larger share of its area, about 20,000 acres, was included within Twelve Towns, it would not be worthwhile for Troy to remain in the project at all, since the cost for the 917 acres that were included would be out of proportion to the benefits that the city as a whole, which would be assessed the cost, would derive from the project. Troy was informed that the gravity flow of the system would not permit taking in the larger area.

On August 9, 1956, the engineering cost estimates became available and were given to the municipalities. By this time five city councils—Oak Park, Ferndale, Royal Oak, Huntington Woods, and Clawson—had formally approved the tentative apportionment. This approval amounted to a vote of confidence, since no formal action was required at this stage. In Troy, on the other hand, the City Commission had instructed its city attorney to find an escape clause that would permit the city to withdraw from the project, and if this withdrawal required legal action, he was authorized to pursue it. It was revealed on August 9 that the cost of the project had risen to $38,000,000. The increase was attributed to a rise in labor and material costs as well as some revisions in the earlier plans and certain unforeseen construction problems. The 27 percent increase came as a jolt to the municipalities, but the Drainage Board believed that they would accept the increase and set November 1 as the target date for signing contracts. On August 13 a new preliminary apportionment schedule based upon the $38,000,-000 figure was distributed to the municipalities. The new apportionment increased acreage—and therefore cost—for one municipality (Southfield), which resulted in changes in the percentage of the total Twelve Towns cost assigned to the other communities. The August 13 apportionment was not "official," but it did serve as the basis for negotiations that took place throughout the remainder of August.

Troy's threat of court action worried the Twelve Towns officials. Court action, even if it were ultimately to prove unsuccessful, would nevertheless delay the sale of bonds. To satisfy bond counsels, any court test would have to be taken to the Michigan Su-

preme Court for a final determination. Having reacted to the preliminary apportionment based upon the $30,000,000 estimate with
a threat to withdraw, Troy's determination to pull out of Twelve
Towns was not cooled by the new apportionment that increased
her share of the cost by over $300,000, to a total of a little over
$2,000,000. Troy's plight was understandable. A newly incorpo-
rated city with a land area of thirty-three square miles, a population of around sixteen thousand, and a 1956 assessed valuation of
a little more than $12,500,000 was being asked to assume a $2,000,-
000 debt, assessed against all the city's taxpayers, to provide for a
drainage system that would serve only 917 acres, about 4 percent,
of the city's territory. Of the 917 acres included in Twelve Towns,
about 500 were within the original drain districts to be relieved
by Twelve Towns, but the remaining acreage was outside any of
the original ten districts. Following the August 13 apportionment,
members of the Drainage Board, their staff, and other officials
from the Twelve Towns municipalities met with the Troy Commission in an attempt to work out a settlement that would avoid
court action. It became clear that the Troy Commission was determined to detach the city from Twelve Towns. A final meeting
between the Drainage Board and the Troy Commission was held
on September 3. The Drainage Board proposed to drop Troy from
Twelve Towns, if Troy would give assurances that it would provide adequate drains to prevent storm waters from the Troy areas
north of Clawson and Royal Oak from flowing into these two
cities. The commission's retort was that it would build such drains
when it chose and when the area could afford to pay for them.
The following day the board met and formally approved a tentative apportionment that included Troy's 917 acres.

As a jurisdiction, Southfield was in a state of limbo. The area
had voted to incorporate as a city, but as yet no charter had been
approved. This left the township officials with the authority to
act for the area. Like Troy, Southfield was on the edge of the
Twelve Towns drainage area, the western edge, and only a part
of Southfield, one-twelfth, was in the Twelve Towns natural drainage basin; the remaining eleven-twelfths was part of the River
Rouge drainage basin. During the early planning stages, Drain
Commissioner Main decided to exclude most of Southfield from

Twelve Towns by providing drains that would drain all of the Southfield area into the River Rouge. Southfield's Twelve Towns neighbors, Berkley, Royal Oak, Huntington Woods and Oak Park, were agreeable to this treatment assuming that the Rouge drains were built. These neighboring communities, especially Berkley and Oak Park, suffered from the Southfield run-off, and their benefits from Twelve Towns would be slight if Southfield continued to flood their territory.

The July 12th apportionment had included only 242.8 acres from Southfield. This area was part of one of the original ten drainage districts Twelve Towns was to relieve, and township officials had agreed to its inclusion in the Twelve Towns project. The new apportionment increased Southfield's acreage by about 440 acres. This increase was made without notice to or the consent of township officials. In later court action, Drainage Board personnel testified that the original 242.8 acres had been the result of an oversight and that the additional acreage was in existing drainage districts to be drained by Twelve Towns and outside the area planned for drainage to the Rouge. The additional acreage increased Southfield's apportionment from $371,925 to $1,268,719, and township supervisors complained that if this were to stand, eighty-two cents out of every tax dollar the township raised under its fifteen-mill tax limit would have to go to pay for a project that would benefit, for the most part, builders and real-estate developers, and would service but a small fraction of the township area. As was the case with Troy, Drainage Board members, their staff, and officials from the other Twelve Towns communities met with Southfield officials and attempted to convince them that they should go along with the project. As a result of these negotiations, Southfield's acreage was cut to 596.3 and its apportionment to $811,046. This reduction meant that the shares of the other municipalities would have to be increased to make up the difference, but this they were willing to do in order to avoid adjudication and delay. This concession, however, proved to be insufficient to appease Southfield officials.

Royal Oak Township was the third jurisdiction that objected to going ahead with the project. Reduced by Madison Height's incorporation to a mere 424 acres, this remaining stub of a town-

ship formed a pocket of low-income Negro families in the southern part of the Twelve Towns area. Unwanted by the wealthy
neighboring cities, this community was in difficult financial straits.
With a 1956 assessed valuation of $2,703,525, it was assigned under
the July apportionment a $560,916 share of Twelve Towns. There
was no question over whether the township belonged in the Twelve
Towns District. Royal Oak Township's objection was that it could
not afford to pay for the drains. The cost would require it to levy
taxes in excess of the state constitution's fifteen-mill tax limitation
on townships. A major adjustment was made to ease the township's plight. Its credit for contributions to existing drains was increased from $346,120 in the July apportionment to $1,048,712 in
the formal tentative apportionment approved by the Drainage
Board on September 4. This reduced the township's share of
Twelve Towns to $344,225, even though the total cost of the project
had increased from $30,000,000 to $38,000,000. This was a major
concession, but it was not enough.

On September 4, 1956, the Drainage Board met and took the
next formal steps. It approved the plans, specifications, and estimates of cost (aggregating $38,581,000), and adopted a tentative
apportionment, setting forth the percentage of the cost to be borne
by each of the public corporations as follows:

Municipality	Percentage of Total Cost
City of Berkley	7.284725
City of Birmingham	4.896367
City of Clawson	5.818323
City of Ferndale	9.986131
City of Hazel Park	3.330601
City of Huntington Woods	3.207309
City of Madison Heights	6.894110
City of Oak Park	12.678732
City of Pleasant Ridge	.907041
City of Royal Oak	32.978951
City of Troy	5.433991
Township of Royal Oak	.892214
Township of Southfield	2.102192
Township of Troy	.093460
County of Oakland	1.567164
State of Michigan	1.928689

The Troy Township area represented a small segment that had not been included in the city when Troy incorporated but was later annexed by adjoining cities. The Oakland County and state of Michigan share was due to drainage of highways. With percentages carried to the sixth place, the board was paying a nice attention to detail that was translated into dollar computations carried to the penny. There was no rounding off. The percentages reported above were those derived after applying the credit for existing drains. Troy's and Madison Heights' shares of the cost were slightly over 1 percent greater than their percentage of the total territory, and Royal Oak Township's and Oak Park's shares were slightly more than 1 percent less than their share of the total territory. For the remaining jurisdictions, the variation between percentage of territory and percentage of Twelve Towns cost was plus or minus less than 1 percent. The board set October 12, 1956 as the date for hearings on the apportionment.

Troy and Southfield Go to Court.   Although negotiations had not succeeded so far in satisfying Troy and Southfield, it was decided to make another try, so a meeting was called for September 11 at a local restaurant. It was hoped that in an informal atmosphere, with representatives of all municipalities present, some form of agreement could be reached. The meeting failed. Troy officials boycotted it, and Southfield sent "observers" instead of representatives. Troy still took the position that if it could not have a large segment of its territory served by Twelve Towns, it did not want to be included at all. Southfield was now determined to fight to get out by challenging the constitutionality of the drain law. On October 3, Southfield filed a bill of complaint with the Oakland County Circuit Court requesting that the Drainage Board be enjoined from further proceedings. The following day Troy filed a similar suit. A temporary injunction was issued, and Circuit Court Judge H. Russel Holland indicated to the parties that he was prepared to cooperate with them in bringing the issue to trial so that an early decision could be had. The trial date was set for October 30.

The Drainage Board did not take advantage of the opportunity for a speedy trial. It requested that the trial date be postponed while it continued to negotiate with Troy and Southfield. The board's attorneys had some doubts about their case and wanted additional time to negotiate. To strengthen their case, Berst and the board's attorneys proposed that the area of Troy included in Twelve Towns but outside existing drainage districts, some four hundred acres, be dropped and that the North Section of the project be redesigned for smaller area coverage. This suggested change, which would require a new tentative apportionment in line with reduced construction costs, aroused the other cities. Royal Oak's mayor complained that he could not understand how the county could negotiate a settlement with Troy that would result in higher apportionment to the other cities without their consent. The mayor announced that Royal Oak would intervene in the suit in order to protect its own interests, since if any city were permitted to withdraw or the areas of coverage changed, it would affect Royal Oak's apportionment. A few days later Oak Park and Ferndale also decided to intervene, and they were eventually joined by Huntington Woods, Hazel Park, Madison Heights, and Berkley. Oak Park now began to insist that all of the Southfield territory in the Clinton drainage basin be included in Twelve Towns to insure that Oak Park would be protected from Southfield run-off.

The negotiations were not proving successful. Troy was not moved to drop its suit even though its area was reduced by four hundred acres, and pressure was mounting to increase the area served in Southfield. Under existing legislation, the Drainage Board was free to change the boundaries of the Twelve Towns District at its own discretion, and it was proceeding to negotiate these changes after issuing the tentative apportionment. Pressure was now developing to change the drain law to require that the board designate the area to be served prior to establishing a tentative apportionment. This requirement would prevent later shifts in area coverage that would affect individual apportionments or extend benefits to areas not required to pay for them. It became law when the necessary change was made in the Drain Code during the 1957 session of the state legislature.

When the trial date came up early in January 1957, the Drainage Board requested another postponement. Drain Commissioner Main had not run for re-election, and the new commissioner elected in the fall of 1956 took office on January 1st. The new drain commissioner, Daniel W. Barry, who automatically became chairman of the Twelve Towns Drainage Board, and the board's attorneys felt that further negotiation with Troy was warranted. One of Troy's strongest objections was that the drain law required that the cost of the drain be assessed against the city at large. Thus all of the city's taxpayers would have to pay, rather than only those in the drain's service area. The board was planning to have the law amended in the 1957 session of the legislature to permit a city to set up a special assessment district consisting of that part of the city deriving special benefit from the project and to assess the cost against this district. This amendment was later adopted, but it did not change the attitude of Troy's policy-makers.

The spring of 1957 was a frustrating period for those cities eager to get on with the Twelve Towns project. Some threatened to form smaller combinations. Hazel Park, under orders from the Michigan Department of Health to stop polluting drains running through Macomb County, proposed that Madison Heights join them in a Two Towns Drainage District. Madison Heights, however, was more interested in considering construction of its own system. Royal Oak and Clawson discussed a joint project, but this, as well as other combinations that were proposed, never went beyond the discussion stage. The logic of the existing system was such that anything less than Twelve Towns would have been but a partial solution to the problem and might, in fact, compound the difficulty. But the Drainage Board refused to be hurried by this show of impatience. It was now clear that negotiations with Troy and Southfield would not result in withdrawal of their suits (Royal Oak township intervened with Southfield in the latter's suit), but there was a case pending before the Michigan Supreme Court involving an intracounty drain in Wayne County that was due to be decided during the summer. The board's counsel, Claude Stevens, was also involved in the Wayne County case, and knowing that the court's decision would settle some of the issues raised by Southfield and Troy, he counseled postponement of the Twelve Towns litigation. The Drainage Board's only formal action during the spring of 1957 was taken on March 15 when it rescinded the tentative apportionment resolution of the previous September. The reduction in Troy's acreage required new cost figures, but before this change was made a more drastic change in plans and in cost estimates would take place.

In April, a heavy rainstorm brought serious flooding to Wayne County when the River Rouge overflowed its banks. The Rouge, taking its rise in southern Oakland County, flowed through a heavily populated section of Detroit and Wayne County and was bordered by industry along its southern reaches, where it empties into the Detroit River. The flooding of the Rouge provoked complaints from Wayne County officials that the development of Oakland County communities was aggravating the situation by increasing the storm run-off into this obviously overloaded natural drain. Subsequent studies conducted by the Wayne County Drain Commission showed that substantial work would have to be done, such as straightening and deepening, in order to permit the Rouge to handle its "natural" load without flooding. These events had a direct bearing upon Twelve Towns. About two thousand acres of Southfield were within the Twelve Towns natural drainage basin, but only about 600 acres were included in the Twelve Towns District in the September 1956 apportionment; the remaining 1400 acres, it will be recalled, were to be drained into the Rouge system. The flooding of the Rouge and Wayne County's threats to sue Oakland County for contributing to the flood damage prompted the Oakland County drain commissioner and his staff to take another look at the Southfield plan. Cost figures were now available on the diversion plan: it would take about $3,000,000 to drain the eastern part of Southfield into the Rouge. By June, the Drainage Board had become convinced that it would have to include 1,948.7 acres of Southfield in Twelve Towns.

There was certain to be a strong reaction from Southfield officials when they heard about the additional acreage. Considering the past juggling of Southfield's acreage, this was understandable. At one period, Drain Commissioner Main had said that only a small portion of the Southfield area would be included, and the first informal apportionment had indeed included small acreage (242 acres). The first formal apportionment had more than doubled that (546.7 acres), resulting in Southfield's suit. Underlying the question of area to be served was Southfield's dubious political status. As a township, Southfield was bound by a fifteen-mill tax limitation. The drain law contained a clause designed to waive the limitation, but it had never been tested in court. As long as Southfield was a township, it made sense to keep its acreage to a minimum. By the summer of 1957, it looked as if Southfield would soon approve a charter, the final step to becoming a city. As a city, Southfield would not be bound by the fifteen-mill limitation, and a higher apportionment could be made to stick. But to the casual observer, unfamiliar with tax laws and drainage basins, the changes in Southfield's acreage indicated that the Drainage Board either did not know what it was doing or was involved in the juggling of acreage in response to pressure brought to bear by the other municipalities in Twelve Towns.

Southfield did not approve its city charter until April 28, 1958, so the proposal to increase its Twelve Towns acreage went before the Township Board of Supervisors early in July 1957. The board reacted as expected; it opposed the increase. Berst, Drain Commissioner Barry, and others attempted to persuade the township officials that they should go along with the increase, but the township supervisors alleged (the Drainage Board denied it) that the increase would bring the cost of the project up to $4,000 per acre of area benefited. This, they said, was too expensive. Earlier plans had not included any actual construction in Southfield. This had been a sore point since it meant paying for construction outside the area served. The revised plan with increased Southfield acreage did call for construction within Southfield. A final meeting between the Drainage Board and Township Board was held on July 23, and the Township Board voted to reject the revised acreage plan. The cost and method of financing were the reasons given for this action. The need for drainage was not denied.

Southfield's neighbors, Berkley, Huntington Woods, and Oak Park, fearing Southfield run-off, were insistent that the increased Southfield area be included, and they threatened to sue Southfield if it withdrew from Twelve Towns. Threats of law suits were as frequent among the Twelve Towns cities as among quarrelsome neighbors, and they were indicative of the annoyance and frustration that continued to build up within the area. The April rains had brought floods to the Twelve Towns as well as the Rouge area, and there was more flooding in July. On July 31, 1957, the

Drainage Board met in a formal session and approved the inclusion of 1,948.714 acres of Southfield Township in the Twelve Towns Drainage District. All of this area had been part of one of the existing drainage districts that Twelve Towns was designed to relieve. By formally incorporating it in the Twelve Towns District, the board was not going outside of the former drainage district boundaries, but, on the contrary, was restoring the project limits to coincide with the original drainage districts that Twelve Towns was designed to relieve. The following day, August 1, it was learned that the decision in the test case would be of no help, for the court had declined the opportunity to use the Wayne County case to settle all outstanding questions concerning the constitutionality of the drain law. The Twelve Towns litigation would have to be resumed.

When the long-awaited decision in the test case failed to clear the way for action, the impatience that had been building up during the summer became vocal. Officials in some of the cities felt that the new drain commissioner was dragging his feet, that he had been relying too much upon the advice of lawyers who had counseled delay and that the cities were not being kept adequately informed of developments. The large, heavily populated cities of the Twelve Towns area (Royal Oak, Oak Park, Ferndale, and Berkley) were especially eager to move. Early in August, the Twelve Towns cities held a meeting and appointed Ferndale's mayor, Bruce Garbutt, chairman of a committee to plan a strategy to expedite the trial. This committee met with the drain commissioner and was told that in order to resume litigation it would be necessary to prepare a new apportionment and call a hearing on it. In order to do this, more money would be needed for redesigning the system to serve the additional Southfield area. Since no bonds could be sold as yet, the Twelve Towns operations were still being financed from county drain funds and from advances from the participating municipalities. These advances were credited to the contributor's share of the project, so that the cities would not be out any funds if the project were approved. Each time a vote on additional funds came before the municipal legislators, the issue of delay and other grievances associated with the project would be brought up and rediscussed. Some cities would contribute their share only after proper warnings and demands had been publicly proclaimed, and one city, Clawson, was chronically late in producing its share. The needed money was forthcoming, however, and by September 23 a new apportionment was ready.

A New Apportionment. On September 25, 1957, the Twelve Towns Drainage Board met in formal session and adopted a new tentative apportionment. A number of revisions to the drain law had been made during the 1957 legislative session, including the aforementioned amending of Section 468, which now provided that:

> Before any tentative apportionment shall hereafter be made, the Drainage Board shall designate the area to be served by the drain project, which may or may not include all of the area in any public corporation to be assessed.

In compliance with this, the Drainage Board proceeded to spell out the precise limits of the Twelve Towns Drainage District, a total of 23,647 acres, including the 1,948 acres in Southfield. The board approved revised engineering estimates which now placed the project cost at $44,092,000. The largest cost increase was in the Middle Section, which had been redesigned to accommodate the Southfield acreage. The cost for this section was about $4,200,000 higher than the 1956 estimate, but the cost estimate for the South Section had increased from $20,042,009 to $20,743,445 during the year without any change in design.

The new tentative apportionment reflected the increase in cost estimates, but the most significant difference resulted from the change in acreage for Troy and Southfield:

	Tentative Apportionment September 1956		Tentative Apportionnment September 1957	
	Acreage	Share of Cost	Acreage	Share of Cost
Troy	917.180	$2,096,488.07	546.664	$1,247,144.63
Southfield	596.336	811,046.80	1,948.714	4,295,893.91

With 8.2 percent of the Twelve Towns area, Southfield was apportioned 9.7 percent of the cost of the relief drains.

The new tentative apportionment included an item that had not appeared before. This was an apportionment to Oakland County for the 246.7 acres comprising Detroit's zoo and golf course located in Huntington Woods. From the beginning, the handling of this area had been a problem. Huntington Woods had refused to have Detroit's property included in its acreage subject to assessment on the ground that there was no way in which it could assess the city of Detroit for the benefits to be derived from the drain. Claude Stevens, the Drainage Board's bond counsel, had advised the board that the city of Detroit could not be included in the apportionment since the property in question was outside its city limits. It was decided to exclude this area from the assessable area of the Twelve Towns District, and Huntington Woods' net area, exclusive of zoo and golf course, was listed as assessable. This arrangement meant that all of the contributors to Twelve Towns were sharing a part of the cost for the zoo and golf course area. Troy had objected to this manner of handling the problem and argued that by the same logic a large cemetery occupying a portion of its Twelve Towns acreage should be similarly excluded.

Apparently concerned over the legality of this treatment, the Drainage Board's attorneys suggested another alternative. Section 468 of the drain law, in dealing with apportionment, provided: "Nothing herein contained shall prohibit the county from assuming any additional cost of said drain if two-thirds of the members-elect of the county board of supervisors shall vote in favor thereof." Pointing out that all of the citizens of Oakland County derived benefit for the zoo and golf course, the attorneys advised that this provision of the statute be used to have the county assume the apportionment for the Detroit properties. This was finally accomplished on March 7, 1957, when the Oakland County Board of Supervisors adopted an appropriate resolution assuming the apportionment by the necessary two-thirds vote. It had taken some hard politicking to accomplish this. The Southfield and Troy supervisors found some support for their contention that county taxpayers should not be forced to pay for a benefit to property owned by Detroit and located in Twelve Towns cities, but the remaining Twelve Towns cities rallied support from other supervisors, and the resolution carried fifty-five to twelve.

The board set October 31, 1957 as the date for the hearing on the new apportionments. With the exception of the three suing jurisdictions—Troy, Southfield, and Royal Oak Township—the new apportionment was accepted without protest. Southfield, on October 14, and Troy, on October 25, filed supplemental bills of complaint. Judge Holland issued a new injunction restraining the board from holding the apportionment hearing, and the trial was set for early in December. In order to save time and avoid repetition, the Troy and Southfield cases were combined. Royal Oak Township had intervened as a plaintiff in the Southfield suit, and all but three of the Twelve Towns cities intervened as defendants. Only Birmingham, Clawson, and Pleasant Ridge took no formal part in the litigation. Arguments in the case were heard during December, and on March 24, 1958, Judge Holland filed his opinion.

Judge Holland's Decision. The Twelve Towns Case was the first comprehensive court test of Chapter XX of the Drainage Code, the chapter dealing with intracounty drains. This legislation had been drafted by the Drainage Board's bond counsel, Claude Stevens, and it had been tailored to the Twelve Towns and other metropolitan drainage situations. The recodification of the state drain laws in 1956 had provided the opportunity for updating earlier legislation, and the delay in litigation from October 1956 to October 1957 had provided an opportunity for amending the new code to accommodate certain objections that had arisen. The 1956 and 1957 legislative sessions had been busy ones for representatives from the Oakland County communities, as they guided through to law many changes in the Drainage Code. Although these were not partisan issues, the legislative relations of predominantly Republican Oakland County were made easier by the fact that the Republicans held a majority in both houses of the state legislature. As an experienced bond counsel and expert in the drainage problems of the metropolis, Stevens had sought to draft legislation that would provide an administrative mechanism through which a number of jurisdictions could be brought together to solve a mutual drainage problem and at the same time provide a means for financing a major project in a manner that would make it possible to raise the funds without recourse to special referenda. The resultant Chapter XX was a powerful tool. Under it, a drainage board could determine how much area of a public corporation would be included in a drain and apportion and assess costs against a public corporation. Judge Holland, who was also, in a way, a specialist in drainage problems, since most of the drainage cases were assigned to him, was conscious of the significance of the case and wrote an opinion that dealt with the key issues. The following quotations are taken from his opinion.

The prime questions fall into two categories, viz.:

1. The constitutionality of the Drainage Code (hereafter referred to as the code);
2. The steps and actions taken by the Drainage Board (hereafter referred to as the board under the code).

An examination of the pleadings, a realization of the number of parties involved, the fact that the taking of testimony consumed three weeks and that exhibits in excess of fifty were introduced, are indicative of the complexities of the problems at hand.

. . . .

This litigation points up the laudatory purpose of said code and emphasizes again the impracticability of attempting to solve this or like drainage problems on an individual corporate or municipal level as opposed to a solution on a natural drainage area or drainage district level. If a legally proper application of this code is not possible, then many municipalities must struggle with the unhappy prospects of solving their problems alone, at an expense that will be exorbitant and out of all proportion to benefits.

The first point of law dealt with in the opinion was whether Section 475 of the code, which exempted assessments made by the board from statutory or charter debt limitations and which exempted taxes levied by a public corporation to pay for the assessment from statutory or charter tax limitations, was in conflict with a provision of the state constitution (Section 21 of Article 10) that limited townships to a fifteen-mill tax unless increased by a two-thirds vote, in which case the limit could rise to fifty mills. The weak taxing power of townships had been a major stumbling block to including them in interjurisdictional projects with cities. The code was drafted with an eye to strengthening this position, but the juggling of Southfield Township's acreage had been motivated by doubts over its ability to finance its share. Judge Holland held that townships were bound by the constitutional tax limitation and that Section 475 of the code did not apply to them, but that this did not mean that they were exempt from the assessments of the board:

> It may well be that the plaintiff township of Southfield and town-ship of Royal Oak (both of which have been partitioned almost be-yond recognition by the formation of cities) may have to effect some economies by discontinuing some service or services to its people for the sake of alleviating a drainage problem which constitutes a health hazard. The fact that a township under the Drain Code may be called upon to pay an apportionment which in turn would necessitate the changing and adjustment of its financial budget or necessitate the increasing of the tax limitation (the electors being willing) or the fact that taxes are already burdensome, does not render Chapter XX of the 1956 Drain Code unconstitutional.

Contrary to the case of townships, municipalities, the court held, that had adopted charters increasing the constitutional tax limita-tion had, in effect, removed the constitutional limit and therefore were subject to Section 475 of the code. In other words, assess-ments by the Drainage Board against cities were not limited by statutory or charter debt or tax limitations.

The court wasted little time over the question of whether Twelve Towns was necessary for the public health:

> . . . a casual perusal of the litigation, past and pending, in this cir-cuit demonstrates that virtually all of southern Oakland County . . . is plagued by drainage and sewage disposal problems. Again, it would seem to be a waste of time to indulge in any reasoning as to whether or not proper drainage and proper disposal of sanitary sewage is necessary to public health.

The relationship of the project to the public health, however, was the key to the court's answer to the question:

> Can the legislature authorize a drain assessment at large against a municipality, which is to be paid by ad valorem taxation, where the drainage area does not include the entire city?
>
> .   .   .   .
>
> This court can only conclude that drains being necessary for the public health, their construction constitutes a public purpose; and that it is within the wide discretion of the legislature to provide the manner of financing the same, which may be by a general tax. Such a tax does not violate the due process clause of the state or federal constitution.
>
> The Drainage Board in the instant cases is acting pursuant to acts of the state legislature. The legislature, as an arm of the state, is supreme when the matter of public health is involved.

The court went on to note that Section 490, which permitted a city legislature to charge back the cost to an area within a city "especially benefited by the drain project," had been added for the benefit of Troy and commented:

> It should be noted first that the legislative body of a public corporation has the choice of electing to charge back the entire tax to the especially benefited area. It is a proper and, this court feels, legal provision to take care of inequities that might arise within a municipality by virtue of the construction of the Twelve Towns system.

Neither Southfield nor Troy had signed the petition that led to setting up the Twelve Towns project, and Southfield, in its case, had argued that it could not be bound by the decisions of the board without having agreed to become participant in the project, but the court held:

> The pertinent part of Section 463 reads as follows: "463. Whenever it shall be necessary for the public health to locate, establish, and construct a county drain, *then a petition therefor may be filed with the county drain commissioner signed by two or more public corporations which will be subject to assessments to pay the cost thereof.*"
>
> For this court to say that all public corporations to be assessed are required to sign the petition would be to put a strained interpretation upon the provisions of the section just quoted. It would be reading something into Section 463 that is not there. The section plainly requires that the petition be signed by *two or more public corporations which will be subject to assessments to pay the cost thereof.* It would seem that had the legislature intended that all must sign, it would have said so.
>
> Again, it is not for this court to pass judgment upon the wisdom of the legislature (or lack of it) for having given to a relatively small board the right to draw many public corporations into a large and expensive drain project, which in turn may be initiated by the petition of only two public corporations to be assessed therefor.

In their bills of complaint, both Troy and Southfield had questioned the legality of the assumption by the county of the assessment for Detroit's zoo and golf course located in Huntington Woods. The court found ample statutory authority to support the county's action.

A more important issue, as later events developed, was the method used by the Drainage Board to apportion costs. The complaining cities had challenged the formula, especially the method used to give credits for existing drains. The court upheld the formula as both equitable and legal.

All the territory in the Twelve Towns Drainage District will be served by the existing drains and the proposed relief drains. Each of the engineers testified that the relief drains were designed so as to supplement the original drains in order to afford equal drainage facilities to all parts of the area for a ten-year frequency storm.

Therefore, after the construction of the Twelve Towns Relief Drains, each municipality will have equal drainage facilities as far as the county drains are concerned. The drains were designed as an area project and without respect to municipal boundary lines. The necessity and wisdom of solving the drainage problem here involved on an *area level* as opposed to township or city levels was amply demonstrated.

. . . .

The plaintiffs object to the . . . [credits] . . . for the old drains. Let us assume two public corporations with the same service area, where one provided more of the original drains. Would it be in accordance with benefits, if both were assessed the same amount for the relief drains where one's need for relief was not as great because of its former larger contributions? Depreciation has no part in the formula. The original drainage districts and not the Twelve Towns area will have to maintain the original drains.

By way of emphasis the following basic facts should be repeated:
1. Credits were granted only for existing county drains which have been paid for, and in some cases are still being paid for, by the citizens of the municipalities in which such county drains are located.
2. The Twelve Towns Drainage System is designed to serve all of the communities within its service area. To do this, both the existing county drains *and* the proposed drains are necessary.

From these two basic premises, it must follow that if credits were not given for existing county drains the residents of relatively less developed communities with few existing county drains, such as Troy and Southfield, would receive the benefit of the existing county drains without paying for them, even though the residents of the communities are paying for them. This being the case, it cannot be said that there has been an abuse of discretion, or that the approach used by the Drainage Board was an unreasonable one. The fact that there may be other possible ways of making the apportionment is immaterial, since the court will not substitute its judgment for that of the members of the Drainage Board.

Both Troy and Southfield questioned the legality of the board's action in changing the routes of the drains from those in the final order of determination, and Southfield questioned the increase of its acreage without a new hearing. The court noted that prior to 1957 the board was not required to fix the limits of the service area but that the service area was defined in the tentative apportionment of September 1957. The Drain Code did not require a hearing prior to the tentative apportionment, but Southfield could be heard when the hearings on the tentative apportionment were held. The court did review the inclusion of the additional Southfield territory and observed that the added territory was part of one of the drainage districts to be relieved and that it belonged in the Clinton River drainage basin. Judge Holland concluded: "The territory encompassed by the proposed Twelve Towns drains in Southfield Township is as it should be."

Judge Holland's decision upheld the Drain Code in all respects as it applied to Twelve Towns, and technically, the decision cleared the way for the resumption of proceedings with the holding of a hearing on the tentative apportionment of September 1957. But before bonds could be sold, Judge Holland's decision would have to be reviewed by the Michigan Supreme Court, which would require an appeal from the Circuit Court decision. Having lost their case, the plaintiffs, Troy and Southfield, would have to initiate the appeal, but if they failed to take this action, the Twelve Towns project would be stymied. For the time being, Troy and Southfield decided not to appeal.

A month after the Twelve Towns decision, Southfield Township ceased to exist. Earlier in the year, on February 3, 1958, the village of Westwood was incorporated, removing four square miles from the township (a year later Westwood changed its name to Beverly Hills), and on April 28, 1958, the remainder of the township area was incorporated as the city of Southfield. Township Supervisor Eugene Swem, a retired schoolteacher who had been leading the township's fight against Twelve Towns, was named acting city manager of the new city of Southfield. These incorporations eliminated the former township's argument concerning the ability to raise the money for the Twelve Towns assessment under the fifteen-mill tax limit on townships, but the two new units continued to oppose Twelve Towns.

Negotiation and Litigation

Provoking an Appeal. While the Twelve Towns project remained stalled in litigation, the State Department of Health continued to be concerned over the pollution of Red Run and thus unintentionally provided an opportunity for ending a legal stalemate.

To Twelve Towns area residents and city officials, the major objective was to eliminate the flooding and damage resulting from storms, and this the relief drains were designed to do. But state health officials were responsible for seeing that the storm relief system in southeastern Oakland County did not contribute to the pollution of drains and rivers in Macomb County. To the health authorities, the Twelve Towns drains were only part of the solution. Even without the addition of the storm relief system, the existing drains were discharging raw sewage into Red Run. From the standpoint of public health, any relief system would be acceptable only if it provided some solution for the handling of sanitary wastes. Before Twelve Towns could be built, it had to be approved by the Michigan Department of Health, and this approval would not be forthcoming unless adequate provisions were made for a sanitary system that would prevent current and future pollution of Red Run. Two additional sanitary works were required: (1) the enclosure of a section of Red Run at the head of the ditch between Campbell Road and Stephenson Highway and various other works that would, in addition to the Twelve Towns drains themselves, provide additional storage capacity for storm water and minimize the discharge of undiluted sanitary sewage into Red Run during the first rush of storm waters; and (2) a new sanitary interceptor sewer running north and south in the vicinity of Dequindre Road, referred to as the Dequindre interceptor. The Twelve Towns area was currently served by a sanitary interceptor that took sanitary sewage from existing drains and transported it to the Detroit system for treatment. Detroit treatment facilities were rated for a capacity in excess of that being used, and the city was willing to contract for additional volume; but the existing interceptor serving the Twelve Towns communities had reached capacity. A new interceptor would have to be built to meet the need of the current as well as additional population. It was the overloading of the existing interceptor that caused the pollution of Red Run by raw sewage even during dry weather, a condition that health officials considered dangerous.

During the early stages of Twelve Towns planning, through 1956, the drain commissioner appeared to disregard the Michigan Department of Health's insistence that a new sanitary interceptor be constructed along with the relief drains, preferring to consider them two independent projects. In a formal, legal sense, they were independent. Twelve Towns had its own organization, Drainage Board and co-ordinator and would be financed through faith and credit bonds, whereas the Dequindre interceptor would be built by the Southeastern Oakland County Sewage Disposal System and financed by revenue bonds. The latter project was a smaller undertaking costing about one-sixth as much as Twelve Towns. But during 1957 it became clear to the new drain commissioner that the State Health Department was not bluffing and intended to insist on a firm construction program for the Dequindre interceptor before approving Twelve Towns. In February 1958, State Health Commissioner Albert E. Heustis notified the communities in the Twelve Towns area that no new sewer permits would be issued by the Health Department until additional capacity was assured. This meant that new homes could be connected to existing sewers, but new sewers could not be constructed. This was a severe sanction for rapidly growing communities that had become accustomed to warnings from health officials but had not expected such drastic action. The reaction to the sewer ban would have been more explosive had not the area been in the midst of an economic recession with a severe reduction in new building starts. Nevertheless, the sanction was sobering, and a month later Drain Commissioner Barry submitted plans for a Dequindre interceptor to the Health Department. By this time the Dequindre project had taken on a new strategic significance in the effort to build Twelve Towns.

In addition to being the principal litigants against Twelve Towns, the cities of Troy and Southfield had many other things in common. Both were new cities with large and sparsely developed land areas; both were on the periphery of the Twelve Towns area, and both were in desperate need of additional sanitary sewers if new industrial and residential developments were to take place. The older Twelve Towns cities had paid for the existing sanitary interceptor, and they derived the most benefit from it. A new interceptor would be of some benefit to the older cities and would certainly diminish pollution in Red Run, but these communities were more concerned with pollution in streets and basements than they were with pollution in Red Run. Storm relief drains held their first priority, but Troy and Southfield, in need of sanitary interceptors, were holding up the relief drains.

The strategy of the Twelve Towns backers was simply to threaten to block the construction of sanitary interceptors until Troy or Southfield appealed Judge Holland's decision. Unless Troy were to build an independent sewage treatment system, which would be expensive, Troy would need the Dequindre interceptor. The Twelve Towns cities to the south of Troy were necessary participants in the Dequindre project, and they were in a position to stall the project or block Troy from being serviced by it. The pressure against Southfield was not as direct. Southfield would benefit from two interceptors, Farmington and Evergreen, planned for construction west of the Twelve Towns Drainage District, but the completion of these two projects required the approval by the Oakland County Board of Supervisors for a drain along Eight Mile Road (the Oakland County–Detroit boundary) that would prevent flooding in Detroit. Detroit refused to permit the two interceptors to be connected with the Detroit system until the flooding condition was corrected. The Twelve Towns cities threatened to block the Eight Mile Road drain with their votes on the Board of Supervisors. In the middle of May 1958, Mayor Garbutt of Ferndale announced these intentions of the Twelve Towns backers, and Drain Commissioner Barry agreed that as far as the projected Dequindre interceptor was concerned, the older Twelve Towns cities could keep it from being expanded to serve Troy. Early in June, the Troy and Southfield councils voted to appeal Judge Holland's decision.

The decision of Troy and Southfield to appeal reopened litigation. The issues in the case related to the taxing power of townships were not relevant to the two jurisdictions, the city of Southfield and the village of Beverly Hills, which had replaced South-field Township, but Royal Oak Township, the last remaining town-ship in the Twelve Towns District, intervened with the appellants to keep this issue alive. At the request of State Health Commis-sioner Heustis, the state attorney general intervened in support of the Twelve Towns Drainage Board because the health commis-sioner had declared "the present sewage system to be a public nuisance and a serious menace to the public health, requiring im-mediate action for correction." But the mills of lawyers, judges, and courts grind slowly: the decision of the Michigan Supreme Court was filed on July 13, 1959, over a year after Troy and South-field had decided to appeal.

Madison Heights Attempts Secession. During the summer of 1958 another threat to Twelve Towns appeared to have been set-tled when Madison Heights decided to go along with the project. Madison Heights completed its incorporation in December 1955, including in its territory all of the eastern segment of Royal Oak Township, a little over eight square miles. The new city was a rapidly growing area both in population (10,458 in 1950 and 33,343 in 1960) and in industry. In terms of family income, residents of Madison Heights were below the average for the other Twelve Towns municipalities, according to 1959 estimates; what remained of Royal Oak Township was the only Twelve Towns jurisdiction with lower family incomes. Local politics in the new city were turbulent. Like its neighbors, Madison Heights had adopted the city-manager form of government, but there was very little evi-dence of the political sophistication necessary to support this form of government.

When the petition establishing Twelve Towns was filed in Octo-ber 1955, Madison Heights was still part of Royal Oak Township, and the township supervisors had joined the other municipalities in endorsing the petition. But as cost estimates, area coverage, drain credits, and apportionments became known in the summer and fall of 1956, opposition developed within Madison Heights. On the eastern edge of the Twelve Towns District, with Red Run Ditch running through its territory, Madison Heights was in the best position of all the Twelve Towns municipalities to provide its own storm drain system, using Red Run for its outlet. About twelve hundred acres, or a little under 25 percent of Madison Heights' area, was included in Twelve Towns, and because of its formerly undeveloped condition, the city received very little credit for existing drains in the apportionment formula. This meant that the city's percentage share of Twelve Towns cost was greater than its percentage share of the Twelve Towns area. Under the September 1957 apportionment, Madison Heights had 5.1 percent of the area and 6.3 percent of the cost, a bill for $2,794,740. Although the percentage difference might appear minor, it was sufficient to cause some residents to feel that Madison Heights was not receiving equitable treatment. Another point of irritation was the fact that, since the Twelve Towns system would enter Red Run in Madison Heights and thus at this point carry the maximum flow from the total system, the size of the works located in Madison Heights were far in excess of what would be needed to handle the city's own storm load. This was cited as evidence that the city was being forced to pay for a system it did not need, thereby subsidizing the other Twelve Towns cities. Finally, there was raised periodically the question of the capacity of Red Run to handle the added flow of Twelve Towns. Engineering data supplied by the drain commissioner and the U.S. Army Corps of Engineers showing the adequacy of Red Run to handle the additional load was produced to quiet doubts, but opponents could photograph Red Run's banks filled to the brim after a heavy rain.

There were strong forces in Madison Heights both for and against Twelve Towns. During 1956, the city supported the project and intervened in the litigation on the side of the Drainage Board, but as the litigation dragged on, the pressure of the opposition increased. In October 1957, shortly after the September 1957 tentative apportionment of the Drainage Board had been announced, Mayor Ferguson pointed to the stalled Twelve Towns project and said that Madison Heights needed its drains right away and would consider going it alone. The mayor contended that Madison Heights could construct drains for the whole city at a cost less than that required to serve part of it under Twelve Towns. Engineering plans for an intracity system were prepared, and the city held a special election on December 9 to vote on a $1,500,000 bond issue for the construction of the system. With only about 17 percent of the eligible voters voting, the bond issue passed by the overwhelming majority of 1,032 to 437. Two days later, the city council passed a resolution to withdraw from Twelve Towns, reasoning that this would not injure any of the other Twelve Towns municipalities, since Madison Heights would be discharging its run-off directly into Red Run and would not be adding it to the Twelve Towns system.

Madison Heights' change of heart came at the very time when the Drainage Board was arguing its case before Judge Holland. If Madison Heights were to succeed in withdrawing from Twelve Towns, the whole project would be further jeopardized. It could necessitate redesigning parts of the system and would certainly require a reapportionment of costs among the remaining municipalities—a move that even the strongest supporters of Twelve Towns would resist. Moreover, the withdrawal of one unit would upset the basic premise upon which the project rested, i.e., that the Twelve Towns District was a drainage system composed of mutually dependent parts, no one of which could be treated independent of the others. As it was apparent that the Madison Heights council was not going to be talked out of its position, the Drainage Board decided to go to court to restrain the withdrawal. With this litigation underway, the political control of Madison Heights changed hands, following a municipal election held April 7, 1958. Mayor Ferguson and his supporters on the commission were defeated by George Horkey and a new council. Before incorporation, Horkey had been a township supervisor, in which capacity he had been familiar with and a supporter of Twelve Towns. Drain Commissioner Barry and Co-ordinator Berst were on good terms with Horkey, who had supported Twelve Towns in his election campaign. Judge Holland's decision upholding the legality of Twelve Towns, which was handed down in March, may have helped Horkey. Other issues were involved in the election, but Horkey's victory was taken as a sign of local support for Twelve Towns.

The new mayor and council did not immediately change the city's policy toward Twelve Towns. They undertook negotiations with Barry and Berst to shift some of the area covered by the project. In the past, area shifts had been the principal medium of negotiation between the drain commissioner and recalcitrant cities, but by now the other cities had lost patience with this maneuver and would not tolerate any area shifts that would affect the apportionment of all the cities. During the second week in June (1958), the new government of Madison Heights voted to sign a consent decree acknowledging the city's part in the Twelve Towns project and thus withdrew from further litigation. The city attorney advised this course, agreeing with the drain commissioner's contention that the city did not have the legal right to withdraw. One councilman and the ousted group protested this decision and demanded that the effort to withdraw from Twelve Towns be pressed in court, but the suit was dropped. Madison Heights was back in the fold.

An Assist from the State Highway Department. In the summer of 1958, prospects for Twelve Towns were more encouraging. By June, the Drainage Board had managed to quell the Madison Heights rebellion and provoke an appeal from Troy and Southfield. The Michigan Supreme Court would soon have the test case. The state health commissioner, at a July meeting with representatives of the Twelve Towns municipalities, reminded his audience of the health hazards created by the sewage system and suggested a timetable of corrective measures. Health officials wanted work begun on the sanitary interceptors, which were not involved in litigation, but Barry reminded them that there were a number of technical details still to be worked out that would cause some delay. The sanitary interceptors were his main lever over the reluctant Twelve Towns participants, and he did not intend to give this up until Twelve Towns was under contract. Another state agency, the Highway Department, was next to give Barry a helping hand.

During the fall of 1958, the Twelve Towns issue remained dormant. In November, Drain Commissioner Barry ran for re-election on the Republican ticket and was re-elected. During the winter, it looked as if the Supreme Court would hand down its decision sometime in April 1959. With a new term of office before him and the court decision in the offing, Commissioner Barry sat down with his aides and re-examined the apportionment formula. The limits of the drainage district had now been formally set by resolution of the Drainage Board and, more important, had become accepted as *the* limits by the core cities supporting the project. There was, however, one variable that could be manipulated which could benefit all of the Twelve Towns municipalities, and that was the apportionment to the State Highway Department for the drainage of state highways.

In the earlier apportionments prepared by Barry's predecessor, the State Highway Department had been apportioned its share of the cost of the relief drains by the same formula as the other public corporations, using as a base the actual acreage owned by the department, some 450 acres. Barry had continued to use this same acreage base in his apportionments, but during the early months of 1959, he began to explore methods by which the state's share could be increased. By the end of March 1959, these efforts had culminated in the negotiation of a new formula whereby the state's contribution for highways was increased from the September 1957 apportionment figure of $754,963 to $3,020,651, and the state's percentage share of Twelve Towns jumped from 1.7 percent to 6.85 percent. This, of course, resulted in a downward readjustment of the shares of all the other participants.

The new highway formula was the result of lengthy discussion and exchange of memoranda between the drain commissioner's office and the State Highway Department. In short, Commissioner Barry pointed out that in the past, the Highway Department's share of county drains had been determined by negotiation for each drain project. In these negotiations, a three-two-one formula was frequently used to determine the benefit that the department derived from the drain. The formula assumed that the run-off from paved areas was three times as great as run-off from seeded areas, and run-off from shoulders was twice that of seeded areas. Recently, what amounted to a six-three-one formula had been used in determining the state's share of an Oakland County drain then under construction, when certain works that the state had agreed to construct on its own were added in. In other words, there was a precedent for using the six-three-one formula for intracounty drains.

In a memorandum to the State Highway Department on March

27, 1959, Commissioner Barry cited two reasons for following this precedent in calculating the state's share of Twelve Towns. First, the state should pay for future use. Barry noted that a proposed expressway would pass through the Twelve Towns Drainage District, and that it was likely that the State Highway Department would construct additional highways in the District in the future and thereby produce additional impervious surfaces creating runoff. "It is most unlikely that the already overloaded drainage facilities existing will be able to handle the increased drainage from improved highway surfaces." Since once the percentage apportionment was confirmed, it was fixed for the life of the project, changing land uses could not be anticipated in it. Only by including future use in the state's apportionment would the state pay its long-term share. His second point concerned past drainage benefits that the state had received:

> ... Over the years, the member municipalities to the Twelve Towns Relief Drains have made such internal improvements as were both necessary and possible. In the planning of the several municipal internal systems, consideration has been given to the drainage from state trunklines located within the individual municipalities. The State Highway Department has utilized applicable individual municipal systems for drainage without (to the knowledge of this office) cost participation for drainage benefit. This has presented problems to several cities, i.e., Pleasant Ridge and Ferndale, where overloading of existing facilities calls for extensive internal modification and expansion to accommodate such drainage. In a sense, therefore, the run-off benefit formula utilized by the Drainage Board in apportioning State Highway Department costs acts as a reimbursement to the several municipalities for facilities already constructed and as a payment toward facilities which it will be necessary to construct to adequately service State Highway Department right-of-way within the District.

In accepting the six-three-one formula, the State Highway Department was, in effect, giving the Twelve Towns project a big assist. Whether department officials were moved by Commissioner Barry's logic or were concerned with the possible threat that lack of drainage in the District would pose to one of the department's expressway programs cannot be precisely determined, but there was no evidence that the Democratic state highway commissioner was acting solely in order to pull a Republican county drain commissioner's chestnuts out of the fire.

The Michigan Supreme Court Decision. On July 13, 1959, the Michigan Supreme Court filed its decision in the Twelve Towns case (*Township of Southfield* v. *Main,* 357 Mich. 59, 97 N.W. 2d 821). In a unanimous opinion, the court upheld the Drainage Board, with the following pertinent holdings as summarized by the board's bond counsel, Claude Stevens:

1. That the Twelve Towns Relief Drains is a health project and that, subject to the constitution, the legislature has supreme power in matters affecting the public health.
2. That in adopting Section 474 of Chapter XX of the Drain Code, the legislature exercised its prerogative that moneys belonging to the townships could be used for a health project, and that this it had the right to do subject only to the Constitution.
3. That Chapter XX of the Drain Code is not in conflict with the constitutional provisions relating to metropolitan districts. .
4. That a petition for an improvement under Chapter XX does not have to be signed by all municipalities to be assessed.
5. That the county of Oakland had the right to assume the apportionment on account of the Detroit Zoological Park and Rackham Golf Course non-taxable properties which are owned and operated by the city of Detroit and located in the cities of Huntington Woods and Royal Oak.
6. That the assessment against the city of Troy at large is valid even though only a small portion of the city lies within the Drainage District, the court saying that the city as a unit is responsible for the health of the entire city and each part thereof, and that contaminations and diseases do not respect lot lines or even city border lines.
7. That the legislature has full power to require a county to pay from its general fund any deficiency accruing on drainage bonds and that this does not operate as a grant of credit in violation of Article X, Section 12 of the constitution.
8. That the change in routes made by the Drainage Board after the entry of its final order of determination, without holding further hearings and without entering a new final order of determination, was valid under the circumstances inasmuch as neither Southfield nor Troy at the trial produced testimony that they had been in any way prejudiced or damaged by reason of such changes.

In dealing with the question of whether all public corporations involved should be required to sign the initiating petition, Judge Thomas M. Kavanagh, who wrote the opinion, echoed Judge Holland's position, holding that:

> If the legislature had intended to require the signatures of all

public corporations to be assessed it would have said so. A public
health question is involved. The legislature had a right to indicate
what type of petition could initiate the procedure. We find no requirement in law that would require all municipalities to join in the
original petition in order to start the action. As long as they have had
notice and an opportunity to be heard prior to assessment, legal
requirements have been met. We believe they are met under this
statute.

In the interest of protecting the public health, the court had thus
sustained the administrative mechanism provided under the Drain
Code to carry out a multi-jurisdictional project.

By upholding the procedures for the establishment of intracounty multi-jurisdictional drainage projects and the authority of
Drainage boards to locate drainage districts and to assess public
corporations, the court sustained a powerful administrative device
for carrying out large-scale metropolitan projects. But the administrative mechanism would be impotent without concomitant
financing power. In drafting Chapter XX, Claude Stevens had
wanted to provide a method of financing projects that would so
bind the county and participating municipalities that faith and
credit bonds could be marketed without difficulty. The court sustained his effort, with one exception. Chapter XX provided (Sect.
474) that the county could advance money to pay bonds in the
case of default of a public corporation and deduct the amount
from funds the county held for allotment to the local jurisdictions
in default. The court's exception to this procedure was explained
in the following excerpt from Stevens' analysis of the decision.

> The Supreme Court also held that in the event the county should
> be required to advance moneys to pay bonds on account of the de-
> fault of a public corporation, it could not reimburse itself from sales
> tax moneys in the hands of its county treasurer for the benefit of such
> public corporation. This holding is based upon the fact that the sales
> tax constitutional amendment of 1954 requires the county treasurer
> to remit the sales tax moneys to the respective cities, townships, and
> villages. This holding, however, does not affect the requirement that
> the county must advance money for the payment of bonds in the
> event of a delinquency on the part of any public corporation. It only
> affects the ability of the county to be reimbursed for such advance-
> ments. Under the decision of the court, all of the cities and villages
> to be assessed for the project have unlimited taxing power to pay
> their at-large drainage assessments. If there is a delinquency on the

part of any city or village, the county can require that a levy be made therefor on the next city or village tax roll. The problem of reimbursement applies to the township of Royal Oak only. . . . The holding of the court, however, does not bar the withholding by the county treasurer of any moneys due the township where such withholding would not be contrary to an express constitutional provision as in the case of the sales tax moneys. . . .

The decision clears the way for the Drainage Board to proceed insofar as legal problems are concerned.

When the Twelve Towns project first got under way in 1952 and 1953, there had been three townships (Troy, Royal Oak, and Southfield) involved, and because townships had a notoriously weak financial status with bond investors, Chapter XX of the Drain Code had been drafted with the objective of strengthening that status. But both Judge Holland's opinion, which held that townships were bound by the constitutional fifteen-mill tax limit unless raised by referendum, and the Supreme Court opinion continued to protect the township, although neither opinion exempted townships from financial participation in the project. The financial provisions of Chapter XX as they related to other public corporations, cities, and villages, were upheld, as Counselor Stevens pointed out. With only one township left in the project, and that a very small one, the Supreme Court decision did open the way for resumption of the project. The next step was the holding of a hearing on the tentative apportionment of costs.

The Final Apportionment and the Final Suit. On August 19, a month after the Supreme Court decision, a new tentative apportionment was adopted (see Table 3) and a hearing set for September 30. The total cost of the project had risen another $3,000,000 and now totaled $47,000,000. Some of the sting of the increase was taken out by the increased share assumed by the Michigan State Highway Department under the six-three-one formula, which resulted in the percentage share for each of the municipalities being reduced from the 1957 apportionment. As can be seen in Table 3, Southfield, Madison Heights, and Troy, new cities with undeveloped areas, were apportioned a larger percentage of the Twelve Towns cost than the percentage of area each had in the District, whereas older, core-area cities, such as Royal Oak, Oak Park, and

Table 3
Twelve Towns Relief Drains Apportionment of August 19, 1959 (Prepared by the Drainage Board)

Public Corporation	Area in Acres	Percent of Area	Share of Complete Drainage System	Share of Benefits Former Drains	Share of Twelve Towns Relief Drains	Approx. Share in Percent Twelve Towns
Cities of:						
Berkley	1,622.643	6.668594	$ 4,235,459.74	$ 1,155,022.09	$ 3,080,437.65	6.539930
Birmingham	1,002.954	4.084766	2,617,933.85	625,000.63	1,992,933.22	4.231101
Clawson	1,365.766	5.562402	3,564,953.41	1,130,462.17	2,434,491.24	5.168552
Ferndale	2,401.495	9.780652	6,268,437.40	2,047,045.43	4,221,391.97	8.962235
Hazel Park	611.067	2.488714	1,595,021.26	263,868.31	1,331,152.95	2.826107
Huntington Woods	706.212	2.876214	1,843,370.71	489,421.99	1,353,948.72	2.874504
Madison Heights	1,207.266	4.916874	3,151,233.36	302,429.76	2,848,803.60	6.048158
Oak Park	3,080.014	12.544080	8,039,523.36	2,701,387.12	5,338,136.24	11.333141
Pleasant Ridge	341.761	1.391902	892,072.49	494,548.22	397,524.27	.843965
Royal Oak	7,328.970	29.848950	19,130,245.55	5,303,094.53	13,827,151.02	29.355762
Southfield	1,810.449	7.373478	4,725,675.27	717,029.30	4,008,645.97	8.510564
Troy	562.797	2.292123	1,469,025.74	166,548.21	1,302,477.53	2.765228
Village of Beverly Hills	154.962	.631119	404,485.30	40,717.58	363,767.72	.772298
Township of Royal Oak	424.408	1.728501	1,107,799.39	704,487.58	403,311.81	.856252
Co. of Oakland—assumed by Co. a/c Zoo & Golf Course	246.730	1.004866	644,020.42	162,020.42	481,568.80	1.022396
Co. of Oakland a/c Highways	315.256	1.283954	822,888.42	299,175.22	523,713.20	1.111870
State of Mich. a/c Highways	453.876*	5.582811	3,578,033.57	385,489.48	3,192,544.09	6.777937
TOTALS	23,636.626†	100.000000	$64,090,179.24	$16,988,179.24	$47,102,000.00	100.000000

* State share based on 6-3-1 benefit formula applied to gross less share of benefits of former drains.
† Total based on expanded area (1,370.777 acres) = 24,553.527.

Ferndale, had a lower percentage of cost than the area percentage each had in the District. This distribution, of course, was the effect of the formula that provided credits for existing drains. In order to show the economic impact of the Twelve Towns apportionment on each jurisdiction, the Twelve Towns assessment is shown as a percentage of the state equalized assessed valuation for each of the jurisdictions in Table 4. This shows that the economic impact of the project upon Troy, Southfield, and Madison Heights was less than it was upon the core-area cities of Royal Oak, Berkley, and Oak Park.

Table 4
Twelve Towns Assessment as Percentage of
State Equalized Assessed Value

Public Corporations*	Assessment	Assessed Value	Percentage
Berkley	$ 3,080,437.65	$ 40,663,628.00	7.5
Birmingham	1,992,933.22	86,275,885.00	2.3
Clawson	2,434,491.24	25,675,261.00	9.5
Ferndale	4,221,391.97	87,843,066.00	4.8
Hazel Park	1,331,152.95	41,311,320.00	3.2
Huntington Woods	1,353,948.72	26,139,021.00	5.2
Madison Heights	2,848,803.60	58,162,763.00	4.9
Oak Park	5,338,136.24	97,251,320.00	5.5
Pleasant Ridge	397,524.27	11,968,950.00	3.3
Royal Oak	13,827,151.02	186,277,573.00	7.4
Southfield	4,008,645.97	121,903,127.00	3.3
Troy	1,302,477.53	51,607,530.00	2.5
Royal Oak Township	403,311.81	5,279,999.00	7.6

*Village of Beverly Hills not included since equalized value is not broken down from the township unit.

As the hearing on the apportionment approached, all but one of the fourteen jurisdictions in Twelve Towns were prepared to accept the apportionment and get on with the project. In Southfield, flooding conditions had finally caught up with the residents, and lack of drains was inhibiting commercial and residential development in the area included in Twelve Towns. City status and the 1957 amendment to the Drain Code, which permitted cities to assess the cost against areas benefiting from the drains, elimi-

nated most of Southfield's objections to the project, and now the
pressure from this community was to move as fast as possible.
Troy, too, was reconciled to having to remain in Twelve Towns
even though its city-wide sewage problems remained unsolved
and were to continue to play a large part in local politics. Royal
Oak Township, the third former litigant, still had its local financial problems, but a solution to its Twelve Towns assessment was
on the horizon. An urban redevelopment project for the area,
financed under the federal Urban Renewal Program, was in its
final stages of approval. Adequate drains, including the relief to
be provided by Twelve Towns, were a necessary part of any redevelopment effort, and part of the cost of the drains could be
charged to the redevelopment program. It thus appeared that most
of Royal Oak Township's share of Twelve Towns would be paid
through the redevelopment financing, thus relieving the township
of the burden. This satisfied the township officials. But there had
been another shift in political control in Madison Heights, and
when the apportionment hearing was held, Madison Heights filed
formal objections.

On September 30, 1959, the first formal hearing on a tentative
apportionment was held by the Drainage Board. It was three years
earlier that the first hearing had been called, and it had been postponed twice because of litigation. It was hoped that this hearing
would be the last formal step before the letting of contracts, but
the Madison Heights Council had instructed its city attorney to
object to the city's apportionment. The gist of the objection was
that in making the apportionment the Drainage Board had ignored
Section 468 of Chapter XX of the Drain Code, which required that:

> . . . there shall be taken into consideration the benefits to accrue to
> each public corporation and also the extent to which each public
> corporation contributes to the conditions which make the drain nec-
> essary . . . .

The statement submitted by Madison Heights cited the following
objections:

> The tentative apportionment apparently has been made on the basis
> of the costs of the entire project, divided among the acreage to be
> served, without consideration being given to the needs of the area
> of the system within the city of Madison Heights. The proposed in-

stallation, in Madison Heights, far exceeds the capacity of a drainage system necessary to serve the city of Madison Heights area within the Twelve Towns Drain System. There seems to be no relationship between the amount of the apportionment and the distance from the outlet that each particular municipality is located [*sic*]. It is submitted that the proximity of Madison Heights to the outlet of the system should be one of the factors considered in the determination of the amount of the apportionment to be charged . . . .

The engineering estimate of cost for the size of system necessary to serve the city of Madison Heights portion of the Twelve Towns System amounts to $1,491,695.00. Any costs chargeable to Madison Heights in excess of that amount are the result of building the system large enough to serve the needs of all the municipalities in the system, and the city . . . ought not be required to pay such excess costs.

The tentative apportionment appears to have been made after allowing certain credits to some of the participating municipalities for benefits from former drains, which will empty into the system, and which were installed many years ago at less than the amount credited. These credits appear to have been given on the basis of present reproduction costs, without depreciation factors, rather than the original costs. No credits have been given to the city of Madison Heights for trunks and connecting arms necessary to be constructed within the city in order to make the Twelve Towns system available to the area charged for its installation.

The complaint concluded with what it considered to be Madison Heights' proper apportionment. It took as the basic cost figure the city's own estimate of $1,500,000 for an intracity system and subtracted from that both the estimated cost of intracity drains to connect with Twelve Towns and the share of benefits for former drains included in the Twelve Towns apportionment for Madison Heights. The remainder, $662,915.24, was given as the proper apportionment for the city as against the $2,848,803.60 under the Drainage Board apportionment.

These were not new arguments, and the Drain Commissioner and his staff had rebutted them at length over the years in the many conferences, meetings, discussions, and debates over the formula. The legality of the formula had been upheld in the Circuit Court proceedings. On appeal, the issue of the formula had not been raised. Madison Heights was the only municipality to raise objections at the hearing. The others accepted their apportionments and urged the Drainage Board to proceed with all haste to let contracts for the construction. The board, by unanimous vote, confirmed the tentative apportionment, and Madison Heights announced that it would go to court, making use of Section 483 of Chapter XX of the Drain Code which provided that:

> Neither the final order of determination nor the final order of apportionment shall be subject to attack in any court, except by proceedings in certiorari brought within twenty days after the filing of such order in the office of the chairman of the board issuing the same. If no such proceeding shall be brought within the time above prescribed, the drain shall be deemed to have been legally established and the legality of the drain and the assessments therefor shall not thereafter be questioned in any suit at law or in equity, either on jurisdictional or non-jurisdictional grounds.

Madison Heights' decision to go to court exasperated nearly all the other participants in Twelve Towns. The action was considered a "nuisance suit" resulting from an internal political struggle within Madison Heights; the other municipalities were angered at what they considered to be an unnecessary delay. To the Twelve Towns attorneys, it appeared that Madison Heights did not have a legal leg to stand on. As noted earlier, Judge Holland had endorsed the concept that Twelve Towns dealt with a drainage system irrespective of municipal boundaries and had upheld the apportionment formula that was based upon a system-wide allocation. The Twelve Towns attorneys considered the issues raised by Madison Heights res judicata, and when Madison Heights filed a petition for a writ of certiorari on October 10, it was expected that the Oakland County Circuit Court would soon dispose of the matter in favor of Twelve Towns. It was anticipated that Judge Holland, who ordinarily was assigned drain cases, would get the case, and since he had had his decision in the original Twelve Towns case upheld by the Supreme Court, there was no reason to expect that he would reverse himself. But the presiding judge, William J. Beer, took the case himself. This came as a surprise in view of Judge Holland's past experience with Twelve Towns, which must have made him one of the most knowledgeable persons on the subject to be found.

By November 18, 1959, arguments had concluded. Madison Heights' arguments were substantially those presented at the hearing, and the Drainage Board's defense was that the issue of the formula was res judicata. On December 16, 1959, Judge Beer issued the following opinion:

> Plaintiff city, within the time allowed by law, filed this action in certiorari. A statute grants to plaintiff right to review by certiorari. Therefore, I rule the plea of res judicata is not a defense.
>
> This being an action of certiorari, the court is confined to the record of the proceedings before the administrative tribunal below. Return of the proceedings have been made to this court. I have read and studied the return in every detail. It is devoid of any evidence, any facts, or any information indicating this administrative tribunal took into consideration the required statutory factors as complained of by the plaintiff. In particular there is a total absence in this return of anything whatsoever showing, in the slightest, defendants considered the statutory requirement of the benefits to accrue to the city of Madison Heights, and the extent to which it contributed to the condition which makes the drain necessary. The taxpayers of the city of Madison Heights had a right to the consideration by defendants of these matters, and there is a total absence of such consideration as reflected from the return, by the administrative tribunal.
>
> Therefore, the proceedings of the defendants determining costs against the city of Madison Heights as returned to this court are quashed.

The judge added an obiter dictum that his decision did not mean the termination of Twelve Towns but that the board was merely required to "proceed to a proper determination of the drain costs to be paid by the taxpayers of Madison Heights." The other cities, he felt, were barred because of the lapse of time from protesting. But if the Drainage Board had proceeded to change Madison Heights' apportionment, it would have changed the percentage contributions of all the other municipalities and required a new apportionment which would be subject to challenge by certiorari.

The day following the Circuit Court's decision, the Drainage Board met and instructed its attorneys to appeal the decision to the Michigan Supreme Court. Explaining their action in a newsletter to the member municipalities, Drain Commissioner Barry said:

> . . . The Drainage Board did not waste the time on calling a meeting of representatives of the municipalities to consult them as to their wishes in this regard. The opinions expressed by the municipal representatives at the apportionment hearing on September 30, 1959 were such that there was no doubt in the minds of the members of

the Drainage Board that this case should be appealed without delay. The Drainage Board has no doubts as to the propriety of its past actions and believes that a Supreme Court appeal of this case will result in reversal.

Indignation probably comes closest to describing the reaction among Twelve Towns supporters to Judge Beer's decision. Some of them were bitter, and many felt that Judge Beer had not understood the complexities of the Twelve Towns project and the history of the development of the formula which all but one city accepted as equitable. But in fairness to the judge, it should be noted that this was an action in certiorari where the judge had to base his decision upon the record of proceedings before the Drainage Board. As an administrative body, the Drainage Board was relatively unsophisticated and had been lax in building a formal record of its action. In any event, by the end of 1959, Twelve Towns, instead of being under contract, was once again in court.

Until the Supreme Court gave its decision, Twelve Towns remained stalled. Much was at stake. If the Supreme Court were to uphold the Drainage Board, then the apportionment confirmed by the board at the September 30 hearing would become final and beyond further attack in court; bonds could be sold, contracts signed, and construction begun. If the Supreme Court were to uphold Judge Beer, then a new apportionment would have to be worked out using a different formula which would in turn require new hearings and open the way for new attacks by certiorari.

On December 1, 1960, the Michigan Supreme Court filed its decision. It upheld the Drainage Board and reversed Judge Beer, but Madison Heights was determined not to let the matter rest and proceeded to appeal to the United States Supreme Court. The Drainage Board attempted to forestall this last appeal by an offer to reduce substantially the Twelve Towns acreage in Madison Heights, with a resultant substantial reduction in Madison Heights' share of the project's cost. By this time the other jurisdictions were willing to accept new adjustments in area coverage and cost allocations in order to end the litigation—at least, this was the board's assumption; but a test of the willingness of the thirteen other jurisdictions to accept major concessions to Madison Heights was avoided by the latter's insistence upon pursuing its case in court. In the spring of 1961, the United States Supreme Court rejected Madison Heights' appeal, and the apportionment formula remained intact.

A final apportionment was released by the Drainage Board on May 16, 1961. The project cost was now estimated at $47,500,000, up $400,000 from the August 1959 apportionment. A second substantial change from the last apportionment was still another increase in the State Highway Department's share. The Highway Department's "expanded" acreage had increased from 1,370.8 acres to 2,068.9, and its share of the costs had increased from $3,192,-544.09 (6.8 percent of the total project cost) to $4,902,774.16 (10.3 percent of the total project cost). The increased share assumed by the Highway Department more than compensated for the overall rise in cost, so that there were small reductions in the assessments to the municipalities. Madison Heights' acreage had been reduced by 105 acres, which meant it received a somewhat larger proportionate reduction than the other municipalities, whose acreage remained the same. Madison Heights' share was now $2,533,-363.83, compared with $2,848,803.60 in 1959. The final figure was much higher than the Drainage Board was reported to have been willing to have settled for if Madison Heights had called off its suit.

The final formal steps preceding the letting of contracts were accomplished during the summer of 1961. Public hearings on the location of the drain and apportionment were held late in June. No verbal objections were raised, nor were formal written objections filed during the twenty-day period following the issuance of the final orders. Construction of the Twelve Towns Relief Drains began early in 1962.

Concluding Comments

Twelve Towns is a case of frustration. The problem to be solved was so evident that during a rainstorm even the casual observer could detect the need, and the technological means for solving the problem were well known and readily available. Taken as a whole, the Twelve Towns District was one of the wealthiest suburban areas in the state and had adequate financial resources to solve its problems. In spite of these conditions, a time-consuming effort was required in order to establish a mechanism whereby the problem of inadequate drains could be solved.

Had the Twelve Towns District encompassed one city instead of fourteen jurisdictions, there would have been no "case." But the facts of life of modern suburbia are such that any suggestion that the Twelve Towns District incorporate into a single city or permit itself to be annexed by Detroit would be met with strong resistance from the people in the Twelve Towns' area. As a matter of fact, the number of jurisdictions increased, as four new municipalities (the cities of Troy, Madison Heights, and Southfield, and the village of Beverly Hills) incorporated in the course of the controversy. There was no evidence of a willingness on the part of suburban cities to abandon their boundaries, even when faced with a major drainage problem. A multi-jurisdictional approach to a solution was considered the only practical route available.

The necessity to revise and codify the state drain law culminating in the Drain Code of 1956 and subsequently to revise Chapter XX, the chapter dealing with intracounty drains, points to one reason for the delay in Twelve Towns. When the project was first discussed in 1952, existing drain legislation was not adequate for a suburban project of the scope of Twelve Towns either in terms of the number of jurisdictions involved or in terms of the amount of financing that would be required. Chapter XX was designed to provide a vehicle through which existing political institutions, the county drain commissioner and municipalities, could be utilized. Drafted by Bond Counsel Claude Stevens, this legislation gave much attention to binding the municipalities to their financial commitments in order to assure the sale of bonds, since this was the key to success for any major project. But as counsel to the Drainage Board, Stevens was in no hurry to push litigation until after the 1957 revisions to the law, which were designed to meet some of the objections of Troy and Southfield and which, by changing the requirement on the annual payments of interest and principal on the bonds (principal payments in the early years when interest was high could be reduced so that payments over the thirty-year period could be equalized), bolstered the support of the other municipalities. In other words, Twelve Towns had to move slowly in order to provide the time to develop, by trial and error, legislation that was, on the one hand, practical from an administrative and financial point of view and, on the other hand, acceptable to the majority of the participating municipalities. This was not accomplished until the end of the 1957 legislative session. To the residents of flooded areas and to many of the city officials, this was a ponderous, time-wasting process consisting of legal hair-splitting, but proof of its effectiveness was the Circuit Court and Michigan Supreme Court decisions upholding Chapter XX and Twelve Towns.

As an administrative body, the Twelve Towns Drainage Board and its major administrative arm, the drain commissioner's office, played by ear. The board members, consisting of the chairman of the Board of Supervisors and chairman of the County Board of Auditors in addition to the drain commissioner, were not professional administrators; they were political officials. The other two members looked to the drain commissioner and his office for direction and guidance, since drains were his area of responsibility. Drain Commissioner Barry was not an engineer; his college major was political science. For technical advice on Twelve Towns, he had his own staff and the reports of the engineering firms that prepared the estimates. Barry and the other board members saw their role as one of persuasion and negotiation. Their principal task was to get all of the municipalities to go along with the project, and in order to do this, they tended to rely on the classic technique of the politician—the award of favors and withholding of benefits. For example, the shifting of the cost of the Detroit zoo and golf course to the county at large was a "favor" to all Twelve Towns members, as was the negotiation of the six-three-one formula with the State Highway Department. The inclusion of various "added" territories was also used as a basis of negotiation, and there were many subtle influences that county officials could bring to bear on municipalities. The threat of delaying the development of sanitary interceptor sewers was the most important penalty that the Drainage Board, with the assistance of a majority of the Twelve Towns municipalities, could impose. This was used effectively to stimulate the appeal from the Circuit Court decision.

While the strength of the Drainage Board lay in its political skill, this was also the source of its weakness. By negotiating the boundaries of the Twelve Towns District, they weakened their own argument that they were dealing with a "natural" drainage district. The early fluctuation in the Troy and Southfield acreage would indicate that either Nature or the board could not make up its mind on the District's boundaries. Many of the city managers in the Twelve Towns municipalities, themselves professional administrators, were suspicious of the dealings of the Drainage Board. These cities maintained their own "watchdog committees" to make sure that they were not hurt by any of the deals. Further evidence of the weakness of the board, or at least its lack of sophistication as an administrative body, was revealed in the course of the litigation. In the first litigation, both the Circuit Court and the Supreme Court pointed to a sparsity of records and a carelessness of procedural niceties that should have been fair warning to the board that in the future its formal proceedings and records would have to consist of something more than a terse formal resolution confirming elaborate but unrecorded negotiations and findings. When interviewed, one Twelve Towns official seemed indignant that the court did not realize that behind the formal resolutions were, in fact, studies and negotiations and the like. The board saw itself more as a legislative body than as an administrative body.

The apportionment formula points up the board's dilemma and its approach to solving it. By treating each acre of land as equal as a source of run-off and a source of benefit for each municipality, it adopted a variable that was easily measured and understood. Although there are many other variables involved in run-off, such as housing density per acre, impervious nature of the soil, natural ponding areas, and so on, by assuming that these differences would average out for each community, the board could argue that area per se was an equitable variable. By allowing credits for existing drains at their appreciated value, the older cities that had paid for these drains and as a consequence were furnishing the drains then in use by the newer communities were somewhat compensated for this earlier investment. Whether they liked it or not, drains paid for by Royal Oak, Oak Park, and Berkley, for example, were providing drainage for Southfield. The older cities had also taken the worst beating from flooding, as newer communities developed around them, and they would enjoy the most immediate direct benefits from Twelve Towns when completed. Without the support of Royal Oak, Oak Park, and Ferndale, which together made up over half of the Twelve Towns area, the project could not be built, but on the other hand these three cities needed the assistance of the other jurisdictions to obtain the relief they needed. The formula was an ingenious device that, while somewhat compensating the three core cities for past investments, still distributed costs in close approximation to the percentage of area that each jurisdiction had in the project and thus was politically feasible.

The political acumen implicit in the apportionment formula is perhaps best illustrated by the formula negotiated with the State Highway Department. When it came to state highways, the drain commissioner had no reservations about abandoning area and credits as the sole basis for calculation and using differential run-off rates for different types of surfaces. Especially interesting in this regard is the treatment accorded county highways, which continued to be apportioned on a straight acreage basis. The reason for the discrepancy is that the state was willing to absorb the additional cost and the county was not in a position to do so. No Twelve Towns member objected to the state assuming a larger share of the cost.

The fact that all of the jurisdictions except Madison Heights (which had endorsed the formula at an earlier date, at least by implication, since it had intervened on the side of the Drainage Board in the Troy-Southfield suit) accepted the apportionment formula was a noteworthy achievement. This success raises some nice questions. If the Drainage Board had not been composed of political officials, would it have been as successful? Could a scientific cost-benefit formula have been developed that would have been more equitable and more readily acceptable? Did the lack of administrative sophistication aid or hinder the Twelve Towns project?

What is the price of delay? This is a key question that cannot be answered. The first firm estimate of the Twelve Towns cost was $38,500,000 (September 1956), and the last estimate, which included works in addition to the 1956 design, was $47,500,000 (May 1959). But the difference between these two figures is no measure of the cost of delay. The true cost would have to include the cost to residents and insurance companies from flood damage and other expenses incurred as a result of the lack of adequate drainage. These expenses would include the cost of special sump pumps and other plumbing arrangements to minimize basement flooding, depreciation of property values, postponement of commercial and industrial development as well as of residential development, and increased insurance rates where flood insurance could be obtained. Add to this the physical discomfort that accompanies flooded streets and basements and the necessary mopping-up operations that follow. These costs may well have amounted to much more than the cost of the Twelve Towns Relief Drains. One can speculate that the odds are against quick agreement among a group of municipalities on the distribution of costs and benefits for a multi-jurisdictional project, and that where construction depends upon such agreement, one of the calculated anticipated costs for employing this procedure is the cost of delay. Whether or not the Twelve Towns type of solution to multi-jurisdictional problems of suburban communities will in the long run prove acceptable might well depend upon the suburbanites' tolerance of delay.

10
Annexation and Incorporation in Farmington Township

Skirmishes on the Metropolitan Frontier

Introduction

Farmington was a Midwestern rural township of classic Jeffersonian proportions—a square made up of thirty-six one-square-mile sections. The gently rolling land must have struck a nostalgic cord for the up-state New Yorkers who settled there in the middle of the nineteenth century. Its center of population and township seat, the village of Farmington, was safely remote, some twenty miles, from the madding urban throngs of downtown Detroit. The early inhabitants were an independent, freethinking lot —the Farmington Universalist Church predated the Civil War, and the village served as a stop on the Underground Railroad.

By mid-twentieth century, Farmington was no longer a rural outpost. Four of Oakland County's southern tier of five townships bordered Wayne County. From east to west they were Royal Oak, Southfield, Farmington and Novi townships. All of Royal Oak's and most of Southfield's southern boundaries formed the northern boundary of the city of Detroit, while Farmington and Novi adjoined rural Wayne townships. The main suburban population thrust had been through Royal Oak Township, and it was within this township that the first major satellite cities developed in south Oakland County. By the late 1950's, the former township territory contained all or part of nine cities, and Royal Oak Township had been reduced to a few hundred acres. The townships to the west of Royal Oak had not grown as rapidly, but by the 1950's, population had begun to spill over into Southfield and Farmington townships. By 1960, the unincorporated territory in Southfield Township had ceased to exist, with the major portion having been incorporated as the city of Southfield and the remaining territory

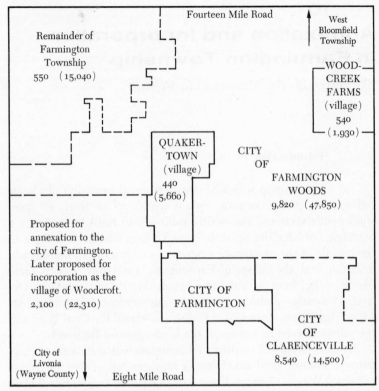

Existing boundaries shown by solid lines.
Numbers in parentheses indicate estimated ultimate population.
Other numbers indicate estimated 1958 population.

7. Existing and Proposed Jurisdictions in Farmington Township

divided among three villages and one small city. Farmington's southern neighbor in Wayne County, the city of Livonia, had grown by leaps and bounds during the fifties and in 1960 had a population of 66,702. Farmington Township continued to maintain its rural status with but one city, the city of Farmington. The townships to the north and west were still predominantly open farm land, as were large segments of Farmington.

Farmington Township was balanced on the edge of the metropolis. The village of Farmington had incorporated as a city in 1925, removing an area of one and three-quarters square miles from the township. The city's last annexation was in 1957, when it succeeded in annexing 190 acres, and with this addition the city had two square miles of territory. The city was the only "urban" area in the township territory, but "small town" would be a more accurate designation. Population was distributed as follows:

Population
(U.S. census data)

	1940	1950	1960
City of Farmington	1,510	2,325	6,881
Farmington Township	5,695	11,224	26,692 (includes two villages)

Farmington Township had four times as many people as the city of Farmington, but they were spread out over eighteen times as much land. Farmington Hills, Biddestone Woods, Ramble Hills, Franklin Knolls, Glen Orchard, Holly Hill Farms, Kendallwood, Normandy Hills, Westbrooke, Old Farm Colony, Woodcreek Farms, Heather Hills, and Woodcroft—these were the names of some of the many subdivisions that speckled the Farmington Township countryside. Most of the subdivisions did, in fact, have "estate-sized lots," modest estates to be sure, and the subdivisions were, for the most part, well sited to take advantage of the rolling terrain, which was a welcome relief from the flat, unassuming plain that made up the terrain in the greater part of the metropolis. Although some of the subdivisions had a longer history, most of them had sprung up during the early fifties. The homes were expensive, with prices in the least expensive developments starting at $20,000, but for many of the developments it would have taken at least twice that amount to buy a foothold. Some of the larger developments had their own sewage treatment systems, which health authorities had required that the developer provide, and some developments had community wells. For the most part, however, each home had its own well and septic tank. In low-density developments where soil conditions and the water table were co-operative, the independent water and sewerage systems worked very well. Some developments were less fortunate, and the seepage from septic tanks ponded in back yards, while in the dry areas, wells ran dry, and water had to be imported.

With the exception of schools, governmental services in the township were minimal and were provided, for the most part, by county agencies such as the Road Commission and the sheriff's office. The township itself was governed by a seven-man board composed of a supervisor, clerk, and treasurer elected for two-year terms and four trustees elected for staggered four-year terms. Candidates ran on partisan tickets.

The people who lived in the elegantly named subdivisions were mainly young middle- or upper-income families—commission salesmen, middle-level executives, or members of a profession, in their thirties and forties, with two or more children. There were exceptions to this, of course. Members of the blue-collar elite, tool and die workers, owners of small businesses or small tool shops, and some white-collar workers had also invaded the area. Many of the residents were mortgaged to the hilt.

In addition to the development dwellers, there were two other types of township residents. First, the true exurbanites—those who sought privacy and seclusion for a way of life lived in their own personal style. Many had found their nook in the township long before the suburban population wave hit, and they were hidden away on dirt roads and at the ends of private lanes. Finally, the township contained pockets of low-income families. Scattered over the area were a few small patches of one-story, cottage-sized frame or cinder-block dwellings, often resembling an overgrown garage, the handiwork of the owner-dweller. The greatest concentration of low-income families was in the south and southeastern part of the township in an unincorporated area known as Clarenceville, which was the part of the township closest to Detroit. Although the township and the city of Farmington had very little work for a wage earner, employment was available in nearby communities. The exact number was not known, but it was estimated that only a small percentage of the township residents earned their living in the township.

The city too had felt the influx of those seeking the suburban life. The population figures show that the period of most rapid growth for the city of Farmington was in the decade of the fifties —mostly before 1958. By 1958, most of the vacant residential lots in the city had been occupied, and an economic recession had slowed down the rate of new construction. Of the total locally assessed property valuation in 1958, 67.7 percent was in residential property, 14.3 percent in commercial, and 4.5 percent in industrial real estate. The city could be divided into pre-1950 and post-1950 periods in terms of both residences and residents. The older residents worked in the community, or nearby, and a few commuted to Detroit. Almost all of the post-1950 population worked outside of Farmington. Local estimates for 1958 rated the city "above average" in family income, but there was a fair representation from both ends of the income continuum. Although some sections of the city had taken on the characteristics of high- or low-income homogeneity, many of the older, tree-lined streets contained modest homes side by side with more expensive dwellings. Like the township, many of the middle- and upper-income breadwinners were in the professional and executive category. Unlike the township, city residents enjoyed a high level of public services under a city-manager form of government, with a council composed of a mayor and four councilmen elected on non-partisan ballots.

A public water supply from community wells, police and fire protection, storm and sanitary sewers, road maintenance, garbage and rubbish collection—these were the major services that the city resident obtained in exchange for a higher tax than that paid by the township resident. The Farmington School District included both the city and township, and the school-tax rate applied equally throughout the district. Another shared service was a city-township library located in the city. As is the case in most small communities, a small group in the city and a small group in the township had controlled these two political jurisdictions in the past.

An occasional exurbanite who might want to make a hobby of local politics or perhaps to further a legal-political career was admitted to the ranks. The local clique, however, could detect the oncoming suburban tide—a market in search of land, goods, and services— and they were intent on holding the reins of political power as the tide swept in. But the tide brought with it new political aspirations to challenge the political grip of the old, and these began to be felt as city and township proceeded to adjust to their new status as part of the metropolis.

Efforts to adjust to the encroaching metropolis came to a head in 1958 when the city of Farmington attempted to annex a part of the township, and a large part of the township attempted to incorporate as a city. The annexation and incorporation moves were related to each other and took place during the time span from March 1958 through November 1958. This case deals with these events.

The City Attempts an Annexation

Annexation Plans. The March 20, 1958 issue of *The Farmington Enterprise,* the weekly newspaper serving the area, headed its front-page story with these paragraphs:

> Many people, for different reasons, are concerned about the future of the Farmington area, both township and city.
>
> They see Novi Township voting to incorporate as a village, what has happened in the city of Livonia, what has happened to older townships which failed to plan ahead and are now a multitude of different kinds of municipalities, all with great problems.
>
> They hear talk of several areas in the township studying possibilities of incorporating as villages, of industrial zones in the townships, of township sewer and water services. Some fear annexation by the city of Farmington.
>
> The problems are many and complicated, and there may be no "black and white" answer as to what would be best for the entire area.

The *Enterprise* had pointed to the key issue disturbing the community—what sort of an urban community would Farmington become. The quickened pace, after 1950, with which Farmington was becoming a part of the metropolis was striking home. The increase in population was most dramatically evident in the rising school population, with a resultant need for new construction, which in turn required higher taxes. High-density developments on small lots would mean many new school children, and if these were not balanced by new inputs of taxpaying industry, taxes would soar. Lack of sewers in the township had provided a natural barrier to high-density development, but the county was in the process of approving the construction of an interceptor sewer that would open a vast amount of acreage to residential development. Another barrier to the area's growth, distance from the hub of the metropolis, was also melting away. As it was, two major arterial roads serviced the area—Grand River Avenue and Northwestern Highway. Grand River Avenue served the city and the southern part of the township, and Northwestern Highway served the northern part of the township. Both provided direct routes to downtown Detroit, and both were due for expressway treatment. When the metropolitan expressway system was completed, Farmington would be one of the most favored communities in the metropolis.

Township residents were faced with the prospect of an urban population demanding urban services which the township, as an economic and political unit, would be ill equipped to provide. The city of Farmington, on the other hand, was rapidly running out of space for expansion. Both the city manager and the council recognized the need for more commercial and industrial development to help balance the city's residential tax base, but if this were to occur, it would be necessary for the city to acquire additional land.

During the spring of 1958, both city and township officials were preparing to take action. The township had engaged a firm of planning consultants to prepare a master plan for the township, and the consultants' recommendation that 7 percent of the township area (1,180 acres) be zoned for industrial use had evoked strong opposition from some of the residents. The city had also sought the advice of outside experts, college professors and consultants, and their advice was that the city should annex additional territory in order to have room to develop a better distribution of residential, commercial, and industrial land uses. Suggestions as to how much territory should be annexed varied from all the remaining township area to some smaller segment.

As the only city in the township, the city of Farmington was the sole nucleus for expansion via the route of annexation. Michigan law permitted a city to annex adjacent unincorporated areas by a majority vote of the city and those in the affected area, each voting as a separate unit. Approval by the township voters as a whole was not required, but only that part of the township affected by the annexation. By applying for an annexation referendum, the city could, in effect, pluck a choice segment from the township's territory as long as the area was contiguous and the residents of the area, as well as those in the city, were willing.

Secrets were no better kept in Farmington than in other small towns. This was particularly true of city-township affairs. Some of those who worked or owned property in the city lived in the township and vice versa. City and township residents attended the same churches, belonged to the same clubs and mixed socially in a variety of ways. It would have been an extraordinary feat if Farmington's city manager, Earl Scherffius, could have kept the city's annexation plans from reaching the local grapevines. The tattered veil of secrecy that was maintained probably intensified rumors about prospective plans, and during the early part of March 1958, rumors were widespread. The word had spread that the city had been sending members of the police force to collect signatures for an annexation petition from township residents in a low-income area adjacent to the city. This area was badly in need of water and sewers—two services which, rumor had it, the police were offering as bait in order to obtain signatures. The city manager was considered to be the instigator of the plot. Rumors differed over the precise boundaries of the area the city intended to annex, but this uncertainty did not prevent quick reactions to the annexation threat.

On Monday, March 24, 1958, a petition was filed at the county seat in Pontiac to incorporate as a village a one-and-one-third-square-mile area north of the city. The village, to be known as Quakertown, included the subdivisions of Quaker Valley, Ramble Hills, Normandy Hills, and Biddestone Woods, and the population of the entire area was about four hundred. This incorporation move was the first response to the annexation rumors, and it was intended to seal off the area from annexation to Farmington. The

Quakertown incorporators had beaten city officials with an annexation petition to the county clerk's office with a bare two minutes to spare. Two days later, on March 26, the city of Farmington filed an annexation petition with boundaries adjusted to exclude the Quakertown area.

Both the city manager and council admitted that the annexation petition had been precipitated by the Quakertown petition. They said that the city had been studying areas to be annexed for the past year and had planned to hold meetings and discussions with people in the affected areas, but the Quakertown petition plus rumors of another petition to incorporate had forced their hand. City officials were embarrassed because the fact that their plan had had no prior publicity made it appear that they had been plotting in secret to take over a portion of the township.

The area chosen for annexation was 7.8 square miles south and west of the city—the entire southwest corner of the township (see map and Tables 5 and 6). About two thousand people inhabited the area, most of them concentrated due south of the city. This was known as the "dry area," since the shallow wells located there were often dry or polluted with surface water, thus requiring importing of water. For the most part, homes were small frame dwellings on dirt or gravel streets, and residents were low-income white families. In the euphemistic language of the other township residents, this type of area was referred to as a "citified" area and the residents as "citified" people. Two very expensive subdivisions, Heather Hills and Woodcroft, were included in the annexation zone, and there was a scattering of farms and farm houses. Most of the land area was vacant, and city officials pointed out that large tracts were ideal for industrial use. The annexation, they said, would permit the city to develop the type of diversity of land use that their planning consultants had recommended as necessary if the city were to continue to develop without putting an "unbearable" tax burden upon residential property. But the area also contained land very desirable for residential development—in fact the bulk of the land fell into this category. Potential industrial land was in the south and southwest portions to be annexed, and residential land in the west and northwest portions. The area, which also included the township's largest industry and largest

Table 5
General Characteristics of Farmington Units
and Areas in Annexation Proposal

Government Unit or Part Thereof	Area in Square Miles	Population (July 1958 est.)	County Equalized Valuations (1958)	Per Capita Valuation
City of Farmington	2.1	5,700	$17,825,034	$3,127
Farmington Township	33.6	22,000	56,960,049	2,589
Section Proposed for Annexation	7.8	2,000	5,509,452	2,755
Remainder of Farmington Township	25.8	20,000	51,450,597	2,573

Table 6
Locally Assessed Farmington Township Property
Valuations by Type of Property (1958)

	Type of Property					
Government Unit or Part Thereof	Residential	Commercial	Industrial	Farm	Personal	Total
			(in dollars)			
City of Farmington	11,115,700	2,343,800	742,800	------	2,221,600	16,423,900
Farmington Township	19,779,300	1,844,300	735,000	2,044,700	3,676,300	28,079,600
Section Proposed for Annexation	1,843,600	110,100	94,000	82,300	586,000	2,716,000
Remainder of Farmington Township	17,935,700	1,734,200	641,000	1,962,400	3,090,300	25,363,600

taxpayer, the Star Cutter Company, was ideal for the city's expansion plans; the big hurdle to its acquisition was getting voter approval in a referendum.

The vote on the annexation proposal was set for August 5, 1958. This provided ample time for views to be aired in public debate and discussion. Voting in the township was limited to the affected area, but township officials and residents in other parts of the township took an active part, since the outcome would affect the township as a whole. By the time the annexation issue came to a vote, two additional incorporation proposals had been formally approved for submission to the voters in November. If approved, these two proposals would incorporate the bulk of the remaining township area into the cities of Farmington Woods and Clarenceville. Although not directly involved in the immediate annexation controversy, the Farmington Woods and Clarenceville proposals were designed to prevent annexation by the city.

The Case for the City. The spokesmen for the city were the manager, the mayor, Robert B. Lindbert, a businessman whose lumber business was located in the city, and the councilmen. In general, the city's businessmen were in favor of annexation, but this support was not organized in any systematic way. The Greater Farmington Chamber of Commerce was a placid organization that remained detached from the controversy. By far the most active proponent of annexation was City Manager Earl Scherffius. Through public meetings, open invitations to residents to visit City Hall with their questions, and a printed brochure, the city hoped to get its points across to city voters as well as to those in the affected area, who were, of course, the main target. The substance of these arguments was best summarized in a brochure distributed among township voters which said:

> On August 5, 1958, your vote will help to decide whether the present two-and-one-quarter-square-mile city of Farmington and a new seven-and-three-quarter-square-mile area of largely undeveloped land shall be united as a city of ten square miles. This is a big decision which will affect each family individually, but more important yet, the future of the entire Farmington community.
>
> Experts on local government, speaking before various community groups, have unanimously voiced their opinions that the entire area needs "incorporated" or "city" status. This is borne out by the many recent moves for incorporation of cities and villages throughout the township. In other townships where sudden and heavy growth occurred earlier than here, the pattern has always been the same—city status.
>
> The problem you are faced with is not "if"—rather, "when" and "with whom" you will form your new city government. We believe

that if each and every one who will vote on this issue will take the time to become informed as to the facts involved, you will overwhelmingly vote to consolidate the two areas.

This consolidation makes good common sense. The present city of Farmington desperately needs new undeveloped land areas into which it can expand and grow. Well-planned development of the surrounding area will provide additional industrial and commercial growth to help carry the tax burden and pay for our schools.

What will be the advantage to you as a resident of the area in question? A comprehensive study of the area made by the city of Farmington reveals:

These municipal services totally lacking and not provided your area at present:

1. Water supply
2. Sewage disposal services
3. Street lighting
4. Weekly garbage and rubbish collection

The city of Farmington can provide these services immediately to the more populated areas. As the need for water, sewer, and street lights develops in other areas, now undeveloped, these services will be extended according to a carefully planned program.

In addition, our study reveals:

These municipal services provided at poor and inadequate standards.

1. ROAD MAINTENANCE

The Oakland County maintenance program covers the entire county. It is a big job and covers many miles of roads. They are the first to admit they are under-staffed, under-financed, and under-equipped to do this job as they would like to. The city of Farmington has the necessary equipment and machinery to maintain your roads. Additional money and manpower would be provided with increased funds from gasoline and weight taxes returned to the city by the State of Michigan. What you need is someone in your own local city government that you can call upon, and get action, for better road maintenance.

2. POLICE AND FIRE PROTECTION

At the present time you have neither full-time police nor fire protection. The city of Farmington maintains a well-staffed, -equipped and -trained Public Safety Department on a twenty-four-hour-a-day basis. This service would be extended to your area immediately and your fire insurance rates would be greatly reduced.

3. ADEQUATE SURFACE AND STORM WATER DRAINAGE

Many areas are now plagued with poor surface-water drainage conditions, and there is no comprehensive plan for improvement. The city has undertaken a plan for this entire area to eliminate these conditions.

There are many other advantages that the city offers, too numerous to list here. Take the time to find out about them.

Those who oppose this consolidation have but one cry to voice against it. "You will be TAXED off your property." This is not true and is a deliberate attempt to confuse and mislead you. Ask them to give you other reasons for their opposition to this move—then call for a representative from the city to come out and give you the true and exact picture of what your taxes would be and you will be in a position to make an "informed" decision as to how you should vote.

These introductory statements were followed, in the brochure, by three pages of questions and answers in which the introductory remarks were elaborated. The only dollar savings promised were from reduced fire insurance rates, from $50.00 to $60.00 less on a three-year policy for a $20,000 house, and it was explained that the city assessed property at 45 percent of the market value and that the tax rate was $10.00 per thousand assessed value. While offering the township resident more services, the city did not imply that this would be accomplished for less money than the township resident was paying in township taxes. The city argument was that the additional services were well worth the additional cost.

The Case for the Township.   Politics in the township were more turbulent than those in the city. Some blamed this on the fact that township elections were partisan, in contrast to the city non-partisan races, but the causes of disturbance went deeper. Covering a wider area, the township also encompassed a wider diversity of people with diverse values and attitudes concerning the role government should play in their lives. Many recent suburbanites, former city dwellers, had only a vague notion of the legal powers of a township government, while the older rural residents not only knew the limits of township government but also were alert to see that township officials did not forget those limits. Historically Republican, the township supervisor, nominally the most important elective township position, was a Democrat, Frank J. Stephenson, but the majority of the township positions were held by Republicans. The presence of the Democrats was in part a reflection of a basic shift in party preference among new arrivals and in part an indication of internal unrest within the township on local issues. The spring and summer of 1958 found the Township Board members divided on many issues, but on one they were united: they opposed the annexation proposed by the city of Farmington.

Unless the township officials were willing to concede that parts of the township were becoming urban and no longer adequately serviced by the township form of government, a position which they did not accept, they would have to make a case for the township form of government. The township had the limited governmental powers appropriate to its historic role of furnishing the county an administrative unit for providing certain minimal services to rural areas. Both the taxing power and the power to borrow were limited, and although these limitations, plus liberal state aid awarded the townships by a friendly, rural-dominated state legislature, meant low township taxes, they also meant a low level of services. For the 1958–59 fiscal year, the township operating budget for serving an estimated population of twenty-two thousand was $217,329, while the city of Farmington had budgeted $269,693 to provide services for its then estimated population of fifty-seven hundred. (The 1960 census showed both these population estimates to have been conservative.) For public safety, the township was spending only $4.53 per capita compared to the city's $17.36, and for services such as street lighting, rubbish collection, recreation, and public buildings, the city per capita figure was $7.46, compared to the township's $.88.

The township's case against annexation was bolstered by a study that the Township Board had done for it by two young political scientists from Wayne State University, Nicholas A. Masters and Deil S. Wright. The hiring was done at its July 8 meeting, and the report was due July 31. This did not permit much time for the research, nor did it permit much time for distribution and discussion of the report prior to the August 5 election. In their discussion of the appropriation for the study, board members made it clear what they thought the results should be: that the township could serve the area as well as the city could, and that the city was merely attempting to add property to the city tax rolls. There was discussion over whether the findings of the report should be publicized if the results favored the city, but the researchers insisted and were assured that their work would be made public, no matter what. The board was not taking much of a risk. The board's main argument was that it cost less in taxes to live in the township, and any objective study would have to show this.

The July 31 deadline for the report was met, and a press release on the results was prepared by the authors for publication in the July 31 edition of the *Enterprise*. Considering the time in which it was prepared, the report itself was quite detailed, but the press release provided the interested voter with his only view of the report. The gist of the release did not differ from that of the full report, but the brief format meant that much explanatory material, such as that dealing with local borrowing and taxing powers and similar complex matters, had to be dropped. The press release appeared in the *Enterprise* and was distributed by the township in pamphlet form. The pamphlet was entitled "Annexation Facts as presented by"—and then came the names of the researchers, identifying them as members of the Department of Political Science at Wayne State University. The pamphlet "was presented . . . through the courtesy of the Farmington Township Board."

The stated purpose of the press release was "to present the pros and cons and to highlight the issues concerning the proposed annexation." First it listed three advantages to residents in the affected area if annexation were to be approved. First, water could be provided by the city "within three to six months," but "this area might be served by the township with Detroit water within nine months to a year." (It had not arrived by January 1962.) Second, the city could provide more intensive services "with respect to roads, public safety, and refuse disposal," but fire insurance rates would not be immediately affected unless a new fire station were immediately built. The third advantage was:

> The city, as contrasted with the township, has had longer and more varied experience in handling the many municipal-type services required by the growing concentrations of population in the township. In terms of providing specific services, this factor cannot be easily measured, but neither can it be ignored. Almost without exception cities operate under fewer legal restrictions than townships as to form

of government, financing, powers to provide services, and general procedures of administration.

To the political scientist this paragraph may have been steeped with the practical implication that the city form of government was better designed to provide the services demanded by an urban population than was township government, but to the average citizen, it may have appeared ambiguous.

There was nothing ambiguous about the first advantage listed for remaining in the township:

> Township taxes are much lower than city taxes—$1.75 per thousand of assessed valuation in the township as contrasted with $10.00 per thousand in the city of Farmington. Differing assessment practices would tend to widen this tax rate differential. For example, real estate assessed at $2,000 in the township would be assessed at approximately $3,850 in the city. In this instance the property owner would pay $3.50 in township taxes as compared with $38.50 if city taxes were levied on the property. Real property assessed at $3,000 in the township and paying $5.25 in township taxes would, if taken into the city, be assessed at about $5,775 and pay city taxes of $57.75. Property owners in the area would, then, pay roughly ten times more than their present *township* taxes if annexed to the city. School and county taxes would be unaffected.

Next, the report stated that "the township is progressive." As evidence of this, the researchers listed "master plans for the controlled development of the entire township with respect to industrial, commercial, and residential land uses as well as plans for additional services, such as water, fire stations, transportation, recreation, and sewage disposal." It was not explained how, in view of the limited financing powers of the township and its low tax rate, these plans could be accomplished, but it was stated that:

> The central question confronting the residents in the area for which annexation is proposed is whether they are willing to pay additional taxes in return for municipal services which, at least potentially, can be extended sooner and on a more intensive scale by the city of Farmington. In making their decision the residents must also carefully weigh the confidence that they place in the ability of the township government, as compared to the city government, to foster and develop the economic potential which exists within the area.

The researchers went on to list three additional disadvantages to the township as a whole if the annexation were to go through. These were aimed as much at the incorporation movements then brewing as at the issue at hand. One of the key issues was hidden within the following sentences:

> In the township area proposed for annexation 21.6 percent of the total property valuations is in the form of personal property. This is considerably higher than the 13.1 percent for the township as a whole and the 15.5 percent for the city. This means that real estate in the area, particularly residential property, bears a smaller proportion of the total tax burden than in any other section of the community.

This was an indirect reference to the fact that the Star Cutter Company, the area's largest taxpayer, was located in the area to be annexed. The release went on to point out that the disadvantage of losing this industrial property from the township tax rolls would be aggravated in the future, if annexation passed, since the area contained vacant land "ideally suited for industrial firms" and the township was preparing to zone eight hundred acres of the area for industrial use. Additional disadvantages were predicted if annexation were to be followed by incorporation of Farmington Woods and Clarenceville. This fragmentation would result in "costly duplication of services; unrealistic boundaries for providing adequate services; inadequate tax bases for financing services." Adoption of both the annexation and incorporation plans would "destroy the planned and integrated development of the township which is called for by the township master plan studies," the press release concluded.

Township officials were obviously pleased with the press release, for they gave it wide distribution. Timed for the last issue of the *Enterprise* prior to the election, city officials had no opportunity to respond to the report through the area's major news medium. If they had been given the opportunity, it was learned later, they would have questioned the implication in the release that township residents could continue to have low taxes and at the same time have urban services provided by the township. They pointed out that there was a big gap between the township's tentative master plan and effectuation of it, especially in view of the erratic nature of township politics. But the report had come too late for the city to counter with an expert's report of its own.

The Election. The city's election strategy was to appeal to the low-income residents south of and adjacent to the city boundary— the "dry area." While dry in respect to well water, this same area was too wet when spring thaws and heavy rains converted dirt roads into bogs. Living within a stone's throw of city services, this group, it was felt, would support annexation. Opposition was expected, and was forthcoming, from the two high-income sub-divisions, Heather Hills and Woodcroft. Both were low-density developments located on high, well-drained land with adequate well-water supplies and individual septic tanks for sewage disposal. The city's appeal to the low-income area was the offer of immediate services: water, sewers, rubbish and garbage collections, paved roads, fire and police protection. The city's appeal to the high-income residents was to convince them that the long-term best interests of the Farmington community as a whole required the extension of the city so as to provide the base for a more prosperous community. This appeal fell on deaf ears. Instead, the high-income areas provided the affected area's leadership against annexation, with assistance from township officials.

The township's election strategy was, on the one hand, to argue that taxes in the township were lower than in the city, and, on the other hand, to imply that the township was preparing to provide urban services to township residents. The researchers' findings bore out these stands. Taxes were indeed less in the township, and plans were being considered for the township's urban development. What the latter would cost was not discussed. Opponents of annexation were critical of the methods used by the city. Police, or more accurately Public Safety personnel (police and fire functions were combined in a Public Safety unit), were said to have circulated the annexation petitions among families in the dry area, and there were hints, but no proof, of coercion. As the election drew near, residents from the high-income areas proposed that if annexation should fail, they would move to incorporate the same area as the village of Woodcroft. If this were an appeal to dry-area residents, it could only be based upon an offer of shared status stemming from the name "Woodcroft," since the prospective village would not be in a position to provide the services available from the city of Farmington. City voters received little attention

from either side. It was presumed—correctly, as it turned out—
that city voters would favor annexation.

The August 5 election was a regular biennial primary for selecting candidates to run for state offices, so there was more than the
annexation issue to attract the voters. Nevertheless, voting was
light. Twenty-five percent of the city's eligible voters went to the
polls and 21 percent of the township's. In the two township precincts where annexation was an issue the percentages were higher,
31 and 37 percent. The city voted in favor of annexation 425 to
206, but the voters in the affected township area defeated it 74
to 391. Township voting precincts were too large to permit pin-
pointing the voting of residents in the low-income area, but observers reported that voting from that area had not been heavy,
although the affirmative votes presumably came from this group.
In Precinct 7, a rural and exurbanite area, the vote went against
annexation 39 to 3.

Second-guessing voter behavior, city officials felt that they had
taken too passive an attitude, relying upon their brochure and
open meetings, and that a more active campaign in the dry area,
including getting out the vote, might have turned the trick. They
conceded that the tax issue had hurt them and that the press release on the study had helped to drive this home. Township officials considered the tax issue their winning point and the hiring
of the political scientists the crowning tactic. At the same election,
the voters in the proposed Quakertown area voted 107 to 13 in
favor of incorporating as a village. The city had lost its battle to
expand.

Farmington Woods Attempts Incorporation

Incorporation Plans. The events in March 1958 that culminated in the filing of petitions to incorporate Quakertown and to
annex territory to the city of Farmington had stirred concern in
other areas of the township. The Quakertown petition had obviously been a maneuver to forestall annexation by the city, and it
had been successful. In petitioning for annexation, a city was free
to set the boundaries of the area to be annexed as long as the
territory did not include incorporated areas, was contiguous with

the city, and contained at least one hundred persons who had indicated their consent by signing an annexation petition. The boundaries had to be approved by the County Board of Supervisors, but this approval was not considered a difficult hurdle. Latitude in boundary-determination gave the city an opportunity to gerrymander by including within the boundary of the area to be annexed a population cluster that was (1) desirous of city services and annexation and (2) large enough to constitute a voting majority in the area and thus able to carry with it large tracts of less densely settled land where residents might be opposed to annexation. In the spring of 1958, that was exactly what the city seemed to have in mind with its proposal to annex the southwest corner of the township. The pro-annexation vote of residents in the dry area, a small fraction of the area to be annexed, would overwhelm the opposition, which was spread thinly throughout the remaining area, and the city would have more than quadrupled its land area. It appeared to some of the township residents that if they were to prevent being swallowed by the city, they would have to act fast. On May 13, 1958, seven weeks after the city filed its annexation petition, the county received a petition requesting a referendum on the incorporation of 14.5 square miles of the township as the city of Farmington Woods.

The petition was the work of a group new to township politics, a group that had emerged from community organizations within the township. Most of the subdivisions had civic associations that had quasi-social and quasi-political functions. These associations afforded neighbors an excuse to meet and gossip over subdivision affairs and provided a mechanism through which subdivision building restrictions could be enforced. To some extent, the civic associations filled the governmental gaps existing under township government, and they provided a structure with which subdivisions could maintain and promote their individual identities and around which loyalties could develop. In June 1956, a move got under way to bring the various civic associations together in some form of federation, and it resulted in the formation of the Farmington Township League of Subdivision Associations. No doubt some of the founders saw the league as a means of furthering their own political careers as well as of exerting political influence in the community. The league functioned as a communications center to which members brought information about what was going on in their area. Its constitution forbade it from taking a stand on issues and provided that it should "not be administered to interfere with the autonomy of members or with the local affairs of members." Elected governmental officials and those in "paid public office" were ineligible "to take or to retain a position as delegate or alternate, or any other league post," in order to insulate the league from politics in carrying out its stated function "to give effective help to members in their efforts to make a good community, both subdivision and township." Sixteen subdivision civic associations had started the organization, and by 1958, there were twenty-five member organizations.

Regardless of the motivation of its founders, the Township League was a natural outgrowth of the pluralistic subdivision civic association structure for dealing with area-wide problems. By 1958, zoning regulations and a prospective interceptor sewer were the major issues facing the league's members, and underlying both of these was growing uneasiness over the future course of the area's development.

The Farmington interceptor sewer was being constructed by Oakland County's newly organized Department of Public Works. The interceptor's route traversed the township from north to south, one mile west of the township's eastern boundary. Assuming that the necessary laterals were built to connect with the interceptor, the entire township area would have sewers available upon completion of the interceptor. This facility would open the township to additional residential and industrial development; how much and of what sort would depend upon township zoning regulations. The township's share of the interceptor's cost would be paid for by a $250 connection fee charged each property holder making a connection. The connection fee was required because townships were not empowered to levy taxes for purposes such as the sewer, and the rate had been determined on the basis of anticipated growth. In addition to the flat-rate connection fee, users would have to pay for trunk arms and laterals through special assessment districts established for this purpose. Locating the interceptor on the eastern edge of the township, which county officials claimed was necessary because of gravity flow, meant that laterals would be long. No township resident would know what the new sewer would cost him until special assessment districts were established, but the variables that would affect his bill were distance from the interceptor and the number, type, and value of properties in the same special assessment district. The exclusively residential, low-density districts would have the largest individual bills.

Many league members had fought the interceptor and continued to criticize its promoters. Some felt that township and county politicians had pushed through the approval of the project by the county and township (it had not required a referendum) in order to open the township to massive residential and industrial development, which would result in the downgrading of residential zoning through reductions in lot-size requirements and the introduction of industry. Similarly, the prospect of annexation by the city of Farmington was looked upon as a threat to the maintenance of a rural-suburban environment. These feelings of threats from without were fertile soil for plans for action that would protect the concerned residents from intrusions on their way of life.

The decision to circulate a petition for a vote on the incorporation of Farmington Woods was made by a group composed of directors and active participants in the league's affairs. (This boiled down, one of the leaders said, to between fifteen and thirty persons. He explained that the league represented over fourten hundred families, that about seventy people came to meetings, that about thirty individuals did the work of the league and that about fifteen did the hard work.) A group headed by Robert Burton, former league president, met on May 1, 1958 to discuss the annexation issue posed by the city of Farmington's effort to expand. Burton lived in a subdivision, Glen Orchard, due north of the city limits, and although this area was not included in the current city annexation proposal, there were rumors that the city was preparing another proposal that would include Burton's subdivision. If the boundaries were properly drawn, such a proposal could include high-value residential areas along with more densely populated, lower-value residential areas east of the city. In a report that was sent to all its members sometime later, the league explained that at this meeting it was decided that in order to prevent the fragmentation of the township into several small village jurisdictions and at the same time prevent annexation by Farmington, "which would result in the development of a citified community," a large area of the township should be incorporated as a city.

This *ad hoc* committee—it could not formally represent the league since the league's constitution forbade it from espousing causes—decided to keep its plans secret in order to prevent the city from initiating an annexation proposal before the incorporation proposal could be filed. Broadening the membership on the committee, the league members were later told, would have lessened the chances for secrecy. In addition to Burton, a past president of the league, the committee included Robert H. Nelson, who was then president of the league and a vocal critic of the township's involvement with the interceptor sewer. Nelson lived in Kendallwood, the township's largest subdivision, which had its own water and sewer system, installed by the developer. He chaired the group's next meeting on May 8, at which detailed plans for drafting an incorporation petition were made. Counterbalancing the youth and the newcomer status of most of the committee members, an older lawyer, who was a lifetime township resident, was retained to aid in drafting the incorporation petition. On May 12, 1958, the committee circulated petitions, and between 7:30 Monday evening and 1:30 Tuesday morning they obtained 326 signatures, well over the necessary 100, and collected $855 to cover the $500 filing fee, legal fees and incidental expenses involved in preparing the petition. The next morning, May 13, 1958, the petition was filed in the county clerk's office.

For most residents of the Farmington area, their first knowledge that a new city was being proposed for incorporation came on May 15 when they read their copies of the *Enterprise*. Next to the story was a map of the area to be included in the proposed city of Farmington Woods (see map). It showed a city of 14.5 square miles which included most of the township area north and northeast of the city of Farmington. Excluded from the new city were the Quakertown area and the area proposed for annexation by the city (votes were pending on both of these); the extreme northwest corner of the township, 4.5 square miles of farm land (which, if it had been included, would have reduced the area's average population density to under the five hundred per square mile required to qualify for incorporation as a city); the village of Wood Creek Farms (a one-square-mile section that had incorporated in 1957 and was thus immune from the 1958 annexation and incorporation efforts); and the southeast corner of the township (which, with an estimated population of 8,540 in a 4.1-square-mile area, was the township's most densely populated area, and its poorest). The Farmington Woods area contained an estimated 9,820 persons.

The vote on the proposed incorporation was set for November 4, 1958, the date of the general election, at which time voters living within the proposed city limits would vote on incorporation and also for members of a charter commission. If incorporation were approved, the charter commission would have ninety days in which to submit a charter to the governor for his approval, after which the charter would be submitted to the voters for final approval. If a charter had not been approved within two years from the date on which incorporation was approved, the incorporation vote would be nullified, and the whole process would have to begin over again or be abandoned. Thus, approval of incorporation on November 4 would not make Farmington Woods a city; Farmington Woods would continue as part of the township until a charter had been approved by the voters of the new city.

The Case for Farmington Woods.   To be a city in order not to be a city was the basic position taken by the supporters of Farmington Woods. The paradoxical nature of this position made for a somewhat confusing campaign, since it meant that supporters of city status were arguing that this was the best method for avoiding having the characteristics of a city.

The men who had led the action to file the incorporation petition formed a group to carry on the campaign, and they called themselves the Farmington Woods Committee. For the most part, these were people who had come to know each other through their active interest and participation in the affairs of the Farmington Township League of Subdivision Associations. Robert Burton continued to head this committee, and Robert Nelson, league president, continued to give active support and leadership to the pro-city cause. The Farmington Woods Committee had no formal association with the league, but the local political aficionados considered the Farmington Woods Committee to be the product of the group who ran the league.

Most of the leaders of the Farmington Woods movement were newcomers to the township who lived in middle- and upper-income subdivisions and were employed outside the township. Nelson, a young lawyer, had his offices in the township. Burton was an automotive engineer. Some were classified by one of their number as "middle executives and up." They were political amateurs in township politics, but some who later ran for elective office may have already had political ambitions. They were an articulate and energetic group, and they were prepared to challenge those who had held power in the township.

The Farmington Woods Committee waged its campaign through speeches, question-and-answer sessions at open meetings, news releases reproduced in detail in the *Enterprise,* and bulletins mailed to residents. From the time of the announcement of filing the petition to incorporate on May 13, 1958, until after the August 5 primary, at which the city of Farmington's annexation proposal was defeated, most attention was focused upon the annexation campaign. There was some speculation that the city's defeat would ease the tension in the township, but the opposite proved to be the case.

The week following the primary, the Township League sent to its members a statement explaining the reasons for the incorporation petition and the role of the committee that had prepared the petition. The statement, which was carried in the August 14 edition of the *Enterprise,* gave the arguments of the supporters of the proposed city of Farmington Woods that were repeated throughout the ensuing campaign. What follows is paraphrased or quoted from it.

The decision to incorporate was made in order to use "the legal status of 'city' as a protection to remain residential-rural," and a vote to incorporate would forestall annexation moves on the part of the city of Farmington and provide up to two years' time in which to decide what type of charter should be adopted. To incorporate as a village had been considered, but "small villages are either far too costly or must do without adequate fire and police protection." Besides, a petition to incorporate as a village would have required a census, so the process could not have been kept secret. Township government was weak and inadequate "because open to annexation, because open to fragmentation into villages, because citified areas are in conflict with residential-rural areas on matters of zoning, municipal services, public works and taxes, because a township's charter is written by the legislature in Lansing rather than by local citizens, because a township lacks some powers desirable to have for purposes of adopting and enforcing the types of ordinances which make for a better community, such as zoning, building codes, trailer camps, gravel and dump pits, etc." The choice of city status was repugnant but necessary: "Although the committee detests the word 'city,' city status enables citizens to write their own charter, to set therein stricter limitations on taxes than can a township, to prevent fragmentation into villages, and to resist more successfully the costly obligations being imposed by Lansing upon local communities." The statement concluded by citing "two moral commitments" that had formed the basis for the committee's action:

(1) To seek a rural charter, i.e., a charter with a strict limitation on taxes, a charter requiring a vote of the electorate in order to add any additional services or to carry out any public works even though state law may authorize it without a vote of the people, a charter requiring special area assessments where residents of a particular area desire a public improvement, a charter providing a simpler, minimum government with better, if not perfect, defenses against taxes for public works, etc.

(2) To offer to the residents of the northwest corner of the township, to the residents of the southwest corner of the township, if they successfully resist annexation, and then excessive fragmentation into villages, and to the residents of Wood Creek Farms and Quakertown the opportunity to send observers to charter commission meetings—with the hope that a charter might result which would be acceptable to all and thus leave oven the door to eventual merger of all residential-rural areas of the township.

Conspicuously omitted from the contemplated "residential-rural" city were the poor and populous southeast corner of the township (Clarenceville) and the dry area south of the city of Farmington.

The Case against Farmington Woods. During the summer of 1958, those interested in preserving the township intact were preoccupied with defeating the city's attempted annexation. Information about the petition to incorporate Farmington Woods had leaked to members of the Township Board, who had informally discussed it before the petition was filed, but no action was taken until after the August 5 primary, which saw the defeat of the annexation proposal. The seven-man Township Board—composed of four trustees, a supervisor, a clerk, and a treasurer, all elective offices—contained two Democrats and five Republicans, but party affiliation did not play a significant role in the incorporation issue. Supervisor Frank J. Stephenson, a Democrat, opposed the incorporation of Farmington Woods along with the rest of the board, but the organized campaign to defeat incorporation was led by Township Trustee Wendell Brown.

Brown, a lawyer with offices in downtown Detroit, had lived in the township for seventeen years, a tenure which set him apart from the newer arrivals. He lived within the boundaries of the proposed city, but in an older neighborhood, and he looked upon the civic association politicos as newcomers seeking political power. Older and experienced in state and county as well as local politics, his approach to political conflict was less amateurish than that of his rivals. Moreover, as president of the Farmington Township Citizens' Committee, Inc., he had the advantage of working with a tightly knit group willing to commit resources to the campaign. The Farmington Township Citizens' Committee was incorporated on August 27, 1958, and the addresses of the twenty-one incorporators showed them to be scattered throughout the proposed city area, with some concentration in the northeast corner, i.e., near Wendell Brown's residence. At least one of the incorporators was reputed to have substantial land interests in the township, and some must have been willing and able to contribute more than a few dollars to a campaign that Brown estimated had cost between $4,000 and $5,000.

The Farmington Township Citizens' Committee's case against the incorporation of Farmington Woods was summarized in a "Home Caller's Fact Book" that was prepared by the committee, under the direction of a professional public-relations expert, for the use of campaign workers and for distribution among residents. The document itself testified to the time and effort that went into the campaign. Approximately thirty pages in length, with colored plastic tabs dividing its three sections, it was offset printed and bound in a cardboard binder. What follows is paraphrased or quoted from the first section of this document entitled "The Case Against Incorporation."

"We like the country style of living we now enjoy under the township." Whenever there is a special need or demand for services, "we can get together with our neighbors and form a special assessment district to meet it. We don't have to wait for the entire community to wake up to our needs, . . . other neighborhoods can't saddle us with the cost of supplying their needs. And we like the low taxes." Cities are expensive because (1) they have ten times the taxing power of a township—"$39.00 per thousand vs. $3.90 on present township valuation"; (2) they can be committed to public improvements without voter approval and "improvements benefiting only one section of the city can be spread over the general tax rolls," whereas township improvements require formation of special assessment districts based upon the petition of residents; (3) they can sell faith and credit bonds in their own name whereas townships cannot; (4) they do not get the free county police, road, and health services given to the township; (5) the "influx of population which always follows on incorporation creates a need for additional expensive city services"; (6) tax limitations written into city charters do not guarantee that they will not be changed or removed at a later date, and by increasing assessments and imposing taxes outside the charter limitations, cities can get around the charter. If Farmington Woods were incorporated, "it would be the most expensive kind of city to administer." It would have to be supported "almost entirely by residential taxation," and population density would be so low, less than one person per acre, that it would cost more to spread city services. Rural characteristics would be destroyed. "Incorporation will be an invitation to row-house builders to move in." Once city services became available, builders would attack in the courts and defeat zoning standards calling for large lots, but this would not happen in the township, where one-third- or one-half-acre lot sizes would be maintained and general improvements to property would not be made at the general taxpayers' expense. Neighborhoods now "zoned residential may be converted to industry," since to maintain a city of residences alone would be too expensive, and with most of the area to be incorporated now zoned residential, it would be necessary to rezone in order to make room for industry.

The Hidden Agenda. The Farmington Woods campaign involved much that did not appear on the surface of the arguments pro and con. Social psychologists have noted the presence of a hidden agenda in group situations where overt behavior often reflects issues and concerns shared by the group but seldom directly referred to or brought out into the open. It would be a rare political campaign that did not have a hidden agenda, and this was not one of those rare occasions. To make sense out of the tone and content of the campaign, it is necessary to attempt to describe the hidden agenda, but this involves certain risks, since it requires dealing with certain "unmentionables" and "unquotables"—the anathemas of research.

Part of the hidden agenda had to do with sewers. Privately, some of the Farmington Woods supporters felt that real-estate developers were behind the interceptor and behind the opposition to Farmington Woods. They felt that township zoning restrictions on lot sizes would crumble, partly because of the cost of the sewer, which would encourage increasing the number of residents to help pay for the cost, and partly because of the political pressure that the developers would exert upon township officials. On the other hand, some opponents of Farmington Woods felt privately that the promoters of Farmington Woods were trying to shift the cost of the sewers from special assessment districts to a general obligation for a city. They were especially suspicious of the Kendallwood area, where the developer had put in a sewage-disposal system that had been turned over to the county for operation. If this system were to become a general obligation of the new city, the new city would relieve Kendallwood residents of the total operating costs while at the same time burdening those not served

by the system. Mutterings of deals and bad motives went much
further on both sides, but these are chronic conditions of a tense
campaign.

The other part of the hidden agenda had to do with the southeast corner of the township, Clarenceville. The Farmington Woods
petition deliberately ignored it. The fact of the matter was that no
one wanted this area, parts of which had the characteristics of a
suburban slum. If any township area needed urban services such
as streets, street lighting, police, welfare and public health, it was
Clarenceville. An estimated 8,500 persons lived in the four-square-
mile area, and it had the lowest assessed valuation per capita of
any area in the township (see Table 7). Slighted by the remainder
of the township, Clarenceville got into the incorporation act when
a group of its citizens filed a petition for incorporation as the city
of Clarenceville. This petition was filed after the Farmington
Woods petition, and the boundaries included all the southeast corner of the township left dangling by the Farmington Woods petition. The vote on Clarenceville was also set for November 4, 1958,
but its potential incorporation was ignored by the remainder of
the township. To the Farmington Woods supporters, their new
city's boundaries would disassociate them from this "citified" section, so whether or not Clarenceville was incorporated was a matter of indifference. Some township officials may have had hopes
that Clarenceville would incorporate and Farmington Woods fail
to, which would leave the township with a "residential-rural" constituency. What seemed to some to be an unhappy prospect was
for Clarenceville to fail to incorporate and Farmington Woods
to succeed. In this event the township would be left with a high
concentration of low-income residents. Like the poor relative,
Clarenceville was not discussed much.

The Citizens' Committee's Campaign. The Farmington Township Citizens' Committee's campaign against the incorporation of
Farmington Woods was launched on schedule on September 9,
1958 with a "Dear Neighbor" letter sent to residents announcing
the formation of the committee. This letter was the first step in
a campaign that had been carefully planned by a professional
public-relations man who had been called in to advise by one of

Table 7

Comparison of Existing and Proposed Units in Farmington Township

	Area in Square Miles	Number of Dwelling Units* (July, 1958)	Estimated Population†	Percent of Total Population	Total Assessed Valuation (dollars)	Percent of Total Assessed Valuation	Per Capita Assessed Valuation (dollars)
Clarenceville (proposed city)	4.1	2,309	8,540	38.836	$ 6,503,564	23.161	$ 762
Farmington Woods (proposed city)	14.5	2,655	9,820	44.657	15,574,636	55.466	1,586
Quakertown (existing village)	2.0	119	440	2.000	1,076,318	3.833	2,446
Wood Creek Farms (existing village)	1.0	145	540	2.456	1,084,149	3.861	2,008
Woodcroft (proposed village)	7.8	568	2,100	9.550	2,715,973	9.673	1,293
Remainder of Township	4.5	149	550	2.501	1,124,951	4.006	2.045
TOTAL TOWNSHIP (at present)	33.9	5,945	21,990‡	100.000	$28,079,591	100.000	$1,277

*Based on a dwelling unit count of Farmington Township made by the Detroit Metropolitan Regional Planning Commission in June 1958.

†Based on 3.7 persons per dwelling unit (from 1950 census).

‡The township population according to the 1950 census was 11,224.

the Citizens' Committee members. A schedule of activities was planned for an eight-week period beginning with the "Dear Neighbor" letter on September 9 and ending with "Final Ads" scheduled for the October 30 edition of the *Enterprise*. For each week of the campaign there was a planned mailing of either a handbill or a letter, and news releases on the mailed material were scheduled for Mondays in order to meet the *Enterprise's* deadline for Thursday publication. A public meeting, a challenge to debate and a debate were also scheduled. Like a good advertising campaign, this campaign was planned to build up to a crescendo as the big event, the November 4 election, drew near. The schedule was adhered to with remarkably few alterations. The tone and quality of workmanship is reflected in the "Dear Neighbor" letter sent to open the campaign, which said:

A group of residents of our community have joined together to prevent a damaging mistake to all of us—incorporation of the proposed city of Farmington Woods.

Practically all of us have homes in the affected area. There are still others with homes in the township who have taken a serious interest in the contemplated action.

We are opposed to incorporation because all of us have many things to gain by remaining a township—preservation of the suburban character of our community, freedom from exorbitant taxes, overcrowded schools, city noise, and numerous other detrimental factors.

To identify ourselves publicly, we have formed the Farmington Township Citizens' Committee, Inc. It is a non-profit corporation. Our ranks are growing every day from among people like yourself who foresee the dangers which would result from incorporation.

We selected the name Farmington Township Citizens' Committee, Inc., because we intend to continue our organization after the November 4 election and to help plan for the betterment of our community. We urge you to join in that planning.

For the present, however, our principal objective is to defeat the proposed incorporation. We urge you to help us defeat it.

The most compelling argument against incorporation is taxes, because the record of other communities has shown that taxes would increase tremendously following incorporation.

We ask you to vote against incorporation. Remember, we have no reason to fear annexation. The vote by which the southwestern part of Farmington Township overwhelmingly rejected annexation at last month's election has made it clear that we can never be annexed unless we want to be.

The September 11 edition of the *Enterprise,* which reported the formation of the Citizen's Committee, also reported that the Township Board, on the motion of Wendell Brown, had hired the two political scientists who had conducted the annexation study to examine the possible effects of incorporation of Farmington Woods and Clarenceville. Only one board member voted against appropriating the $1,000 for the study, objecting that there was no money in the budget for it; and Robert Burton, chairman of the Farmington Woods Committee, was on hand protesting that the researchers had produced a biased study of the annexation issue and would again favor the township. The report was to be completed ten days before the election and was, in fact, completed on October 27, in time for the last pre-election issue of the *Enterprise.*

In the meantime the Citizens' Committee mailed to residents a series of handbills purporting to show "what happens when a township incorporates," based upon "research by . . . , predoctoral fellow in political science, Wayne State University." (This was an exaggerated designation, for the student held no fellowship, and Wayne, at that time, did not offer the Ph.D. in political science, but the mistake seems to have been the result of some misunderstanding or misinterpretation of the student's status rather than a deliberate attempt to misinform.) Three handbills included a total of five "case histories" comparing township taxes with various cities in the metropolis that had incorporated. As opponents were quick to point out, the comparisons left something to be desired in the way of objective research. In the handbills comparing Oak Park with Farmington Township and Madison Heights with Farmington Township, the percentage increase in population, taxes, and the like for the cities was given for the period since incorporation, but the figures for Farmington Township were all for the year 1957; thus no comparison in rates of change could be made. Since Oak Park's incorporation had taken place in 1946 when the area had a population of 1,703, its 1957 figures for a population of 33,419 (used in the handbill) showed fantastic percentage increases. In the first handbill the Farmington Township school-tax rate appeared as $24.34 per $1,000 and in the second, $44.80 per $1,000, a discrepancy which did not promote confidence in the data. Two handbills ended with the same "Conclusion: Incorporation is followed by an immense influx of population and industry, destroying the suburban character of the community. Public payrolls and TAXES shoot up and up."

Fodder for another handbill came from developments on the sewer issue. During the second week in October, the Michigan Supreme Court, in a four-to-four decision, upheld the legality of the financing of the Farmington interceptor sewer, and any remaining doubts over whether or not the project would be built were removed. On October 16, at the invitation of Township Supervisor Stephenson, Oakland County's director of public works, Harold Schone, held a public meeting in the Farmington High School to answer questions about the interceptor. In view of the assumed interest in the issue, the turnout, estimated at under one hundred, was disappointing. The Citizens' Committee used the meeting to get answers to questions which they felt the Farmington Woods supporters were raising by implication in their campaign, and following the meeting, they released a handbill headed "The Interceptor Sewer Issue Exploded." In this they reported that Schone and a representative of the Michigan Department of Health had made it clear that even if Farmington Woods had been a city, it could not have prevented the interceptor, since once it was determined by the Michigan Department of Health that a sewer was required for the public health, no city charter restriction could prevent it from being built. The handbill went on to attack the Farmington Woods supporters' claim that all township residents would have to pay for the sewer for the benefit of those who needed it and that owners of septic tanks could be forced to tie in with the sewer. The meeting had made clear, according to the handbill, that users alone would pay through special assessment districts, and that these districts could not be formed without a majority vote in the district. (The handbill did not make clear whether this was to be a majority vote of subdivision residents, regardless of the amount of land each owned, or of lots, regardless of the number or even the presence of residents. One person could conceivably own over half of the lots. After the interceptor was built, this became an issue.) The hidden agenda seeped to the surface in one of the handbill's concluding paragraphs:

As a matter of fact, under all the smoke of the Woods Committee's discussion of the interceptor sewer, there is some fire. Some of the committee have a very personal interest in getting a city to meet the sewer costs by a general tax, rather than a township which would make the users and potential users pay for the sewer.

If the committee's campaign had left a stone unturned, it was not deliberate.

The Farmington Woods Committee's Campaign. There was no evidence that the Farmington Woods supporters had the same degree of professional planning of their campaign as that enjoyed by the Citizens' Committee. But the Farmington Woods Committee was composed of intelligent people, most of them college-educated, who remembered enough about their political science courses to feel that they had some knowledge about political campaigns, and whose business and professional training and experience protected them from too much naïveté. Early in August they heard that a group headed by Wendell Brown was being formed to oppose incorporation, but they could not pry out information about it before the first "scheduled" releases in early September. Lacking active opposition and with the election several months off, campaign activity was limited to a single public meeting held for the purpose of explaining why the incorporation move had been initiated. At this meeting, held on July 1, speakers devoted much time to explaining why it was necessary to incorporate as a city in order to prevent becoming one. As committee members had anticipated in their earliest discussions of incorporation, the word "city" was one of their major problems.

When the Citizens' Committee opened its campaign in early September, the Farmington Woods Committee could finally locate its opposition in its sights, and both sides commenced discharging their broadsides. Instead of "Dear Neighbor," the Farmington Woods Committee's mailed missives were addressed to "Mr. and Mrs. Homeowner." These letters, or bulletins, and news releases printed in the *Enterprise*, were the principal media for presenting to residents the arguments for incorporation. The letters were simple, one-page affairs printed on both sides, folded and stapled, and mailed without an envelope at bulk rates. It is

not known for certain whether this format was a necessary economy, as claimed, or a strategic display of lack of funds to contrast
with the Citizens' Committee's printed letterheads, envelopes, and
first-class postage; but it did provide an invidious comparison of
the resources of the two committees. The letters were sent during
the last weeks of the campaign.

The first letter set the stage: "A fog of confusion is never desirable at election time. Especially this coming election. *To help
pierce this fog of confusion the Farmington Woods Committee
will provide beacons.*" The promised beacons were to appear in
successive letters and cover three "focal points." These were: "The
Danger We Face; The Farmington Woods Proposal Will Meet
This Danger; How and Why Many Cons Are Trying to Blind Us
to This Danger." On this latter point the Farmington Woods Committee's letters never got very specific. No doubt the lawyers among
them perused the missives with one eye on the libel laws, but this
did not prevent broad hints such as those in the following paragraph, taken from one of the letters:

> The cons are using many confusion tactics to achieve a "no" vote.
> Their financing and other facts indicate profit and other special incen-
> tives on the part of several cons. Several cons will profit from de-
> generation, and many of them have aided and abetted the rapid
> degeneration overtaking us. In claiming they seek a low-tax, sub-
> urban-rural community, many cons are wolves in sheep's clothing.

All of one letter and part of another was devoted to "the danger
we face" because "our township form of government and township
area are woefully inadequate to resist the strong forces causing the
rapid degeneration of our community and ever increasing taxes."
Both elements of the hidden agenda came to the surface in the elaboration of the contention that township government was too weak
to resist urbanization. The letter argued that the township charter
was a product of a state legislature, which was "content to give us
statutes permitting costly public works without a vote of the people." These statutes undoubtedly referred to the enabling legislation for the interceptor sewer, which was "being forced upon us
and will cause an explosive building boom. . . ." The letter went
on to say that the township area was itself a "force for degeneration" because "township officials seeking *high budgets* and

public works have had strong support from the *citified* portion of the township to the *south*." It continued:

> With our present township *area*, any official seeking to carry out the will of the people will have *political schizophrenia*. In trying to be *all things to all men*, our township officials will *sometimes* please *northern* constituents with low budgets and strong zoning enforcement and sometimes they will please *southern* constituents with increased municipal services, high budgets, and public works. And every time *this* happens our community degenerates.

How the Farmington Woods proposal would meet these prospects is best summarized in the following excerpt:

> Use of the highest legal status, with certain charter provisions, will provide the additional democracy, local self-determination, and greater power necessary to resist all of these strong forces facing us. Exclusion of the SE [southeast] area will provide protection against undesirable charter amendments, budget contests, and other rural-area–citified-area disputes.

These ends would be accomplished through a "bill-of-rights charter" which would "prevent the council from imposing, *without a vote of the people,* any tax of any type, any assessment, any bonded indebtedness, any additional municipal services, any additional public works, *regardless of any state legislation permitting it.*"

In all of its mailings, the Farmington Woods Committee emphasized that a vote for incorporation would prevent further piecemeal incorporations or annexation for at least two years, a delay which would provide "a calm opportunity for further investigation and a look at a charter." Most letters also included a plea for money to support the committee's campaign; the implication was that the "cons" were much better off.

The Report of the Experts. On Monday, October 27, the Farmington Township League of Subdivision Associations sponsored a debate between a team led by Wendell Brown, representing the Citizens' Committee, and a team led by Robert Burton, representing the Farmington Woods Committee, with an Oakland County judge as moderator. Both sides welcomed the debate, as much for the stimulant it would give to public interest in the issues as for the opportunity to present the by now well-established positions. Well attended, the debate covered old ground with a good deal of heat and was warmly received by the audience. Unfortunately, from the point of view of enlightened public debate, the study of the two political scientists was not completed in time to allow both sides and the public an opportunity to study it before the debate. As it was, the researchers had to rush to complete a final draft by the twenty-seventh. The Farmington Woods backers complained that they did not have enough time to study it and accused the researchers of having prepared a slanted summary of the report for the press.

After the debate, having studied the complete report, the Farmington Woods supporters felt that it contained much that was favorable to their position, so they went before the Township Board on Tuesday, October 28, at which time the report was formally submitted, and insisted that an additional one hundred copies of the full thirty-nine-page report be reproduced (the researchers had filed twenty-five copies) and made available to the subdivision associations and interested citizens. The report dominated the *Enterprise*'s pre-election edition coverage of the incorporation issue on October 30. Printed in full was a press release summarizing the report prepared by the researchers, accompanied by two detailed analyses of the report, printed side by side, one prepared by the Farmington Woods supporters and the other by the Citizens' Committee.

The report itself was a carefully prepared document that attempted to show "the effects of incorporation" of Clarenceville and Farmington Woods, and to accomplish this, special attention was given to the level and cost of services under the township as compared to the estimated cost and tax rate to provide similar services under each of the proposed cities. In addition, estimated costs and tax rates were shown "if services were equal to the average level of services provided by cities in the 5,000-to-10,000 population class." The introduction noted: "Because of the number and complexity of the factors considered, we found it impossible to give a simple 'yes' or 'no' answer to the question whether these units should incorporate. Our report is presented in order to make public all factors, pro and con, on each incorporation."

The key finding of the study for both sides of the incorporation controversy was how much would incorporation cost. The threat of higher taxes, both city and township officials agreed, had been the crucial factor in defeating the city of Farmington's annexation proposal. By allocating service benefits currently supplied to the proposed cities by the township on the basis of population, land area, and assessed valuation, the researchers found that Clarenceville was receiving $63,122 in service benefits and Farmington Woods $103,609. When the amount received in state aid and building permit revenues each would receive as cities was deducted from this total, it left Clarenceville with a property-tax rate of .79 mills and Farmington Woods with a rate of .84 mills. The township rate was 1.75 mills. The researchers commented that these data presupposed current levels of services. If ". . . after incorporation the residents desired and obtained additional services, . . . a reasonable assumption might be that the level of services to be provided would be at the average service level for other units of similar population size." Basing their estimates upon the average city-government employment figures of the U.S. Bureau of the Census (for 1956 for cities in the 5,000-to-10,000 population class), the costs and tax rates were recalculated. On the basis of this projection, the Clarenceville tax rate was estimated at 10.79 mills and Farmington Woods at 3.64 mills. In summarizing these data in their press release, the researchers concluded:

> In view of the experiences of a majority of other newly incorporated units, it would be rather unusual if Clarenceville and Farmington Woods, as incorporated units, were able to maintain the present modest rates of property taxation in Farmington Township.

The fact that both sides could put together in the *Enterprise* extracts from the report which they felt led to the conclusion that their position was correct was testimony to the researchers' skill in preparing a report that did examine the pros and cons. The Citizens' Committee selected this extract, among others, as support for their cause:

> Population growth, for example, might result in the reorientation of attitudes in the area. Moreover, an increase in the number of people may pyramid the needs and costs of water, sewers, roads, police, fire, etc., that it would be impossible to "hold the line" in terms of

taxes, and the existence of restrictive charter provisions would serve to accentuate the community's problems or prevent the solution of the problems.

While the Farmington Woods Committee took comfort from words such as these:

> Farmington Woods takes in an area more than three times as large as Clarenceville. . . . Its estimated population . . . is slightly larger than that of Clarenceville, but because of large area it is not nearly so densely settled. . . . Its per capita assessed valuation doubles that of Clarenceville, the figure being $1,586. These figures would seem to indicate that Farmington Woods has a more favorable tax base for incorporation than does Clarenceville.
>
> Compared with the 1.75 mills presently levied on a township-wide basis, the millage rates after incorporation of Clarenceville and Farmington Woods are lower in those areas provided that the existing modest level of services presently extended by the township is retained.

The Citizens' Committee pointed to the report's warning that the "irregularity of (Farmington Woods) boundaries would seriously limit any economies that might otherwise be achieved in the performance of public works functions," and the Farmington Woods Committee quoted from the report that "a lower interest rate on special assessment bonds might be secured by a city because of the more favorable financial position of cities generally when contrasted with the position of townships."

The Farmington Woods Committee's final "Mr. and Mrs. Homeowner" letter indicated that they felt that the research report had backfired on Wendell Brown, because the calculations had shown that it would cost less than the current township tax to provide the same services to the proposed city. As for the projected 3.64 mills which the researchers had estimated that it would cost if the city were to provide services comparable to other cities of its population, the letter cited that this was less than the tax of 3.90 mills proposed by the township supervisor for the current year. The letter noted that the report had shown that as a city the Farmington Woods area would receive substantially more funds for road construction through gas- and weight-tax refunds than had been spent in the area by the county for roads.

The Citizens' Committee did not prepare a special handbill

or letter on the report. If Wendell Brown was disappointed in the results, he did not let it be known. On the contrary, he said, some time later, that he felt that the report had helped his committee's cause.

The Final Shots. The *Farmington Enterprise,* which had remained neutral throughout the controversy and had scrupulously allocated equal coverage to both sides, permitted each group to issue a final statement. The two statements were printed side by side in the October 30 issue. They amounted to a reprise in which former arguments were underscored, although one new note may have been added within the image-laden prose of the following paragraph taken from the Farmington Woods Committee's statement:

> We also saw that the already apparent cancer of fragmentation of our area through numerous tiny village incorporations and annexations needed only to be fed a little of the food called "Destruction of Rural Character" in order to become a raging menace which would leave the township only a hollow shell to be buried to "rest in peace," as has been done with what was once Royal Oak Township.

The allusion here is difficult to establish. What was left of Royal Oak Township, after many incorporations, was a small area, less than one square mile, composed mainly of low-income Negroes. Perhaps the supporters of Farmington Woods were suggesting that this was likely to happen in the southeast corner of the township and that the Farmington Woods area should incorporate to insulate against it, but from the language used, it would be difficult to pin down the meaning with any precision.

The final letter sent by the Farmington Woods Committee also struck a slightly histrionic tone, with underscored, capitalized headings to statements extolling city status such as these: "Greater Resistance to Ever Increasing Taxes; Greater Resistance to the Spread of Commercial Blight; Greater Resistance to Foul and Dangerous Industrial Operation in Residential Zones and Any Other Zones; and Greater Resistance to Building Booms." This last heading was followed by this statement:

> This will be tough, but "city" status will free us from the avaricious and overpowering tentacles and nets of Oakland County. An entire subdivision *will not* be condemned because *one* lot lacks percolation.

Knowing the hideous consequences of half-day sessions and school-tax increases never before nightmared, Farmington Woods officials will not make the road easy, except where existing residents want the sewer or the water. *Land developers* will find the road paved with losses instead of profits. A bond issue will require a vote, and in Farmington Woods this will not be a vote of a few politicians but a vote of all the people.

If there *is* a health order . . . and none has been issued yet . . . or if the sewer comes otherwise, an OBSTACLE COURSE will lie in the path of the perpetrators of mass housing. Villages could not afford this, but Farmington Woods could; it's really a very large area, and an OBSTACLE COURSE Fund will be built up.

The reference to the health order was a reply to the Citizens' Committee's assertion in one of its letters that sewers could be ordered by the Michigan Department of Health—a position confirmed by a Health Department representative at the open meeting on the interceptor sewer. From the Farmington Woods Committee's final campaign letter, it was obvious that sewers and housing developments were considered to be the key issues. A parting shot struck a nautical note:

We'll welcome those who want what we want. As for mass-housing land developers and builders—*they're* not out to ruin our community for the fun of ruining it, *they're* doing it for *profit*. Our OBSTACLE COURSES will take the profit out of it. Two or three cases may be sufficient to those who navigate by the sign of the dollar, to show that Farmington Woods is a rock-strewn coast.

Wendell Brown's Citizens' Committee had fought a counter-punching campaign—meeting every argument for incorporation with counterarguments. The city of Farmington's failure to annex a part of the township was cited as proof that annexation was not to be feared and could not be used as an argument for incorporation. Much was made of the fact that the Farmington Woods campaign for a city consisted of arguments against cities, and the Citizens' Committee raised the question in their letters: "What are the Farmington Woods promoters' real motives for pushing their city?" It was pointed out that township taxes were already limited by state law to a 2-mill rate that worked out at 3.90 mills on current equalized valuations. "Townships are the least expensive and most democratic units of government. . . . Outside the field of taxing and spending, a city has no greater power than a township. A city could not protect against industry, mass housing, or gravel pits any better than the township—and probably not as well" said the Citizens' Committee in its summary.

At the public debate, Wendell Brown had emphasized that the Farmington Woods supporters could not produce firm estimates of what it would cost to run the proposed city—evidence, he indicated, of the lack of experience in government of the Farmington Woods promoters. This theme, that the Farmington Woods incorporation proposal was the work of amateurs, was again emphasized in the Citizens' Committee's summary in the October 30 *Enterprise:*

> The Farmington Woods incorporation plan was conceived in haste and secrecy and never submitted to public study before the petitions were filed. It's jigsaw shape would be impractical as a city. . . .·
>
> .   .   .   .
>
> The argument that this proposed city will be somehow different is made by men who have never had any experience in government and who cannot point to an example of a city which is different.

The Citizens' Commiteee's final "Dear Neighbor" letter went out on schedule on October 29 and said:

> We like our country way of life in Farmington Township.
>
> We like the clean air, the ample play space for our children, the freedom from traffic on residential streets, the good schools, the quiet, spacious neighborhoods, the absence of industrial neighbors.
>
> We like the democracy of the annual township meeting.
>
> We like the assurance that we'll never have to pay for improvements to someone else's property. And we like the township machinery which enables us to join with our neighbors to provide desired public improvements at our own expense.
>
> And we like the low taxes.
>
> We moved to the country to get away from the city. We don't propose to bring the city here after us.
>
> THAT IS WHY WE ARE WORKING FOR A "NO" VOTE ON INCORPORATION; TUESDAY, NOV. 4.
>
> Join us in preserving our country way of life in Farmington Township. Help defeat the incorporation proposal so overwhelmingly there will be no more city schemes to disturb the peace of our community for a long time to come.

The letter contained a P.S. saying that the Citizens' Committee "will remain in business after the election to work for the continuing betterment of our township," and extending an invitation from "our more than three hundred members" to join.

The Voters' Decision. The November 4, 1958 ballot was a full one for Farmington Township voters in the proposed Clarenceville and Farmington Woods area, for it contained, in addition to candidates for Congress and for state and county offices, the incorporation propositions and slates of candidates to form a charter commission, should incorporation be approved. The Citizens' Committee had held a meeting in Clarenceville prior to the election, at which speakers had urged that the incorporation be defeated, but no vigorous campaign, pro or con, had been waged in Clarenceville. The only argument that seems to have been made in support of incorporation was that it would forestall, for at least two years, any annexation attempt on the part of the city of Farmington. The Clarenceville voters' response to incorporation was a resounding "No"—1,061 against, 342 in favor. In no precinct was the vote close. The voters in the southeastern corner of the township were not eager to form a city of their own.

The outcome of the Farmington Woods vote was not as one-sided, but incorporation lost—1,367 in favor of incorporation to 1,906 against it. The Farmington Woods proposal thus lost by 539 votes; the opponents of incorporation received 58 percent of the vote. The pattern of voting varied among the five precincts. In Precinct 6, incorporation won, 294 to 243, but in Precinct 3 it lost by its largest margin, 172 to 521. Precinct 3, in the northeast corner of the township, was where Wendell Brown had received much of his initial support. The area included a large subdivision, Franklin Knolls, that had had serious problems disposing of sewage through individual septic tanks. The area was committed to tie into the interceptor sewer, and the cost was to be met through a special assessment district, regardless of whether the area remained in the township or became part of a city. Precinct 6 was not as densely settled nor were its subdivisions committed to the interceptor. It may have been that in this area residents felt that city status would help them remain out of the interceptor. In the remaining three precincts the vote was closer than in Precinct 3, but incorporation lost in each of them, including the one in which Chairman Burton of the Farmington Woods Committee lived.

Interest is difficult to measure, but the *Enterprise* reported that in the city of Farmington, with no annexation issue on the ballot, 73 percent of the registered voters had voted on November 4, whereas only 68 percent of the township's registered voters had voted. This comparison was not a true indicator of intensity of interest in incorporation, since not all township voters were voting on that issue. In Precinct 4, with the Farmington Woods area's highest concentration of large subdivisions, 80 percent of the registered voters voted; incorporation lost, 475 to 607.

Whether the defeat of incorporation met the Citizens' Committee's aspiration of being so "overwhelming" as to discourage future "city schemes to disturb the peace of our community," only the future can tell. But the defeat of annexation in August and incorporation in November terminated any immediate plans for boundary changes. By the end of 1958, the suburban building boom had slowed to the point where very little pressure was being exerted to extend the boundaries of the metropolis, and in spite of all of the activity, no significant change in the political boundaries within Farmington Township had taken place during 1958. The incorporation of Quakertown as a village had not removed that area from the township's jurisdiction, and the proposed incorporation of the annexation area as the village of Woodcroft had been dropped. The township had won its battle to remain intact.

Post Mortem. One leader of the Farmington Woods incorporation movement gave this analysis of the reasons for the defeat of incorporation. The word "city" had been one major obstacle. He felt that if they had heeded the precedent of another suburb in the metropolis that had incorporated as a city with the name "City of Lathrup Village" and had adopted a name such as "City of Farmington Woods Village," they might have picked up an additional five hundred votes. But he also conceded that the tax issue had hurt his cause. The township tax was, in fact, low, and many were fearful that a change to city status would make taxes go up. Then, too, he admitted that the Citizens' Committee's contention that the new city would have no industry to share the tax load, whereas the township did have some and had zoned for more at a safe distance away from the Farmington Woods area, strengthened the township's tax argument. He felt that if his group had succeeded in making clear that the purpose of the proposed city was the reverse of what was commonly associated with the purpose of organizing a city, they would have won. Like many who suffer political defeat, he attributed it to failure to communicate. Another Farmington Woods leader felt that their campaign had been amateurish in comparison with their opponents. He estimated that the Farmington Woods campaign had cost about $1,000, which, he felt, was considerably less than the amount spent by the Citizens' Committee. The sample budget for the proposed city that had been prepared by the proponents was cited as a project that had backfired, since it was easy for the political pros to poke holes in it and use it as evidence of the ineptitude of the Farmington Woods promoters. Both leaders felt that the incorporation movement had been opposed by "tremendous forces."

Having won, Wendell Brown was probably less concerned with diagnosing why, but he did attribute a decisive role to the report of the political scientists in pointing to the impracticability of the proposed city. He also felt that the vote against incorporation had been a vote of confidence in the township officials and reflected a lack of confidence in the leaders of the Farmington Woods movement. Brown said, however, that if the researchers' reports had definitely come out against the township, the Farmington Woods incorporation supporters would have won.

The incorporation controversy demonstrated the intensity of the zoning issue and the consensus, at least in the northern two-thirds of the township, that the suburban-rural characteristics of that area should be maintained. Neither side had questioned that goal; both had argued that their chosen means, city or township government, was the best way to achieve it. Regardless of its reasonableness or economic feasibility in the face of the growing metropolis, neither of which was discussed or debated, the suburban-rural image had been accepted as public policy.

Concluding Comments

Frontier politics, as we have seen, still involves boundary disputes, but the weapons are now words—spoken and written in letters, handbills, newspaper accounts, and reports by experts. The stakes in the boundary settlement are often difficult to discern, but that stakes are involved can be deduced from the amount of energy devoted to the struggle to maintain or change the boundary. Unlike an earlier period in our history, however, the losers on the metropolitan frontier live on to fight new battles. The defeat of incorporation of Farmington Woods shifted the battle over zoning and retention of the suburban-rural characteristics of the area to the arena of township politics.

Some of the original members of the Farmington Woods Committee, those who had masterminded the incorporation project, went on to win township elective office. Robert Nelson was elected justice of the peace, not an unrewarding position for a lawyer in a suburban community, and two other committee members, Raymond B. Wilcox and Arthur S. Bassette, were elected as trustees on the Township Board. Wilcox and Bassette ran on a "community-preservation" platform sponsored by the Farmington Township Association for Community Preservation. As might be expected from the label, this was a strict-zoning, minimum-service, low-tax program. Other aspirants for office, such as Robert Burton, running under the Community Preservation label in a Republican primary, were defeated.

But township politics, although employing the partisan ballot, are personal, and it would be a mistake to assume that later political success or failure could be attributed solely to participation in the incorporation campaign. A candidate's fate was as likely to be determined by his personal popularity or his acceptance by a currently dominant clique as by any public statements concerning policy. Among the odd folk-beliefs of American politics, especially strong in suburbia, is the notion that the "non-partisan" and "non-political" person makes the most acceptable candidate for public office. This type of Orwellian doublethink forces the aspiring suburban politician to seek roles that help spread his personal popularity and at the same time establish his deep (but "non-political") concern with public issues. The Farmington Township League of Subdivision Associations as well as the Farmington Woods Committee provided bases from which the political newcomers could launch their political careers and challenge those holding political power.

But the political newcomers, while meeting some success at the polls, did not overwhelm the older group. Wendell Brown continued to serve on the Township Board. Although he was unsuccessful in a bid for a county judgeship, he ran well in his own township, and his township political position remained intact. The Farmington Township Citizens' Committee, the "non-partisan" organization which Brown headed to defeat incorporation and which was to continue to work for community "betterment" after the election, lapsed into a dormant state. It had served the purpose, as had the Farmington Woods Committee, of providing a short-lived *ad hoc* political organization in a township lacking sophisticated political institutions. No doubt it could be reactivated, if needed, to fight another battle.

Fusion of the old blood and the new blood in the township political structure signified both the accommodation of new political forces and ambitions and the acceptance of the township form of government as the means of preserving the suburban-rural image. This acceptance was Farmington's answer to the questions concerning the role of suburban government which underlay the annexation and incorporation controversies. The controversies stemmed from different premises concerning the function of suburban governmental units, and the choices made will influence the future shape of governmental institutions in the metropolis.

The city of Farmington's annexation move was based upon the premise that the suburban city should have an economic tax base sufficient to support the services and amenities associated with city life. This assumption implied the need for a variety of land uses, commercial and industrial as well as residential. It also meant that the city would provide employment for at least some of its residents and not be an exclusively bedroom community. Since a large amount of land was to be annexed and most of it was vacant, it was expected that the anticipated uses could be distributed and protected by zoning so as to create a desirable as well as an economically viable community. Professional and academic planners endorsed this approach.

The Farmington Woods incorporation plan was based upon the premise that the function of that city should be to enforce zoning restrictions and provide certain minimum services in order to maintain the exclusive suburban-rural characteristics of the area. Modern technology, which provides the private transportation that permitted the midde-class urban dweller a wide choice in selecting a place to live, also provided the electricity, pumps, septic tanks, and ancillary gadgets that made it possible to live on the metropolitan frontier and still enjoy all of the "modern conveniences." With each home a self-sufficient unit, why pay for city services? City status was proposed as a way to prevent city services. If a service were forced upon residents, such as the interceptor sewer, it would be paid for through special assessment districts, but the implication was that such districts would seldom be approved. A "bill-of-rights charter" would require a referendum on almost every decision involving the expenditure of money. This suburban city would be an exclusive neighborhood in which to live, not a place in which to work.

Township government was the alternative chosen by those afforded the opportunity to annex with the city of Farmington and by those afforded the opportunity to incorporate as the city of Farmington Woods. What can a city do that a township cannot do, supporters of the township had asked rhetorically in their campaign literature, and the answer was "tax up to ten times as much" and "make public improvements and sell bonds as a general obligation of the city." The township's answer for those who wanted services was the special assessment district. With the possible exception of future projects, such as the interceptor sewer, that might be undertaken by an expanding county bureaucracy or by an *ad hoc* multi-jurisdictional authority, minimum government and minimum service was guaranteed under the township. As an alternative form of minimum government, the city of Farmington Woods was rejected; but it is an alternative that will lurk in the background and be revived if the township should renege on its commitment to the suburban-rural image.

The economically integrated, satellite suburban city, the residential-exclusive suburban city, the township–special-assessment-district suburban jurisdiction—each of these types of adjustment to suburban status can be found on the edges of American metropolises. From the narrowest perspective, the best type of adjustment would be that which is most satisfying to the residents within a given jurisdiction. The use of the referendum to determine whether a given boundary or governmental form should be changed is based upon this method of evaluation. Each of these three alternatives has limitations. The satellite city, even with a sound tax base, would still be drawing wealth from the core city and the surrounding metropolis where salaries and wages were earned, and the resultant governmental unit would still not be the optimum size for providing services through a professional bureaucracy. The residential-exclusive suburban city merely compounds the problems of the metropolis by luring those most able to pay for city services to jurisdictions with low taxes and minimal services, leaving the core city and older suburban cities with high concentrations of problems and meager resources with which to meet them. The township–special-assessment-district alternative is a temporary expedient with neither the institutional structure nor the powers to carry out efficient urban services.

In spite of these limitations, these three alternatives continue to be the prevailing choices. Suburban areas have traditionally provided a field for the clustering of those with similar social and economic status, and as these clusters develop into political enclaves as villages or cities, they harden into impregnable jurisdictions. In Farmington Township the clustering and hardening process has not been completed, but it is well under way. Chances are good that as the clustering proceeds, the township area will break up into smaller jurisdictions, in spite of the efforts of citizens' committees. If this happens, the jurisdictional boundaries will include a smaller, more homogeneous area than that represented by the proposed Farmington Woods, and the metropolis will have spawned a new brood of satellite jurisdictions.

Epilog

The cautious can avoid the embarrassment of possible error by refusing to make predictions. But our study of the Detroit metropolis emboldens us to identify those of its existing major characteristics that we believe will continue to condition its growth and development. To the extent that other metropolises share these characteristics, their futures will be similarly influenced.

The most conspicuous and most often attacked characteristic of the metropolis is its multiplicity of governmental jurisdictions. The metropolis includes not only cities, villages, townships, counties, and various *ad hoc* multi-jurisdictional local units, but also state and federal agencies. All operate under certain restrictions—local governmental units being limited to a particular area in the metropolis, while state and federal agencies along with *ad hoc* units have a wider territorial range but are restricted to a particular function. Decision-making within the metropolitan jurisdictional complex requires a variety of intergovernmental relationships, such as applications from a city to a federal agency for urban renewal funds and tripartite contracts binding city, county, and state to a metropolitan expressway program. Not as perceptible but nevertheless present are numerous informal contacts and relationships among governmental officers from the proliferating jurisdictions of the metropolis.

The variety of intergovernmental relations may be viewed as adaptive behavior by which demands for highways, water, airports, and other needs that are multi-jurisdictional or metropolitan in scope are met within a pluralistic governmental structure. The adjustments made within this system do produce results: express-

ways are built, slum areas are cleared, and relief drains are constructed. Since the adjustments by which these results are achieved,
such as the formation of the Twelve Towns Drainage District and
the expanded service area of the Detroit water works, fortify the
maintenance of existing local units by removing a particular pressure for change, these changes strengthen, rather than weaken,
the pluralistic governmental structure of the metropolis. The present system also has the advantage of a system in being, has a very
proper lineage in hallowed institutions of local self-government,
and is considered satisfactory by large numbers of citizens and
almost all local officials.

A hallowed institution of the Detroit metropolis is non-partisanship in local decision-making. Although county elections are partisan, the non-partisan election of city officials has established a
non-partisan tradition for the metropolis. The absence of party
organization as a channel for citizen action on local issues has not
left the metropolitan dweller without organizational resources for
dealing with his government. The cases are replete with instances
where existing community groups, such as civic associations, were
brought into play to contest a policy or where new *ad hoc* groups
were formed to further an issue. Whether this is a more adequate
or less adequate means of obtaining citizen participation in public
affairs than that offered by party organization is debatable. But
the organized political activity generated around issues in a non-
partisan setting does result in public debate prior to decision-
making and does provide an opportunity for communication between citizens and public officers. Citizen preference for non-
partisan city government persists, as newly incorporated suburban
cities continue to adopt it.

Lacking party organization, one might expect the power gap
to be filled by some person, organization, or group. Our cases have
not turned up a single master decision-maker for the Detroit metropolis in the form of a person, group, or organization. Detroit's
most prominent political officers, mayor and councilmen, can, at
most, extend their influence into Wayne County affairs, where
they have a formal role on the Board of Supervisors; but non-
partisan urban political support has not been automatically trans-
ferable to the partisan political arena. The Board of Commerce

plays a prominent role in metropolitan decision-making, much more prominent than any equivalent representative of organized labor, but there is ample evidence from the cases that the board is but one important factor in a pluralistic power system. The success with which the various competing organizations and groups have prevented power from becoming concentrated in the hands of a ruling elite makes it unlikely that the pluralistic power balance will be significantly tipped in the future.

Stripped of partisan overtones, the focus of metropolitan politics is clearly upon the extension or retention of specific benefits to the metropolitan dweller. Unlike many who write about the metropolis, the metropolitan dweller tends to be ideologically neutral and pragmatic in his approach to urban problems. Whether his water is furnished by Wayne County, by Detroit, or by some other jurisdiction concerns him less than the fact that he wants enough water to preserve his lawn; or if he has his own well and septic tank, he wants no part of an urban water and sewerage system, regardless of who furnishes it. The presence or absence of a service or function, and, at times, the cost and manner of performance are key issues, not who provides it. A similar attitude was apparent in the cases involving annexation and incorporation. City, township, or village status was accepted or rejected because of the practical advantage it was expected to entail rather than because of an ideological commitment to a particular form of government.

Without doubt, the metropolitan dweller's acceptance of governmental forms that satisfy particular substantive needs or demands is resulting in a drastic change in the role of traditional forms of local general government (cities, townships, villages, and counties) in the metropolis. While narrowing the functional range of many general governmental units, the demand for services has also resulted in: (1) the expansion of certain county functions to include services for the whole metropolis, such as the Detroit-Wayne County Metropolitan Airport; (2) the extraterritorial expansion of core-city agencies, such as the Detroit water works; and (3) the development of *ad hoc* units, such as the Twelve Towns Drainage District. Multi-jurisdictional units such as these will continue to develop from city and county agencies or to be specially created as limited-function units. These functionally based organizations are here to stay, and they will play an increasingly important role in the politics of the metropolis.

The expansion of functional agencies enhances the importance of their bureaucracies. Our cases show the prominent decision-making role now played by bureaucracies, and both the airport and water-supply cases reveal bureaucratic struggles to gain the right to be the exclusive providers of certain services. As functional activities become more firmly grounded in science and technology, the lay citizen will encounter increasing difficulty in challenging policies and decisions based upon technical determinations of the bureaucracy. At the same time, his demand for services will continue to provide the impetus for increasingly powerful bureaucracies.

Bureaucracies are, of course, subject to the controls exercised by legislators and by elected and appointed executives, and, in addition, are subject to the checks resulting from the pluralism of the metropolitan system. Expanding bureaucracies operating in the same functional area but in different governmental units compete for new territory, and rival bureaucracies operating within a single governmental unit vie to expand or protect their functional jurisdictions. To the citizen, certain internal bureaucratic struggles are subliminal, but conflicts involving crucial values spill over into the political consciousness of the citizenry and are dealt with in the political arena. Since, as our cases show, forms of political activity tend to adjust to new organizational arrangements, the citizen's capacity to hold governmental officers responsible is not necessarily weakened by the growth of functional bureaucracies. Encroachments by governmental bureaucracies upon the private economic sector are guarded against by organizations such as the Board of Commerce, which can hire experts to challenge the expertise of the governmental bureaucracy. Lacking a consensus on policy, the political arena will continue to function as it did in the port case, as a restraint upon the plans of the bureaucracy.

The pluralistic, functionally oriented system imposes one important condition upon decision-making in the metropolis. This condition is sluggishness in reacting to a changing environment.

Reaching the required agreement for joint action among a number of separate units takes time, whether the agreement be along vertical functional lines, such as the agreement among local, state, and federal highway officials, or along horizontal lines, such as among the Twelve Towns jurisdictions. Rivalries among bureaucracies blossom into time-consuming battles, while the particular need goes unfulfilled. If the set of circumstances calling for the initial decision has significantly changed by the time that decision is made, the decision may have little relationship to the changed circumstances. The ever increasing rate with which science and technology develop and convert information into usable forms which affect the economic and social structure of the metropolis assure a metropolitan environment in a constant state of change. The lag in response to demonstrable needs (for example, urban renewal, water, sewers, and transportation facilities) is the price which a complex industrial society pays for functioning through a pluralistic political system.

Lacking some form of metropolitan super-cost-accounting that would permit an evaluation of the economic, social, and political costs and benefits of the present metropolitan system, the metropolitan dweller is understandably reluctant to abandon a system in being, with a modest capacity for adapting to change, for some new arrangement such as a single governmental unit for the whole metropolis. We find no dominant political values upon which such a metropolitan super-government is likely to be built, nor do we find any perceptible demand for a single government for the metropolis. On the contrary, as the functional bureaucracies continue to grow in size and power, they will guard their enclaves against being brought within the orbit of a single metropolitan government.

Any major change in the political structure of the metropolis must await a more precise accounting of its costs and benefits or a major breakdown in the capacity of the current structure to satisfy demands made upon it. The metropolitan dweller views local government as a means for achieving social and economic ends, and only when he is deprived of a convenience or benefit does his focus shift to the governmental devices for correcting the deprivation. Thus deliberate attempts to reorganize the metropolis would require a convincing assessment of the costs and benefits of the present system, a firm grasp of the values that the altered system would be designed to achieve, and some evidence that the altered system would perform as predicted. Lacking these conditions, and short of a major economic or thermo-nuclear disaster, we believe that the present system will continue to retain its basic pluralistic structure.

Appendix

General Characteristics of the Detroit Metropolis

Population

According to the 1960 census, Detroit was the fifth largest Standard Metropolitan Area (SMA) in the United States.. (Beginning with the 1960 census, the designation was changed from SMA to Standard Metropolitan Statistical Area, SMSA, which designation is used in the following tables.) Detroit's metropolitan growth of 24.7 percent over the past decade is close to the 26.4 percent rate for all SMSA's. The decline in the population of the central city is also typical of most of the larger and older cities.

Population of the Fifteen Largest U.S. Standard Metropolitan Statistical Areas and Percent of Increase Inside and Outside Central City or Cities—1950–1960

Source: 1960 Census of Population, Supplementary Reports PC (S1)-1, U.S. Department of Commerce, Bureau of the Census.

Standard Metropolitan Statistical Area	1960	1950	Percent Increase 1950–1960
New York, New York	10,694,633	9,555,943	11.9
New York			− 1.4
Outside Central City			75.0
Los Angeles–Long Beach	6,742,696	4,367,911	54.4
In Central Cities			27.1
Outside Central Cities			82.6
Chicago, Illinois	6,220,913	5,177,868	20.1
Chicago			− 1.9
Outside Central City			71.5
Philadelphia, Pa.–N.J.	4,342,897	3,671,048	18.3
Philadelphia			− 3.3
Outside Central City			46.3
Detroit, Michigan	3,762,360	3,016,197	24.7
Detroit	1,670,144	1,849,568	− 9.7
Outside Central City	2,092,216	1,166,629	79.3
San Francisco–Oakland	2,783,359	2,240,767	24.2
In Central Cities			− 4.5
Outside Central Cities			55.0
Boston, Massachusetts	2,589,301	2,410,572	7.4
Boston			−13.0
Outside Central City			17.6
Pittsburgh, Pennsylvania	2,405,435	2,213,236	8.7
Pittsburgh			−10.7
Outside Central City			17.2
St. Louis, Mo.–Ill.	2,060,103	1,719,288	19.8
St. Louis			−12.5
Outside Central City			51.9
Washington, D.C.–Md.–Va.	2,001,897	1,464,089	36.7
Washington, D.C.			− 4.8
Outside Central City			87.0

(*continued*)

Standard Metropolitan Statistical Area	1960	1950	Percent Increase 1950–1960
Cleveland, Ohio	1,796,595	1,465,511	22.6
Cleveland			— 4.2
Outside Central City			41.6
Baltimore, Maryland	1,727,023	1,405,399	22.9
Baltimore			— 1.1
Outside Central City			72.9
Newark, New Jersey	1,689,420	1,468,458	15.0
Newark			— 7.6
Outside Central Cities			24.7
Minneapolis–St. Paul	1,482,030	1,151,053	28.8
In Central Cities			— 4.4
Outside Central Cities			115.7
Buffalo, New York	1,306,957	1,089,230	20.0
Buffalo			— 8.2
Outside Central City			52.1
All SMSA's	112,885,178	89,316,903	26.4
All Central Cities			10.7
Outside Central Cities			48.6
Outside SMSA's	66,437,997	62,008,895	7.1

Population of Major Jurisdictions in the Detroit Metropolis 1940, 1950, and 1960

SOURCE: 1960 Census of Population, Number of Inhabitants. PC (1)-24A Michigan and Advance Reports, General Population Characteristics PC (A2)-24.

Jurisdiction	1940	1950	1960	Percent Increase 1950–1960	Percent Non-white 1960
Detroit	1,623,452	1,849,568	1,670,144	— 9.7	29.2
Wayne County*	2,015,623	2,435,235	2,666,297	9.5	20.1
Oakland County	254,068	396,001	690,259	74.3	3.5
Macomb County	107,638	184,961	405,804	119.4	1.7

*Includes Detroit population

Population Density in the Detroit Standard Metropolitan Statistical Area—1960

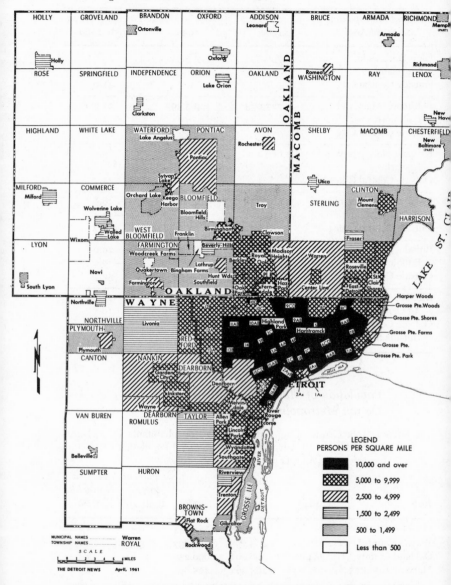

LEGEND
PERSONS PER SQUARE MILE

- 10,000 and over
- 5,000 to 9,999
- 2,500 to 4,999
- 1,500 to 2,499
- 500 to 1,499
- Less than 500

MUNICIPAL NAMES .... Warren
TOWNSHIP NAMES .... ROYAL

SCALE

0 1 2 3 4 5 6 MILES

THE DETROIT NEWS   April, 1961

Housing Growth in the Detroit Standard Metropolitan Statistical Area, 1950–1960

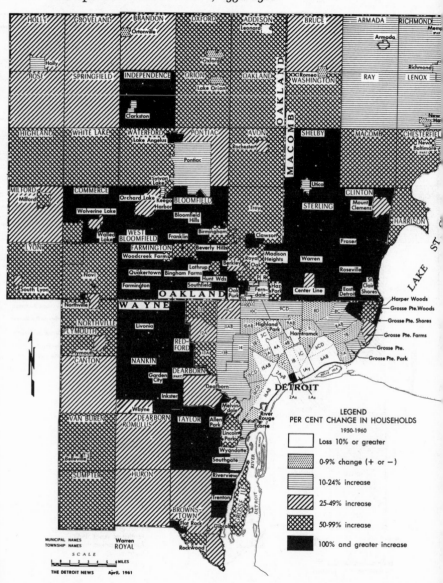

LEGEND
PER CENT CHANGE IN HOUSEHOLDS
1950-1960

Loss 10% or greater

0-9% change (+ or −)

10-24% increase

25-49% increase

50-99% increase

100% and greater increase

MUNICIPAL NAMES   Warren
TOWNSHIP NAMES   ROYAL

SCALE

THE DETROIT NEWS   April, 1961

Economic Map of the Detroit Standard
Metropolitan Statistical Area

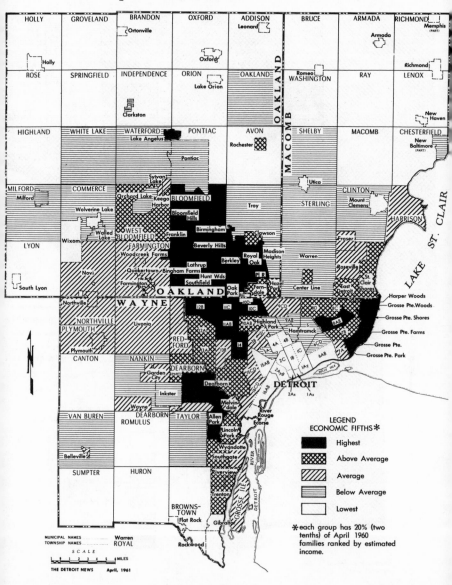

LEGEND
ECONOMIC FIFTHS *

- ■ Highest
- ▨ Above Average
- ▥ Average
- ≡ Below Average
- □ Lowest

* each group has 20% (two tenths) of April 1960 families ranked by estimated income.

MUNICIPAL NAMES .... Warren
TOWNSHIP NAMES .... ROYAL

SCALE

THE DETROIT NEWS   April, 1961

Economic Characteristics

Land Use. In 1958, the Detroit Metropolitan Area Regional Planning Commission surveyed land use within the region, and the following data are taken from the report of the commission's findings.

Land Use in the SMSA Counties

Land Use	Macomb County Sq. Mi.	Percent	Oakland County Sq. Mi.	Percent	Wayne County Sq. Mi.	Percent
Commercial	5.6	1.2	9.7	1.1	13.1	2.1
Industrial	6.5	1.4	6.7	0.7	27.0	4.3
Industrial *extractive*	2.6	0.5	8.3	0.9	1.9	0.3
Residential *urban*	37.8	7.9	76.0	8.4	131.8	21.1
Residential *rural non-farm*	26.1	5.4	71.8	8.0	61.1	9.8
Public and Semi-public	7.0	1.5	25.7	2.8	26.2	4.2
Airports	4.7	1.0	2.5	0.3	9.3	1.5
Recreational	6.6	1.3	41.5	4.6	19.1	3.1
Major Streets	16.6	3.5	29.3	3.3	58.6	9.4
TOTAL DEVELOPED AREA	113.5	23.7	271.5	30.1	348.1	55.8
Vacant and Agri-cultural	365.9	76.3	604.6	67.1	268.5	43.0
Water Area (lakes)	0.0	0.0	25.1	2.8	7.4	1.2
TOTAL AREA	479.4	100.0	901.2	100.0	624.0	100.0

Increase in Developed Areas 1949–1958

	Developed Area 1949 Sq. Mi.	1958 Sq. Mi.	1949–1958 Increase Area Sq. Mi.	Percent
Macomb County	68.9	113.5	44.6	65
Oakland County	163.2	271.5	108.3	66
Wayne County	257.8	348.1	90.3	35

The major features of the existing land use were summarized by the Regional Planning Commission as follows:

The current land-use picture in the Detroit Region presents various types of urban expansion. In some cases, a patchwork pattern of development has left both large and small islands of undeveloped land while moving into the outer areas of the region. Certain other salient features can also be recognized. Some of these are:

(1) a continuing industrial corridor development along major rail lines and traffic arteries;

(2) concentrated urban development surrounding the city of Detroit where water and sewer services are available;

(3) intensive development around the many lakes located in Oakland County;

(4) many of the cities once separated from the central urban complex of Detroit by open spaces are now joined by nearly continuous development;

(5) strip commercial development along the major arteries as evidence of earlier construction; and

(6) large regional recreation areas located mostly in the northwestern section of the region where resources for this type of use are most abundant.

Economy. In January 1960 the Detroit Metropolitan Area Regional Planning Commission issued a report on the "Economy of the Detroit Area" based upon "study of the characteristics, trends, regional mix of basic and non-basic industries." The quotations that follow were taken from the summary of this report.

The Detroit-area economic pattern differs from that of many other metropolitan areas. One principal difference is the degree to which manufacturing employment is lodged in a single industry—motor vehicle production. In 1954 approximately 40 percent of all manufacturing employment was concentrated in the motor vehicle industry.

Since 1929, however, the transportation equipment industry has continued to take a smaller share of all manufacturing employment. In contrast, the machinery and metals industries have increased their proportionate share of all manufacturing employment.

Along with the motor vehicle industry, Detroit-area employment in the metal working machinery, iron and steel foundries, tools and hardware, inorganic chemicals, drugs and medicines, and the nonferrous metals industries ranks first or second in the nation.

.   .   .   .

Non-manufacturing employment in the Detroit areas has been obscured by the significance of the area as a leading manufacturing center. Since 1947, however, non-manufacturing industries here have been gradually employing a greater proportion of the labor force. The importance of the retail, wholesale and service trades in the non-manufacturing economy is illustrated by the fact that in 1958 these industries accounted for almost two-thirds of the 681,000 employees in this segment of the economy.

The Detroit area is a relatively unimportant retail trade center in the sense of serving a large population in the area beyond the counties of Macomb, Oakland, and Wayne. This fact is revealed in part by its per capita sales of $1,240 in 1954 as compared with $1,450 in Cleveland and $1,360 in Chicago. Employment in this industry in 1954 was 167,500.

A study of the retail trade structure of the Detroit area from 1948 to 1954 shows a greater proportionate increase in employment and sales than stores. The end result has been a greater centralization of retail employment. The future retailing pattern will contain more retail-owned warehousing activities. Such activities will service outlying points through branch stores, with the central office located in the Detroit area.

. . . .

Based on a measure of employment to population ratios, the Detroit area in 1954 had six basic industries. By definition basic industries are those which produce goods or services in excess of local demand. In a sense they may be termed "export" industries which generate income that in turn stimulates the development of local service industries. The six industries that contributed to basic employment in the area in 1954 were: transportation equipment, fabricated metals, machinery, retail food, general retail merchandising and automotive retailing. Since 1950 general merchandise and food retailing have been added to the list of basic industries in the Detroit area. It is significant to note that the area is not only increasing the number of its basic industries but also is diversifying them in terms of its manufacturing—non-manufacturing base.

In spite of the fact that the Detroit area increased the number of its basic industries, it still ranked eighteenth out of twenty-seven metropolitan areas studied in the number of such industries in 1955. The high areas were Chicago, Kansas City, and Indianapolis with fifteen basic industries each, and the low areas were Birmingham and Boston with four basic industries each.

. . . .

Fluctuations in industrial output (and employment levels) have been one of the most important characteristics of the Detroit area's manufacturing industrial structure. Since 1920 trade and service employment have shown a high degree of relative employment stability. On the other hand, the manufacturing, construction, and transportation industries have shown the greatest degree of cyclical sensitivity.

A comparison of the Detroit area's labor force with that of other major metropolitan areas shows that this area ranks relatively high in skilled and semi-skilled workers, and low in unskilled workers, clerks, professional persons, managers and officials. Changes are taking place in the occupational structure of the area, however. From 1920 to 1950 skilled and unskilled workers as a proportion of the labor force decreased from 26 percent to 18 percent and 21 percent to 15 percent, respectively. Semi-skilled and professional workers during this same period rose from 22 percent to 27 percent and 5 percent to 9 percent of the labor force, respectively. In general, technological advancements, a rising level of living, and increased specialization have been the cause of these occupational shifts.

In spite of the fact that the Detroit area is a high-wage center, a substantial percentage of the labor force (42 percent) received less than the median annual income of $6,000 in 1955. The continued growing demand for semi-skilled workers will tend to perpetuate this income distribution, especially in light of the fact that the need for skilled workers has been declining. It is expected, therefore, any future rise in the level of incomes will come principally from higher wage and salary scales.

. . . .

Employment in the Detroit area is expected to reach 1,650,000 by 1970. This figure raises some implications. With current employment in the vicinity of 1,300,000, it in effect means that another 300,000 jobs will have to be provided in the next eleven years to insure continued growth of the area. The extent to which these jobs will be provided in the Detroit area depends on many factors. Among such factors are (1) the future of the automobile industry in the Detroit area, (2) trends in manufacturing employment, (3) trends in non-manufacturing employment, (4) the potential for new economic activity, and (5) the economic implications of the St. Lawrence Seaway.

Government

Political Jurisdictions in Wayne, Oakland, and Macomb Counties in 1960

	Wayne County	Oakland County	Macomb County	Total
Cities	23	22	10	55
Villages	6	17	4	27
Townships	14	25	13	52
	43	64	27	134

Government of the City of Detroit

Structure of Detroit's Government

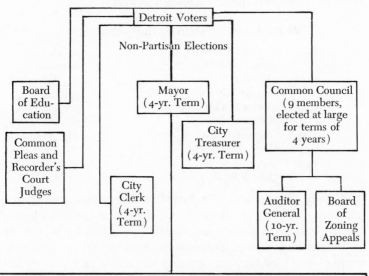

Under the mayor there are thirty-three different offices, departments, boards or commissions making up the operating agencies of the city. The controller, corporation counsel, commissioners of Departments of Public Works, Police, Building and Safety Engineering, Purchases and Supplies, Assessors, and the members of the various boards and commissions are appointed by the mayor and with the exception of the civil service commissioners and Board of Assessors, who have four-year terms, serve at the pleasure of the mayor.

The deputies and secretaries of the various departments are appointed by the commissioners or department heads. The assistants and clerks and other employees are appointed by the respective department heads subject to civil service regulations. The merit system is comprehensive in coverage and nationally recognized as being well administered.

In spite of the large number of boards and commissions, the mayor, through his appointive and removal power, can function as a strong mayor. He may veto the action of the Common Council, and it requires a two-thirds vote of the council to override the veto.

Over half of these jurisdictions are beyond the immediate range of the metropolis but are within its long-term potential grasp. Cities in Oakland and Macomb counties favor the city-manager form of government, with all but two of Oakland County's cities employing city managers; but only seven of the Wayne County cities have adopted the city-manager system.

Vote for Mayor of Detroit, 1947–1961

1947	Edward J. Jeffries, Jr.	205,543
	Eugene VanAntwerp	224,310
1949	Albert E. Cobo	313,136
	George Edwards	206,134
1951	Albert E. Cobo	168,453
	Edgar M. Branigin	113,284
1953	Albert E. Cobo	237,357
	James Lincoln	159,330
1957	Louis Miriani	290,947
	John J. Beck	48,074

County Government. "A board of supervisors, consisting of one from each organized township, shall be established in each county, with such powers as may be prescribed by law. Cities shall have such representation in the board of supervisors of the counties in which they are situated as may be provided by law" (Article 8, Section 7, Constitution of the State of Michigan). The law provides that each city may determine how it will select its representatives on the Board of Supervisors, and the number of representatives from each city is determined by population. None of the supervisors is elected at large by the county voters, but many of the supervisors representing cities hold elective office as mayor or councilman, or appointive office such as city manager or department head. Many city representatives hold no other elective or appointive public office but are selected by a council to represent a city. The perennial chairman of the Oakland County Board of Supervisors, a most influential position, is the appointed representative of one of the county's smallest cities, and he never has to account directly to an electorate in order to maintain this powerful position. Chairmanship of the Wayne County Board of Supervisors rotates between Detroit and out-county supervisors, with Detroit's turn going to a councilman.

In 1960, the Wayne County Board of Supervisors had one hundred and eleven members; fifty-eight from Detroit, thirty-nine from the remaining cities and fourteen township supervisors. Detroit's delegation included twelve elected officials (mayor, clerk, treasurer and councilmen), eighteen appointive city officials (agency heads or commissioners), and twenty-eight citizens, appointed by the mayor and council, representing major interest groups, such as labor and business, in the community. Oakland County's 1960 Board of Supervisors roster contained eighty-three names. The cities of Pontiac (seven representatives) and Royal Oak (six representatives) had the largest delegations. Macomb County had fifty-four supervisors in 1960 with the city of Warren leading the city delegations with eight members.

The county boards of supervisors have both legislative and administrative functions and responsibilities that are carried out through standing committees and the various boards, agencies, and commissions appointed by the supervisors and responsible to them. The key standing committee is the one dealing with finance (the Ways and Means Committee in Oakland and Wayne counties and the Finance Committee in Macomb County). One significant difference among the three counties is the organization of certain fiscal and service functions, which in Wayne County are carried out by a three-man elective Board of Auditors, in Oakland County by a three-man Board of Auditors appointed by the supervisors, and in Macomb County by a single officer, the controller, appointed by the Board of Supervisors.

Structure of Wayne County Government

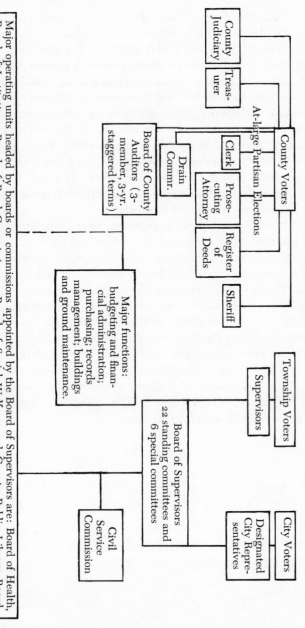

Major operating units headed by boards or commissions appointed by the Board of Supervisors are: Board of Health, Board of Institutions, Board of Road Commissioners, Board of Social Welfare, and County Public Library Board. Some agencies function through the budget and fiscal mechanism of the Board of Auditors; others, such as the Road Commission, are virtually autonomous, since most of their operating funds come from state gas and weight taxes not subject to the supervisor's control.

Structure of Oakland County Government

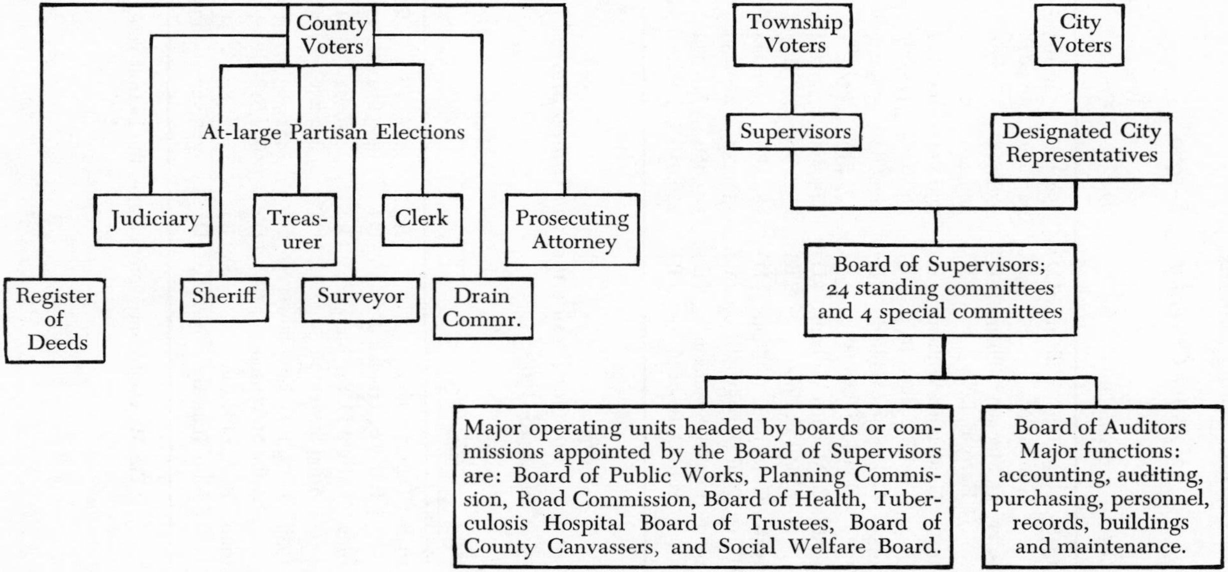

Partisan Voting Patterns

Vote for Governor 1948–1960

Date	Candidate		Detroit	Wayne County*	Oakland County	Macomb County
1948	G. Mennen Williams	(D)	432,426	540,105	58,268	27,612
	Kim Sigler	(R)	227,032	303,078	59,371	18,652
1950	G. Mennen Williams	(D)	358,595	448,296	47,569	23,582
	Harry F. Kelly	(R)	209,240	280,772	56,085	18,407
1952	G. Mennen Williams	(D)	536,851	693,111	89,815	43,779
	Fred M. Alger, Jr.	(R)	287,828	415,867	106,447	33,904
1954	G. Mennen Williams	(D)	429,662	569,298	75,625	41,161
	Donald S. Leonard	(R)	179,549	266,284	76,210	22,163
1956	G. Mennen Williams	(D)	545,595	759,704	124,004	75,406
	Albert E. Cobo	(R)	232,786	377,177	127,173	44,204
1958	G. Mennen Williams	(D)	384,386	547,044	93,621	61,601
	Paul D. Bagwell	(R)	159,537	266,233	101,104	34,095
1960	John B. Swainson	(D)	503,880	740,942	130,087	101,497
	Paul D. Bagwell	(R)	226,056	408,287	164,559	63,254

Vote for President of the United States 1948–1960

Date	Candidate		Wayne County*	Oakland County	Macomb County
1948	Thomas Dewey	(R)	321,516	62,516	21,205
	Harry S. Truman	(D)	489,654	51,491	25,265
1952	Dwight D. Eisenhower	(R)	456,371	115,503	37,474
	Adlai Stevenson	(D)	622,236	73,871	36,544
1956	Dwight D. Eisenhower	(R)	481,783	152,990	58,337
	Adlai Stevenson	(D)	664,618	99,901	62,816
1960	Richard Nixon	(R)	394,485	162,026	61,989
	John Kennedy	(D)	773,327	135,531	105,681

*The Wayne County vote includes the Detroit vote.

Case Index of
Major Participants

This index classifies the cases according to their major participants. The first two sections are complementary: Section A classifies governmental participants by *jurisdiction* or level of government; Section B by *unit* of government. (For example, in Chapter 1, the Gratiot Redevelopment Project, the core city and the federal government were the chief jurisdictional participants, and the Plan Commission, Housing Commission, mayor, and Housing and Home Finance Agency were the governmental agencies involved.) Sections C and D show the cases in which nongovernmental power groups and other participants affected decision-making. Chapter numbers are used to identify the cases.

County:
    Board of Supervisors   3, 4, 5, 6
    Drain commissioner   9
    Port Commission   5
    Road Commission   4, 6
Township officers   6, 9, 10
State:
    Aeronautics Commission   6
    Department of Health   9
    Highway Department   7, 8
Federal:
    Civil Aeronautics Administration   6
    Housing and Home Finance Agency   1, 2

C. Non-Governmental Power Groups:
    Business and/or labor groups   1, 2, 4, 5, 6
    Greater Detroit Board of Commerce   2, 4, 5, 6
    Local political organizations   6, 8, 10
    Neighborhood civic associations   2, 7, 8, 10

D. Other Participants:
    Courts   1, 3, 4, 9
    Experts   2, 4, 5, 6, 7, 10
    Newspapers   5, 8, 10

INDEX

272–274, 280–281, 282; and Port Director Stettin, 261, 264, 265, 267, 269, 289; and first public port plan, 264, 270, 272; and proposal for private port development, 275–276, 277–278; and second public port plan, 277, 278, 279, 282; reduction in staff of, 285–286; appraisal of role of, 290–292; mentioned, 243, 257, 262, 266, 272, 280, 284, 294

Port of Detroit District: establishment of, 238–239; study of, 240–241; mentioned, 246, 290

Port of New York Authority, 284, 291

Pouder, G. H., 254

Precious Blood Roman Catholic Church: opposes expressway, 428–429; mentioned, 441

President's Air Co-ordinating Committee, 353, 356, 359, 376, 393. *See also* Airport Use Panel

President's Airport Commission, 351, 357

Preuett, Leonard, 502

Price, William, 109

Propeller Club of Detroit, 267, 280

Public hearing: on Gratiot redevelopment project, 65; discussion of function of, 116–117, 136–137; on Corktown redevelopment project, 100, 124–126, 130–131; on northwest airport site, 301; on northeast airport site, 337, 339; on Lodge Expressway route, 419; on double-deck expressway plan, 429–434; on cantilever expressway plan, 452–455; on Ford Expressway route through Harper Woods, 476–477, 513; on Twelve Towns drains, 573

Public housing: objections to, 15; opposed by Mayor Cobo, 19–20; related to slum clearance, 21–23; plans for, in Detroit, 25–27, 53; and relocation of families from Gratiot site, 28, 30, 34, 36–38, 40, 41, 45; effect of Citizens' Redevel-

opment Committee plan on, 68–69, 73–74; considered for Corktown, 85, 90–94; mentioned, 21, 23, 133

Public Housing Act, 14

Public Housing Administration, 25, 26, 53

Public Works Administration, 296

Quakertown: petition to incorporate, 586–587; vote on incorporation of, 597; mentioned, 601, 623

Rackham Golf Course: and Twelve Towns cost apportionment, 547; mentioned, 531, 532, 551, 563, 575

Rago, Bernard, 502, 508

Reese, C. J., 383

Reid, Thomas, 267–268

Remus, Gerald: appointed head of Water Department, 189; policies of, 189–191, 229–230; reports water-supply expansion plans, 192–193; defends expansion plans, 198, 199–201, 211–212; and Maiullo suit, 213–214; appraisal of role of, in water controversy, 231; mentioned, 185, 199, 203, 204, 205, 210, 215, 222, 223, 228, 234

Rentzel, D. W., 326

Residents for Political Alliance, 502, 503

Reuther, Walter: opposes Detroit Plan, 19; and Citizens Redevelopment Committee, 64–65, 67, 71, 77; supports international airport site, 323; mentioned, 468

Reves, Haviland: opposes double-deck expressway plan, 428, 429, 432, 433; loses anti-expressway leadership position, 437–439; mentioned, 445, 449, 461

Richards, Glenn: and northeast airport site, 300; comments on Horner-Shifrin report, 304; opposes international airport, 314, 323–324; and DMAA, 320, 321, 325; designated

The manuscript was edited by Faith S. Schmidt. The book was designed by Richard Kinney. The text type face is Linotype Caledonia, designed by W. A. Dwiggins in 1940. The display face is Venus Bold Extended, cut by Bauer between 1907 and 1913 and based on a nineteenth-century face.

This book is printed on Warren's 1854 Text regular finish paper. The book is bound in Warren's Lustro Gloss for the soft-cover books and Joanna Mills Parchment for the hard-cover edition. Manufactured in the United States of America.